駿台

2025
大学入学共通テスト
実戦問題集

英語 リーディング

駿台文庫編

は　じ　め　に

　2021 年度より始まった大学入学共通テストは，2020 年度までのセンター試験とは出題内容や形式が大きく変わりました。英語の 4 技能と呼ばれる「読む」，「聞く」，「書く」，「話す」のうち，リーディング問題においては，「読む」ことに関する能力が試されるわけですが，共通テストにおいて重視される能力は，極端に難しい英文を読む能力ではなく，実際のコミュニケーションにおける，様々な目的や場面，状況に対応できる読解力です。このような出題方針から，従来のセンター試験で出題されていたような，発音・文法・語法・語句整序などを単独で問うような問題は廃止され，すべてが「読解問題」の形式になりました（ただし発音や文法などの知識は，リスニングやリーディングの問題の中で重要なポイントとなることもあるので，軽視せずに学習を続けていくことが大事です）。そして設問内容は，与えられた文章の要点を把握したり，必要な情報を読み取ったりする力を見るものが中心となります。より具体的には，以下のような特徴があります。

　英文の難易度は，従来のセンター試験と大きな変化はなく，極端に難しいものはありません。現状の共通テストの大問数は 6 題ですが，その中の 4 題は A と B の 2 つのセクションに分かれているため，問題の分量はかなり多めです。そのため，時間配分を誤ると，すべての問題に取り組むことができなくなるおそれがあります。一言で言えば，「難しくはないが，分量が多い」というのが，共通テストの特徴と言えます。したがって，時間配分に十分留意しつつ，各問題を手際よく片付けていく必要があります。そのため，本問題集を活用して，各問題の形式・特徴を掴み，効率よく解答する方法を探ることは，間違いなく本番で大きな助けになることでしょう。

　出題される英文のジャンルは，高校生から大学生ぐらいの日本人が日常生活や学業の中で触れる機会が多い SNS，メール，ブログ，行事などの案内文，討論や発表のための記事や資料などが中心となります（会話文を素材とする問題はリーディングからはなくなりました。会話の内容を理解する力はリスニング問題で問われることになります）。加えて，一部の問題文ではイギリス英語が使用されるなど，現代のグローバルな状況に対する意識が反映されていることにも注意しておきましょう。

　形式的な特徴としては，本文や問いの中に，図表・イラスト・グラフが数多く用いられていることが挙げられます。また，すべての問題で“You are planning …”などの場面が設定されており，受験者に当事者意識を持たせ，あたかも実際のコミュニケーションにおける目的・場面・状況などに応じて英語の理解力を考査しているような作りになっているのも，共通テスト独自の特徴と言えるでしょう。さらに問いの中には，「事実と意見を区別するもの」，「図表中の空所を埋めるもの」，「本文の内容と一致する図（表）を選ぶもの」など，他の試験にはほとんど見られない独特の形式が含まれるため，本番で戸惑うことがないよう，本問題集を活用して慣れておくことが大事です。

　このように，出題される英文のジャンルや問いの形式は独特なものが多いので，共通テストに向けての対策としては，確実な英文読解力を養成していくことは言うまでもありませんが，それに加えて，各設問に合わせた情報検索スキルを高めていくことも非常に重要なものとなります。そのことを忘れずに日々の学習を積み重ねていってください。そうすれば必ずや良い結果が得られることでしょう。本問題集がその一助となれば幸いです。

（編集責任者）　鈴木貴之

本書の特長と利用法

特　長

1　オリジナル予想問題＆過去問を掲載

　　共通テスト「英語（リーディング）」対策のために，オリジナル予想問題５回分と，大学入試センター公表の令和７年度（2025 年度）大学入学共通テスト試作問題および２年分の共通テスト過去問題を掲載しています。予想問題は，大学入試センターが令和４年12 月に実施した「試作問題モニター調査」の問題をもとにした８題構成で作成されています。形式・分量はもちろん，題材・レベルに至るまで，実戦力が身に着くよう工夫を凝らしてあります。

2　傾向と対策をわかりやすく解説

　　「共通テスト英語　攻略のポイント」では，本試験の問題例を具体的に示しながら，リーディングの学習方法や解き方のポイントを簡潔に解説しています。

3　重要事項の総復習ができる

　　解答冊子の巻頭には，共通テストの英語（リーディング）における重要事項をまとめた「直前チェック総整理」を掲載しています。コンパクトにまとめてありますので，限られた時間で効率よく重要事項をチェックすることができます。

4　学力の客観的評価が可能

　　2024・2023 年度共通テスト（本試験）の扉には「得点別偏差値表」を掲載していますので，「自分の得点でどの程度のレベルになるのか」が一目でわかります。

5　試験関連情報が満載

　　① 2025 年度大学入学共通テスト出題教科・科目，② 2019 〜 2024 年度共通テスト・センター試験の受験者数・平均点の推移，③ 2024 年度共通テストのデータネット自己採点集計による得点別人数グラフを掲載しました。

利用法

1　問題は，本番の試験に臨むつもりで，マークシート解答用紙を用いて，必ず制限時間を設けて取り組んでください。マークシート解答用紙は本冊の巻末にありますので，切り取って使用してください。

2　解答したあとは，自己採点をし（結果は解答ページの自己採点欄に記入しておく），ウイークポイントの発見に役立ててください。ウイークポイントがあったら再度解き，わからないところを教科書や辞書で調べるなどして克服しましょう！

2025年度　大学入学共通テスト　出題教科・科目

以下は，大学入試センターが公表している大学入学共通テストの出題教科・科目等の一覧表です。

最新の情報は，大学入試センター web サイト（http://www.dnc.ac.jp）でご確認ください。

不明点について個別に確認したい場合は，下記の電話番号へ，原則として志願者本人がお問い合わせください。

●問い合わせ先　大学入試センター　TEL　03-3465-8600　（土日祝日，5月2日，12月29日〜1月3日を除く　9時30分〜17時）

教科	グループ	出題科目	出題方法 （出題範囲，出題科目選択の方法等） 出題範囲について特記がない場合，出題科目名に含まれる学習指導要領の科目の内容を総合した出題範囲とする。	試験時間（配点）
国語		『国　語』	・「現代の国語」及び「言語文化」を出題範囲とし，近代以降の文章及び古典（古文，漢文）を出題する。	90分（200点）（注1）
地理歴史		『地理総合，地理探究』 『歴史総合，日本史探究』 『歴史総合，世界史探究』→(b) 『公共，倫理』 『公共，政治・経済』 『地理総合／歴史総合／公共』→(a) ※(a)：必履修科目を組み合わせた出題科目 (b)：必履修科目と選択科目を組み合わせた出題科目	・左記出題科目の6科目のうちから最大2科目を選択し，解答する。 ・(a)の『地理総合／歴史総合／公共』は，「地理総合」，「歴史総合」及び「公共」の3つを出題範囲とし，そのうち2つを選択解答する（配点は各50点）。 ・2科目を選択する場合，以下の組合せを選択することはできない。 　(b)のうちから2科目を選択する場合 　　『公共，倫理』と『公共，政治・経済』の組合せを選択することはできない。 　(b)のうちから1科目及び(a)を選択する場合 　　(b)については，(a)で選択解答するものと同一名称を含む科目を選択することはできない。（注2） ・受験する科目数は出願時に申し出ること。	1科目選択 60分（100点） 2科目選択 130分（注3） （うち解答時間120分） （200点）
公民				
数学	①	『数学Ⅰ，数学A』 『数学Ⅰ』	・左記出題科目の2科目のうちから1科目を選択し，解答する。 ・「数学A」については，図形の性質，場合の数と確率の2項目に対応した出題とし，全てを解答する。	70分（100点）
	②	『数学Ⅱ，数学B，数学C』	・「数学B」及び「数学C」については，数列（数学B），統計的な推測（数学B），ベクトル（数学C）及び平面上の曲線と複素数平面（数学C）の4項目に対応した出題とし，4項目のうち3項目の内容の問題を選択解答する。	70分（100点）
理科		『物理基礎／化学基礎／生物基礎／地学基礎』 『物　理』 『化　学』 『生　物』 『地　学』	・左記出題科目の5科目のうちから最大2科目を選択し，解答する。 ・『物理基礎／化学基礎／生物基礎／地学基礎』は，「物理基礎」，「化学基礎」，「生物基礎」及び「地学基礎」の4つを出題範囲とし，そのうち2つを選択解答する（配点は各50点）。 ・受験する科目数は出願時に申し出ること。	1科目選択 60分（100点） 2科目選択 130分（注3） （うち解答時間120分） （200点）
外国語		『英　語』 『ドイツ語』 『フランス語』 『中国語』 『韓国語』	・左記出題科目の5科目のうちから1科目を選択し，解答する。 ・『英語』は「英語コミュニケーションⅠ」，「英語コミュニケーションⅡ」及び「論理・表現Ⅰ」を出題範囲とし，【リーディング】及び【リスニング】を出題する。受験者は，原則としてその両方を受験する。その他の科目については，『英語』に準じる出題範囲とし，【筆記】を出題する。 ・科目選択に当たり，『ドイツ語』，『フランス語』，『中国語』及び『韓国語』の問題冊子の配付を希望する場合は，出願時に申し出ること。	『英　語』 【リーディング】 80分（100点） 【リスニング】 60分（注4） （うち解答時間30分）（100点） 『ドイツ語』『フランス語』『中国語』『韓国語』 【筆記】 80分（200点）
情報		『情報Ⅰ』		60分（100点）

（備考）　『　』は大学入学共通テストにおける出題科目を表し，「　」は高等学校学習指導要領上設定されている科目を表す。

　　　また，『地理総合／歴史総合／公共』や『物理基礎／化学基礎／生物基礎／地学基礎』にある“／”は，一つの出題科目の中で複数の出題範囲を選択解答することを表す。

（注１） 『国語』の分野別の大問数及び配点は，近代以降の文章が３問110点，古典が２問90点（古文・漢文各45点）とする。

（注２） 地理歴史及び公民で２科目を選択する受験者が，(b)のうちから１科目及び(a)を選択する場合において，選択可能な組合せは以下のとおり。
・(b)のうちから『地理総合，地理探究』を選択する場合，(a)では「歴史総合」及び「公共」の組合せ
・(b)のうちから『歴史総合，日本史探究』又は『歴史総合，世界史探究』を選択する場合，(a)では「地理総合」及び「公共」の組合せ
・(b)のうちから『公共，倫理』又は『公共，政治・経済』を選択する場合，(a)では「地理総合」及び「歴史総合」の組合せ

［参考］地理歴史及び公民において，(b)のうちから１科目及び(a)を選択する場合に選択可能な組合せについて

○：選択可能　×：選択不可

		(a)	
	「地理総合」「歴史総合」	「地理総合」「公共」	「歴史総合」「公共」
(b) 『地理総合，地理探究』	×	×	○
『歴史総合，日本史探究』	×	○	×
『歴史総合，世界史探究』	×	○	×
『公共，倫理』	○	×	×
『公共，政治・経済』	○	×	×

（注３） 地理歴史及び公民並びに理科の試験時間において２科目を選択する場合は，解答順に第１解答科目及び第２解答科目に区分し各60分間で解答を行うが，第１解答科目及び第２解答科目の間に答案回収等を行うために必要な時間を加えた時間を試験時間とする。

（注４） 【リスニング】は，音声問題を用い30分間で解答を行うが，解答開始前に受験者に配付したICプレーヤーの作動確認・音量調節を受験者本人が行うために必要な時間を加えた時間を試験時間とする。
　　　なお，『英語』以外の外国語を受験した場合，【リスニング】を受験することはできない。

2019〜2024年度 共通テスト・センター試験 受験者数・平均点の推移（大学入試センター公表）

センター試験←｜→共通テスト

科目名	2019年度 受験者数	平均点	2020年度 受験者数	平均点	2021年度第1日程 受験者数	平均点	2022年度 受験者数	平均点	2023年度 受験者数	平均点	2024年度 受験者数	平均点
英語 リーディング（筆記）	537,663	123.30	518,401	116.31	476,173	58.80	480,762	61.80	463,985	53.81	449,328	51.54
英語 リスニング	531,245	31.42	512,007	28.78	474,483	56.16	479,039	59.45	461,993	62.35	447,519	67.24
数学Ⅰ・数学A	392,486	59.68	382,151	51.88	356,492	57.68	357,357	37.96	346,628	55.65	339,152	51.38
数学Ⅱ・数学B	349,405	53.21	339,925	49.03	319,696	59.93	321,691	43.06	316,728	61.48	312,255	57.74
国　語	516,858	121.55	498,200	119.33	457,304	117.51	460,966	110.26	445,358	105.74	433,173	116.50
物理基礎	20,179	30.58	20,437	33.29	19,094	37.55	19,395	30.40	17,978	28.19	17,949	28.72
化学基礎	113,801	31.22	110,955	28.20	103,073	24.65	100,461	27.73	95,515	29.42	92,894	27.31
生物基礎	141,242	30.99	137,469	32.10	127,924	29.17	125,498	23.90	119,730	24.66	115,318	31.57
地学基礎	49,745	29.62	48,758	27.03	44,319	33.52	43,943	35.47	43,070	35.03	43,372	35.56
物　理	156,568	56.94	153,140	60.68	146,041	62.36	148,585	60.72	144,914	63.39	142,525	62.97
化　学	201,332	54.67	193,476	54.79	182,359	57.59	184,028	47.63	182,224	54.01	180,779	54.77
生　物	67,614	62.89	64,623	57.56	57,878	72.64	58,676	48.81	57,895	48.46	56,596	54.82
地　学	1,936	46.34	1,684	39.51	1,356	46.65	1,350	52.72	1,659	49.85	1,792	56.62
世界史B	93,230	65.36	91,609	62.97	85,689	63.49	82,985	65.83	78,185	58.43	75,866	60.28
日本史B	169,613	63.54	160,425	65.45	143,363	64.26	147,300	52.81	137,017	59.75	131,309	56.27
地理B	146,229	62.03	143,036	66.35	138,615	60.06	141,375	58.99	139,012	60.46	136,948	65.74
現代社会	75,824	56.76	73,276	57.30	68,983	58.40	63,604	60.84	64,676	59.46	71,988	55.94
倫　理	21,585	62.25	21,202	65.37	19,954	71.96	21,843	63.29	19,878	59.02	18,199	56.44
政治・経済	52,977	56.24	50,398	53.75	45,324	57.03	45,722	56.77	44,707	50.96	39,482	44.35
倫理，政治・経済	50,886	64.22	48,341	66.51	42,948	69.26	43,831	69.73	45,578	60.59	43,839	61.26

（注1）2020年度までのセンター試験『英語』は，筆記200点満点，リスニング50点満点である。
（注2）2021年度以降の共通テスト『英語』は，リーディング及びリスニングともに100点満点である。
（注3）2021年度第1日程及び2023年度の平均点は，得点調整後のものである。

2024年度 共通テスト本試「英語（リーディング）」「英語（リスニング）」
データネット（自己採点集計）による得点別人数

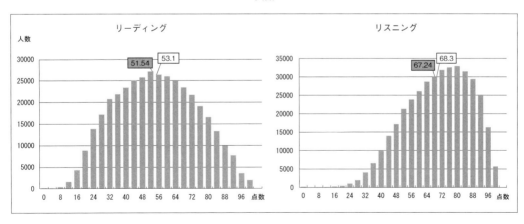

　上のグラフは，2024年度センター試験データネット（自己採点集計）に参加したリーディング：377,676名，リスニング：376,819名の得点別人数をグラフ化したものです。
　2024年度データネット集計による平均点は リーディング 53.1 ／リスニング 68.3 ，2024年度大学入試センター公表の本試験平均点は リーディング 51.54 ，リスニング 67.24 です。

共通テスト英語　攻略のポイント

2024年度　本試験：**英語（リーディング）**

1. 英語（リーディング）の概要

2024年度本試験の概要と，各問題の内容は，以下のとおりです：

・試験時間：80分　　・配点：100点　　・平均点：51.54点（前年度の平均点は53.81点）
・問題数　大問：6題　小問：39題（マーク箇所は49ヵ所）
・問題構成：

大問 （配点）	状況設定	素材	内容	*総語数	小問数	難易度	解答時間 （目安）
第1問 （10点）	案内文を読み，希望する活動を申し込む	A：案内広告	イベントの案内書	271語	2題	易	8分程度
		B：案内広告	ツアーの案内書	367語	3題	標準	
第2問 （20点）	自分の関心や必要に合う情報を読む	A：入部案内文 （コメント付き）	戦略ゲーム部への勧誘	367語	5題	標準	12分程度
		B：レビュー記事	海外旅行保険についてのレビュー	526語	5題	標準	
第3問 （15点）	身近なイベントへの参加体験談を読む	A：ブログ	フォトラリーの体験記	340語	2題	標準	10分程度
		B：学校新聞の記事	イングリッシュデーの体験記	510語	3題	標準	
第4問 （16点）	関係資料を読んで，身近な問題を解決する	記事とアンケート	部室改善プロジェクト	843語	5題	標準	10分程度
第5問 （15点）	ストーリーを読んで紹介する	ストーリー	マキのキッチン	1,222語	5題	標準	15分程度
第6問 （24点）	記事を読んで討論や発表のためにまとめる	A：記事	時間の知覚	821語	4題	標準	25分程度
		B：ウェブサイトからの抜粋	チリ・ペッパー：生活のスパイス	1,044語	5題	やや難	

*「総語数」とは，指示文・問題文・設問に含まれるすべての語の合計です。

—8—

上の表からもわかるように，リーディングの問題はその名の通り，すべて読解問題で，設問も英文の内容に関する理解を問うものからなり，文法・語法・熟語の知識のみを問う問題は原則として出題されません。各問題に用いられる英文の素材は，高校生や大学生が日常生活や学校生活の中で触れる英文という想定のもとに選ばれます。そのため，各問題の冒頭には，上の表の「状況設定」にあるように，受験者（状況説明文の中では you で示されます）が置かれている状況を説明する英文が付され，そこでは以下の本文が，自分の生活や学業とどのような関わり合いを持っているかが説明されます。自分がその状況に置かれていると想定して本文に取り組みましょう。また，状況説明文の中に本文や設問を理解するのに有用な情報が含まれていることもあるので，必ず目を通して，状況を把握してください。

設問は，すべて英語で出題されます。原則として本文中には，空所や下線など，設問との対応箇所を示す記号は設けられません。第4問以降では，本文の後にその内容を整理したノートやスライドなどが与えられ，それらの中に空所が設けられます。設問内容は上で述べたように，すべて英文の理解度を問うものですが，さまざまな形式が用いられます。以下に各問題の主な特徴を紹介していきます。

2．各問題の特徴

第1問：

第1問は，AとBの2部構成です。どちらも実用的な文書を素材とする問題で，本年度はイベントやツアーの案内書が素材となりました。設問は，質問に対する適切な解答文を選択するいわゆる英問英答形式と，本文の内容と一致する英文を完成させる空所補充形式からなります。

Aは，本文は比較的短く平易ですが，情報量は多く，必要な情報を素早く的確に選び取る力が求められます。「あなた（you）」自身がイベントに参加するという想定で，参加の仕方やイベントでできることなどを問う問題が出されます（**例1**）。設問数は2題と少ないことから，短時間で解答することが大事ですが，細かい情報を正しく読み取らないと間違える恐れがあるので注意が必要です。

例1

| 問1　To join the event free of charge, you must ◻1 . |

Bは，Aよりも長めの文書を素材とする問題です。情報量も増え，設問数も1題多いことから，速く読み，必要な情報を的確に見つけることがさらに重要となります。第1問の解答時間の目安は，AとB合わせて8分です。これ以上時間をかけると，第2問以降で時間不足になる可能性が出てくるので注意しましょう。

第2問：

第2問もAとBの2部構成です。ここでは自分の関心や必要に合う文書を読むという状況を想定して問題が出されます。また，本文には複数の人物によるレビューやコメントが添えられることがあるのも1つの特徴です。第2問の解答目標時間は12分です。

Aは高校のクラブへの入部勧誘のチラシが素材で，本文は「クラブ活動の説明」と「部員のコメント」の2つの部分からなっています。設問形式は，第1問と同様に，「英問英答問題」と「空所補充による英文完成問題」ですが，問3では「（客観的な事実ではなく）意見」を問う問題が出題されているのが特徴的です（**例2**）。解答の手がかりとなる情報が，本文中の各所に分散していることが多く，本問でもやはり本文中の必要な情報を素早く見つけ出す力が鍵となります。

例2

| 問3　One **opinion** stated by a member is that ◻8 . |

Bは，米国留学を経験した女子大学生が書いた旅行保険についてのレビューが素材です。設問は，本文中で紹介される3つの保険プランの補償内容に関するものに加えて，筆者の「意見」（問4：Aの問3と同形式）や考え方（問5）を問う問題が出されます。また，問3では同一の選択肢群から2つの正解を選ぶ形式が採用されています（**例3**）。

例3

| 問5　Which is the best combination that describes TravSafer International? ◻13

A：They allow monthly payments.
B：They design scholarship plans for students.
C：They help you remember your medication.
D：They offer an Internet-based registration system.
E：They require a few days to process the application form. |

— 9 —

①	A and D
②	A and E
③	B and D
④	B and E
⑤	C and D

第3問：

第3問もＡとＢの2部構成です。どちらの問題文も，自分にとって身近なイベントについて，他者が書いた参加体験談を読むという状況設定です。この問題の解答時間の目安は 10 分です。

Ａは，日本で外国人旅行者向けのイベントに参加した英国人が書いたブログ記事が素材で，記事には参加時の出来事を綴った文章と，イベントのルール表からなっています。設問は2題で，そのうち1題はブログの内容を正しく表しているイラストを選択するという形式です（問1）。

Ｂは，学校新聞の記事が素材で，学校の行事である「イングリッシュデー」への参加体験記が素材です。設問は3題です。問1では，参加学生のコメントを読み，それが表すイベントを起こった順序通りに並べるという問題が出されました（例4）。また，問3の内容一致文完成問題は，本文中の異なる2つの箇所で示される情報を組み合わせることで正解が決まる問題なので，注意が必要です。

		例4

問1　Yuzu's article also included ...

第4問：

第4問は，「部室の改善」という問題に取り組むために，必要な資料を読み，問題解決のための討論用のレジュメを作成するという状況設定です。素材となる資料は，論説記事とアンケート結果の2つです。設問内容は，レジュメの中の空欄を埋める形式で，論説記事やアンケート結果の内容が問われます。問3のように，レジュメの中で削除すべき項目を選ばせる問題（例5）や，アンケートの回答者名を答えさせる問題（問4・5）もあるのが特徴です。この問題は 10 分以内に回答するのが目安です。

		例5

問3　You are checking the handout. ...

第5問：

長めの英文を読み，その要点をまとめることを主な狙いとする問題です。問題は「本文」とその要点をまとめた「ノート」の2つからなり，メモの中に空所が設けられ，それを適切な表現で埋めるという出題形式です。本文の素材はストーリーで，メモは「ストーリーのアウトライン」，「主人公の紹介」，「重要な節目の解釈」からなっています。設問の中には，起こった出来事を時系列に沿った順序に並べることを問う問題が含まれます（例6）。これは第3問Ｂの問1と似ていますが，本文における出来事の記述の順序は，必ずしもそれらが起こった順序と同じではなく，また空所よりも選択肢の数が多い（つまりいずれの空所にも入らない選択肢が1つ含まれる）ので，より一層の注意が必要です。また，本文中には明確な形で書かれていないストーリーの教訓や解釈などが問われることもあります。本文の分量が本試験の問題の中では最も多いことから，設問との対応箇所をいかに速くかつ的確に見つけられるかどうかが大きな鍵となります。この問題の解答時間の目標は 15 分です。

		例6

問1　Choose four out of the five events ...

第6問：

第6問はＡとＢの2部構成です。第5問と同様に，長い文章を読んで，その要点をまとめたメモやスライドの中の空所を埋めるという形式の問題ですが，この問題では論説調の記事が素材となります。この問題は 25 分で解答するのが目安です。

Ａの素材文は，「時間の知覚」というタイトルの記事です。本文の後の「ノート」には，段落別のアウトラインと，本文の内容に基づいて「あなた」が作成した具体例が記されていて，その中の空所を適切な表現で埋めていきます。アウトライン中の空所を埋める問題（問1・2）は，空所に該当する段落を読んだ時点で解答すればよいので，取り組みやすい形式です。具体例として適切なものを選ばせる問3・4も，本文が正しく読めていれば，正解を選ぶのは難しくありません。

Ｂの素材文は，「チリ・ペッパー」などの香辛料をテーマにした解説調の文章です。本文を読んだ後で，発表用のスライドを作成するという設定で，本文の要点をまとめたスライド内の空所を埋めることが求められます。出題内容には，素材文は情報量のかなり多い英文で，細かい情報を読み取って整理・比較する力が求められます（例7）。第4問の問3と同じように，削除すべき項目を選

ぶ問題も出されます（問2）。かなり分量の多い問題ですが，本文を1段落読むごとに，スライドの内容を確認しながら取り組んでいけば，効率よく解答できるでしょう。

ないようにしましょう。こういった学習を日々積み重ねた上で，本書を利用して，過去に出題された問題の形式，特徴，効率のよい取り組み方などを頭に入れておけば，制限時間内に全ての問題に正解するのは不可能ではありません。本書がその一助となれば幸いです。

例7

問1　What is the first characteristics ... ?

Characteristics

chili peppers	wasabi

・oil-like elements ・ 44

・triggering TRPV1 ・changing to vapor

・persistent feeling ・spicy rush

2

---

3. 学習対策

教科書レベルの英文を速く正確に読める力をつけよう。

　共通テストのリーディング問題の最大の特徴を一言で言えば，「難解ではないが分量が多い」ということです。どの問題の英文も，極端に難しいものはなく，設問についても，本文が正しく読めれば正誤の判断に迷うものは少ないので，標準的な学力がある受験生が落ち着いて時間をかけて取り組めば，かなりの高得点が取れると思います。しかしながら，80分という制限時間の中で，すべての問題に取り組んで正解を出すのはかなり難しいことです。したがって，「平易な英文を速く正確に読めるようにする」ことが，リーディング問題への最大の対策であることは間違いありません。そのためには，まず高校の教科書レベルの英文をしっかり理解した上で，止まったり戻ったりすることなくスピーディーに読めるようになるまで読み込むことが大事です。このような訓練を日々繰り返して，習熟した英文の量を増やしていくことが，共通テストで高得点が取れる学力を養うための最大の鍵となります。そしてそのプロセスで語彙力を自然に身につけていくのが，望ましい単語の覚え方です。なお，文法や語法や熟語の知識のみを問う問題は出題されませんが，これらの知識を間接的な形で問う問題もあり，英文を正しく読む上でも文法や語法や熟語の知識は大切ですから，これらの分野の標準的なレベルの学習は怠ら

第 1 回
（80分）

実 戦 問 題

英　　語（リーディング）

各大問の英文や図表を読み，解答番号 $\boxed{1}$ ～ $\boxed{46}$ にあてはまるものとして最も適当な選択肢を選びなさい。

第 1 問 （配点　6）

You are an exchange student in Canada, and your homestay family wants to take you on a day trip. Your homestay mother has given you some information about the available tours.

Prince Edward Island (PEI) Sightseeing Tours
Choose from three Maple Tours itineraries

The Montgomery Tour

Learn about Lucy Maud Montgomery, the author of *Anne of Green Gables*, whose writing was inspired by the island's nature and people. Start the tour at the Cavendish United Church, built in 1901, where Montgomery was buried in 1940. Next, visit  the Anne of Green Gables Museum and see items belonging to Montgomery. The museum was originally a house built by Montgomery's relatives in 1872. Finally, visit the school where Montgomery taught. The tour will be conducted by tour guides who were all brought up on PEI.

PEI Scenic Drive

Let's experience the island's beautiful scenery and nature. Your local guide will pick you up directly from your accommodation. First, we will drive down Charlottetown's main street, passing Province House, completed in 1847, and the site of the Charlottetown Conference in 1864, which led to the formation of Canada. Then we will visit the Prince Edward Island National Park, before stopping at North Rustico, a lobster fishing village. Try some delicious lobster at a restaurant there.

第1回 英語（リーディング）

Charlottetown Food Highlights Walking Tour

Let's explore Charlottetown on foot. Your guide has lived on PEI his entire life, and he will introduce Charlottetown's historical sights, while pointing out delicious local food to sample. Start the tour at Peake's Wharf, by the sea. These warehouse buildings were built in 1872, and are now restaurants and gift shops. Try some ice cream before moving on to the Farmer's Market. Meet local farmers and buy delicious fresh produce. After wandering the streets, we'll eat at the Canton Café, the island's longest-running restaurant. The owners moved to Canada in the 1950s and opened their Chinese restaurant in 1970.

問1 Prince Edward Island has ☐ 1 ☐ .

① a place where a historically important conference was held

② a school that was founded by Canada's most famous female writer

③ the first Chinese restaurant that opened in Canada

④ warehouses that have been used to store goods since the 18th century

問2 On all three tours, you will ☐ 2 ☐ .

① be taken around by a guide who lives on the island

② learn about famous people from the island

③ see the center of the largest city, Charlottetown

④ try various examples of local food

問3 Which is the oldest building you will see on these tours? ☐ 3 ☐

① Province House

② the Anne of Green Gables Museum

③ the Canton Café, Chinese restaurant

④ the Cavendish United Church

— 3 —

第2問 (配点 10)

You will soon move to the UK to study at a university there. You are reading an article about bank accounts for students written by a recent graduate of that university.

Almost all banks these days offer special "student bank accounts," and I strongly recommend signing up because they offer services not available to regular account holders.

My account is with Alpha Bank. To attract new customers, they offer a 3-year student railcard if you open an account in September. These railcards are worth £120, and holders can get 30% off train fares. Other banks give cash gifts. For example, Waverly Bank puts £50 in every new student account, while Phoenix Bank gives £40.

In addition to online banking and a debit card, all student accounts provide low-interest credit cards and offer zero-interest short-term loans. Last month, the salary from my part-time job was late, but I borrowed £100 from Alpha at zero interest for a week. Some banks allow higher limits. Customers of Waverly Bank and Phoenix Bank can borrow up to £200 and £300 interest-free respectively.

Most adult bank accounts charge a fee of up to £10 a month, but student bank accounts are usually cheap or free to use. My bank charges £2 a month, but Waverly and Phoenix are free. However, my bank does not charge at all for ATM cash withdrawals, unlike the other two.

The unique benefit of Alpha bank is that it offers free travel insurance until I graduate. This is great for me because I like to travel. I took a trip to Paris last month and my camera was stolen. I was able to get some money back to buy a new camera, although I wish the money had arrived faster and the procedure was simpler.

Each account offers different benefits and services, so think about your own needs before choosing a student bank account.

第 1 回　英語（リーディング）

問 1　According to the article, which of the following is true?　4

　　① All bank accounts mentioned allow free ATM withdrawals.
　　② Alpha Bank's gift to new student clients is the most valuable.
　　③ Both Alpha Bank and Waverly Bank provide travel insurance.
　　④ Only Waverly Bank and Phoenix Bank offer interest-free loans.

問 2　Which is **not** offered by the author's bank?　5

　　① A debit card
　　② ATM services
　　③ Free-of-charge banking
　　④ Free travel insurance

問 3　Which is the features of student bank accounts described in this article?　6

　　A : Loans and services are cheaper than adult accounts.
　　B : They allow students to withdraw cash without charge only weekdays.
　　C : They help students find part-time jobs.
　　D : They insist new account holders pay £40 into their account.
　　E : They offer incentives to new customers.

　　① A and D
　　② A and E
　　③ B and C
　　④ B and D
　　⑤ C and E

問4　One **opinion** the writer has of her student account is that ☐ 7 ☐ .

   ① her insurance claim took too long to process

   ② the banking app is too complicated to use

   ③ the free gift was not very useful for her

   ④ the limit for the zero-interest loan is too low

問5　Which of the following best describes the writer's attitude? ☐ 8 ☐

   ① She believes opening a student account will generate various monetary profits.

   ② She considers there to be little difference between student and regular accounts.

   ③ She hopes that more banks will offer similar financial services to students.

   ④ She thinks it is better to buy separate travel insurance when going abroad.

第1回　英語（リーディング）

（下 書 き 用 紙）

英語（リーディング）の試験問題は次に続く。

第3問 (配点 9)

You and the other members of your school English Club are going to take part in a volunteering day. You are reading a report written by Junya, a member who took part in a similar event last year.

River Cleaning and Nature Survey Day

For last year's volunteering day, we worked with the River Clean Up Association (RCUA). Volunteers come to the river each month and pick up all the trash that has built up. Because of the recent typhoon, there was more trash than usual. We also took part in a nature survey and recorded the flowers we found.

First, we met the RCUA members. Although it was sunny, the ground was very wet and muddy, so we wore boots and waterproof pants. We wore gloves to protect our hands, and had plastic bags in which to collect the trash. We formed two groups. One group collected the trash, and the other group checked it for recyclable  items. By lunchtime, we had collected 30 large bags of trash.

We stopped for lunch at midday. Most of us had packed lunches, but some students forgot theirs, so they went to a convenience store to buy food. We felt sorry for them because they were already tired after the morning's work.

After lunch, Mika, an RCUA member, taught us how to collect information about flowers. The RCUA was helping some university ecology experts collect research data. We formed pairs and threw large hoops at random into the grass. We then counted the numbers and species of the flowers inside the hoop. We all felt proud to contribute to university research. Mika told us that we would be able to read about our work in a famous ecology journal next year.

Finally, we loaded the trash into the RCUA truck. They planned to take it to the city's trash disposal facility later. They also invited us to dinner at a nearby restaurant. We enjoyed talking about environmental issues. We practiced our English with the two foreign members in the group.

This year, I will join the volunteer day again. The experience inspired me in many ways. Writing this report also reminded me of what Mika had said about the ecology journal. I decided to go to the library to see if she was right.

問 1 Junya's article also included student comments (①〜④) describing the events during the volunteering day. Put the comments in the order in which the events happened.

① I wish I had brought lunch! It was hard walking all the way to the store to buy food after cleaning up the riverbank.

② Speaking to the RCUA members over dinner was my favorite experience. Learning to communicate with people of different ages and backgrounds is important.

③ The highlight of the day was collecting research data. I'm interested in plants and I hope to become a biologist in the future.

④ We were surprised to see how much work we had to do when we arrived. The strong wind had blown a lot of things into the water.

問2 During the volunteering day, the students did **not** [13].

① carry out information gathering regarding flowers
② go to the trash disposal facility
③ have conversations with volunteers in English
④ take a break between activities

問3 What did Junya most likely find when he went to the library? [14]

① a book about wild flowers
② a guide to the local river ecology
③ a journal article based on their data
④ a news report about the typhoon

第1回　英語（リーディング）

（下 書 き 用 紙）

英語（リーディング）の試験問題は次に続く。

第4問 (配点 12)

In English class you are writing an essay about a science issue you are interested in. This is your most recent draft. You are now working on revisions based on comments from your teacher.

How to Improve Your Sleep	Comments
Scientific research tells us that most adults need around 7 to 9 hours of sleep a night to stay healthy. Long-term lack of sleep can cause many health problems, including heart disease, high blood pressure, and obesity. It also affects our brains, making us less alert and less able to retain information. Despite the importance of sleep, many people find themselves unable to sleep well at night. ⁽¹⁾<u>For instance,</u> there are many things we can do to make our sleep better.	*(1) You have used the wrong connecting expression here. Please change it.*
First, it is important to expose ourselves to natural light in the morning. This is because our natural daily rhythm is set by exposure to light. ⁽²⁾∧ Hormones are released from inside our brains which stop us from feeling sleepy. The first exposure to light also instructs our bodies to make the sleep hormone melatonin around 14 hours later.	*(2) This sentence does not connect well with the previous sentence. Add more information to improve the flow of your writing.*
Second,⁽³⁾ <u>where do you sleep?</u> The best temperature for sleep is said to be between 18 and 20 degrees Celsius. In addition to light, the human sleep cycle is regulated by other environmental triggers such as temperature. Therefore, by lowering the temperature of our bedrooms, we can signal to the body that we are ready to sleep and that helps us fall asleep quicker and improve the quality of our sleep.	*(3) The topic sentence does not explain the following paragraph well. Rewrite it.*

第1回　英語（リーディング）

Finally, it is known that using electronic devices late in the evening can negatively affect the quality of our sleep. Devices such as smartphones and tablets emit blue light, which can delay the production of melatonin.

In summary, there are a number of things we can do to get better sleep, as we have seen above. ⁽⁴⁾∧

(4) I think you should add a final, concluding sentence.

Teacher's Comment

Good job! I definitely need to get more sleep, so I will take on your advice! ☺

問1　Based on comment (1), which is the best expression to use instead?
15

① However
② In contrast
③ In short
④ Therefore

問2　Based on comment (2), which is the best expression to add? 16

① After falling asleep,
② By spending time in the dark,
③ If we protect our eyes against this,
④ When sunlight enters our eyes,

— 13 —

問3 Based on comment (3), which is the best replacement? 17

① it is important to sleep in a dark environment.
② make sure you are tired enough to sleep.
③ sleeping in a cool room is recommended.
④ try to relax your body before going to bed.

問4 Which sentence should you add, based on comment (4)? 18

① In conclusion, people in our society are still not doing these things properly.
② In this way, we can not only improve our sleep quality, but also our overall health.
③ Therefore, we should spend less time working, and more time sleeping.
④ These points show the importance of getting more sleep for young people.

第1回　英語（リーディング）

（ 下 書 き 用 紙 ）

英語（リーディング）の試験問題は次に続く。

第5問 （配点　16）

You and some friends have decided to start a new club at your high school — an English debate club. You have made a handout about the topic based on the following article and the results of a questionnaire given to students who had recently taken part in an English debate in class.

What Makes a Successful Debate?

Lucy Gonzalez, debate team captain at Skyrock College

Debate is a tool used to discuss important topics. Debating allows students to explore difficult subjects, express their opinions logically, and challenge their prejudices. All debates start with a resolution — the statement to be discussed — which is chosen in advance.

A debate requires three groups: the affirmative team, the opposing team, and the judges. The affirmative team starts by presenting arguments supporting the resolution and their reasons. They should also anticipate reasons for disagreeing with the resolution, and explain why those reasons are false.

Next, the opposing team presents their opposing arguments. The speaker answers questions raised by the other team, and presents further reasons for opposing the resolution. Researching both sides of the topic and guessing what your opponent will say brings success.

Both teams speak again in the rebuttal section. Here, the speakers can comment on what the other team said, and give further counter-arguments. Finally, the judges listen to the final statements. The judges look for two main points — clarity and relevance. Clarity means that the arguments were clear and logical, while relevance means that the speakers stuck to the topic and gave appropriate evidence. Judges should base their judgment on these points regardless of their own personal opinions.

A debate should be fun. Although participants should take their roles seriously, everyone should remain polite. Through this activity, members can improve their skills and knowledge.

— 16 —

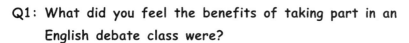
Results of the Questionnaire

Q1: What did you feel the benefits of taking part in an English debate class were?

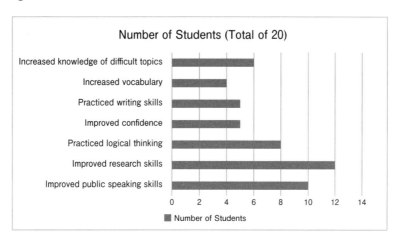

Number of Students (Total of 20)

Q2: Give your opinions about the debate class.

Main comments:

Student 1 (S1): Although I was assigned to the opposition team, I actually agreed with the resolution personally. It was difficult for me to think of opposing arguments.

S2: I was a member of one of the debate groups, but my friend was a judge. She didn't do any research at all. I think judges have to research the topics too. She also said it was difficult to remember the key points each team made.

S3: The debate was difficult for me because I didn't know the necessary English words. I wish we had had a vocabulary list before starting the activity.

S4: The opposition team found statistics and data to support their opinion. The affirmative team did not come up with logical reasons or evidence, so they lost.

S5: I think we needed more time in class to prepare for the debate and understand the topic I didn't have enough time to investigate.

S6: My knowledge of the subject was really poor and I didn't have any opinions before doing the debate. However, not only did I gain knowledge about the topic, I learned about other related issues.

Your discussion handout:

Organizing a Formal Debate

■ **Debate Structure**
- Resolution: [19]
- Three groups: affirmative team, opposing team, and judges

■ **Recommendations for the team members based on expert advice and questionnaire results**
- Affirmative Team:
  Research and present reasons [20].

- Opposing Team:
  Give the opposing view on the topic, even if you personally disagree.
  Giving hints to the team in advance may help them prepare opposing arguments.

- Judges:
  [21]
  A. Decide your opinion before the debate starts.
  B. Learn about the topic in advance.
  C. Look for clear and logical arguments.
  D. Look for evidence that supports arguments.
  E. Take notes during the debate to avoid forgetting.

■ **Other issues to discuss**
- The lowest number of students said that [22] as [23]'s comment mentioned. What should we do about this?
- Based on both the graph and [24]'s comment, should we assign club time to understanding the topic and planning the arguments? How much time do we think the teams will need?
- S1 said that he already had a fixed opinion about the topic they debated in class. Perhaps we should have a large group brainstorming session before being divided into teams so everyone can see all sides of the argument. What do you think?

第1回　英語（リーディング）

問1　Choose the best option for ⬚ 19 ⬚.

① A statement to which both teams should prepare opposing arguments

② A view about an issue to be debated

③ An opinion about a controversial subject that most people agree with

④ The first argument of the opposing team that the affirmative team opposes

問2　Choose the best option for ⬚ 20 ⬚.

① agreeing with the resolution, backed up with data you researched

② disagreeing with the topic, using advanced English vocabulary

③ for both sides of the argument, allowing the judges to decide

④ for your personal opinion of the topic, to convince the other team

問3　You are checking the handout. You notice an error in recommendations under Judges. Which of the following should you **remove**? ⬚ 21 ⬚

① A

② B

③ C

④ D

⑤ E

— 19 —

問4　Choose the best options for ┃ 22 ┃ and ┃ 23 ┃.

┃ 22 ┃

① it was difficult to speak in front of friends

② there was little time to prepare

③ they were able to acquire new words

④ they had little knowledge of the topic

⑤ writing practice was not included

┃ 23 ┃

① S1

② S2

③ S3

④ S4

⑤ S5

⑥ S6

問5　Choose the best option for ┃ 24 ┃.

① S1

② S2

③ S3

④ S4

⑤ S5

⑥ S6

第1回　英語（リーディング）

（下 書 き 用 紙）

英語（リーディング）の試験問題は次に続く。

第6問 （配点 18）

You are working on an essay about whether the voting age in a state of the U.S. should be lowered to 16. You will follow the steps below.

Step 1: Read and understand various viewpoints about lowering the voting age.

Step 2: Take a position about whether or not the voting age should be lowered.

Step 3: Create an outline for an essay using additional sources.

[Step 1] Read various sources

Author A (High school student)

Some of my friends feel that we should have the right to vote at age 16. However, I don't feel ready to become a voter yet. I still have another two years of high school until I graduate, so I still feel like a child in many ways. I also don't know enough about the political system to have a strong opinion about who to vote for. I'd probably just vote for the same party as my parents.

Author B (Teacher)

Many people believe that 16-year-olds are still children, and therefore, should not have the right to vote. I actually believe that 16 is the ideal age for young people to start taking an interest in politics and society. If they are given enough information to make an informed choice, I think they are capable of doing so. However, while we must teach them about politics at school, as teachers we must be careful not to influence them too much with our own personal political opinions.

Author C (Voting station staff)

I've noticed that the number of people who come to vote is dropping every year. That's why I'm in favor of lowering the voting age. Now, the majority of voters are elderly people, with young adults in the minority. If we allow younger people to vote, they will hopefully take a deeper interest in politics and become voters for the rest of their lives. However, if we allow 16-year-olds to vote, we must make sure that they have the motivation to do so, and that they receive a balanced political education. I don't know if schools have the time or experience to do that.

第 1 回　英語 （リーディング）

Author D (Psychologist)

Most developmental psychologists agree that the human brain does not finish maturing until we are in our mid-twenties. Therefore, 16-year-olds are still children in a developmental sense. However, this is not the main reason why I disagree with lowering the voting age. Probably there are many 16-year-olds who are mature enough, but I think they lack the knowledge of both politics and society to make a good choice. We cannot do this without huge changes in our education system. I do not support lowering the voting age until school students have enough knowledge to be able to make important decisions.

Author E (Politician)

Statistics show that the majority of voters in my state are in the 45-64 age group. That means that politicians tend to make policies aimed at pleasing older voters. Times are hard for young people now, and I think that if they were able to vote, they could make choices for a brighter future. Some politicians are against lowering the voting age because 16-year-olds will be strongly influenced by the political choices of their teachers or parents, but I believe we should make a better society for everyone, not just our older voters.

問 1　Both Authors B and E mention that ☐ 25 ☐.

① 16-year-olds are far too young to take an active interest in politics

② high school students do not work or pay taxes so they cannot understand politics

③ it is mainly the middle-aged and elderly that are politically active

④ young people's political opinions could be influenced by their teachers

— 23 —

問2   The main argument of Author D is that 26 .

① information about the political system is not adequately taught in schools now

② people under the age of about 25 are immature and should lose the right to vote

③ there are no school students who are wise enough to make good political decisions

④ those people whose brains are not fully developed should not be able to vote

[Step 2] Take a position

問3   Now that you understand the various viewpoints, you have taken a position on lowering the voting age to 16, and have written it out as below.   Choose the best options to complete 27 , 28 , and 29 .

Your position: The voting age should not be lowered to 16.

- Authors 27 and 28 support your position.
- The main argument of the two authors: 29 .

Options for 27 and 28 (The order does not matter.)

① A

② B

③ C

④ D

⑤ E

— 24 —

第 1 回　英語（リーディング）

Options for ☐ 29

① Parents are likely to tell their teenage children to vote for the political parties they support

② Some students under 18 have the maturity to be able to vote

③ Students under 18 are likely to be influenced by their friends' decisions

④ Young people aged 16 to 18 do not have the knowledge or experience to vote

[Step 3] Create an outline using sources A and B

Outline of your essay:

Lowering the voting age is not a good idea

Introduction

These days, the number of people who vote in elections is decreasing. Therefore, some people believe the voting age should be lowered to 16 to encourage more people to vote. However, this is not a good idea.

Body

Reason 1: (From Step 2)

Reason 2: (Based on Source A) ⋯⋯ ☐ 30

Reason 3: (Based on Source B) ⋯⋯ ☐ 31

Conclusion

The voting age should not be lowered to 16.

Source A

In most countries of the world, the age of adulthood has been set as 18 years old, while others set an even higher age as the age of adulthood. The reason why 18-year-olds are considered adults in most countries is because it is the age where young people are developmentally able to make important decisions about their own lives. That is, they can marry without permission, and they can sign legal contracts. Some of them are also likely to be working full-time. It also follows that most countries have matched the age of adulthood with the age of fitness to vote. In fact, the average voting age around the world is just over 18. Most governments believe that anyone not legally considered an adult should not have the right to vote in an election and affect the politics of a country.

Source B

A survey conducted in the US asked people of different age groups whether or not they supported voting rights for 16- and 17-year-olds. Just over 1,000 people who were supporters of various political parties answered the survey questions. There was also a fair balance of genders, ethnic groups, and income.

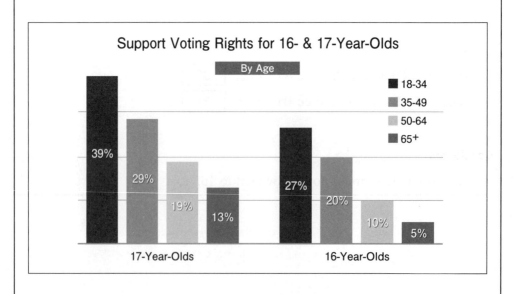

第１回　英語（リーディング）

問４　Based on Source A, which of the following is the most appropriate for
Reason 2?　 30

① 18-year-olds are still studying in school, so they are not considered
old enough to vote and influence politics.

② Even 18 is too young to be able to vote, because some countries
have decided people are children until around 20.

③ Since people over 18 work full-time in most countries, they're
expected to be able to vote.

④ We should keep the voting age at 18 because that is considered the
age of adulthood in most countries.

問５　For Reason 3, you have decided to write, "Lowering the voting age is
not supported by Americans." Based on Source B, which option best
supports this statement?　 31

① 18-34 people are the most likely to disagree that 16-year-olds should
be able to vote, but just under a third support it for 17-year-olds.

② Almost three-quarters of 18- to 34-year-olds are not for lowering the
voting age to 16, and 5% of people over 64 agree.

③ Although the majority of people aged 34 and younger believe the
voting age should be lowered, this is not supported by people in the
other age groups.

④ Most people aged 18-34 support the voting age being lowered to 17,
but just 27% of them are for the voting age being lowered to 16.

― 27 ―

第7問 （配点 15）

You are in English class preparing for a presentation about a story. You have found an interesting story in a magazine and you are taking notes about the story for your presentation.

Sam's School

The phone rang. Sam Hawkin woke up from a deep sleep and looked at the clock next to his bed. It was 4:00 a.m. Still half asleep, he picked up the phone.

"Hello?"

"Sam. It's Mom. Your dad is sick again. He's in the hospital. I think you need to come home this time."

When his wife Hiroko woke up a couple of hours later, he told her the news.

"I'm going to book a flight back to Canada for tomorrow. Dad's very sick. Can you stay here and take care of the children?"

"Sure. I hope your dad gets well soon. I'll take care of everything here. Go as soon as you can." Hiroko replied. Later that morning, she told their children, Mina and Karen, that Dad was going to visit Granny and Grandpa in Canada for a while.

Sam had enjoyed his time at university so much that he didn't want to graduate. Not only did he not want to give up his fun student life, he also didn't know what he wanted to do as a job. Most of his friends had already decided on their careers — John was going to be a lawyer, Chris was going to be a journalist, and Mike was going to work in his father's company. It was just Sam who didn't know what he wanted to do. His parents were high school teachers, and they had suggested the same career to him many times, but he wasn't sure. However, one day just before graduation at the age of 22, he noticed a poster on the wall of his dormitory building. "Teach English in

Japan!" it said. Sam made a note of the website address printed on the poster. That evening, he applied.

"But Sam, you've never even left Canada! Why are you going to Japan?" His mother asked, surprised.

"You suggested I become a teacher, Mom. I'll be a teacher in Japan! I'll just go there for a year, then if I like teaching, I'll come back and become a high school teacher here in Canada."

"It will be a big culture shock for you. If you feel lonely, you can come back here whenever you like," said his father. The month after that, Sam flew to Tokyo.

That was 15 years ago. Despite knowing little about Japan before leaving Canada, it had become home for him. He was still working at the same school he had applied for after graduating, and he was loved by his students and colleagues. He had also taught himself to read, speak, and write Japanese. Three years after arriving in Japan, he married Hiroko, whom he had met at an international party. Their girls were born a few years after their wedding. Hiroko was a writer, and she had had several novels published. Even after becoming a mother, she continued writing in her spare time at home. They were a happy family and Sam was considering spending the rest of his life in Japan.

Back in Canada, Sam was surprised to see how sick his father was. The doctors told him he could be in the hospital for a long time. Seeing his mother's sad face, Sam wondered if he should change his plans and move back to Canada to take care of his mother until his father had recovered. That evening, Sam met up with his old friends, John, Chris and Mike. They talked about their university days and their lives now. All of them were married and had children. They showed Sam pictures of their families, and Sam thought it would be nice for his girls and his friends' children to play together. He told them about his father.

"Come back, Sam," his friends said.

"I'd love to live here again, but I don't want to go back to college to get my teacher's certificate. I have a family — I need to work right away."

"You could start a Japanese school," suggested Chris, the journalist. "I just wrote an article for a magazine about the popularity of anime and Japanese culture. Many people want to learn Japanese these days."

"Right! Our company has plenty of space in our building. You can use that space for free," offered Mike.

"And I'll help you with all the paperwork for Hiroko's visa," said John, the lawyer.

That night, Sam called Hiroko in Tokyo and told her his idea. To his delight, she agreed.

Sam returned to Japan, but six months later, the Hawkin family's move to Canada was complete. There was enough space in Sam's parents' home for everyone to live together. Hiroko was able to continue her writing work remotely. Mina and Karen were enjoying life in their Canadian school. They had been sad to leave all of their friends in Japan, but they loved spending time with their Canadian Granny and Grandpa. Their English was improving all the time. Grandpa was still very weak, but he was getting stronger every day thanks to the love of his family. When Sam saw his family together, he thought it was a shame they hadn't thought of doing this earlier.

Sam's school was a success from the start. His friends had helped him just as they had promised. One day, Mike dropped by the Japanese school.

"Hey, Sam. We didn't have a welcome home party for you. Why don't we do that this weekend?" Mike suggested.

"No, Hiroko and I should hold a thank-you party for you, John and Chris. It's thanks to you that our move went so smoothly. Come to our house on Saturday with your families, and Hiroko and I will cook some delicious Japanese food for you all."

And so they did.

Your notes:

Sam's School

Story outline

Sam graduates from university.

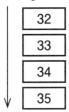

| 32 |
| 33 |
| 34 |
| 35 |

Sam and Hiroko hold a thank-you party.

About Sam

- Nationality: Canadian
- Age: | 36 |
- Occupation: Teacher
- How his friends and family supported him:

    His old friend John | 37 |.

    Sam's mother and father | 38 |.

Interpretation of key moments

- Sam was delighted when he spoke to Hiroko on the phone from Canada because | 39 |.
- At his home in Canada, Sam thought that something was "a shame." It was that | 40 |.

問 1   Choose **four** out of the five events (① ~ ⑤) and rearrange them in the order they happened. | 32 | → | 33 | → | 34 | → | 35 |

① Hiroko and Sam get married.

② Hiroko becomes a high school teacher in Canada.

③ Mike offers Sam space for his language school.

④ Sam moves to Japan.

⑤ Sam's father becomes sick.

問 2   Choose the best option for | 36 | .

① early 20s

② late 20s

③ late 30s

④ early 40s

問 3   Choose the best options for | 37 | and | 38 | .

① allowed Sam, Hiroko and the children to live with them

② gave Sam money to start his new business in Canada

③ prepared the documents Hiroko needed to live in Canada

④ showed Sam a poster about teaching jobs in Japan

⑤ wrote a marketing article to advertise Sam's new school

— 32 —

第1回　英語（リーディング）

問4　Choose the best option for [39] .

   ① she accepted his plan of returning to Canada together

   ② she gave him good news about their two children

   ③ she told him that his father would get better quickly

   ④ she told him that she had published another novel

問5　Choose the best option for [40] .

   ① his children were not settling into their new school life

   ② his family had missed out on a lot of time together

   ③ his father was still sick and unable to leave the hospital

   ④ his wife was not enjoying her life in Canada anymore

第8問 (配点 14)

You are preparing a presentation for your science class, using the following information from a health website.

Dietary Fiber: the Forgotten Hero

Health experts are always encouraging us to eat more fruit and vegetables. We know that these foods contain a large variety of vitamins, minerals, and nutrients that are vital for keeping our bodies healthy. However, one other reason for encouraging the consumption of fruit and vegetables is because they contain fiber. In fact, we can only get the fiber our bodies need through eating fruit, vegetables, and other plant-based foods. Other foods such as meat, fish, and dairy products contain many nutrients, but they completely lack fiber.

In Western countries, fiber intake has decreased, while consumption of processed foods has risen. It is difficult for busy people to take the time to cook meals from fresh ingredients for themselves and their families, so more and more people are relying on ready-made food. According to the UK National Health Service, the average adult should eat at least 30g of fiber each day. However, research shows that the current average is just 20g. Unfortunately, a lack of fiber in one's diet can lead to numerous health problems.

It is important to note that there are two main types of fiber — soluble fiber and insoluble fiber. Each type of fruit or vegetable contains a different amount of each. Soluble fiber is fiber that dissolves in liquid to form a gel inside the digestive system. This gel is not absorbed by the body itself, but is used as food by the bacteria that live inside us. These bacteria play a very important role in not only digestion, but also our brain health. That is because these bacteria release certain compounds that act as signaling chemicals in our nervous system. Recent evidence suggests that increasing consumption of soluble fiber can lower the risk of developing diseases of the brain such as Alzheimer's disease. When we eat, we should think not only about our needs, but also the needs of our "good" gut bacteria.

Soluble fiber also blocks or slows the absorption of the fat and sugars that we eat. This means that by consuming more soluble fiber, we can stop

— 34 —

第１回　英語（リーディング）

high amounts of fat and sugar from suddenly entering our blood stream after a meal. Sharp rises in blood sugar over a long period of time can eventually lead to diabetes, while too much fat and cholesterol can lead to heart disease. In reducing our intake of fat and sugar, weight gain is slowed down. It is known that gaining too much weight can also lead to high blood pressure and pain in our joints. Soluble fiber is found in all plant foods but it is particularly high in oats, beans, and carrots.

Insoluble fiber, on the other hand, is not broken down at all in the body and does not dissolve in water. It is a physical material that moves through our digestive system and cleans it. It attracts water and sticks to other waste products of the digestion process, eventually helping to form the waste we release when we use the toilet. It helps us use the toilet regularly, preventing stomach pain and discomfort, and prevents harmful waste products remaining in our digestive system for too long. Without insoluble fiber, we would be more likely to develop cancers of the digestive system, such as intestinal cancer. These cancers are rising in young people around the world, and one reason for this may be a lack of insoluble fiber in our diets. To increase our intake of insoluble fiber, we should eat foods like nuts, apples and potatoes. Eating the skin of apples and potatoes helps us consume even more of this type of fiber.

Although there are many important benefits to increasing our intake of both types of fiber, there are some negative effects of eating too much. First, people who suddenly increase their fiber intake may suffer from gas and stomachache. This is because the bacteria living in the digestive system produce gas when they break down the fiber. The pressure of the gas inside the digestive system may be painful. Second, because fiber binds to water, we may become dehydrated if we do not drink enough water. This can make it difficult to get rid of waste regularly. Finally, because fiber slows down the absorption of nutrients, we may not be able to absorb the nutrients our body needs if we consume too much fiber.

Despite the risks of taking in too much fiber, it is a problem that is unlikely to occur in most people. Around 90% of people do not eat enough fiber, so the general advice is for everyone to increase their intake of fruits, vegetables, beans, and nuts.

Presentation slides:

| Dietary Fiber: the Forgotten Hero  1 | Characteristics
Soluble fiber   Insoluble Fiber
• dissolves in water   • attracts water
• [41]   • binds to waste
• not absorbed   • cleans digestive system
• food for bacteria   2 |

Health Benefits of Fiber Consumption

Increasing fiber consumption to the recommended amount can ... [42]
  A. lower risk of diabetes.
  B. result in weight gain.
  C. prevent brain diseases.
  D. make us use the toilet regularly.
  E. reduce risk of developing cancer.

3

Side Effects of Too Much Fiber

• [43]
• Dehydration
• [44]

4

Gut Bacteria

[45]

5

Final Remarks

[46]

6

第 1 回　英語（リーディング）

問 1　What is the second characteristic of soluble fiber on Slide 2?　| 41 |

① enhances fat and sugar absorption

② forms a gel-like substance

③ speeds up digestion

④ works as a signaling chemical

問 2　Which is an **error** you found on Slide 3?　| 42 |

① A

② B

③ C

④ D

⑤ E

問 3　Choose two options for Slide 4.　(The order does not matter.)
| 43 |・| 44 |

① death of useful gut bacteria

② inability to take in sufficient nutrients

③ stomach pain or discomfort

④ too much water in our waste

⑤ using the toilet too often

— 37 —

問4 What can we say about the bacteria living in our digestive systems for Slide 5? 45

① Eating too much insoluble fiber causes bacteria to grow, which may lead to the development of cancer in young people in Western countries.

② It is important that we do not eat the wrong kind of fiber, because it will cause too many bacteria to grow and produce gas.

③ We should avoid too much fiber because it helps bad bacteria grow in our gut that may cause diseases such as Alzheimer's.

④ We should feed our gut bacteria with fiber because they break down the food and produce important chemicals.

問5 Choose the most appropriate remark for Slide 6? 46

① Everyone should increase their consumption of plant-based foods, but always peel vegetables because the skin contains harmful fiber.

② Not all people can tolerate large amounts of fiber, so people should consult a doctor before changing their diet.

③ Since most people do not eat enough fiber, it's better to increase our consumption of both types of fiber without thinking about the possible negative effects.

④ There is no evidence to suggest fiber supports brain health, but some people say it may reduce cancer risk in young people.

⑤ We should choose foods that contain soluble fiber, but avoid those that contain insoluble fiber because of the risk of health problems.

— 38 —

第 2 回
（80分）

実 戦 問 題

英　　語（リーディング）

各大問の英文や図表を読み，解答番号 1 ～ 46 にあてはまるものとして最も適当な選択肢を選びなさい。

第1問（配点　6）

You are looking at the website for a shopping mall near your university, and you find information on an environmentally-friendly program it will be carrying out.

  Reuse your clothes & reboot your life!
Special coupons for your old favorites

It takes a lot of natural resources to make the clothes we wear every day. However, last year the amount of dumped clothes was 11 million tons in America alone — worse than ever!
So how can we tackle this issue? Reuse!

Our project

Our clothing-collecting project just started three years ago. You can help us like this:

1. Instead of throwing your unwanted clothes away, please bring them to us at **Silver Sky Mall**.
2. Turn in your clothes (any brands, in any condition) at the register.
    ※ We accept items bought at shops other than ours.
3. We will give you a $5 coupon per one item to make your next purchase at our mall. (You can bring up to three items at one time; if you bring a member's card or sign up for one, you can donate one more item.)

Last year, thanks to you, we collected one ton of textiles and successfully reused them. Collected garments will be reworn by someone, remade into new clothes, or recycled into other products like shopping bags or machine parts.

第2回　英語（リーディング）

Date

Sat. April 20th – Tues. April 23rd, 9:00 a.m. - 4:00 p.m.

※ You can participate in this campaign <u>once per person</u> during this period.

Want items at special prices?

Some collected clothes will be sold as secondhand clothing at our mall from May. During this event, if you want to look at pictures of the items, please visit the special website.

https://silversky.trade-in.example

問1　If you have a member's card, you can get coupons for a maximum of ⬛1⬛ .

① $10

② $15

③ $20

④ $25

問2　Last year was ⬛2⬛ .

① the beginning of the distribution of coupons on the website

② the first time Silver Sky Mall had collected more than 1,000 kg of unwanted garments

③ the first year of this clothes-collecting program

④ the worst year for the amount of wasted clothes in the US

問3　During this program, you **cannot** ⬛3⬛ .

① bring clothes purchased from other countries

② check on the Internet what items will be sold

③ send in the clothes you want to sell by mail

④ use the coupon next time you come to the mall

— 3 —

第2問 (配点 10)

You are a member of the student council. The members have been discussing a project helping students to clear the town of trash. To get ideas, you are reading a report about a school challenge. It was written by an assistant language teacher who taught at a junior high school in Japan.

Cleanup Challenge

In response to the town's environmental beautification campaign, our junior high school worked on the town's cleanup activity. I also felt that there was a lot of litter, such as empty bottles or pieces of paper, on the road the school is on, so I thought this would be a good opportunity to improve the environment near our school. We started this activity to help students understand the importance of keeping the community clean. A total of 250 students participated every Friday from January 10th to February 10th. They picked up litter on their way to school, put it in a special plastic bag and brought it to school. What was interesting was that students from the western part of the town picked up more litter than students from other areas. What was the cause of this? Based on the feedback (given below), there seems to be an answer to this question:

Feedback from participants

AS: Thanks to this project, I realized the importance of cleaning. It seemed that when the road was clean, my heart was also clean.

BK: Some of my friends seemed to find it difficult to pick up litter because they commuted to school by bicycle.

SC: I made a map of where I found a lot of litter. There seems to be no significant relationship between distance from the station and amounts of trash.

JD: We separated trash carefully. Cigarette butts were the most common objects, followed by plastic trash, wastepaper, and empty cans. Smoking on the street is prohibited in our town, so I was very upset.

ML: One of my classmates commuting from the western area of our city picked up more litter than I did. This may be related to the fact that there is a busy shopping area there.

— 4 —

第2回　英語（リーディング）

問1　The aim of the Cleanup Challenge was to help students to ☐4☐ .

① appreciate the need for a clean environment

② be worthy members of the community

③ recognize regional trash connections

④ understand different types of litter

問2　One **fact** about the Cleanup Challenge is that ☐5☐ .

① it lasted for two months during the winter

② it was held at least four times during a set period

③ most of the students came from the western side of town

④ students had to use homemade bags

問3　From the feedback, ☐6☐ were activities reported by participants.

A : examining different types of litter

B : recording where litter was found

C : taking litter home

D : warning people not to smoke

① A and B

② A and C

③ A and D

④ B and C

⑤ B and D

⑥ C and D

問4　One of the participants' opinions about the Cleanup Challenge is that
    　7　.

　① 　it was more efficient for students commuting by bicycle
　② 　many students got into the habit of picking up litter
　③ 　smoking should be prohibited as soon as possible
　④ 　the cleaner the town was, the better the participant felt

問5　The author's question is answered by 　8　.

　① 　AS
　② 　BK
　③ 　JD
　④ 　ML
　⑤ 　SC

第2回　英語（リーディング）

（下 書 き 用 紙）

英語（リーディング）の試験問題は次に続く。

第3問 （配点 9）

You found the following article about success in a magazine that one of your friends lent you.

From Rags to Riches

(By Sally Ellis)

You may have never heard of Howard Schultz, but most likely you know the company he transformed. Born into a poor family in New York in 1953, his number one goal in life was to succeed and build a brighter future, and he fought hard at school to achieve good grades.

Schultz later proved to be a natural at sports, and was offered a free place at university because of his ability. After graduation Schultz did sales for a small coffee-maker company, as well as for other companies, and was promoted quickly there. Eventually he became an advertising manager for a coffee bean company with a few stores in Seattle. The name of this small chain? Starbucks.

On an Italian trip, Schultz was impressed by the café culture there, and suggested Starbucks open coffee shops where people could socialize and chat comfortably. Even when the top managers doubted that ideas would suit their organization, they sometimes allowed their staff to carry them out; and the American public loved Schultz's idea. He then left and returned to Starbucks twice, eventually becoming president of the enterprise, expanding it across the USA and further, incorporating it into 39 countries by 2012. Ironically, some neighboring Starbucks stores have closed because they were competing with each other. Soon after, Schultz was listed in Forbes Magazine as one of America's richest.

—8—

第2回　英語（リーディング）

Schultz has used any power he had in positive ways since he climbed to the top of his company, and once famously criticized an investor for being against gay marriage, even suggesting he spend his money boosting another company. He received an award for never lying at work, and was invited to teach a course on fair business practices at an American university. He supports the concept of an environmentally friendly business world, and wants oil and gas to be taxed more harshly.

問1　Put the following events (① ～ ④) into the order in which they happened. ⎡ 9 ⎤ → ⎡ 10 ⎤ → ⎡ 11 ⎤ → ⎡ 12 ⎤

① Schultz became the head of Starbucks.

② Schultz proposed introducing a new business style to Starbucks.

③ Schultz quit working at Starbucks.

④ Schultz started using his influence constructively.

問2　One **fact** we know about Schultz's life is that he ⎡ 13 ⎤ .

① caused constant trouble at school

② preferred traditional American customs

③ used expensive energy sources

④ was among the wealthiest persons in the USA

問3　From this story, you learned that Starbucks ⎡ 14 ⎤ .

① began as a cheap store accessible to people living in poverty

② faced considerable challenges early on and almost went out of business

③ itself collected ideas from restaurants worldwide to build an international chain

④ listened to proposals of employees and was willing to try new things

— 9 —

第4問 （配点 12）

In English class you are writing an essay about an environmental issue you are interested in. This is your most recent draft. You are now working on revisions based on comments from your teacher.

Reducing Paper Use	Comments
In 2021, people around the world used 417 million tons of paper. Producing this much paper has major environmental effects, including deforestation, use of energy and water, and pollution. ⁽¹⁾In contrast, paper makes up around 26% of all waste in landfill sites. Although much of this paper waste is produced in the workplace, we can also try to reduce paper use in our daily lives.	*(1) You have used the wrong expression here. Please change it.*
First, we should reduce our use of disposable paper towels and tissues. Many people use single-use paper towels and tissues to clean their homes. This is particularly true in the kitchen, especially when cleaning up spilled liquids. ⁽²⁾∧ Wherever possible, you should do this instead of using paper towels.	*(2) You are missing an important sentence. What do you recommend we do?*
Second, ⁽³⁾do you do a lot of reading? The publishing industry in the US uses around 32 million trees a year to produce books. While it is the responsibility of that industry to use more recycled paper, you can help by borrowing books from the library instead of buying them, or by purchasing electronic books instead of printed versions.	*(3) Change the style of the topic sentence.*
Finally, we should change our bills and bank statements to digital versions. Until recently, most families received paper bills, which not only wastes paper but also uses energy during delivery. By accessing your bills and bank information online, you can save paper, time, and energy.	

— 10 —

第2回　英語（リーディング）

In conclusion, there are many things you can do to save paper. We can reduce our reliance on single-use paper products, change the way we consume books ⁽⁴⁾∧. By doing this, we can help to protect the environment.

(4) Please summarize your third point here.

Teacher's Comment
Great effort! I should do some of these things too. ☺

問1　What is the best expression to replace the one you used, based on comment (1)? ☐ 15 ☐

① As a result
② In addition
③ In other words
④ On the other hand

問2　What is the best sentence to add, based on comment (2)? ☐ 16 ☐

① However, this job could be done using reusable.
② I believe it is important that we use better quality towels.
③ It is important that you avoid spilling drinks in the kitchen.
④ Therefore, you should be much more careful at home.

問3　What expression should you replace the question with, according to comment (3)? ☐ 17 ☐

① you should buy books that use less paper
② you should change the way you read books
③ you should reduce the number of books you throw away
④ you should think about reading fewer books

— 11 —

問4 Which expression should you add, according to comment (4)? 18

① and avoid having letters delivered
② and change the banks you use
③ and have your bills delivered digitally
④ and reduce the energy you consume

第2回　英語（リーディング）

（下 書 き 用 紙）

英語（リーディング）の試験問題は次に続く。

第5問 (配点 16)

You have been asked by your teacher to make a presentation on effective reading strategies and you are reading two articles and are planning to present what you have learned in your next class.

Useful Practice: Rereading
James King
Librarian at Mount City Middle School

Rereading is the act of reading a book, article, or any written material again after having already read it once. It is a common practice among readers who wish to gain a deeper understanding of a text, refresh their memory, or simply enjoy a book they love once again. Rereading is also beneficial for language learners. By rereading a text, learners can improve their vocabulary, comprehension, and fluency. Rereading can also be used as a tool for academic or professional purposes, such as studying for an exam, writing a paper, or preparing for a presentation.

When rereading a text, readers may notice things they missed during their first reading. This is because rereading allows the reader to focus on the details of the text rather than on the plot or overall structure. The reader may find new insights, connections, or meanings that were not apparent before. Additionally, rereading often helps readers identify patterns or themes that were not obvious during their initial reading. Thus readers can also develop their critical thinking skills by analyzing the text and forming their own opinions and interpretations.

However, rereading also has its downsides. It is time-consuming, especially for longer texts. It can also become monotonous or boring because it is not active. Moreover, rereading is not necessarily effective in proportion to frequency, as the graph shows.

In conclusion, though it may not always be necessary or effective, rereading is a useful practice that helps readers gain a deeper understanding of a text, improve their language skills, and develop their critical thinking ability.

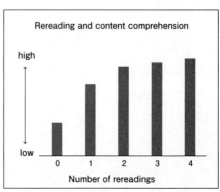

Effective Reading Strategy: Interactive Reading
Eric Brier
Professor at Mount City University

Interactive reading refers to the process of engaging with a text through active participation and dialogue. Unlike passive reading, where one simply consumes the words on the page, interactive reading requires the reader to think critically, ask questions, and form connections with the material.

To read interactively, one must approach the text with an open and curious mind. Rather than simply accept the information presented, the reader should actively seek to understand and interpret it. This involves asking questions, making predictions, and connecting the material to one's own experiences and knowledge.

One effective way to engage in interactive reading is through annotation (making a mark or a note), as with the examples below. By doing so, the reader can better remember the material and make deeper connections to it. Annotation also helps the reader to identify key themes and ideas in the text, which can aid in comprehension.

Examples of annotation	
Highlighting:	marking important parts with a colored pen
Underlining:	drawing a line beneath key words or phrases
Margin notes:	writing comments or questions in the text
Sticky notes:	attaching small notes

Another way to engage in interactive reading is through discussion with others, which involves book clubs, classroom discussions, or informal conversations with friends. By discussing the text with others, readers can gain new perspectives and insights, as well as reinforce their own understanding of the material.

However, there are also some disadvantages to interactive reading. Firstly, it takes a lot of time, especially if the discussion or activities are extensive. This is not favorable for individuals with busy schedules or limited time. Secondly, interactive reading can also be distracting to the reading process itself, as it often shifts the focus away from the text and towards the discussion or activity. Lastly, the interpretation and analysis of the text may be influenced by the opinions and perspectives of the group, which can limit individual understanding and critical thinking.

問1　King thinks that 19 .

① getting insights at the first reading is important

② reading books brings us back to reality

③ repetition can deepen our understanding of a text

④ rereading the same text is very exciting

問2　In the reading method discussed by Brier, readers can 20 .

① accept the information as it is

② gain a new way of looking at things

③ make their language skills better

④ understand the text more quickly

問3　Both reading strategies have their disadvantages. King says that rereading tends not to be very 21 , while one disadvantage of interactive reading, Brier says, is that other people's views may affect the reader's 22 thinking. (Choose the best one for each box from options ① ~ ⑥.)

① academic

② critical

③ extensive

④ interesting

⑤ logical

⑥ positive

第2回　英語（リーディング）

問4　Both writers agree that effective reading requires ☐23☐ .

① a competitive environment

② considerable time

③ high intelligence

④ personal information

問5　Which additional information would be the best to further support Brier's argument for interactive reading? ☐24☐

① How to absorb as much information from a book as possible

② The most effective way to make annotations while reading

③ The reasons why many people don't read the same books again

④ Whether or not debating skills are important for your life

— 17 —

第6問 (配点 18)

You are working on an essay about whether high school students should be allowed to have part-time jobs. You will follow the steps below.

Step 1: Read and understand various viewpoints about working students.
Step 2: Take a position about whether or not high school students should be allowed to work part-time jobs.
Step 3: Create an outline for an essay using additional sources.

[Step 1] Read various sources

Author A (Teacher)

A few of the students in my high school class are now working part-time jobs. Some work in restaurants, some work in cafes, and one student works in a convenience store. Certainly, they can learn some important lessons about the real world, but I worry about their health. Once they start earning money, they try to pick up more hours to earn even more, and this impacts their sleep. There are not enough hours in the day for students to work, study, play, and rest.

Author B (Parent)

My son worked in a café last year, but I had to ask him to quit. At first, I was very proud that he was taking on lots of shifts and earning lots of money, but he started to become very stressed. He was trying to pass the entrance exam for medical school, but he underestimated the amount of work he had to do. It was impossible for him to combine studying with work. I won't allow his sister to work part-time when she is a high school student.

Author C (Restaurant owner)

I employ several high school students in my restaurant. I value them as important members of staff. They are eager, willing to learn, and they also work hard. I think working from a young age has taught them responsibility. I have seen my young employees blossom into responsible adults. Students who don't work seem childish to me. I also worked from a young age and it helped me become a successful businessman. Not all people want or have the ability to succeed in an academic environment, so I think it is important that high school students have the opportunity to enter the world of work.

— 18 —

第2回　英語（リーディング）

Author D (Police officer)

I can understand why high school students want to work. They want to start earning money so they can socialize with their friends. I also believe it is good to learn about how society works. On the other hand, I am concerned about safety. Many young people have to walk home late at night after a shift at their work places. I have seen many car or bike accidents involving students who are too tired to concentrate after a hard day. I have forbidden my own children from working until they graduate from high school and become university students.

Author E (Student)

I have always been a shy person, but my parents encouraged me to start working at a supermarket near my home. I only work on weekends, but I have already become less quiet and more confident. I have to speak to customers and colleagues of all ages and backgrounds, so I think this job has helped me become a better communicator and a more responsible person. I have also managed to save over $2,000, which I intend to use to pay my university fees next year.

問1　Both Authors A and D mention that 　25　 .

① part-time jobs offer students the chance to experience the real world

② students need to learn about the value of work and money from a young age

③ they do not allow their own children to take part-time jobs after school

④ working in a part-time job improves motivation for high-school students

— 19 —

問2　Author C says that 　26　 .

① a part-time job is an especially positive experience for students who are not good at studying

② he tries to employ high school students at his restaurant as they are cheap employees

③ high school students are too young and too inexperienced to be valuable employees

④ if students start working at a young age, they are more likely to become businesspeople

[Step 2] Take a position

問3　Now that you understand the various viewpoints, you have taken a position on allowing high school students to work part-time, and have written it out as below.　Choose the best options to complete 　27　 , 　28　 , and 　29　 .

　　Your position: High school students should be allowed to get part-time jobs.

- Authors 　27　 and 　28　 support your position.
- The main argument of the two authors: 　29　 .

Options for 　27　 and 　28　 (the order does not matter)

① A
② B
③ C
④ D
⑤ E

第2回　英語（リーディング）

Options for [29]

① It is important for students to start earning and saving money as soon as possible

② One way to improve communication skills is to work with much older people

③ Working at a café, restaurant, or supermarket is a good way to make new friends

④ Working from a young age is a valuable experience because it teaches responsibility

[Step 3] Create an outline using sources A and B

Outline of your essay:

High school students should be allowed to do part-time jobs

Introduction

School work is extremely important for high school students. However, there are many positive aspects to working part-time for them.

Body

Reason 1: (From Step 2)

Reason 2: (Based on Source A) ······ [30]

Reason 3: (Based on Source B) ······ [31]

Conclusion

In summary, high school students should be permitted to take part-time jobs.

Source A

One reason why many young university graduates struggle to find a suitable job immediately is that many jobs require several years of work experience. However, that is exactly what new graduates lack. A recent survey of jobs listed on a popular employment website showed that 35% of entry-level jobs required at least three years of relevant work experience. These are not technical or specialist jobs, they are jobs that require very few skills. It is this requirement that prevents many capable young people from entering the job market. In times of recession, or when applying for jobs in competitive markets, a few years of work experience can make the difference. This is why teachers and parents should encourage teenagers to take on some work as early as possible. In particular, communication and customer service skills are popular with employers, so a part-time job in a customer-facing role is ideal.

Source B

A study found giving high school students part-time jobs had an effect on their likelihood of committing crimes. Students in a poor, high-crime neighborhood were chosen randomly and given jobs. The graph below shows the change in numbers of arrests for violent crime and theft during and after the program.

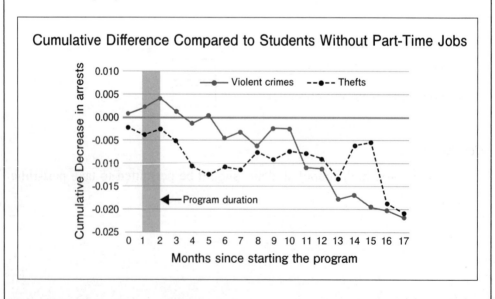

第2回　英語（リーディング）

問4　Based on Source A, which of the following is the most appropriate for Reason 2?　30

① A part-time job as a high-school student will give young people an advantage in the job market even after graduating from university.

② Entry-level graduate jobs only employ people who worked in customer service jobs during high school.

③ Graduates who enter jobs in specialist careers are more likely to have worked as high school students.

④ Students are more likely to be successful at university if they have had some kind of work experience at high school.

問5　For reason 3, you have decided to write, "Working part-time can improve youth crime situations." Based on Source B, which option supports this statement?　31

① Arrests for both theft and violent crime rise slightly during the working period, but crime rates start to improve a year later.

② Even after their part-time jobs finished, students who were employed were less likely to get arrested for both violent crime and theft.

③ While both types of crime drop during the working period, arrests for theft start to rise when the part-time work has finished.

④ Working part-time can cut violent crime dramatically, but theft is not affected.

— 23 —

第7問 (配点 15)

In your English writing course, you are required to choose one short story to read. You are reading the following story and making a summary of it to help other students to understand the story line.

The Restructuring that Changed Everything

Isabella Andrews

"Sit still, please," Emily says to her two daughters, smiling. "With you moving so much, I can't paint a picture of you." "I'm sorry, Mum," Marianne replies, with a gentle smile on her face. "Look how far I've come," Emily says to herself.

Five years ago today, Emily had to make an important but difficult decision about her career. She had been working for a well-known advertising firm for six years. Unfortunately, in order to escape bankruptcy, the company was going through restructuring and her position was going to be eliminated. She was offered a new role within the company.

Of course, she was grateful for the opportunity to stay with the company. After all, it was far easier to work where she knew what she was doing. But at the same time, she couldn't help feeling she was being taken advantage of. The new role would mean a significantly lower salary and she would have to work harder to earn as much as she used to.

After contemplating for what felt like forever, Emily decided to turn down the offer and began job-searching. However, it was an incredibly difficult path. She was met with one rejection after another, and her confidence began to fall.

As if that wasn't bad enough, Emily had trouble communicating with her children at home. One day, when she got back home from one of the job interviews, she asked Sarah, her older daughter, what she had done at school, to which she didn't reply. Totally shocked and disappointed, she asked her husband, Nick, why Sarah had behaved the way she did. "It seems your whole life has been revolving around your work, and you've paid far less attention to our daughters than they deserve," he said.

— 24 —

Maybe he was right, she thought. Looking back, she had always told herself that it was her duty to make a decent amount of money for the sake of her daughters, but she now realized that all she was doing was making an excuse for not fulfilling her role as a mother.

"Do you remember you had a dream of becoming an artist?" Nick said. "They would often say that they wanted you to follow your dream." Then, suddenly, she remembered how she had liked art but given up her long-held dream in favor of making money. "If you still have a passion for art, isn't this a good time to pursue it? Don't worry about money." "Thank you, Nick," she said, her eyes brimming with tears.

The next day, Emily told her daughters how sorry she felt, apologizing for her complete failure as a mother. Also she told them about her idea of drawing and painting pictures again. They looked confused at first, but soon their expressions softened. "I guess it'd be good," Sarah said.

After a lot of twists and turns, two years later, she eventually landed a job as an art director for a small advertising agency, which allowed her to combine her passion for art with her experience in advertising. Her salary was not so good, but she found the work considerably more satisfying and fulfilling than in her previous job.

Today, the construction of Emily's small home studio is finally complete. Now, sitting in it with her beloved family, Emily is flooded with a sense of great happiness that would have been unattainable had she not made the difficult decision to change careers. The restructuring, however hard it seemed at that time, was in fact a blessing. Of that, she is absolutely sure.

Your notes:

The Restructuring that Changed Everything

1. Characters
- Emily (main character)
  - ► She was offered a new position, but she was worried that [32] .
- Sarah and Marianne (Emily's daughters)
- Nick (Emily's husband)
  - ► He suggested that Emily [33] .

2. What happens in the story
Emily is offered a new position in the advertising company.

→ [34] → [35] → [36] → [37]

3. Some important lessons
- [38]
- [39]
- Considering one's personal fulfillment when making career decisions is essential.

4. An idiomatic expression we can learn
"Look how far I've come" (first paragraph)
This can be roughly paraphrased as " [40] !"

— 26 —

第2回　英語（リーディング）

問1　Choose the best option for ☐32☐.

   ① she might make less money than she deserved

   ② she would be transferred to another branch

   ③ the company might go bankrupt before long

   ④ the job offered would be very boring

問2　Choose the best option for ☐33☐.

   ① become a full-time mother to compensate for her past mistake

   ② consult with their daughters about job hunting

   ③ stop looking for a job and take a good rest

   ④ try pursuing what she originally wished to do

問3　Choose **four** out of the five options (① ～ ⑤) and rearrange them in the order they happened. ☐34☐ → ☐35☐ → ☐36☐ → ☐37☐

   ① Emily decides to start job-hunting.

   ② Emily paints her daughters' picture at home.

   ③ Emily starts to work as a professional painter.

   ④ Nick talks about Emily neglecting her duty as a mother.

   ⑤ Sarah ignores Emily's question about her day at school.

問4 Choose the best two options for ⬚38⬚ and ⬚39⬚ . (The order does not matter.)

① A good balance between work and family life is crucial.
② A restructuring is the best option for employees in a struggling company.
③ An unfortunate situation sometimes turns out to be beneficial.
④ Pursuing your original goal leads to a higher salary in the end.
⑤ Spending more time with children than at work is the key to success.

問5 Choose the best option for ⬚40⬚ .

① How distant my dream seems
② How much time I've wasted
③ What an exciting life I've had
④ What great progress I've made

第2回　英語（リーディング）

（下 書 き 用 紙）

英語（リーディング）の試験問題は次に続く。

第8問 （配点 14）

You are in a student group preparing for an international presentation contest. You are using the following passage to create your part of the presentation on a popular mushroom.

The earth contains more species of organisms than animal species, including us humans. Typical examples are fungi, of which there are estimated to be 1.5 to 5 million species, compared to only about 1.5 million animal species. This is partly due to the fact that fungi are highly adapted to their environment and can live in a wider range of places than animals. Fungi are also able to reproduce both sexually and non-sexually, which gives them a greater capacity to evolve and diversify. Of all the fungi, perhaps the most familiar to us are mushrooms.

When we were young, we may have seen red and white mushrooms in fairy tales and other stories. There are different opinions as to what these mushrooms are, but the most promising is fly agaric. It has a red pileus (cap) that is typically between 5-15 cm wide and a white stem that can grow up to 20 cm tall. This makes it one of the most easily recognizable types of mushrooms. It is originally from northern Europe, but now it is found in many different regions around the world, ranging from temperate forests to the cold and damp forests of the northern areas.

Fly agaric has played an important role in many cultures and traditions, from being depicted in folklore and fairy tales to being used in religious ceremonies. In some cultures, it was believed to have spiritual and healing powers. The Vikings are said to have used it to feel brave before battle. In Hindu texts, it is mentioned as "soma" and believed to have been used in religious rituals to communicate with the gods.

Fly agaric is attracting attention for its medicinal properties. One of the chemicals that have been recently studied in fly agaric is ibotenic acid. This substance has been linked to learning and memory, and it could be helpful in treating various nervous disorders such as Parkinson's and Alzheimer's

— 30 —

diseases. In addition, fly agaric contains several substances that are being studied for their potential usefulness in the treatment of various organ diseases, including cancer and liver disease.

Fly agaric is also known as *Amanita muscaria* in scientific terms. It is part of the genus *Amanita*, which includes other well-known species like death cap. Fly agaric is a type of fungus called mycorrhizal, which means that it needs a tree to survive. They need each other to exist because the tree absorbs nutrients from the soil through the fungus, while the fungus receives sugars and other nutrients from the tree.

The fly agaric fungus grows beneath the ground, and only the mushrooms, or fruiting bodies, can be seen above ground. It is considered to be an annual fungus, which usually grows once a year and then dies, but the mycelium remains underground and is able to produce new fruiting bodies the following year. The growth and reproduction of fly agaric is closely tied to environmental factors such as temperature, moisture, and light.

The body mechanics of the fly agaric are unique. It has a bright red pileus, which is covered with white spots called scales. It releases tiny single-celled structures called spores that spread into the environment to settle on new growth areas. The spores are white and located on the gills under the pileus. The mushroom stands tall on a thick stem, which is usually white or cream in color, and has a cup-like structure at the base called a volva. It also has a distinctive ring-like structure around the stem called the annulus, which also serves as one of the main characteristics of the mushroom.

Although fly agaric has cultural significance and potential medicinal benefits, it's important to remember that it is a poisonous mushroom. Eating too much of it can lead to serious illness or even death. Therefore, it's essential to be careful and seek advice from professionals before attempting to use fly agaric for any purpose. Nevertheless, the unique qualities of this fungus will continue to fascinate and inspire scientists and mushroom fans alike.

Your presentation slides:

```
┌─────────────────────────┐  ┌─────────────────────────────┐
│                         │  │     1. Basic Information    │
│      Fly Agaric :       │  │ • 5 cm to 15 cm in diameter │
│  Red and White Mushroom │  │ • up to 20 cm in height     │
│     Known Worldwide     │  │ •                           │
│                         │  │ •  [ 41 ]                   │
│                         │  │ •                           │
└─────────────────────────┘  └─────────────────────────────┘
```

```
┌─────────────────────────┐  ┌─────────────────────────────┐
│    2. Use as Medicine   │  │      3. Classification      │
│  • [ 42 ]               │  │ • Amanita muscaria          │
│  • [ 43 ]               │  │ • mycorrhizal               │
│                         │  │ • annual                    │
└─────────────────────────┘  └─────────────────────────────┘
```

4. Mechanism [44]   5. Final Statement   [45]

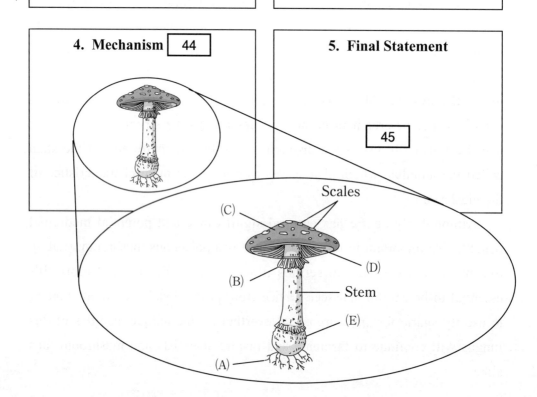

第2回　英語（リーディング）

問 1 Which of the following should you **not** include for ☐ 41 ?

① appears in folk and fairy tales

② approximately 5 million species have been found

③ found in both warm and cold forests

④ used in religious ceremonies

⑤ very easy to recognize

問 2 For the **Use as Medicine** slide, select two features of the fly agaric which are most likely true. (The order does not matter.) ☐ 42 ・ ☐ 43

① Fly agaric has been proved to have positive effects on stress and fatigue.

② Fly agaric is studied for its possible usefulness in treating some nervous disorders.

③ It was believed in some religions that fly agaric was a medicine brought by the gods.

④ Some substances in fly agaric might be effective against certain organ diseases.

⑤ The Vikings are said to have eaten fly agaric to feel relaxed after fighting.

— 33 —

問3 Complete the missing labels on the illustration of a fly agaric for the **Mechanism** slide. 44

① (A) Annulus   (B) Mycelium   (C) Volva
   (D) Pileus   (E) Gills

② (A) Mycelium   (B) Annulus   (C) Pileus
   (D) Gills   (E) Volva

③ (A) Mycelium   (B) Gills   (C) Pileus
   (D) Annulus   (E) Volva

④ (A) Pileus   (B) Mycelium   (C) Volva
   (D) Gills   (E) Annulus

⑤ (A) Volva   (B) Pileus   (C) Gills
   (D) Annulus   (E) Mycelium

問4 Which is the best statement for the final slide? 45

① Fly agaric has traditionally been used as a medicine because it is agreeable to the human sense of taste.

② Fly agaric should be more widely used on a daily basis because of its proven healing effects.

③ Fly agaric will most likely be used more because it is easily found due to its visual characteristics.

④ While fly agaric may be effective for some diseases, it can cause serious health problems if consumed in large quantities.

第2回　英語（リーディング）

問5　According to the passage, which statement is true?　46

① Fly agaric grows in a square shape mostly underground, with only the fruiting bodies visible above ground. This means that it is probably stronger than any other fungus.

② The life cycle of fly agaric is generally not affected by the environment. This enables it to live even in the harsh environment of the northern hemisphere.

③ The mycelium can produce new fruiting bodies once a year; fly agaric normally reproduces itself several times a year.

④ Trees get nutrients from the soil through fly agaric, and the fly agaric obtains sugars and other nutrients from the trees, so they are dependent on each other for survival.

第 3 回

（80分）

実 戦 問 題

第3回　実戦問題

英　　語（リーディング）

各大問の英文や図表を読み，解答番号 1 ～ 46 にあてはまるものとして最も適当な選択肢を選びなさい。

第１問 （配点　6）

You are a university student in the US and you are interested in joining a creative writing summer course. You find a website for such a course.

Join YCW's fifth annual intensive creative writing course. Stay with other young writers in the camp and learn from published writers and artists.

One Week Intensive Course

Dates：August 20th to 27th 2023
Location：Camp YCW, Lake Washington, Seattle
Course Price：$750 – accommodation and food provided (bring cash to use in the camp store)
Optional Activities：hiking, lake cruise

Courses Available

◆ **Shakespeare Course**：You will analyze two Shakespeare plays with the help of an award-winning screenwriter. You will also work in small groups to write a short play which will be performed on the final morning of the course in front of your campmates.
◆ **Bronte Course**：Karen Nelson, a published novelist, will lead this course. She will teach you the basics of writing, techniques for storytelling, and how to get your work published. Your short stories will be made into a book, which you will receive in the mail a week after the course.
◆ **Lee Course**：Named after Stan Lee, the creator of some of the world's most famous comics, this course will teach you the basics of comic writing. You will also learn about Japanese manga from published manga artist Kana Kagawa. Your work will be shown as a slide presentation to your campmates on the final evening.

— 2 —

第3回　英語（リーディング）

▲ **How to Apply**

1. Complete the **online application form** by June 7th, 2023. Please state your preferred course.

2. You will receive email confirmation of your place after June 8th.

*Please note that places are limited to 20 students for each course. If too many students apply for one course, places will be given at random. Students who do not get their preferred course may cancel their application or join a less popular course.

問1　All camp instructors are ☐ 1 ☐ .

① experts whose work has been published or highly evaluated

② knowledgeable about the Japanese language

③ qualified teachers of literature

④ writers who have been awarded a prize for their novels

問2　On the last morning of the camp, campers will ☐ 2 ☐ .

① enjoy a slide presentation of Japanese manga

② go fishing in Lake Washington

③ read a book created by the Bronte Course students

④ watch a play written during the camp

問3　What will happen if a course is too popular? ☐ 3 ☐

① Each student will have an equal chance of being chosen.

② Each student's writing skills will be checked.

③ Students who applied earlier will be chosen.

④ Students will have to take a placement test.

— 3 —

第2問 (配点 10)

You are a member of your school's student council. You and the other members have been discussing how to help the younger students in the school become more active. To get ideas, you are reading an article about a school fitness program a school in the US started.

Walk-to-School Project

Studies have shown that the activity levels of school students are dropping each year. In addition, fewer students are walking or cycling to school than in previous years. This lack of exercise means that students are becoming unhealthy and overweight.

Although many parents want their children to walk to and from school, they are worried about safety. For that reason, they drive their children to school or put them on a school bus, even though they live within walking distance of school.

Our school started the Walk-to-School project on November 1st on a trial basis. We had a group of students living in the same neighborhood walk to school together with adult supervisors. Three walking routes were organized, with two adult volunteers per route. Seventy-five students from grades 1 and 2 participated in the beginning, but only 60 students were using the Walk-to-School program by the start of the winter vacation in December. Let's look at feedback from students and parents to find out why.

Student/Parent Feedback

M.M. Thanks to this project, many students, including my daughter, have made new friends from different classes. They have also begun to enjoy exercise more. I consider it a success.

K.J. I enjoyed the walking in the beginning, but I didn't like it on rainy days. It rains a lot in winter so I'm thinking of taking the bus on rainy days.

R.B. A few weeks after the project began, both volunteers on my son's route had to retire for family reasons. I didn't trust the students to walk to school by themselves so I started driving my son to school again, as did other parents.

V.K. My friend wanted to join too but she lives in an area not covered by the project. I wish she could join too.

W.L. I love the Walk-to-School project because I can talk to my friends before school and it motivates me to get up early and leave the house on time.

第3回　英語（リーディング）

問1　The aim of the Walk-to-School Project was to ⬚4 .

① allow parents free time in the morning

② cut transportation costs for parents

③ give students the chance to exercise

④ help students get to school on time

問2　One **fact** about the Walk-to-School Project is that ⬚5 .

① every student participated

② fifteen students quit the project

③ it is a permanent project

④ it was canceled on rainy days

問3　From the feedback, ⬚6 were problems reported by students or parents.

A : lack of interest by parents

B : limited areas included in the project

C : road conditions in winter

D : too few volunteers

① **A** and **B**

② **A** and **C**

③ **A** and **D**

④ **B** and **C**

⑤ **B** and **D**

⑥ **C** and **D**

問4　One of the opinions about the Walk-to-School Project is that 　7　 .

① it helped many students to get to know other students
② it started too early in the morning
③ it was faster than taking the bus
④ parents started to trust their children more

問5　The author's question was answered by 　8　 .

① K.J.
② M.M.
③ R.B.
④ V.K.
⑤ W.L.

第3回　英語（リーディング）

（下 書 き 用 紙）

英語（リーディング）の試験問題は次に続く。

第3問 (配点 9)

You share an apartment with other exchange students. Your kitchen is messy, so you have decided to clean and organize it. You read the following article written by an expert home organizer.

Maximizing Kitchen Efficiency

When I first returned to work after having my children, I realized that I needed to make my life as organized and efficient as possible, to stay on schedule, and to maximize the time I could spend with my children. I noticed that so much of my time involved preparing food, so I decided to organize my kitchen first. Here is how I succeeded in making my kitchen easier to use, and decreasing the amount of time I spent cooking and tidying up.

The first step to organizing a kitchen is to get rid of clutter. I decided that any items such as plates, dishes or pans that I hadn't used for a year could be sold, recycled, or thrown away. This freed up a lot of storage space. Next, I put all the equipment I use most often near the places I use it. For example, frying pans that I use daily I put in the shelves to the right of the cooker. As a right-handed person, this means I can easily pull the pans out with my right hand and use them on the cooker immediately. Coffee cups were placed next to the coffee machine, while storage containers were put on the shelf above the fridge.

第3回　英語（リーディング）

After that, I focused on food. Sometimes when food is in boxes or packages, it is difficult to see how much is left. I often felt disappointed when I realized a package was almost empty and I had forgotten to buy a replacement. To solve that problem, I bought clear glass jars for items such as cereal, flour, pasta, and sugar so that I can easily see how much is left. Now, I use my smartphone to take a photo of my shelves before I go to the store so that I can easily check what I need to buy.

Finally, I made a virtual library of my favorite recipes. I often wrote down good meal ideas on scraps of paper or in notepads, but this not only created a pile of paper, it also made it difficult to find what I wanted quickly. Instead, I photographed all my recipes and stored them on my tablet. I threw away all the old paper and now everything is available at the touch of a button. I can even e-mail them to my husband when it's his turn to cook!

問1　Put the following events (① ~ ④) into the order they happened.

| 9 | → | 10 | → | 11 | → | 12 |

① The writer changed the location of her utensils.

② The writer created digital copies of her recipes.

③ The writer disposed of unused equipment.

④ The writer purchased transparent containers.

問2　If you follow the writer's advice to create an efficient kitchen, you should 13 .

① avoid throwing away items that are rarely used

② make sure items are stored in logical locations

③ use things for a year before getting rid of them

④ wait until food has run out before buying it

— 9 —

問3 From this article, you understand that the writer 14 .

① spends less money on groceries than before

② wants her husband to do more cooking

③ wastes less time in the kitchen these days

④ would like her children to help with housework

第3回　英語（リーディング）

（下 書 き 用 紙）

英語（リーディング）の試験問題は次に続く。

第4問 （配点 12）

In English class you are writing about a social issue you are interested in. This is your most recent draft. You are now working on revisions based on comments from your teacher.

The Benefits of Playing Computer Games	**Comments**
Video games have a bad reputation among parents and teachers. They often believe that video games have no benefits at all and are a bad influence on a child's studies and social life. ⁽¹⁾∧ Some studies show that there are multiple benefits to game playing for young people.	*(1) Add a linking sentence to introduce the main topic of the essay.*
First, research by psychologists has shown that playing certain types of video games improves the thinking skills of the players. These thinking skills include navigation skills, memory, and reasoning. This is particularly true for shooting games, which involve a player finding and shooting targets while trying to avoid being attacked. In fact, gamers polish these skills just as much by playing video games as they would on a real-life course designed to teach these skills.	
Second, a long-term study has found that games may develop problem-solving skills. Role-playing games are especially good for developing this skill. The study found that the longer a student plays role-playing video games, the greater the improvement in school grades the following year. In short, playing role-playing games can ⁽²⁾<u>improve school grades</u>.	*(2) Avoid words you used in the previous sentences and try to use a different phrase.*

— 12 —

第3回 英語（リーディング）

(3) ∧ Games that are short and easy to play can encourage relaxation and make the player feel happier than before. Put simply, playing video games can make young people feel good. This is important in a society where depression and mental health problems are becoming more common.

(3) Insert the topic sentence for this paragraph.

In summary, video games have many positive points. (4) ∧ Of course, there are negative points as well, but if people use games in moderation, they can benefit them in many ways.

(4) Summarize those positive points here.

Teacher's Comment
Very interesting! Maybe I should play video games to make myself smarter! ^^

問1　Based on comment (1), which is the most appropriate linking sentence to add?　15

① Actually, this is probably correct.

② However, this is not always the case.

③ In fact, most studies support this.

④ In short, this is not supported at all.

問2　Based on comment (2), which is the most appropriate phrase to use instead?　16

① cause school performance to decline

② lead to higher academic results

③ make students do more school work

④ result in a drop in achievement

— 13 —

問3 Which is the most appropriate topic sentence to add based on comment (3)? 　17

① Finally, it is better for a person's mood and mental health to play long and difficult video games.

② Finally, playing video games has little effect in either direction on a person's happiness or moods.

③ Finally, the longer a person plays video games, the more their mental health is negatively affected.

④ Finally, video games help to improve a person's moods and prevent them from feeling anxious.

問4 Which sentence should you add, based on comment (4)? 　18

① They develop a person's ability to design, work hard, and socialize with other young people.

② They improve cognitive ability, polish solution-finding skills, and make a person feel good.

③ They protect a person's mind, and their ability to study, and increase depression.

④ They refine the shooting skills of the players, their ability to concentrate, and their energy levels.

第3回　英語（リーディング）

（下書き用紙）

英語（リーディング）の試験問題は次に続く。

第5問 (配点 16)

You have decided to volunteer as an assistant Japanese language teacher in Australia next year. To prepare, you are reading two articles about language teaching techniques.

Task-Based Learning
K. Matsui
English Teacher, Iwahashi High School

When I was a high school student many years ago in Japan, all my classes were taught using the "grammar-translation method." In fact, even when I became an English teacher myself, that was the method I used. I taught my students an English grammar rule and its meaning in Japanese, then we practiced translating Japanese into English using this rule. The students learned grammar in great detail, and they were able to pass their exams. It was boring but effective.

However, when I took a break from my career and studied at a language school in Australia, I realized there was another way to learn a language. My teacher used "task-based learning." This means that instead of focusing on a grammar rule, we were given a task to complete in English, then we looked at the language after we had finished the task. For example, we were given the task of planning a travel schedule for a friend. We had to research accommodations and activities, role-play calling a hotel to make a reservation, then write an email to a friend. During this task we used reading, writing, speaking and listening skills, and practiced language without feeling it was "work." When the project or "task" was over, our teacher gave us advice about our English without using any Japanese at all.

I decided to use this technique more when I returned to Japan. Now, as a high school teacher, I use task-based learning as much as I can in my English lessons. I have noticed that my students are more engaged and their ability to actually use the language they have learned has improved. I believe it is time that the old-fashioned grammar-translation method was retired. I also think that the use of Japanese by English teachers in the classroom should not be encouraged.

The Grammar-Translation Method
M. Suzuki
Researcher, Kanto Language University

I enjoyed reading Ms. Matsui's experience of task-based language learning, and I agree that it can be very beneficial to intermediate language learners. It encourages communication and allows the students to understand that language is a tool for everyday life.

However, I do not believe we should completely get rid of grammar translation as a method of language teaching, particularly when we teach beginners. For example, take a class of 12-year-old Japanese students. They have very limited exposure to English, so they know few words and even less grammar. It would be impossible for them to complete any kind of meaningful task in English. It would be even more difficult to explain the task to them in English because they would not understand the teacher's instructions. We need to give them the tools of vocabulary and grammar and explain it to them in language they understand while they are at the beginner stage.

In one study conducted at a school in Jordan, researchers compared test results of students taught an English grammar point in the source language (their native language: Arabic), with the results of students taught only in the target language (English). They randomly divided students into two groups of ten of equal academic ability. Group A was taught a specific grammar point using the grammar-translation method, with instructions in their native language. Group B was taught the same grammar point using just English and a number of example sentences. The two groups were then given the same grammar test. As you can see, there is a significant difference in the average test scores of the two groups.

Therefore, while I agree that task-based learning is a great teaching tool, we should not give up on grammar translation if we want our students to accurately learn how to read and write English and pass the all-important university entrance exams. I believe a good English course incorporates a number of different teaching techniques to give students a thorough understanding of the language and motivate them in a way that grammar translation does not.

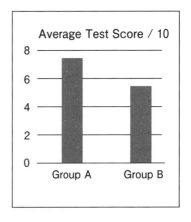

問 1　Matsui believes that ☐19☐ .

① grammar translation is ineffective in preparing for exams
② task-based learning is the best way to pass exams
③ teaching grammar is boring for English teachers
④ teaching in Japanese is not helpful for students

問 2　In the study introduced by Suzuki, students were ☐20☐ .

① compared after being taught using different methods
② divided into two groups of different levels
③ not able to produce better results after the experiment
④ taught example sentences in their native language

問 3　Suzuki explains that while task-based language learning is effective in improving intermediate students' ☐21☐ skills, grammar translation ensures that students learn the ☐22☐ language accurately, and is therefore an important method when teaching beginners. (Choose the best one for each box from options ① ～ ⑥.)

① communication
② job
③ source
④ study
⑤ target
⑥ writing

— 18 —

第3回　英語（リーディング）

問4　Both writers agree that grammar translation is helpful for 23 .

① learning how to write creatively
② motivating intermediate students
③ scoring well in exams
④ seeing English as a tool

問5　Which additional information would be the best to further support Suzuki's argument? 24

① How to combine the task-based method and the grammar-translation method most successfully
② What makes grammar-translation learning more enjoyable for advanced students
③ Whether foreign language teachers should use their native language in class
④ Why task-based language learning is effective at the beginner stage

第6問 (配点 18)

You are working on an essay about whether self-driving cars should be permitted on roads. You will follow the steps below.

Step 1: Read and understand various viewpoints about self-driving cars.
Step 2: Take a position about whether or not self-driving cars should be allowed.
Step 3: Create an outline for an essay using additional sources.

[Step 1] Read various sources

Author A (Elderly Person)

I'm excited about this new technology. As I get older, my reactions are getting worse, so it's too dangerous for me to drive a regular car now. However, if I had a self-driving car, I would be able to keep my independence for many more years. This technology will be very useful for disabled people, too. Anything that allows the elderly and disabled people to move around safely by themselves is a good thing. The only thing that worries me is how expensive these cars are!

Author B (Driving Instructor)

I'm not worried about an increase in self-driving cars. Rather, my concern is that we will see more unsuitable drivers on the road. There are certain situations where a car will switch from self-driving to driver-operated, and we still need everyone to be sufficiently good at driving without artificial intelligence. On the other hand, this technology benefits people who can't drive normal cars now, such as senior citizens or people with disabilities. They will be able to stay independent for longer.

Author C (Car Engineer)

As an engineer for a car company, I have no worries about the safety of self-driving vehicles. In fact, we specifically design these cars to be safer than human-operated cars. In my country, 85% of car accidents are caused by human error. If we can reduce this human error, we can save hundreds of lives every year. Of course, I worry a little about computer security, as there is always a chance that the vehicle's internal computer can get hacked, but I am confident that we have the skills and knowledge to deal with this quickly.

— 20 —

第3回　英語（リーディング）

Author D (Police officer)

A lot of my daily work involves warning or arresting people for road offenses, such as speeding, drunk driving, or dangerous driving. I have heard that when this new technology becomes available, it may reduce traffic accidents. However, I don't believe this will actually happen, because there are so many things that can go wrong, causing more accidents. Overall, I don't think it is a good idea to bring this new technology in. The answer to the problems I mentioned is stricter driving tests and better laws.

Author E (Taxi driver)

I have been following this new technology with interest because I work as a taxi driver and my industry will be greatly impacted. I worry that not only private vehicles but also taxis and buses will eventually be replaced by driverless cars. Although the cars themselves will be more expensive than a regular car at first, they will start to become cheaper. At that point, transportation companies will decide that drivers are an unnecessary expense. I'm afraid taxi and bus drivers might not be able to work as we do now.

問1　Both Authors A and B mention that ☐ 25 ☐ .

① cars with this technology will become more expensive, so the elderly cannot use them

② families will be positively affected by self-driving cars because grandparents can help more

③ fewer people will take driving lessons because these new cars can drive themselves

④ self-driving cars will allow certain groups of people to become drivers and maintain independence

— 21 —

問2　Author C states that 　26　 .

① although many people worry about the safety of these cars, they are no different to regular cars

② by removing the need for human drivers, these new cars will help reduce the number of accidents

③ people will become better drivers with these new cars because the controls are much easier to operate

④ the cars are designed so that if there is the risk of an accident, the car switches to driver-operated mode

[Step 2] Take a position

問3　Now that you understand the various viewpoints, you have taken a position on the introduction of self-driving cars, and have written it out as below. Choose the best options to complete 　27　 , 　28　 , and 　29　 .

Your position: Self-driving cars should be allowed on the road.

- Authors 　27　 and 　28　 support your position.
- The main argument of the two authors: 　29　 .

Options for 　27　 and 　28　 (the order does not matter):

① A
② B
③ C
④ D
⑤ E

— 22 —

第3回　英語（リーディング）

Options for 29

① Accidents will now be the responsibility of car manufacturers, rather than human drivers

② Introducing self-driving technology will allow people to safely operate cars regardless of their driving skills

③ Self-driving cars are much less likely to get hacked by dangerous people than regular cars

④ The number of people who are arrested for drinking alcohol and driving will drop dramatically

[Step 3] Create an outline using sources A and B

Outline of your essay:

Self-driving cars are the future

Introduction

In recent years, more car manufacturers are developing self-driving cars. Although many people are worried about this technology, they should be allowed on the roads.

Body

Reason 1: [From Step 2]

Reason 2: [Based on Source A] ······ 30

Reason 3: [Based on Source B] ······ 31

Conclusion

For these reasons, people should be permitted to buy and use self-driving cars.

— 23 —

Source A

Cars and vans currently account for about 10% of the world's carbon emissions. Therefore, it is very important that every step is taken to reduce this amount. One way to do this is by moving toward self-driving cars. Now, cars burn a large amount of energy when driven at high speeds, when braking, and when accelerating too quickly. Self-driving cars, on the other hand, are smart enough to optimize speed and acceleration to burn as little fuel as possible. They can also choose the most efficient route for journeys. In addition, if these cars eventually become completely driverless, households will need fewer vehicles because the same car can drive all the family members to work or school by itself, without needing lots of short journeys in different cars. Finally, as technology improves, the weight of the car will decrease, leading to even less burning of fuels. Now, batteries are heavy, but they are likely to get lighter over time.

Source B

A study by an insurance company in the US show that the amount we pay for insurance is likely to change if self-driving cars become more common. The calculations show the amount people pay currently for insurance for different types of car, compared to future estimates if the car becomes self-driving. This is because self-driving cars are less likely to have accidents.

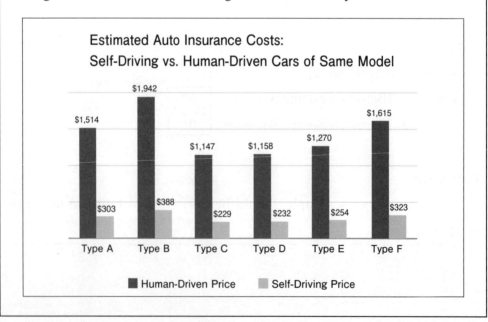

第3回　英語（リーディング）

問4　Based on Source A, which of the following is the most appropriate for Reason 2? 　30

① Human-driven cars are about 10% more inefficient than self-driving cars.

② Newer self-driving cars have lighter batteries and brake faster than older ones, so they are more efficient to drive.

③ Self-driving cars can move faster for longer and have lighter batteries than human-driven cars, so they use less CO_2-emitting fuel.

④ Self-driving cars may be better for the environment because they are more fuel efficient and can cut down the number of car journeys.

問5　For Reason 3, you have decided to write, "Self-driving vehicles are likely to save people money". Based on Source B, which option best supports this statement? 　31

① Around 50% of self-driving cars will have cheaper insurance than human-driven cars because they are cheaper to repair if they get damaged.

② Insurance costs for self-driving cars are half the price of human-driven cars due to changes in the car insurance industry.

③ More people will switch to smaller cars and self-driving cars because they are both cheaper to insure than regular ones.

④ Owners of self-driving cars may save around $1,000 each year in insurance costs because these cars are less likely to be involved in accidents.

第7問 （配点 15）

Your science teacher has asked everyone to research an important woman in science and present your research to the class, using notes. You have found an article about Mileva Marić, Albert Einstein's first wife.

The Life of Mileva Marić

Everyone knows the name "Albert Einstein." He is considered the most important physicist of the 20th century, winning the Nobel Prize in Physics in 1921. However, few people know about his first wife, Serbian physicist Mileva Marić. She was associated with Einstein between 1896, when they first met, and 1919, when they divorced. It is believed by many that Mileva was the key to Einstein's success.

Mileva Marić was born in Serbia in 1875 to a wealthy family. All of her education before university was completed in her home country. At that time, only boys were allowed to attend physics lectures at her high school, but her father recognized her ability and obtained special permission for her to participate. In 1886, she entered Zurich Polytechnic in Switzerland, where she enrolled at the same time as Albert Einstein. She was the only woman in her course, which indicates she must have been very talented because opportunities for female scientists at that time were very limited. Mileva and Albert spent many years studying together. It is clear from the letters they exchanged at the time that she greatly influenced his studies. Mileva and Albert finished their classes with very similar grades, except in applied physics, where Mileva achieved much higher grades than Albert.

Albert's parents opposed his relationship with Mileva because of her nationality, her religion, and her high intellect. They believed she would not make a suitable wife for him. However, they continued their relationship and married in 1903.

— 26 —

第3回　英語（リーディング）

Even before their marriage, the couple worked together on research. In 1900, they submitted their first research paper which was signed only by Albert. Despite this, both Mileva and Albert referred to it as "our article" in letters to each other and friends. Why did Mileva not add her name to the article? It is believed there are two main reasons. The first is that Mileva wanted Albert to make a name for himself so that his parents would allow him to marry her, and the second is that there was great prejudice against women at that time. By having their research published only in a man's name, it was more likely to be received positively.

1905 was Einstein's most productive year. He published five major articles in that year, one of which led to his Nobel Prize in 1921. Mileva mentioned to friends at the time that she and her husband would stay up late every night working on these papers. In addition, Einstein's biographer stated that Mileva was the one who checked the articles and sent them out while Einstein rested. Albert himself said to a friend, "I need my wife. She solves for me all my mathematical problems." Despite this, it was Albert who became the celebrated physicist while Mileva quietly worked in the background.

In 1912, Albert began a secret relationship with Elsa Lowenthal, his cousin. He also lived in different European cities during this time for work. This caused the collapse of his marriage to Mileva, and they divorced in 1919. Albert and Mileva were not on good terms after their divorce, and there is evidence that Albert's lawyers were worried that the truth of Mileva's input would be revealed after her death and the "Einstein myth" be destroyed.

Mileva Marić is just one of many female scientists in history whose work has been hidden. It is only recently that her influence on Einstein has been acknowledged. As with many women of her time, she abandoned her own wishes in order to support her husband's success. In fact, without Mileva Marić, Albert Einstein would probably not have become the household name he is today.

Your notes:

The Life of Mileva Marić

About Mileva Marić

- Spent her youth in her home country of Serbia.
- Met Albert Einstein at university in Switzerland.
- Evidence of her talent in physics is that [32] .

Influential people in Mileva's life

- Her father, who fought for her to study alongside boys.
- Albert's parents, who opposed their marriage, which probably caused her to [33] .

Influential events

Enrolled at Zurich Polytechnic → [34] → [35] → [36] → [37]

Mileva and Albert's legacy

Albert's lawyers were concerned that [38] .

What we can learn from Mileva's story

- [39]
- [40]

第3回　英語（リーディング）

問1　Choose the best option for ☐ 32 ☐.

   ① she got a scholarship to Zurich Polytechnic

   ② she got the best grades in her high school

   ③ she was acknowledged by Einstein in college

   ④ she was the sole female admitted to her college course

問2　Choose the best option for ☐ 33 ☐.

   ① avoid writing her name on joint research papers

   ② complete her own research with no input from Albert

   ③ move to various European cities without Albert

   ④ stop helping Albert write his physics research papers

問3　Choose **four** out of the five events (① ～ ⑤) and rearrange them in the order they happened. ☐ 34 ☐ → ☐ 35 ☐ → ☐ 36 ☐ → ☐ 37 ☐

   ① Albert and his cousin started a secret romantic relationship.

   ② Albert got better grades than Mileva in applied physics.

   ③ Albert published the paper that led to his Nobel Prize.

   ④ Mileva and Albert finally became husband and wife.

   ⑤ Mileva and Albert finished and published their first article.

問4 Choose the best option for 38 .

① Mileva had not supported Albert as much as she had told friends

② Mileva would not get the recognition she deserved for her work

③ Mileva's contribution would become known, ruining Albert's reputation

④ papers the couples published together would not be found after her death

問5 Choose the best two options for 39 and 40 . (The order does not matter.)

① Albert would have been more successful without his parent's strong opposition.

② Einstein was a very important physicist, but his wife's influence may be greater than believed.

③ Mileva is an example of a female scientist whose work has not been fully recognized.

④ More Nobel Prizes should be awarded to female scientists than to male scientists.

⑤ Most of Albert Einstein's work was completed by his wife and not him.

— 30 —

第3回　英語（リーディング）

（下 書 き 用 紙）

英語（リーディング）の試験問題は次に続く。

第8問 (配点 14)

You are in a student group preparing for a university biology presentation. You are using the following passage to create your part of the presentation on useful viruses.

When you think of viruses, you probably think of disease. After all, viruses are responsible for many of the illnesses that regularly affect humans. Influenza, the common cold, COVID-19, and countless other diseases are caused by viruses that specifically infect humans. For that reason, many people believe that all viruses are bad and must be avoided at all costs. However, that is not strictly true. There are many viruses that live inside us that are not responsible for disease at all. In fact, the opposite is true, because many viruses that live inside our digestive systems actually keep us healthy by killing harmful bacteria. Those viruses are called "bacteriophages," and they do not harm human cells at all. Moreover, scientists have also been researching other types of viruses that can kill cancer cells. These cancer-killing viruses have already been used to treat skin cancer in patients, and it is hoped that more treatment of this kind will be developed in the future.

The interesting thing about viruses is that they are not really "alive." They are not made out of cells, and they cannot make energy or reproduce by themselves. In simple terms, they are just a small piece of genetic material, such as DNA, surrounded by a protein case. Because viruses are very simple structures, they are very small. In fact, most viruses are 100-times smaller than a human cell. They are so small that they cannot be seen under a standard microscope. However, it's a virus's size and structure that allows it to bind to the outside of a host cell, insert its genetic instructions, then use the host cell's machinery to make copies of itself. The attack on a cell by a virus in this way usually results in the death of the host cell.

It is a virus's ability to kill a host cell that has allowed researchers to develop cancer treatments using viruses. In 2015, the first virus treatment

— 32 —

第3回　英語（リーディング）

for cancer was approved by the US government for use on patients. Scientists used a herpes virus, which usually causes mouth sores in humans. They modified the outer protein case of the virus so that it ignored healthy cells and attached itself to the outside of cancer cells. They also modified the genetic material of the virus so that it produced molecules called antigens that would attract human immune cells to the site of the cancer. Doctors could then inject these modified viruses into the site of the cancer every two weeks. The viruses would use the cancer cells to reproduce, killing the host cells in the process. The body's immune system would also attack the cancer cells itself. In this way, large skin cancer tumors have been destroyed.

There are many benefits of this treatment compared to standard medicine. First, there are fewer bad side effects because the virus only attacks cancer cells and leaves healthy cells alone. It is also a good way to treat skin tumors that cannot be removed by surgery. In addition, the viruses are injected directly into the tumor, so the treatment is targeted by location. This treatment is also easier for patients because it involves short visits to a doctor instead of long stays in hospital. On the other hand, there may be mild side effects such as fever and tiredness. In addition, this treatment cannot be used on patients with weak immune systems.

Currently, scientists are testing a similar treatment for patients with an eye disease that causes vision to gradually decline. Scientists have altered the genetic information in a virus so that it can deliver treatment to the eyes of patients with this disease to stop the vision loss. This treatment has been successful on laboratory mice, and it is hoped that it can be used in humans in the near future. However, one of the biggest challenges associated with this type of therapy is preventing the body's own immune system from identifying and killing the virus before it can deliver its important package to the cells that need it.

In summary, viruses can be used for good. They can be used to fight cancer and deliver important genes to the site of genetic disease. In the future, many other human diseases may be cured by specially adapted viruses.

Your presentation slides:

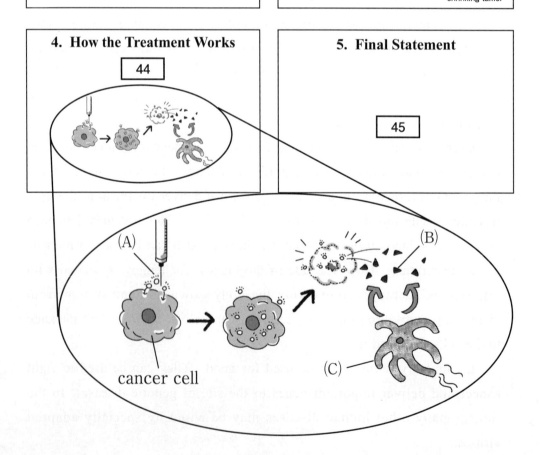

第3回　英語（リーディング）

問1　Which of the following should you **not** include for ⬚41⬚ ?

① Help human cells reproduce quickly

② Most viruses are one-hundredth the size of a human cell

③ No reproduction without a host

④ Reproduction usually kills the host cell

⑤ Simple genetic material in a protein case

問2　For the **Benefits of This Treatment** slide, select two aspects of this treatment that are beneficial to the patient. (The order does not matter.) ⬚42⬚ · ⬚43⬚

① By using modified herpes viruses, the patient also becomes immune to future herpes infections.

② It is not so hard on the patient because it only requires short visits to a doctor.

③ It is usually used to make the removal of tumors by surgery much easier and faster.

④ The modified herpes viruses are adapted to attack only cancer cells, so healthy cells do not die.

⑤ This treatment causes no side effects, unlike cancer medicine which causes fever.

問3　Complete the missing labels on the illustration for the **How the Treatment Works** slide. ⬚44⬚

① (A) antigens　　　　　(B) immune cell
　 (C) modified virus

② (A) antigens　　　　　(B) modified virus
　 (C) immune cell

③ (A) immune cell　　　 (B) modified virus
　 (C) antigens

④ (A) modified virus　　 (B) antigens
　 (C) immune cell

⑤ (A) modified virus　　 (B) immune cell
　 (C) antigens

問4　Which is the best statement for the final slide?　45

①　Although many viruses cause disease, some are actually beneficial to humans. Furthermore, some viruses can be adapted so that they target and kill unhealthy cells.

②　In the future, our knowledge of viruses will help us cure diseases such as cancer. However, until this technology develops, viruses are dangerous to humans.

③　The number of viruses that cure diseases is greater than the number that cause them, so their negative reputation is no longer deserved.

④　Viruses that cause disease and illness have sometimes evolved to cure diseases such as cancer in humans.

問5　Why is the body's own immune system a barrier to the effectiveness of virus-based treatments?　46

①　The body's immune system may find the virus and kill it before it can treat the disease.

②　The human immune system is not good at reacting to viruses that enter the body.

③　Viruses cannot be recognized by the human immune system so the treatment is useless.

④　Viruses may cause the body's immune system to kill healthy cells instead of cancer cells.

第 4 回
（80分）

実 戦 問 題

英　　語（リーディング）

各大問の英文や図表を読み，解答番号 1 〜 45 にあてはまるものとして最も適当な選択肢を選びなさい。

第１問 （配点　6）

You are looking at an advertisement for an art gallery in Wellington, New Zealand and notice information about a competition for college students. You are considering taking part.

College Students — Transform Your Trash!

Time to clean out your room and get rid of your trash? Read on!

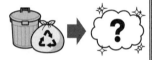

Your task is to keep a seven-day diary of all the rubbish from your big clean-up and make something 'cool' or useful!

Rules of Entry

◆ Record your trash every day for one week between April 1 and May 19.
◆ Make a piece of art or something useful using your trash.
◆ Take 3 to 5 pictures of your work after the seven days and upload them on the relevant link with your trash diary by 23:59 May 26.

→ **Upload Art**
→ **Upload Something Useful**

◆ Explain in under 30 words why you made your entry.

Vote for the Best!

◆ You can only vote once in each of the categories, and not for your own work. Click the link to look at all the entries and vote from May 27 until the last day of the month at 20:00.

→ **Vote**

◆ Each vote costs 1.5 NZD, which will be donated to recycling awareness.

第4回　英語（リーディング）

Winners

The winner of the 'Art' category will have his / her piece exhibited in our gallery until January 5 next year!

The winner of the 'Something Useful' category will have his / her work reproduced by a professional local artist and sold in our gift shop!

Those in first, second and third place will each get two free tickets for our summer 'It's Trash?' exhibition!

問1　You can upload your work between 　1　 .

① April 1 and May 19

② April 8 and May 26

③ May 27 and May 31

④ June 1 and January 5

問2　When entering this competition you have to 　2　 .

① buy something you want at the gift shop

② collect different kinds of trash

③ create something with your unwanted things

④ vote for two different entries

問3　If you come in second or third place you will be able to 　3　 .

① meet an artist who works in Wellington

② select something from the gift shop

③ take someone to see a summer exhibition

④ visit the gallery whenever until January

— 3 —

第2問　(配点　10)

You are a member of staff for your school English magazine. Paula, an assistant teacher from the UK, has submitted an article.

Do you believe in aliens? A recent survey showed people in Mexico in particular are believers, but not as many as Russia where around 70% of people think we humans are not the only intelligent lifeform. Whereas just under half of people in China think so, in Holland about one in four people would agree.

So, should we spend more time studying space?

A well-known science magazine states the pros and cons of exploring space.

Advantages of space exploration are:
- Many technologies designed to let us go into space now improve our lives at home.
- Most of our studies are done from Earth, so we don't even need to travel outside our planet.
- It is important for finding another planet where humans can survive after using all of Earth's resources.

However, researching about space is incredibly expensive, and it is necessary to use a lot of natural resources as fuels. We are also turning space into a huge trash can, with all the garbage we are leaving up there.

Men and younger generations tend to believe in aliens the most, perhaps because of their love of alien movies and the high-tech special effects today which seem so real. Religious people often believe that humans are unique because they were created by God. Though more than half of us think that there must be life beyond Earth, more than three out of five people, myself included, don't think anything is likely to be as intelligent as humans. I wonder if it is worth trying to find out the truth.

第4回 英語 (リーディング)

問1 In terms of the ratio of people who believe in aliens, which shows the countries' ranking from **highest to lowest**? ⬚4

① China — Holland — Russia
② China — Russia — Holland
③ Holland — China — Russia
④ Holland — Russia — China
⑤ Russia — China — Holland
⑥ Russia — Holland — China

問2 According to the well-known scientific magazine, one advantage of exploring space is that ⬚5 .

① we can make life more exciting
② we go to outer space more easily
③ we have more advanced technology
④ we will find a healthier planet

問3 One way of thinking mentioned in Paula's article is ⬚6

① 'Humans, made by God, are a special lifeform.'
② 'Men like science fiction movies best.'
③ 'More study on our own planet is necessary.'
④ 'Space is a good place to put trash.'

— 5 —

問4 Which best summarises Paula's opinion about aliens? 7

　　① It is unlikely that they exist.

　　② People might never know the truth.

　　③ Real aliens are unlikely to be very intelligent.

　　④ Whether you believe doesn't depend on your culture.

問5 Which is the most suitable title for the article? 8

　　① God or Science?

　　② Protecting Our Planet

　　③ Space — Should We Know More?

　　④ The Human Imagination

第4回　英語（リーディング）

（下 書 き 用 紙）

英語（リーディング）の試験問題は次に続く。

第 3 問 （配点 9 ）

You are interested in joining a worthwhile project and have found a story in a catalogue about volunteering.

Building for the Future

Last July, I headed to a small town in Romania, with seven other students from my school and two former students who graduated last year. Our destination was a rural town in a poor part of this developing nation, and our goal was to help as volunteers for Habitat for Humanity. We would spend two weeks as part of a project designed to bring about permanent, lasting changes to a struggling community. I had absolutely no building experience except for painting, which I finally put into practice the day before I left Romania.

After a short flight and a long bus ride through beautiful countryside, interrupted only by a group of sheep being driven along a narrow road, we arrived. Not long after being shown the basic accommodation where we would stay, we were handed a hard protective hat and a schedule. Some 200 people from various parts of the world had been there weeks or days and would tell newcomers what to do.

I arrived at the site to find neat holes dug in the ground, building materials organized and laid out with the necessary tools for the job, and a tent for breaks. The first day my team's task was to cut wood to a certain size, and then build an outside wall of a house with bricks. My motivation was soon lost when a team member began shouting at me. I'd measured the wood wrongly and the pieces were too small. To make matters worse I'd been unprepared for the heat and had had to take a long break in the morning after feeling ill.

Considering quitting, I found new drive when the angry woman from the first day calmy explained to me that any mistake could delay the

第4回　英語（リーディング）

completion of the homes for those waiting for them.　I realized I needed to be more serious.　On the night before I started working, my team had been introduced to teen sisters who would get one of the homes and when our job was complete, I spoke to them.　They explained that they had lost their parents in farming accidents as small kids and had had to drop out of school to earn money, staying in a home packed with parentless kids. Though a tough two weeks, as I saw their tears of happiness, it was all worth it.

問1　Put the following events (① ～ ④) into the order they happened.

$$\boxed{9} \rightarrow \boxed{10} \rightarrow \boxed{11} \rightarrow \boxed{12}$$

① Some sheep delayed the group.

② The team first met two sisters who would get a home.

③ The writer did some painting.

④ The writer got sick because of the hot weather.

問2　Why did one of the team members get so angry with the writer?　$\boxed{13}$

① The writer behaved in too unfriendly a manner.

② The writer didn't cut the wood to the right size.

③ The writer failed in health care.

④ The writer lied about her building experience.

問3　From this story, you learned that the project's aim was to $\boxed{14}$.

① build a center for kids without parents

② help make basic homes more comfortable

③ provide people with long-term accommodation

④ teach people with little education new skills

— 9 —

第4問 （配点 12）

In English class you are writing an essay on IT problems you are interested in. This is your most recent draft. You are now working on revisions based on comments from your teacher.

AI art generators should be used properly	Teacher's Comments
In recent years, artificial intelligence (AI) has developed rapidly. AI is used for many things, such as generating music, translating foreign languages, and analyzing data. AI can be used in many positive ways. However, many artists are worried about AI programs that generate art. They believe these programs should be limited or restricted.	
First, AI art generators steal the work of real artists. These programs must be trained on thousands of examples of real art made by human artists. (1) ∧ Many artists don't consent to AI programs using their art this way. They believe their work has been stolen and is being used illegally.	(1) Can you tell me how the AI programs do that? Add more information here.
Second, AI art takes jobs from real artists. AI art generators can make photographs or pictures at a much lower price than a human artist and in much less time. This (2) changes the demand for real artists and leaves them with less work. In the future, this may cause artists to lose their jobs, even though they are highly skilled and have spent years perfecting their skills.	(2) Changes the demand in what way? Be more specific.
Finally, (3) let's consider learning art. Drawing, painting, and photography are all creative forms of expression, and are important to us as human beings. Practicing art develops the small muscles in our hands and encourages imagination and creativity. If art becomes something we can make at the click of a button, we will lose this important part of our culture.	(3) The topic sentence doesn't adequately summarize your point. Rewrite it.

— 10 —

第4回　英語（リーディング）

In conclusion, AI programs sample the work of artists without permission, they reduce work opportunities for artists, and they discourage people from making art themselves. Many artists believe that despite the advantages of AI art, it has a negative influence on our culture overall. (4) ∧

(4) Add a concluding sentence here.

Overall Comment

This is very interesting. I had never thought about the problems with AI art generators before. Good work!

問1　Based on comment (1), which sentences should you insert here?
　　　　15

① AI programs analyze these images and sample them to make new ones.

② AI programs can make original art without using other people's images.

③ AI programs use art or photography bought from professional artists.

④ AI programs use pictures donated for free by human artists.

問2　Based on comment (2), which word or expression should you use here instead?　16

① expands

② magnifies

③ reduces

④ replaces

— 11 —

問3　Based on comment (3), which topic sentence should be inserted here?　17

① AI art generators are better at making drawings and photographs than humans

② an increase in AI art will discourage people from studying and practicing art

③ children who use AI art use their imaginations in a way that is different from artists

④ using AI art is a different form of creativity, so it should be encouraged

問4　Which sentence should you add, based on comment (4)?　18

① As a result, artists should use AI art generators more carefully.

② Consequently, AI technology is still not effective enough.

③ In summary, AI should be developed more.

④ Therefore, the use of AI art generators should be limited.

第4回　英語（リーディング）

（ 下 書 き 用 紙 ）

英語（リーディング）の試験問題は次に続く。

第5問 （配点 16）

You are going to study at Wyatt University in the US from September and need accommodation. You are looking at the blogs of two students, Olivia and Rob, to see what options are available.

See You at Wyatt University!
Posted by Olivia at 3:32 p.m. on July 17, 2022

Need a place to live for your college adventure? One thing to consider is what your rent includes, and other spending costs. Look at the average amount of money students spent on necessities not included in their rents this year.

Added Costs — Be Aware!

Groceries $110 a month   Electricity $20 a month   Internet $15 a month   Transportation $20~30 a month   Laundry $38 a month

Naturally where, and the kind of place you live make a difference. Living in a campus dormitory or a private campus room, you won't need to travel. If you stay with a family, freshly cooked food is usually included, but one problem is that you can't always expect privacy. I'd advise selecting a no-food plan in a private campus room for $95 a month less than a food plan. There aren't student discounts for buses, so I'd recommend a place in Zone 1 so you can walk to classes.

By the way, don't forget hidden savings or costs! In off-campus accommodation, both apartments and families, the deposits are at least double those of accommodation in private campus rooms. If you live in an on-campus dormitory you must move out in summer, but that saves you money!

第4回　英語（リーディング）

Join Us at Wyatt!
Posted by Rob at 11:03 a.m. on July 18, 2022

I remember the tough time I had finding accommodation on starting at Wyatt University.

I spent my first year in a private campus room, where everything except laundry fees was included, though paying for food service separately is probably better. I often missed meals because of studying or hanging out with friends. And, from my room commuting to class was quick, but the bus service in Zones 2 and 3 is also efficient. The journey from Zone 3 is more time-consuming, and if you consider the extra price of buses and relatively small differences in rents between these two areas, I'd prefer to live nearer the city center.

If you pay each time you wash clothes, money disappears soon! But if you live in an apartment house with three other students, you can pick up a washing machine for around $120 per person, and you'll save almost all laundry fees. In the on-campus dormitory, everything is included except food and laundry, but this definitely isn't for someone who enjoys time alone!

Type	Monthly Rent		
	Zone 1 (City Center)	Zone 2	Zone 3
Staying with Families A, B, and C	$240 (A)	$198 (B)	$182 (C)
Campus dormitory	$66		
Private campus room with food included	$270		
Off-campus students' apartments X, Y, and Z	$220 (X)	$170 (Y)	$150 (Z)

https://helpwithaccommodationwu.example.com

Don't forget deposits! If you live on-campus, it is $150 for the dormitory, and $300 for private rooms on moving in.

— 15 —

問 1 Olivia recommends living close to the university because ☐ 19 ☐.

① the city bus doesn't offer student rates

② the city bus service is unreliable

③ walking to class is good exercise

④ you can save time commuting on foot

問 2 Rob suggests purchasing ☐ 20 ☐.

① a washing machine with other students if possible

② extra food because campus meals are small

③ some kind of wi-fi router for faster Internet access

④ your own desk so that you can study more easily

問 3 Both Olivia and Rob recommend that you ☐ 21 ☐.

① choose accommodation in Zone 2

② choose accommodation without food included

③ live with a family if possible

④ live with roommates you can get along well with

第4回　英語（リーディング）

問4　If you want your privacy ensured but wish to pay the cheapest monthly rent, you should choose to ☐22☐ among the four options.

① live in a campus dormitory
② live in a campus private room without food included
③ live in off-campus students' apartment Y
④ live with Family C

問5　Among the four options, ☐23☐ is likely to be your choice if you want to pay the least deposit; and if you need to live in a place in Zone 1 for the whole year, the monthly rent is likely to be the most inexpensive by living in ☐24☐ . (Choose one for each box from options ① ～ ④.)

① Campus dormitory
② Off-campus students' apartment X
③ Private campus room with food included
④ Staying with Family A

第6問 (配点 18)

You are working on an essay about whether financial education (knowledge about personal finance) classes should be taught in schools. You will follow the steps below.

Step 1: Read and understand various viewpoints about financial education.
Step 2: Take a position about whether or not financial education should be taught in schools.
Step 3: Create an outline for an essay using additional sources.

[Step 1] Read various sources

Author A (student)

When I heard my school was going to introduce personal finance lessons, I was annoyed, because we already have so much academic work. Despite that, I began to change my mind after a few classes. I learned so much important information that will help me in my future. My parents are immigrants from South America, and they work hard but they don't have much money. I want to build a better future for myself, and these classes have given me the knowledge to make wise decisions about my money.

Author B (high school principal)

I was thinking about adding personal finance lessons to our curriculum like some schools in our district. However, we don't have enough time or qualified teachers available to do this properly. I believe life skills such as personal finance should be taught at home. I understand that some students don't have the opportunity to learn these skills from their family members. That is why we'll have a counsellor who can speak to students about their individual problems including financial matters.

Author C (parent)

I have always taught my children about how to take care of their money. Even from a young age, I gave them pocket money and opened savings accounts for them. When they start university, I will help them get the best deal on a student loan, and encourage them to get a part-time job. This is why I don't believe personal finance classes in school are necessary. I'm also concerned about who will teach the subject. I think teachers generally aren't qualified to talk about financial issues for now.

— 18 —

第4回　英語（リーディング）

Author D (finance journalist)

Before I answer this question, I have to ask what "financial education" is. What do schools intend to teach? It is a very wide-ranging subject and much of the basics are common sense. I believe even young children understand that they need to save money and not borrow money they can't pay back. Of course, my job is to write about pensions and investments, but the information is constantly changing. If you want to know where to put your money, I recommend reading the financial pages of a newspaper, not asking a school teacher.

Author E (university counsellor)

Due to my job, I know a large number of students start university in a bad financial situation because they made a poor decision about which student loan to take out. Of course, some students have very knowledgeable parents, or rich parents, so they don't get into trouble in this way. On the other hand, some very intelligent students get into trouble because they simply weren't prepared by their parents. I think that schools should help these students out by giving them the knowledge that their parents or families can't give.

問1　Both Authors C and D mention that | 25 | .

① it is too difficult to teach information about pensions and investments, so students should consult experts

② students can learn more about finance by going to university and earning money in a part-time job

③ teachers may not have the knowledge or experience necessary to teach classes about personal finance

④ there is not enough time to teach personal finance in schools because of the students' busy schedule

— 19 —

問2 Author B implies that ⬚26⬚ .

① she wants to add personal finance classes to the schedule but the teachers and students are against it

② some students are at a disadvantage because their families do not teach them about personal finance

③ the students want to have personal finance classes but the teachers do not have the knowledge to teach it

④ young people are more likely to make risky decisions than adults, so should not handle money early

[Step 2] Take a position

問3 Now that you understand the various viewpoints, you have taken a position on teaching personal finance in schools, and have written it out as below. Choose the best options to complete ⬚27⬚ , ⬚28⬚ , and ⬚29⬚ .

Your position: Classes about personal finance should be taught in high schools.

- Authors ⬚27⬚ and ⬚28⬚ support your position.
- The main argument of the two authors: ⬚29⬚ .

Options for ⬚27⬚ and ⬚28⬚ (the order does not matter):

① A
② B
③ C
④ D
⑤ E

第4回　英語（リーディング）

Options for ☐ 29

① Learning about money while at high school will allow students to get better careers in the future

② Parents who are poor can learn about finance and money from their children, which improves their lives

③ Students who learn about finance at school are more motivated to study hard to improve their prospects

④ Teaching personal finance in school will reduce the inequality between students of different backgrounds

[Step 3] Create an outline using sources A and B

Outline of your essay:

Schools should introduce personal finance classes for their students

Introduction

In recent years, more schools in various countries around the world are introducing classes about personal finance for their students. This is a good idea for the following reasons.

Body

Reason 1: (From Step 2)

Reason 2: (Based on Source A)　……　☐ 30

Reason 3: (Based on Source B)　……　☐ 31

Conclusion

High school teachers should teach their students about money and personal finance.

— 21 —

Source A

One advantage of giving high school students classes in personal finance is that they are less likely to engage in risky financial behavior later in life. One measure of this is the likelihood of taking out payday loans. A payday loan is a loan that has a very high interest rate and needs to be repaid within a short period of time, such as a couple of weeks. People who take out these loans and cannot pay them back often get into legal trouble or even get involved in crime in order to find the money they need. However, studies show that young people who took part in personal finance education while at school were much less likely to become involved in taking out payday loans. They were also less likely to delay repaying their debts such as credit card debt. We can assume that this will lead to fewer legal problems and a lower likelihood of getting involved in crime when these students become adults and are responsible for their own financial decisions.

Source B

A research study in the US tracked the credit scores of students in three states who had undergone personal finance lessons at high school. Credit scores are important because they help banks and other organizations determine how trustworthy a person is regarding money. People with high credit scores are more likely to get good interest rates on loans and credit cards, and are more likely to be approved for a home loan.

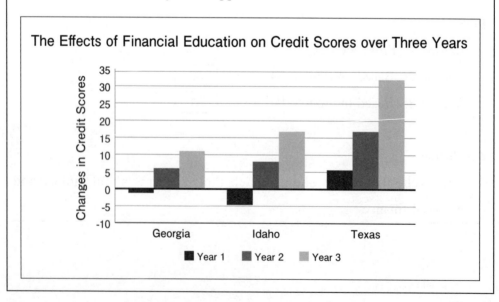

第4回　英語（リーディング）

問4　Based on Source A, which of the following is the most appropriate for Reason 2?　30

① Crime rates went down among students who had taken finance classes at school because they earned more money.

② Students were less likely to use credit cards and loans after taking classes in personal finance at high school.

③ Those students who went into a legal or finance career were more likely to have had finance classes at high school.

④ Young people who had received financial education at school were less likely to make high-risk financial decisions.

問5　For Reason 3, you have decided to write, "Personal finance classes make students more financially responsible." Based on Source B, which option best supports this statement?　31

① All of the students in the three states managed to raise their credit scores after three years. However, Idaho was the least successful state in terms of teaching financial education.

② In some states, there was a drop in credit scores a year after taking finance classes. This means that young people always make bad financial decisions that affect their long-term future.

③ In two of the states, there was a negative effect on credit scores because of taking finance classes. After that, their credit scores rose, which shows that credit scores always rise over time.

④ Three years after taking finance classes at schools, students in all three states had considerably improved their credit scores. This shows that they are making good financial decisions.

第7問 (配点 15)

In your English class, you will give a presentation about a professional inventor. You found the following article and prepared notes for your presentation.

Many people at sea have been saved by lifeboats — boats whose purpose is to rescue people in trouble on our oceans. In 1790 after a boat sank near the coast of England, a local businessman who saw the disaster decided something had to be done. He designed a rescue boat made partly of a light wood, which would be difficult to turn upside-down. Though it did save many people, there was one huge problem. It was only useful for accidents near land.

Maria Beasley

Around 1840, Maria Beasley was born in the USA to a miller — someone who processes flour. She was extremely interested in her father's machines and would examine how they worked. When she was thirteen, she successfully designed and made a boat to use on a lake, and perhaps this later inspired her to improve designs of lifeboats in 1880.

Visiting one of her grandfathers, who owned a drink factory, during her school summer vacation, she became fascinated by the wooden barrels made for transportation and learned about the barrel-making machines. This curiosity later led her to invent a tool to speed up the barrel-making process, which she patented in 1881 and 1882. Due to its ability to produce more barrels, and so naturally to sell more product, business owners from everywhere wanted this machine. Making various improvements to the machine over the years, her business flourished, and she sold it for about $1.4 million dollars about ten years before she died. That's more than $40 million today!

第4回　英語（リーディング）

Beasley probably decided to make a career of her love of engineering when she moved to the city of Philadelphia for her sons' education. This city held a world fair in 1876 for nations worldwide to show off their latest achievements. She was a frequent visitor, and it inspired her to invent a foot warmer and a roasting pan at the end of that same decade.

In 1895, Beasley was living in Chicago when a major rail project to link both coasts of America by rail through Chicago was announced. Beasley became involved, exploring ways to make trains faster and, more importantly, safer. Beasley was acknowledged as the key designer of the new trains, whose shape allowed them to move faster and made them less likely to come off the rails at high speeds. Built with windows that allowed the train drivers to see more clearly, they were safer forms of transport than previous models.

Nevertheless, Beasley is most remembered for her lifeboat designs. Her boats were strong in rough seas and apparently fireproof. They could be folded, which meant that they were much easier to store on ships. In the late 1800s and early 1900s immigration by ship to the US by people in search of better lives was booming, and there is no doubt that Beasley's lifeboats and train improvements saved hundreds of lives.

Maria Beasley's family strongly supported her. In an era in which wives' earnings and possessions legally belonged to their husbands, her husband John refused to take credit. Her son worked closely with her before she died in 1913. Her determination to make life-changing machines was extraordinary, and her works were displayed at a Chicago world fair in 1893. It is hard to believe that she started out as a dressmaker!

Your presentation notes:

Maria Beasley (Around 1840~1913)

— [32] —

From Birth to School Days
— born to a miller
— [33]
— [34]

Sequence of Life Events

A world fair caused her engineering interest.

[35]

Beasley got a patent for her barrel-making machine.

[36]

[37]

[38]

Train Design
— The trains Beasley designed [39] .

Lifeboat Design
— Early lifeboats were only useful for accidents near land.
— [40]

第4回　英語（リーディング）

問1　Which is the best subtitle for your presentation? ☐32

① Amazing Family and Life-changing Designs

② Engineering Designs to Save Lives

③ Inventions of Various Shapes and Sizes

④ Selfish Businesswoman and Inventor

問2　Choose the best two options for ☐33 and ☐34 to complete From Birth to School Days.　(The order does not matter.)

① built her own boat for sailing on a lake

② entered and won a nationwide invention competition

③ helped some sailors who were in trouble

④ hit on a totally new way of processing flour

⑤ studied the machines at a relative's business

問3　Choose **four** out of the five events (① ～ ⑤) in the order they happened to complete Sequence of Life Events.

☐35 → ☐36 → ☐37 → ☐38

① A rail project hired Beasley to improve the design of trains.

② Beasley moved to Philadelphia in order to educate her sons there.

③ Beasley sold her business for a fortune.

④ Some of Beasley's inventions were displayed at a world fair.

⑤ The design of lifeboats was made better by Beasley.

— 27 —

問4　Choose the best option for 　39　 to complete Train Design.

① had better engines that didn't overheat after long hours of use

② had stronger windows that would rarely break if hit with something

③ were able to stay firmly on train tracks when moving at high speeds

④ were far less dangerous than other types of public transport

問5　Choose the best option for 　40　 to complete Lifeboat Design.

① Her boats could also help put out fires.

② Her boats' size could be reduced for storage.

③ New US citizens arrived on her boats.

④ The design of her lifeboats remains unchanged until today.

第4回　英語（リーディング）

（下 書 き 用 紙）

英語（リーディング）の試験問題は次に続く。

第8問 (配点 14)

You are in a group of students preparing a poster for a presentation contest with the theme "Popular health concerns in society." You have been using the following passage to create the poster.

Doing Battle with Allergies
～ A Common Health Worry Today ～

Nowadays millions of people suffer from allergies. Indeed, allergies are a modern phenomenon, and the number of people having to deal with them — whether they are chemical, plant, food, or medicine-related — is growing higher as cities spread and industry progresses. In remote areas of Africa and South America, it is still rare to find someone with allergies. Though they are seldom life-threatening, they can make us miserable. Around 6% of young kids in the USA have a food allergy, and today manufacturers are required by law to print on packaging when something contains ingredients that harm many of us — namely nuts, milk, eggs, fish, soy and flour. Some children with severe allergies must eat at different tables from their classmates or even be educated at home in order to avoid them getting sick from an item in another child's lunch.

So why are we developing allergies to everyday things? The reason is, unfortunately, unclear. One day the body meets a harmless ingredient, such as flour in a cake, and for some reason flags it as an enemy. At first nothing happens, but the body, remembering it, starts making plans to do battle. Our immune systems, which protect us from poisons and illnesses, begin producing 'soldiers' that attach to cells and wait for the offensive material to enter the body again. When it does, even months later, the 'soldiers' fight it with chemicals, which actually irritate our skin, or make us cough or our noses run. The battle, and our physical reaction, can become more intense over time.

— 30 —

第4回　英語（リーディング）

Though allergies can be passed down from parents, the rise in the number of sufferers is so rapid that this clearly isn't the only cause. Our environments and behavior must have something to do with the increase. There are theories that babies who are raised on factory milk-substitutes may be more at risk of getting allergies than those who drink their mother's milk. The same could be true for consuming processed foods more than natural foods like fruits and vegetables. Some scientists argue that children living near busy roads may have worse allergies, most likely due to what passing traffic puts into the air.

Being too clean, ironically, is also presumably a factor. Technology provides us with effective medicines, spotless hospitals, and solid homes that not only keep cold and bad weather out but also guard us from dirt. Not playing in nature or getting dirty can mean children's developing bodies lose the chance to practice attacking things that damage our health and therefore grow lazy and become insufficiently prepared. When cases of people with plant-related allergies began to surface in 1819, none of them were uneducated poor people. Today even families in developed nations who aren't wealthy can lead clean lives, and the dirt we need to encounter, such as soil from fields and animal waste is practically nowhere in urban areas.

Some scientists believe that exposing kids to the right kinds of dirt at a young age could be a key solution, though with evolution and our forever changing bodies, this could do more harm when we get older and live cleanly. While some professionals believe we should expose children to popular sources of allergies like flour as much as possible when young to build up their defenses, others feel we should distance them from them totally. Obviously, we don't know enough yet. We are more aware of allergies now, though, and many hotels offer rooms with special fans to keep air free of dust and wash sheets with products that don't contain substances likely to hurt our skin. Through engineering genetics, we can take some ingredients out of foods without changing the taste. But how much should we change nature through science? And even if we do, what new things will our bodies object to in the future?

Your presentation poster draft:

Why do allergies occur?

41

Suggested causes for various allergies

Type	Cause	Theory	Origins
1	Diet	Children who consume manufactured foods 42 may be at high risk.	foods, drinks, etc.
2	Transportation	In areas where there is a lot of traffic, children's allergies may get worse.	chemicals in gasoline, etc.
3	Nature	Lack of contact with dirt and waste may 43 .	soil, animals, etc.

Possible solutions to allergies:

44

45

— 32 —

第4回　英語（リーディング）

問1　Under the first poster heading, your group wants to introduce the reason why allergies occur, as explained in the passage.　Which of the following is most appropriate?　41

① They appear because of more newly developed medicines being used in modern life.

② They are unexplained violent reactions by our bodies to supposedly safe things.

③ They begin when we suddenly make complete changes to our living environments.

④ They develop when technology advances so much that it causes changes in our brains.

問2　You have been asked to write theories for possible allergy cause Type 1 and 3.　Choose the best options for　42　and　43　.

Type 1　42
① and drink processed baby milk
② and eat lots of sweets
③ but avoid nutritious juices
④ but no nuts or fish

Type 3　43
① cause us to be unaware of their dangers
② deny us enough fresh country air
③ lead to our difficulties in standing cold temperatures
④ make us vulnerable to unhealthy elements

— 33 —

問3 You are making statements about possible ways allergies could be tackled. According to the article, which two of the following are appropriate? (The order does not matter.) ⬚44 ・ ⬚45

① Children ought to be kept away from foods that are often the cause of allergies.

② Families with young children ought to put air-cleaning appliances in bedrooms.

③ People should have the chance to encounter the right type of dirt early in life.

④ Plants and foods that commonly make children feel ill should be scientifically altered.

⑤ Special bed sheets made from natural materials should be sold for children.

⑥ Vitamins that help children develop healthily ought to be added to certain foods.

第 5 回

（80分）

実 戦 問 題

第5回 実戦問題

英　　語（リーディング）

各大問の英文や図表を読み，解答番号 1 ～ 45 にあてはまるものとして最も適当な選択肢を選びなさい。

第1問 （配点　6）

You are the chief leader of the English club at your school, and the club is going to attend a contest explained in a flyer as follows:

The 1st Youth English Drama Contest

　　The Youth English Drama Society will have its first contest. We aim to encourage young Japanese people to learn English through drama, which is one of the best forms of entertainment.

　There are three stages to this competition. Winners will be selected at each stage, and if you pass all three stages, you can participate in the Grand Final.

The Grand Final	Place: Century Hall Date:　February 5, 2023

GRAND PRIZE

　　The winning team can join The International English Camp in Canberra, Australia in March 2023.

Contest information:

Stages	Things to Upload & Events	Details	2022 Deadlines & Dates
Stage 1	Answers to a questionnaire, and an English essay	Number of words for the essay: 150 - 200	Upload by 12 p.m. on August 13
Stage 2	A video of your team giving its performance	Time: 25-30 minutes	Upload by 12 p.m. on October 25

― 2 ―

第5回　英語（リーディング）

Stage 3	Regional Contests	On this site we'll show you the winners, who will go on to the Grand Final.	Held on December 23

Grand Final Grading Information

Pronunciation & Intonation, etc.	Gestures & Performance	Voice & Eye Contact	Teamwork	Answering Questions from Judges
40%	10%	10%	30%	10%

◆ You must download the questionnaire as well as the title of your English essay and the script for your play online.

click here.

◆ You must upload your materials online. All dates and times are Japan Standard Time (JST).

◆ You can get to know the results of Stage 1 and 2 on the website seven days after the deadline for each stage.

For more details, **click here**.

問1　To take part in the first stage, you should ☐ 1 ☐ .

① answer the questions and make a video of your performance

② answer the questions and write an essay in English

③ write an English essay and make a video of your performance

④ write an English essay and write a play

問2　When can you start to check the result of the first stage? ☐ 2 ☐

① August 6

② August 13

③ August 20

④ August 27

— 3 —

問3　You should put the greatest effort into speaking natural English and

　　　[3] to earn a high score in the Grand Final.

　① controlling your voice and expressions

　② explaining your story carefully to the judges

　③ using dramatic gestures

　④ working better as a group

第5回　英語（リーディング）

（下 書 き 用 紙）

英語（リーディング）の試験問題は次に続く。

第2問 （配点 10）

You and John, an exchange student from the UK, are the editors of a school English paper. He has written an article for the paper.

Do you like using a tablet in class? The UK has been promoting ICT (Information and Communication Technology) education, but I don't think it's going smoothly. How about in Japan? Results of some surveys about Japanese high schools give us some answers.

> - The number of schools which didn't provide a tablet for each student was about five times as large as that of schools which did in 2018.
>
> In 2020, the situation was as follows:
> - The number of schools which didn't think of introducing tablets was more than three times as large as that of schools which did.
> - 43.8% of private high schools got tablets for each of their students, while only 5.4% of public ones provided each student with one.
> - There were many more private than public high schools which planned to give all students tablets.

As you know, in our school we are luckily provided with individual tablets. However, I wonder if they are properly and fully used by each student. Are the teachers skillful enough to use one? Are they trying to have each student make the most of his or her tablet in their everyday classes? I've got some information from the head teacher; four in ten of our math teachers are eager to promote ICT education. This is higher than the number of English teachers. Three in eleven of them are having their students use their tablets. And the lowest percentage goes to the Japanese teachers.

第5回　英語（リーディング）

In fact, I wonder whether we will need to depend on such electronic tools more or not in the future. I think we've got to give questionnaires or something to the students and teachers at our school, and we may get hints about the usage of tablets which will lead to the improvement of the present situation.

問1　In terms of the ratios of your school's teachers who are trying ICT education eagerly, which shows the subject teachers' ranking from **highest to lowest**?　4

① English teachers — Japanese teachers — math teachers

② English teachers — math teachers — Japanese teachers

③ Japanese teachers — English teachers — math teachers

④ Japanese teachers — math teachers — English teachers

⑤ math teachers — English teachers — Japanese teachers

⑥ math teachers — Japanese teachers — English teachers

問2　John's comments on the current ICT education at his school show that　5　.

① he feels ICT education in his own country is inferior

② he is satisfied with the effective way of using tablets at the school

③ he is skeptical about whether tablets are being used effectively at the school

④ he wants to see more kinds of online learning

—7—

問3　The statement that best reflects one finding from the survey is ⬚6

① 'I wish I were a public school student because I could get my own tablet.'
② 'My school is public and isn't planning to promote ICT education now.'
③ 'One out of three schools provided tablets for each student in 2018.'
④ 'The majority of schools intend to improve their ICT education classes.'

問4　Which best summarises John's opinions about ICT education at his school? ⬚7

① Some surveys are necessary to make the situation better.
② Tablets are not as useful as we expected.
③ We have to hold classes for teachers to teach them how to use tablets.
④ We need to make it easier for students to use tablets.

問5　Which is the most suitable title for the article? ⬚8

① Cost and Performance of Tablets
② Introducing Tablets and Their Future
③ Strategy for Distributing Tablets to Public Schools
④ Usefulness of and Problems with Tablets

― 8 ―

第５回　英語（リーディング）

（ 下 書 き 用 紙 ）

英語（リーディング）の試験問題は次に続く。

第3問 （配点 9）

Your friend in the U.S. introduced his favorite musician to you. Wanting to learn more, you found the following article in a music magazine.

Bob Marley, the Soul of Reggae

Bob Marley was born on February 6, 1945. He was a Jamaican reggae singer, songwriter, musician, and guitarist who achieved international fame and is still highly praised by his enthusiastic fans. Starting out in 1963 with the group *The Wailers*, he created a distinctive songwriting and vocal style that would soon be received with admiration by audiences worldwide. After *The Wailers* broke up in 1974, Marley pursued a solo career that reached its peak with the release of the album *Exodus* in June, 1977. It is certain that the album established his worldwide reputation and led to his status as one of the world's best-selling artists of all time, with sales of more than 75 million records.

Bob Marley was a committed Rastafarian, an Abrahamic religion which developed in Jamaica in the 1930s. This religion inspired him and filled his music with a sense of spirituality. The *Rastafari movement* was a key element in the development of reggae. As a passionate supporter of Rastafari, Bob Marley took reggae music out of the socially deprived areas of Jamaica and onto the international music scene.

In July, 1977, Marley was found to be suffering from a type of a fatal disease under the nail of one of his toes. His doctors strongly advised him to have an operation on it. However, Marley turned down their advice, citing his religious beliefs. In spite of his illness, he continued touring until his health grew worse as the cancer spread throughout his body. He died on

第５回　英語（リーディング）

11 May 1981 at Cedars of Lebanon Hospital in Miami (now University of Miami Hospital) at the age of 36. The spread of the cancer to his lungs and brain caused his death. His final words to his son Ziggy were: "Money can't buy life."

問 1　Put the following events (①〜④) into the order in which they happened.

　　 9 　→　 10 　→　 11 　→　 12

　　① 　Marley began to sing solo.

　　② 　Marley didn't stop his tours after he discovered his disease.

　　③ 　Marley joined the group *The Wailers*.

　　④ 　The album *Exodus* was released.

問 2　Marley refused to be taken care of by his doctors because 　 13 　 .

　　① 　he thought it was too late to have an operation

　　② 　he was busy doing concert tours

　　③ 　he was following his faith

　　④ 　his cancer was at an early stage

問 3　From this story, you learned that 　 14 　 .

　　① 　a religion had an influence on Marley's music

　　② 　a religion made Marley move to Jamaica

　　③ 　Marley didn't get along with his band members

　　④ 　Marley's music deprived his country of money

— 11 —

第4問 (配点 12)

In English class you are writing an essay on a social issue you are interested in. This is your most recent draft. You are now working on revisions based on comments from your teacher.

The Benefits of Taxing High-Sugar Drinks	Teacher's Comments
Sweet drinks such as fruit juice and soda are very popular with young people around the world. However, we know that consuming these drinks is bad for the health. Taking in too much sugar can lead to obesity and other health problems, such as heart disease and diabetes. ⁽¹⁾ <u>For example</u>, many governments around the world are trying to get their citizens to reduce their sugar intake by adding a so-called "sugar tax" to sweet drinks. This new tax has produced some positive results.	*(1) You have used the incorrect word here. Please choose a different word or expression.*
First, a tax on sweet drinks reduces consumption. When a tax was added to sweet drinks in five cities in the US, ⁽²⁾ <u>it</u> declined by 33%. That means that people stopped buying sweet drinks, and bought healthier alternatives instead. This is a particularly important effect in poor areas, because people in poor areas tend to be less healthy and consume more sugary drinks.	*(2) What does "it" mean here? Write out the sentence in full.*
Second, raising the price of sweet drinks reduces obesity ⁽³⁾ ∧. Elementary school-aged children benefit the most from this. When a sugar tax was added to drinks on sale in England, there was a large drop in the number of obese children in the higher grades of elementary school. In addition, the number of children entering the hospital for the removal of teeth declined.	*(3) Your topic sentence doesn't summarize the other effect you mention in this passage. Please add it.*

— 12 —

第5回　英語（リーディング）

Finally, sugar taxes help the government save money on healthcare. When people become healthier, they use public hospitals less often, live longer, and spend more time at work. This means that the government has to spend less money on healthcare and unemployment benefits. That money can be used to benefit society in many other ways, such as investing in education or improving cities.

In conclusion, applying a tax on sweet drinks has many benefits. It makes people drink fewer sweet beverages, improves the health of children, and (4) helps hospitals. More countries around the world should do this to improve the health and well-being of their citizens.

(4) *This does not really summarize what you wrote in the fourth paragraph. Please rewrite this.*

問1　Based on comment (1), which is the best word to use instead?　15

① In addition

② In contrast

③ On the contrary

④ Therefore

問2　Based on comment (2), which is the best expression to use here?　16

① the amount of tax paid

② the amount people ate

③ the number of people paying tax

④ purchases of these drinks

— 13 —

問3 Based on comment (3), which expression should you add here? 17

① and helps children avoid dental problems

② and improves academic grades

③ and makes children work harder

④ and raises school attendance

問4 Based on comment (4), which is the best replacement? 18

① allows governments to spend money on projects that benefit society

② helps schools receive more money for education from the government

③ makes our cities easier to live in by improving infrastructure

④ stops hospitals and schools from wasting money on unnecessary things

第5回 英語（リーディング）

（下 書 き 用 紙）

英語（リーディング）の試験問題は次に続く。

第5問 （配点 16）

You are now studying at Robert University in the US. In a social studies class, you are asked to report on how smartphones affect people. You found the blogs of two students, Paul and Linda, who are discussing the usage of smartphones.

Smartphone Addiction?

Posted by Paul at 4:52 p.m. on September 5, 2022

Since the world saw the first iPhone in 2007, smartphone usage has steadily become an accepted part of our daily lives — and the smartphone addiction statistics prove it. Now, in 2022, we are glued to our phones. Because we rely on our phones for communication and connection, it can be hard to determine when excessive smartphone use becomes an addiction. However, it's necessary to know the following statistics:

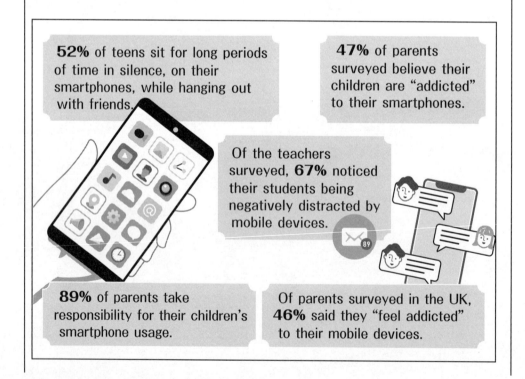

52% of teens sit for long periods of time in silence, on their smartphones, while hanging out with friends.

47% of parents surveyed believe their children are "addicted" to their smartphones.

Of the teachers surveyed, **67%** noticed their students being negatively distracted by mobile devices.

89% of parents take responsibility for their children's smartphone usage.

Of parents surveyed in the UK, **46%** said they "feel addicted" to their mobile devices.

In fact, I once suffered from sleep deprivation, increased stress levels, depression, and anxiety because of, I believe, my smartphone. And I've stopped using it. While being addicted to your digital devices doesn't negatively impact your health as seriously as other types of addiction, it does indeed impact not only your mental health but your physical wellbeing. Why don't you stop and think about how you use YOUR smartphone?

Smartphone (over)usage in school

Posted by Linda at 11:22 a.m. on September 6, 2022

If there's anything that most deserves the claim to being a man's best friend in the modern age, it has got to be the smartphone. Mobile devices have penetrated every type of human activity. Nearly everyone uses one at home, school, work, and during times of leisure. So much so that not having access to a mobile phone has paved the way for "nomophobia", the fear of being out of mobile phone contact. As such, understanding the current smartphone addiction statistics is important to get a grasp of how serious it really is.

Here, I'd like to shine a light on smartphone usage and habits in school. Given that smartphones are mini-computers, they can take on a wide variety of functions which can be useful in class. This allows users to enjoy their devices in a lot of different ways. Unfortunately, too much enjoyment can be counterproductive. As the smartphone addiction statistics suggest, mobile phones prove to be huge distractions in schools. This causes dips in productivity.

Percentage	What does the percentage show?
20%	The time spent by students in class texting and checking social media
45%	Students who are constantly online. This includes the time that they are in class.
46%	Parents who want educators to find ways to integrate the use of smartphones into lessons more
49%	Students who are distracted by smartphones and other digital gadgets in class
80%	Schools which have a policy that restricts the use of mobile phones in class

If you're uncomfortable with your attachment to your smartphone, there are ways to cultivate a healthier relationship with the technology in your life. Try limiting the time spent on your smartphone by using an app that tracks your daily usage and sends reminders to log off. You can also access your average screen time in the settings of your phone. Another trick that helps limit smartphone use is to turn your color settings to black and white. Late night scrolling isn't as stimulating when you're seeing black and white visuals, which encourages putting down your device.

問1　Paul recommends stopping using smartphones because　19 .

① they are harmful to our health

② they can damage human relationships

③ they cost a lot of money

④ they prevent face-to-face communication

問2　Linda suggests that　20 .

① you should be careful about your physical health being affected by your smartphone

② you should change the color of the screen of your smartphone

③ you should install an app which turns off your smartphone automatically

④ you should limit the time you use your smartphone using other digital gadgets

— 18 —

第5回　英語（リーディング）

問3　Both Paul and Linda recommend that you ☐21☐ .

① appreciate the advance of communication technologies

② look into how effectively smartphones are utilized by people

③ realize how dangerous using social networking services is

④ understand how affected people are by smartphones through statistics

問4　The percentage of students who are distracted by digital gadgets in class is higher than the percentage of students who ☐22☐ .

① are always connected to the Internet

② are using their smartphones properly

③ use apps that limit their phone use

④ use their smartphones late at night

問5　In ☐23☐ blog, you can find that less than half of parents ☐24☐ . (Choose the best one for each box from options ① ～ ④.)

① are satisfied with the way smartphones are used at school

② think their children are using their smartphones too much

③ Linda's

④ Paul's

— 19 —

第6問 （配点 18）

You are working on an essay about whether we should be encouraged to eat food that has been grown or produced locally. You will follow the steps below.

Step 1: Read and understand various viewpoints about locally-produced food.

Step 2: Take a position about whether people should try to eat food that was produced locally.

Step 3: Create an outline for an essay using additional sources.

[Step 1] Read various sources

Author A (environmental campaigner)

In 2005 some food activists in San Francisco challenged people to eat only locally grown food for a month. I joined in that challenge and I found it really difficult. We don't always realize how much we rely on imported food. However, I decided that instead of imported food, I should actively look for local products. They are fresher, and I can support local farmers, and less greenhouse gases are released during food transportation. Everyone should try doing this.

Author B (scientist)

I had believed that it was more environmentally friendly to buy locally-produced food. However, this idea isn't always backed up by data. When I looked at the data related to the life cycle of food, the majority of greenhouse gases are not released during the transportation phases but during the production phase. Therefore, in my opinion, if you are concerned about the environmental impact of your food, then you should not worry about where your food comes from, but how it is produced.

Author C (small grocery store owner)

I have family members who own farms in my local area, so it is easy for me to support them by stocking locally-produced food in my store. Of course, it is not possible to do this all year round, because fresh food is very seasonal. However, my customers are willing to pay a little extra for fresh local food, and I try to give them what they want. Some of my stock is imported, but I try to limit this as much as possible. I worry about the impact imported food has on the environment, so I want to buy locally-grown fruit and vegetables as much as I can.

— 20 —

第5回　英語（リーディング）

Author D (farmer)

A lot of the food I grow is sold at a low price to big supermarket chains. Supermarkets are very powerful, and I can't really negotiate high prices for my food. However, I often sell my own vegetables at local farmers markets, too. By doing this, I can charge higher prices and I like selling to local people in my community because they value the work that I put into producing high-quality food. I would definitely encourage more people to support their local community by buying from the farmers in the area in which they live.

Author E (mother)

Buying locally-produced food sounds like a great idea, but this can lead to a very unbalanced diet. I live in the north of the country, where the weather is poor so we can't get enough food without relying on imported foods. In addition, local farmers markets sell very high-quality local produce, but it can be quite expensive. Most families don't have enough money to do that. I know some people worry about the environmental costs of importing food, but I read that transportation accounts for only a small proportion of greenhouse gas emissions in food production.

問1　Both Authors D and E mention that 25 .

① food grown locally often costs more than food that has been imported from other places

② food sold in large supermarkets is of poor quality compared to food sold at markets

③ it is hard to eat a variety of foods if you are limited to buying things that have been grown locally

④ people appreciate the work of farmers more if the food has been grown near where they live

— 21 —

問2 Author B implies that 26 .

① food production is not as bad for the environment as many people believe

② if major organizations recommend people to do something, it must be based on research

③ the stage of food production that is worst for the environment is transportation

④ things that may seem correct may be proved wrong when studied in depth by scientists

[Step 2] Take a position

問3 Now that you understand the various viewpoints, you have taken a position on whether buying only locally-produced food should be encouraged, and have written it out as below. Choose the best options to complete 27 , 28 , and 29 .

Your position: People should not be encouraged to buy only locally-produced food.

• Authors 27 and 28 support your position.

• The main argument of the two authors: 29 .

Options for 27 and 28 (the order does not matter):

① A

② B

③ C

④ D

⑤ E

— 22 —

第5回 英語（リーディング）

Options for 29

① In places where the climate is poor, it is impossible to eat locally grown food

② People generally eat too much meat, which is bad for the environment

③ Transporting food is not as bad for the environment as many people believe

④ Very little food is transported between countries , so it has no impact on the environment

[Step 3] Create an outline using sources A and B

Outline of your essay:

We should not encourage people to only eat locally-produced food.

Introduction

Many people these days try to avoid imported food and buy locally-produced food to help the environment and to improve their health. However, there are many problems with this idea.

Body

Reason 1: (From Step 2)

Reason 2: (Based on Source A) 30

Reason 3: (Based on Source B) 31

Conclusion

People should not be encouraged to buy and eat only locally-grown food.

― 23 ―

Source A

Food production is very seasonal, and the harvesting season for each type of fruit and vegetable is very short. That means that if we try to eat only local foods, there will be times of over-production and under-production. In times of over-production, the food must be stored so that it can be used for as long as possible and does not get wasted. For example, the British apple season is at its peak in autumn. Each year, up to 610,000 tons of apples are produced there in that season. For these apples to stay fresh and meet demand from customers over the year, they would have to be placed in cold storage. A study showed that it would cost more and produce twice the level of emissions to keep local British apples in cold storage for 10 months than to import apples from South America by sea to the UK when they are needed. It is far more sustainable and energy efficient to meet a country's food requirements by importing food than to store large amounts of food and keep it fresh.

Source B

A study conducted by an agriculture magazine looked at the amount of food produced in the UK compared to the total available supply of that food in stores. The graph below shows the findings of that study. Many of these foods are difficult to produce in the local climate, and have to be grown in greenhouses, making them more expensive than imported foods.

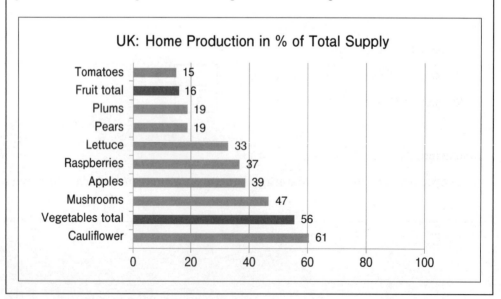

第5回　英語（リーディング）

問4　Based on Source A, which of the following is the most appropriate for Reason 2? ☐30☐

① Because most food is seasonal, it is more energy-efficient to transport it from abroad when needed than to store it.

② Food can only be stored for around 10 months, so it is better for our health to import food than to refrigerate it.

③ Fruit cannot usually be stored for long, so we can get fresher and tastier fruit if we import it from abroad.

④ South America is more efficient at growing apples than the UK, so British people should try to eat imported apples.

問5　For Reason 3, you have decided to write, "It would not be possible for people in certain countries to eat healthily by buying only locally-produced food." Based on Source B, which option best supports this statement? ☐31☐

① Most of the foods grown locally are disliked by many adults and children, so they would be more likely to buy unhealthy food because it is much cheaper.

② Most people cannot afford to buy the healthiest foods like tomatoes and other fruits because they are up to 15% more expensive when they are grown locally.

③ Only around half of the vegetables and one-sixth of the fruits available to buy in the UK were grown in the country. Avoiding imported foods would cost more and probably lead to an unbalanced diet.

④ While people in the UK could eat mostly locally-grown fruits, eating locally-grown vegetables would be much more difficult and expensive, leading to an unbalanced diet.

— 25 —

第7問 (配点 15)

In your English class, you will give a presentation about a great writer in the world. You found the following article and prepared notes for your presentation.

Edgar Allan Poe was born on January 19, 1809 in Boston, Massachusetts. He was an American author, poet, editor, and literary critic. He is widely regarded as a central figure of Romanticism in the United States, and of American literature. Poe is best known for his tales of mystery. He was one of the earliest American practitioners of the short story, and is generally considered the inventor of the detective fiction genre.

Edgar Allan Poe

Both Poe's father and mother were professional actors. They died before the poet was three years old. John and Frances Allan never formally adopted him but raised him as a foster child in Richmond, Virginia. Poe attended the University of Virginia for one semester but left due to lack of money. Poe quarreled with John over the funds for his education and his gambling debts. In 1827, he enlisted in the United States Army under a false name. It was at this time his writing career began with his first publication, although humbly, with an anonymous collection of poems, *Tamerlane and Other Poems* (1827), credited only to "a Bostonian". With the death of Frances Allan in 1829, Poe and John Allan reached a temporary reestablishing of good relations. Poe later failed as a military officer's trainee at West Point. He firmly stated his strong wish to be a poet and writer and parted ways with John Allan.

Although Poe began earnestly in his attempts to start his career as a poet, he chose a difficult time to do so. The American publishing industry was particularly hurt by the Panic of 1837, a financial crisis in

第5回　英語（リーディング）

the United States: profits, prices, and wages went down. Unemployment went up, and pessimism prevailed. Publishers often refused to pay their writers or paid them much later than they had promised. Poe had to have had a hard time. After his early attempts at poetry, Poe turned his attention to prose. He spent the next several years working for literary journals and periodicals. He became well-known, acting as a critic of literature in his own unique way. His work forced him to move between several cities, including Baltimore, Philadelphia, and New York City. In Baltimore in 1835, he married his cousin Virginia Clemm, which may have inspired some of his writing.

In January 1845 Poe published the poem, "*The Raven*", which became a popular sensation. It made Poe a household name almost instantly, though he was paid only $9 for its publication. His wife died of tuberculosis two years after its publication. For years, he had been planning to produce his own journal, *The Penn* (later renamed *The Stylus*), though he died before it could be published. On October 7, 1849, at age 40, Poe died in Baltimore; the cause of his death is unknown and has been variously attributed to alcohol, brain disease, cholera, drugs, heart disease, suicide, tuberculosis, and other causes.

Edgar Allan Poe and his works influenced literature in the United States and around the world, as well as being responsible for the start of specialized areas of writing. He is considered as one of the originators of both horror and detective fiction. He is also credited as the "architect" of the modern short story. As a critic he was one of the first writers to put emphasis on the effect of style and structure. He was thus a forerunner in the "art for art's sake" movement. Poe is particularly respected in France, in part due to early translations by Charles Baudelaire. Baudelaire's translations became definitive artistic performances of Poe's work throughout Europe.

Poe and his work appear throughout popular culture in literature, music, films, and television. A number of his homes are dedicated as museums today. The Mystery Writers of America present an annual award known as the Edgar Award for distinguished work in the mystery genre.

Your presentation notes:

Edgar Allan Poe

He was born on January 19, 1809 and is considered the inventor of the detective fiction genre.

Early Life
— He was taken care of by John and Frances Allan.
— He argued with John but, later, made up with him.
— [32]

A New Life and Marriage
— He switched his focus to [33] .
— He became famous for his own style of [34] .
— He married his cousin, Virginia Clemm.

Success and Death

[35]

He joined the Army under a false name.

[36]

[37]

[38]

He died in Baltimore from an unknown cause.

Influence
— He and his work appear throughout popular culture in literature, music, films, and television.
— [39]

Achievements and Recognition
— He invented the field of horror and detective fiction.
— He first focused on how style and structure affect a story.
— [40]

第5回　英語（リーディング）

問1　Choose the best statement for ☐32☐ .

① He cut off contact with John, declaring that he would be a poet and writer.

② His father abandoned the family and left home.

③ His first collection of poems made his name well-known to people.

④ Poe became on bad terms with John again just after he joined the army.

問2　Choose the best two items for ☐33☐ and ☐34☐ to complete A New Life and Marriage.

① detective stories

② editing magazines

③ literary criticism

④ plotting mysteries

⑤ prose writing

問3　Choose **four** out of the five events (① ～ ⑤) in the order they happened to complete Success and Death.

☐35☐ → ☐36☐ → ☐37☐ → ☐38☐

① An anonymous collection of poems was published.

② He entered the University of Virginia.

③ His wife passed away because of a disease.

④ *The Penn* was published.

⑤ "*The Raven*" was published and was a big hit.

— 29 —

問4 Choose the best option for 39 to complete Influence.

① He improved the style and structure of fiction which was popular at
  that time.

② He inspired Baudelaire, whose works were translated by him.

③ His literary criticism on short stories made an impact on mysteries.

④ His work was translated into French and became highly valued in
  Europe.

問5 Choose the best option for 40 to complete Achievements and
Recognition.

① A prominent mystery writer is honored in the name of Poe every
  year.

② As an architect, he changed his homes into museums.

③ He established the Mystery Writers of America organization.

④ He was against the trend of criticizing mysteries artistically.

第5回　英語（リーディング）

（ 下 書 き 用 紙 ）

英語（リーディング）の試験問題は次に続く。

第8問 (配点 14)

You are in a group preparing for a poster presentation whose title is "How we can Send Messages." Your group is interested in pictograms, a way of sending messages through pictorial symbols, and is planning to use the following passage to create the poster.

Hazard Pictograms
— Symbols Quick to Send a Message —

Pictograms introduced here are graphic images that immediately show the user of a hazardous product what type of hazard is present. With a quick glance you can see, for example, if the product is flammable (capable of burning quickly), or if it might be a health hazard in another way.

Some pictograms have a diamond shape. Inside this diamond is a symbol that represents the potential hazard (e.g., fire, harmful if eaten, strong acid, etc.). Together, the symbol and the design of the diamond are referred to as a pictogram. Pictograms are assigned specific hazard classes or categories.

Hazard pictograms form part of the international Globally Harmonized System of Classification and Labelling of Chemicals (GHS). Two sets of pictograms are included within the GHS: one for the labeling of containers and for workplace hazard warnings, and a second for use during the transport of dangerous goods. Either one or the other is chosen, depending on the target audience, but the two are not used together. The two sets of pictograms use the same symbols for the same hazards, although certain symbols are not required for transport pictograms. Transport pictograms come in a wider variety of colors and may contain additional information such as a subcategory number.

Hazard pictograms are one of the key elements for the labeling of containers under GHS, along with other information such as:

— 32 —

- a description of the product
- a signal word – either 'Danger' or 'Warning' — where necessary
- hazard statements, indicating the nature and degree of the risks posed by the product
- precautionary statements, indicating how the product should be handled to minimize risks to the user (as well as to other people and the general environment)
- the identity of the supplier (who might be a manufacturer or importer)

The GHS chemical hazard pictograms are intended to provide the basis for or to replace national systems of hazard pictograms. In fact, GHS transport pictograms are the same as those recommended in the UN Recommendations on the Transport of Dangerous Goods, widely implemented in national regulations in many countries.

The figure below shows some examples of hazard pictograms.

Figure 1. Hazard Pictograms

Can you guess what each pictogram means? They are divided into two groups. One group (numbers 1 and 2) shows the first set of pictograms mentioned above, physical hazards pictograms. On the other hand, the other group (numbers 3, 4, 5, 6 and 7) contains the second set, transport pictograms. Now, we will look at each of them, beginning with the first group.

The pictograms of the first group have their own names; No. 1 is called "Flame," and No. 2 is named "Flame over Circle." The former means flammable materials or substances liable to catch fire by themselves when exposed to water or air, or which emit flammable gas and cause other materials to burn, while the latter identifies oxidizers, which are chemicals that help something burn or make fires burn hotter and last longer.

Next, let us move on to the second group. No. 3 shows flammable solids or self-reactive substances. Under conditions encountered in transport, they could possibly catch fire, may cause or contribute to fire through friction, or may explode if not treated carefully. No. 4 means flammable liquids — liquids which have a flash point of less than 60℃ and which are capable of sustaining burning. No. 5 means substances liable to burn spontaneously — substances which are liable to spontaneously heat up under normal conditions encountered in transport, or to heat up due to contact with air, and are then liable to catch fire. No. 6 shows influential substances — substances which, while in themselves not necessarily burnable, may, generally by releasing oxygen, cause, or contribute to, the burning of other material. Finally, No. 7 means organic poisons — organic substances which contain harmful matter or hazardous materials with certain chemical structures.

Each pictogram covers a specific type of hazard and is designed to be immediately recognizable to anyone handling hazardous material, though those pictograms are not so easy for general people to understand.

第5回　英語（リーディング）

Your presentation poster draft:

> ## Do you know hazard pictograms?
>
> ### What are hazard pictograms?
>
> · They are graphic images that show what type of hazard is present in a product.
>
> · [41]
>
> ### Some kinds of hazard pictograms
>
> | No. | Pictogram | Hazards | General Meaning |
> |-----|-----------|---------|-----------------|
> | 1 | | · flammable materials or substances | They are materials or substances which can burn or [42] . |
> | 2 | | · oxidizers | They are chemicals which [43] . |
> | 3 | | · flammable solids
· self-reactive substances | They are materials or substances which can catch fire easily due to friction. |
>
> ### Pictograms with common messages
>
> [44]
>
> [45]

問1 Under the first poster heading, your group wants to introduce hazard pictograms as explained in the passage. Which of the following is the most appropriate? ☐ 41 ☐

① The same hazards may be represented by different symbols.

② There are two sets, and you can use both sets at the same time.

③ They are accompanied by other information about a product.

④ They were invented by the UN and are widely accepted around the world.

問2 You have been asked to write general meanings of No. 1 and No. 2 pictograms. Choose the best options for ☐ 42 ☐ and ☐ 43 ☐ .

No. 1 ☐ 42 ☐

① contain a deadly poison

② explode near a fire

③ melt even in low temperatures

④ release gases that burn

No. 2 ☐ 43 ☐

① can be active and catch fire without proper controls

② can shorten the time in which materials explode

③ contain substances which can absorb oxygen

④ increase the temperature and length of fire

第5回　英語（リーディング）

問3　You are making statements about some pictograms which share common messages. According to the article, which two of the following are appropriate? (The order does not matter.) ⬚44⬚ ・ ⬚45⬚

① No.1 and 5 can be dangerous when air is brought into contact with them.

② No.1 and 6 release gases that can cause a fire.

③ No. 1, 6, and 7 mean that they can emit poisonous gas.

④ No. 1, and No. 7 mean that they burn easily and produce harmful gas.

⑤ No. 2 and No. 6 indicate that they are flammable and can cause big fires.

⑥ No. 3, 4 and 6 show that they start to burn at low temperatures.

試作問題

2022年度大学入試センター公表

令和7年度（2025年度）大学入学共通テスト

試作問題

英語（リーディング）

（30点）

第Ａ問

You are working on an essay about whether high school students should be allowed to use their smartphones in class. You will follow the steps below.

    Step 1: Read and understand various viewpoints about smartphone use.

    Step 2: Take a position on high school students' use of their smartphones in class.

    Step 3: Create an outline for an essay using additional sources.

[Step 1] Read various sources

Author A (Teacher)

My colleagues often question whether smartphones can help students develop life-long knowledge and skills. I believe that they can, as long as their use is carefully planned. Smartphones support various activities in class that can enhance learning. Some examples include making surveys for projects and sharing one's learning with others. Another advantage is that we do not have to provide students with devices; they can use their phones! Schools should take full advantage of students' powerful computing devices.

Author B (Psychologist)

It is a widespread opinion that smartphones can encourage student learning. Being believed by many, though, does not make an opinion correct. A recent study found that when high school students were allowed to use their smartphones in class, it was impossible for them to concentrate on learning. In fact, even if students were not using their own smartphones, seeing their classmates using smartphones was a distraction. It is clear that schools should make the classroom a place that is free from the interference of smartphones.

Author C (Parent)

I recently bought a smartphone for my son who is a high school student. This is because his school is located far from our town. He usually leaves home early and returns late. Now, he can contact me or access essential information if he has trouble. On the other hand, I sometimes see him walking while looking at his smartphone. If he is not careful, he could have an accident. Generally, I think that high school students are safer with smartphones, but parents still need to be aware of the risks. I also wonder how he is using it in class.

— 2 —

Author D (High school student)

At school, we are allowed to use our phones in class. It makes sense for our school to permit us to use them because most students have smartphones. During class, we make use of foreign language learning apps on our smartphones, which is really helpful to me. I am now more interested in learning than I used to be, and my test scores have improved. The other day, though, my teacher got mad at me when she caught me reading online comics in class. Occasionally these things happen, but overall, smartphones have improved my learning.

Author E (School principal)

Teachers at my school were initially skeptical of smartphones because they thought students would use them to socialize with friends during class. Thus, we banned them. As more educational apps became available, however, we started to think that smartphones could be utilized as learning aids in the classroom. Last year, we decided to allow smartphone use in class. Unfortunately, we did not have the results we wanted. We found that smartphones distracted students unless rules for their use were in place and students followed them. This was easier said than done, though.

問1　Both Authors A and D mention that ☐ 1 ☐ .

① apps for learning on smartphones can help students perform better on exams
② one reason to use smartphones as an educational tool is that most students possess one
③ smartphones can be used to support activities for learning both at school and at home
④ smartphones make it possible for students to share their ideas with classmates

問2　Author B implies that ☐ 2 ☐ .

① having time away from digital devices interferes with students' motivation to learn
② sometimes commonly held beliefs can be different from the facts that research reveals
③ students who do not have smartphones are likely to consider themselves better learners
④ the classroom should be a place where students can learn without the interference of teachers

— 3 —

[Step 2] Take a position

問3　Now that you understand the various viewpoints, you have taken a position on high
school students' use of their smartphones in class, and have written it out as below. Choose
the best options to complete ⃞3⃞ , ⃞4⃞ , and ⃞5⃞ .

Your position: High school students should not be allowed to use their smartphones in class.
- Authors ⃞3⃞ and ⃞4⃞ support your position.
- The main argument of the two authors: ⃞5⃞ .

Options for ⃞3⃞ and ⃞4⃞ (The order does not matter.)
① A
② B
③ C
④ D
⑤ E

Options for ⃞5⃞
① Making practical rules for smartphone use in class is difficult for school teachers
② Smartphones may distract learning because the educational apps are difficult to use
③ Smartphones were designed for communication and not for classroom learning
④ Students cannot focus on studying as long as they have access to smartphones in class

試作問題

[Step 3] Create an outline using Sources A and B

Outline of your essay:

Using smartphones in class is not a good idea

Introduction

    Smartphones have become essential for modern life, but students should be prohibited from using their phones during class.

Body

    Reason 1: [From Step 2]

    Reason 2: [Based on Source A]   ········· **6**

    Reason 3: [Based on Source B]   ········· **7**

Conclusion

    High schools should not allow students to use their smartphones in class.

Source A

Mobile devices offer advantages for learning. For example, one study showed that university students learned psychology better when using their interactive mobile apps compared with their digital textbooks. Although the information was the same, extra features in the apps, such as 3D images, enhanced students' learning. It is important to note, however, that digital devices are not all equally effective. Another study found that students understand content better using their laptop computers rather than their smartphones because of the larger screen size. Schools must select the type of digital device that will maximize students' learning, and there is a strong argument for schools to provide computers or tablets rather than to have students use their smartphones. If all students are provided with computers or tablets with the same apps installed, there will be fewer technical problems and it will be easier for teachers to conduct class. This also enables students without their own smartphones to participate in all class activities.

— 5 —

Source B

A study conducted in the U.S. found that numerous teenagers are addicted to their smartphones. The study surveyed about 1,000 students between the ages of 13 and 18. The graph below shows the percentages of students who agreed with the statements about their smartphone use.

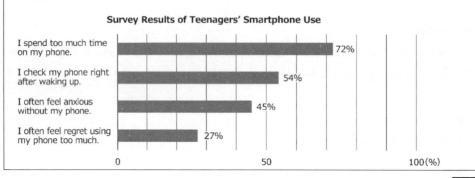

問4　Based on Source A, which of the following is the most appropriate for Reason 2?　6

① Apps that display 3D images are essential for learning, but not all students have these apps on their smartphones.

② Certain kinds of digital devices can enhance educational effectiveness, but smartphones are not the best.

③ Students should obtain digital skills not only on smartphones but also on other devices to prepare for university.

④ We should stick to textbooks because psychology studies have not shown the positive effects of digital devices on learning.

問5　For Reason 3, you have decided to write, "Young students are facing the danger of smartphone addiction." Based on Source B, which option best supports this statement?　7

① Although more than half of teenagers reported using their smartphones too much, less than a quarter actually feel regret about it. This may indicate unawareness of a dependency problem.

② Close to three in four teenagers spend too much time on their phones. In fact, over 50% check their phones immediately after waking. Many teenagers cannot resist using their phones.

③ Over 70% of teenagers think they spend too much time on their phones, and more than half feel anxious without them. This kind of dependence can negatively impact their daily lives.

④ Teenagers are always using smartphones. In fact, more than three-quarters admit to using their phones too much. Their lives are controlled by smartphones from morning to night.

試作問題

（下 書 き 用 紙）

英語（リーディング）の問題は次に続く。

— 7 —

第Ｂ問

In English class you are writing an essay on a social issue you are interested in. This is your most recent draft. You are now working on revisions based on comments from your teacher.

Eco-friendly Action with Fashion	**Comments**
Many people love fashion. Clothes are important for self-expression, but fashion can be harmful to the environment. In Japan, about 480,000 tons of clothes are said to be thrown away every year. This is equal to about 130 large trucks a day. We need to change our "throw-away" behavior. This essay will highlight three ways to be more sustainable.	
First, when shopping, avoid making unplanned purchases. According to a government survey, approximately 64% of shoppers do not think about what is already in their closet. (1)∧So, try to plan your choices carefully when you are shopping.	*(1) You are missing something here. Add more information between the two sentences to connect them.*
In addition, purchase high-quality clothes which usually last longer. Even though the price might be higher, it is good value when an item can be worn for several years. (2)∧Cheaper fabrics can lose their color or start to look old quickly, so they need to be thrown away sooner.	*(2) Insert a connecting expression here.*
Finally, (3)<u>think about your clothes</u>. For example, sell them to used clothing stores. That way other people can enjoy wearing them. You could also donate clothes to a charity for people who need them. Another way is to find a new purpose for them. There are many ways to transform outfits into useful items such as quilts or bags.	*(3) This topic sentence doesn't really match this paragraph. Rewrite it.*
In conclusion, it is time for a lifestyle change. From now on, check your closet before you go shopping, (4) <u>select better things,</u> and lastly, give your clothes a second life. In this way, we can all become more sustainable with fashion.	*(4) The underlined phrase doesn't summarize your essay content enough. Change it.*

Overall Comment:
Your essay is getting better. Keep up the good work. (Have you checked your own closet? I have checked mine! ☺)

— 8 —

試作問題

問 1　Based on comment (1), which is the best sentence to add? 　1

　① As a result, people buy many similar items they do not need.

　② Because of this, customers cannot enjoy clothes shopping.

　③ Due to this, shop clerks want to know what customers need.

　④ In this situation, consumers tend to avoid going shopping.

問 2　Based on comment (2), which is the best expression to add? 　2

　① for instance

　② in contrast

　③ nevertheless

　④ therefore

問 3　Based on comment (3), which is the most appropriate way to rewrite the topic sentence?
　　　3

　① buy fewer new clothes

　② dispose of old clothes

　③ find ways to reuse clothes

　④ give unwanted clothes away

問 4　Based on comment (4), which is the best replacement? 　4

　① buy items that maintain their condition

　② choose inexpensive fashionable clothes

　③ pick items that can be transformed

　④ purchase clothes that are second-hand

— 9 —

'24 本試験問題

2024年度

大学入学共通テスト

本試験

英語（リーディング）

（100点　80分）

● 標 準 所 要 時 間 ●

第1問　8分程度	第4問　10分程度
第2問　12分程度	第5問　15分程度
第3問　10分程度	第6問　25分程度

英　　語（リーディング）

各大問の英文や図表を読み，解答番号 1 ～ 49 にあてはまるものとして最も適当な選択肢を選びなさい。

第1問 （配点 10）

A　You are studying English at a language school in the US. The school is planning an event. You want to attend, so you are reading the flyer.

The Thorpe English Language School

International Night

Friday, May 24, 5 p.m.-8 p.m.

Entrance Fee: $5

The Thorpe English Language School (TELS) is organizing an international exchange event. TELS students don't need to pay the entrance fee. Please present your student ID at the reception desk in the Student Lobby.

- **Enjoy foods from various parts of the world**
  Have you ever tasted hummus from the Middle East? How about tacos from Mexico? Couscous from North Africa? Try them all!

- **Experience different languages and new ways to communicate**
  Write basic expressions such as "hello" and "thank you" in Arabic, Italian, Japanese, and Spanish. Learn how people from these cultures use facial expressions and their hands to communicate.

- **Watch dance performances**
  From 7 p.m. watch flamenco, hula, and samba dance shows on the stage! After each dance, performers will teach some basic steps. Please join in.

Lots of pictures, flags, maps, textiles, crafts, and games will be displayed in the hall. If you have some pictures or items from your home country which can be displayed at the event, let a school staff member know by May 17!

問 1 To join the event free of charge, you must **1** .

① bring pictures from your home country

② consult a staff member about the display

③ fill out a form in the Student Lobby

④ show proof that you are a TELS student

問 2 At the event, you can **2** .

① learn about gestures in various cultures

② participate in a dance competition

③ read short stories in foreign languages

④ try cooking international dishes

B You are an exchange student in the US and next week your class will go on a day trip. The teacher has provided some information.

Tours of Yentonville
The Yentonville Tourist Office offers three city tours.

The History Tour
The day will begin with a visit to St. Patrick's Church, which was built when the city was established in the mid-1800s. Opposite the church is the early-20th-century Mayor's House. There will be a tour of the house and its beautiful garden. Finally, cross the city by public bus and visit the Peace Park. Opened soon after World War II, it was the site of many demonstrations in the 1960s.

The Arts Tour

The morning will be spent in the Yentonville Arts District. We will begin in the Art Gallery where there are many paintings from Europe and the US. After lunch, enjoy a concert across the street at the Bruton Concert Hall before walking a short distance to the Artists' Avenue. This part of the district was developed several years ago when new artists' studios and the nearby Sculpture Park were created. Watch artists at work in their studios and afterwards wander around the park, finding sculptures among the trees.

The Sports Tour
First thing in the morning, you can watch the Yentonville Lions football team training at their open-air facility in the suburbs. In the afternoon, travel by subway to the Yentonville Hockey Arena, completed last fall. Spend some time in its exhibition hall to learn about the arena's unique design. Finally, enjoy a professional hockey game in the arena.

Yentonville Tourist Office, January, 2024

2024 本試 英語（リーディング）

問 1　Yentonville has ☐ 3 .

① a church built 250 years ago when the city was constructed

② a unique football training facility in the center of the town

③ an art studio where visitors can create original works of art

④ an arts area with both an art gallery and a concert hall

問 2　On all three tours, you will ☐ 4 .

① learn about historic events in the city

② see people demonstrate their skills

③ spend time both indoors and outdoors

④ use public transportation to get around

問 3　Which is the newest place in Yentonville you can visit on the tours?
☐ 5

① The Hockey Arena

② The Mayor's House

③ The Peace Park

④ The Sculpture Park

― 5 ―

第 2 問 (配点 20)

A You are an exchange student at a high school in the UK and find this flyer.

 Invitation to the Strategy Game Club

Have you ever wanted to learn strategy games like chess, *shogi*, or *go*? They are actually more than just games. You can learn skills such as thinking logically and deeply without distractions. Plus, these games are really fun! This club is open to all students of our school. Regardless of skill level, you are welcome to join.

We play strategy games together and...

- learn basic moves from demonstrations by club members
- play online against club friends
- share tips on our club webpage
- learn the history and etiquette of each game
- analyse games using computer software
- participate in local and national tournaments

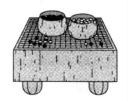

Regular meetings: Wednesday afternoons in Room 301, Student Centre

Member Comments

- My mind is clearer, calmer, and more focused in class.
- It's cool to learn how some games have certain similarities.
- At tournaments, I like discussing strategies with other participants.
- Members share Internet videos that explain practical strategies for chess.
- It's nice to have friends who give good advice about *go*.
- I was a complete beginner when I joined, and I had no problem!

2024 本試 英語（リーディング）

問 1 According to the flyer, which is true about the club? 6

① Absolute beginners are welcome.
② Members edit computer programs.
③ Professional players give formal demonstrations.
④ Students from other schools can join.

問 2 Which of the following is **not** mentioned as a club activity? 7

① Having games with non-club members
② Playing matches against computers
③ Sharing game-playing ideas on the Internet
④ Studying the backgrounds of strategy games

問 3 One **opinion** stated by a member is that 8 .

① comparing different games is interesting
② many videos about *go* are useful
③ members learn tips at competitions
④ regular meetings are held off campus

問 4　The club invitation and a member's comment both mention that | 9 | .

    ① new members must demonstrate experience

    ② online support is necessary to be a good player

    ③ *shogi* is a logical and stimulating game

    ④ strategy games help improve one's concentration

問 5　This club is most likely suitable for students who want to | 10 | .

    ① create their own computer strategy games

    ② improve their skill level of playing strategy games

    ③ learn proper British etiquette through playing strategy games

    ④ spend weekends playing strategy games in the club room

B You are a college student going to study in the US and need travel insurance. You find this review of an insurance plan written by a female international student who studied in the US for six months.

There are many things to consider before traveling abroad: pack appropriate clothes, prepare your travel expenses, and don't forget medication (if necessary). Also, you should purchase travel insurance.

When I studied at Fairville University in California, I bought travel insurance from TravSafer International. I signed up online in less than 15 minutes and was immediately covered. They accept any form of payment, usually on a monthly basis. There were three plans. All plans include a one-time health check-up.

The Premium Plan is $100/month. The plan provides 24-hour medical support through a smartphone app and telephone service. Immediate financial support will be authorized if you need to stay in a hospital.

The Standard Plan worked best for me. It had the 24-hour telephone assistance and included a weekly email with tips for staying healthy in a foreign country. It wasn't cheap: $75/month. However, it was nice to get the optional 15% discount because I paid for six months of coverage in advance.

If your budget is limited, you can choose the Economy Plan, which is $25/month. It has the 24-hour telephone support like the other plans but only covers emergency care. Also, they can arrange a taxi to a hospital at a reduced cost if considered necessary by the support center.

I never got sick or hurt, so I thought it was a waste of money to get insurance. Then my friend from Brazil broke his leg while playing soccer and had to spend a few days in a hospital. He had chosen the Premium Plan and it covered everything! I realized how important insurance is—you know that you will be supported when you are in trouble.

問 1 According to the review, which of the following is true? 11

① Day and night medical assistance is available with the most expensive plan.

② The cheapest plan includes free hospitalization for any reason.

③ The mid-level plan does not include the one-time health check-up.

④ The writer's plan cost her over $100 every month.

問 2 Which is **not** included in the cheapest option? 12

① Email support

② Emergency treatment

③ Telephone help desk

④ Transport assistance

2024 本試 英語（リーディング）

問 3　Which is the best combination that describes TravSafer International?
　　　13

　　　A : They allow monthly payments.
　　　B : They design scholarship plans for students.
　　　C : They help you remember your medication.
　　　D : They offer an Internet-based registration system.
　　　E : They require a few days to process the application form.

　　　① 　A and D
　　　② 　A and E
　　　③ 　B and D
　　　④ 　B and E
　　　⑤ 　C and D

問 4　The writer's **opinion** of her chosen plan is that 　14　.

　　　① 　it prevented her from being health conscious
　　　② 　she was not satisfied with the telephone assistance
　　　③ 　the option for cost reduction was attractive
　　　④ 　the treatment for her broken leg was covered

問 5　Which of the following best describes the writer's attitude?　15

　　　① 　She believes the smartphone app is useful.
　　　② 　She considers travel preparation to be important.
　　　③ 　She feels the US medical system is unique in the world.
　　　④ 　She thinks a different hospital would have been better for her friend.

— 11 —

第3問 (配点 15)

A Susan, your English ALT's sister, visited your class last month. Now back in the UK, she wrote on her blog about an event she took part in.

Hi!

I participated in a photo rally for foreign tourists with my friends: See the rules on the right. As photo rally beginners, we decided to aim for only five of the checkpoints. In three minutes, we arrived at our first target, the city museum. In quick succession, we made the second, third, and fourth targets. Things were going smoothly! But, on the way to the last target, the statue of a famous samurai from the city, we got lost. Time was running out and my feet were hurting from walking for over two hours. We stopped a man with a pet monkey for help, but neither our Japanese nor his English were good enough. After he'd explained the way using gestures, we realised we wouldn't have enough time to get there and would have to give up. We took a photo with him and said goodbye. When we got back to Sakura City Hall, we were surprised to hear that the winning team had completed 19 checkpoints. One of our photos was selected to be on the event website (click here). It reminds me of the man's warmth and kindness: our own "gold medal."

> **Sakura City Photo Rally Rules**
>
> - Each group can only use the **camera** and **paper map**, both provided by us
> - Take as many photos of **25 checkpoints** (designated sightseeing spots) as possible
> - **3-hour** time limit
> - Photos must include **all 3 team members**
> - All members must move **together**
> - **No** mobile phones
> - **No** transport

— 12 —

問 1　You click the link in the blog. Which picture appears?　16

問 2　You are asked to comment on Susan's blog. Which would be an appropriate comment to her?　17

① I want to see a picture of you wearing the gold medal!
② You did your best. Come back to Japan and try again!
③ You reached 19 checkpoints in three hours? Really? Wow!!
④ Your photo is great! Did you upgrade your phone?

B You are going to participate in an English Day. As preparation, you are reading an article in the school newspaper written by Yuzu, who took part in it last year.

Virtual Field Trip to a South Sea Island

This year, for our English Day, we participated in a virtual science tour. The winter weather had been terrible, so we were excited to see the tropical scenery of the volcanic island projected on the screen.

First, we "took a road trip" to learn about the geography of the island, using navigation software to view the route. We "got into the car," which our teacher, Mr Leach, sometimes stopped so we could look out of the window and get a better sense of the rainforest. Afterwards, we asked Mr Leach about what we'd seen.

Later, we "dived into the ocean" and learnt about the diversity of marine creatures. We observed a coral reef via a live camera. Mr Leach asked us if we could count the number of creatures, but there were too many! Then he showed us an image of the ocean 10 years ago. The reef we'd seen on camera was dynamic, but in the photo it was even more full of life. It looked so different after only 10 years! Mr Leach told us human activity was affecting the ocean and it could be totally ruined if we didn't act now.

In the evening, we studied astronomy under a "perfect starry sky." We put up tents in the gymnasium and created a temporary planetarium on the ceiling using a projector. We were fascinated by the sky full of constellations, shooting stars, and the Milky
Way. Someone pointed out one of the brightest lights and asked Mr Leach if it was Venus, a planet close to Earth. He nodded and explained that humans have created so much artificial light that hardly anything is visible in our city's night sky.

On my way home after school, the weather had improved and the sky was now cloudless. I looked up at the moonless sky and realised what Mr Leach had told us was true.

問 1　Yuzu's article also included student comments (①~④) describing the events in the virtual tour. Put the comments in the order in which the events happened.

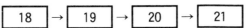

①
I was wondering how dangerous the island was. I saw beautiful birds and a huge snake in the jungle.

②
It was really shocking that there had been many more creatures before. We should protect our beautiful oceans!

③
Setting up a camping site in the gymnasium was kind of weird, but great fun! Better than outside, because we weren't bitten by bugs!

④
We were lost for words during the space show and realised we often don't notice things even though they're there.

問 2　From the tour, Yuzu did **not** learn about the　22　of the south sea island.

① marine ecosystem

② night-time sky

③ seasonal weather

④ trees and plants

問 3　On the way home, Yuzu looked up and most likely saw　23　in the night sky.

① a shooting star

② just a few stars

③ the full moon

④ the Milky Way

2024 本試 英語 (リーディング)

（下 書 き 用 紙）

英語 (リーディング) の試験問題は次に続く。

第 4 問 (配点 16)

Your college English club's room has several problems and you want to redesign it. Based on the following article and the results of a questionnaire given to members, you make a handout for a group discussion.

What Makes a Good Classroom?

Diana Bashworth, writer at *Trends in Education*

As many schools work to improve their classrooms, it is important to have some ideas for making design decisions. SIN, which stands for *Stimulation, Individualization*, and *Naturalness*, is a framework that might be helpful to consider when designing classrooms.

The first, Stimulation, has two aspects: color and complexity. This has to do with the ceiling, floor, walls, and interior furnishings. For example, a classroom that lacks colors might be uninteresting. On the other hand, a classroom should not be too colorful. A bright color could be used on one wall, on the floor, window coverings, or furniture. In addition, it can be visually distracting to have too many things displayed on walls. It is suggested that 20 to 30 percent of wall space remain free.

The next item in the framework is Individualization, which includes two considerations: ownership and flexibility. Ownership refers to whether the classroom feels personalized. Examples of this include having chairs and desks that are suitable for student sizes and ages, and providing storage space and areas for displaying student works or projects. Flexibility is about having a classroom that allows for different kinds of activities.

Naturalness relates to the quality and quantity of light, both natural and artificial, and the temperature of the classroom. Too much natural light may make screens and boards difficult to see; students may have difficulty reading or writing if there is a lack of light. In addition, hot summer classrooms do not promote effective study. Schools should install systems allowing for the adjustment of both light and temperature.

While Naturalness is more familiar to us, and therefore often considered the priority, the other components are equally important. Hopefully, these ideas can guide your project to a successful end.

— 18 —

Results of the Questionnaire

Q1: Choose any items that match your use of the English club's room.

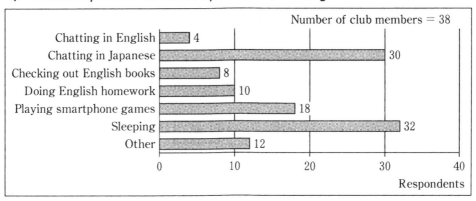

Q2: What do you think about the current English club's room?

Main comments:

Student 1 (S 1): I can't see the projector screen and whiteboard well on a sunny day. Also, there's no way to control the temperature.

S 2: By the windows, the sunlight makes it hard to read. The other side of the room doesn't get enough light. Also, the books are disorganized and the walls are covered with posters. It makes me feel uncomfortable.

S 3: The chairs don't really fit me and the desks are hard to move when we work in small groups. Also, lots of members speak Japanese, even though it's an English club.

S 4: The pictures of foreign countries on the walls make me want to speak English. Everyone likes the sofas — they are so comfortable that we often use the room for sleeping!

S 5: The room is so far away, so I hardly ever go there! Aren't there other rooms available?

S 6: There's so much gray in the room. I don't like it. But it's good that there are plenty of everyday English phrases on the walls!

Your discussion handout:

Room Improvement Project

■ **SIN Framework**
- What it is: [24]
- SIN = Stimulation, Individualization, Naturalness

■ **Design Recommendations Based on SIN and Questionnaire Results**
- Stimulation:

  Cover the floor with a colorful rug and [25].

- Individualization:

  Replace room furniture.

  (tables with wheels → easy to move around)

- Naturalness:

  [26]

  A. Install blinds on windows.

  B. Make temperature control possible.

  C. Move projector screen away from windows.

  D. Place sofas near walls.

  E. Put floor lamp in darker corner.

■ **Other Issues to Discuss**
- The majority of members [27] the room as [28]'s comment mentioned. How can we solve this?
- Based on both the graph and [29]'s comment, should we set a language rule in the room to motivate members to speak English more?
- S5 doesn't like the location, but we can't change the room, so let's think about how to encourage members to visit more often.

— 20 —

2024 本試 英語（リーディング）

問 1　Choose the best option for ｜　24　｜.

① A guide to show which colors are appropriate to use in classrooms

② A method to prioritize the needs of students and teachers in classrooms

③ A model to follow when planning classroom environments

④ A system to understand how classrooms influence students' performance

問 2　Choose the best option for ｜　25　｜.

① move the screen to a better place

② paint each wall a different color

③ put books on shelves

④ reduce displayed items

問 3　You are checking the handout. You notice an error in the recommendations under Naturalness. Which of the following should you **remove**? ｜　26　｜

① A
② B
③ C
④ D
⑤ E

— 21 —

問 4　Choose the best options for　27　and　28　.

　　27

① borrow books from

② can't easily get to

③ don't use Japanese in

④ feel anxious in

⑤ take naps in

　　28

① S 1

② S 2

③ S 3

④ S 4

⑤ S 5

⑥ S 6

問 5　Choose the best option for　29　.

① S 1

② S 2

③ S 3

④ S 4

⑤ S 5

⑥ S 6

2024 本試 英語（リーディング）

（下 書 き 用 紙）

英語（リーディング）の試験問題は次に続く。

第5問 (配点 15)

You are in an English discussion group, and it is your turn to introduce a story. You have found a story in an English language magazine in Japan. You are preparing notes for your presentation.

Maki's Kitchen

"*Irasshai-mase*," said Maki as two customers entered her restaurant, Maki's Kitchen. Maki had joined her family business at the age of 19 when her father became ill. After he recovered, Maki decided to continue. Eventually, Maki's parents retired and she became the owner. Maki had many regular customers who came not only for the delicious food, but also to sit at the counter and talk to her. Although her business was doing very well, Maki occasionally daydreamed about doing something different.

"Can we sit at the counter?" she heard. It was her old friends, Takuya and Kasumi. A phone call a few weeks earlier from Kasumi to Takuya had given them the idea to visit Maki and surprise her.

Takuya's phone vibrated, and he saw a familiar name, Kasumi.

"Kasumi!"

"Hi Takuya, I saw you in the newspaper. Congratulations!"

"Thanks. Hey, you weren't at our 20th high school reunion last month."

"No, I couldn't make it. I can't believe it's been 20 years since we graduated. Actually, I was calling to ask if you've seen Maki recently."

Takuya's family had moved to Kawanaka Town shortly before he started high school. He joined the drama club, where he met Maki and Kasumi. The three became inseparable. After graduation, Takuya left Kawanaka to become an actor, while Maki and Kasumi remained. Maki had decided she wanted to study at university and enrolled in a preparatory school. Kasumi, on the other hand, started her career. Takuya tried out for various acting roles but was constantly rejected; eventually, he quit.

Exactly one year after graduation, Takuya returned to Kawanaka with his dreams destroyed. He called Maki, who offered her sympathy. He was surprised to learn that Maki had abandoned her plan to attend university because she had to manage her family's restaurant. Her first day of work had been the day he called. For some reason, Takuya could not resist giving Maki some advice.

"Maki, I've always thought your family's restaurant should change the coffee it serves. I think people in Kawanaka want a bolder flavor. I'd be happy to recommend a different brand," he said.

"Takuya, you really know your coffee. Hey, I was walking by Café Kawanaka and saw a help-wanted sign. You should apply!" Maki replied.

Takuya was hired by Café Kawanaka and became fascinated by the science of coffee making. On the one-year anniversary of his employment, Takuya was talking to Maki at her restaurant.

"Maki," he said, "do you know what my dream is?"

"It must have something to do with coffee."

"That's right! It's to have my own coffee business."

"I can't imagine a better person for it. What are you waiting for?"

Maki's encouragement inspired Takuya. He quit his job, purchased a coffee bean roaster, and began roasting beans. Maki had a sign in her restaurant saying, "We proudly serve Takuya's Coffee," and this publicity helped the coffee gain popularity in Kawanaka. Takuya started making good money selling his beans. Eventually, he opened his own café and became a successful business owner.

Kasumi was reading the newspaper when she saw the headline: *TAKUYA'S CAFÉ ATTRACTING TOURISTS TO KAWANAKA TOWN.* "Who would have thought that Takuya would be so successful?" Kasumi thought to herself as she reflected on her past.

In the high school drama club, Kasumi's duty was to put make-up on the actors. No one could do it better than her. Maki noticed this and saw that a cosmetics company called Beautella was advertising for salespeople. She encouraged Kasumi to apply, and, after graduation, she became an employee of Beautella.

The work was tough; Kasumi went door to door selling cosmetics. On bad days, she would call Maki, who would lift her spirits. One day, Maki had an idea, "Doesn't Beautella do make-up workshops? I think you are more suited for that. You can show people how to use the make-up. They'll love the way they look and buy lots of cosmetics!"

Kasumi's company agreed to let her do workshops, and they were a hit! Kasumi's sales were so good that eight months out of high school, she had been promoted, moving to the big city of Ishijima. Since then, she had steadily climbed her way up the company ladder until she had been named vice-president of Beautella this year.

"I wouldn't be vice-president now without Maki," she thought, "she helped me when I was struggling, but I was too absorbed with my work in Ishijima to give her support when she had to quit her preparatory school." Glancing back to the article, she decided to call Takuya.

"Maki wasn't at the reunion. I haven't seen her in ages," said Takuya.

"Same here. It's a pity. Where would we be without her?" asked Kasumi.

The conversation became silent, as they wordlessly communicated their guilt. Then, Kasumi had an idea.

The three friends were talking and laughing when Maki asked, "By the way, I'm really happy to see you two, but what brings you here?"

"Payback," said Takuya.

"Have I done something wrong?" asked Maki.

"No. The opposite. You understand people incredibly well. You can identify others' strengths and show them how to make use of them. We're proof of this. You made us aware of our gifts," said Takuya.

"The irony is that you couldn't do the same for yourself," added Kasumi.

"I think Ishijima University would be ideal for you. It offers a degree program in counseling that's designed for people with jobs," said Takuya.

"You'd have to go there a few times a month, but you could stay with me. Also, Takuya can help you find staff for your restaurant," said Kasumi.

Maki closed her eyes and imagined Kawanaka having both "Maki's Kitchen" and "Maki's Counseling." She liked that idea.

Your notes:

Maki's Kitchen

Story outline

Maki, Takuya, and Kasumi graduate from high school.

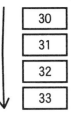

Maki begins to think about a second career.

About Maki

- Age: [34]
- Occupation: restaurant owner
- How she supported her friends:

    Provided Takuya with encouragement and [35].

    〃   Kasumi   〃   〃   and [36].

Interpretation of key moments

- Kasumi and Takuya experience an uncomfortable silence on the phone because they [37].
- In the final scene, Kasumi uses the word "irony" with Maki. The <u>irony</u> is that Maki does not [38].

問 1　Choose **four** out of the five events (① ~ ⑤) and rearrange them in the order they happened. $\boxed{30}$ → $\boxed{31}$ → $\boxed{32}$ → $\boxed{33}$

① Kasumi becomes vice-president of her company.

② Kasumi gets in touch with Takuya.

③ Maki gets her university degree.

④ Maki starts working in her family business.

⑤ Takuya is inspired to start his own business.

問 2　Choose the best option for $\boxed{34}$.

① early 30s

② late 30s

③ early 40s

④ late 40s

問 3　Choose the best options for $\boxed{35}$ and $\boxed{36}$.

① made the product known to people

② proposed a successful business idea

③ purchased equipment for the business

④ suggested moving to a bigger city

⑤ taught the necessary skills for success

問 4 Choose the best option for 37 .

① do not want to discuss their success

② have not spoken in a long time

③ regret not appreciating their friend more

④ think Maki was envious of their achievements

問 5 Choose the best option for 38 .

① like to try different things

② recognize her own talent

③ understand the ability she lacks

④ want to pursue her dreams

第6問 (配点 24)

A Your English teacher has assigned this article to you. You need to prepare notes to give a short talk.

Perceptions of Time

When you hear the word "time," it is probably hours, minutes, and seconds that immediately come to mind. In the late 19th century, however, philosopher Henri Bergson described how people usually do not experience time as it is measured by clocks (**clock time**). Humans do not have a known biological mechanism to measure clock time, so they use mental processes instead. This is called **psychological time**, which everyone perceives differently.

If you were asked how long it had taken to finish your homework, you probably would not know exactly. You would think back and make an estimate. In a 1975 experiment, participants were shown either simple or complex shapes for a fixed amount of time and asked to memorize them. Afterwards, they were asked how long they had looked at the shapes. To answer, they used a mental process called **retrospective timing**, which is estimating time based on the information retrieved from memory. Participants who were shown the complex shapes felt the time was longer, while the people who saw the simple shapes experienced the opposite.

Another process to measure psychological time is called **prospective timing**. It is used when you are actively keeping track of time while doing something. Instead of using the amount of information recalled, the level of attention given to time while doing the activity is used. In several studies, the participants performed tasks while estimating the time needed to complete them. Time seemed shorter for the people doing more challenging mental activities which required them to place more focus on the task than on time.

— 30 —

2024 本試 英語 (リーディング)

Time felt longer for the participants who did simpler tasks and the longest for those who were waiting or doing nothing.

Your emotional state can influence your awareness of time, too. For example, you can be enjoying a concert so much that you forget about time. Afterwards, you are shocked that hours have passed by in what seemed to be the blink of an eye. To explain this, we often say, "Time flies when you're having fun." The opposite occurs when you are bored. Instead of being focused on an activity, you notice the time. It seems to go very slowly as you cannot wait for your boredom to end. Fear also affects our perception of time. In a 2006 study, more than 60 people experienced skydiving for the first time. Participants with high levels of unpleasant emotions perceived the time spent skydiving to be much longer than it was in reality.

Psychological time also seems to move differently during life stages. Children constantly encounter new information and have new experiences, which makes each day memorable and seem longer when recalled. Also, time creeps by for them as they anticipate upcoming events such as birthdays and trips. For most adults, unknown information is rarely encountered and new experiences become less frequent, so less mental focus is required and each day becomes less memorable. However, this is not always the case. Daily routines are shaken up when drastic changes occur, such as changing jobs or relocating to a new city. In such cases, the passage of time for those people is similar to that for children. But generally speaking, time seems to accelerate as we mature.

Knowledge of psychological time can be helpful in our daily lives, as it may help us deal with boredom. Because time passes slowly when we are not mentally focused and thinking about time, changing to a more engaging activity, such as reading a book, will help ease our boredom and speed up the time. The next occasion that you hear "Time flies when you're having fun," you will be reminded of this.

— 31 —

Your notes:

Perceptions of Time

Outline by paragraph

1. ☐ 39
2. Retrospective timing
3. Prospective timing
4. ☐ 40
   ➤ Skydiving
5. Effects of age
   ➤ Time speeds up as we mature, but a ☐ 41 .
6. Practical tips

My original examples to help the audience

A. Retrospective timing
   Example: ☐ 42
B. Prospective timing
   Example: ☐ 43

問 1　Choose the best options for ☐ 39 and ☐ 40 .

① Biological mechanisms

② Effects of our feelings

③ Kinds of memory

④ Life stages

⑤ Ongoing research

⑥ Types of time

— 32 —

2024 本試 英語 (リーディング)

問 2　Choose the best option for [41].

    ① major lifestyle change at any age will likely make time slow down

    ② major lifestyle change regardless of age will likely make time speed up

    ③ minor lifestyle change for adults will likely make time slow down

    ④ minor lifestyle change for children will likely make time speed up

問 3　Choose the best option for [42].

    ① anticipating a message from a classmate

    ② memorizing your mother's cellphone number

    ③ reflecting on how many hours you worked today

    ④ remembering that you have a meeting tomorrow

問 4　Choose the best option for [43].

    ① guessing how long you've been jogging so far

    ② making a schedule for the basketball team summer camp

    ③ running into your tennis coach at the railway station

    ④ thinking about your last family vacation to a hot spring

B You are preparing a presentation for your science club, using the following passage from a science website.

Chili Peppers: The Spice of Life

Tiny pieces of red spice in chili chicken add a nice touch of color, but biting into even a small piece can make a person's mouth burn as if it were on fire. While some people love this, others want to avoid the painful sensation. At the same time, though, they can eat sashimi with wasabi. This might lead one to wonder what spiciness actually is and to ask where the difference between chili and wasabi comes from.

Unlike sweetness, saltiness, and sourness, spiciness is not a taste. In fact, we do not actually taste heat, or spiciness, when we eat spicy foods. The bite we feel from eating chili peppers and wasabi is derived from different types of compounds. Chili peppers get their heat from a heavier, oil-like element called capsaicin. Capsaicin leaves a lingering, fire-like sensation in our mouths because it triggers a receptor called TRPV1. TRPV1 induces stress and tells us when something is burning our mouths. Interestingly, there is a wide range of heat across the different varieties of chili peppers, and the level depends on the amount of capsaicin they contain. This is measured using the Scoville Scale, which is also called Scoville Heat Units (SHU). SHUs range from the sweet and mild *shishito* pepper at 50-200 SHUs to the Carolina Reaper pepper, which can reach up to 2.2 million.

Wasabi is considered a root, not a pepper, and does not contain capsaicin. Thus, wasabi is not ranked on the Scoville Scale. However, people have compared the level of spice in it to chilis with around 1,000 SHUs, which is on the lower end of the scale. The reason some people cannot tolerate chili spice but can eat foods flavored with wasabi is that the spice compounds in it are low in density. The compounds in wasabi vaporize easily, delivering a blast of spiciness to our nose when we eat it.

Consuming chili peppers can have positive effects on our health, and much research has been conducted into the benefits of capsaicin. When capsaicin activates the TRPV1 receptor in a person's body, it is similar to what happens when they experience stress or pain from an injury. Strangely, capsaicin can

2024 本試 英語（リーディング）

also make pain go away. Scientists found that TRPV1 ceases to be turned on after long-term exposure to chili peppers, temporarily easing painful sensations. Thus, skin creams containing capsaicin might be useful for people who experience muscle aches.

Another benefit of eating chili peppers is that they accelerate the metabolism. A group of researchers analyzed 90 studies on capsaicin and body weight and found that people had a reduced appetite when they ate spicy foods. This is because spicy foods increase the heart rate, send more energy to the muscles, and convert fat into energy. Recently, scientists at the University of Wyoming have created a weight-loss drug with capsaicin as a main ingredient.

It is also believed that chili peppers are connected with food safety, which might lead to a healthier life. When food is left outside of a refrigerated environment, microorganisms multiply on it, which may cause sickness if eaten. Studies have shown that capsaicin and other chemicals found in chili peppers have antibacterial properties that can slow down or even stop microorganism growth. As a result, food lasts longer and there are fewer food-borne illnesses. This may explain why people in hot climates have a tendency to use more chili peppers, and therefore, be more tolerant of spicier foods due to repeated exposure. Also, in the past, before there were refrigerators, they were less likely to have food poisoning than people in cooler climates.

Chili peppers seem to have health benefits, but can they also be bad for our health? Peppers that are high on the Scoville Scale can cause physical discomfort when eaten in large quantities. People who have eaten several of the world's hottest chilis in a short time have reported experiencing upset stomachs, diarrhea, numb hands, and symptoms similar to a heart attack. Ghost peppers, which contain one million SHUs, can even burn a person's skin if they are touched.

Luckily the discomfort some people feel after eating spicy foods tends to go away soon—usually within a few hours. Despite some negative side effects, spicy foods remain popular around the world and add a flavorful touch to the table. Remember, it is safe to consume spicy foods, but you might want to be careful about the amount of peppers you put in your dishes.

Presentation slides:

Chili Peppers: **The Spice of Life**  1	**Characteristics** chili peppers wasabi • oil-like elements • [44] • triggering TRPV1 • changing to vapor • persistent feeling • spicy rush 2

Positive Effects
 Capsaicin can...   [45]
   A. reduce pain.
   B. give you more energy.
   C. speed up your metabolism.
   D. make you feel less stress.
   E. decrease food poisoning.
 	
 3
	Negative Effects
	 When eating too many strong chili peppers in a short time,
	
	 • [46]
	 • [47]
	
	 4

Spice Tolerance [48] 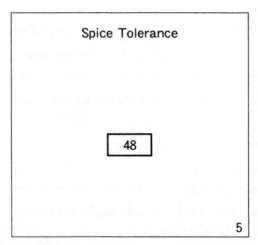 5	**Closing Remark** [49] 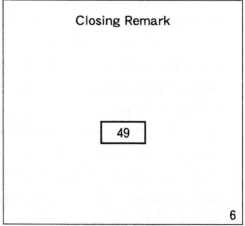 6

2024 本試 英語（リーディング）

問 1　What is the first characteristic of wasabi on Slide 2?　44

① burning taste

② fire-like sensation

③ lasting feeling

④ light compounds

問 2　Which is an **error** you found on Slide 3?　45

① A

② B

③ C

④ D

⑤ E

問 3　Choose two options for Slide 4.　(The order does not matter.)
46 ・ 47

① you might activate harmful bacteria.

② you might experience stomach pain.

③ you might lose feeling in your hands.

④ your fingers might feel like they are on fire.

⑤ your nose might start hurting.

— 37 —

問 4　What can be inferred about tolerance for spices for Slide 5?　48

① People with a high tolerance to chili peppers pay attention to the spices used in their food.

② People with a high tolerance to wasabi are scared of chili peppers' negative effects.

③ People with a low tolerance to chili peppers can get used to their heat.

④ People with a low tolerance to wasabi cannot endure high SHU levels.

問 5　Choose the most appropriate remark for Slide 6.　49

① Don't be afraid. Eating spicy foods will boost your confidence.

② Next time you eat chili chicken, remember its punch only stays for a second.

③ Personality plays a big role in our spice preference, so don't worry.

④ Unfortunately, there are no cures for a low wasabi tolerance.

⑤ When someone offers you some spicy food, remember it has some benefits.

2023年度

大学入学共通テスト

本試験

英語（リーディング）

（100点　80分）

---●　標 準 所 要 時 間　●---

第1問　7 分程度	第4問 12 分程度
第2問 13 分程度	第5問 14 分程度
第3問 12 分程度	第6問 22 分程度

'23
本試験問題

英 語(リーディング)

各大問の英文や図表を読み，解答番号 | 1 | ～ | 49 | にあてはまるものとして
最も適当な選択肢を選びなさい。

第1問 （配点 10）

A You are studying in the US, and as an afternoon activity you need to choose
one of two performances to go and see. Your teacher gives you this handout.

Performances for Friday

Palace Theater	**Grand Theater**
Together Wherever	***The Guitar Queen***
A romantic play that will make you laugh and cry	A rock musical featuring colorful costumes
▶ From 2:00 p.m. (no breaks and a running time of one hour and 45 minutes)	▶ Starts at 1:00 p.m. (three hours long including two 15-minute breaks)
▶ Actors available to talk in the lobby after the performance	▶ Opportunity to greet the cast in their costumes before the show starts
▶ No food or drinks available	▶ Light refreshments (snacks & drinks), original T-shirts, and other goods sold in the lobby
▶ Free T-shirts for five lucky people	

Instructions: Which performance would you like to attend? Fill in the form
below and hand it in to your teacher today.

✂ -

Choose (✔) one: *Together Wherever* ☐   *The Guitar Queen* ☐
Name: _____

— 2 —

2023 本試 英語 (リーディング)

問 1　What are you told to do after reading the handout?　1

 ① Complete and hand in the bottom part.

 ② Find out more about the performances.

 ③ Talk to your teacher about your decision.

 ④ Write your name and explain your choice.

問 2　Which is true about both performances?　2

 ① No drinks can be purchased before the show.

 ② Some T-shirts will be given as gifts.

 ③ They will finish at the same time.

 ④ You can meet performers at the theaters.

— 3 —

B You are a senior high school student interested in improving your English during the summer vacation. You find a website for an intensive English summer camp run by an international school.

Intensive English Summer Camp

Galley International School (GIS) has provided intensive English summer camps for senior high school students in Japan since 1989. Spend two weeks in an all-English environment!

Dates: August 1-14, 2023
Location: Lake Kawaguchi Youth Lodge, Yamanashi Prefecture
Cost: 120,000 yen, including food and accommodation (additional fees for optional activities such as kayaking and canoeing)

Courses Offered

◆**FOREST**: You'll master basic grammar structures, make short speeches on simple topics, and get pronunciation tips. Your instructors have taught English for over 20 years in several countries. On the final day of the camp, you'll take part in a speech contest while all the other campers listen.

◆**MOUNTAIN**: You'll work in a group to write and perform a skit in English. Instructors for this course have worked at theater schools in New York City, London, and Sydney. You'll perform your skit for all the campers to enjoy on August 14.

◆**SKY**: You'll learn debating skills and critical thinking in this course. Your instructors have been to many countries to coach debate teams and some have published best-selling textbooks on the subject. You'll do a short debate in front of all the other campers on the last day. (Note: Only those with an advanced level of English will be accepted.)

2023 本試 英語（リーディング）

▲**Application**

Step 1: Fill in the online application **HERE** by May 20, 2023.

Step 2: We'll contact you to set up an interview to assess your English ability and ask about your course preference.

Step 3: You'll be assigned to a course.

問 1　All GIS instructors have ⬚3⬚ .

① been in Japan since 1989

② won international competitions

③ worked in other countries

④ written some popular books

問 2　On the last day of the camp, campers will ⬚4⬚ .

① assess each other's performances

② compete to receive the best prize

③ make presentations about the future

④ show what they learned at the camp

問 3　What will happen after submitting your camp application? ⬚5⬚

① You will call the English instructors.

② You will take a written English test.

③ Your English level will be checked.

④ Your English speech topic will be sent.

— 5 —

第2問 (配点 20)

A　You want to buy a good pair of shoes as you walk a long way to school and often get sore feet. You are searching on a UK website and find this advertisement.

Navi 55 presents the new *Smart Support* shoe line

Smart Support shoes are strong, long-lasting, and reasonably priced. They are available in three colours and styles.

nano-chip

Special Features

Smart Support shoes have a nano-chip which analyses the shape of your feet when connected to the *iSupport* application. Download the app onto your smartphone, PC, tablet, and/or smartwatch. Then, while wearing the shoes, let the chip collect the data about your feet. The inside of the shoe will automatically adjust to give correct, personalised foot support. As with other Navi 55 products, the shoes have our popular Route Memory function.

Advantages

Better Balance: Adjusting how you stand, the personalised support helps keep feet, legs, and back free from pain.

Promotes Exercise: As they are so comfortable, you will be willing to walk regularly.

Route Memory: The chip records your daily route, distance, and pace as you walk.

Route Options: View your live location on your device, have the directions play automatically in your earphones, or use your smartwatch to read directions.

2023 本試 英語（リーディング）

Customers' Comments

● I like the choices for getting directions, and prefer using audio guidance to visual guidance.

● I lost 2 kg in a month!

● I love my pair now, but it took me several days to get used to them.

● As they don't slip in the rain, I wear mine all year round.

● They are so light and comfortable I even wear them when cycling.

● Easy to get around! I don't need to worry about getting lost.

● They look great. The app's basic features are easy to use, but I wouldn't pay for the optional advanced ones.

問 1　According to the maker's statements, which best describes the new shoes?

　　　6

① Cheap summer shoes

② High-tech everyday shoes

③ Light comfortable sports shoes

④ Stylish colourful cycling shoes

問 2　Which benefit offered by the shoes is most likely to appeal to you?

　　　7

① Getting more regular exercise

② Having personalised foot support

③ Knowing how fast you walk

④ Looking cool wearing them

－7－

問 3　One **opinion** stated by a customer is that 　8　.

① the app encourages fast walking

② the app's free functions are user-friendly

③ the shoes are good value for money

④ the shoes increase your cycling speed

問 4　One customer's comment mentions using audio devices.　Which benefit is this comment based on?　　9

① Better Balance

② Promotes Exercise

③ Route Memory

④ Route Options

問 5　According to one customer's opinion, 　10　 is recommended.

① allowing time to get accustomed to wearing the shoes

② buying a watch to help you lose weight

③ connecting to the app before putting the shoes on

④ paying for the *iSupport* advanced features

B You are a member of the student council. The members have been discussing a student project helping students to use their time efficiently. To get ideas, you are reading a report about a school challenge. It was written by an exchange student who studied in another school in Japan.

Commuting Challenge

Most students come to my school by bus or train. I often see a lot of students playing games on their phones or chatting. However, they could also use this time for reading or doing homework. We started this activity to help students use their commuting time more effectively. Students had to complete a commuting activity chart from January 17th to February 17th. A total of 300 students participated: More than two thirds of them were second-years; about a quarter were third-years; only 15 first-years participated. How come so few first-years participated? Based on the feedback (given below), there seems to be an answer to this question:

Feedback from participants

HS: Thanks to this project, I got the highest score ever in an English vocabulary test. It was easy to set small goals to complete on my way.

KF: My friend was sad because she couldn't participate. She lives nearby and walks to school. There should have been other ways to take part.

SS: My train is always crowded and I have to stand, so there is no space to open a book or a tablet. I only used audio materials, but there were not nearly enough.

JH: I kept a study log, which made me realise how I used my time. For some reason most of my first-year classmates didn't seem to know about this challenge.

MN: I spent most of the time on the bus watching videos, and it helped me to understand classes better. I felt the time went very fast.

— 9 —

問 1 The aim of the Commuting Challenge was to help students to ⬚ 11 ⬚ .

① commute more quickly

② improve their test scores

③ manage English classes better

④ use their time better

問 2 One **fact** about the Commuting Challenge is that ⬚ 12 ⬚ .

① fewer than 10% of the participants were first-years

② it was held for two months during the winter

③ students had to use portable devices on buses

④ the majority of participants travelled by train

問 3 From the feedback, ⬚ 13 ⬚ were activities reported by participants.

A : keeping study records

B : learning language

C : making notes on tablets

D : reading lesson notes on mobile phones

① A and B

② A and C

③ A and D

④ B and C

⑤ B and D

⑥ C and D

— 10 —

2023 本試 英語 (リーディング)

問 4 One of the participants' opinions about the Commuting Challenge is that 14 .

① it could have included students who walk to school

② the train was a good place to read books

③ there were plenty of audio materials for studying

④ watching videos for fun helped time pass quickly

問 5 The author's question is answered by 15 .

① HS

② JH

③ KF

④ MN

⑤ SS

— 11 —

第 3 問 (配点 15)

A You are studying at Camberford University, Sydney. You are going on a class camping trip and are reading the camping club's newsletter to prepare.

Going camping? Read me!!!

Hi, I'm Kaitlyn. I want to share two practical camping lessons from my recent club trip. The first thing is to divide your backpack into three main parts and put the heaviest items in the middle section to balance the backpack. Next, more frequently used daily necessities should be placed in the top section. That means putting your sleeping bag at the bottom; food, cookware and tent in the middle; and your clothes at the top. Most good backpacks come with a "brain" (an additional pouch) for small easy-to-reach items.

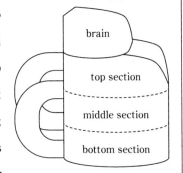

Last year, in the evening, we had fun cooking and eating outdoors. I had been sitting close to our campfire, but by the time I got back to the tent I was freezing. Although I put on extra layers of clothes before going to sleep, I was still cold. Then, my friend told me to take off my outer layers and stuff them into my sleeping bag to fill up some of the empty space. This stuffing method was new to me, and surprisingly kept me warm all night!

I hope my advice helps you stay warm and comfortable. Enjoy your camping trip!

問 1 If you take Kaitlyn's advice, how should you fill your backpack? 16

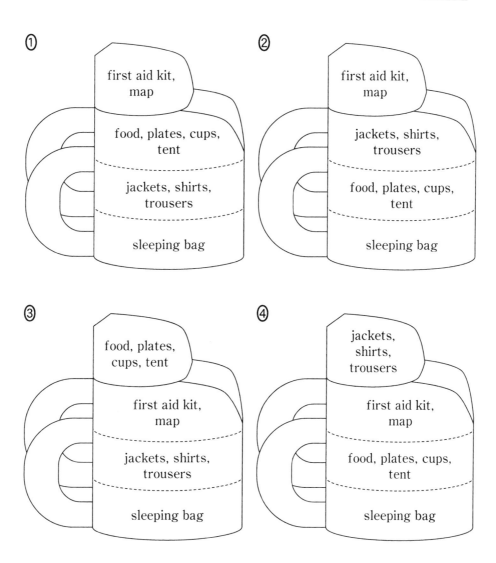

問 2 According to Kaitlyn, 17 is the best method to stay warm all night.

① avoiding going out of your tent
② eating hot meals beside your campfire
③ filling the gaps in your sleeping bag
④ wearing all of your extra clothes

B Your English club will make an "adventure room" for the school festival. To get some ideas, you are reading a blog about a room a British man created.

Create Your Own "Home Adventure"

Last year, I took part in an "adventure room" experience. I really enjoyed it, so I created one for my children. Here are some tips on making your own.

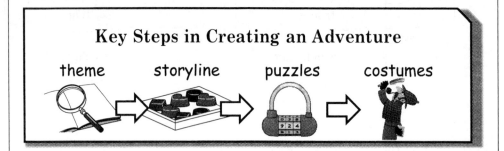

First, pick a theme. My sons are huge Sherlock Holmes fans, so I decided on a detective mystery. I rearranged the furniture in our family room, and added some old paintings and lamps I had to set the scene.

Next, create a storyline. Ours was *The Case of the Missing Chocolates*. My children would be "detectives" searching for clues to locate the missing sweets.

The third step is to design puzzles and challenges. A useful idea is to work backwards from the solution. If the task is to open a box locked with a three-digit padlock, think of ways to hide a three-digit code. Old books are fantastic for hiding messages in. I had tremendous fun underlining words on different pages to form mystery sentences. Remember that the puzzles should get progressively more difficult near the final goal. To get into the spirit, I then had the children wear costumes. My eldest son was excited when I handed him a magnifying glass, and immediately began acting like Sherlock Holmes. After that, the children started to search for the first clue.

This "adventure room" was designed specifically for my family, so I made some of the challenges personal. For the final task, I took a couple of small cups and put a plastic sticker in each one, then filled them with yogurt. The "detectives" had to eat their way to the bottom to reveal the clues. Neither of my kids would eat yogurt, so this truly was tough for them. During the adventure, my children were totally focused, and they enjoyed themselves so much that we will have another one next month.

問 1 Put the following events (①~④) into the order in which they happened.

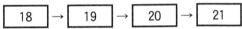

- ① The children ate food they are not fond of.
- ② The children started the search for the sweets.
- ③ The father decorated the living room in the house.
- ④ The father gave his sons some clothes to wear.

問 2 If you follow the father's advice to create your own "adventure room," you should 22 .

- ① concentrate on three-letter words
- ② leave secret messages under the lamps
- ③ make the challenges gradually harder
- ④ practise acting like Sherlock Holmes

問 3 From this story, you understand that the father 23 .

① became focused on searching for the sweets

② created an experience especially for his children

③ had some trouble preparing the adventure game

④ spent a lot of money decorating the room

2023 本試 英語（リーディング）

（下 書 き 用 紙）

英語（リーディング）の試験問題は次に続く。

第4問 (配点 16)

Your teacher has asked you to read two articles about effective ways to study. You will discuss what you learned in your next class.

How to Study Effectively: Contextual Learning!
Tim Oxford
Science Teacher, Stone City Junior High School

As a science teacher, I am always concerned about how to help students who struggle to learn. Recently, I found that their main way of learning was to study new information repeatedly until they could recall it all. For example, when they studied for a test, they would use a workbook like the example below and repeatedly say the terms that go in the blanks: "Obsidian is igneous, dark, and glassy. Obsidian is igneous, dark, and glassy...." These students would feel as if they had learned the information, but would quickly forget it and get low scores on the test. Also, this sort of repetitive learning is dull and demotivating.

To help them learn, I tried applying "contextual learning." In this kind of learning, new knowledge is constructed through students' own experiences. For my science class, students learned the properties of different kinds of rocks. Rather than having them memorize the terms from a workbook, I brought a big box of various rocks to the class. Students examined the rocks and identified their names based on the characteristics they observed.

Thanks to this experience, I think these students will always be able to describe the properties of the rocks they studied. One issue, however, is that we don't always have the time to do contextual learning, so students will still study by doing drills. I don't think this is the best way. I'm still searching for ways to improve their learning.

Rock name	Obsidian
Rock type	igneous
Coloring	dark
Texture	glassy
Picture	

— 18 —

How to Make Repetitive Learning Effective
Cheng Lee
Professor, Stone City University

Mr. Oxford's thoughts on contextual learning were insightful. I agree that it can be beneficial. Repetition, though, can also work well. However, the repetitive learning strategy he discussed, which is called "massed learning," is not effective. There is another kind of repetitive learning called "spaced learning," in which students memorize new information and then review it over longer intervals.

The interval between studying is the key difference. In Mr. Oxford's example, his students probably used their workbooks to study over a short period of time. In this case, they might have paid less attention to the content as they continued to review it. The reason for this is that the content was no longer new and could easily be ignored. In contrast, when the intervals are longer, the students' memory of the content is weaker. Therefore, they pay more attention because they have to make a greater effort to recall what they had learned before. For example, if students study with their workbooks, wait three days, and then study again, they are likely to learn the material better.

Previous research has provided evidence for the advantages of spaced learning. In one experiment, students in Groups A and B tried to memorize the names of 50 animals. Both groups studied four times, but Group A studied at one-day intervals while Group B studied at one-week intervals. As the figure to the right shows, 28 days after the last learning session, the average ratio of recalled names on a test was higher for the spaced learning group.

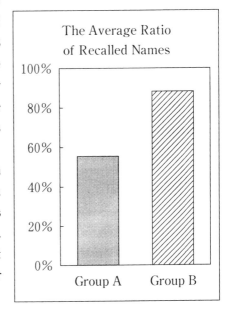

I understand that students often need to learn a lot of information in a short period of time, and long intervals between studying might not be practical. You should understand, though, that massed learning might not be good for long-term recall.

問 1　Oxford believes that 　24　 .

　① continuous drilling is boring

　② reading an explanation of terms is helpful

　③ students are not interested in science

　④ studying with a workbook leads to success

問 2　In the study discussed by Lee, students took a test 　25　 after their final session.

　① four weeks

　② immediately

　③ one day

　④ one week

問 3　Lee introduces spaced learning, which involves studying at 　26　 intervals, in order to overcome the disadvantages of 　27　 learning that Oxford discussed.　(Choose the best one for each box from options ①~⑥.)

　① contextual

　② extended

　③ fixed

　④ irregular

　⑤ massed

　⑥ practical

2023 本試 英語（リーディング）

問 4 Both writers agree that | 28 | is helpful for remembering new information.

① experiential learning
② having proper rest
③ long-term attention
④ studying with workbooks

問 5 Which additional information would be the best to further support Lee's argument for spaced learning? | 29 |

① The main factor that makes a science class attractive
② The most effective length of intervals for spaced learning
③ Whether students' workbooks include visuals or not
④ Why Oxford's students could not memorize information well

— 21 —

第 5 問 (配点 15)

Your English teacher has told everyone in your class to find an inspirational story and present it to a discussion group, using notes. You have found a story written by a high school student in the UK.

Lessons from Table Tennis

Ben Carter

The ball flew at lightning speed to my backhand. It was completely unexpected and I had no time to react. I lost the point and the match. Defeat... Again! This is how it was in the first few months when I started playing table tennis. It was frustrating, but I now know that the sport taught me more than simply how to be a better athlete.

In middle school, I loved football. I was one of the top scorers, but I didn't get along with my teammates. The coach often said that I should be more of a team player. I knew I should work on the problem, but communication was just not my strong point.

I had to leave the football club when my family moved to a new town. I wasn't upset as I had decided to stop playing football anyway. My new school had a table tennis club, coached by the PE teacher, Mr Trent, and I joined that. To be honest, I chose table tennis because I thought it would be easier for me to play individually.

At first, I lost more games than I won. I was frustrated and often went straight home after practice, not speaking to anyone. One day, however, Mr Trent said to me, "You could be a good player, Ben, but you need to think more about your game. What do you think you need to do?" "I don't know," I replied, "focus on the ball more?" "Yes," Mr Trent continued, "but you also need to study your opponent's moves and adjust your play accordingly. Remember, your opponent is a person, not a ball." This made a deep impression on me.

— 22 —

I deliberately modified my style of play, paying closer attention to my opponent's moves. It was not easy, and took a lot of concentration. My efforts paid off, however, and my play improved. My confidence grew and I started staying behind more after practice. I was turning into a star player and my classmates tried to talk to me more than before. I thought that I was becoming popular, but our conversations seemed to end before they really got started. Although my play might have improved, my communication skills obviously hadn't.

My older brother Patrick was one of the few people I could communicate with well. One day, I tried to explain my problems with communication to him, but couldn't make him understand. We switched to talking about table tennis. "What do you actually enjoy about it?" he asked me curiously. I said I loved analysing my opponent's movements and making instant decisions about the next move. Patrick looked thoughtful. "That sounds like the kind of skill we use when we communicate," he said.

At that time, I didn't understand, but soon after our conversation, I won a silver medal in a table tennis tournament. My classmates seemed really pleased. One of them, George, came running over. "Hey, Ben!" he said, "Let's have a party to celebrate!" Without thinking, I replied, "I can't. I've got practice." He looked a bit hurt and walked off without saying anything else.

Why was he upset? I thought about this incident for a long time. Why did he suggest a party? Should I have said something different? A lot of questions came to my mind, but then I realised that he was just being kind. If I'd said, "Great idea. Thank you! Let me talk to Mr Trent and see if I can get some time off practice," then maybe the outcome would have been better. At that moment Patrick's words made sense. Without attempting to grasp someone's intention, I wouldn't know how to respond.

I'm still not the best communicator in the world, but I definitely feel more confident in my communication skills now than before. Next year, my friends and I are going to co-ordinate the table tennis league with other schools.

Your notes:

Lessons from Table Tennis

About the author (Ben Carter)
- Played football at middle school.
- Started playing table tennis at his new school because he 30 .

Other important people
- Mr Trent: Ben's table tennis coach, who helped him improve his play.
- Patrick: Ben's brother, who 31 .
- George: Ben's classmate, who wanted to celebrate his victory.

Influential events in Ben's journey to becoming a better communicator
Began playing table tennis → 32 → 33 → 34 → 35

What Ben realised after the conversation with George
He should have 36 .

What we can learn from this story
- 37
- 38

2023 本試 英語 (リーディング)

問 1　Choose the best option for ☐30☐.

　　① believed it would help him communicate

　　② hoped to become popular at school

　　③ thought he could win games easily

　　④ wanted to avoid playing a team sport

問 2　Choose the best option for ☐31☐.

　　① asked him what he enjoyed about communication

　　② encouraged him to be more confident

　　③ helped him learn the social skills he needed

　　④ told him what he should have said to his school friends

問 3　Choose **four** out of the five options (①～⑤) and rearrange them in the order they happened.　☐32☐ → ☐33☐ → ☐34☐ → ☐35☐

　　① Became a table tennis champion

　　② Discussed with his teacher how to play well

　　③ Refused a party in his honour

　　④ Started to study his opponents

　　⑤ Talked to his brother about table tennis

— 25 —

問 4　Choose the best option for ☐36☐ .

① asked his friend questions to find out more about his motivation

② invited Mr Trent and other classmates to the party to show appreciation

③ tried to understand his friend's point of view to act appropriately

④ worked hard to be a better team player for successful communication

問 5　Choose the best two options for ☐37☐ and ☐38☐ .　(The order does not matter.)

① Advice from people around us can help us change.

② Confidence is important for being a good communicator.

③ It is important to make our intentions clear to our friends.

④ The support that teammates provide one another is helpful.

⑤ We can apply what we learn from one thing to another.

2023 本試 英語 (リーディング)

（下 書 き 用 紙）

英語（リーディング）の試験問題は次に続く。

第6問 (配点 24)

A You are in a discussion group in school. You have been asked to summarize the following article. You will speak about it, using only notes.

Collecting

Collecting has existed at all levels of society, across cultures and age groups since early times. Museums are proof that things have been collected, saved, and passed down for future generations. There are various reasons for starting a collection. For example, Ms. A enjoys going to yard sales every Saturday morning with her children. At yard sales, people sell unwanted things in front of their houses. One day, while looking for antique dishes, an unusual painting caught her eye and she bought it for only a few dollars. Over time, she found similar pieces that left an impression on her, and she now has a modest collection of artwork, some of which may be worth more than she paid. One person's trash can be another person's treasure. Regardless of how someone's collection was started, it is human nature to collect things.

In 1988, researchers Brenda Danet and Tamar Katriel analyzed 80 years of studies on children under the age of 10, and found that about 90% collected something. This shows us that people like to gather things from an early age. Even after becoming adults, people continue collecting stuff. Researchers in the field generally agree that approximately one third of adults maintain this behavior. Why is this? The primary explanation is related to emotions. Some save greeting cards from friends and family, dried flowers from special events, seashells from a day at the beach, old photos, and so on. For others, their collection is a connection to their youth. They may have baseball cards, comic books, dolls, or miniature cars that they have kept since they were small.

2023 本試 英語 (リーディング)

Others have an attachment to history; they seek and hold onto historical documents, signed letters and autographs from famous people, and so forth.

For some individuals there is a social reason. People collect things such as pins to share, show, and even trade, making new friends this way. Others, like some holders of Guinness World Records, appreciate the fame they achieve for their unique collection. Cards, stickers, stamps, coins, and toys have topped the "usual" collection list, but some collectors lean toward the more unexpected. In September 2014, Guinness World Records recognized Harry Sperl, of Germany, for having the largest hamburger-related collection in the world, with 3,724 items; from T-shirts to pillows to dog toys, Sperl's room is filled with all things "hamburger." Similarly, Liu Fuchang, of China, is a collector of playing cards. He has 11,087 different sets.

Perhaps the easiest motivation to understand is pleasure. Some people start collections for pure enjoyment. They may purchase and put up paintings just to gaze at frequently, or they may collect audio recordings and old-fashioned vinyl records to enjoy listening to their favorite music. This type of collector is unlikely to be very interested in the monetary value of their treasured music, while others collect objects specifically as an investment. While it is possible to download certain classic games for free, having the same game unopened in its original packaging, in "mint condition," can make the game worth a lot. Owning various valuable "collector's items" could ensure some financial security.

— 29 —

This behavior of collecting things will definitely continue into the distant future. Although the reasons why people keep things will likely remain the same, advances in technology will have an influence on collections. As technology can remove physical constraints, it is now possible for an individual to have vast digital libraries of music and art that would have been unimaginable 30 years ago. It is unclear, though, what other impacts technology will have on collections. Can you even imagine the form and scale that the next generation's collections will take?

Your notes:

Collecting

Introduction
◆ Collecting has long been part of the human experience.
◆ The yard sale story tells us that ☐ 39 ☐ .

Facts
◆ ☐ 40 ☐
◆ Guinness World Records
  ◇ Sperl: 3,724 hamburger-related items
  ◇ Liu: 11,087 sets of playing cards

Reasons for collecting
◆ Motivation for collecting can be emotional or social.
◆ Various reasons mentioned: ☐ 41 ☐ , ☐ 42 ☐ , interest in history, childhood excitement, becoming famous, sharing, etc.

Collections in the future
◆ ☐ 43 ☐

問 1   Choose the best option for ☐39☐ .

① a great place for people to sell things to collectors at a high price is a yard sale

② people can evaluate items incorrectly and end up paying too much money for junk

③ something not important to one person may be of value to someone else

④ things once collected and thrown in another person's yard may be valuable to others

問 2   Choose the best option for ☐40☐ .

① About two thirds of children do not collect ordinary things.

② Almost one third of adults start collecting things for pleasure.

③ Approximately 10% of kids have collections similar to their friends.

④ Roughly 30% of people keep collecting into adulthood.

問 3   Choose the best options for ☐41☐ and ☐42☐ . (The order does not matter.)

① desire to advance technology

② fear of missing unexpected opportunities

③ filling a sense of emptiness

④ reminder of precious events

⑤ reusing objects for the future

⑥ seeking some sort of profit

問 4   Choose the best option for ☐43☐ .

① Collections will likely continue to change in size and shape.

② Collectors of mint-condition games will have more digital copies of them.

③ People who have lost their passion for collecting will start again.

④ Reasons for collecting will change because of advances in technology.

— 32 —

2023 本試 英語（リーディング）

B You are in a student group preparing for an international science presentation contest. You are using the following passage to create your part of the presentation on extraordinary creatures.

Ask someone to name the world's toughest animal, and they might say the Bactrian camel as it can survive in temperatures as high as 50℃, or the Arctic fox which can survive in temperatures lower than −58℃. However, both answers would be wrong as it is widely believed that the tardigrade is the toughest creature on earth.

Tardigrades, also known as water bears, are microscopic creatures, which are between 0.1 mm to 1.5 mm in length. They live almost everywhere, from 6,000-meter-high mountains to 4,600 meters below the ocean's surface. They can even be found under thick ice and in hot springs. Most live in water, but some tardigrades can be found in some of the driest places on earth. One researcher reported finding tardigrades living under rocks in a desert without any recorded rainfall for 25 years. All they need are a few drops or a thin layer of water to live in. When the water dries up, so do they. They lose all but three percent of their body's water and their metabolism slows down to 0.01% of its normal speed. The dried-out tardigrade is now in a state called "tun," a kind of deep sleep. It will continue in this state until it is once again soaked in water. Then, like a sponge, it absorbs the water and springs back to life again as if nothing had happened. Whether the tardigrade is in tun for 1 week or 10 years does not really matter. The moment it is surrounded by water, it comes alive again. When tardigrades are in a state of tun, they are so tough that they can survive in temperatures as low as −272℃ and as high as 151℃. Exactly how they achieve this is still not fully understood.

Perhaps even more amazing than their ability to survive on earth — they have been on earth for some 540 million years — is their ability to survive in space. In 2007, a team of European researchers sent a number of living

— 33 —

tardigrades into space on the outside of a rocket for 10 days. On their return to earth, the researchers were surprised to see that 68% were still alive. This means that for 10 days most were able to survive X-rays and ultraviolet radiation 1,000 times more intense than here on earth. Later, in 2019, an Israeli spacecraft crashed onto the moon and thousands of tardigrades in a state of tun were spilled onto its surface. Whether these are still alive or not is unknown as no one has gone to collect them — which is a pity.

Tardigrades are shaped like a short cucumber. They have four short legs on each side of their bodies. Some species have sticky pads at the end of each leg, while others have claws. There are 16 known claw variations, which help identify those species with claws. All tardigrades have a place for eyes, but not all species have eyes. Their eyes are primitive, only having five cells in total — just one of which is light sensitive.

Basically, tardigrades can be divided into those that eat plant matter, and those that eat other creatures. Those that eat vegetation have a ventral mouth — a mouth located in the lower part of the head, like a shark. The type that eats other creatures has a terminal mouth, which means the mouth is at the very front of the head, like a tuna. The mouths of tardigrades do not have teeth. They do, however, have two sharp needles, called stylets, that they use to pierce plant cells or the bodies of smaller creatures so the contents can be sucked out.

Both types of tardigrade have rather simple digestive systems. The mouth leads to the pharynx (throat), where digestive juices and food are mixed. Located above the pharynx is a salivary gland. This produces the juices that flow into the mouth and help with digestion. After the pharynx, there is a tube which transports food toward the gut. This tube is called the esophagus. The middle gut, a simple stomach/intestine type of organ, digests the food and absorbs the nutrients. The leftovers then eventually move through to the anus.

— 34 —

Your presentation slides:

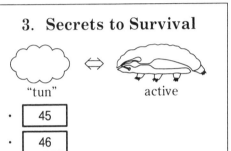
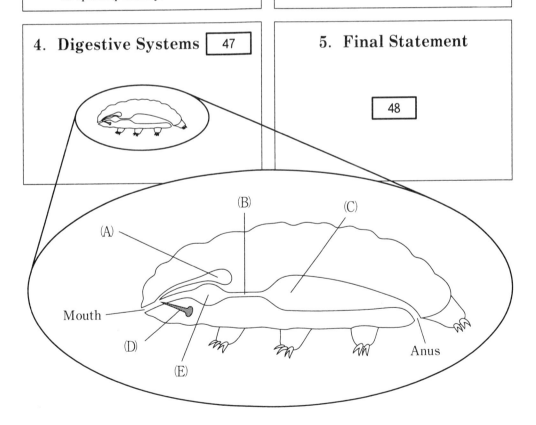

問 1 Which of the following should you **not** include for 44 ?

① eight short legs

② either blind or sighted

③ plant-eating or creature-eating

④ sixteen different types of feet

⑤ two stylets rather than teeth

問 2 For the **Secrets to Survival** slide, select two features of the tardigrade which best help it survive. (The order does not matter.) 45 · 46

① In dry conditions, their metabolism drops to less than one percent of normal.

② Tardigrades in a state of tun are able to survive in temperatures exceeding 151℃.

③ The state of tun will cease when the water in a tardigrade's body is above 0.01%.

④ Their shark-like mouths allow them to more easily eat other creatures.

⑤ They have an ability to withstand extreme levels of radiation.

問 3 Complete the missing labels on the illustration of a tardigrade for the **Digestive Systems** slide. 47

① (A) Esophagus (B) Pharynx (C) Middle gut
  (D) Stylets (E) Salivary gland

② (A) Pharynx (B) Stylets (C) Salivary gland
  (D) Esophagus (E) Middle gut

③ (A) Salivary gland (B) Esophagus (C) Middle gut
  (D) Stylets (E) Pharynx

④ (A) Salivary gland (B) Middle gut (C) Stylets
  (D) Esophagus (E) Pharynx

⑤ (A) Stylets (B) Salivary gland (C) Pharynx
  (D) Middle gut (E) Esophagus

— 36 —

2023 本試 英語（リーディング）

問 4 Which is the best statement for the final slide? 48

① For thousands of years, tardigrades have survived some of the harshest conditions on earth and in space. They will live longer than humankind.

② Tardigrades are from space and can live in temperatures exceeding the limits of the Arctic fox and Bactrian camel, so they are surely stronger than human beings.

③ Tardigrades are, without a doubt, the toughest creatures on earth. They can survive on the top of mountains; at the bottom of the sea; in the waters of hot springs; and they can also thrive on the moon.

④ Tardigrades have survived some of the harshest conditions on earth, and at least one trip into space. This remarkable creature might outlive the human species.

問 5 What can be inferred about sending tardigrades into space? 49

① Finding out whether the tardigrades can survive in space was never thought to be important.

② Tardigrades, along with other creatures that have been on earth for millions of years, can withstand X-rays and ultraviolet radiation.

③ The Israeli researchers did not expect so many tardigrades to survive the harsh environment of space.

④ The reason why no one has been to see if tardigrades can survive on the moon's surface attracted the author's attention.

— 37 —

2025－駿台　大学入試完全対策シリーズ
大学入学共通テスト実戦問題集
英語リーディング

2024 年 7 月 11 日　2025 年版発行

編　　者	駿 台 文 庫
発 行 者	山 﨑 良 子
印刷・製本	日 経 印 刷 株 式 会 社
発 行 所	駿台文庫株式会社

〒 101-0062　東京都千代田区神田駿河台 1-7-4
小畑ビル内
TEL. 編集 03（5259）3302
販売 03（5259）3301
《共通テスト実戦・英語リーディング 560pp.》

Ⓒ Sundaibunko 2024

許可なく本書の一部または全部を，複製，複写，
デジタル化する等の行為を禁じます。
落丁・乱丁がございましたら，送料小社負担にて
お取り替えいたします。
ISBN978-4-7961-6463-4　Printed in Japan

駿台文庫 Web サイト
https://www.sundaibunko.jp

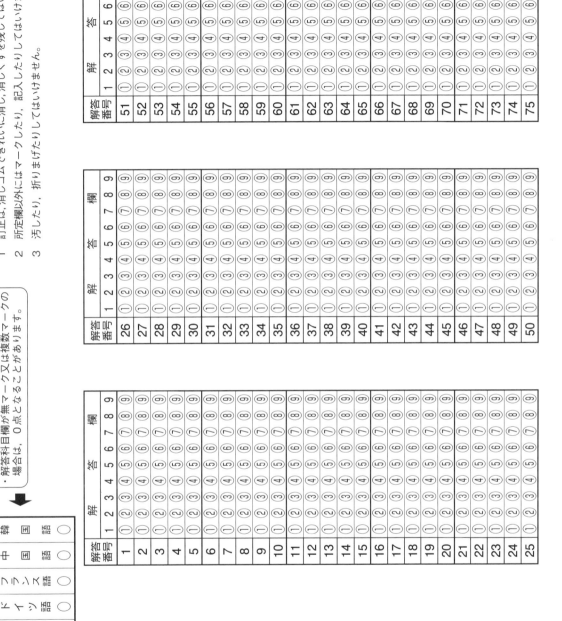

外国語 解答用紙

マーク例

良い例	悪い例
●	⊙ ⊗ ◖ ○

①

受験番号を記入し、その下のマーク欄にマークしなさい。

受験番号欄

千位	百位	十位	一位	英字
—	—	—	—	
	⓪	⓪	⓪	Ⓐ
①	①	①	①	Ⓑ
②	②	②	②	Ⓒ
③	③	③	③	Ⓗ
④	④	④	④	Ⓚ
⑤	⑤	⑤	⑤	Ⓜ
⑥	⑥	⑥	⑥	Ⓡ
⑦	⑦	⑦	⑦	Ⓤ
⑧	⑧	⑧	⑧	Ⓧ
⑨	⑨	⑨	⑨	Ⓨ
				Ⓩ

②

氏名・フリガナ、試験場コードを記入しなさい。

フリガナ	
氏 名	

試験場コード	十万位	万位	千位	百位	十位	一位

③

解答科目欄

英語	ド イ ツ 語	フ ラ ン ス 語	中 国 語	韓 国 語
○	○	○	○	○

注意事項

1. 1科目だけマークしなさい。
   解答科目欄が無マーク又は複数マークの場合は、0点となることがあります。

注意事項

1 訂正は、消しゴムできれいに消し、消しくずを残してはいけません。

2 所定欄以外にはマークしたり、記入したりしてはいけません。

3 汚したり、折りまげたりしてはいけません。

解答欄 (解答番号 1〜25)

解答番号	解 答 欄
1	① ② ③ ④ ⑤ ⑥ ⑦ ⑧ ⑨
2	① ② ③ ④ ⑤ ⑥ ⑦ ⑧ ⑨
3	① ② ③ ④ ⑤ ⑥ ⑦ ⑧ ⑨
4	① ② ③ ④ ⑤ ⑥ ⑦ ⑧ ⑨
5	① ② ③ ④ ⑤ ⑥ ⑦ ⑧ ⑨
6	① ② ③ ④ ⑤ ⑥ ⑦ ⑧ ⑨
7	① ② ③ ④ ⑤ ⑥ ⑦ ⑧ ⑨
8	① ② ③ ④ ⑤ ⑥ ⑦ ⑧ ⑨
9	① ② ③ ④ ⑤ ⑥ ⑦ ⑧ ⑨
10	① ② ③ ④ ⑤ ⑥ ⑦ ⑧ ⑨
11	① ② ③ ④ ⑤ ⑥ ⑦ ⑧ ⑨
12	① ② ③ ④ ⑤ ⑥ ⑦ ⑧ ⑨
13	① ② ③ ④ ⑤ ⑥ ⑦ ⑧ ⑨
14	① ② ③ ④ ⑤ ⑥ ⑦ ⑧ ⑨
15	① ② ③ ④ ⑤ ⑥ ⑦ ⑧ ⑨
16	① ② ③ ④ ⑤ ⑥ ⑦ ⑧ ⑨
17	① ② ③ ④ ⑤ ⑥ ⑦ ⑧ ⑨
18	① ② ③ ④ ⑤ ⑥ ⑦ ⑧ ⑨
19	① ② ③ ④ ⑤ ⑥ ⑦ ⑧ ⑨
20	① ② ③ ④ ⑤ ⑥ ⑦ ⑧ ⑨
21	① ② ③ ④ ⑤ ⑥ ⑦ ⑧ ⑨
22	① ② ③ ④ ⑤ ⑥ ⑦ ⑧ ⑨
23	① ② ③ ④ ⑤ ⑥ ⑦ ⑧ ⑨
24	① ② ③ ④ ⑤ ⑥ ⑦ ⑧ ⑨
25	① ② ③ ④ ⑤ ⑥ ⑦ ⑧ ⑨

解答欄 (解答番号 26〜50)

解答番号	解 答 欄
26	① ② ③ ④ ⑤ ⑥ ⑦ ⑧ ⑨
27	① ② ③ ④ ⑤ ⑥ ⑦ ⑧ ⑨
28	① ② ③ ④ ⑤ ⑥ ⑦ ⑧ ⑨
29	① ② ③ ④ ⑤ ⑥ ⑦ ⑧ ⑨
30	① ② ③ ④ ⑤ ⑥ ⑦ ⑧ ⑨
31	① ② ③ ④ ⑤ ⑥ ⑦ ⑧ ⑨
32	① ② ③ ④ ⑤ ⑥ ⑦ ⑧ ⑨
33	① ② ③ ④ ⑤ ⑥ ⑦ ⑧ ⑨
34	① ② ③ ④ ⑤ ⑥ ⑦ ⑧ ⑨
35	① ② ③ ④ ⑤ ⑥ ⑦ ⑧ ⑨
36	① ② ③ ④ ⑤ ⑥ ⑦ ⑧ ⑨
37	① ② ③ ④ ⑤ ⑥ ⑦ ⑧ ⑨
38	① ② ③ ④ ⑤ ⑥ ⑦ ⑧ ⑨
39	① ② ③ ④ ⑤ ⑥ ⑦ ⑧ ⑨
40	① ② ③ ④ ⑤ ⑥ ⑦ ⑧ ⑨
41	① ② ③ ④ ⑤ ⑥ ⑦ ⑧ ⑨
42	① ② ③ ④ ⑤ ⑥ ⑦ ⑧ ⑨
43	① ② ③ ④ ⑤ ⑥ ⑦ ⑧ ⑨
44	① ② ③ ④ ⑤ ⑥ ⑦ ⑧ ⑨
45	① ② ③ ④ ⑤ ⑥ ⑦ ⑧ ⑨
46	① ② ③ ④ ⑤ ⑥ ⑦ ⑧ ⑨
47	① ② ③ ④ ⑤ ⑥ ⑦ ⑧ ⑨
48	① ② ③ ④ ⑤ ⑥ ⑦ ⑧ ⑨
49	① ② ③ ④ ⑤ ⑥ ⑦ ⑧ ⑨
50	① ② ③ ④ ⑤ ⑥ ⑦ ⑧ ⑨

解答欄 (解答番号 51〜75)

解答番号	解 答 欄
51	① ② ③ ④ ⑤ ⑥ ⑦ ⑧ ⑨
52	① ② ③ ④ ⑤ ⑥ ⑦ ⑧ ⑨
53	① ② ③ ④ ⑤ ⑥ ⑦ ⑧ ⑨
54	① ② ③ ④ ⑤ ⑥ ⑦ ⑧ ⑨
55	① ② ③ ④ ⑤ ⑥ ⑦ ⑧ ⑨
56	① ② ③ ④ ⑤ ⑥ ⑦ ⑧ ⑨
57	① ② ③ ④ ⑤ ⑥ ⑦ ⑧ ⑨
58	① ② ③ ④ ⑤ ⑥ ⑦ ⑧ ⑨
59	① ② ③ ④ ⑤ ⑥ ⑦ ⑧ ⑨
60	① ② ③ ④ ⑤ ⑥ ⑦ ⑧ ⑨
61	① ② ③ ④ ⑤ ⑥ ⑦ ⑧ ⑨
62	① ② ③ ④ ⑤ ⑥ ⑦ ⑧ ⑨
63	① ② ③ ④ ⑤ ⑥ ⑦ ⑧ ⑨
64	① ② ③ ④ ⑤ ⑥ ⑦ ⑧ ⑨
65	① ② ③ ④ ⑤ ⑥ ⑦ ⑧ ⑨
66	① ② ③ ④ ⑤ ⑥ ⑦ ⑧ ⑨
67	① ② ③ ④ ⑤ ⑥ ⑦ ⑧ ⑨
68	① ② ③ ④ ⑤ ⑥ ⑦ ⑧ ⑨
69	① ② ③ ④ ⑤ ⑥ ⑦ ⑧ ⑨
70	① ② ③ ④ ⑤ ⑥ ⑦ ⑧ ⑨
71	① ② ③ ④ ⑤ ⑥ ⑦ ⑧ ⑨
72	① ② ③ ④ ⑤ ⑥ ⑦ ⑧ ⑨
73	① ② ③ ④ ⑤ ⑥ ⑦ ⑧ ⑨
74	① ② ③ ④ ⑤ ⑥ ⑦ ⑧ ⑨
75	① ② ③ ④ ⑤ ⑥ ⑦ ⑧ ⑨

駿 台 文 庫

外国語　解答用紙

マーク例

良い例	悪い例
●	⊙ ⊗ ◐ ○

① 受験番号を記入し、その下のマーク欄にマークしなさい。

受験番号欄

千位	百位	十位	一位	英字
				Ⓐ Ⓑ Ⓒ Ⓗ Ⓚ Ⓜ Ⓡ Ⓤ Ⓧ Ⓨ Ⓩ

② 氏名・フリガナ、試験場コードを記入しなさい。

フリガナ	
氏　名	

試験場コード	十万位	万位	千位	百位	十位	一位

③ 解答科目欄

解答科目欄				
リ英 語（ティング語	ド イ ツ 語	フ ラ ン ス 語	中 国 語	韓 国 語
○	○	○	○	○

・1科目だけマークしなさい。
・解答科目欄が無マーク又は複数マークの場合は、0点となることがあります。

注意事項

1　訂正は、消しゴムできれいに消し、消しくずを残してはいけません。
2　所定欄以外にはマークしたり、記入したりしてはいけません。
3　汚したり、折り曲げたりしてはいけません。

解答番号	解　答　欄
1	① ② ③ ④ ⑤ ⑥ ⑦ ⑧ ⑨
2	① ② ③ ④ ⑤ ⑥ ⑦ ⑧ ⑨
3	① ② ③ ④ ⑤ ⑥ ⑦ ⑧ ⑨
4	① ② ③ ④ ⑤ ⑥ ⑦ ⑧ ⑨
5	① ② ③ ④ ⑤ ⑥ ⑦ ⑧ ⑨
6	① ② ③ ④ ⑤ ⑥ ⑦ ⑧ ⑨
7	① ② ③ ④ ⑤ ⑥ ⑦ ⑧ ⑨
8	① ② ③ ④ ⑤ ⑥ ⑦ ⑧ ⑨
9	① ② ③ ④ ⑤ ⑥ ⑦ ⑧ ⑨
10	① ② ③ ④ ⑤ ⑥ ⑦ ⑧ ⑨
11	① ② ③ ④ ⑤ ⑥ ⑦ ⑧ ⑨
12	① ② ③ ④ ⑤ ⑥ ⑦ ⑧ ⑨
13	① ② ③ ④ ⑤ ⑥ ⑦ ⑧ ⑨
14	① ② ③ ④ ⑤ ⑥ ⑦ ⑧ ⑨
15	① ② ③ ④ ⑤ ⑥ ⑦ ⑧ ⑨
16	① ② ③ ④ ⑤ ⑥ ⑦ ⑧ ⑨
17	① ② ③ ④ ⑤ ⑥ ⑦ ⑧ ⑨
18	① ② ③ ④ ⑤ ⑥ ⑦ ⑧ ⑨
19	① ② ③ ④ ⑤ ⑥ ⑦ ⑧ ⑨
20	① ② ③ ④ ⑤ ⑥ ⑦ ⑧ ⑨
21	① ② ③ ④ ⑤ ⑥ ⑦ ⑧ ⑨
22	① ② ③ ④ ⑤ ⑥ ⑦ ⑧ ⑨
23	① ② ③ ④ ⑤ ⑥ ⑦ ⑧ ⑨
24	① ② ③ ④ ⑤ ⑥ ⑦ ⑧ ⑨
25	① ② ③ ④ ⑤ ⑥ ⑦ ⑧ ⑨

解答番号	解　答　欄
26	① ② ③ ④ ⑤ ⑥ ⑦ ⑧ ⑨
27	① ② ③ ④ ⑤ ⑥ ⑦ ⑧ ⑨
28	① ② ③ ④ ⑤ ⑥ ⑦ ⑧ ⑨
29	① ② ③ ④ ⑤ ⑥ ⑦ ⑧ ⑨
30	① ② ③ ④ ⑤ ⑥ ⑦ ⑧ ⑨
31	① ② ③ ④ ⑤ ⑥ ⑦ ⑧ ⑨
32	① ② ③ ④ ⑤ ⑥ ⑦ ⑧ ⑨
33	① ② ③ ④ ⑤ ⑥ ⑦ ⑧ ⑨
34	① ② ③ ④ ⑤ ⑥ ⑦ ⑧ ⑨
35	① ② ③ ④ ⑤ ⑥ ⑦ ⑧ ⑨
36	① ② ③ ④ ⑤ ⑥ ⑦ ⑧ ⑨
37	① ② ③ ④ ⑤ ⑥ ⑦ ⑧ ⑨
38	① ② ③ ④ ⑤ ⑥ ⑦ ⑧ ⑨
39	① ② ③ ④ ⑤ ⑥ ⑦ ⑧ ⑨
40	① ② ③ ④ ⑤ ⑥ ⑦ ⑧ ⑨
41	① ② ③ ④ ⑤ ⑥ ⑦ ⑧ ⑨
42	① ② ③ ④ ⑤ ⑥ ⑦ ⑧ ⑨
43	① ② ③ ④ ⑤ ⑥ ⑦ ⑧ ⑨
44	① ② ③ ④ ⑤ ⑥ ⑦ ⑧ ⑨
45	① ② ③ ④ ⑤ ⑥ ⑦ ⑧ ⑨
46	① ② ③ ④ ⑤ ⑥ ⑦ ⑧ ⑨
47	① ② ③ ④ ⑤ ⑥ ⑦ ⑧ ⑨
48	① ② ③ ④ ⑤ ⑥ ⑦ ⑧ ⑨
49	① ② ③ ④ ⑤ ⑥ ⑦ ⑧ ⑨
50	① ② ③ ④ ⑤ ⑥ ⑦ ⑧ ⑨

解答番号	解　答　欄
51	① ② ③ ④ ⑤ ⑥ ⑦ ⑧ ⑨
52	① ② ③ ④ ⑤ ⑥ ⑦ ⑧ ⑨
53	① ② ③ ④ ⑤ ⑥ ⑦ ⑧ ⑨
54	① ② ③ ④ ⑤ ⑥ ⑦ ⑧ ⑨
55	① ② ③ ④ ⑤ ⑥ ⑦ ⑧ ⑨
56	① ② ③ ④ ⑤ ⑥ ⑦ ⑧ ⑨
57	① ② ③ ④ ⑤ ⑥ ⑦ ⑧ ⑨
58	① ② ③ ④ ⑤ ⑥ ⑦ ⑧ ⑨
59	① ② ③ ④ ⑤ ⑥ ⑦ ⑧ ⑨
60	① ② ③ ④ ⑤ ⑥ ⑦ ⑧ ⑨
61	① ② ③ ④ ⑤ ⑥ ⑦ ⑧ ⑨
62	① ② ③ ④ ⑤ ⑥ ⑦ ⑧ ⑨
63	① ② ③ ④ ⑤ ⑥ ⑦ ⑧ ⑨
64	① ② ③ ④ ⑤ ⑥ ⑦ ⑧ ⑨
65	① ② ③ ④ ⑤ ⑥ ⑦ ⑧ ⑨
66	① ② ③ ④ ⑤ ⑥ ⑦ ⑧ ⑨
67	① ② ③ ④ ⑤ ⑥ ⑦ ⑧ ⑨
68	① ② ③ ④ ⑤ ⑥ ⑦ ⑧ ⑨
69	① ② ③ ④ ⑤ ⑥ ⑦ ⑧ ⑨
70	① ② ③ ④ ⑤ ⑥ ⑦ ⑧ ⑨
71	① ② ③ ④ ⑤ ⑥ ⑦ ⑧ ⑨
72	① ② ③ ④ ⑤ ⑥ ⑦ ⑧ ⑨
73	① ② ③ ④ ⑤ ⑥ ⑦ ⑧ ⑨
74	① ② ③ ④ ⑤ ⑥ ⑦ ⑧ ⑨
75	① ② ③ ④ ⑤ ⑥ ⑦ ⑧ ⑨

駿　合　文　庫

外国語　解答用紙

マーク例

良い例	悪い例

注意事項

1　訂正は、消しゴムできれいに消し、消しくずを残してはいけません。
2　所定欄以外にはマーク又は記入したりしてはいけません。
3　汚したり、折りまげたりしてはいけません。

① 受験番号を記入し、その下のマーク欄にマークしなさい。

受験番号欄

千位	百位	十位	一位	英字

③
・1科目だけマークしなさい。
・解答科目欄が無マーク又は複数マークの場合は、0点となることがあります。

解答科目欄

英 語	ド イ ツ 語	フ ラ ン ス 語	中 国 語	韓 国 語

② 氏名・フリガナ、試験場コードを記入しなさい。

フリガナ	
氏　名	
試験場コード	十万位　万位　千位　百位　十位　一位

解答欄

解答番号 1〜25, 26〜50, 51〜75

解　答　欄　1 2 3 4 5 6 7 8 9

駿台文庫

外国語　解答用紙

マーク例

良い例	悪い例
●	⊙ ⊗ ◕ ○

① 受験番号を記入し，その下のマーク欄にマークしなさい。

受験番号欄				
千位	百位	十位	一位	英字
－	⓪	⓪	⓪	Ⓐ
①	①	①	①	Ⓑ
②	②	②	②	Ⓒ
③	③	③	③	Ⓗ
④	④	④	④	Ⓚ
⑤	⑤	⑤	⑤	Ⓜ
⑥	⑥	⑥	⑥	Ⓡ
⑦	⑦	⑦	⑦	Ⓤ
⑧	⑧	⑧	⑧	Ⓧ
⑨	⑨	⑨	⑨	Ⓨ
－	－	－	－	Ⓩ

② 氏名・フリガナ，試験場コードを記入しなさい。

フリガナ						
氏　名						
試験場コード	十万位	万位	千位	百位	十位	一位

解答科目欄				
英語（リーディング）	ドイツ語	フランス語	中国語	韓国語
○	○	○	○	○

③ ・１科目だけマークしなさい。
・解答科目欄が無マーク又は複数マークの場合は，０点となることがあります。

注意事項

1　訂正は，消しゴムできれいに消し，消しくずを残してはいけません。

2　所定欄以外にはマークしたり，記入したりしてはいけません。

3　汚したり，折りまげたりしてはいけません。

解答番号	解答欄								
	1	2	3	4	5	6	7	8	9
1	①	②	③	④	⑤	⑥	⑦	⑧	⑨
2	①	②	③	④	⑤	⑥	⑦	⑧	⑨
3	①	②	③	④	⑤	⑥	⑦	⑧	⑨
4	①	②	③	④	⑤	⑥	⑦	⑧	⑨
5	①	②	③	④	⑤	⑥	⑦	⑧	⑨
6	①	②	③	④	⑤	⑥	⑦	⑧	⑨
7	①	②	③	④	⑤	⑥	⑦	⑧	⑨
8	①	②	③	④	⑤	⑥	⑦	⑧	⑨
9	①	②	③	④	⑤	⑥	⑦	⑧	⑨
10	①	②	③	④	⑤	⑥	⑦	⑧	⑨
11	①	②	③	④	⑤	⑥	⑦	⑧	⑨
12	①	②	③	④	⑤	⑥	⑦	⑧	⑨
13	①	②	③	④	⑤	⑥	⑦	⑧	⑨
14	①	②	③	④	⑤	⑥	⑦	⑧	⑨
15	①	②	③	④	⑤	⑥	⑦	⑧	⑨
16	①	②	③	④	⑤	⑥	⑦	⑧	⑨
17	①	②	③	④	⑤	⑥	⑦	⑧	⑨
18	①	②	③	④	⑤	⑥	⑦	⑧	⑨
19	①	②	③	④	⑤	⑥	⑦	⑧	⑨
20	①	②	③	④	⑤	⑥	⑦	⑧	⑨
21	①	②	③	④	⑤	⑥	⑦	⑧	⑨
22	①	②	③	④	⑤	⑥	⑦	⑧	⑨
23	①	②	③	④	⑤	⑥	⑦	⑧	⑨
24	①	②	③	④	⑤	⑥	⑦	⑧	⑨
25	①	②	③	④	⑤	⑥	⑦	⑧	⑨

解答番号	解答欄								
	1	2	3	4	5	6	7	8	9
26	①	②	③	④	⑤	⑥	⑦	⑧	⑨
27	①	②	③	④	⑤	⑥	⑦	⑧	⑨
28	①	②	③	④	⑤	⑥	⑦	⑧	⑨
29	①	②	③	④	⑤	⑥	⑦	⑧	⑨
30	①	②	③	④	⑤	⑥	⑦	⑧	⑨
31	①	②	③	④	⑤	⑥	⑦	⑧	⑨
32	①	②	③	④	⑤	⑥	⑦	⑧	⑨
33	①	②	③	④	⑤	⑥	⑦	⑧	⑨
34	①	②	③	④	⑤	⑥	⑦	⑧	⑨
35	①	②	③	④	⑤	⑥	⑦	⑧	⑨
36	①	②	③	④	⑤	⑥	⑦	⑧	⑨
37	①	②	③	④	⑤	⑥	⑦	⑧	⑨
38	①	②	③	④	⑤	⑥	⑦	⑧	⑨
39	①	②	③	④	⑤	⑥	⑦	⑧	⑨
40	①	②	③	④	⑤	⑥	⑦	⑧	⑨
41	①	②	③	④	⑤	⑥	⑦	⑧	⑨
42	①	②	③	④	⑤	⑥	⑦	⑧	⑨
43	①	②	③	④	⑤	⑥	⑦	⑧	⑨
44	①	②	③	④	⑤	⑥	⑦	⑧	⑨
45	①	②	③	④	⑤	⑥	⑦	⑧	⑨
46	①	②	③	④	⑤	⑥	⑦	⑧	⑨
47	①	②	③	④	⑤	⑥	⑦	⑧	⑨
48	①	②	③	④	⑤	⑥	⑦	⑧	⑨
49	①	②	③	④	⑤	⑥	⑦	⑧	⑨
50	①	②	③	④	⑤	⑥	⑦	⑧	⑨

解答番号	解答欄								
	1	2	3	4	5	6	7	8	9
51	①	②	③	④	⑤	⑥	⑦	⑧	⑨
52	①	②	③	④	⑤	⑥	⑦	⑧	⑨
53	①	②	③	④	⑤	⑥	⑦	⑧	⑨
54	①	②	③	④	⑤	⑥	⑦	⑧	⑨
55	①	②	③	④	⑤	⑥	⑦	⑧	⑨
56	①	②	③	④	⑤	⑥	⑦	⑧	⑨
57	①	②	③	④	⑤	⑥	⑦	⑧	⑨
58	①	②	③	④	⑤	⑥	⑦	⑧	⑨
59	①	②	③	④	⑤	⑥	⑦	⑧	⑨
60	①	②	③	④	⑤	⑥	⑦	⑧	⑨
61	①	②	③	④	⑤	⑥	⑦	⑧	⑨
62	①	②	③	④	⑤	⑥	⑦	⑧	⑨
63	①	②	③	④	⑤	⑥	⑦	⑧	⑨
64	①	②	③	④	⑤	⑥	⑦	⑧	⑨
65	①	②	③	④	⑤	⑥	⑦	⑧	⑨
66	①	②	③	④	⑤	⑥	⑦	⑧	⑨
67	①	②	③	④	⑤	⑥	⑦	⑧	⑨
68	①	②	③	④	⑤	⑥	⑦	⑧	⑨
69	①	②	③	④	⑤	⑥	⑦	⑧	⑨
70	①	②	③	④	⑤	⑥	⑦	⑧	⑨
71	①	②	③	④	⑤	⑥	⑦	⑧	⑨
72	①	②	③	④	⑤	⑥	⑦	⑧	⑨
73	①	②	③	④	⑤	⑥	⑦	⑧	⑨
74	①	②	③	④	⑤	⑥	⑦	⑧	⑨
75	①	②	③	④	⑤	⑥	⑦	⑧	⑨

外国語 解答用紙

注意事項

1 訂正は、消しゴムできれいに消し、消しくずを残してはいけません。

2 所定欄以外にはマークしたり、記入したりしてはいけません。

3 汚したり、折りまげたりしてはいけません。

③

- 1科目だけマークしなさい。
- 解答科目欄が無マーク又は複数マークの場合は、0点となることがあります。

解答科目欄					
英語（リーディング）	ドイツ語	フランス語	中国語	韓国語	
○	○	○	○	○	

マーク例

良い例	悪い例
●	◑ ⊗ ◓

①

受験番号を記入し、その下のマーク欄にマークしなさい。

受験番号欄				
千位	百位	十位	一位	英字
－	－	－	－	－
①	⓪	⓪	⓪	Ⓐ
②	①	①	①	Ⓑ
③	②	②	②	Ⓒ
④	③	③	③	Ⓗ
⑤	④	④	④	Ⓚ
⑥	⑤	⑤	⑤	Ⓜ
⑦	⑥	⑥	⑥	Ⓡ
⑧	⑦	⑦	⑦	Ⓤ
⑨	⑧	⑧	⑧	Ⓧ
	⑨	⑨	⑨	Ⓨ
				Ⓩ

②

氏名・フリガナ、試験場コードを記入しなさい。

フリガナ	
氏名	
試験場コード	十万位 万位 千位 百位 十位 一位

解答番号 1〜25

解答番号	解 答 欄
1	① ② ③ ④ ⑤ ⑥ ⑦ ⑧ ⑨
2	① ② ③ ④ ⑤ ⑥ ⑦ ⑧ ⑨
3	① ② ③ ④ ⑤ ⑥ ⑦ ⑧ ⑨
4	① ② ③ ④ ⑤ ⑥ ⑦ ⑧ ⑨
5	① ② ③ ④ ⑤ ⑥ ⑦ ⑧ ⑨
6	① ② ③ ④ ⑤ ⑥ ⑦ ⑧ ⑨
7	① ② ③ ④ ⑤ ⑥ ⑦ ⑧ ⑨
8	① ② ③ ④ ⑤ ⑥ ⑦ ⑧ ⑨
9	① ② ③ ④ ⑤ ⑥ ⑦ ⑧ ⑨
10	① ② ③ ④ ⑤ ⑥ ⑦ ⑧ ⑨
11	① ② ③ ④ ⑤ ⑥ ⑦ ⑧ ⑨
12	① ② ③ ④ ⑤ ⑥ ⑦ ⑧ ⑨
13	① ② ③ ④ ⑤ ⑥ ⑦ ⑧ ⑨
14	① ② ③ ④ ⑤ ⑥ ⑦ ⑧ ⑨
15	① ② ③ ④ ⑤ ⑥ ⑦ ⑧ ⑨
16	① ② ③ ④ ⑤ ⑥ ⑦ ⑧ ⑨
17	① ② ③ ④ ⑤ ⑥ ⑦ ⑧ ⑨
18	① ② ③ ④ ⑤ ⑥ ⑦ ⑧ ⑨
19	① ② ③ ④ ⑤ ⑥ ⑦ ⑧ ⑨
20	① ② ③ ④ ⑤ ⑥ ⑦ ⑧ ⑨
21	① ② ③ ④ ⑤ ⑥ ⑦ ⑧ ⑨
22	① ② ③ ④ ⑤ ⑥ ⑦ ⑧ ⑨
23	① ② ③ ④ ⑤ ⑥ ⑦ ⑧ ⑨
24	① ② ③ ④ ⑤ ⑥ ⑦ ⑧ ⑨
25	① ② ③ ④ ⑤ ⑥ ⑦ ⑧ ⑨

解答番号	解 答 欄
26	① ② ③ ④ ⑤ ⑥ ⑦ ⑧ ⑨
27	① ② ③ ④ ⑤ ⑥ ⑦ ⑧ ⑨
28	① ② ③ ④ ⑤ ⑥ ⑦ ⑧ ⑨
29	① ② ③ ④ ⑤ ⑥ ⑦ ⑧ ⑨
30	① ② ③ ④ ⑤ ⑥ ⑦ ⑧ ⑨
31	① ② ③ ④ ⑤ ⑥ ⑦ ⑧ ⑨
32	① ② ③ ④ ⑤ ⑥ ⑦ ⑧ ⑨
33	① ② ③ ④ ⑤ ⑥ ⑦ ⑧ ⑨
34	① ② ③ ④ ⑤ ⑥ ⑦ ⑧ ⑨
35	① ② ③ ④ ⑤ ⑥ ⑦ ⑧ ⑨
36	① ② ③ ④ ⑤ ⑥ ⑦ ⑧ ⑨
37	① ② ③ ④ ⑤ ⑥ ⑦ ⑧ ⑨
38	① ② ③ ④ ⑤ ⑥ ⑦ ⑧ ⑨
39	① ② ③ ④ ⑤ ⑥ ⑦ ⑧ ⑨
40	① ② ③ ④ ⑤ ⑥ ⑦ ⑧ ⑨
41	① ② ③ ④ ⑤ ⑥ ⑦ ⑧ ⑨
42	① ② ③ ④ ⑤ ⑥ ⑦ ⑧ ⑨
43	① ② ③ ④ ⑤ ⑥ ⑦ ⑧ ⑨
44	① ② ③ ④ ⑤ ⑥ ⑦ ⑧ ⑨
45	① ② ③ ④ ⑤ ⑥ ⑦ ⑧ ⑨
46	① ② ③ ④ ⑤ ⑥ ⑦ ⑧ ⑨
47	① ② ③ ④ ⑤ ⑥ ⑦ ⑧ ⑨
48	① ② ③ ④ ⑤ ⑥ ⑦ ⑧ ⑨
49	① ② ③ ④ ⑤ ⑥ ⑦ ⑧ ⑨
50	① ② ③ ④ ⑤ ⑥ ⑦ ⑧ ⑨

解答番号	解 答 欄
51	① ② ③ ④ ⑤ ⑥ ⑦ ⑧ ⑨
52	① ② ③ ④ ⑤ ⑥ ⑦ ⑧ ⑨
53	① ② ③ ④ ⑤ ⑥ ⑦ ⑧ ⑨
54	① ② ③ ④ ⑤ ⑥ ⑦ ⑧ ⑨
55	① ② ③ ④ ⑤ ⑥ ⑦ ⑧ ⑨
56	① ② ③ ④ ⑤ ⑥ ⑦ ⑧ ⑨
57	① ② ③ ④ ⑤ ⑥ ⑦ ⑧ ⑨
58	① ② ③ ④ ⑤ ⑥ ⑦ ⑧ ⑨
59	① ② ③ ④ ⑤ ⑥ ⑦ ⑧ ⑨
60	① ② ③ ④ ⑤ ⑥ ⑦ ⑧ ⑨
61	① ② ③ ④ ⑤ ⑥ ⑦ ⑧ ⑨
62	① ② ③ ④ ⑤ ⑥ ⑦ ⑧ ⑨
63	① ② ③ ④ ⑤ ⑥ ⑦ ⑧ ⑨
64	① ② ③ ④ ⑤ ⑥ ⑦ ⑧ ⑨
65	① ② ③ ④ ⑤ ⑥ ⑦ ⑧ ⑨
66	① ② ③ ④ ⑤ ⑥ ⑦ ⑧ ⑨
67	① ② ③ ④ ⑤ ⑥ ⑦ ⑧ ⑨
68	① ② ③ ④ ⑤ ⑥ ⑦ ⑧ ⑨
69	① ② ③ ④ ⑤ ⑥ ⑦ ⑧ ⑨
70	① ② ③ ④ ⑤ ⑥ ⑦ ⑧ ⑨
71	① ② ③ ④ ⑤ ⑥ ⑦ ⑧ ⑨
72	① ② ③ ④ ⑤ ⑥ ⑦ ⑧ ⑨
73	① ② ③ ④ ⑤ ⑥ ⑦ ⑧ ⑨
74	① ② ③ ④ ⑤ ⑥ ⑦ ⑧ ⑨
75	① ② ③ ④ ⑤ ⑥ ⑦ ⑧ ⑨

駿 台 文 庫

駿 合 文 庫

マーク例
良い例 ●
悪い例 ⊙ ⊗ ◐ ◑

① 受験番号を記入し、その下のマーク欄にマークしなさい。

受験番号欄

千位	百位	十位	一位	英字

② 氏名・フリガナ、試験場コードを記入しなさい。

フリガナ
氏　名

試験場コード	十万位	万位	千位	百位	十位	一位

③
・1科目だけマークしなさい。
・解答科目欄が無マーク又は複数マークの場合は、0点となることがあります。

解答科目欄

英語	ドイツ語	フランス語	中国語	韓国語
○	○	○	○	○

外国語　解答用紙

注意事項
1　訂正は、消しゴムできれいに消し、消しくずを残してはいけません。
2　所定欄以外にはマークしたり、記入したりしてはいけません。
3　汚したり、折りまげたりしてはいけません。

外国語 解答用紙

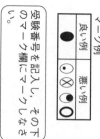

注意事項
1 訂正は、消しゴムできれいに消し、消しくずを残してはいけません。
2 所定欄以外にはマークしたり、記入したりしてはいけません。
3 汚したり、折りまげたりしてはいけません。

駿 台 文 庫

外国語　解答用紙

注意事項

1　訂正は、消しゴムできれいに消し、消しくずを残してはいけません。
2　所定欄以外にはマークしたり、記入したりしてはいけません。
3　汚したり、折りまげたりしてはいけません。

③
・1科目だけマークしなさい。
・解答科目欄が無マーク又は複数マークの場合は、0点となることがあります。

解答科目欄

| 英語 | ドイツ語 | フランス語 | 中国語 | 韓国語 |
| ○ | ○ | ○ | ○ | ○ |

マーク例

| 良い例 | 悪い例 |
| ● | ⊙ ⊗ ○ |

① 受験番号を記入し、その下のマーク欄にマークしなさい。

受験番号欄

千位	百位	十位	一位	英字
-	0	0	0	A
1	1	1	1	B
2	2	2	2	C
3	3	3	3	H
4	4	4	4	K
5	5	5	5	M
6	6	6	6	R
7	7	7	7	U
8	8	8	8	X
9	9	9	9	Y
-	-	-	-	Z

② 氏名・フリガナ、試験場コードを記入しなさい。

フリガナ	
氏　名	
試験場コード	十万位　万位　千位　百位　十位　一位

駿台文庫

外国語　解答用紙

マーク例

良い例	悪い例
●	⊙ ⊗ ◑ ○

① 受験番号を記入し、その下のマーク欄にマークしなさい。

受験番号欄

千位	百位	十位	一位	英字

② 氏名・フリガナ、試験場コードを記入しなさい。

フリガナ		
氏　名		
試験場コード	十万位 万位 千位 百位 十位 一位	

③

解答科目欄

英語	ドイツ語	フランス語	中国語	韓国語
リスニング語				
○	○	○	○	○

・1科目だけマークしなさい。
・解答科目欄が無マーク又は複数マークの場合は、0点となることがあります。

注意事項

1　訂正は、消しゴムできれいに消し、消しくずを残してはいけません。
2　所定欄以外にはマーク、記入したりしてはいけません。
3　汚したり、折りまげたりしてはいけません。

駿台文庫

外国語　解答用紙

マーク例

良い例	悪い例
●	◐ ⊗ ◑ ◔

注意事項

1 訂正は、消しゴムできれいに消し、消しくずを残してはいけません。

2 所定欄以外にはマークしたり、記入したりしてはいけません。

3 汚したり、折りまげたりしてはいけません。

③
- 1科目だけマークしなさい。
- 解答科目欄が無くマーク又は複数マークの場合は、0点となることがあります。

解答科目欄

英語 リーディング	ドイツ語	フランス語	中国語	韓国語
○	○	○	○	○

① 受験番号を記入し、その下のマーク欄にマークしなさい。

② 氏名・フリガナ、試験場コードを記入しなさい。

駿　合　文　庫

外国語　解答用紙

駿台文庫

マーク例

良い例	悪い例
●	◑ ⊗ ◓ ○

① 受験番号を記入し、そのマーク欄にマークしなさい。

受験番号欄

千位	百位	十位	一位	英字
－	－	－	－	Ⓩ

② 氏名・フリガナ、試験場コードを記入しなさい。

フリガナ					
氏名					
試験場コード	十万位	万位	千位	百位	十位	一位

③ 解答科目欄

解答科目欄				
英（リーディング）語	ド イ ツ 語	フ ラ ン ス 語	中 国 語	韓 国 語
○	○	○	○	○

注意事項

1 訂正は、消しゴムできれいに消し、消しくずを残してはいけません。
2 所定欄以外にはマークしたり、記入したりしてはいけません。
3 汚したり、折りまげたりしてはいけません。

・1科目だけマークしなさい。
・解答科目欄が無マーク又は複数マークの場合は、0点となることがあります。

解答欄 1〜25

解答番号	解 答 欄 1 2 3 4 5 6 7 8 9
1	① ② ③ ④ ⑤ ⑥ ⑦ ⑧ ⑨
2	① ② ③ ④ ⑤ ⑥ ⑦ ⑧ ⑨
3	① ② ③ ④ ⑤ ⑥ ⑦ ⑧ ⑨
4	① ② ③ ④ ⑤ ⑥ ⑦ ⑧ ⑨
5	① ② ③ ④ ⑤ ⑥ ⑦ ⑧ ⑨
6	① ② ③ ④ ⑤ ⑥ ⑦ ⑧ ⑨
7	① ② ③ ④ ⑤ ⑥ ⑦ ⑧ ⑨
8	① ② ③ ④ ⑤ ⑥ ⑦ ⑧ ⑨
9	① ② ③ ④ ⑤ ⑥ ⑦ ⑧ ⑨
10	① ② ③ ④ ⑤ ⑥ ⑦ ⑧ ⑨
11	① ② ③ ④ ⑤ ⑥ ⑦ ⑧ ⑨
12	① ② ③ ④ ⑤ ⑥ ⑦ ⑧ ⑨
13	① ② ③ ④ ⑤ ⑥ ⑦ ⑧ ⑨
14	① ② ③ ④ ⑤ ⑥ ⑦ ⑧ ⑨
15	① ② ③ ④ ⑤ ⑥ ⑦ ⑧ ⑨
16	① ② ③ ④ ⑤ ⑥ ⑦ ⑧ ⑨
17	① ② ③ ④ ⑤ ⑥ ⑦ ⑧ ⑨
18	① ② ③ ④ ⑤ ⑥ ⑦ ⑧ ⑨
19	① ② ③ ④ ⑤ ⑥ ⑦ ⑧ ⑨
20	① ② ③ ④ ⑤ ⑥ ⑦ ⑧ ⑨
21	① ② ③ ④ ⑤ ⑥ ⑦ ⑧ ⑨
22	① ② ③ ④ ⑤ ⑥ ⑦ ⑧ ⑨
23	① ② ③ ④ ⑤ ⑥ ⑦ ⑧ ⑨
24	① ② ③ ④ ⑤ ⑥ ⑦ ⑧ ⑨
25	① ② ③ ④ ⑤ ⑥ ⑦ ⑧ ⑨

解答欄 26〜50

解答番号	解 答 欄 1 2 3 4 5 6 7 8 9
26	① ② ③ ④ ⑤ ⑥ ⑦ ⑧ ⑨
27	① ② ③ ④ ⑤ ⑥ ⑦ ⑧ ⑨
28	① ② ③ ④ ⑤ ⑥ ⑦ ⑧ ⑨
29	① ② ③ ④ ⑤ ⑥ ⑦ ⑧ ⑨
30	① ② ③ ④ ⑤ ⑥ ⑦ ⑧ ⑨
31	① ② ③ ④ ⑤ ⑥ ⑦ ⑧ ⑨
32	① ② ③ ④ ⑤ ⑥ ⑦ ⑧ ⑨
33	① ② ③ ④ ⑤ ⑥ ⑦ ⑧ ⑨
34	① ② ③ ④ ⑤ ⑥ ⑦ ⑧ ⑨
35	① ② ③ ④ ⑤ ⑥ ⑦ ⑧ ⑨
36	① ② ③ ④ ⑤ ⑥ ⑦ ⑧ ⑨
37	① ② ③ ④ ⑤ ⑥ ⑦ ⑧ ⑨
38	① ② ③ ④ ⑤ ⑥ ⑦ ⑧ ⑨
39	① ② ③ ④ ⑤ ⑥ ⑦ ⑧ ⑨
40	① ② ③ ④ ⑤ ⑥ ⑦ ⑧ ⑨
41	① ② ③ ④ ⑤ ⑥ ⑦ ⑧ ⑨
42	① ② ③ ④ ⑤ ⑥ ⑦ ⑧ ⑨
43	① ② ③ ④ ⑤ ⑥ ⑦ ⑧ ⑨
44	① ② ③ ④ ⑤ ⑥ ⑦ ⑧ ⑨
45	① ② ③ ④ ⑤ ⑥ ⑦ ⑧ ⑨
46	① ② ③ ④ ⑤ ⑥ ⑦ ⑧ ⑨
47	① ② ③ ④ ⑤ ⑥ ⑦ ⑧ ⑨
48	① ② ③ ④ ⑤ ⑥ ⑦ ⑧ ⑨
49	① ② ③ ④ ⑤ ⑥ ⑦ ⑧ ⑨
50	① ② ③ ④ ⑤ ⑥ ⑦ ⑧ ⑨

解答欄 51〜75

解答番号	解 答 欄 1 2 3 4 5 6 7 8 9
51	① ② ③ ④ ⑤ ⑥ ⑦ ⑧ ⑨
52	① ② ③ ④ ⑤ ⑥ ⑦ ⑧ ⑨
53	① ② ③ ④ ⑤ ⑥ ⑦ ⑧ ⑨
54	① ② ③ ④ ⑤ ⑥ ⑦ ⑧ ⑨
55	① ② ③ ④ ⑤ ⑥ ⑦ ⑧ ⑨
56	① ② ③ ④ ⑤ ⑥ ⑦ ⑧ ⑨
57	① ② ③ ④ ⑤ ⑥ ⑦ ⑧ ⑨
58	① ② ③ ④ ⑤ ⑥ ⑦ ⑧ ⑨
59	① ② ③ ④ ⑤ ⑥ ⑦ ⑧ ⑨
60	① ② ③ ④ ⑤ ⑥ ⑦ ⑧ ⑨
61	① ② ③ ④ ⑤ ⑥ ⑦ ⑧ ⑨
62	① ② ③ ④ ⑤ ⑥ ⑦ ⑧ ⑨
63	① ② ③ ④ ⑤ ⑥ ⑦ ⑧ ⑨
64	① ② ③ ④ ⑤ ⑥ ⑦ ⑧ ⑨
65	① ② ③ ④ ⑤ ⑥ ⑦ ⑧ ⑨
66	① ② ③ ④ ⑤ ⑥ ⑦ ⑧ ⑨
67	① ② ③ ④ ⑤ ⑥ ⑦ ⑧ ⑨
68	① ② ③ ④ ⑤ ⑥ ⑦ ⑧ ⑨
69	① ② ③ ④ ⑤ ⑥ ⑦ ⑧ ⑨
70	① ② ③ ④ ⑤ ⑥ ⑦ ⑧ ⑨
71	① ② ③ ④ ⑤ ⑥ ⑦ ⑧ ⑨
72	① ② ③ ④ ⑤ ⑥ ⑦ ⑧ ⑨
73	① ② ③ ④ ⑤ ⑥ ⑦ ⑧ ⑨
74	① ② ③ ④ ⑤ ⑥ ⑦ ⑧ ⑨
75	① ② ③ ④ ⑤ ⑥ ⑦ ⑧ ⑨

外国語　解答用紙

マーク例

良い例	悪い例
●	⊗ ◐ ○

③
- 1科目だけマークしなさい。
- 解答科目欄が無くマーク又は複数マークの場合は、0点となることがあります。

解答科目欄

英語 （リーディング）	ド イ ツ 語	フ ラ ン ス 語	中 国 語	韓 国 語
○	○	○	○	○

① 受験番号を記入し、その下のマーク欄にマークしなさい。

受験番号欄

千位	百位	十位	一位	英字
—	⓪	⓪	⓪	Ⓐ
①	①	①	①	Ⓑ
②	②	②	②	Ⓒ
③	③	③	③	Ⓗ
④	④	④	④	Ⓚ
⑤	⑤	⑤	⑤	Ⓜ
⑥	⑥	⑥	⑥	Ⓡ
⑦	⑦	⑦	⑦	Ⓤ
⑧	⑧	⑧	⑧	Ⓧ
⑨	⑨	⑨	⑨	Ⓨ
—	—	—	—	Ⓩ

② 氏名・フリガナ、試験場コードを記入しなさい。

フリガナ	
氏　名	

試験場コード	十万位	万位	千位	百位	十位	一位

駿　台　文　庫

注意事項

1　訂正は、消しゴムできれいに消し、消しくずを残してはいけません。

2　所定欄以外にはマークしたり、記入したりしてはいけません。

3　汚したり、折りまげたりしてはいけません。

解答欄（1〜25）

解答番号	1	2	3	4	5	6	7	8	9
1	①	②	③	④	⑤	⑥	⑦	⑧	⑨
2	①	②	③	④	⑤	⑥	⑦	⑧	⑨
3	①	②	③	④	⑤	⑥	⑦	⑧	⑨
4	①	②	③	④	⑤	⑥	⑦	⑧	⑨
5	①	②	③	④	⑤	⑥	⑦	⑧	⑨
6	①	②	③	④	⑤	⑥	⑦	⑧	⑨
7	①	②	③	④	⑤	⑥	⑦	⑧	⑨
8	①	②	③	④	⑤	⑥	⑦	⑧	⑨
9	①	②	③	④	⑤	⑥	⑦	⑧	⑨
10	①	②	③	④	⑤	⑥	⑦	⑧	⑨
11	①	②	③	④	⑤	⑥	⑦	⑧	⑨
12	①	②	③	④	⑤	⑥	⑦	⑧	⑨
13	①	②	③	④	⑤	⑥	⑦	⑧	⑨
14	①	②	③	④	⑤	⑥	⑦	⑧	⑨
15	①	②	③	④	⑤	⑥	⑦	⑧	⑨
16	①	②	③	④	⑤	⑥	⑦	⑧	⑨
17	①	②	③	④	⑤	⑥	⑦	⑧	⑨
18	①	②	③	④	⑤	⑥	⑦	⑧	⑨
19	①	②	③	④	⑤	⑥	⑦	⑧	⑨
20	①	②	③	④	⑤	⑥	⑦	⑧	⑨
21	①	②	③	④	⑤	⑥	⑦	⑧	⑨
22	①	②	③	④	⑤	⑥	⑦	⑧	⑨
23	①	②	③	④	⑤	⑥	⑦	⑧	⑨
24	①	②	③	④	⑤	⑥	⑦	⑧	⑨
25	①	②	③	④	⑤	⑥	⑦	⑧	⑨

解答欄（26〜50）

解答番号	1	2	3	4	5	6	7	8	9
26	①	②	③	④	⑤	⑥	⑦	⑧	⑨
27	①	②	③	④	⑤	⑥	⑦	⑧	⑨
28	①	②	③	④	⑤	⑥	⑦	⑧	⑨
29	①	②	③	④	⑤	⑥	⑦	⑧	⑨
30	①	②	③	④	⑤	⑥	⑦	⑧	⑨
31	①	②	③	④	⑤	⑥	⑦	⑧	⑨
32	①	②	③	④	⑤	⑥	⑦	⑧	⑨
33	①	②	③	④	⑤	⑥	⑦	⑧	⑨
34	①	②	③	④	⑤	⑥	⑦	⑧	⑨
35	①	②	③	④	⑤	⑥	⑦	⑧	⑨
36	①	②	③	④	⑤	⑥	⑦	⑧	⑨
37	①	②	③	④	⑤	⑥	⑦	⑧	⑨
38	①	②	③	④	⑤	⑥	⑦	⑧	⑨
39	①	②	③	④	⑤	⑥	⑦	⑧	⑨
40	①	②	③	④	⑤	⑥	⑦	⑧	⑨
41	①	②	③	④	⑤	⑥	⑦	⑧	⑨
42	①	②	③	④	⑤	⑥	⑦	⑧	⑨
43	①	②	③	④	⑤	⑥	⑦	⑧	⑨
44	①	②	③	④	⑤	⑥	⑦	⑧	⑨
45	①	②	③	④	⑤	⑥	⑦	⑧	⑨
46	①	②	③	④	⑤	⑥	⑦	⑧	⑨
47	①	②	③	④	⑤	⑥	⑦	⑧	⑨
48	①	②	③	④	⑤	⑥	⑦	⑧	⑨
49	①	②	③	④	⑤	⑥	⑦	⑧	⑨
50	①	②	③	④	⑤	⑥	⑦	⑧	⑨

解答欄（51〜75）

解答番号	1	2	3	4	5	6	7	8	9
51	①	②	③	④	⑤	⑥	⑦	⑧	⑨
52	①	②	③	④	⑤	⑥	⑦	⑧	⑨
53	①	②	③	④	⑤	⑥	⑦	⑧	⑨
54	①	②	③	④	⑤	⑥	⑦	⑧	⑨
55	①	②	③	④	⑤	⑥	⑦	⑧	⑨
56	①	②	③	④	⑤	⑥	⑦	⑧	⑨
57	①	②	③	④	⑤	⑥	⑦	⑧	⑨
58	①	②	③	④	⑤	⑥	⑦	⑧	⑨
59	①	②	③	④	⑤	⑥	⑦	⑧	⑨
60	①	②	③	④	⑤	⑥	⑦	⑧	⑨
61	①	②	③	④	⑤	⑥	⑦	⑧	⑨
62	①	②	③	④	⑤	⑥	⑦	⑧	⑨
63	①	②	③	④	⑤	⑥	⑦	⑧	⑨
64	①	②	③	④	⑤	⑥	⑦	⑧	⑨
65	①	②	③	④	⑤	⑥	⑦	⑧	⑨
66	①	②	③	④	⑤	⑥	⑦	⑧	⑨
67	①	②	③	④	⑤	⑥	⑦	⑧	⑨
68	①	②	③	④	⑤	⑥	⑦	⑧	⑨
69	①	②	③	④	⑤	⑥	⑦	⑧	⑨
70	①	②	③	④	⑤	⑥	⑦	⑧	⑨
71	①	②	③	④	⑤	⑥	⑦	⑧	⑨
72	①	②	③	④	⑤	⑥	⑦	⑧	⑨
73	①	②	③	④	⑤	⑥	⑦	⑧	⑨
74	①	②	③	④	⑤	⑥	⑦	⑧	⑨
75	①	②	③	④	⑤	⑥	⑦	⑧	⑨

マーク例

良い例	悪い例
●	⊙ ⊗ ◐ ○

① 受験番号を記入し、その下のマーク欄にマークしなさい。

受験番号欄

千位	百位	十位	一位	英字
－	－	－	－	

② 氏名・フリガナ、試験場コードを記入しなさい。

フリガナ					
氏 名					
試験場コード	十万位	万位	千位	百位	十位	一位

駿 台 文 庫

③

外国語　解答用紙

解答科目欄

英 語	ド イ ツ 語	フ ラ ン ス 語	中 国 語	韓 国 語	（リーディング語）
○	○	○	○	○	○

注意事項

1　訂正は、消しゴムできれいに消し、消しくずを残してはいけません。
2　所定欄以外にはマークしたり、記入したりしてはいけません。
3　汚したり、折りまげたりしてはいけません。

・1科目だけマークしなさい。
・解答科目欄が無マーク又は複数マークの場合は、0点となることがあります。

解答番号 1〜25、解答欄 1〜9
解答番号 26〜50、解答欄 1〜9
解答番号 51〜75、解答欄 1〜9

駿台

2025
大学入学 共通テスト

実戦問題集

英語 リーディング
【解答・解説編】

駿台文庫編

直前チェック総整理

英語（リーディング）試作問題の特徴と解答のポイント

　令和7年度大学入学共通テストに向けて，大学入試センターより試作問題が公表された。英語の試験問題は「リーディング」・「リスニング」の形式を通して総合的な英語力を評価することが基本的な作成方針とされているが，試作問題については特に「情報や自分の考えを適切に表現したり伝え合ったりするために，理解した情報や考えを整理したり，何をどのように取り上げるかなどを判断したりする力を重視する」ための問題の具体例として示されている。ここではリーディング（第A問・第B問）について，問題の特徴と解答に際してのポイントを見ていく。

＜第A問：3つのステップでエッセイを作成する＞

試作問題　第A問
　この問題では，高校生である「あなた(you)」がエッセイを作成するという状況で問題が出されている。ただし，完成したエッセイが出題されるのではなく，エッセイ作成の過程に焦点を当てた問題となっており，まず以下のような状況設定文が与えられる。

設定文　You are working on an essay about whether high school students should be allowed to use their smartphones in class. You will follow the steps below.「あなたは高校生が授業中にスマートフォンを使うのを許されるべきかどうかについてのエッセイを作成中で，以下のステップを踏もうとしています」

Step 1 : Read and understand various viewpoints about smartphone use.
Step 2 : Take a position on high school students' use of their smartphones in class.
Step 3 : Create an outline for an essay using additional sources.

ステップ1：スマートフォンの使用についてのさまざまな見解を読んで理解する。
ステップ2：高校生が授業中にスマートフォンを使用することについて1つの立場をとる。
ステップ3：さらにいろいろな情報源を利用して，エッセイのアウトラインを作成する。

　この問題では，「授業中のスマートフォン使用の是非」というトピックが与えられ，それについてのエッセイを作成する作業が3つのステップに分けられている。具体的には，「関連資料の読解（ステップ1）」，「自分の意見の形成（ステップ2）」，「追加の情報源の読解とアウトラインの作成（ステップ3）」となっており，それぞれのステップに関して問題が出されている。

ステップ１は，「トピックに関連するさまざまな資料を読む」という作業である。試作問題では，トピックに関する５つの異なる意見が資料として出題された。これらの意見を読み，２つの問いに答える（**問１・２**）。これらの問いでは，それぞれの意見の趣旨や，いくつかの意見に見られる共通点（**例１**）や相違点が問われている。

例１［ステップ１］

設問文　**問１**　Both Authors A and D mention that ⬚1⬚ .　「著者 A と D はいずれも ⬚1⬚ と述べている」

　① apps for learning on smartphones can help students perform better on exams
　② one reason to use smartphones as an educational tool is that most students possess one
　③ smartphones can be used to support activities for learning both at school and at home
　④ smartphones make it possible for students to share their ideas with classmates

　① スマートフォンの学習用アプリは，生徒が試験の成績を上げるのに役立てられる
　② 教育の道具としてスマートフォンを使う理由の１つは，ほとんどの生徒がそれを持っているということだ
　③ スマートフォンは学校でも家庭でも，学習活動を支援するために使うことができる
　④ スマートフォンは，生徒が自分の考えをクラスメートと共有するのを可能にする

　ステップ２（**問３**）では，まず「自分の立場（your position）」が指定され，ステップ１の５つの意見の中から，自分の立場に合う意見を２つ選び，それらの意見に共通する論点を選ぶことが求められる（**例２**）。ここでも，ステップ１に出てきた各意見の主旨とその論拠が把握できているかどうかが鍵となる。それぞれの意見の「トピックへの賛否」と「その主たる根拠」を迅速かつ的確に把握することが大きなポイントとなるので，「トピックへの賛否」について各意見ごとに印（○，×，△など）を付けておくと，問いに効率よく答えることができるだろう。

例２［ステップ２］

設問文　**問３**　Now that you understand the various viewpoints, you have taken a position on high school students' use of their smartphones in class, and have written it out as below.　Choose the best options to complete ⬚3⬚ , ⬚4⬚ , and ⬚5⬚ .　「あなたはさまざまな見解を理解したので，高校生の授業でのスマートフォンの使用に関する立場を決めて，それを以下のように書き出してみた。 ⬚3⬚ , ⬚4⬚ , ⬚5⬚ を埋めるのに最適な選択肢を選びなさい」

Your position: High school students should not be allowed to use their smartphones in class.
　・Authors ⬚3⬚ and ⬚4⬚ support your position.
　・The main argument of the two authors: ⬚5⬚ .

あなたの立場：高校生は授業中のスマートフォンの使用を許されるべきではない。
　・著者 ⬚3⬚ と ⬚4⬚ はあなたの立場を支持している。
　・この２人の著者の主要な論点： ⬚5⬚ 。

― 英 R 2 ―

ステップ3は,「追加資料の読解」と「エッセイのアウトラインの作成」という作業になる。与えられるアウトラインは「序論 (Introduction)」,「本論 (Body)」,「結論 (Conclusion)」の3部からなり,その中の空所を埋める問題が2題出される(**問4・5**)。試作問題では,「本論」となる3つの根拠の中の2つを選ばせる問いが出題された(**例3**)。このステップでは,関連する情報源 (Source) が2つ追加される (A と B)。情報源 A は論説調の文章で,情報源 B は図表を含む文章である。これらを読み,自分がとる立場の根拠 (Reason) として,情報源の内容と合っている英文を選ぶことが求められる。これらの資料を読む際には,自分がとる立場の根拠になりうる適切な事項を探しながら読むことで,正解を見抜きやすくなるだろう。また,情報源 B に関する問題(**問5**)では,選択肢中の英文の「差」や「増減」に関する表現を正しく読み取ることが大きなポイントとなる。

例3 [ステップ3]

Body

Reason 1：[From Step 2]

Reason 2：[Based on Source A]　……　6

Reason 3：[Based on Source B]　……　7

本論

　理由1：[ステップ2から]

　理由2：[情報源 A を根拠に]　……　6

　理由3：[情報源 B を根拠に]　……　7

― 英 R 3 ―

＜第Ｂ問：エッセイの草稿を修正する＞

> **試作問題　第Ｂ問**
>
> 　第Ｂ問では，「あなた」は英語の授業でエッセイを書いており，先生があなたの作成した草稿（draft）の中に４つのコメントを付けているので，それに従って適切な文章に直していく，という設定で問題が出題された。

> 設定文　　In English class you are writing an essay on a social issue you are interested in. This is your most recent draft. You are now working on revisions based on comments from your teacher.
> 「英語の授業であなたは関心のある社会問題についてのエッセイを書いています。これが最も新しい草稿です。あなたは今，先生からのコメントに基づいて，修正を行っています」

　先生のコメントは，基本的に内容上の不備を指摘するもので，文法や語法などの誤りを指摘するものではない。試作問題においては，「論の飛躍している箇所に適切な文を補充する（**問１／例４**）」，「前後の文との論理関係を示す適切な語句を補充する（**問２**）」，「パラグラフの主題を示す文（トピックセンテンス）を適切なものに訂正する（**問３**）」，「まとめの表現をより適切なものに訂正する（**問４**）」ことを求める問題が出されていた。高校生が授業で書くエッセイが素材文なので，英文自体は平易だが，文と文との論理的なつながり，パラグラフの構造，内容の整合性などに注意を向けて読むことがポイントとなる。適切な組み立ての英文の書き方を理解しているかどうかを見るための問題とも言えるだろう。

例４

Comments

⑴　You are missing something here. Add more information between the two sentences to connect them.
「ここは何かが足りません。２つの文をつなぐために，間にさらに情報を追加してください」

設問文　**問１**　Based on comment ⑴, which is the best sentence to add?　「コメント⑴に基づくと，どの文を加えるのが最も良いか」

① As a result, people buy many similar items they do not need.
② Because of this, customers cannot enjoy clothes shopping.
③ Due to this, shop clerks want to know what customers need.
④ In this situation, consumers tend to avoid going shopping.

① その結果，人々は必要のない似た品物をたくさん買ってしまうのです。
② このために，お客さんは衣服のショッピングを楽しむことができません。
③ このせいで，店員はお客さんが何を必要としているかを知りたいのです。
④ この状況では，消費者は買い物に行くのを避ける傾向があります。

― 英Ｒ４ ―

情報収集能力

　これまでに実施された共通テスト・リーディング問題の特徴は，英語の読解力そのものというよりむしろ，読解力をツールとして正解に必要な情報を引き出す「情報検索能力」にある。そのためには本文とイラストや図表といった視覚情報のさまざまな箇所に目を向けなければならず，その正確さと迅速さが高得点への鍵となろう。以下では2022年に出題された3つの問題を通して「情報処理」の過程を具体的に見ていくことで，注意するべきポイントを明示し，共通テスト対策における必要不可欠なステップとしていきたい。

　まず，2022年度第4問を検討してみる。

2022年度（本試）第4問：2つのブログ記事とイラストおよび図表からなる

　　　　　　問5：最安値の電子レンジが購入できる店と5年保証付きの最安値のテレビが購入できる
　　　　　　　　　店を問う問題

設問文　　　You have decided to buy microwave from ⬚28⬚ because it is the cheapest. You have decided to buy a television from ⬚29⬚ because it is the cheapest with a five-year warranty. (Choose one for each box from options ①～④.) 「あなたは最も値段が安いという理由で ⬚28⬚ で電子レンジを購入することにした。あなたは5年保証つきで最も値段が安いという理由で ⬚29⬚ でテレビを購入することにした。(それぞれの空欄に対し選択肢①～④から1つずつ選べ)」

① Cut Price　　　「カットプライス」
② Great Buy　　　「グレートバイ」
③ Second Hand　　「セカンドハンド」
④ Value Saver　　「バリューセーバー」

⬚28⬚　（電子レンジを最安値で購入できる店）

＜第1段階：イラストと図表に掲載されている電子レンジの価格＞
　それぞれの店における電子レンジの価格は以下の通り。

① 「カットプライス」(シンディのブログに掲載された図表)：$88
② 「グレートバイ」(シンディのブログに掲載された図表)：$90
③ **「セカンドハンド」(レンのブログに掲載されたチラシのイラスト)：$85**
　(イラストと図表に掲載されている価格だけを比較すると最安値)
④ 「バリューセーバー」(シンディのブログに掲載された図表)：$95

― 英R5―

レンのブログに掲載された図表　　　　シンディのブログに掲載された図表

<第2段階：本文中の割引情報>
　シンディのブログの第4段落第5文で，グレートバイでは学生証を提示すれば図表に掲載されている価格から10%割引される，と述べられている。リード文から「あなた」はロビンソン大学の新入生であるとわかるので，この学生割引が適用され，グレートバイでは電子レンジを提示価格 $90 の 10% 引き = $81 で購入できることになる。この価格は ③「セカンドハンド」の $85 を下回って最安値となるので，正解は ②「グレートバイ」となる。

[29]　（テレビを5年保証付きの最安値で購入できる店）

<第1段階：イラストと図表に掲載されているテレビの価格>
　それぞれの店におけるテレビの価格は以下の通り。

① 「カットプライス」（シンディのブログに掲載された図表）：$300
② 「グレートバイ」（シンディのブログに掲載された図表）：$295
③ 「セカンドハンド」（レンのブログに掲載されたチラシのイラスト）：$250
　　（5年保証付きという条件を抜きにして，イラストと図表に掲載されている価格だけを比較すると最安値）
④ 「バリューセーバー」（シンディの記事に掲載された図表）：$305

レンのブログに掲載された図表　　　　シンディのブログに掲載された図表

＜第２段階：５年保証付きという条件を加味する＞

それぞれの店における保証に関する条件は以下の通り。

① 「カットプライス」：シンディのブログの第４段落最終文で，カットプライスでは<u>５年保証をつけるには商品ごとに $10 払わなければならない</u>，と述べられていることから，５年保証付きのテレビの価格は提示価格 $300 ＋ $10 ＝ <u>$310</u> ということになる。

② 「グレートバイ」：シンディのブログの第４段落第５文で，グレートバイではすべての家庭用品に１年保証を付与している，と述べられているだけで５年保証に関する言及はないために条件から外れる。

③ 「セカンドハンド」：セカンドハンドはレンのブログで紹介されているが，保証に関する言及はないために条件から外れる。

④ 「バリューセーバー」：シンディのブログの第４段落第３～４文で，バリューセーバーはすべての家庭用品に<u>無料で１年保証を付与し</u>，さらに<u>$300 以上の商品は保証期間をさらに４年延長している</u>，と述べられている。バリューセーバーのテレビの提示価格は $305 であるので，この特典が利用できることになり，保証期間が１年から４年延長されて５年となり，価格は提示価格である <u>$305</u> のままということになる。この価格は ① 「カットプライス」の $310 を下回って最安値となるので，正解は ④ 「バリューセーバー」となる。

>   Note that warranties are available for all items. So, if anything stops working, replacing it will be straightforward. Value Saver provides one-year warranties on all household goods for free. If the item is over $300, the warranty is extended by four years. Great Buy provides one-year warranties on all household goods, and students with proof of enrollment at a school get 10% off the prices listed on the table above. Warranties at Cut Price are not provided for free. You have to pay $10 per item for a five-year warranty.
>
>   Things go fast! Don't wait or you'll miss out!

第２段階

（シンディのブログ第４段落）

2021 年度（第１日程）第３問Ａはさらに手の込んだ問題となっていたので，こちらもあわせて検討してみたい。

2021 年度 第３問Ａ：Q&A 形式になっている英語の本文とイラストからなる
（第１日程） 問２：バクストン空港からホリーツリーホテルまで最も速く行く方法を問う問題

[設問文] You are departing on public transport from the airport at 2.00 pm on 15 March 2021. What is the fastest way to get to the hotel? 「あなたは 2021 年３月 15 日の午後２時に空港から公共の交通機関に乗って出発するところだ。ホテルまで最も速く行く方法はどれか」

① By express bus and city bus 「高速バスと市バス」
② By express bus and on foot 「高速バスと徒歩」
③ By underground and city bus 「地下鉄と市バス」
④ By underground and on foot 「地下鉄と徒歩」

<第1段階：アクセス図>
　バクストン空港からホリーツリーホテルまでの交通アクセスを図示したイラストがあることから，まずはイラスト内で示されている情報を検討する。

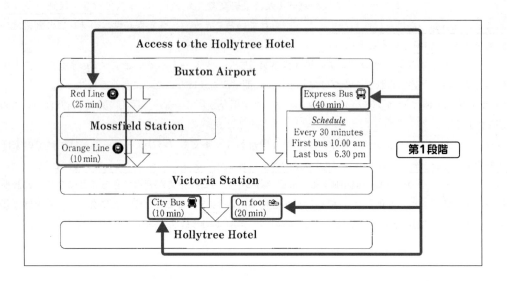

① 高速バスでヴィクトリア駅まで40分，ヴィクトリア駅からホテルまで市バスで10分，合計**50分**。
② 高速バスでヴィクトリア駅まで40分，ヴィクトリア駅からホテルまで徒歩で20分，合計**60分**。
③ 地下鉄でモスフィールド駅まで25分，さらに地下鉄を乗り換えてヴィクトリア駅まで10分，ヴィクトリア駅からホテルまで市バスで10分，合計**45分**（この時点で**最速**）。
④ 地下鉄でモスフィールド駅まで25分，さらに地下鉄を乗り換えてヴィクトリア駅まで10分，ヴィクトリア駅からホテルまで徒歩で20分，合計**55分**。

<第2段階：本文中の道路工事情報>

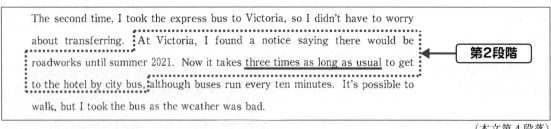

（本文第4段落）

　設問文に「2021年3月15日」と日付が記されているが，本文から，2021年夏までは道路工事が行われるために市バスを使うと通常よりも3倍の時間（30分）がかかる，ということがわかる。よって市バスを利用する選択肢①と③には20分加算されることになる。

① 50分 + 20分 = **70分**
② 60分

③ 45分 + 20分 = <u>65分</u>

④ 55分（この時点で最速）

　この第2段階までを考慮すると最速の行き方は④となり，本試で正解として④をマークした受験生は少なくなかったのではないかと思われる。センター試験でも複数箇所の情報統合は2箇所であることが多かったために，その印象が影響を及ぼしたということもあるかも知れない。だが，共通テストで大学入試センターが用意したハードルはこれだけにとどまらなかったのである。

<第3段階：本文中の地下鉄乗り換え情報>

On my first visit, I used the underground, which is cheap and convenient. Trains run every five minutes.　From the airport, I took the Red Line to Mossfield. Transferring to the Orange Line for Victoria should normally take　◀━━ 第3段階

about seven minutes, but the directions weren't clear and I needed an extra　要注意！ここは無関係！

five minutes.　From Victoria, it was a ten-minute bus ride to the hotel.

（本文第3段落）

　本文から，地下鉄の乗り換えには通常7分ほどかかる，ということがわかる。よって地下鉄の乗り換えを含む選択肢③と④には7分加算され，この時点での最速の選択肢は②となり，これが正解となる。

① 70分

② **60分（この時点で最速）**

③ 65分 + 7分 = <u>72分</u>

④ 55分 + 7分 = <u>62分</u>

情報判断能力

大学入試センターが用意した「これでもか」というほどの仕掛けはさらにあり、乗り換え時間に関する記述の直後では、このQ&A解答者のアレックス (Alex) の場合、乗り換え案内がはっきりしなかったためにさらに5分多くかかった、と述べられていた。しかしこれはアレックスの個人的な経験に属するもので、正解を得るのに必要な情報ではなく、結果としてかなりやっかいな情報検索が求められたことになる。

2021年度　第3問B：交換留学生のクラスメートが学校新聞に書いたボランティア募集の記事
（第1日程）　問1：交換留学生が参加することになった、ある施設を維持するための募金活動にまつわる出来事の順番を問う問題

設問文　Put the following events (①〜④) into the order in which they happened.
「以下の出来事 (①〜④) を発生した順番に並べよ」

① Sarah attended a centre event.　　　「セーラはセンターのあるイベントに参加した」
② Sarah donated money to the centre.　「セーラはセンターにお金を寄付した」
③ Sarah made a suggestion to Katy.　　「セーラはケイティにある提案をした」
④ The campaigners asked the mayor for help.　「募金運動をしている人たちは町長に援助を求めた」

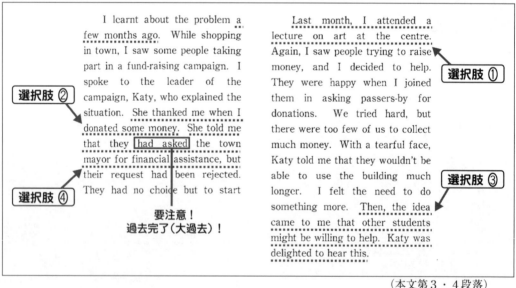

(本文第3・4段落)

本文で述べられている出来事を追っていくと、数ヵ月前のことを述べた第3段落で「私 [交換留学生のセーラ] がいくらかのお金を寄付すると彼女 [募金運動のリーダーであるケイティ] は私に感謝してくれた (She thanked me when I donated some money.)」と述べられており、これが選択肢 ② にあたると判断できる。その直後の文には「ケイティが私に語ったところによると、彼女たちは町長に経済的援助を求めたが…(She told me that they had asked the town mayor for financial assistance, but …)」とあり，この内容が選択肢 ④ と対応するので，早合点して ② → ④ と続くと判断してしまった受験生も少なくなかったかもしれないが，もちろん had asked は過去完了形で大過去を示しているので，実際は ④ → ② という順番になる。さらに，第4段落の冒頭(Last month, I …)で述べられている「先月，私はセンターの美術に関する講演に参加した」という内容が選択肢 ① にあたり，最後の2つの文（Then, the idea …）(Katy was delighted …) で述べられている「そのとき，他の学生が進んで援助してくれるかもしれないという考えが私の頭に浮かんだ。そのことを聞いてケイティは喜んだ」ということが選択肢 ③ を示唆していると推測できるので，正解は ④ → ② → ① → ③ という順番になるとわかる。

　センター試験から共通テストに変わって文法問題がなくなったが，今後もリーディング問題においてこのような形で文法的知識が問われていくのではないだろうか。

　以上実際の問題に沿って具体的に見てきたように，共通テストのリーディング問題の特徴が読解力をツールとしての「情報検索能力」にあることはわかっていただけただろうか。こうした問題への対策としては，「複数箇所の情報を統合する問題が出題される可能性が高い」という，さらに「検索した情報を正しく判断することを求める問題が出題される可能性が高く，その中には文法要素も含まれうる」という意識を常に持ち，十分な練習を積んでいくことが重要だろう。相手の出方を知り，戦略を立て，十分な練習を積むことでこそ，本番でベストパフォーマンスを発揮することができるだろう。諸君の健闘を心から祈る。

第1回　解答・解説

第 1 回　　実戦問題　解答・解説

☆下記の表は，「解答・解説」の中で用いた記号・略語の一覧表です。

S	主語または主部（Subject）	－	動詞の原形
S′	意味上の主語	to－	to 不定詞
V	動詞（Verb）	－ing	現在分詞または動名詞
O	目的語（Object）	p.p.	過去分詞
C	補語（Complement）	[　]	置換可能な語句
M	修飾語句（Modifier）	（　）	省略可能な語句
名動副.etc.	名詞，動詞，副詞，etc.	〈　〉	つながりのある語句

英語（リーディング） 第1回 （100点満点）

（解答・配点）

問題番号（配点）	設問	解答番号	正解	配点	自己採点欄
第1問（6）	1	1	①	2	
	2	2	①	2	
	3	3	①	2	
	小　計				
第2問（10）	1	4	②	2	
	2	5	③	2	
	3	6	②	2	
	4	7	①	2	
	5	8	①	2	
	小　計				
第3問（9）	1	9	④	3*	
		10	①		
		11	③		
		12	②		
	2	13	②	3	
	3	14	③	3	
	小　計				
第4問（12）	1	15	①	3	
	2	16	④	3	
	3	17	③	3	
	4	18	②	3	
	小　計				
第5問（16）	1	19	②	3	
	2	20	①	3	
	3	21	①	3	
	4	22	③	2	
		23	③	2	
	5	24	⑤	3	
	小　計				

問題番号（配点）	設問	解答番号	正解	配点	自己採点欄
第6問（18）	1	25	④	3	
	2	26	①	3	
	3	27 － 28	① － ④	3*	
		29	④	3	
	4	30	④	3	
	5	31	②	3	
	小　計				
第7問（15）	1	32	④	3*	
		33	①		
		34	⑤		
		35	③		
	2	36	③	3	
	3	37	③	3*	
		38	①		
	4	39	①	3	
	5	40	②	3	
	小　計				
第8問（14）	1	41	②	2	
	2	42	②	3	
	3	43 － 44	② － ③	3*	
	4	45	④	3	
	5	46	③	3	
	小　計				

（注）
1　＊は，全部正解の場合のみ点を与える。
2　－（ハイフン）でつながれた正解は，順序を問わない。

第1問

解答 問1 - ① 問2 - ① 問3 - ① （各2点）

出典 *Original Material*

全訳

あなたはカナダにいる交換留学生で，ホームステイ先の家族はあなたを日帰り旅行に連れて行きたいと思っています。ホームステイ先の母親があなたに利用可能なツアーについての情報を提供してくれました。

プリンスエドワード島（PEI）観光ツアー
メイプルツアーズの３つの旅行計画から選択する

モンゴメリツアー

『赤毛のアン』の作者であるルーシー・モード・モンゴメリ — 彼女の著作はこの島の自然と人々に触発されました — について学びます。1901 年に建てられ，1940 年にモンゴメリが埋葬されたキャベンディッシュ・ユナイテッド・チャーチからツアーは出発します。次に「赤毛のアン博物館」を訪れ，モンゴメリの所持品を見学します。博物館はもともとモンゴメリの親戚の人たちにより 1872 年に建てられた家屋でした。最後に，モンゴメリが教鞭を執った学校を訪問します。このツアーは，みんなこの PEI で育ったガイドたちが案内します。

PEI の景観を眺めながらのドライブ

この島の美しい風景と自然を体験しましょう。地元のガイドが宿泊先から直接あなたを車に乗せてくれます。まず，チャールストン大通りを通って，1847 年完成のプロビンスハウスと，カナダの建国につながった 1864 年のシャーロットタウン会議跡地を通ります。それからプリンスエドワード島国立公園を訪れ，その後，ロブスター漁の村であるノースラスティコに立ち寄ります。そこのレストランでおいしいロブスターを食べてみてください。

シャーロットタウンの食のハイライトをめぐるウォーキングツアー

シャーロットタウンを歩いて探検しましょう。ガイドは生まれてからずっと PEI で暮らしてきたので，おいしい地元の食べ物に目を留めて試食しながら，シャーロットタウンの史跡を紹介してくれます。海に近いピークスワーフからツアーに出発します。この倉庫群は 1872 年に建てられ，今ではレストランやギフトショップになっています。アイスクリームを食べてみてから，ファーマーズマーケットに移動しましょう。地元の農家に会って新鮮でおいしい農産物を手に入れてください。通りを散策してから，この島で最も長く営業しているレストランであるカントンカフェで食事をします。各オーナーは 1950 年代にカナダへと移住してきて，1970 年にそれぞれの中華レストランを開きました。

— 英 R 15 —

設問解説

問1 **1** 正解①

「プリンスエドワード島には **1** がある」

① 歴史的に重要な会議が開かれた場所
② カナダのもっとも有名な女性作家によって創立された学校
③ カナダで開店した最初の中華レストラン
④ 18世紀以来商品を貯蔵するために使用されてきた倉庫群

　正解は①。2つ目のツアーである「PEIの景観を眺めながらのドライブ」の第3文（First, we will ...）に「まず，チャールストン大通りを通って，1847年完成のプロビンスハウスと，カナダの建国につながった1864年のシャーロットタウン会議跡地を通ります」とあるが，シャーロットタウン会議跡地は選択肢①の「歴史的に重要な会議が開かれた場所」と考えられることから，正解は①となる。

　②に関しては，カナダの女性作家である『赤毛のアン』の作者ルーシー・モード・モンゴメリと彼女が教鞭を執った学校のことは1つ目のツアーである「モンゴメリツアー」で言及されているが，モンゴメリが創立した学校については述べられていないので不可。

　③に関しては，中華レストランは3つ目のツアーである「シャーロットタウンの食のハイライトをめぐるウォーキングツアー」で言及されているが，「カナダで開店した最初の中華レストラン」であるとは述べられていないので不可。

　④に関しては，倉庫群は3つ目のツアーである「シャーロットタウンの食のハイライトをめぐるウォーキングツアー」で言及されているが，その第4文（These warehouse buildings ...）で「この倉庫群は1872年に建てられ，今ではレストランやギフトショップになっています」と述べられていることから，今では商品を貯蔵するために使用されているわけではないことがわかるので不可。

問2 **2** 正解①

「3つのツアーのすべてで，あなたは **2** ことになる」

① この島に住んでいるガイドに案内してもらう
② この島の出身である有名な人々について学ぶ
③ もっとも大きな都市であるシャーロットタウンの中心部を見学する
④ さまざまな代表的な地元の食べ物を試食する

　正解は①。1つ目のツアーである「モンゴメリツアー」の最終文（The tour will ...）では「このツアーは，みんなこのPEIで育ったガイドたちが案内します」と述べられ，2つ目のツアーである「PEIの景観を眺めながらのドライブ」の第2文（Your local guide ...）では「地元のガイドが宿泊先から直接あなたを車に乗せてくれます」と，そして3つ目のツアーである「シャーロットタウンの食のハイライトをめぐるウォーキングツアー」の第2文（Your guide has ...）では「ガイドは生まれてからずっとPEIで暮らしてきたので，おいしい地元の食べ物に目を留めて試食しながら，シャーロットタウンの史跡を紹介してくれます」と述べられていることから，3つのツアーすべてにおいて地元出身のガイドが案内してくれることがわかる。よって正解は①となる。

　②に関しては，1つ目のツアーである「モンゴメリツアー」ではカナダの有名な女性作家である『赤毛のアン』の作者ルーシー・モード・モンゴメリについて学ぶことがわかるが，他の2つのツアーでは「この島の出身である有名な人々について学ぶ」ことが述べられていないので不可。

　③に関しては，1つ目の「モンゴメリツアー」がシャーロットタウンで行われるとの記述がないので不可。

　④に関しては，2つ目のツアーである「PEIの景観を眺めながらのドライブ」ではロブスターを食べること，また3つ目のツアーである「シャーロットタウンの食のハイライトをめぐるウォーキングツアー」では地元の食べ物やアイスクリームを試食することやカ

— 英 R 16 —

フェで食事をすることが述べられているが、1つ目のツアーである「モンゴメリツアー」では試食に関する記述はないので不可。

問3　　3　　正解①

「これらのツアーで見学することになる中で最も古い建物はどれか」　　3

① プロビンスハウス
② 赤毛のアン博物館
③ カントンカフェという中華レストラン
④ キャベンディッシュ・ユナイテッド・チャーチ

正解は①。1つ目のツアーである「モンゴメリツアー」では、1901年に建てられたキャベンディッシュ・ユナイテッド・チャーチから出発することと、「赤毛のアン博物館」がもともとモンゴメリの親戚の人たちにより1872年に建てられた家屋であったことが述べられている。2つ目のツアーである「PEIの景観を眺めながらのドライブ」では、カナダの建国につながった、1847年完成のプロビンスハウスについて言及されている。そして3つ目のツアーである「シャーロットタウンの食のハイライトをめぐるウォーキングツアー」では、1970年に開店した中華レストランについての言及がある。以上の中で最も古い建物は1847年完成のプロビンスハウスであるとわかるので正解は①ということになる。

主な語句・表現　・問題冊子を参照のこと。

[リード文]
◇ exchange student「交換留学生」　　　　◇ available 形「利用可能な」

[本文]
◇ sightseeing 名「観光」　　　　　　　　◇ itinerary 名「旅程表；旅行計画」
◇ *Anne of Green Gables* はルーシー・モード・モンゴメリ作の長編小説『赤毛のアン』の原題。
◇ be inspired by ...「…に触発される」　　◇ bury 動「…を埋葬する」
◇ relative 名「親戚；親類」　　　　　　　◇ conduct 動「…を案内する」
◇ bring up ...「…を育てる」　　　　　　◇ scenic 形「景色の（すばらしい）」
◇ scenery 名「風景」　　　　　　　　　　◇ pick ... up「…を車に乗せる」
◇ accommodation 名「宿泊施設」　　　　　◇ conference 名「会議」
◇ formation 名「設立」　　　　　　　　　◇ on foot「徒歩で」
◇ point out ...「…に注目させる」　　　　◇ sample 動「…を試食する」
◇ warehouse 名「倉庫」　　　　　　　　　◇ produce 名「農産物」

[設問文・選択肢]
◇ found 動「…を創設［創立］する」　　　◇ be used to−「−するために用いられる」
◇ take ... around「…を案内して回る」

— 英 R 17 —

第２問

解答　　問1 - ②　　問2 - ③　　問3 - ②　　問4 - ①　　問5 - ①　　（各2点）

出典　*Original Material*

全訳

あなたはまもなくイギリスへ行き，そこの大学で勉強することになります。あなたは，その大学を最近卒業した人によって書かれた学生用銀行預金口座についての記事を読んでいるところです。

最近のほぼすべての銀行は特別な「学生銀行口座」を提供しており，そうした口座は通常の口座保持者では利用できないサービスを提供しているので，私は申請することを強く勧めます。

私の口座はアルファ銀行にあります。新規の顧客を呼び込むために，9月に口座を開設すると，3年間の鉄道の学生割引証を提供しています。この鉄道割引証は120ポンド分の価値があり，保持者は鉄道料金を30％引きにすることができます。他には現金のギフトを提供してくれるところもあります。たとえば，ウェイバリー銀行はすべての新しい学生用口座に50ポンドを入れてくれますし，フェニックス銀行は40ポンドを提供しています。

オンライン銀行やデビットカードに加えて，すべての学生用口座は低金利のクレジットカードを支給し，金利ゼロの短期ローンを提供しています。先月，私のアルバイトの給料が遅れましたが，私はアルファ銀行から1週間，利息なしで100ポンドを借りました。銀行の中にはもっと高い上限を認めているところもあります。ウェイバリー銀行とフェニックス銀行の顧客はそれぞれ利息なしで最大200ポンドと300ポンドを借りることができます。

ほとんどの成人用銀行口座は毎月最大10ポンドの手数料を請求しますが，学生用銀行口座はたいてい安い価格か無料で利用できます。私の銀行は月に2ポンド請求しますが，ウェイバリー銀行とフェニックス銀行は無料です。しかし，私の銀行はATMでの現金引き出しには，その2つの他の銀行とは異なり，まったく料金を請求しません。

アルファ銀行独自の利点は，卒業まで無料の旅行保険を提供してくれることです。これは，私が旅行好きであることから，私にとってはすばらしいものです。私は先月，パリへ旅行に行き，カメラを盗まれてしまいました。私は新しいカメラを買うためにいくらかのお金を取り戻すことができました。もっとも，そのお金がもっと速く届いて，手続きがもっと簡単であればよかったのですけれども。

それぞれの口座がさまざまな利点やサービスを提供していますので，学生用銀行預金口座を選ぶ前に自分自身に必要なものについて考えておいてください。

— 英 R 18 —

設問解説

問1 ┃ 4 ┃ 正解 ②

「記事によれば，以下のどれが本当か」 ┃ 4 ┃
① 言及されているすべての銀行預金口座は ATM の無料引き出しを認めている。
② アルファ銀行の新しい学生の顧客へのギフトがもっとも金銭的価値がある。
③ アルファ銀行とウェイバリー銀行は共に旅行保険を提供している。
④ ウェイバリー銀行とフェニックス銀行だけが金利ゼロのローンを提供している。

　正解は ②。第2段落第1文（My account is ...）～第3文（These railcards are ...）から，筆者が利用しているアルファ銀行は 120 ポンドに相当する鉄道の学生割引証を新規の顧客に提供していることがわかる。また最終文（For example, Waverly ...）には，ウェイバリー銀行はすべての新しい学生用口座に 50 ポンドを入れてくれ，フェニックス銀行は 40 ポンドを提供していると述べられている。以上から，銀行が新たに銀行口座を開設した学生に提供するものの中でもっとも価値が高いのは，アルファ銀行の 120 ポンドに相当する鉄道の学生割引証であることがわかるので，正解は ② となる。

　① に関しては，第4段落最終文（However, my bank ...）からわかるように，ATM の無料引き出しを認めているのは筆者が利用しているアルファ銀行だけであるので不可。

　③ に関しては，第5段落第1文（The unique benefit ...）で筆者が利用しているアルファ銀行が無料の旅行保険を提供していることが言及されているが，ウェイバリー銀行が旅行保険を提供していることは述べられていないので不可。

　④ に関しては，第3段落第1文（In addition to ...）から，すべての学生用口座がゼロ金利のローンを提供していることがわかるので不可。

問2 ┃ 5 ┃ 正解 ③

「筆者の銀行によって提供されていないものはどれか」 ┃ 5 ┃
① デビットカード
② ATM サービス
③ 無料の銀行取引業務
④ 無料の旅行保険

　正解は ③。第3段落第1文（In addition to ...）から，すべての学生用口座がオンライン銀行とデビットカードを提供していることがわかる。また第4段落最終文（However, my bank ...）に「ATM での現金引き出し」の言及があるので ATM サービスが提供されていることもわかる。さらに第5段落第1文（The unique benefit ...）で筆者が利用しているアルファ銀行が無料の旅行保険を提供していることが言及されている。一方，第4段落第1文（Most adult bank ...）～第2文（My bank charges ...）から，筆者が利用している銀行（アルファ銀行）は月に 2 ポンドの銀行口座利用手数料を請求しており，銀行取引業務は無料ではないことがわかる。以上から正解は ③ となる。

　①，②，④ に関しては，上で述べたように，筆者の銀行が提供しているものなので不可。

問3 ┃ 6 ┃ 正解 ②

「この記事の中で説明されている学生用銀行預金口座の特徴はどれか」 ┃ 6 ┃
A：ローンとサービスが成人用口座よりも安い。
B：学生が平日のみ無料で現金を引き出すことを可能にしている。
C：学生がアルバイトの仕事を探す手助けをしている。
D：新しい口座保持者が自分の口座に 40 ポンド入れることを要求している。
E：新しい顧客に奨励金を提供している。

① ＡとＤ
② ＡとＥ
③ ＢとＣ
④ ＢとＤ
⑤ ＣとＥ

　正解は②。第3段落第1文（In addition to ...）から，すべての学生用口座はゼロ金利の短期ローンを提供していることがわかり，第4段落第1文（Most adult bank ...）から，学生用銀行口座は成人用口座よりも安い価格か無料で利用できることがわかるので，Aが学生用口座のことを説明していると判断できる。また，第2段落第4文（Other banks give ...）～最終文（For example, Waverly ...）から，たとえばウェイバリー銀行やフェニックス銀行のように新しい学生の顧客に奨励金を提供している銀行もあることがわかるので，Eが学生用口座のことを説明していると判断できる。以上から正解は②ＡとＥとなる。

問4　　7　　正解①

「自身の学生用口座に関して筆者が抱いている1つの意見は　7　ということである」
　① 保険請求は処理するための時間があまりに長くかかりすぎた
　② 銀行業務アプリは使用するにはあまりに複雑すぎる
　③ 無料ギフトは彼女にはあまり役に立たなかった
　④ ゼロ金利ローンの上限があまりに低すぎる

　正解は①。筆者は，第5段落第1文（The unique benefit ...）で「（筆者が利用している）アルファ銀行独自の利点は，卒業まで無料の旅行保険を提供してくれることです」と述べ，第3文（I took a ...）では旅行先のパリでカメラの盗難被害にあったことに言及し，最終文（I was able ...）においては「私は新しいカメラを買うためにいくらかのお金を取り戻すことができました。もっとも，そのお金がもっと速く届いて，手続きがもっと簡単であればよかったのですけれども」と，銀行の保険手続きに時間がかかりすぎたことに関する不満を述べていることから，正解は①とわかる。

　②に関しては記述がないので不可。

　③に関しては，「無料ギフト」と考えられるものは鉄道の割引証，ATM引き出し手数料，旅行保険などがあるが，いずれも「役に立たなかった」という記述はないので誤り。

　④に関しては，第3段落第3文（Some banks allow ...）で，銀行の中にはゼロ金利ローンの上限額を筆者が利用しているアルファ銀行よりも高くしているところもあることが言及されているが，アルファ銀行のゼロ金利ローンの上限があまりに低すぎるとは述べていないので不可。

問5　　8　　正解①

「以下のどれが筆者の考えをもっともよく表しているか」　8
　① 彼女は学生用口座を開設することはさまざまな金銭上の利益を生むだろうと考えている。
　② 彼女は，学生用口座と通常の口座にはほとんど違いはないと考えている。
　③ 彼女は，学生に同様の金銭的サービスを提供する銀行が増えることを期待している。
　④ 彼女は，外国に行くときには別の旅行保険を購入した方がいいと考えている。

　正解は①。第1段落第1文（Almost all banks ...）から，最近のほぼすべての銀行は特別な「学生銀行口座」を提供しており，そうした口座は通常の口座保持者では利用できないサービスを提供していることがわかり，第2段落～第5段落では，そうしたさまざまなサービスには金銭的な価値があることが紹介されている。よって正解は①となる。

　②，③，④に関しては，筆者が述べている内容にはなっていないので不可。

― 英 R 20 ―

主な語句・表現	・問題冊子を参照のこと。

[リード文]
◇ bank account「銀行預金口座」　　　◇ graduate 名「卒業生」

[本文]
◇ recommend -ing「－することを勧める」　◇ sign up「申し込む；申請する」
◇ available to ...「…に利用できる」　not available 以下は直前の services にかかる形容詞句
　となっている。
◇ attract 動「…を引きつける」　　　　◇ railcard 名「鉄道の割引証」
◇ be worth ...「…の価値がある」　　　◇ fare 名「運賃」
◇ banking 名「銀行取引業務」
◇ debit card「デビットカード」　預金口座の残額や，あらかじめ定めた金額の範囲内で買い
　物に使用できる即時払い式のカード。
◇ low-interest 形「金利の低い」　　　◇ allow 動「…を許可する；…を認める」
◇ up to ...「最大［最高］…」　　　　　◇ interest-free 形「利息なしで」
◇ respectively 副「それぞれ」　　　　◇ charge 動「…を請求する」
◇ fee 名「料金；手数料」　　　　　　◇ cash withdrawal「現金引き出し」
◇ travel insurance「旅行保険」　　　◇ procedure 名「手続き」

[設問文・選択肢]
◇ without charge「無料で」　　　　　◇ incentive 名「奨励金」
◇ claim 名「請求」　　　　　　　　　◇ financial 形「金銭的な」

第3問

解答	問1 –	9	④,	10	①,	11	③,	12	②	（完答で3点）

問2 – ②　　　問3 – ③　　　　　　　　　　　　　　　　　　　　（各3点）

出典　*Original Material*

全訳

あなたと学校の英語クラブの他のメンバーたちがボランティアの日に参加することになっています。あなたは昨年同様のイベントに参加したメンバーであるジュンヤによって書かれた報告書を読んでいます。

川の清掃と自然調査の日

去年のボランティアの日，私たちは河川浄化協会（RCUA）と一緒に働きました。ボランティアの人たちは毎月川に来て，蓄積したごみをすべて拾っています。最近の台風のために，いつもよりも多くのごみがありました。私たちはまた自然調査にも参加して，自分たちが見つけた花を記録しました。

まず初めに，私たちは RCUA のメンバーたちと会いました。よく晴れていましたが，地面はとても濡れてぬかるんでいたので，私たちは長靴と防水性のズボンを履きました。手の保護のために手袋をして，ごみを集めるポリ袋を持ちました。私たちは2つのグループを作りました。1つのグループはごみを集め，もう1つのグループが再生利用できるものがないかとそのごみを点検しました。お昼時までに，私たちは大きな袋30個分のごみを集めていました。

正午になると昼食のために手を休めました。私たちのほとんどが弁当を持っていましたが，中には自分の分を忘れた人もいたので，そうした人たちは食べ物を買いにコンビニに行きました。彼らは午前中の仕事の後ですでに疲れていたので，私たちは気の毒に思いました。

昼食後，RCUA のメンバーであるミカが私たちに，花に関する情報の集め方を教えてくれました。RCUA は一部の大学における生態学の専門家が研究データを集める手助けをしていたのです。私たちはペアを作って，大きな輪を無作為に草の中に投げました。それからその輪の中の花の数と種類を数えました。大学の研究に貢献して，私たちは皆誇らしく感じました。ミカは私たちに，来年，有名な生態学の専門誌で自分たちの仕事について読むことができるだろう，と教えてくれました。

最後に，私たちはごみを RCUA のトラックに積み込みました。RCUA の人たちは後でそれを市のごみ処理施設に持って行く計画でした。彼らはまた，私たちを近くのレストランでの夕食に招待してくれました。私たちは楽しく環境問題についての話をしました。私たちは RCUA のグループの中にいた2人の外国人のメンバーと英語の練習をしました。

今年，私はまたボランティアの日に参加するつもりです。多くの点で，経験したことが私をやる気にさせたのです。この報告書を書きながらも，私はミカが生態系の専門誌について言ったことを思い出しました。私は，彼女が正しかったかどうかを確かめるために図書館に行こうと心に決めました。

— 英 R 22 —

設 問 解 説　問1　9　正解 ④,　10　正解 ①,　11　正解 ③,　12　正解 ②

「ジュンヤの記事には，ボランティアの日の出来事について述べた学生たちのコメント（①～④）も含まれていた。各コメントを出来事が起きた順番通りにしなさい」

① 昼食を持ってきていたらなあ！　土手を掃除した後で，食べ物を買いに店までずっと歩いて行くのはつらいことでした。

② 夕食を食べながら RCUA のメンバーたちと話したことは，私のお気に入りの経験でした。年齢や経歴が異なる人たちとコミュニケーションをとれるようになるのは重要なことです。

③ この日のハイライトは研究データを集めることでした。私は植物に興味があるので，将来は生物学者になることを希望しています。

④ 到着した時には，いかに多くの仕事をしなければならないのかを知って，私たちは驚きました。強風がたくさんの物を水の中へと吹き飛ばしてしまっていたのです。

このボランティアの日の出来事を時系列で追っていくと，まず第1段落第3文（Because of the ...）に「最近の台風のために，いつもよりも多くのごみがありました」とあるが，これは川の清掃作業前の光景の記述であると推測できるので，最初に ④ が来る。午前中の清掃作業を終えた後，昼食をとることになるのだが，第3段落第2文（Most of us ...）～最終文（We felt sorry ...）から，一部の人たちは昼食を持ってくるのを忘れたので，午前中の作業で疲れていたがコンビニまで食べ物を買いに行かなければならなかったことがわかる。① はその昼食を持ってくるのを忘れた人たちの1人のコメントであると推測できるので，2番目には ① が来る。「昼食後」で始まる第4段落（After lunch, Mika, ...）には，午後に自然調査を行った経緯が述べられている。③ はその自然調査に関するコメントであると判断できるので，3番目には ③ が来る。「最後に」で始まる第5段落（Finally, we loaded ...）から，その日の作業を終えた後，近くのレストランで RCUA（河川浄化協会）の人たちと夕食を食べたことがわかる。② はその夕食時に関するコメントであると判断できるので，最後の4番目には ② が来るとわかる。以上から，正解は ④ → ① → ③ → ② の順となる。

問2　13　正解 ②

「ボランティアの日の間，学生たちは 13 ことはなかった」

① 花に関する情報収集を行う

② ごみ処理施設に行く

③ ボランティアの人たちと英語で会話する

④ 活動の間に休憩をとる

正解は ②。第4段落（After lunch, Mika, ...）には，学生たちは RCUA のメンバーからやり方を教わりながら花に関する情報収集を行ったことが述べられているので，① は学生たちが行った行動である。また，第5段落には，RCUA のメンバーたちとレストランで夕食を食べた時のことが述べられているが，その最終文（We practiced our ...）に「RCUA のグループの中にいた2人の外国人のメンバーと英語の練習をしました」とあることから，③ も学生たちが行った行動である。さらに，第3段落第1文（We stopped for ...）に「正午になると昼食のために手を休めました」とあることから，午前中の川の清掃活動と午後の自然調査の活動の間に昼食をとるための休憩をとったことがわかるので，④ も学生たちが行った行動である。しかし，第5段落第1文（Finally, we loaded ...）～第2文（They planned to ...）で「最後に，私たちはごみを RCUA のトラックに積み込みました。RCUA の人たちは後でそれを市のごみ処理施設に持って行く計画でした」と述べられていることから，<u>学生たちはごみ処理施設には行かなかった</u>ことがわかるので，正解は ② となる。

— 英 R 23 —

問3 　14　 正解 ③

「ジュンヤは図書館に行った時に，おそらくのところ何を見つけたか」　14

① 野生の花に関する本
② 地元の川の生態系の案内書
❸ **自分たちのデータに基づいた専門誌の記事**
④ 台風に関する報道

　正解は ③。第4段落最終文（Mika told us ...）では，RCUA のメンバーであるミカがジュンヤたちに，来年，有名な生態学の専門誌で自分たちの仕事について読むことができるだろう，と教えてくれたことが述べられ，最終段落最終文（I decided to ...）には「私［この記事の筆者であるジュンヤ］は，彼女が正しかったかどうかを確かめるために図書館に行こうと心に決めました」とあることから，ジュンヤは図書館に行き，おそらくのところ自分たちのデータに基づいた専門誌の記事を探して見つけた，と推測できるので，正解は ③ となる。

　①，②，④ に関しては，いずれも本文からはジュンヤが図書館に行って見つける可能性のあるものと考えることはできないので不可。

（主な語句・表現）
・問題冊子を参照のこと。

[リード文]
◇ take part in ...「…に参加する」

[本文]
◇ survey 图「調査」　　　　　　　　　　◇ trash 图「ごみ；くず；がらくた」
◇ build up「増大する」　　　　　　　　　◇ muddy 形「泥だらけの；ぬかるんでいる」
◇ waterproof pants「防水性のズボン」　　◇ plastic bag「ポリ袋；ビニール袋」
◇ in which to - は〈前置詞＋関係代名詞＋ to -〉という形で直前の名詞にかかる形容詞句となっている。
◇ recyclable 形「再生利用できる」　　　　◇ midday 图「正午」
◇ pack 動「…を詰める；…を入れる」　　　◇ feel sorry for ...「…を気の毒に思う」
◇ ecology expert「生態学の専門家」　　　◇ hoop 图「大きな輪」
◇ at random「無作為に」
◇ feel proud to -「- することで誇らしく感じる」
◇ contribute to ...「…に貢献する」　　　◇ journal 图「専門誌」
◇ load A into B「A を B〈車など〉に積む」　◇ trash disposal facility「ごみ処理施設」
◇ inspire 動「…を鼓舞する；…を奮起させる」
◇ in many ways「多くの点で」　　　　　　◇ remind〈人〉of ...「人に…を思い出させる」
◇ see if ...「…かどうかを確かめる」

[設問文・選択肢]
◇ It was hard walking all the way ... の walking 以下は形式主語 It の真主語となる動名詞句となっている。
◇ riverbank 图「川岸；土手」　　　　　　◇ over dinner「夕食を食べながら」
◇ learn to -「- する［できる］ようになる」◇ background 图「背景；経歴」
◇ blow A into B「A を B の中に吹き飛ばす」◇ carry out ...「…を実行する」
◇ information gathering「情報収集」　　　◇ regarding 前「…に関する」
◇ take a break「休憩をとる」　　　　　　◇ most likely「おそらく」
◇ based on ...「…に基づいた」　　　　　　◇ news report「報道」

— 英 R 24 —

第4問

解答　　問1 - ①　　　問2 - ④　　　問3 - ③　　　問4 - ②　　　　　（各3点）

出典　Original Material

全訳

英語の授業であなたは関心のある科学的問題についてのエッセイを書いています。これが最も新しい草稿です。あなたは今，先生からのコメントに基づいて，修正に取り組んでいます。

睡眠を改善する方法	コメント
科学的研究によれば，ほとんどの成人は，健康を維持するには一晩に7～9時間ほどの睡眠が必要です。長期間にわたって睡眠が不足すると，心臓病や高血圧や肥満を含め，多くの健康上の問題を引き起こす可能性があります。それはまた脳にも影響を及ぼし，頭の回転や，情報保持の能力を低下させます。睡眠の重要性にもかかわらず，多くの人々は夜，十分に眠ることができていません。(1)たとえば，睡眠を改善するために，私たちにできることはたくさんあります。 　第一に，朝，自然の光に触れることが重要です。自然な生活リズムは光に触れることによって作られるからです。(2)∧眠気を感じることを防ぐホルモンが脳の内部から放出されます。また最初に光に触れたときに，身体に約14時間後にメラトニンという睡眠ホルモンを作る指示が出されます。 　第二に，(3)どこで眠っているでしょうか？　睡眠に最適な温度は摂氏18～20度と言われています。光に加えて，人間の睡眠周期は温度のような環境的な要因によって調節されます。したがって，寝室の温度を下げることによって，身体に眠る準備をする指示を出すことができ，それが寝つく時間を早め，睡眠の質を改善することに役立ちます。 　最後に，夜に電子機器を使用すると睡眠の質に悪影響を及ぼす可能性があることが知られています。スマートフォンやタブレットといった機器はブルーライトを放射し，それがメラトニンの生成を遅らせることになりうるのです。 　要約すると，以上見てきたように，よりよい睡眠をとるためにできることはたくさんあります。(4)∧	⑴ ここには間違った接続表現が用いられています。変更してください。 ⑵ この文は前の文とうまくつながっていません。記述の流れを良くするためにさらに情報を追加してください。 ⑶ この主題文は後に続く文章をうまく説明していません。書き直してください。 ⑷ 最終的な結論となる文を追加するべきだと思います。
先生のコメント 上出来です！　私は，確実にもっと多くの睡眠をとる必要があるので，あなたのアドバイスを取り入れるつもりです！ ☺	

— 英 R 25 —

設問解説

問1 15 **正解①**

「コメント(1)に基づくと，代わりに使う最もよい表現はどれか」 15

① しかし
② 対照的に
③ 要するに
④ したがって

正解は①。下線部(1)の前文では，睡眠は重要であるけれども，多くの人々が睡眠不足に陥っていることが述べられ，下線部(1)に続く文では，睡眠を改善するためにできることはたくさんあると述べられているが，これは前文の例示ではなく，前文で述べられている<u>好ましくない状況を，それとは逆の好ましい状況にするための方法</u>に関する言及であるとみなせる。すなわち，「睡眠の重要性にもかかわらず，多くの人々は夜，十分に眠ることができていません。<u>しかし（ながら）</u>，睡眠を改善するために，私たちにできることはたくさんあります」というつながりにすれば自然な文脈となる。以上から①の However「しかし（ながら）」が正解となる。

②，③，④はいずれも自然な文脈とはならないので不可。

問2 16 **正解④**

「コメント(2)に基づくと，追加するのに最もよい表現はどれか」 16

① 寝ついた後，
② 暗い所で時間を過ごすことによって，
③ 私たちがそのことから目を守れば，
④ **日光が目に入ってくると，**

正解は④。下線部(2)を含む文の前文には「自然な生活リズムは<u>光に触れること</u>によって作られるからです」とあり，下線部(2)を含む文ではそれを具体的に説明して「(2)∧眠気を感じることを防ぐホルモンが脳の内部から放出されます」と述べられていると推測できる。よって下線部(2)には眠気を感じることを防ぐホルモンが放出される「<u>光に触れること</u>」を含む前提となる表現が入ると自然な文脈となる。以上から④の When sunlight enters our eyes,「日光が目に入ってくると，」が正解となる。

①，②，③はいずれも自然な文脈とはならないので不可。

問3 17 **正解③**

「コメント(3)に基づくと，置き換えたものとしてどれが最適か」 17

① 暗い環境で眠ることが重要です。
② 必ず十分に疲れた状態で眠るようにしましょう。
③ **涼しい部屋で眠ることを推奨します。**
④ 寝る前に身体をリラックスさせるようにしましょう。

正解は③。空所(3)の後には，睡眠に最適な温度は摂氏18〜20度であると言われているので，<u>寝室の温度を調節することで睡眠の質が改善される</u>，といった内容が述べられているとわかる。よってこの段落の主題文としては選択肢③「涼しい部屋で眠ることを推奨します」が最適であると判断できるので，③が正解となる。

①，②，④はいずれもこの段落で述べられている内容ではないので不可。

問4 18 **正解②**

「コメント(4)に基づくと，どの文を追加するべきか」 18

① 結論として，私たちの社会の人々はいまだにこうしたことを適切に行っていません。
② **このようにして，私たちは睡眠の質ばかりでなく，健康全般を改善することができます。**

— 英 R 26 —

③　したがって，私たちは労働時間を減らし，睡眠時間を増やすべきです。
④　これらの点は，若者たちにとってより多くの睡眠をとることの重要性を示しています。

　正解は②。コメント(4)には「最終的な結論となる文を追加するべきだと思います」とある。空所(4)を含む段落の前までの段落構成は以下のようになっている（［　］内の数字は段落番号を表す）。
　　[1] 序論　「睡眠改善と健康改善のためにできること」
　　[2] 本論1「朝，日光に触れること」
　　[3] 本論2「寝室の温度を下げること」
　　[4] 本論3「夜，電子機器の利用を控えること」
　以上の内容を受けて，[5] では「要約すると，以上見てきたように，よりよい睡眠をとるためにできることはたくさんあります。(4)」と述べられているので，空所(4)に②「このようにして，私たちは睡眠の質をばかりでなく，健康全般を改善することができます」という文を追加すれば，最終的な結論を示す適切な結びとなると判断できる。よって正解は②となる。
　①，③，④はいずれも最終的な結論を示す内容とはなっていないので不可。

主な語句・表現	・問題冊子を参照のこと。

[リード文]
◇ draft 名「草稿」　　　　　　　　　◇ work on ...「…に取り組む」
◇ revision 名「改訂；修正」　　　　　◇ based on ...「…に基づいて［た］」

[第1段落]
(Scientific research tells ...)
◇ long-term 形「長期にわたる」　　　◇ including ...「…を含めて」
◇ high blood pressure「高血圧」　　　◇ obesity 名「肥満」
◇ affect 動「…に影響を及ぼす」　　　◇ alert 形「機敏な；頭の回転が速い」
◇ retain 動「…を保持する」

[第2段落]
(First, it is ...)
◇ expose A to B「AをBに触れさせる」　◇ hormone 名「ホルモン」
◇ release 動「…を放出する」　　　　　◇ from inside ...「…の内部から」
◇ instruct O to −「Oに−するよう指示を与える」

[第3段落]
(Second, [3] where do ...)
◇ degree 名「(温度・角度などの) 度」　◇ Celsius 名「摂氏」
◇ in addition to ...「…に加えて」　　　◇ regulate 動「…を調節する」
◇ trigger 名「引き金；要因」
◇ signal to A that ...「Aに…と指示［合図］する」
◇ fall asleep「寝つく；眠りに落ちる」

[第4段落]
(Finally, it is ...)
◇ electronic device「電子機器」
◇ negatively 副「否定的に；悪い方へ」　negatively affect ... で「…に悪影響を及ぼす」。
◇ emit 動「…を放射［放出］する」　　◇ delay 動「…を遅らせる」

[最終段落]
(In summary, there ...)
◇ in summary「要約すると」
◇ a number of 複数形「多くの［いくつかの］複数形」

[先生のコメント]
◇ definitely 副「確かに；確実に」　　◇ take on ...「…を採用する［取り入れる］」

[コメント]
◇ connect with ...「…とつながる」　　◇ topic sentence「主題文」
◇ rewrite 動「…を書き直す」　　　　　◇ concluding 形「結論となる；結びの」

[設問文・選択肢]
◇ protect A against [from] B「B から A を守る」
◇ make sure (that) ...「必ず［確実に］…する」
◇ recommend 動「…を勧める；推奨する」
◇ in conclusion「結論として」
◇ properly 副「適切に」
◇ in this way「このようにして」
◇ overall 形「全般的な」
◇ spend A −ing「−して A〈時間・お金など〉を費やす」

第5問

解 答

問1 − ②　　問2 − ①　　問3 − ①　　　　　　　　　　　　　　　　（各3点）

問4　22 − ③　　23 − ③　　　　　　　　　　　　　　　　　　　（各2点）

問5 − ⑤　　　　　　　　　　　　　　　　　　　　　　　　　　　　（3点）

出 典　*Original Material*

全 訳

あなたと何人かの友人は高校で新しいクラブ―英語によるディベートクラブ―を始めることにしました。あなたは，以下の記事に基づいた主題と，授業で最近英語によるディベートに参加した生徒に対して行ったアンケート結果についての配布資料を作りました。

ディベートを成功させるのは何か
スカイロック大学ディベートチームのキャプテンである，ルーシー・ゴンザレス

ディベートは重要な主題について議論するための道具です。ディベートを行うことによって，学生は難解な主題を探求し，自分の意見を論理的に表現し，自分が抱いている先入観に疑問を投げかけることができるのです。すべてのディベートは，前もって選ばれる1つの決議案―議論されるべき意見―から始まります。

ディベートは，賛成チーム，反対チーム，そして審査団という3つのグループを必要とします。賛成チームは，決議案を支持する主張とその理由を発表することから始めます。また彼らは決議案に対する反対理由を予測し，その理由がなぜ間違っているのかを説明しなければなりません。

次に，反対チームが反対である主張を発表します。発表者は相手チームによって提起された疑問に答え，決議案に反対するさらなる理由を発表します。主題の両面を調査し，相手チームがどういう発言をするかを推測することが成功をもたらします。

両チームは反論セクションで再び発言します。ここでは，発表者は相手チームが言ったことに関する見解を述べ，さらなる反論を述べます。最後に，審判団が最終的な意見を聴きます。審判団は主要な2つの点―明晰さと妥当性―を探ります。明晰さとは主張が明快で論理的であったことを意味し，一方，妥当性とは発表者が主題からそれることなく適切な証拠をあげたことを意味します。審判団は，自分たち自身の個人的意見とは関係なく，そうした点に自分たちの判断の基盤を置かなければなりません。

ディベートは楽しくあるべきです。参加者は自分たちの役割を真剣に引き受けなければなりませんが，全員が礼儀正しいままでいるべきです。こうした活動を通して，メンバーたちは自分の技術と知識をよりよいものにしていくことができるのです。

— 英 R 29 —

アンケート結果

質問1：英語のディベートの授業に参加することの利点はどういうことだと感じましたか。

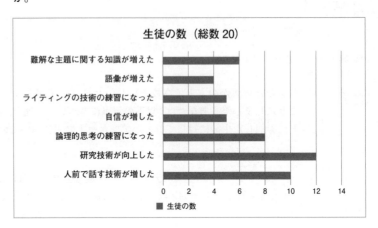

質問2：ディベートの授業に関する意見を述べてください。

主な意見：

生徒1（S1）：私は反対チームに割り当てられましたが，実際のところは個人的には決議案に賛成でした。反対の主張を考えるのは私にとって難しいことでした。

S2：私はディベートグループの1つの一員でしたが，私の友だちは審判でした。彼女はまったく研究をしませんでした。私は審判団も主題の研究をしなければならないと思います。彼女はまたそれぞれのチームが述べていた要点を覚えておくことは難しかったと言っていました。

S3：私は必要な英単語がわからなかったので，私にとってディベートは難しいものでした。活動を始める前に語彙リストがあればよかったと思います。

S4：反対チームは自分たちの意見を支持する統計とデータを見つけました。賛成チームは論理的な理由や証拠を見つけることができなかったので，負けたのです。

S5：私は，私たちには授業中に，ディベートの準備をし，調査する時間が十分とれなかった主題を理解するための時間がもっと必要だったと思います。

S6：主題に関する私の知識は本当に貧弱で，私はディベートを行う前にはどんな意見も持っていませんでした。しかし，私は主題に関する知識を得たばかりでなく，関連する他の問題についてもたくさん学びました。

あなたの議論に関する配布資料：

正式なディベートを計画すること

■ ディベートの構成
－決議案： 19
－3つのグループ：賛成チーム，反対チーム，審判団

■ 専門家のアドバイスとアンケート結果に基づくチームメンバーへの助言
－賛成チーム：
  20 理由を研究し発表する。

－反対チーム：
たとえ個人的には同意していないとしても，主題に関する反対意見を述べる。
前もってチームに有益な情報を与えることは，反対である主張を準備するのに役立つ
かもしれない。

－審判団：
  21
A. ディベートが始まる前に自分の意見を決める。
B. 前もって主題に関して学ぶ。
C. 明晰で論理的な主張を探す。
D. 主張を支持する証拠を探す。
E. 忘れてしまわないように，ディベートの間にメモをとる。

■ 話し合うべきその他の問題
－ 23 の意見が言及していたように， 22 と言っていた学生の数はもっとも少な
かった。そのことに関して，我々はどうすべきか。
－グラフと 24 の意見の両方に基づけば，我々はクラブの時間を，主題を理解し，
主張の計画を立てることに割り当てるべきなのだろうか。我々はそれぞれのチームが
どれだけの時間を必要とすると考えているのだろうか。
－S1 は，授業中に議論された主題に関する自分の意見はすでに決まっていたと述べて
いた。おそらく，我々は，全員が主張のあらゆる側面を理解できるようにするために，
各チームに分かれる前に，グループでのブレーンストーミングのための時間を多く持
つべきである。あなたはどう思うか。

設問解説

問1 　19　　正解②

「　19　に入れるのにもっとも適切な選択肢を選びなさい」

① 両チームが反対の主張を準備するべきである意見
❷ ディベートするべき問題に関する意見
③ 議論の余地のある主題についてのほとんどの人々が賛成する意見
④ 賛成チームが反対する，反対チームの最初の主張

　正解は②。「ディベートを成功させるのは何か」という記事の第1段落最終文（All debates start ...）で「すべてのディベートは，前もって選ばれる1つの決議案―議論されるべき意見―から始まります」と述べられていることから，「決議案」とは「議論されるべき意見」であることがわかるので，正解は②と考えることができる。

　①，③，④はいずれも決議案の定義として記事で述べられている内容ではないので不可。

問2 　20　　正解①

「　20　に入れるのにもっとも適切な選択肢を選びなさい」

❶ あなたが研究したデータで裏づけられる，決議案に同意する
② 上級の英語語彙を使って，主題に反対する
③ 審判団が決断を下すことを可能にする，主張に関する双方の側にとっての
④ 相手チームを説得するための，主題に関する個人的な意見の

　正解は①。「ディベートを成功させるのは何か？」という記事の第2段落第2文（The affirmative team ...）で「賛成チームは，決議案を支持する主張とその理由を発表することから始めます」と述べられている。賛成チームが行うこととして　20　に①を入れると「あなたが研究したデータで裏づけられる。決議案に同意する理由を研究し発表する」という意味になり，記事で述べられていることとほぼ同じ意味を表すことになると判断できるので，正解は①となる。

　②，③，④はいずれも，　20　に続けても賛成チームが行うこととして記事で述べられている内容とはならないので不可。

問3 　21　　正解①

「あなたは配布資料を点検しているところである。審判団の下にある助言の中に誤りを見つけた。以下のどれを取り除くべきか」　21

① A
② B
③ C
④ D
⑤ E

　正解は①。「ディベートを成功させるのは何か」という記事の第4段落第3文（Finally, the judges ...）以降に審判団が行うことの説明がなされているが，最終文（Judges should base ...）に「審判団は，自分たち自身の個人的意見とは関係なく，そうした点に自分たちの判断の基盤を置かなければなりません」とあるので，Aの「ディベートが始まる前に自分の意見を決める」は誤りであるとわかる。

　②Bは S2 のコメントにある「審判団も主題の研究をしなければならないと思います」という意見を反映させたものであると考えることができる。③Cと④Dは第4段落第4文（The judges look ...）と第5文（Clarity means that ...）で述べられている，「審判団は主要な2つの点―明晰さと妥当性―を探ります。明晰さとは主張が明快で論理的であったことを意味し，一方，妥当性とは発表者が主題からそれることなく適切な証拠をあげたことを意味します」という内容に対応していると考えられる。⑤Eは S2 のコメントにある「彼女［審判の1人］はまたそれぞれのチームが述べていた要点を覚えておくことは難

― 英 R 32 ―

しかったと言っていました」という意見を反映させたものであると考えることができる。

問4　[22]　正解③　　[23]　正解③
「[22]と[23]に入れるのにもっとも適切な選択肢を選びなさい」
　[22]
①　友人たちの前で話すのは難しかった
②　準備のための時間がほとんどなかった
③　**新しい単語を身につけることができた**
④　主題に関する知識がほとんどなかった
⑤　ライティングの練習が含まれていなかった

　[23]
①　S1
②　S2
③　S3
④　S4
⑤　S5
⑥　S6

　正解は[22]が③，[23]が③。
　空所[22]と[23]を含む箇所は，話し合うべきその他の問題の1つとして「[23]の意見が言及していたように，[22]と言っていた学生の数はもっとも少なかった。そのことに関して，我々はどうすべきか」という意味を表している。空所[22]に関し，グラフより，学生の数がもっとも少なかった項目は「語彙が増えた」であるので，[22]には③「新しい単語を身につけることができた」が入ることになる。空所[23]に関し，アンケート結果の質問2における各生徒の意見の中でS3は「私は必要な英単語がわからなかったので，私にとってディベートは難しいものでした。活動を始める前に語彙リストがあればよかったと思います」とコメントしている。「必要な英単語がわからなかった」ということは「新しい単語を身につけることができたと言っていた学生の数はもっとも少なかった」というグラフが示していることと呼応していると判断できるので，[23]には③S3が入ると考えることができる。

問5　[24]　正解⑤
「[24]に入る最も適切な選択肢を答えなさい」
①　S1
②　S2
③　S3
④　S4
⑤　**S5**
⑥　S6

　正解は⑤。空所[24]を含む箇所は「グラフと[24]の意見の両方に基づけば，我々はクラブの時間を，主題を理解して主張の計画を立てることに割り当てるべきなのだろうか。我々はそれぞれのチームがどれだけの時間を必要とすると考えているのだろうか」という意味を表している。アンケート結果の質問2における各生徒の意見の中で，S5は「私は，私たちには授業中に，ディベートの準備をし，調査する時間が十分とれなかった主題を理解するための時間がもっと必要だったと思います」とコメントしているが，そのコメントに基づいて「主題を理解して主張の計画を立てることに割り当てるべきなのだろうか」という問題提起がなされていると判断できるので，[24]には⑤S5が入ることになる。

主な語句・表現	・問題冊子を参照のこと。

［リード文］
◇ handout 名「配布資料；プリント」
◇ based on ...「…に基づいて」 base A on B「A の基礎を B に置く」
◇ questionnaire 名「アンケート」　　　　◇ take part in ...「…に参加する」

［記事］
◇ allow O to －「O が－することを可能にする」
◇ challenge 動「…を疑問視する」　　　　◇ prejudice 名「先入観；偏見」
◇ resolution 名「決議案」　　　　　　　　◇ statement 名「声明；陳述；意見」
◇ affirmative 形「賛成の；肯定の」　　　　◇ oppose 動「反対する」
◇ judge 名「審判」　　　　　　　　　　　◇ present 動「…を発表する」
◇ argument 名「主張」　　　　　　　　　◇ support 動「…を支持する」
◇ anticipate 動「…を予想する」　　　　　◇ raise 動「〈問題など〉を提起する」
◇ opponent 名「相手；敵」　　　　　　　◇ rebuttal 名「反論；反駁」
◇ counter-argument 名「反対の主張［意見］；反論」
◇ clarity 名「明晰さ」　　　　　　　　　◇ relevance 名「妥当性；適合性；適切さ」
◇ logical「論理的な」　　　　　　　　　◇ stick to ...「…に固執する；…から外れない」
◇ regardless of ...「…とは無関係に」

［アンケート結果］
◇ confidence 名「自信」　　　　　　　　　◇ be assigned to ...「…に割り当てられる」
◇ come up with ...「…を思いつく；…を見つける」
◇ I didn't have enough time 以下は直前の the topic を先行詞とする関係代名詞節であるが，
　 関係代名詞は目的格であるために省略されている。
◇ investigate 動「…を調べる」

［配布資料］
◇ recommendation for ...「…への助言」　　◇ take notes「メモを取る」
◇ brainstorming 名「ブレーンストーミング」 集団の自発的あるいは自由な発案・議論によ
　 る問題解決法のこと。
◇ session 名「集団活動；（集団活動のための）時間」

［設問文・選択肢］
◇ declaration 名「発表」　　　　　　　　◇ controversial 形「議論の余地のある」
◇ back up ...「…を裏づける」　　　　　　◇ convince 動「…を説得する」

— 英 R 34 —

第6問

解答

問1 - ④	問2 - ①	（各3点）
問3 - 27 · 28 - ①·④		（順不同・両方正解で3点）
29 - ④		（3点）
問4 - ④	問5 - ②	（各3点）

出典 *Original Material*

全訳

あなたはアメリカのある州において選挙年齢が16歳に下げられるべきかどうかについてのエッセイに取り組んでいます。以下の各ステップに従っていきます。

　　ステップ1：選挙年齢を下げることに関するさまざまな見解を読んで理解する。
　　ステップ2：選挙年齢が下げられるべきかどうかについての判断を下す。
　　ステップ3：追加の情報源を使って，エッセイの概要を作成する。

[ステップ1] さまざまな情報源を読む
筆者A（高校生）
私の友人の中には，私たちは16歳で投票する権利を持つべきである，と感じている人たちもいます。しかし，私はまだ有権者になる準備ができていないと感じています。卒業するまで高校はまだ2年あるので，多くの点で私はまだ子どものように感じているのです。また私は誰に投票すべきかに関する確固とした意見をもつほど政治制度について十分わかっていません。おそらく両親と同じ政党に投票するだけでしょう。

筆者B（教師）
多くの人たちは，16歳はまだ子どもである，したがって投票権を持つべきではない，と信じています。実際のところ，私は，16歳は若者が政治や社会に関心を持ち始める理想的な年齢だ，と思います。彼らに情報に基づく選択を行うための十分な情報が与えられるならば，そうすることができる，と私は思います。しかし，私たちは彼らに学校で政治について教えなければならないのですが，私たちは教師として自分たち自身の個人的な政治的意見に関し，彼らにあまり影響を与えすぎないように注意しなければなりません。

筆者C（投票所職員）
私は，投票に来る人の数が毎年減っていることに気づきました。そういうわけで，私は選挙年齢を下げることには賛成です。今，有権者の大多数はお年寄りで，若者は少数派です。より若い人々が投票することを可能にすれば，彼らは期待を込めて政治にもっと深く興味を持ち，これからの人生において有権者となってくれるでしょう。しかし，16歳の者たちが投票することを可能にした場合，確実に彼らが投票する動機を抱き，バランスの取れた政治教育を受けるようにしなければなりません。学校にそういったことをする時間や経験があるかどうかわかりませんが。

筆者D（心理学者）
ほとんどの発達心理学者は，人間の脳は20代半ばまでは成熟が終わらないということで意見が一致しています。したがって，16歳の者たちは発達という意味ではまだ子どもです。しかし，これが私が選挙年齢を下げることに反対する主要な理由ではありません。おそらく十分に成熟している16歳はたくさんいるでしょうが，私は彼らには適切な選択を行う

— 英 R 35 —

ための政治と社会の両方に関する知識が欠けていると思います。教育制度を大きく変えることなしにこのことを行うことは不可能です。私は，学校の生徒が重要な決断をすることを可能にする十分な知識を持つまで，選挙年齢を下げることを支持しません。

筆者 E（政治家）
統計によると，私の州における有権者の大部分は 45 歳から 64 歳にかけての年齢層です。それはつまり，政治家が高齢の有権者が気にいることに向けた政策決定を行う傾向にあるということです。今は若者にとっては困難な時代ですので，もし彼らが投票することができれば，もっと明るい未来のための選択をすることができる，と私は思うのです。政治家の中には，16 歳の者たちは教師や親の政治的選択に強い影響を受けることになるので，選挙年齢を下げることに反対する者もいますが，私は，高齢の有権者ばかりでなく，すべての人のためのよりよい社会を作るべきだと思います。

設問解説

問1　　25　　正解 ④
「筆者 B と E は両者とも　25　と言及している」
　① 16 歳の者たちは，政治に積極的な関心を持つにはあまりに若すぎる
　② 高校生は仕事をしたり税金を払ったりしていないので，政治を理解することができない
　③ 政治に積極的であるのは，主に中高年の人たちである
　④ 若者の政治的意見は教師の影響を受ける可能性がある
　　正解は ④。教師である筆者 B は最終文（However, while we ...）で「しかし，私たちは彼らに学校で政治について教えなければならないのですが，私たちは教師として自分たち自身の個人的な政治的意見に関し，彼らにあまり影響を与えすぎないように注意しなければなりません」と述べているということは，それは若者は教師の意見に影響を受ける可能性が高いという根拠に立っての発言であると推測できる。また政治家である筆者 E は最終文（Some politicians are ...）で「政治家の中には，16 歳の者たちは教師や親の政治的選択に強い影響を受けることになるので，選挙年齢を下げることに反対する者もいますが，私は，高齢の有権者ばかりでなく，すべての人のためのよりよい社会を作るべきだと思います」と述べている。以上から著者 B と E は両者とも「若者の政治的意見は教師の影響を受ける可能性がある」ことに言及しているので，正解は ④ となる。
　　①，②，③ に関しては，いずれも筆者 B と E の両者が言及している内容ではないので不可。

問2　　26　　正解 ①
「筆者 D の主な主張は　26　ということである」
　① 現在，学校では政治制度に関する情報は適切に教えられてはいない
　② 大体 25 歳になっていない人々は未熟であり，投票権を持つべきでない
　③ 適切な政治的決断を行うほど十分に賢明である学校の生徒はいない
　④ 脳が十分に発達していない人々は投票することができるようになるべきではない
　　正解は ①。心理学者である筆者 D は第 4 文（Probably there are ...）後半で「私は彼ら［16 歳の者たち］には適切な選択を行うための政治と社会の両方に関する知識が欠けていると思います」と述べ，続く第 5 文（We cannot do ...）で「教育制度を大きく変えることなしにこのことを行うことは不可能です」と述べている。以上のことから筆者 D は「現在，学校では政治制度に関する情報は適切に教えられてはいない」ことを示唆していると判断できるので，正解は ① となる。
　　③ に関しては，筆者 D が示唆している内容とは言えないので不可。
　　②，④ に関しては，筆者 D は第 1 文（Most developmental psychologists ...）〜第 2 文

— 英 R 36 —

(Therefore, 16-year-olds ...) で，16歳の者たちの脳はまだ十分には発達していないのでまだ子どもである，ということが述べられているが，その直後の第3文（However, this is ...）で筆者Dは「しかし，これが私が選挙年齢を下げることに反対する主要な理由ではありません」と述べているので，正解とはならない。

[ステップ2] 判断を下す
問3　[27]・[28]　正解①・④　　[29]　正解④
　「さまざまな見解を理解したので，選挙年齢を16歳まで下げることに関して判断を下し，それを以下のように書き出した。[27]，[28]，[29]を完成させるのにもっとも適切な選択肢を選びなさい」

あなたの判断：選挙年齢は16歳まで下げられるべきではない。
　・　筆者[27]と[28]があなたの判断を支持している。
　・　その2人の筆者の主要な論拠：[29]。

　　　[27]と[28]に入る選択肢（順序は問わない）
　　①　A
　　②　B
　　③　C
　　④　D
　　⑤　E
　正解は①と④。筆者Aは第1文(Some of my friends ...)～第2文(However, I don't ...)で「私の友人の中には，私たちは16歳で投票を行う権利を持つべきである，と感じている人たちもいます。しかし，私はまだ有権者になる準備ができていないと感じています」と述べ，筆者Dは第3文（However, this is ...）で「しかし，これが私が選挙年齢を下げることに反対する主要な理由ではありません」と述べていることから，筆者AとDが「選挙年齢は16歳まで下げられるべきではない」という判断を支持していると推測できるので，[27]・[28]の正解は①　Aと④　Dということになる。

　　　[29]に入る選択肢
　　①　親は10代の子どもたちに，自分たちが支持する政党に投票するように言う可能性が高い
　　②　18歳未満の生徒の中には，投票を行うことができるほど成熟している者もいる
　　③　18歳未満の生徒は友人の決定に影響を受ける可能性が高い
　　④　16歳から18歳の若者は投票するための知識や経験を持っていない
　正解は④。筆者Aは第3文（I don't also ...）で「また私は誰に投票すべきであるかに関する確固とした意見を持つほど政治制度についてわかっていません」と述べ，筆者Dは第4文（Probably there are ...）で「おそらく十分に成熟している16歳はたくさんいるでしょうが，私は彼らには適切な選択を行うための政治と社会の両方に関する知識が欠けていると思います」と述べていることから，「あなた」の判断を支持している筆者AとDの主要な論拠は選択肢④の「16歳から18歳の若者は投票するための知識や経験を持っていない」ことであるとわかる。

[全訳]

[ステップ3] 情報源AとBを使って，概要を作成する。
あなたのエッセイの概要：

選挙年齢を下げることは適切な考えではない

序論
　最近，選挙で投票する人々の数が減っている。したがって，より多くの人たちに投票を行うよう促すために選挙年齢を16歳まで下げるべきであると考える者もいる。しかし，それは適切な考えではない。

本論
　理由1：（ステップ2から）
　理由2：（情報源Aに基づく）……　30
　理由3：（情報源Bに基づく）……　31

結論
　選挙年齢は16歳まで下げられるべきではない。

情報源A
世界のほとんどの国では，成人年齢は18歳に設定されてきている一方，成人年齢としてずっと高い年齢を設定している国もある。ほとんどの国で18歳が成人とみなされている理由は，発達段階において若者が自分自身の人生に関して重要な決断を行うことができる年齢だからである。すなわち，彼らは許可を得ずに結婚できるし，法的契約書にサインすることができるのである。フルタイムで働いている可能性のある者もいる。したがって，ほとんどの国は成人年齢を投票するのに適した年齢に合わせることにもなっている。実際のところ，世界中の平均的な選挙年齢は18歳を少し上回るところである。ほとんどの政府は，法的に成人とみなされない者は，選挙における投票権を持ち国の政治に影響を及ぼすべきではないと考えている。

情報源B
米国で行われた調査は，さまざまな年齢層の人たちに16歳と17歳の者たちの投票権を支持するかどうかを尋ねた。さまざまな政党の支持者である1,000人を少し上回る人たちが調査の質問に回答した。ジェンダー，民族集団，収入といった公正なバランスも存在していた。

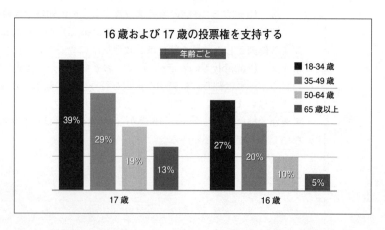

設問解説

問4 　30　 正解 ④

「情報源 A に基づけば，以下のどれが理由 2 としてもっとも適切か」 　30

① 18 歳の者たちはまだ学校で勉強しているので，投票を行い政治に影響を及ぼすほど十分な年齢になっているとはみなされない。

② 国の中には人は大体 20 歳になるまでは子どもであると判断しているところもあるので，18 歳でもあまりに若すぎるので投票を行うことはできない。

③ ほとんどの国では 18 歳より上の人々は教育を終えているので，彼らは投票を行うことができると期待されている。

④ ほとんどの国では 18 歳が成人年齢とみなされているので，我々は選挙年齢を 18 歳のままに留めておくべきである。

正解は ④。情報源 A の第 2 文（The reason why ...）で「ほとんどの国で 18 歳が成人とみなされている理由は，発達段階において若者が自分自身の人生に関して重要な決断を行うことができる年齢だからである」と述べられ，さらに最終文（Most governments believe ...）で「ほとんどの政府は，法的に成人とみなされない者は，選挙における投票権を持ち国の政治に影響を及ぼすべきではないと考えている」と述べられていることから，正解は ④ であると判断できる。

①，② に関しては，情報源 A で述べられている内容ではないので不可。

③ に関しては，エッセイの概要である「選挙年齢を下げることは適切な考えではない」ということの理由とみなすことはできないので不可。

問5 　31　 正解 ②

「理由 3 として，あなたは『選挙年齢を下げることはアメリカ人によって支持されていない』と書くことにした。情報源 B に基づけば，どの選択肢がこの記述をもっともよく支持しているか」 　31

① 18 歳から 34 歳の人々は，16 歳の者たちが投票を行うことができるようにするべきだということに反対する可能性がもっとも高いが，3 分の 1 を少し下回る人々は 17 歳に対してはこのことを支持している。

② 18 歳から 34 歳の人々のほぼ 4 分の 3 が選挙年齢を 16 歳に下げることに賛成してはおらず，64 歳より上の 5 ％は賛成している。

③ 34 歳以下の人々の大多数が選挙年齢は下げられるべきであると考えているが，これは他の年齢層の人々には支持されていない。

④ 18 歳から 34 歳のほとんどの人々は選挙年齢が 17 歳に下げられることを支持しているが，その人たちのうち 27％ だけが選挙年齢を 16 歳に下げることに賛成している。

正解は ②。グラフでは選挙年齢を 16 歳とすることを支持する 18 歳から 34 歳の人々は 27％ となっているので，そうではない人は 73％，すなわちほぼ 4 分の 3 であることがわかる。また 65 歳以上の人々は 5 ％が賛成していることがわかるので，正解は ② となる。

① に関しては，グラフより最も反対する可能性が高いのは 65 歳以上であり，また 18 歳から 34 歳の人々においては 3 分の 1 を少し上回る人々が 17 歳という年齢を支持していることがわかるので不可。

③ に関しては，グラフから 34 歳以下の人々のうち選挙年齢を 17 歳にすることを支持する者は 39％，16 歳にすることを支持する者は 27％ であることがわかるので，34 歳以下の人々の大多数が選挙年齢は下げられるべきであると考えていることにはならないので不可。

④ に関しては，上の ③ が不可の理由で述べたように，選挙年齢を 17 歳にすることを支持する者は 39％ であり，「18 歳から 34 歳のほとんどの人々は選挙年齢が 17 歳に下げられることを支持している」ことにはならないので不可。

— 英 R 39 —

主な語句・表現	・問題冊子を参照のこと。

[リード文]
◇ work on ...「…に取り組む」　　　　　◇ voting age「選挙年齢；投票年齢」
◇ take a position about ...「…についての判断を下す」
◇ outline 名「概要」

[ステップ1]
◇ the right to vote「投票権」　　　　　◇ in many ways「多くの点で」
◇ vote for ...「…に投票する」　　　　　◇ party 名「政党」
◇ ideal 形「理想的な」
◇ take an interest in ...「…に興味［関心］を持つ」
◇ informed 形「情報に基づく」　　　　◇ be careful not to −「−しないよう注意する」
◇ voting station「投票所」
◇ that's why ...「そういうわけで…；したがって…」
◇ in favor of ...「…に賛成して；…を支持して」
◇ elderly people「お年寄り；高齢者」
◇ with young adults in the minority「若者は少数派である」　with はここでは付帯状況を表している。
◇ allow + O + to −「O が−することを許す［可能にする］」
◇ make sure (that) ...「確実に…する」　　◇ motivation 名「動機」
◇ developmental psychologist「発達心理学者」
◇ mature 動「〈自動詞〉成熟する」　形「成熟した」⇔ immature 形「未熟な」
◇ in ... sense「…の意味で」　　　　　◇ statistics 名「統計（の数字）」
◇ aimed at ...「…に向けた」　aimed at pleasing older voters は直前の policies にかかる過去分詞句。
◇ against ...「…に反対して」　⇔ for ...「…に賛成して」

[設問文・選択肢]
◇ mention that ...「…に言及している」
◇ middle-aged and elderly (people)「中高年（の人々）」
◇ imply that ...「…と示唆している」　　◇ adequately 副「適切に」

[ステップ2]
◇ now that ...「（今や）…なので」　　　◇ as below「以下のように」
◇ be likely to −「−する可能性が高い」　◇ have the maturity「成熟している」
◇ aged ...「…歳の」　aged 16 to 18 は直前の Young people にかかる過去分詞句。

[ステップ3]
◇ election 名「選挙」
◇ encourage + O + to −「O に−するよう勧める」
◇ be set as ...「…に［として］設定されている」
◇ be considered ...「…とみなされる」　◇ that is「すなわち」
◇ permission 名「許可」　　　　　　◇ legal contract「法的契約書」
◇ it follows that ...「（したがって）…ということになる」
◇ match A with B「A を B に合わせる」
◇ not legally considered an adult「法的に成人とみなされない」　直前の anyone にかかる過去分詞句。
◇ affect 動「…に影響を及ぼす」
◇ conducted in the US「米国で行われた」　直前の A survey にかかる過去分詞句。
◇ gender 名「ジェンダー」　歴史的・文化的・社会的に形成される男女の差異。
◇ ethnic group「民族集団」

[設問文・選択肢]
◇ be expected to −「−することを期待される」　　◇ a third「3 分の 1」
◇ three-quarters「4 分の 3」

— 英 R 40 —

第7問

解 答

問1 — 32 ④, 33 ①, 34 ⑤, 35 ③ （全部正解で3点）
問2 — ③ （3点）
問3　37 — ③　38 — ① （両方正解で3点）
問4 — ①　　問5 — ② （各3点）

出 典　*Original Material*

全 訳

あなたは英語の授業である物語に関する発表のための準備をしているところです。あなたはある雑誌で興味深い物語を見つけて，自分の発表のためにその物語についてのメモを取っているところです。

　　　　　　　　　　サムの学校

　電話が鳴った。サム・ホーキンは深い眠りから目覚めて，ベッド脇の時計を見た。午前4時。まだ寝ぼけたまま，彼は受話器を取り上げた。
「もしもし？」
「サム。ママだけど。パパがまた病気になってね。パパは病院にいるわ。今回はあなたは家に帰ってくる必要があると思っているわ」
　2, 3時間後にサムの妻であるヒロコが起きた時，彼は彼女にその知らせを伝えた。
「僕は明日カナダへ帰る飛行機を予約するつもりだ。パパが重病なんだ。君はここにいて子どもたちの面倒を見てくれるかい？」
「もちろんよ。あなたのパパがすぐによくなることを願っているわ。こっちの方はすべて私がやっておくから。できるだけ早く行ってあげて」とヒロコは応じた。その朝遅く，彼女は子どもたちのミナとカレンに，パパがしばらくカナダのおばあちゃんとおじいちゃんのところに行くことになる，と伝えた。

　サムは大学時代は自分の時間を非常に楽しんでいたので，卒業したくなかった。サムは，楽しい学生生活をあきらめたくなかったばかりでなく，また仕事として自分が何をしたいのかがわかってもいなかった。彼の友人のほとんどはすでに仕事に関する決断を下していた ― ジョンは弁護士になるつもりだったし，クリスはジャーナリストに，そしてマイクは父親の会社で働くつもりだった。何をしたいのかがわかっていなかったのはサムだけだった。彼の両親は高校の教師で，彼らは彼に同じ仕事をしてはどうかと何度も提案していたが，彼にはよくわからなかった。しかし，22歳で卒業する直前のある日，彼は寮の建物の壁に貼ってあったポスターに気がついた。そこには「日本で英語を教えませんか！」と書いてあった。サムはポスターに印刷されていたウェブサイトのアドレスをメモした。その夜，彼は応募したのだった。

「でもサム，あなたはカナダを離れたことさえ一度もないじゃない！ なぜ日本に行くの？」 彼の母親は驚いて尋ねた。

「ママ，ママたちは僕が教師になってはどうかと勧めてたよね。僕は日本で教師になるんだよ！ 僕はまず１年間そこに行って，それで教えることが好きだったら，戻ってきてカナダで高校の教師になるよ」

「お前にとっては大きなカルチャーショックになるぞ。もし寂しくなったら，好きなときにはいつでも戻ってきていいからな」と彼の父親が言った。その翌月に，彼は日本へ飛んだ。

それが15年前のことだった。カナダを出る前は日本のことはほとんど知らなかったけれども，日本はサムにとって故郷となった。彼は卒業後に応募したのと同じ学校でいまだに働いており，生徒や同僚たちに愛されていた。彼はまた日本語を読み，話し，書くことを独学で勉強していた。日本に来て３年後，彼は国際交流パーティーで出会ったヒロコと結婚した。結婚して数年後に娘たちが生まれた。ヒロコは作家で，いくつかの小説が出版されていた。母親になった後も，ヒロコは家で空いた時間に執筆を続けていた。彼らは幸せな家族であり，サムは残りの人生は日本で過ごすと思っていた。

カナダに戻り，サムは父親の病気がいかに重いかを知って驚いた。医者は彼に，父親は長く入院する可能性がある，と伝えた。母親の悲しい顔を見て，サムは計画を変更し，父親が快復するまで母親を見守るためにカナダに戻ってくるべきなのかと思った。その晩，サムは旧友のジョン，クリス，マイクに会った。彼らは大学時代の日々や現在の生活について話した。彼らはみな結婚して，子どもがいた。サムは彼らの家族の写真を見せてもらい，自分の娘たちと友人の子どもたちが一緒に遊べたらすばらしいだろうと思った。彼は友人たちに父親のことについて話した。

「戻って来いよ，サム」と友人たちが言った。

「僕はまたここに住みたいけど，教員免許を取りに大学に戻りたくはないな。僕には家族がいる ― すぐにでも働く必要がある」

「日本語学校を始めることだってできる」とジャーナリストのクリスが提案した。「僕はある雑誌にアニメや日本文化の人気についての記事を書いたところだ。最近は日本語を習いたいと思っている人は多いよ」

「その通りだ！ うちの会社にはビルの中に空いている場所がたくさんある。君はその場所をただで使うことができるよ」とマイクが申し出てくれた。

「そして僕はヒロコのビザの文書業務全般を手伝うよ」と弁護士のジョンが言った。

その夜，サムは東京のヒロコに電話し，彼女に自分の考えを伝えた。嬉しかったことに，ヒロコは同意した。

サムは日本に戻ったが，６ヵ月後，ホーキン一家のカナダへの引っ越しが完了した。サムの両親の家にはみんなで一緒に暮らすための十分な場所があった。ヒロコはリモートで執筆の仕事を続けることができた。ミナとカレンはカナダの学校生活を楽しんでいた。彼女たちは日本の友だちのみんなと離れて悲しかったが，

カナダのおばあちゃんやおじいちゃんと一緒に時間を過ごすことが大好きになった。彼女たちの英語はずっと上達していた。おじいちゃんはまだとても病弱だったが，家族の愛情のおかげで日に日に体力が回復しつつあった。家族が一緒にいるところを見た時，サムは，もっと早くこうすることを考えなかったのは残念だと思った。

　サムの学校は当初から成功した。彼の友人たちは約束通りに彼を助けてくれた。ある日，マイクは日本語学校に立ち寄った。
　「やあ，サム。僕たちはまだ君のための歓迎会をしてなかったね。今週末に歓迎会をしようよ」とマイクが提案した。
　「ダメだな，ヒロコと僕が君とジョンとクリスのために感謝の会を開くべきなんだ。僕たちの引っ越しがこんなに順調に進んだのは君たちのおかげだよ。土曜日に家族と一緒にうちへ来てくれないか。そうしたらヒロコと僕は君たちみんなのためにおいしい日本食を作るから」
　それで彼らはそのようにしたのであった。

あなたのメモ：

サムの学校

物語の概略

サムが大学を卒業する
↓
| 32 |
| 33 |
| 34 |
↓
| 35 |

サムとヒロコが感謝の会を開く

サムに関して
- 国籍：カナダ
- 年齢：| 36 |
- 職業：教師
- 友人たちと家族はどのように彼を援助したか：
    旧友のジョンは | 37 |。
    サムの母親と父親は | 38 |。

重要な時の説明
- サムがカナダから電話でヒロコと話したときに喜んだのは，| 39 | からだった。
- カナダの彼の家で，サムはあることが「残念」だと思った。それは | 40 | ということだった。

設問解説

問1　[32]　正解 ④,　[33]　正解 ①,　[34]　正解 ⑤,　[35]　正解 ③

「5つの出来事（①～⑤）から4つを選び，それらが起きた順に並べ替えなさい」

① ヒロコとサムが結婚する。
② ヒロコがカナダで高校教師になる。
③ マイクがサムに，サムの語学学校のための場所を提供する。
④ サムが日本に渡る。
⑤ サムの父親が病気になる。

正解は ④ → ① → ⑤ → ③。

　物語の第2ブロック第6文（However, one day ...）～最終文（That evening, he ...）から，サムは22歳で大学を卒業する直前に，日本で教師を募集するポスターを見つけ，その夜に応募したことがわかる。そしてそのことを両親に話した後で，第3ブロック最終文（The month after ...）に，その翌月にサムが日本に渡った，と述べられている（サム22歳）ので，選択肢の中では ④ が最初に来ることになる。その後，第4ブロック第5文（Three years after ...）で「日本に来て3年後，彼は国際交流パーティで出会ったヒロコと結婚した（サム25歳）」と述べられていることから，① が次に来る。第4ブロック第1文（That was 15 ...）から，大学を卒業して日本に渡って来たのが15年前のことであるとわかり，15年後（サム37歳）のある朝早く，第1ブロック（The phone rang. ...）で述べられているように，カナダの母親から電話があり，父親がまた病気になり，今回はサムがカナダに戻る必要がある，と告げられることになるので，次に来るのは ⑤ となる。第5ブロック（Back in Canada, ...）で，カナダに戻り，重病の父親を見舞い，母親の悲しい顔を見たサムはカナダに戻ってくるべきだろうかと考える。その夜，3人の旧友に会った時に，旧友たちから，カナダに戻って来て日本語学校を開けばいいのではないかという提案を受けるが，その時に旧友の1人であるマイクが自分が働いている父親の会社のビルには空いている場所が多くあるから，そこならただで使うことができると申し出たことがわかる。よって，③ が最後に来ることになる。以上から正解は ④ → ① → ⑤ → ③ となる。

　② は物語では述べられていない内容なので，選ぶべき4つの選択肢には入らない。

問2　[36]　正解 ③

「[36] に入れるのに最も適切な選択肢を選びなさい」

① 20代の初め
② 20代の終わり
③ 30代の終わり
④ 40代の初め

　正解は ③。この物語が始まる時点，つまりある朝早くカナダの母親から電話を受けた時点は，問1の解説でも触れたように，第4ブロック第1文（That was 15 ...）から，サムが22歳で大学を卒業して日本に渡ってきた15年後であるとわかるので，サムは37歳になっていると判断できる。よって正解は ③ となる。

問3　[37]　正解 ③　　[38]　正解 ①

「[37] と [38] に入れるのに最も適切な選択肢を選びなさい」

① サムとヒロコと子どもたちが自分たちと一緒に住むことを認めた
② サムにカナダで新しい事業を始めるためのお金を渡した
③ ヒロコがカナダで暮らすために必要な文書を準備した
④ サムに日本で教師の仕事をすることに関するポスターを見せてくれた
⑤ サムの新しい学校を宣伝するためのマーケティング記事を書いた

　[37] に関しては，第5ブロック（Back in Canada, ...）から，サムがカナダに戻り，旧友たちと再会した夜に，旧友たちがサムにカナダで日本語学校を開けばいいのではない

― 英 R 44 ―

かと提案した時に，「『そして僕はヒロコのビザの文書業務全般を手伝うよ』と弁護士のジョンが言った」とあることから，「旧友のジョンは」に続くのは，③「ヒロコがカナダで暮らすために必要な文書を準備した」ということになる。

　　　38　に関しては，第6ブロック第1文（Sam returned to ...）～第2文（There was enough ...）から，サムの一家が6ヵ月後にカナダへの引っ越しを完了し，「サムの両親の家にはみんなで一緒に暮らすための十分な場所があった」と述べられている。また第5文（They had been ...）後半で「（彼女たち［娘たち］は）カナダのおばあちゃんやおじいちゃんと一緒に時間を過ごすことが大好きになった」とあることから実際に一緒に暮らすようになったことがわかるので，「サムの母親と父親は」に続くのは，①「サムとヒロコと子どもたちが自分たちと一緒に住むことを認めた」ということになる。

　　その他の選択肢については，本文中で述べられていない。

問4　　39　　正解①

　　「　39　に入れるのに最も適切な選択肢を選びなさい」

　　　①　彼女が一緒にカナダへ戻るという彼の計画を受け入れた
　　　②　彼女が彼に2人の子どもについてのよい知らせを伝えた
　　　③　彼女が彼に彼の父親はすぐによくなるだろうと言った
　　　④　彼女が彼に自分はもう1つ小説を出版したと言った

　　正解は①。第5ブロック最後の2文（That night, Sam ...・To his delight, ...）に「その夜，サムは東京のヒロコに電話し，彼女に自分の考えを伝えた。嬉しかったことに，ヒロコは同意した」と述べられているが，「自分の考え」とは第5ブロックで述べられている旧友3人とのやりとりから，「（家族で）一緒にカナダへ戻る」ことであると判断でき，そのサムの発言に「嬉しかったことに，ヒロコは同意した」とあるので，正解は①となる。

　　その他の選択肢については，本文中で述べられていない。

問5　　40　　正解②

　　「　40　に入れるのに最も適切な選択肢を選びなさい」

　　　①　彼の子どもたちは新しい学校生活に慣れていない
　　　②　彼の家族が一緒にいる多くの時間を逃してしまっていた
　　　③　彼の父親がいまだ病気で，退院することができない
　　　④　彼の妻がカナダでの生活をもはや楽しんでいない

　　正解は②。第6ブロック最終文（When Sam saw ...）で「家族が一緒にいるところを見た時，サムは，もっと早くこうすることを考えなかったのは残念だと思った」と述べられているが，「こうすること」とはここまでの内容から「（サムの両親を含めて）家族が一緒にいること」であるとみなせるので，正解は②ということになる。

　　その他の選択肢については，本文中で言及されている箇所はない。

【主な語句・表現】

・問題冊子を参照のこと。

[リード文]　　◇ presentation 图「発表」　　　　　　　　◇ take a note「メモを取る」

[第1ブロック]　◇ half asleep「寝ぼけている」　　　　　◇ a couple of ...「2，3の…；いくつかの…」
（The phone　　◇ book 動「…を予約する」　　　　　　◇ get well「よくなる；快復する」
rang. ...）

[第2ブロック]　◇ Not only did he not want to –「–したくなかったばかりでなく」　Not only「…ばかりで
（Sam had　　　なく」は否定の副詞句であるため，後には倒置の形（疑問文の語順）が続いている。
enjoyed ...）　　◇ decide on ...「…について決める」

— 英 R 45 —

◇ It was just Sam who ... は just Sam を強調する強調構文だが，人を強調しているので，that の代わりに who が用いられている。

◇ suggest 動「…を提案する；…を勧める」　◇ dormitory 名「寮；寄宿舎」

◇ apply (for ...)「（…に）応募［志願］する」

[第4ブロック]
(That was 15 ...)

◇ home 名「本拠地；故郷」

◇ teach oneself to −「−することを独学で学ぶ」

◇ international party「国際交流パーティー」

◇ have several novels published「いくつかの小説が出版される」　have O p.p. は「O が−してもらう［される］」という意味を表す構文。

◇ consider −ing「−することを考える」

[第5ブロック]
(Back in Canada, ...)

◇ meet up with ...「…と（約束して）会う」　◇ teacher's certificate「教員免許」

◇ right away「すぐに」　◇ article 名「記事」

◇ plenty of ...「たくさんの…」　◇ for free「ただで；無料で」

◇ paperwork 名「文書［書類］業務」

◇ to one's ＋感情を表す名詞「人が…したことには」

[第6ブロック]
(Sam returned to ...)

◇ remotely 副「リモートで；遠く離れて」　◇ thanks to ...「…のおかげで」

◇ it is a shame (that) ...「…ことは残念である」

[第7ブロック]
(Sam's school was ...)

◇ drop by ...「…に立ち寄る」　◇ why don't we ...?「…しよう」

◇ hold a party「会を開く」

◇ It's thanks to you that ... は，thanks to you という副詞句を強調した強調構文。

[メモ]

◇ outline 名「概略」　◇ nationality 名「国籍」

◇ occupation 名「職業」　◇ interpretation 名「説明」

◇ key 形「重要な」

[設問文・選択肢]

◇ rearrange 動「…を並び替える」

◇ they happened は直前の the order「順番」にかかる関係副詞節。

◇ allow O to −「O が−することを認める」　◇ document 名「文書」

◇ Hiroko needed 以下は直前の the documents を先行詞とする関係代名詞節だが，関係代名詞自体は目的格であるために省略されている。

◇ advertise 動「…を宣伝する」　◇ settle into ...「…に慣れる；…に落ち着く」

◇ miss out on ...「〈楽しみなど〉を逃す」　◇ not ... anymore「もはや…ない」

第8問

解答

問1 - ②		（2点）
問2 - ②		（3点）
問3 - ②・③		（順不同・両方正解で3点）
問4 - ④	問5 - ③	（各3点）

出典 *Original Material*

全訳

あなたは，ある健康に関するウェブサイトから得た以下の情報を使って，理科の授業のための発表の準備をしています。

食物繊維―忘れられたヒーロー

　健康の専門家はいつも私たちに果実や野菜をもっと多く食べるように勧めている。こうした食べ物には，自分たちの身体を健康に保つのにきわめて重要である多種多様なビタミンやミネラルや栄養素が含まれていることを私たちは知っている。しかし，果実や野菜の摂取を促す他の理由の1つは，それらには食物繊維が含まれているということである。実際のところ，私たちは身体が必要としている食物繊維を果実や野菜やその他の植物性食品を通してしか得ることができない。肉や魚や乳製品といった他の食べ物にも多くの栄養素は含まれているが，それらには食物繊維はまったくのところ欠けているのである。

　西洋諸国では，食物繊維の摂取が減少した一方で，加工食品の消費が増加した。自分自身と家族のために新鮮な材料から時間をかけて食事を作ることは忙しい人々にとっては難しいので，既製食品に頼る人々がますます増えている。イギリス国民保健サービスによれば，平均的な成人は毎日少なくとも30gの食物繊維を摂るべきである。しかし，研究が示すところでは，現在の平均は20gだけである。残念なことに，食事において食物繊維が不足すると，多くの健康上の問題につながる可能性がある。

　2種類の主要な食物繊維―水溶性食物繊維と不溶性食物繊維―があることに注意しておくことは重要である。各種の果実や野菜には異なる量のそれぞれの食物繊維が含まれている。水溶性食物繊維は液体に溶けて，消化器系の内部でゼリー状の物質を形成する食物繊維である。このゼリー状物質は身体そのものによっては吸収されず，私たちの中にいるバクテリアによって食糧として用いられる。これらのバクテリアは，消化ばかりでなく，脳の健康においても非常に重要な役割を果たしている。なぜなら，これらのバクテリアはある種の化合物を放出し，それが私たちの神経系においてシグナル伝達化学物質として働くからである。最近の証拠が示唆するところでは，水溶性食物繊維の摂取が増えると，アルツハイマー病といった脳の病気を発症するリスクが低くなる可能性がある。ものを食べるとき，私たちは自分たちが必要としているものばかりでなく，自分たちの「優秀な」腸バクテリアが必要としているもののことも考えるべきである。

　水溶性食物繊維はまた私たちが摂取する脂肪分と糖分の吸収を防いだり，遅らせたりもする。これはつまり，水溶性食物繊維をより多く摂取することによって，私たちは食事の後で大量の脂肪分と糖分が血流の中へ急に入って来ないようにすることができるということである。長期にわたる血糖の急激な増加は最終的に糖尿病を引き起こす可能性がある一方で，脂肪分とコレステロールを取りすぎると心臓病につながることもある。脂肪分と糖分の摂取量を減らすことで，体重増加は鈍化する。体重が増えすぎることはまた高血圧や関節痛を引き起こす可能性がある。水溶性食物繊維はすべての植物性食品の中に見出されるが，特にオーツ麦や豆類やニンジンの中に多く見出される。

— 英 R 47 —

一方，不溶性食物繊維は身体の中で分解されることはまったくなく，水分の中に溶けていかない。不溶性食物繊維は物理的な物質であり，私たちの消化器系を通って移動し，掃除する。この食物繊維は水分を引きつけ，消化過程の他の老廃物に固着し，最終的にトイレを使用するときに排出する老廃物を形成するのに役立つ。それは私たちが定期的にトイレを使用することを助け，胃の痛みや不快感を予防し，有害な老廃物が消化器系内にあまりにも長く留まるのを防いでくれる。不溶性食物繊維がなければ，腸がんといった消化器系のがんを発症する可能性がより高くなるだろう。こうしたがんは世界中の若者の間でも増加しつつあり，その1つの理由は私たちの食事に不溶性食物繊維が不足しているからかもしれない。不溶性食物繊維の摂取量を増やすために，私たちはナッツ類やリンゴやジャガイモといった食物を食べるべきである。リンゴやジャガイモの皮を食べることは，この種の食物繊維をさらに多く摂取することに役立つ。

　両方の種類の食物繊維の摂取量を増やすことには多くの重要な利点があるが，あまりにも摂りすぎることがもたらす悪影響もいくつかある。まず第一に，食物繊維の摂取量を急激に増やす人々はガスや胃痛に悩むことになるかもしれない。これは，消化器系内に存在しているバクテリアが食物繊維を分解するときに，ガスを生み出すからである。消化器系内のガスの圧力が痛みを伴うのかもしれない。第二に，食物繊維は水分と結合するので，十分な水分を摂らないと，脱水状態になることもある。そのせいで，定期的に老廃物を除去することが困難になりかねない。最後に，食物繊維は栄養素の吸収を鈍化させるので，食物繊維を摂取しすぎた場合，身体が必要とする栄養素を吸収できなくなる可能性がある。

　食物繊維を摂りすぎるということにリスクはあるものの，それはほとんどの人々においては発生する可能性は低い問題である。約90%の人々は十分な食物繊維を摂っていないので，一般的なアドバイスは，すべての人は果実や野菜や豆類やナッツ類の摂取量を増やすようにするということになる。

発表用スライド：

<table>
<tr><td>

食物繊維：
忘れられたヒーロー

1
</td><td>

特徴

水溶性食物繊維 | 不溶性食物繊維
- 水分に溶ける
- 　41
- 吸収されない
- バクテリアにとっての食糧

- 水分を引きつける
- 老廃物と結合する
- 消化器系を掃除する

2
</td></tr>
<tr><td>

食物繊維摂取の健康上の利益

食物繊維の摂取を推奨される量まで増加させることは 42 可能性がある。
A. 糖尿病のリスクを低下させる
B. 体重増加という結果を招く
C. 脳の病気を予防する
D. トイレを定期的に使用するようにする
E. がんを発症するリスクを減らす　3
</td><td>

食物繊維を摂りすぎることの副作用

- 　43
- 脱水症状
- 　44

4
</td></tr>
</table>

— 英 R 48 —

腸バクテリア	最終的な意見
45	46
5	6

設問解説

問1　　41　　正解 ②

「スライド2での水溶性食物繊維の2つ目の特徴は何か」　　41

① 脂肪分と糖分の吸収を高める
② **ゼリー状の物質を形成する**
③ 消化を早める
④ シグナル伝達化学物質として機能する

　正解は②。第3段落第3文（Soluble fiber is ...）で「水溶性食物繊維は液体に溶けて，消化器系の内部でゼリー状の物質を形成する」と述べられていることから，正解は②となる。

　①，③に関しては，水溶性食物繊維の特徴として本文で述べられている内容ではないので不可。④に関しては，第3段落第6文（That is because ...）において「なぜなら，これらのバクテリアはある種の化合物を放出し，それが私たちの神経系においてシグナル伝達化学物質として働くからである」で述べられているように，シグナル伝達化学物質として働くのはバクテリアが放出する化合物であり，水溶性食物繊維自体ではないことがわかるので不可。

問2　　42　　正解 ②

「スライド3であなたが見つけた間違いはどれか」　　42

① A
② **B**
③ C
④ D
⑤ E

　正解は②。第4段落（Soluble fiber also ...）では，水溶性食物繊維は脂肪分と糖分の吸収を防いだり，遅らせたりし，そのようにして脂肪分と糖分の摂取量が減れば体重増加は鈍化する，ということが述べられている。食物繊維の消費を増加させることは，脂肪分と糖分の摂取量が減ることになるので体重増加にはつながらないと判断できるので，Bが間違いで，したがって②が正解だとわかる。

　①のAに関しては，第4段落第3文（Sharp rises in ...）で糖尿病に関して「長期にわたる血糖の急激な増加は最終的に糖尿病を引き起こす可能性がある」と述べられているが，上でも触れたように，水溶性食物繊維は脂肪分と糖分の吸収を防ぎ，遅らせる働きがあるので糖尿病を引き起こす可能性が低くなると判断できるので，本文の内容に合致している。

　③のCに関しては，第3段落第7文（Recent evidence suggests ...）で「最近の証拠が示唆するところでは，水溶性食物繊維の消費が増えると，アルツハイマー病といった脳の病気を発症するリスクが低くなる可能性がある」と述べられていることから，本文の内容に合致している。

　④のDに関しては，第5段落第3文（It attracts water ...）～第4文（It helps us ...）

— 英 R 49 —

で「この食物繊維は水分を引きつけ，消化過程の他の老廃物に固着し，最終的にトイレを使用するときに排出する老廃物を形成するのに役立つ。それは私たちが定期的にトイレを使用することを助け，胃の痛みや不快感を予防し，有害な老廃物が消化器系内にあまりにも長く留まるのを防いでくれる」と述べられていることから，本文の内容に合致している。

⑤のEに関しては，第5段落第5文（Without insoluble fiber, ...）～第6文（These cancers are ...）で「不溶性食物繊維がなければ，腸がんといった消化器系のがんを発症する可能性がより高くなるだろう。こうしたがんは世界中の若者の間でも増加しつつあり，その1つの理由は私たちの食事に不溶性食物繊維が不足しているからかもしれない」と述べられていることから，本文の内容に合致している。

問3　43・44　正解②・③
「スライド4に入る2つの選択肢を選べびなさい（順番は問わない）」　43・44
① 有益な腸バクテリアの死滅
② 十分な栄養素を摂取できないこと
③ 胃の痛みや不快感
④ 老廃物内の水分が多すぎること
⑤ トイレを使用する回数が多すぎること

正解は②と③。②に関しては，第6段落最終文（Finally, because fiber ...）で「最後に，食物繊維は栄養素の吸収を鈍化させるので，食物繊維を摂取しすぎた場合，身体が必要とする栄養素を吸収できなくなる可能性がある」と述べられていることから，②が正解の1つとなることがわかる。③に関しては，第6段落第2文（First, people who ...）で「まず第一に，食物繊維の摂取量を急激に増やす人々はガスや胃痛に悩むことになるかもしれない」と述べられていることから，③がもう1つの正解となることがわかる。

①，⑤に関しては，本文で述べられている内容ではないので不可。

④に関しては，第6段落第5文（Second, because fiber ...）～第6文（This can make ...）で「第二に，食物繊維は水分と結合するので，十分な水分を摂らないと，脱水状態になることもある。そのせいで，定期的に老廃物を除去することが困難になりかねない」と述べられているが，この内容に合致しないので不可。

問4　45　正解④
「スライド5として，私たちの消化器系に存在するバクテリアについてどういったことが言えるか」　45
① 不溶性食物繊維をあまりに多く摂りすぎることはバクテリアが成長する原因となり，それが西洋諸国の若者におけるがんの発症を引き起こす可能性がある。
② 私たちが間違った種類の食物繊維を摂取しないことが重要であるのは，それがあまりに多くのバクテリアが成長し，ガスを生み出す原因になるからだ。
③ 私たちがあまりに多くの食物繊維を避けるべきであるのは，それがアルツハイマー病のような病気を引き起こすかもしれない悪いバクテリアが腸内で成長することを助長するからだ。
④ 私たちが腸バクテリアに食物繊維を与えるべきであるのは，腸バクテリアが食物を分解し，重要な化学物質を生み出すからだ。

正解は④。第3段落第3文（Soluble fiber is ...）～第6文（That is because ...）において，水溶性食物繊維はゼリー状の物質を形成し，この物質が体内のバクテリア，すなわち腸バクテリアの食糧となり，このバクテリアは私たちが食べる物の消化を助け，ある種の化合物を放出し，それが私たちの神経系においてシグナル伝達化学物質として働く，ということが述べられている。よって正解は④であるとわかる。

①，②，③に関しては，本文で述べられている内容ではないので不可。

— 英 R 50 —

問5 46 正解 ③

「スライド6に入る，最も適切な意見を選びなさい」 46

① すべての人が植物性食品の摂取を増やすべきであるが，野菜の皮は有害な食物繊維を含んでいるので，常に皮をむくべきだ。

② すべての人々が多量の食物繊維に耐えられるわけではないので，人々は食事を変える前には医者に相談するべきである。

③ ほとんどの人々は十分な食物繊維を摂取していないので，私たちは発生しうる悪影響のことは考慮せず，両方の種類の食物繊維の消費を増やすべきである。

④ 食物繊維が脳の健康を支援するということを示唆する証拠はないが，中には食物繊維が若者におけるがんのリスクを減らす可能性があると言う人々もいる。

⑤ 私たちは，水溶性食物繊維を含んでいる食品を選ぶべきであるが，健康上のリスクがあるために不溶性食物繊維を含む食品は避けるべきである。

　正解は③。第6段落第1文（Although there are ...）の前半では「両方の種類の食物繊維の摂取量を増やすことには多くの重要な利点があるが，あまりにも摂りすぎることがもたらす悪影響もいくつかある」と述べられているが，最終段落第1文（Despite the risks ...）で「食物繊維を摂りすぎるということにリスクはあるものの，それはほとんどの人々においては発生する可能性は低い問題である」と述べられていることから，この文章の最終的な意見としては③が最も適切な選択肢であると判断できる。

　①，②，④，⑤に関しては，本文で述べられている内容ではないので不可。

（主な語句・表現）

・問題冊子を参照のこと。

[リード文]
◇ presentation 名「発表」　　　◇ science class「理科の授業」

[第1段落]
(Health experts ...)
◇ dietary fiber「食物繊維」
◇ encourage O to -「O が-することを勧める［促す］」
◇ a large variety of ...「たくさんの種類の…；多種多様な…」
◇ nutrient 名「栄養物；栄養素」　　◇ vital 形「きわめて重要な；必要不可欠な」
◇ consumption 名「摂取；消費」　　◇ plant-based food「植物性食品」
◇ dairy product「乳製品」

[第2段落]
(In Western countries, ...)
◇ intake 名「摂取」　　　　　　　◇ processed food「加工食品」
◇ ingredient 名「（主に料理の）材料」　◇ ready-made food「既製食品」
◇ lead to ...「…につながる；…を引き起こす」　◇ numerous 形「多くの」

[第3段落]
(It is important ...)
◇ note that ...「…に注意する；…を覚えておく」
◇ soluble 形「水溶性の」⇔ insoluble 形「非水溶性の」
◇ dissolves in ...「…に溶ける」　　◇ liquid 名「液体」
◇ gel 名「ゼリー状の物質」　　　　◇ digestive system「消化器系」
◇ absorb 動「…を吸収する」　　　◇ bacteria 名「バクテリア；細菌」
◇ digestion 名「消化」　　　　　　◇ release 動「…を放出［排出］する」
◇ compound 名「化合物」　　　　　◇ signaling chemical「シグナル伝達化学物質」
◇ develop diseases of ...「…の病気を発症する」
◇ Alzheimer's disease「アルツハイマー病」　◇ gut bacteria「腸バクテリア；腸細菌」

[第4段落]
(Soluble fiber also ...)
◇ absorption 名「吸収」　　　　　◇ fat and sugar「脂肪分と糖分」
◇ stop O from -ing「O が-することを止める」
◇ high amounts of ...「多量の…」　◇ blood stream「血流」

— 英 R 51 —

◇ blood sugar「血糖」　　　　　　　　　◇ diabetes 名「糖尿病」
◇ high blood pressure「高血圧」　　　　◇ joint 名「関節」
◇ oats 名「オーツ麦」

[第5段落]　　　◇ break down ...「…を分解する」　　◇ physical material「物理的な物質」
(Insoluble fiber,　◇ stick to ...「…に固着する；…にくっつく」◇ waste (product)「老廃物」
on ...)　　◇ prevent O (from) -ing「O が-することを防ぐ[妨げる]」
　　　　　◇ intestinal cancer「腸がん」　　　◇ skin 名「(野菜などの) 皮；皮膚」

[第6段落]　　　◇ benefit 名「利点；利益」　　　　◇ negative effect「悪影響」
(Although there　◇ suffer from ...「…で苦しむ；…に悩む」◇ bind to ...「…と結合する」
are ...)　　◇ dehydrated 形「脱水状態の」　　◇ get rid of ...「…を除去する」

[最終段落]　　　◇ take in ...「…を摂取する」
(Despite the ...)

[設問文・選択肢]　◇ recommend…「…を推奨する」　　◇ dehydration 名「脱水 (症状)」
　　　　　◇ enhance 動「…を高める」　　　　◇ substance 名「物質」
　　　　　◇ inability to -「-することができないこと」
　　　　　◇ cause O to -「O が-する原因となる」
　　　　　◇ feed A with B「A に B〈食料・餌など〉を与える」
　　　　　◇ peel 動「… (の皮) をむく」　　　◇ harmful 形「有害な」

第2回 実戦問題 解答・解説

英語（リーディング） 第2回 （100点満点）

（解答・配点）

問題番号（配点）	設問	解答番号	正解	配点	自己採点欄
第1問（6）	1	1	③	2	
	2	2	④	2	
	3	3	③	2	
小計					
第2問（10）	1	4	①	2	
	2	5	②	2	
	3	6	①	2	
	4	7	④	2	
	5	8	④	2	
小計					
第3問（9）	1	9	②	3*	
		10	③		
		11	①		
		12	④		
	2	13	④	3	
	3	14	④	3	
小計					
第4問（12）	1	15	②	3	
	2	16	①	3	
	3	17	②	3	
	4	18	③	3	
小計					
第5問（16）	1	19	③	3	
	2	20	②	3	
	3	21	④	2	
		22	②	2	
	4	23	②	3	
	5	24	②	3	
小計					

問題番号（配点）	設問	解答番号	正解	配点	自己採点欄
第6問（18）	1	25	①	3	
	2	26	①	3	
	3	27 － 28	③ － ⑤	3*	
		29	④	3	
	4	30	①	3	
	5	31	②	3	
小計					
第7問（15）	1	32	①	3	
	2	33	④	3	
	3	34	①	3*	
		35	⑤		
		36	④		
		37	②		
	4	38 － 39	① － ③	3*	
	5	40	④	3	
小計					
第8問（14）	1	41	②	2	
	2	42 － 43	② － ④	3*	
	3	44	②	3	
	4	45	④	3	
	5	46	④	3	
小計					

（注）
1 ＊は，全部正解の場合のみ点を与える。
2 －（ハイフン）でつながれた正解は，順序を問わない。

— 英 R 54 —

第1問

解答 | 問1 - ③　　　問2 - ④　　　問3 - ③ | (各2点)

出典 | *Original Material*

全訳 |

あなたは自分の通う大学の近くにあるショッピングモールのウェブサイトを見ています。そこで，ショッピングモールが行う環境保護プログラムについての情報を見つけます。

服を再利用して，新生活を始めよう！
昔大好きだった服を，特別なクーポンに

私たちが毎日着ている服をつくるために，天然資源が多く使用されています。しかし，昨年捨てられた服の量は，アメリカだけでも1,100万トンにのぼりました。これは過去最悪の数字です！

そこで，この問題に対して私たちにできることは何でしょうか？　それは，再利用です！

私たちの取り組み

私たちの服回収計画は，ちょうど3年前に開始されました。以下のようにして参加していただくことが可能です：

1. 不要な服は，捨てるのではなく，私たち**シルバースカイモール**にお持ちください。
2. 服（ブランドや状態は問いません）をレジまでお持ちください。
   ※シルバースカイモール以外の店舗で購入されたアイテムも受け付けています。
3. 1点につき，当モールでの次のお買い物時に使える5ドルのクーポンを1枚差し上げます。（一度に3点までご持参いただけます。もしメンバーズカードをお持ちになるか，メンバーズカードにお申し込みいただければ，追加でもう1点寄付いただくことが可能です）

昨年は皆様のおかげで，1トン分の服地が回収でき，その再利用に成功しました。回収された服は，他のどなたかが再び着る場合，新しい服に作り変えられる場合，そして買い物袋や機械の部品など他の製品にリサイクルされる場合があります。

日程
4月20日土曜日～4月23日火曜日　午前9時～午後4時
　※このキャンペーンには，上記の期間中<u>おひとり様につき1回のみ</u>ご参加可能です。

特別な価格で衣服を手に入れたい？
回収された衣服の一部は，古着として5月から私たちのショッピングモールで売りに出されます。このイベントの開催中，もし品物の写真を見たい場合は，特設ウェブサイトをご覧ください。
https://silversky.trade-in.example

設問解説

問1　　1　　正解 ③

「もしメンバーズカードを持っていれば，最大で　1　分のクーポンを取得できる」

① 10 ドル
② 15 ドル
③ 20 ドル
④ 25 ドル

正解は ③。Our project の 3 の項目（We will give... ）に，「服 1 点につき 5 ドル分のクーポンがもらえる」，「一度に 3 点まで服を持ってくることが可能」，「メンバーズカードがあれば 1 点追加で持ってくることが可能」とあるため，5 ドル × 4 で 20 ドル。Date の項目に「期間中おひとり様につき 1 回のみご参加可能です」とあり，これ以上追加でクーポンを取得することはできないため，正解は ③。

問2　　2　　正解 ④

「昨年は　2　だった」

① ウェブサイト上でのクーポンの配布を開始した年
② シルバースカイモールが初めて 1,000kg を上回る不要な衣服を回収した年
③ この衣服回収計画が始まった年
④ **アメリカで捨てられた服の量が最悪だった年**

正解は ④。表の一番上の説明の第 2 文（However, last year ...）に，昨年はアメリカで 1,100 万トンの服が捨てられ，それは過去最悪だったと記述があるため，④ が正解。

ウェブサイト上でのクーポン配布については記述がないため，① は誤り。② は，「初めて」や「1,000kg を上回る」という部分が，本文の内容と合わない。この衣服回収計画は 3 年前に始まったという記述があるため ③ も誤り。

問3　　3　　正解 ③

「このプログラム中，あなたは　3　ことは<u>できない</u>」

① 他の国から購入した服を持ってくる
② どんな服が売りに出されるかをインターネットで調べる
③ **自分が売りたい服を郵送する**
④ 次にモールに来た時にクーポンを使用する

正解は ③。「売りたい服を郵送できる」という記述は本文中にないため，③ が正解。

他の場所で買った衣服を持ってきても良いと書いてあるため，① は誤り。古着として売りに出される品物はウェブサイトで写真が見られるとあるため，② は誤り。クーポンは次にモールで買い物をするときに使用できると書いてあるため，④ は誤り。

主な語句・表現

・問題冊子を参照のこと。

[リード文]
◇ environmentally-friendly 形「環境にやさしい」
◇ carry O out「O を実行する」

[本文]
◇ clothes 名「衣服」
◇ natural resource「天然資源」
◇ dump 動「…を捨てる」
◇ issue 名「問題」
◇ instead of O「O ではなく」
◇ unwanted 形「不要な」
◇ condition 名「状態」
◇ donate 動「…を寄付する」

◇ reboot 動「…を再起動する」
◇ amount 名「量」
◇ tackle 動「…に取り組む」
◇ clothing 名「衣服」
◇ throw O away「O を捨てる」
◇ turn in O「O を提出する」
◇ purchase 名「購入」 動「…を購入する」
◇ textile 名「服；布」

— 英 R 56 —

◇ garment 图 「衣服」　　　　　　　　◇ product 图 「製品」
◇ secondhand 形 「中古の」　　　　　　◇ available 形 「利用可能な」

[設問文・選択肢]　◇ distribution 图 「配布」　　　　　　◇ worst 形 「最悪の」
◇ send in 「〈郵便・メールなどで〉提出する；送る」

第２問

| 解答 | 問1 - ① | 問2 - ② | 問3 - ① | 問4 - ④ | 問5 - ④ | （各2点） |

出典   *Original Material*

全訳

あなたは生徒会のメンバーです。メンバーたちは生徒が町のごみを清掃するのを手助けするプロジェクトについて話し合ってきました。アイデアを得るため，あなたはスクール・チャレンジに関するレポートを読んでいます。それは日本のある中学校で教えている外国語指導助手が書いたものです。

クリーンアップ・チャレンジ

　町の環境美化運動に呼応して，私たちの中学校では地域清掃活動に取り組みました。私も通学路に空き瓶や紙くずなどのごみが多いと感じていたので，学校周辺の環境を改善する良い機会だと思いました。私たちがこの活動に取り組み始めたのは，生徒たちに町を清潔に保つ大切さを理解させる手助けをするためでした。合計250名の生徒が1月10日から2月10日まで毎週金曜日に参加しました。彼らは通学途中に拾ったごみを特製のビニール袋に入れて学校に持ち運びました。興味深かったのは，町の西部の生徒たちの方が他の地域の生徒たちよりも多くのごみを拾ったということでした。この原因は何だったのでしょうか？　（以下の）フィードバックに基づけば，この問いに対する答えがあるようです。

参加者からのフィードバック

AS：このプロジェクトのおかげで清掃の大切さを実感しました。道がきれいになると自分の心もきれいになるようでした。

BK：私の友人の一部は自転車で通学しているため，ごみを拾うことが難しかったようです。

SC：私はどこに多くのごみが落ちているのかに関する地図を作りました。駅からの距離とごみの量の間には，顕著な関連性はないようです。

JD：慎重にごみの分別をしました。たばこの吸い殻が一番多く，次にプラスチックごみ，紙くず，空き缶の順でした。路上でタバコを吸うことは私たちの町では禁止されているので，大変頭にきました。

ML：私たちの町の西部から通ってくる1人のクラスメートの方が私より多くのごみを拾っていました。これは，そちらの方ににぎやかな商店街があることと関係しているのかもしれません。

— 英 R 58 —

設問解説

問1　　4　　正解 ①

「クリーンアップ・チャレンジの目的は，生徒が　4　ことを手助けすることだった」
　① 清潔な環境の必要性を理解する
　② 地域社会の価値ある一員となる
　③ 地域のごみの関係性を認識する
　④ さまざまな種類のごみを理解する

　　正解は①。クリーンアップ・チャレンジに関する本文の第3文（We started this ...）に「私たちがこの活動に取り組み始めたのは，生徒たちに町を清潔に保つ大切さを理解させる手助けをするためでした」とあり，①が適切だとわかる。
　　②は文章中に記述がない。③，④はフィードバック中に該当すると考えられる記述があるが，この運動が行われた目的とは言えないため，不適切である。

問2　　5　　正解 ②

「クリーンアップ・チャレンジに関する1つの事実は　5　ということだ」
　① 冬の間に2ヵ月間行われた
　② 設定期間中に少なくとも4回行われた
　③ 生徒の大半は町の西部から来ていた
　④ 生徒は自家製の袋を使わなければならなかった

　　正解は②。クリーンアップ・チャレンジに関する本文の第4文（A total of ...）に「合計250名の生徒が1月10日から2月10日まで毎週金曜日に参加しました」とあり，この活動が1ヵ月間続き，週1回の参加で少なくとも4回は行われたことがわかるため，②が適切である。
　　①は本文内容と矛盾する。③は本文中に記述がない。④は本文中に「特製のビニール袋を使う」という記述があるが，自家製とは明示されていないため不適切である。

問3　　6　　正解 ①

「フィードバックによると，　6　は参加者によって報告された活動だった」
　A：さまざまな種類のごみを調べること
　B：ごみがどこで見つかったのか記録すること
　C：ごみを家に持ち帰ること
　D：人々に喫煙しないように注意すること

　① AとB
　② AとC
　③ AとD
　④ BとC
　⑤ BとD
　⑥ CとD

　　正解は①。フィードバック中のSCのコメントに「私はどこに多くのごみが落ちているのかに関する地図を作りました」とあり，ごみが落ちている場所に関する記録をつけていたことがわかるため，Bは適切である。また，JDのコメントに「慎重にごみの分別をしました」とあり，落ちているごみの内訳を調べたという内容があるため，Aも適切である。以上より，①AとBが正解である。
　　CとDは本文中に記述がない。

問4　　7　　正解 ④

「クリーンアップ・チャレンジに関する参加者の意見の1つは　7　ということだ」

— 英 R 59 —

① 自転車で通学する生徒にはより効率が良かった
② 生徒の多くはごみを拾うことが習慣となった
③ タバコを吸うことをできるだけ早く禁止すべきだ
④ 町がきれいになればなるほど，ますます参加者の気分も良くなった

　正解は④。フィードバック中の AS のコメントに「道がきれいになると自分の心もきれいになるようでした」とあるため，④が適切である。

　①は，BK のコメントに，自転車通学者はごみを拾うのが難しかったとあるため，不適切である。②は，本文中に記述がない。③は，JD のコメントに，路上喫煙は禁止されているとあるため，不適切である。

問5　│　8　│　正解④

　「筆者の問いは │　8　│ によって答えられている」
　　　① AS
　　　② BK
　　　③ JD
　　　④ ML
　　　⑤ SC

　正解は④。クリーンアップ・チャレンジに関する本文の第6文（What was interesting ...），第7文（What was the ...）に「興味深かったのは，町の西部の生徒たちの方が他の地域の生徒たちよりも多くのごみを拾ったということでした。この原因は何だったのでしょうか？」とあり，西部の生徒たちがより多くのごみを拾った事実に筆者は疑問を抱いている。それに対して，フィードバック中の ML のコメントに「私たちの町の西部から通ってくる1人のクラスメートの方が私より多くのごみを拾っていました。これは，そちらの方ににぎやかな商店街があることと関係しているのかもしれません」とその疑問に対する回答が述べられているため，④が適切である。

　他の選択肢はこの疑問に対して回答を述べていないため，不適切である。

| 主な語句・表現 | ・問題冊子を参照のこと。 |

[リード文]
◇ student council「生徒会」　　　　　　　◇ trash 图「ごみ；くず」
◇ assistant language teacher「外国語指導助手」

[本文]
◇ in response to ...「…に応じて」　　　　　◇ beautification 图「美化」
◇ campaign 图「運動；キャンペーン」　　　◇ work on ...「…に取り組む」
◇ litter 图「ごみ；くず」　　　　　　　　◇ empty 形「空の；中身のない」
◇ opportunity 图「機会」　　　　　　　　◇ a total of ...「総数…」
◇ participate 動「参加する」　　　　　　　◇ pick up ...「…を拾う」
◇ on one's way to ...「…に行く途中で」　　◇ plastic bag「ビニール袋」
◇ based on ...「…に基づけば」　　　　　　◇ feedback 图「反応；フィードバック；意見」

[フィードバック]
◇ thanks to ...「…のおかげで」　　　　　　◇ commute 動「通勤する；通学する」
◇ amount 图「量；総額；総計」　　　　　　◇ separate 動「…を分ける」
◇ cigarette butt「タバコの吸い殻」　　　　◇ common 形「ありふれた；よく見られる」
◇ object 图「物；物体」　　　　　　　　　◇ ..., followed by ～「…，その後に～が続く」
◇ prohibit 動「…を禁止する」　　　　　　◇ upset 形「取り乱している；腹を立てている」
◇ be related to ...「…に関係［関連］のある」
◇ busy 形「にぎやかな」

― 英 R 60 ―

第3問

解答

問1 ─ ② 9 ②. 10 ③. 11 ①. 12 ④　　　　　　　　　（完答で3点）
問2 ─ ④　　　問3 ─ ④　　　　　　　　　　　　　　　　（各3点）

出典　*Original Material*

全訳

あなたは，友人の1人が貸してくれた雑誌の中に，成功に関する以下の記事を見つけました。

ぼろから富へ

サリー・エリス

ハワード・シュルツについてあなたは聞いたことがないかもしれないが，彼が変革した会社のことはおそらく知っているだろう。1953年にニューヨークの貧しい家庭に生まれた彼の人生における第一の目標は成功してより明るい未来を築くことであり，彼は良い成績を収めようと学校で奮闘した。

シュルツは後にスポーツの天才であると判明し，またその能力ゆえに大学では学費免除を受けた。卒業後シュルツは，他の会社と並んでコーヒーメーカーを扱う小さな会社でも販売業務を行い，そこで急速に昇進した。最終的に彼は，シアトルにいくつか店舗のあるコーヒー豆の会社の広告部長になった。この小さなチェーン店の名前はと言えば，スターバックスだった。

イタリア旅行に行った際，シュルツは当地のカフェ文化に感銘を受け，人々が居心地良く集まっておしゃべりできる喫茶店を開くようスターバックスに提案した。着想が組織に合わないのではないかと最高経営者たちが疑うときでさえ，彼らはスタッフにその実行を許可する場合があった。そしてアメリカの大衆はシュルツの着想が大いに気に入ったのである。彼はそれからスターバックスから離れては戻ることを二度行い，最終的には企業の頭取となってそれをアメリカ合衆国中に広め，さらには2012年までに39ヵ国へと出店した。皮肉にも，隣接するスターバックスの店舗が互いに競合し閉店する場合もあった。ほどなくシュルツは，アメリカでトップの金持ちの1人としてフォーブズ誌に載った。

シュルツは自分の会社のトップに上りつめて以来，持てる力のすべてを良い方向へと使ってきた。そしてよく知られているようにかつてある投資家を同性婚に反対していることについて批判し，その投資家に自分の金を別の会社を後援するために使うよう提案さえした。彼は職場で決して嘘をつかないことに対して賞を与えられ，公正な商慣習に関する講座を教えるようあるアメリカの大学に招かれた。彼は環境に優しい実業界という理念を支持しており，石油やガスへの課税がより厳しくなるよう望んでいる。

— 英 R 61 —

設問解説

問1 | 9 | 正解 ②, | 10 | 正解 ③, | 11 | 正解 ①, | 12 | 正解 ④
「以下の出来事 (①～④) を起きた順に並べよ」
　① シュルツはスターバックスの頭取になった。
　② シュルツはスターバックスへの新たなビジネス形態の導入を提案した。
　③ シュルツはスターバックスで働くのをやめた。
　④ シュルツは自分の影響力を建設的に使い始めた。
　第3段落第1文 (On an Italian ...) にあるように「喫茶店を開くよう提案」した後，同段落第3文 (He then left ...) にあるように「スターバックスから離れては戻ることを二度行い」，さらに同文にあるように「最終的には企業の頭取」となってそれ以来，最終段落第1文 (Schultz has used ...) にあるように「持てる力のすべてを良い方向に使ってきた」のであるから，それぞれに対応する ②, ③, ①, ④ が，それぞれ | 9 |, | 10 |, | 11 |, | 12 | に対する正解となる。

問2 | 13 | 正解 ④
「シュルツの人生についてわかっている1つの事実は，彼が | 13 | ということである」
　① 学校で絶えず面倒を引き起こした
　② 伝統的なアメリカの慣習を好んだ
　③ 高価なエネルギー源を使用した
　④ アメリカで最も富裕な人々のうちの1人だった
　正解は ④。第3段落最終文 (Soon after, Schultz ...) に「シュルツはアメリカでトップの金持ちの1人としてフォーブズ誌に載った」という記述が見られるので，④ が正解。
　他の選択肢はいずれも，本文に書かれていない内容。

問3 | 14 | 正解 ④
「この話から，スターバックスは | 14 | ということがわかった」
　① 貧しい暮らしの人にとって利用しやすい，安く利用できる店として始まった
　② 早い時期に相当の難題に直面し，廃業しかかった
　③ 国際的なチェーン店を作り上げるために，自ら世界中のレストランからアイディアを集めた
　④ 従業員の提案に耳を傾け，新しいことを試すことを厭わなかった
　正解は ④。第3段落第2文 (Even when the ...) に「着想が組織に合わないのではないかと最高経営者が疑うときでさえ，彼ら [＝スターバックスの最高経営者たち] はスタッフにその実行を許可する場合があった」とあるため，④ が正解。
　他の選択肢はいずれも，本文に書かれていない内容。

主な語句・表現
・問題冊子を参照のこと。
[本文]
◇ rag 图「ほろ（きれ）」　　　　　　　　　◇ riches 图「富；財産」　通例複数扱いされる。
◇ most likely「たぶん；十中八九」
◇ Born into ...「…に生まれて」　分詞構文。意味上の主語である he [＝ Howard Schultz] が文の主語である his number one goal in life と一致していない点で厳密に言えば文法から外れているが，現実の英語ではそう珍しいことではない。
◇ natural 图「生来の達人；天才」　　　　　◇ free place「授業料免除の学籍」
◇ coffee-maker 图「コーヒーメーカー」　ここでは形容詞的に company を修飾している。
◇ socialize 動「うち解けて [社交的に] 交際 [おしゃべり] する」
◇ incorporate 動「…を組み入れる」　　　　◇ soon after「すぐ後に」
◇ list 動「…を名簿に載せる」
◇ Forbes Magazine「フォーブズ誌」　アメリカの経済雑誌。

— 英 R 62 —

◇ famously 圖「よく知られているように」　◇ criticize O for ...「O を…のことで批判する」
◇ gay marriage「同性愛［間］結婚」
◇ even suggesting ...「…と提案しさえして」　分詞構文。
◇ boost 動「…を後援［宣伝］する」　　　◇ business practice「商慣習」
◇ concept 名「概念；（基本）理念」　　　◇ harshly 圖「厳しく」

[設問文・選択肢]　◇ constructively 圖「建設的に」
◇ accessible to ...「…にとって利用［入手］しやすい」
◇ in poverty「貧困のうちに」　　　　　　◇ early on「早い時期［段階］に」
◇ go out of business「廃業する」

第4問

| 解答 | 問1 − ② 　　問2 − ① 　　問3 − ② 　　問4 − ③ 　　　　　　　　（各3点） |

出典　*Original Material*

全訳

英語の授業であなたは関心のある環境問題についてのエッセイを書いています。これが最も新しい草稿です。あなたは今,先生からのコメントに基づいて,修正に取り組んでいます。

紙の使用を減らすこと	コメント
2021年,世界中の人々は4億1,700万トンの紙を使用しました。これほどの多量の紙を生産することは,森林伐採やエネルギーと水の使用や汚染を含め,環境に大きな影響を及ぼします。(1)<u>対照的に</u>,紙はゴミの埋立地におけるすべての廃棄物の約26％を構成しています。こうした紙の廃棄物の多くは仕事場で生み出されていますが,私たちは日常生活の中で紙の使用を減らす努力をすることもできます。 　第一に,私たちは使い捨てのペーパータオルやティッシュの使用を減らすべきです。多くの人たちが使い捨てのペーパータオルやティッシュを使って家を掃除しています。これはとりわけ,特にこぼれた液体を掃除するときに,台所において言えることです。(2)∧ 可能なところはどこででも,ペーパータオルを使わずにこうしたことを行うべきです。 　第二に,(3)<u>みなさんは読書をたくさんするでしょうか？</u>　アメリカの出版業界は,本を生産するために1年に約3,200万本の木を使用しています。再生紙の使用を増やすことがこの業界の責任なのですが,本を買う代わりに図書館から本を借りることによって,あるいは印刷された本ではなく電子書籍を購入することによって,みなさんも貢献することができます。 　最後に,請求書や銀行取引明細書をデジタル版に変えるべきです。最近まで,ほとんどの家庭は紙の請求書を受け取っていましたが,それは紙を浪費するばかりでなく,配達する間にエネルギーを使用してもいます。請求書や銀行情報をオンラインで入手することで,紙と時間とエネルギーを節約することができます。 　結論として,紙を節約するためにできることはたくさんあります。私たちは,使い捨ての紙製品に対する依存を減らし,本の消費の仕方を変えることができます (4)∧ 。そうしたことをすることで,私たちは環境保護を助けることができるのです。	(1) ここには間違った表現が使用されました。変更してください。 (2) 重要な1文が欠けています。あなたは私たちが何をすることを推奨しているのですか。 (3) 主題文の文体を変更してください。 (4) ここで3番目のポイントを要約してください。
先生のコメント 大変努力しましたね！　私もそうしたことのいくつかを行った方がいいでしょう。☺	

— 英 R 64 —

設問解説

問1　15　正解②

「コメント(1)に基づくと，使用した表現に取って代わる最もよい表現はどれか」　15
- ①　結果として
- **②　加えて**
- ③　言い換えれば
- ④　一方

　正解は②。下線部(1)の直前では，多量の紙を使用することによる，森林伐採・エネルギーと水の使用・汚染といった環境に及ぼされる悪影響が言及され，下線部(1)の直後でも，紙がゴミの埋立地における廃棄物の約 26 ％を構成しているという，廃棄物となった紙の好ましからぬ面，言い換えれば悪影響が言及されている。つまり，下線部(1)の前後の内容はともに紙のもたらす悪影響であることから，「対比対照」ではなく「添加」の関係にあると判断できる。よって正解は②の「加えて」となる。

　①，③，④はいずれも自然な文脈とはならないので不可。

問2　16　正解①

「コメント(2)に基づくと，追加するのに最もよい文は何か」　16
- **①　しかし，この仕事は再利用できるものを使って行うことができるでしょう。**
- ②　私はより品質の良いタオルを使うことが重要だと考えます。
- ③　台所で飲み物をこぼすのを避けることが重要です。
- ④　したがって，家庭では一層気をつけるべきです。

　正解は①。第1段落では，環境保護のために日常生活の中で紙の使用を減らすことが可能である，と述べられ，その第1の方法として，第2段落の(2)の前では，使い捨てのペーパータオルやティッシュの使用を減らすべきであるという提案がなされている。さらに(2)の後では，第1の方法に代わるものとしてペーパータオルを使わずにこうしたこと［掃除をすること］を行うべきであるという提案がなされている。したがって，(2)に，使い捨てのペーパータオル以外のもの，すなわち再利用できるものを使うことができるという内容が入れば，筆者が推奨していることを表す文になる。よって正解は①となる。

　②，③，④はいずれも自然な文脈とはならないので不可。

問3　17　正解②

「コメント(3)によれば，どんな表現を疑問文と取り替えるべきか」　17
- ①　紙の使用量が少ない本を購入するべきです
- **②　本を読む方法を変えるべきです**
- ③　捨てる本の数を減らすべきです
- ④　読む本の数を減らすことについて考えるべきです

　正解は②。下線部(3)の2文後では「再生紙の使用を増やすことがこの業界の責任なのですが，本を買う代わりに図書館から本を借りることによって，あるいは印刷された本ではなく電子書籍を購入することによって，みなさんも貢献することができます」と述べられているが，それは本を読む方法を変えることによって私たちも紙の使用を減らすことに貢献できることを意味していると判断できる。よって，下線部(3)を②の「本を読む方法を変えるべきです」にすれば疑問文を肯定文の文体に変えてこの段落の主題を表現できる。

　①，③，④はいずれもこの段落で述べられている内容ではないので不可。

問4　18　正解③

「コメント(4)に基づくと，どの表現を追加するべきか」　18
- ①　そして手紙を配達してもらうことを避けます
- ②　そして利用する銀行を変えます

— 英 R 65 —

③　そして請求書をデジタル方式で配信してもらう
　　④　そして消費するエネルギーを減らす

　正解は③。コメント(4)には「ここで3番目のポイントを要約してください」とある。(4)を含む段落の前までの段落構成は以下のようになっている（カッコ内の数字は段落番号を表す）。

　　[1]　主題　「日常生活の中で紙の消費を減らすことができる」
　　[2]　例示1「使い捨ての清掃用品の使用量を減らしたり，そうしたものを使わないこと」
　　[3]　例示2「読書の仕方を変えること」
　　[4]　例示3「請求書や銀行明細書をデジタル版に変えること」

　以上から，この文章全体の主題である「紙の消費量を減らすこと」における3番目のポイントは第4段落の内容である「請求書や銀行明細書をデジタル版に変えること」であるとわかる。したがって，正解は③となる。
　①，②，④はいずれも第4段落の内容とはなっていないので不可。

主な語句・表現
・問題冊子を参照のこと。

[リード文]
◇ draft 名「草稿；下書き」　　　　　◇ work on ...「…に取り組む」
◇ revision 名「修正」　　　　　　　◇ based on ...「…に基づいて [た]」

[第1段落]
(In 2021, people ...)
◇ major 形「大きな；重大な」　　　◇ effect 名「影響」
◇ including ...「…を含めて」　　　　◇ deforestation 名「（森林の）伐採」
◇ in contrast「対照的に」　　　　　◇ make up ...「…を構成する」
◇ landfill site「（ゴミの）埋立地」

[第2段落]
(First, we should ...)
◇ disposal 形「使い捨ての」　　　　◇ single-use 形「1回使用の；使い捨ての」
◇ spilled 形「こぼれた」　　　　　　◇ liquid 名「液体」
◇ wherever possible「可能なところはどこででも」

[第3段落]
(Second, (3)do ...)
◇ publishing industry「出版業界」　◇ recycled paper「再生紙」
◇ purchase 動「…を購入する」　　　◇ electronic book「電子書籍」

[第4段落]
(Finally, we should ...)
◇ bill 名「請求書」　　　　　　　　◇ bank statement「銀行取引明細書」
◇ delivery 名「配達；配送」　　　　◇ access 動「…を入手する」
◇ bank information「銀行情報」

[最終段落]
(In conclusion, there ...)
◇ in conclusion「結論として」　　　◇ reliance on ...「…への依存」
◇ consume 動「…を消費する」

[コメント]
◇ recommend 動「推奨する；勧める」　◇ style 名「文体」
◇ topic sentence「主題文」　　　　　◇ summarize 動「…を要約する」

[設問文・選択肢]
◇ replace 動「…に取って代わる」　　◇ reusable 名「再利用できるもの」
◇ avoid － ing「－することを避ける」　◇ spill 動「…をこぼす」
◇ much more careful「一層気をつける[注意する]」　much は直後の比較級を強調している。
◇ replace A with B「A を B に取り替える」
◇ having letters delivered「手紙を配達してもらうこと」　have O p.p.「O を…してもらう；O を…される」
◇ digitally 形「デジタル方式で」

第5問

解答

問1 − ③　　問2 − ②　　　　　　　　　　　　　　　　　　（各3点）
問3　21 − ④　　22 − ②　　　　　　　　　　　　　　　　　（各2点）
問4 − ②　　問5 − ②　　　　　　　　　　　　　　　　　　（各3点）

出典　*Original Material*

全訳

あなたは先生から効果的な読書法についての発表をするように言われ，2つの記事を読んでいて，学んだことを次の授業で発表しようと考えています。

役に立つ習慣：再読
ジェームズ・キング
マウントシティ中学校図書館司書

　再読とは，本や記事や何であれ書かれたものを，すでに一度読んだ後でもう一度読むことだ。文章をより深く理解したい，記憶をよみがえらせたい，単に好きな本をもう一度読みたいといった読者たちの間では，一般的な習慣である。再読は，言語学習者にとっても有益だ。文章を再読することで，学習者は語彙力，理解力，流暢さを向上させることができる。また，試験勉強や論文執筆，プレゼンテーションの準備など，学術的・職業的な目的を達する手段としても再読は利用できる。

　文章を再読すると，読者は最初に読んだときに見落としたことに気づくかもしれない。これは，再読によって，読者が筋書きや全体的な構造ではなく，文章の細部に集中できるようになるからだ。読者は以前は明らかではなかった新たな理解やつながり，意味を見つけるかもしれない。さらに，再読することで，読者が最初に読んだときにははっきりしなかったパターンやテーマがわかることも多い。このようにして，文章を分析し，自分なりの意見や解釈を形成することで，読者は批判的思考力を養うこともできる。

　しかし，再読にはデメリットもある。特に長い文章の場合，多くの時間が必要となる。また，能動的でないため，単調になったり，退屈になったりすることもある。その上，グラフが示すように，再読は必ずしも頻度に比例して効果を発揮するわけではない。

　結論として，再読は必ずしも必要ではないし，効果的でないかもしれないが，読者が文章をより深く理解し，言語能力を向上させ，批判的思考能力を開発するのに役立つ習慣である。

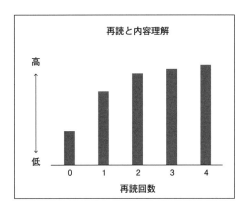

効果的な読書戦略：インタラクティブ・リーディング

エリック・ブライアー

マウントシティ大学教授

　インタラクティブ・リーディングは，積極的な参加と対話を通してテキストに取り組むプロセスのことをいう。ページ上の言葉をただ読むだけの受動的な読書とは異なり，インタラクティブ・リーディングでは，読者が批判的に考え，質問し，読むものとのつながりを形成することが求められる。

　インタラクティブに読むためには，偏見のない好奇心旺盛な精神で文章に向かう必要がある。提示された情報をただ受け入れるのではなく，読者は積極的にその情報を理解し，解釈しようとしなければならない。このようなことには，質問をしたり，予測を立てたり，読むものを自分の経験や知識と結びつけたりすることが必要だ。

　インタラクティブ・リーディングをするための効果的な方法の1つに，下の例のようなアノテーション（印やメモをつけること）がある。そうすることで，読者はその内容をよりよく記憶し，より深く関わり合うことができる。また，アノテーションを行うことで，読者が文章中の重要なテーマやアイデアを特定することも助長され，理解度を高めることができる。

アノテーションの例

目立たせる：	重要な部分にカラーペンで印をつける
下線を引く：	重要な単語やフレーズの下に線を引く
余白ノート：	文章中にコメントや質問を書き込む
付箋：	小さなメモを貼る

　インタラクティブ・リーディングのもう1つの方法は，読書クラブ，教室での議論，友人との日常的な会話などを含む，他者との議論を通じて行うことだ。他の人と文章について話し合うことで，読者は新しい視点や洞察を得ることができ，また読むものへの自分自身の理解を深めることができる。

　しかし，インタラクティブ・リーディングにはいくつかのデメリットもある。1つ目に，特に議論や活動が広範囲に及ぶ場合，多くの時間を要する。これは，スケジュールが多忙な人や時間の限られた人には好ましくない。2つ目に，インタラクティブ・リーディングは，テキストから議論や活動に焦点を移すことが多いため，読書プロセスそのものに対して注意が散漫になる可能性もある。最後に，テキストの解釈や分析が，集団の意見や見解に影響される可能性があり，個人の理解や批判的思考を制限する可能性がある。

設問解説

問1　19　正解 ③

「キングは　19　と考えている」

① 一読して理解することが重要である

② 本を読むと現実に引き戻される

③ 繰り返し読むことで文章への理解を深めることができる

④ 同じ文章を読み返すのはとてもわくわくする

　正解は③。キングは自身のレポートの第1段落から第2段落までで，再読することの利点について述べ，第3段落では再読の欠点を述べてはいるが，最終段落は，「再読は必ずしも必要ではないし，効果的でもないかもしれないが，読者が文章をより深く理解し，言語能力を向上させ，批判的思考能力を開発するのに役立つ習慣である」と結論づけているので，再読つまり繰り返し読むことで理解が深まるという内容の③が正解となる。

①は再読を評価するキングの立場に矛盾している。②のようなことはキングのレポートでは述べられていない。④は第3段落第3文（It can also ...）に「単調になったり，退屈になったりすることもある」と述べられているのと矛盾する。

問2 　20 　正解②
「ブライアーが提唱する読書法においては，読者は 　20 　ことができる」
　　①　情報をありのままに受け止める
　　②　新しいものの見方を得る
　　③　言語能力を向上させる
　　④　文章をより速く理解する
　正解は②。ブライアーは自身のレポートの第4段落最終文（By discussing the ...）で，「読者は新しい視点や洞察を得ることができ」と述べており，これと合致する②が正解となる。
　①は第2段落第2文（Rather than simply ...）に「提示された情報をただ受け入れるのではなく」とあるのと矛盾する。③はキングのレポートの第1段落第4文（By rereading a ...）に記述されている内容であり，ブライアーの提唱する読書法に関することではない。④は，ブライアーのレポートの最終段落第2文（Firstly, it takes ...）に「多くの時間を要する」とあるのと矛盾する。

問3 　21 　正解④　　22 　正解②
「いずれの読書法にも，それぞれ欠点がある。キングは，再読はあまり 　21 　ない傾向があると言い，その一方でブライアーは，インタラクティブ・リーディングの1つの欠点として，他人の見解が読者の 　22 　思考に影響する可能性があると言う。（それぞれの空所に，選択肢①～⑥の中から最適なものを1つずつ選びなさい）」
　　①　学術的
　　②　批判的
　　③　広範囲
　　④　興味深く
　　⑤　論理的
　　⑥　積極的
　正解は 　21 　が④， 　22 　が②。キングが再読の欠点として挙げていることはキングのレポートの第3段落にあり，「時間を要すること」，「単調で退屈であること」そして「再読回数に比例して効果があるわけではないこと」が述べられている。よって 　21 　は④に決まる。一方ブライアーがインタラクティブ・リーディングの欠点として挙げていることは，ブライアーのレポートの最終段落に「長時間を要すること」，「読書そのものへの集中力が削がれること」そして「他人の意見や考えに左右され，理解や批判的思考が制限されることがあること」が述べられている。よって 　22 　は②に決まる。

問4 　23 　正解②
「両筆者とも，効果的な読書には 　23 　が必要であることに同意している」
　　①　競争的な環境
　　②　かなりの時間
　　③　高い知性
　　④　個人の情報
　正解は②。前問の解説にもあるように，キングは自身のレポートの第3段落第2文（It is time-consuming ...）で再読には時間がかかるということを述べ，ブライアーは自身のレポートの最終段落第2文（Firstly, it takes ...）でインタラクティブ・リーディングは多くの時間がかかると述べていることから正解は②となる。

— 英 R 69 —

問5 24 正解 ②

「インタラクティブ・リーディングに関するブライアーの主張をさらに支持するのに最適な追加情報はどれか」 24

① 1冊の本からできるだけ多くの情報を吸収する方法
② 読書中にアノテーションを行う最も効果的な方法
③ 同じ本を読み返さない人が多い理由
④ ディベートスキルは人生にとって重要かどうか

正解は ②。ブライアーは自身のレポートの最終段落においてインタラクティブ・リーディングの欠点について述べてレポートを終えているが，ブライアーのレポートの表題にもあるとおり，ブライアーはインタラクティブ・リーディングに関して，効果的な読書戦略であると評価している。よって「ブライアーの主張をさらに支持する」のに必要な情報は，ブライアーがインタラクティブ・リーディングを行うためにするべきことの1つとしてアノテーションを挙げていることを考慮すると，選択肢の中では ② の「アノテーションを行う最も効果的な方法」を加えれば良いとわかる。

① に関しては多くの情報を吸収することがインタラクティブ・リーディングの目的や効果であるとは本文中に述べられてはいないので不適切。③ はキングのレポートに関する内容である。④ はブライアーのレポートの第4段落には他人と文章について議論するという内容は出てくるが，これはディベートスキルについて述べているわけではないので不適切である。

主な語句・表現

・問題冊子を参照のこと。

[リード文]
◇ presentation 名「発表；プレゼンテーション」
◇ effective 形「効果的な」　　　　　　　　◇ present 動「…を提示する」

[キングのレポート]
[第1段落]
◇ practice 名「行為；やること；習慣」　　◇ reread 動「…を再読する」
◇ article 名「記事」　　　　　　　　　　◇ common 形「普通の」
◇ refresh 動「…をよみがえらせる」　　　　◇ beneficial 形「利益がある」
◇ improve 動「…を改善する」　　　　　　◇ vocabulary 名「語彙」
◇ comprehension 名「理解」　　　　　　　◇ fluency 名「流暢さ」
◇ tool 名「道具」　　　　　　　　　　　◇ academic 形「学術的な」
◇ paper 名「論文；レポート」

[第2段落]
◇ miss 動「…を見逃す」
◇ allow O to − 「O が−することを可能にする」
◇ focus on ...「…に集中する」　　　　　◇ detail 名「詳細」
◇ plot 名「筋書き」　　　　　　　　　　◇ overall 形「全体の」
◇ structure 名「構造」　　　　　　　　　◇ insight 名「深く正しい理解；洞察」
◇ apparent 形「明らかな」　　　　　　　◇ additionally 副「それに加えて」
◇ identify 動「…の正体を明らかにする」　◇ theme 名「テーマ」
◇ obvious 形「明らかな」　　　　　　　　◇ initial 形「最初の」
◇ critical 形「批判的な」　　　　　　　　◇ analyze 動「…を分析する」
◇ interpretation 名「解釈」

[第3段落]
◇ time-consuming 形「時間を消費する」　◇ monotonous 形「単調な」
◇ boring 形「つまらない」
◇ not necessarily「必ずしも…とは限らない」　部分否定。
◇ proportion 名「割合」　　　　　　　　◇ frequency 名「頻度」

— 英 R 70 —

[最終段落]　◇ in conclusion「結論として」

[ブライアーのレポート]

[第1段落]
◇ interactive 形「相互の」　　　　　　◇ refer to ...「…に言及する」
◇ engage 動「関わる；携わる」　　　　◇ participation 名「参加」
◇ dialogue 名「対話」　　　　　　　　◇ unlike 前「…とは違って」
◇ passive 形「受動的な；消極的な」
◇ consume 動「…を消費する」　この箇所では「読む」くらいの意味。
◇ critically 副「批判的に」　　　　　　◇ material 名「題材；素材」

[第2段落]
◇ approach 動「…に向かう；…に取り組む」◇ open 形「偏見のない」
◇ curious 形「好奇心旺盛な」
◇ information presented「提示された情報」　presented は過去分詞で，information を修飾
　している。
◇ seek to −「−しようとする」　　　　◇ involve 動「…に関わる」
◇ prediction 名「予想」

[第3段落]
◇ annotation 名「注釈をつけること」　◇ aid 動「一助となる」
◇ highlight 動「強調する」　　　　　　◇ beneath 前「…の下に」
◇ margin 名「余白」　　　　　　　　　◇ sticky 形「貼り付く」
◇ attach 動「…を貼り付ける」

[第4段落]
◇ informal 形「非公式な；日常の」　　◇ perspective 名「ものの見方」
◇ ～ as well as ...「…と同様に～」　　◇ reinforce 動「…を強化する」

[最終段落]
◇ disadvantage 名「欠点」　　　　　　◇ extensive 形「広い」
◇ favorable 形「好ましい」　　　　　　◇ schedule 名「スケジュール」
◇ distracting 形「気を逸らすような」
◇ shift away ... / shift ... away「…を遠ざける」
◇ analysis 名「分析」

[設問文・選択肢]
◇ repetition 名「繰り返し」　　　　　　◇ deepen 動「…を深める」
◇ method 名「方法論」　　　　　　　　◇ affect 動「…に影響する」
◇ logical 形「論理的な」　　　　　　　◇ competitive 形「競争の」
◇ considerable 形「かなりの」　　　　　◇ intelligence 名「知性」
◇ additional 形「追加の；さらなる」　　◇ further 副「さらに」
◇ argument 名「主張」　　　　　　　　◇ absorb 動「…を吸収する」
◇ whether or not ...「…かどうか」

第6問

解答

問1 - ① 問2 - ①	（各3点）
問3 - 27 ・ 28 - ③・⑤	（順不同・両方正解で3点）
29 - ④	（3点）
問4 - ① 問5 - ②	（各3点）

出典 *Original Material*

全訳

あなたは高校生がアルバイトをすることを許されるべきかどうかについてのエッセイに取り組んでいます。以下の各ステップに従っていきます。

ステップ1：働いている学生に関するさまざまな見解を読んで理解する。
ステップ2：高校生がアルバイトをすることを許されるべきかどうかについての判断を下す。
ステップ3：追加の情報源を使って，エッセイの概要を作成する。

［ステップ1］さまざまな情報源を読む

筆者A（教師）

私が受け持つ高校のクラスの生徒の何人かが今アルバイトをしています。レストランで働いている者もいれば，カフェで働く者も，またある生徒はコンビニエンスストアで働いています。確かに，彼らは実世界に関していくつかの重要な教訓を学ぶことはできますが，私は彼らの健康を心配しています。彼らはいったんお金を稼ぎ始めると，さらに多くのお金を稼ぐためにより多くの時間をかけようとし，これが彼らの睡眠に影響を及ぼします。1日の間に，学生が働き，勉強し，遊び，休息を取るための十分な時間はないのです。

筆者B（親）

私の息子は去年，カフェで働いていましたが，私は彼に仕事をやめるよう求めざるを得ませんでした。初め私は，彼がたくさんの交代勤務時間を引き受け，たくさんのお金を稼ぐことをとても誇らしく思っていましたが，彼は非常にストレスを受けるようになりました。息子は医科大学の入試に合格しようと努力していましたが，自分がしなければならない仕事量を少なく見積りすぎていました。勉強と仕事を両立させることは彼には不可能でした。私は，彼の妹が高校時代にアルバイトをすることは許可しないでしょう。

筆者C（レストラン経営者）

私は自分のレストランで高校生を何人か雇っています。私は彼らをスタッフの重要なメンバーとして評価しています。彼らは熱心にそして進んで学び，また一生懸命に仕事をしています。私は，若い年から仕事をすることは彼らに責任というものを教えてきたと思っています。私は若い従業員たちが責任ある大人に成長するのを見てきました。働いていない学生は私には子どもっぽく見えます。私も若い年から働き，それは私が実業家として成功することに役立ちました。すべての人たちが学業に関わる環境で成功する能力を望んでいたり，持っていたりするわけではないので，私は高校生が仕事の世界に入っていく機会を持つことは大事であると思うのです。

— 英 R 72 —

筆者 D（警官）

私にはなぜ高校生が働きたいのかがわかります。彼らは，友人たちと付き合うためにお金を稼ぎ始めたいと思っているのです。また，社会がどのように機能しているのかを学ぶことはよいことだと私は信じています。一方，私は安全性については心配しています。多くの若者は仕事場での交代勤務時間が終わった後，夜遅く歩いて帰宅しなければなりません。私は，大変な１日の後であまりに疲れすぎていて集中できなくなっている学生を巻き込んだ車や自転車の事故を数多く見てきました。私は自分の子どもには高校を卒業して大学生になるまでは働くことを禁じています。

筆者 E（学生）

私はずっと内気な人間でしたが，私の両親が私に自宅近くのスーパーマーケットで働き始めることを勧めてくれました。私が働くのは週末だけですが，すでに寡黙ではなくなり，より自信を持つようになりました。私はあらゆる年代の，そしてあらゆる背景を持ったお客さんや同僚たちと話さなければならないので，この仕事のおかげでよりうまくコミュニケーションを取り，より責任のある人間になれたと思います。また何とか 2,000 ドルを越すお金を貯めることができ，私はそれを来年大学の授業料を支払うために使うつもりです。

設 問 解 説

問 1　　25　　正解 ①

「筆者 A と D は両者とも　25　と言及している」

① アルバイトは学生に実世界を経験する機会を与える

② 学生は若い年から労働とお金の価値について学ぶ必要がある

③ 彼らは自分の子どもたちが放課後にアルバイトの仕事をすることを許していない

④ アルバイトの仕事をすることは高校生にとって動機を向上させる

　　正解は ①。教師である筆者 A は第 3 文（Certainly, they can ...）で「確かに，彼ら［アルバイトをする高校生］は実世界に関していくつかの重要な教訓を学ぶことはできますが，私は彼らの健康を心配しています」と述べ，警官である筆者 D は高校生がアルバイトをするよい点として第 3 文（I also believe ...）で「また，社会がどのように機能しているのかを学ぶことはよいことだと私は信じています」と述べている。以上から，筆者 A と D は両者とも「アルバイトは学生に実世界を経験する機会を与える」ことに言及していることがわかるので，正解は ① となる。

　　②，④ に関しては，いずれも筆者 A と D が言及している内容ではないので不可。

　　③ に関しては，筆者 D は最終文（I have forbidden ...）で「私は自分の子どもには高校を卒業して大学生になるまでは働くことを禁じています」と言及しているものの，筆者 A は言及していないので不可。

問 2　　26　　正解 ①

「筆者 C は　26　と言っている」

① アルバイトは，勉強が得意でない学生にとっては特に有益な経験である

② 高校生は安く使える従業員なので，彼は自分のレストランでは高校生を雇おうとしている

③ 高校生はあまりに若く経験も乏しいので，貴重な従業員にはなれない

④ 学生が若い年で働き始めるならば，実業家になる可能性がより高くなる

　　正解は ①。レストラン経営者である筆者 C は最終文（Not all people ...）で「すべての人たちが学業に関わる環境で成功する能力を望んでいたり，持っていたりするわけではないので，私は高校生が仕事の世界に入っていく機会を持つことは大事であると思うのです」と述べているが，これは人々の中には学業で成功する能力を望んでいたり持っていたりするわけではない者たち，すなわち勉強が得意でない学生たちもいて，そういった学生［高

— 英 R 73 —

校生〕にとって「仕事の世界に入っていく機会を持つことは大事である」，言い換えれば「アルバイトは特に有益な経験である」ということを意味しているので，正解は①とわかる。
②，③，④はいずれも筆者Cが述べている内容となっていないので不可。

［ステップ2〕判断を下す
問3　　27　・　28　　正解③・⑤　　29　　正解④
「さまざまな見解を理解したので，高校生がアルバイトをすることを許可することに関して判断を下し，それを以下のように書き出した。　27　，　28　，　29　を完成させるのにもっとも適切な選択肢を選びなさい」

あなたの判断：高校生はアルバイトの仕事をすることを許されるべきだ。
・　筆者　27　と　28　があなたの判断を支持している。
・　その2人の筆者の主要な論拠：　29　

　　27　と　28　に入る選択肢（順序は問わない）
①　A
②　B
③　C
④　D
⑤　E

正解は③と⑤。レストラン経営者である筆者Cは最終文（Not all people ...）の後半で「私は高校生が仕事の世界に入っていく機会を持つことは大事であると思うのです」と述べている。また学生である筆者Eは両親の勧めでアルバイトを始めたが，それが自分の性格や将来にとって有益であるとわかったことを第3文(I have to ...)〜最終文(I have also ...)で「私はあらゆる年代の，そしてあらゆる背景を持ったお客さんや同僚たちと話さなければならないので，この仕事のおかげでよりうまくコミュニケーションを取り，より責任のある人間になれたと思います。また何とか2,000ドルを越すお金を貯めることができ，私はそれを来年大学の授業料を支払うために使うつもりです」と述べていることから，筆者CとEは「高校生はアルバイトの仕事をすることを許されるべきだ」という判断を支持する意見を述べていることがわかる。よって　27　と　28　には③と⑤が入るとわかる。

　　29　に入る選択肢
①　できる限り早くお金を稼いで貯め始めることは学生にとって重要である
②　コミュニケーション能力を向上させる方法の1つは，ずっと年上の人たちと一緒に働くことである
③　カフェやレストランやスーパーマーケットで働くことは新しい友人を作るよい方法である
④　若い年から働くことは，それが責任というものを教えてくれるので，貴重な経験である

正解は④。筆者Cは第4文（I think working ...）で「私は，若い年から仕事をすることは彼らに責任というものを教えてきたと思っています」と述べ，筆者Eは上でも触れたように第3文（I have to ...）の後半で「この仕事のおかげでよりうまくコミュニケーションを取り，より責任のある人間になれたと思います」と述べていることから，あなたの判断を支持している筆者CとEの論拠は選択肢④の「若い年から働くことは，それが責任というものを教えてくれるので，貴重な経験である」ということであるとわかる。

— 英 R 74 —

(全訳)

[ステップ3] 情報源AとBを使って，概要を作成する
あなたのエッセイの概要：

> **高校生はアルバイトをすることを許されるべきだ**
>
> **序論**
> 学校の勉強は高校生にとってきわめて重要である。しかし，高校生にとってアルバイトをすることには多くの有益な側面がある。
>
> **本論**
> 　理由1：[ステップ2から]
> 　理由2：[情報源Aに基づく] …… 30
> 　理由3：[情報源Bに基づく] …… 31
>
> **結論**
> 要するに，高校生はアルバイトをすることを許されるべきである。

情報源A
多くの若い大学卒業生が適した仕事をすぐに見つけることに苦労している1つの理由は，多くの仕事が数年間の労働経験を要求しているということである。しかし，それがまさに新たに卒業する者たちに欠けているものなのである。人気のある就職のウェブサイトに列挙されている仕事に関する最近の調査が示すところでは，初歩的な仕事の35％が少なくとも3年間の関係のある労働経験を要求するものであった。それらは技術的な，あるいは専門的な仕事ではなく，技術をほとんど要しない仕事である。多くの有能な若者が労働市場に参加することを妨げているのは，この要件なのである。不況の時代においては，あるいは競争の激しい市場で仕事を志望するときには，数年の仕事の経験が影響する可能性がある。そういうわけで，教師と親は10代の若者たちにできるだけ早い時期にいくらかの仕事を引き受けるよう勧めるべきなのである。特にコミュニケーションと顧客に対するサービスの能力は雇用者が好意的に受け止めるので，お客さんと面と向かう役割を担うアルバイトは理想的である。

情報源B
ある研究によって，高校生にアルバイトをさせることは彼らが犯罪を犯す可能性に影響を及ぼすことがわかった。貧しく犯罪の多い地域の学生が無作為に選ばれ，仕事を与えられた。以下のグラフはこの計画の間とその後における暴力犯罪と窃盗のために逮捕された数の変化を示している。

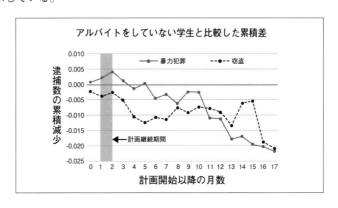

設問解説

問4 | 30 | 正解 ①

「情報源 A に基づけば，以下のどれが理由2としてもっとも適切か」 | 30 |

① 高校生としてのアルバイトは，大学卒業後においてさえ労働市場において若者を有利にする。

② 大学卒業生の初歩的仕事は，高校生の間に顧客サービスの仕事をしていた者たちだけを採用する。

③ 専門的な職業における仕事に就く卒業生は，高校生時代に働いていた可能性がより高くなっている。

④ 高校で何らかの種類の仕事の経験を持っていた場合，学生が大学で成功する可能性はより高くなる。

正解は ①。情報源 A の第 1 文（One reason why ...）では「多くの若い大学卒業生が適した仕事をすぐに見つけることに苦労している 1 つの理由は，多くの仕事が数年間の労働経験を要求しているということである」と述べられ，そうした労働経験を積む有効な手段として第 7 文（This is why ...）で「そういうわけで，教師と親は 10 代の若者たちにできるだけ早い時期にいくらかの仕事を引き受けるよう勧めるべきなのである」と提言されている。10 代の若者たちができるだけ早い時期に引き受ける仕事が高校生のアルバイトであり，それが大学卒業生が仕事を見つけることにおいて有利に働くことになると判断できるので，正解は ① となる。

②，③，④ に関しては，情報源 A で述べられている内容ではないので不可。

問5 | 31 | 正解 ②

「理由3として，あなたは『アルバイトをすることは若者の犯罪状況を改善する可能性がある』と書くことにした。情報源 B に基づけば，どの選択肢がこの記述をもっともよく支持しているか」 | 31 |

① 窃盗と暴力犯罪の両方における逮捕は，働いている間にはわずかに増加するが，犯罪率は 1 年後に改善し始める。

② アルバイトを終えた後でさえ，雇用を受けた学生は暴力犯罪と窃盗の両方において逮捕される可能性がより低くなっていた。

③ 働いている間に両方の種類の犯罪は減少するが，窃盗における逮捕はアルバイトが終わった時に増加し始める。

④ アルバイトは暴力犯罪を劇的に減らすことがあるが，窃盗は影響を受けない。

正解は ②。情報源 B のグラフより，「計画継続期間」が過ぎた後でも，暴力犯罪と窃盗における逮捕数が減少していることがわかるので，正解は ② ということになる。

① に関しては，グラフは「犯罪率は（計画継続期間の）1 年後に低下し始める」ことを示していないので不可。

③ に関しては，グラフは，計画継続期間に両方の犯罪が減少することも，その後に窃盗における逮捕が増加し始めることも示してはいないので不可。

④ に関しては，グラフは窃盗が影響を受けないことを示してはいないので不可。

主な語句・表現

・問題冊子を参照のこと。

[リード文]
◇ work on ...「…に取り組む」
◇ allow [permit] O to −「O が−することを許す」
◇ part-time job「アルバイト」
◇ take a position about ...「…についての判断を下す」
◇ outline 图「概要」

[ステップ1]

◇ pick up ...「…を手に入れる［得る］」

◇ even more の後には money が省略されている。even は後の比較級を強調している。

◇ impact動「…に影響を及ぼす」　　　　◇ quit動「辞める」

◇ be proud that ...「…を誇りに思う」　　◇ take on ...「…を引き受ける」

◇ shift名「交代勤務時間；シフト」

◇ underestimate動「…を過小評価する；…を少なく見積りすぎる」

◇ combine A with B「（A を B と組み合わせる→）A を B と両立させる」

◇ value A as B「A を B として評価する」

◇ be eager to -「熱心に - する」　　　　◇ be willing to -「進んで - する」

◇ blossom into ...「成長して…になる」

◇ not all ...「（部分否定を表して）すべての…が～するというわけではない」

◇ academic形「学業に関する」

◇ so (that) S can ...「（目的を表して）S が…するために」

◇ socialize with ...「…と付き合う［交際する］」

◇ be concerned about ...「…を心配している」

◇ involving ...「…を巻き込む」　この現在分詞句は直前の many car or bike accidents にか
　かっている。

◇ forbid O from -ing「O が - することを禁じる」

◇ encourage O to -「O が - することを勧める［奨励する］」

◇ confident形「自信がある」　　　　　　◇ colleague名「同僚」

◇ background名「背景；素性；経歴」　　◇ manage to -「何とか - することができる」

[設問文・選択肢]

◇ positive形「有利な；プラスの」　　　◇ inexperienced形「経験不足の」

◇ be likely to -「- する可能性が高い」

[ステップ2]

◇ now that ...「（今や）…なので」　　　◇ as below「以下のように」

[ステップ3]

◇ aspect名「側面」　　　　　　　　　　◇ in summary「要するに；要約すると」

◇ struggle to -「- することに苦労する」　◇ suitable形「（自分に）適した」

◇ immediately副「すぐに」

◇ listed on a popular employment website は直前の A recent survey of jobs にかかる過去
　分詞句。

◇ entry-level形「初歩的な」　　　　　　◇ relevant形「関係［関連］のある」

◇ It is this requirement that ... は this requirement を強調した強調構文。

◇ requirement名「要件」

◇ prevent O from -ing「O が - することを妨げる」

◇ job market「労働市場」　　　　　　　◇ recession名「不況」

◇ apply for ...「…を志願する」　　　　　◇ competitive形「競争の激しい」

◇ make the difference「違いを作る；影響する」

◇ this is why ...「そういうわけで…；したがって…」

◇ ideal形「理想的な」　　　　　　　　　◇ have an effect on ...「…に影響を及ぼす」

◇ likelihood名「可能性」　　　　　　　◇ commit a crime「犯罪を犯す」

◇ randomly副「無作為に」　　　　　　　◇ arrest名「逮捕」

◇ theft名「窃盗」

◇ compared to ...「…と比較した［比較して］」

◇ duration名「継続期間」　　　　　　　◇ affect動「…に影響を及ぼす」

第7問

解 答

問1 – ①	問2 – ④	（各3点）

問3 – 34 ①, 35 ⑤, 36 ④, 37 ②　　　　　（全部正解で3点）

問4 – ①・③　　　　　　　　　　　　　　（順不同・両方正解で3点）

問5 – ④　　　　　　　　　　　　　　　　（3点）

出 典　*Original Material*

全 訳

英語のライティングのクラスでショートストーリーを1つ選んで読まなくてはなりません。あなたは次の物語を読んで，他の生徒が話の流れを理解するのを助けるために物語を要約しています。

すべてを変えたリストラ

イザベラ・アンドルーズ

「お願いだからじっとして座っていてちょうだい」　エミリーは笑顔で2人の娘たちに言った。「そんなに動いたら，あなたたちの絵を描けないわ」「ごめんねお母さん」マリアンナが優しい笑顔を浮かべながら応えた。「ここまできたのね」　エミリーは心の中でそう思った。

5年前の今日，エミリーは重要だが難しい，そんな仕事上の決断を迫られていた。彼女は有名な広告会社に6年ほど勤めてきた。運悪く，倒産を免れるために，その会社はリストラを行うことになり，彼女の役職はなくなってしまうことになっていた。彼女は社内の新しい仕事をオファーされた。

もちろん，会社に残る機会を与えられたことには感謝していた。だって，自分の仕事をよく理解している環境で働く方がはるかに簡単なのだから。でも同時に，上手く利用されているように感じずにはいられなかった。新しい仕事を引き受けるということは，給料がはるかに下がり，以前と同じくらい稼ぐためにはより一生懸命に働かなくてはならないということを意味していた。

永遠とも思えるくらいに長い時間じっくり考えた後，エミリーはオファーを断るという決断をして，職探しを始めた。とはいえ，信じられないくらいに険しい道のりだった。次から次へと採用を断られ，彼女は自信をなくし始めた。

この大変さにさらに追い打ちをかけるかのように，エミリーは家庭での子どもたちとのコミュニケーションにも苦労していた。ある日就職面接の1つを終えて帰ってきたとき，長女であるサラに学校で何をしたの，と尋ねたら，無視されてしまった。すっかりショックでがっかりしてしまい，夫のニックになんでサラはあんな態度をとったのか尋ねた。「君の人生全ては仕事を中心に回っているみたいで，君が娘たちに払ってきた関心は，とても十分とは言えないね」と彼は言った。

彼が言っていることはたぶんその通りだ，と彼女は思った。振り返ってみると，彼女は娘たちのために十分なお金を稼ぐことが自分の責務だと自分に常に言い聞かせていたけれど，自分はただ母親としての役割を全うしないことの言い訳をしているだけだったとこの時気づいたのだった。

— 英 R 78 —

「アーティストになるという夢があったことを覚えている？」 ニックは尋ねた。「彼女たちはお母さんにその夢を追いかけてほしいとよく言っていたんだ」 それを聞いたとたん，自分はとても芸術が好きだったけれど，お金を稼ぐために長年の夢を諦めたんだ，ということを彼女は思い出した。「芸術へ情熱がまだあるなら，それを追求するいい機会なんじゃない？　お金のことは心配しなくていいから」「ありがとう，ニック」 そう言う彼女の眼には涙があふれていた。

次の日，エミリーは娘たちに母親としての役割を一切果たせてこなかったことを謝り，とても申し訳なく思っているということを伝えた。そして，もう一度絵を描こうと思っているということも伝えた。彼女たちは最初は困惑したようだったが，すぐに2人の表情は和らいだ。「いいんじゃないかな」とサラは言った。

紆余曲折を経て，彼女は2年後，最終的に小さな広告会社のアートディレクターの職を得た。その仕事では，広告業界での経験と芸術への情熱をどちらも生かすことができた。給料はそんなに良くないけれど，前職よりも，その仕事の方がはるかに満足のいく充実したものだと感じた。

今日，エミリーの小さなホームスタジオの工事がついに終了した。今，愛する家族とともにスタジオの中で座りながら，エミリーは大きな幸福感に浸っていた。仕事を変えるという難しい決断をしなかったら，こんな幸せは手に入らなかっただろう。たとえあの時はどんなに辛い状況に思えたにしても，実のところあのリストラは恩恵だったのだ。そのことを，彼女は強く確信している。

あなたのメモ：

すべてを変えたリストラ

1．登場人物
●エミリー（主人公）
　▶ 新しい役職をオファーされたが， 32 ことを心配していた。
●サラとマリアンナ（エミリーの娘）
●ニック（エミリーの夫）
　▶ 彼はエミリーが 33 ことを提案した。

2．物語での出来事
エミリーは広告会社で新しい役職をオファーされる。
→ 34 → 35 → 36 → 37

3．いくつかの重要な教訓
・ 38
・ 39
・ 職業上の決定をする際は自分の充実感を考慮することが必要不可欠である。

4．物語から学べるよくある言い回し
"Look how far I've come" （第1段落）
この表現はおおよそ " 40 !" と言い換えられる。

— 英 R 79 —

設問解説

問1 | 32 | 正解 ①

「 32 に入る最適な選択肢を選びなさい」
① **本来もらってしかるべきよりも少ない給料しかもらえないかもしれない**
② 別の部署に異動させられるかもしれない
③ まもなく会社は倒産してしまうかもしれない
④ オファーを受けた仕事は非常に退屈かもしれない

正解は①。第3段落第4文（The new role ...）に「給料がはるかに下がり，以前と同じくらい稼ぐためにはより一生懸命に働かなくてはならない」と書かれている。元々もらっている給料が「本来もらってしかるべき給料」と考えれば，結局「本来彼女が値するよりも少ない給料しかもらえない」ということになるので，①が正しい。

③に関しては第2段落第3文（Unfortunately, in order ...）に「倒産を免れるためにリストラをする」とあるが，「実際に倒産した」とはどこにも書かれていないし，それをエミリーが心配していたという内容も本文からは読み取れないので誤りと判断できる。②と④に該当する内容は書かれていないので誤り。

問2 | 33 | 正解 ④

「 33 に入る最適な選択肢を選びなさい」
① 過去の過ちの埋め合わせのために専業主婦になる
② 就職活動について娘たちに相談する
③ 職探しをやめて十分な休息をとる
④ **もともとやりたかったことを追求してみる**

正解は④。第7段落でエミリーが芸術を愛しており，その分野で仕事に就くことがもともとの夢であったという趣旨のことが書かれている。さらに同段落第5文（"If you still ...）は「芸術へ情熱がまだあるなら，それを追求するいい機会なんじゃない？」というニックの発言であり，ここからニックは「アーティストになるというもともとの夢を追求すること」をエミリーに提案しているとわかるので，④が正しい。

①は確かに第6段落でエミリーが母親の役目を果たしていなかったという趣旨のことが書かれているが，「専業主婦になること」を提案していると読み取れる記述は一切ないので誤り。②と③は本文に書かれていない。

問3 | 34 | 正解 ①， | 35 | 正解 ⑤， | 36 | 正解 ④， | 37 | 正解 ②

「5つの選択肢（① ～ ⑤）から4つ選び，起きた順序に並び替えなさい」
① エミリーが就職活動をすることに決める。
② エミリーが娘たちの絵を家で描く。
③ エミリーがプロの画家として仕事を始める。
④ エミリーが母親としての責務をないがしろにしているとニックが言う。
⑤ サラが学校での出来事についてのエミリーの質問を無視する。

正解は① → ⑤ → ④ → ②。

①は第4段落第1文（After contemplating for ...）に「エミリーはオファーを断るという決断をして，職探しを始めた」とある部分が該当する。②は第1段落第2文（"With you moving ...）の「そんなに動いたら，あなたたちの絵を描けないわ」というエミリーの発言が該当箇所である。③に関しては本文に書かれていない。第9段落第1文（After a lot ...）から，実際に就いた職はアートディレクターとあり，プロの画家ではない。④に関しては第5段落最終文（"It seems your ...）のニックの発言が該当する。⑤に関しては同じく第5段落第2文（One day, when ...）の「長女であるサラに学校で何をしたの，と尋ねたら，無視されてしまった」という部分が該当する。

本文は基本的に時系列に沿ってストーリーが展開しているが，第1段落と最終段落が現

— 英 R 80 —

在を描き，第2段落から第9段落にかけては昔を振り返った描写になっている。よって，第1段落の②の内容は最後に来ることに注意し，その他は本文の登場順に並べれば良いことになる。よって，①→⑤→④→②が正しい。

問4 ┃ 38 ┃・┃ 39 ┃ 正解①・③

「┃ 38 ┃と┃ 39 ┃に入る最適な選択肢を2つ選びなさい（順番は問わない）」

  ① 仕事と家族生活の良いバランスが重要である。

  ② リストラは大変な状況に置かれた会社の従業員にとって最善の選択肢である。

  ③ 不運な状況が時にありがたいものであることがわかる。

  ④ 元々の目標を追求することは最後にはより高い給料を得ることにつながる。

  ⑤ 職場にいるよりも子どもと一緒にいることに多くの時間をかけることが成功への鍵である。

    正解は①と③。第5段落及び第6段落の内容から，エミリーが仕事に没頭するあまり母親としての責任を全うできていなかったことが読み取れる。続く第7段落で娘たちに謝罪をしたことで関係性が改善する方向性が読みとれる。そして第1段落および最終段落から仲睦まじい家族の描写と共に，エミリーが幸福感を感じていることが読み取れる。よって，仕事に没頭するだけではなく，家族生活との両立が大切であるというメッセージを読み取ることができるので，①は正しい。また，最終段落第3文（The restructuring, however ...）で「たとえあの時はどんなに辛い状況に思えたにしても，実のところあのリストラは恩恵だったのだ」と言っているが，これが③の選択肢と一致する。ストーリー全体の流れを考えても，難しい決断に迫られたが，それがあったからこそ仕事の面でも家庭の面でも良い方向に向かった，ということが読み取れるので，③は正しいと言える。

    ②は該当する記述がない。リストラが重要なきっかけになったと書かれているが，あくまで本文ではエミリー個人の話をしているので，会社や従業員一般に当てはまると言える根拠はない。④に関しては，第9段落最終文（Her salary was ...）で「給料はそんなに良くない」と書いてあるので，誤りであると判断できる。⑤に関しては，職場や家庭で過ごす具体的な時間の長さの話は本文では言及されていないので正解とは言えない。

問5 ┃ 40 ┃ 正解④

「┃ 40 ┃に入る最適な選択肢を選びなさい」

  ① 自分の夢はいかに遠く思えるか

  ② 自分はいかに多くの時間を無駄にしてきたか

  ③ 自分の人生はいかに面白かったか

  ④ 自分はなんと大きな進歩をしたのだろうか

    正解は④。look は疑問詞や感嘆詞が作る節を目的語にとって，命令文の形で「…を見てみなさい；注目しなさい；考えなさい」という意味で使う。how far I've come は直訳すると「どれほど遠くに来たか」となるが，これは文字通り旅などで遠くに来たことを表現することもあるが，比喩的に「大変な道のりでずいぶん前進した」という，要するに「かなり進歩した；改善した」という意味合いで使われることも多い。ここでは，仕事で苦労していた過去や娘との関係性が悪かった過去に比べ，現在はとても充実している，ということを表している。よって全体で「見てよ，私はここまで頑張ってきたわ」ということを表している。この意味合いに合致する④が正解である。

(主な語句・表現)	・問題冊子を参照のこと。

[第1段落]
("Sit still, please," ...)

◇ sit still「じっとしている；じっと座っている」
◇ smiling「微笑みながら」 小説ではよく smiling / laughing / surprised などの表情・感情を表す分詞が一語で文末に置かれる形が用いられる。
◇ with you moving so much「あなたたちがそんなに動いていたら」 you が意味上の主語，moving が意味上の動詞で，「あなたたちがそんなにたくさん動く状態では」ということ。この with はいわゆる付帯状況と言われる用法である。

[第2段落]
(Five years ago ...)

◇ five years ago today「5年前の今日」 X ago は「X前」という意味だが，後ろに today をつけると，「X前の今日」という意味になる。類例として，ten years ago this month「10年前の今月」など。要するに，X ago Y は「Yからさかのぼって X前」という意味を表す。
◇ well-known 形「よく知られた；有名な」　　◇ go through「経験する；経る；受ける」
◇ restructuring 名「リストラ；企業再構築」◇ eliminate 動「…を消す；除去する」

[第3段落]
(Of course, she ...)

◇ grateful 形「感謝している」　　　　　　◇ stay with ...「…にとどまる」
◇ after all「だって；なんだかんだ言っても（やはり）」 この表現は前言の理由を述べる「だって」という意味合いで使われることが多い。
◇ where 接「…するところで」
◇ at the same time「（しかし）一方では」 文字通りには「同時に」の意味だが，but を伴い「しかしその一方」という意味合いで使うことが多い。
◇ couldn't help -ing「-せずにはいられない；ついつい-してしまう」
◇ take advantage of ...「…をいいように使う」 人を目的語にとると，「人をいいように使う；人を不当に扱う」の意味合いで使われる。
◇ significantly 副「はるかに」

[第4段落]
(After contemplating ...)

◇ contemplate 動「じっくり考える」
◇ for what felt like forever「永遠にも思えるくらいの（時）間」
◇ turn down「断る」　　　　　　　　　　◇ a difficult path「険しい道のり；いばらの道」
◇ one ... after another「次から次の…」　◇ rejection 名「拒絶；不採用」

[第5段落]
(As if that ...)

◇ as if that wasn't bad enough「すでに良くない状況なのにそれに追い打ちをかけるように」 文字通りには「それはまだ十分に悪くは言えないかのように」ということで，「さらに悪い事には」の意味合いで使われる表現。wasn't の代わりに weren't のこともある。また，bad がなくてもおおよそ同じ意味合いで使われる。
◇ why S had behaved the way S did「なぜSはあんな振る舞いをしたのか」
◇ revolve around ...「…を中心に回っている；…中心である」
◇ deserve 動「…に値する」

[第6段落]
(Maybe he was ...)

◇ looking back「振り返ってみると」　　◇ duty 名「責務」
◇ decent 形「満足のいく；まともな；きちんとした」
◇ for the sake of ...「…のために」　　◇ fulfill 動「…を満たす；全うする」

[第7段落]
("Do you remember ...)

◇ remember how ...「…ということを思い出す」 この how は「どのように」ではなく，実質的に that 節と同じような意味合いになる。
◇ in favor of ...「…を優先して」　　　◇ brim with ...「…で溢れる」

[第9段落]	◇ twists and turns「紆余曲折」	◇ land 動「〈仕事など〉を得る」
(After a lot ...)	◇ considerably 副「かなり」	◇ satisfying 形「満足のいく」
	◇ fulfilling 形「充実した」	

[最終段落]
(Today, the construction ...)

◇ beloved 形「愛する」　　　　　　　◇ be flooded with ...「…に満たされている」
◇ unattainable 形「手に入れられない」
◇ had she not made　これは仮定法の条件節 if she had not made の倒置形である。
◇ blessing 名「ありがたいこと：恩恵」　　◇ absolutely 副「絶対的に」

第8問

解答

問1 － ②　　　　　　　　　　　　　　　　　　　　　　　　　　　（2点）
問2 － ②・④　　　　　　　　　　　　　　　（順不同・両方正解で3点）
問3 － ②　　　問4 － ④　　　問5 － ④　　　　　　　　　　（各3点）

出典　*Original Material*

全訳

　あなたは国際的なプレゼンテーションコンテストの準備をしている学生グループに所属しています。あなたは，ある人気のキノコについてのプレゼンテーションの，自分の担当部分を作成するために次の文章を使用しています。

　地球上には私たち人間を含む動物種より多くの生物の種が存在している。代表的な例が菌類で，150万種程度しかいない動物種に対し，菌類は150万から500万種存在すると推定されている。この理由の一部には，菌類が環境に非常に適応しており，動物よりも広い範囲で生息できるという事実がある。また，菌類は有性，無性のどちらでも繁殖することができるため，進化や多様化する能力がより高い。すべての菌類の中で，私たちに最も身近なものはおそらくキノコであろう。

　幼い頃，私たちはおとぎ話やその他の物語で赤と白のキノコを見たことがあるかもしれない。そのキノコが何なのかということに関してはさまざまな意見があるが，最も有力なのはハエキノコだ。それは一般的に幅5cmから15cmの赤い菌傘（かさ）と，高さ20cmにまで成長することもある白い柄を持っている。このことにより，ハエキノコはキノコの中でも最も見分けがつきやすい種類の1つとなっている。その原産地は北欧だが，現在では温帯林から北部地域の寒くてじめじめした森まで，世界中のさまざまな地域で見られる。

　ハエキノコは，民話やおとぎ話に描かれたり宗教的な儀式に使われたりと，多くの文化や伝統の中で重要な役割を果たしてきた。一部の文化では霊的な力や癒しの力があると信じられていた。バイキングはそれを戦いの前に勇気を出すために使ったと言われている。ヒンドゥー教の文書では，それは「ソーマ」という名で言及されており，神々と交信するための宗教儀式に用いられたと考えられている。

　ハエキノコはその薬効で注目を集めている。最近研究されているハエキノコ中の化学物質の1つはイボテン酸である。この物質は学習や記憶に関連性があり，パーキンソン病やアルツハイマー病などさまざまな神経疾患の治療に役立つかもしれない。それに加えてハエキノコは，がんや肝臓病を含むさまざまな臓器疾患の治療に役立つ可能性に関して研究されている，いくつかの物質を含んでいる。

　ハエキノコは学術的にはベニテングダケとしても知られている。それはタマゴテングダケのような他の有名な種を含むテングダケ属の一種である。ハエキノコは生存のために木を必要とすることを意味する菌根菌と呼ばれる菌類の一種である。木はこの菌を通して土から栄養を吸収し，一方でこの菌は木から糖分や他の栄養を受け取るので，それらは生存のためにお互いを必要としている。

　ハエキノコ菌は地中で成長し，地上ではキノコ，つまり子実体しか見ることができない。それは一年菌と考えられており，通常は1年に1度成長し，その後枯れるが，菌糸は地中に残り翌年には新しい子実体を作ることができる。ハエキノコの成長と繁殖は温度，水分，光などの環境因子と密接に関係している。

　ハエキノコの構造は独特である。鱗片と呼ばれる白い斑点に覆われた真っ赤な菌傘がある。それは新しい生育場所に定着するため，周囲の環境に広まる胞子と呼ばれる小さな単細胞構造物を放出している。胞子は白色で菌傘の下のひだのところにある。キノコは大抵

― 英 R 84 ―

白色かクリーム色の太い柄に支えられてまっすぐ立っており，根元にはつぼと呼ばれるカップ状の構造物がついている。また柄の周囲には，つばと呼ばれる特徴的な環状構造物があり，これもこのキノコの大きな特徴の1つとなっている。

ハエキノコには文化的な意義と潜在的な薬としての恩恵があるが，毒キノコであることを覚えておくことが重要だ。それを食べすぎると重病や死に至ることもある。したがって，ハエキノコをいかなる目的であれ活用しようとする前には注意し，専門家のアドバイスを求めることが不可欠だ。それでもなお，この菌類の独特の性質は，科学者だけでなくキノコ好きな人も魅了し，彼らにインスピレーションを与え続けることだろう。

あなたのプレゼンテーションのスライド：

ハエキノコ：
世界中で知られている
赤と白のキノコ

1．基本的な情報

- 直径は 5 cm から 15 cm
- 高さは最大で 20 cm
-
- 41
-
-

2．薬としての使用

- 42
- 43

3．分類

- ベニテングダケ
- 菌根類
- 一年菌

4．構造 44

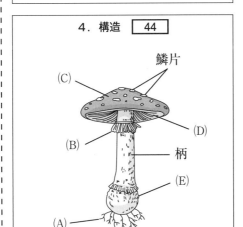

5．最後に

45

設問解説　問1　41　正解②

「 41 に含めるべきではないものは次のうちのどれか」

① 民話やおとぎ話に登場する
② およそ 500 万種が見つかっている
③ 温かい森と寒い森の両方で見られる
④ 宗教的な儀式で使われる
⑤ 非常に識別しやすい

正解は②。 41 を含むスライドの見出しになっている，ハエキノコの「基本的な情報」は，本文の第2段落から第3段落で述べられている。

②はハエキノコの種類に関する内容だが，これについては本文では述べられていない。第1段落第2文（Typical examples are ...）の中に，「150 万から 500 万種」という表現があるが，これは菌類（fungi）全体のことであって，ハエキノコに関する記述ではないことに注意。したがって正解は②となる。

①と④は，第3段落第1文（Fly agaric has ...）の「ハエキノコは，民話やおとぎ話に描かれたり宗教的な儀式に使われたり」という部分に一致する。③は第2段落最終文（It is originally ...）の「（ハエキノコの）その原産地は北欧だが，現在では温帯林から北部地域の寒くてじめじめした森まで，世界中のさまざまな地域で見られる」という内容に一致する。⑤に関しては，第2段落第3文（It has a ...）で「幅 5 cm から 15 cm の赤い菌傘（かさ）と，高さ 20 cm にまで成長することもある白い柄を持っている」，続く第4文（This makes it ...）に「このことにより，ハエキノコはキノコの中でも特に見分けがつきやすい種類の1つとなっている」とあり，色やサイズの点からハエキノコは非常に識別しやすいことがわかる。したがって，本文の内容に一致している。

問2　42 ・ 43　正解②・④

「『薬としての使用』スライドに関して，ハエキノコの特徴で最も正しいと思われるものを2つ選びなさい（順番は問わない）」 42 ・ 43

① ハエキノコはストレスや疲労に好影響を及ぼすことが証明されている。
② ハエキノコはいくつかの神経疾患の治療に有効だという可能性があるため研究されている。
③ いくつかの宗教で，ハエキノコは神々によってもたらされた薬だと信じられていた。
④ ハエキノコに含まれるいくつかの物質が，ある種の臓器疾患に有効であるかもしれない。
⑤ バイキングは，戦いの後にリラックスするためにハエキノコを食べたと言われている。

42 ・ 43 を含むスライドの見出しになっている「薬としての使用」に関しては，第4段落で述べられている。

②に関しては，第4段落第2文（One of the ...）に「最近研究されているハエキノコ中の化学物質の1つはイボテン酸である」とあり，イボテン酸については続く第3文（This substance has ...）で「学習や記憶に関連性があり，パーキンソン病やアルツハイマー病などさまざまな神経疾患の治療に役立つかもしれない」と述べられているので，本文の内容に一致していることがわかる。④については，第4段落最終文（In addition, fly ...）で「ハエキノコは，がんや肝臓病を含むさまざまな臓器疾患の治療に役立つ可能性に関して研究されている，いくつかの物質を含んでいる」とあるので，こちらも本文の内容に一致している。

①のようなことは本文では述べられていない。③の「神々によってもたらされた薬」という内容は，本文中に書かれていない。⑤については，第3段落第3文（The Vikings are ...）に「バイキングはそれ（ハエキノコ）を戦いの前に勇気を出すために使ったと言われている」とあるが，⑤のように「戦いの後にリラックスするため」とは述べられていないので，本文の内容と一致しているとは言えない。

問3　44　正解②

「『構造』のスライドに関して，ハエキノコのイラストに欠けているラベルを完成させなさい」　44

① (A) つば　(B) 菌糸　(C) つぼ　(D) 菌傘　(E) ひだ

② (A) 菌糸　(B) つば　(C) 菌傘　(D) ひだ　(E) つぼ

③ (A) 菌糸　(B) ひだ　(C) 菌傘　(D) つば　(E) つぼ

④ (A) 菌傘　(B) 菌糸　(C) つぼ　(D) ひだ　(E) つば

⑤ (A) つぼ　(B) 菌傘　(C) ひだ　(D) つば　(E) 菌糸

　　正解は②。　44　を含むスライドの見出しになっているハエキノコの「構造」に関しては，第6段落及び第7段落で述べられている。

　　まず，第6段落第1文（The fly agaric ...）に「ハエキノコ菌は地中で成長し，地上ではキノコ，つまり子実体しか見ることができない」とあり，続く第2文（It is considered ...）に「それは一年菌と考えられており，通常は1年に1度成長し，その後枯れるが，菌糸（mycelium）は地中に残り翌年には新しい子実体を作ることができる」とあることから，Mycelium は地上からは見えない地中にある部分であることがわかる。したがってイラストの最も下にある(A)が Mycelium だと見当がつくが，(A)が地中にあるかどうかはイラストからはわからないので，この時点で Mycelium の位置を断定する必要はない。次に，第7段落第2文（It has a ...）の「鱗片と呼ばれる白い斑点に覆われた真っ赤な菌傘（pileus）がある」という内容から，Pileus は(C)の部分であることがわかる。その後，第7段落第4文（The spores are ...）では「胞子は白色で菌傘の下のひだ（gills）のところにある」とあるので，Gills は(D)の部分となり，続く第5文（The mushroom stands ...）には「キノコは大抵白色かクリーム色の太い柄に支えられてまっすぐ立っており，根元にはつぼ（volva）と呼ばれるカップ状の構造物がついている」とあるので，Volva は(E)であるとわかる。さらに，第7段落最終文（It also has ...）で「また柄の周囲には，つば（annulus）と呼ばれる特徴的な環状構造物があり，これもこのキノコの大きな特徴の1つとなっている」と述べられており，Annulus は(B)ということがわかる。以上の内容から，正解は②に決まる。

問4　45　正解④

「最後のスライドに最も適切な文はどれか」　45

① ハエキノコは人間の味覚に合うので，伝統的に薬として使用されてきた。

② ハエキノコは癒し効果が証明されているので，日常的により幅広く使われるべきだ。

③ ハエキノコは見た目の特徴から見つけやすいので，より多く利用されていく可能性がかなり高い。

④ ハエキノコはいくつかの病気に効果があるかもしれないが，大量に摂取すると深刻な健康問題を引き起こすこともありえる。

　　正解は④。「ハエキノコはいくつかの病気に効果があるかもしれない」という部分は，第4段落第3文（This substance has ...），及び同段落最終文（In addition, fly ...）で，ハエキノコがいくつかの病気の治療に有効である可能性があることが述べられていることに一致する。「大量に摂取すると深刻な健康問題を引き起こすこともありえる」については，最終段落第1文（Although fly agaric ...）の「ハエキノコには文化的な意義と潜在的な薬としての恩恵があるが，毒キノコであることを覚えておくことが重要だ」，続く第2文

— 英 R 87 —

（Eating too much ...）の「それを食べすぎると重病や死に至ることもある」という内容に一致している。

①の「ハエキノコは人間の味覚に合うので」，②の「ハエキノコは癒し効果が証明されているので」という内容は本文中に書かれていないため，誤り。③は「ハエキノコは見た目の特徴から見つけやすい」という内容は第2段落第4文（This makes it ...）に述べられてはいるものの，この性質によって「より多く利用されていく可能性がかなり高い」と判断する材料を本文中から見つけることはできない。したがって，誤りとなる。

問5 　46　 正解④

「この文章によると，次の中で正しいことを述べているのはどれか」 　46

① ハエキノコは，ほとんどが地中で四角いかたちで成長し，地上では子実体しか見えない。このことは他のどの菌よりもおそらく強いことを意味している。

② ハエキノコのライフサイクルは，一般的に環境に影響されない。このことにより，それは北半球の厳しい環境下でも生息できる。

③ 菌糸は1年に1度新しい子実体を作ることができる。ハエキノコは通常1年に数度繁殖する。

④ 樹木はハエキノコを通して土から栄養をとり，ハエキノコは樹木から糖分などの栄養を得るので，生存のことで互いに依存し合っている。

正解は④。第5段落最終文（They need each ...）の「木はこの菌を通して土から栄養を吸収し，一方でこの菌は木から糖分や他の栄養を受け取るので，それらは生存のためにお互いを必要としている」という内容と一致する。

①のハエキノコの地中での成長に関しては，第6段落第1文（The fly agaric ...）で述べられているものの，①のように「地中で四角いかたちで成長する」ということは本文中で書かれておらず，「（ハエキノコが）他のどの菌よりもおそらく強い」という部分も本文の情報からは判断できないため，誤り。②の「（ハエキノコは）北半球の厳しい環境下でも生息できる」という内容は，第2段落最終文（It is originally ...）の「（ハエキノコは）その原産地は北欧だが，現在では温帯林から北部地域の寒くてじめじめした森まで，世界中のさまざまな地域で見られる」という内容には一致しているが，「ハエキノコのライフサイクルは，一般的に環境に影響されない」の部分は，第6段落最終文（The growth and ...）の「温度，水分，光などの環境因子と密接に関係している」という内容と矛盾しているため，誤り。③については，第6段落第2文（It is considered ...）に「それは一年菌と考えられており，通常は1年に1度成長し，その後枯れるが，菌糸は地中に残り翌年には新しい子実体を作ることができる」とあるので，「菌糸は1年に1度新しい子実体を作ることができる」という部分は正しいが，「ハエキノコは通常1年に数度繁殖する」の部分が本文の内容と一致しないため誤りとなる。

（主な語句・表現）・問題冊子を参照のこと。

[リード文]　◇ prepare for ...「…の準備をする」　　　◇ create 動「…を作る」
◇ mushroom 名「キノコ」

[第1段落]　◇ contain 動「…を含んでいる」　　　　◇ species 名「（生物の）種」
（The earth　◇ organism 名「生物」　　　　　　　　◇ typical 形「典型的な」
contains ...）◇ fungi 名「菌」（fungus の複数形）
◇ be estimated to be ...「…と推定されている」
◇ compared to ...「…と比べて；…に対し」　◇ partly 副「一部には；1つには」
◇ due to ...「…が原因で；…のせいで」　◇ highly 副「非常に；大いに」
◇ be adapted to ...「…に適応している」　◇ a wide range of ...「広い範囲の…」

— 英 R 88 —

◇ reproduce 動「繁殖する」　　　　　　　◇ sexually 副「性的に」
◇ capacity 名「能力」　　　　　　　　　◇ evolve 動「進化する」
◇ diversify 動「多様化する」　　　　　　◇ familiar 形「身近である；馴染みがある」

[第2段落]　◇ fairy tale 名「おとぎ話」　　　　　　◇ as to ...「…に関して」
(When we were　◇ promising 形「有力な」　　　　　　　◇ typically 副「一般的に；典型的に」
...)　◇ up to ...「(最大で) …まで」
　◇ recognizable 形「見分けがつく；識別できる」
　◇ originally 副「もともと；最初に」　　　◇ region 名「地域」
　◇ range from ... to 〜「…から〜まで (の範囲に) 及んでいる」
　◇ temperate 形「温暖な」　　　　　　　◇ forest 名「森林 (地帯)；山林」
　◇ damp 形「湿った；じめじめした」　　　◇ northern 形「北の；北にある」

[第3段落]　◇ play a 〜 role in ...「… (の中) で〜役割を果たす」
(Fly agaric has ...)　◇ tradition 名「伝統」　　　　　　　　◇ depict 動「…を描く」
　◇ folklore 名「民話」　　　　　　　　　◇ religious 形「宗教的な」
　◇ ceremony 名「儀式」　　　　　　　　◇ spiritual 形「霊的な」
　◇ healing 形「癒しの；(人を) 癒すような」◇ brave 形「勇敢な；勇気のある」
　◇ text 名「文書」
　◇ mention 動「… (の名) を挙げる […に言及する]」
　◇ ritual 名「儀式」

[第4段落]　◇ attract 動「…を引く；…を集める」　◇ attention 名「注目」
(Fly agaric is ...)　◇ medicinal 形「薬用の」　　　　　　　◇ property 名「特性；効能」
　◇ chemical 名「化学物質」　　　　　　　◇ substance 名「物質」
　◇ be linked to ...「…と関連がある」　　　◇ helpful 形「役に立つ」
　◇ treat 動「…を治療する」　　　　　　　◇ various 形「さまざまな」
　◇ nervous 形「神経の」　　　　　　　　◇ disorder 名「疾患」
　◇ such as ...「(たとえば) …のような」　　◇ disease 名「病気」
　◇ in addition「(それに) 加えて」　　　　◇ potential 形「潜在的な」
　◇ usefulness 名「有用性」　　　　　　　◇ treatment 名「治療」
　◇ organ 名「臓器」　　　　　　　　　　◇ cancer 名「がん」
　◇ liver 名「肝臓」

[第5段落]　◇ be known as ...「…として知られている」◇ term 名「(専門) 用語」
(Fly agaric is ...)　◇ survive 動「生存する」　　　　　　　◇ each other「お互い」
　◇ exist 動「存在する」　　　　　　　　◇ absorb 動「…を吸収する」
　◇ nutrient 名「栄養物；栄養素」　　　　◇ soil 名「土」
　◇ receive 動「…を受け取る」　　　　　　◇ sugar 名「糖分」

[第6段落]　◇ beneath 前「…の下で」　　　　　　　◇ ground 名「地面」
(The fly agaric　◇ fruiting body「子実体」　菌類が胞子を生じるための器官。
...)　◇ annual 形「年1回の」　　　　　　　　◇ underground 副「地中に」
　◇ growth 名「成長」　　　　　　　　　◇ reproduction 名「繁殖」
　◇ be tied to ...「…に関係している」　　　◇ closely 副「密接に」
　◇ environmental 形「環境の」　　　　　　◇ factor 名「要因」
　◇ moisture 名「水分」

[第7段落] (The body mechanics ...)	◇ mechanics 图「構造;しくみ」	◇ be covered with ...「…で覆われている」
	◇ spot 图「斑点」	◇ release 動「…を放出する」
	◇ tiny 形「小さな」	◇ single-celled 形「単細胞の」
	◇ structure 图「構造物」	◇ spread 動「広まる」
	◇ settle on ...「…に定着する[定住する]」	◇ be located「ある;位置する」
	◇ stand tall「まっすぐ立っている」	
	◇ stem 图「(草木の) 茎;(花・葉・果実などの) 柄」	
	◇ base 图「土台;根元」	◇ distinctive 形「特徴的な」
	◇ ring-like 形「環状の」	◇ serve 動「役立つ」
	◇ characteristic 图「特徴」	

[最終段落] (Although fly agaric ...)	◇ significance 图「意義;重要性」	◇ benefit 图「利益;恩恵」
	◇ poisonous 形「有毒の」	◇ lead to ...「…につながる」
	◇ essential 形「不可欠な」	◇ attempt to -「-しようとする」
	◇ purpose 图「目的」	◇ nevertheless 副「それでもなお」
	◇ quality 图「性質」	◇ fascinate 動「…を魅了する」
	◇ inspire 動「…にインスピレーションを与える」	
	◇ A and B alike「AだけでなくBも同様に」	

[スライド]	◇ X in diameter「直径がXである」	◇ X in height「高さがXである」

[設問文・選択肢]	◇ appear 動「登場する」	◇ folk tale「民話」
	◇ recognize 動「…を見分ける[識別する]」	◇ be proved to -「-すると証明されている」
	◇ have a ~ effect on ...「…に~な影響を与える」	
	◇ possible 形「可能性のある」	◇ effective 形「効果がある;効果的だ」
	◇ certain 形「ある;特定の」	◇ relaxed 形「リラックスしている」
	◇ be agreeable to ...「…に合っている」	◇ sense of taste「味覚」
	◇ widely 副「幅広く」	◇ on a daily basis「日常的に」
	◇ effect 图「影響;効果」	◇ likely 副「おそらく;たぶん」
	◇ consume 動「…を消費する;…を摂取する」	
	◇ quantity 图「量」	◇ in a ... shape「…かたちで」
	◇ visible 形「目に見える」	◇ affect 動「…に影響を与える」
	◇ enable O to -「Oが-するのを可能にする」	
	◇ harsh 形「厳しい;過酷な」	◇ hemisphere 图「半球」
	◇ be dependent on ... for ~「~のことで…に頼っている」	

| 第3回 | 実戦問題　解答・解説 |

英語（リーディング） 第3回 （100点満点）

（解答・配点）

問題番号 （配点）	設問	解答番号	正解	配点	自己採点欄	問題番号 （配点）	設問	解答番号	正解	配点	自己採点欄
第1問 （6）	1	1	①	2		第6問 （18）	1	25	④	3	
	2	2	④	2			2	26	②	3	
	3	3	①	2			3	27 — 28	① — ③	3*	
小計								29	②	3	
第2問 （10）	1	4	③	2			4	30	④	3	
	2	5	②	2			5	31	④	3	
	3	6	⑤	2		小計					
	4	7	①	2		第7問 （15）	1	32	④	3	
	5	8	③	2			2	33	①	3	
小計							3	34	⑤	3*	
第3問 （9）	1	9	③	3*				35	④		
		10	①					36	③		
		11	④					37	①		
		12	②				4	38	③	3	
	2	13	②	3			5	39 — 40	② — ③	3*	
	3	14	③	3		小計					
小計						第8問 （14）	1	41	①	2	
第4問 （12）	1	15	②	3			2	42 — 43	② — ④	3*	
	2	16	②	3			3	44	④	3	
	3	17	④	3			4	45	①	3	
	4	18	②	3			5	46	①	3	
小計						小計					
第5問 （16）	1	19	④	3							
	2	20	①	3							
	3	21	①	2							
		22	⑤	2							
	4	23	③	3							
	5	24	①	3							
小計											

（注）
1 ＊は，全部正解の場合のみ点を与える。
2 －（ハイフン）でつながれた正解は，順序を問わない。

第1問

| 解 答 | 問1 - ① 問2 - ④ 問3 - ① | （各2点） |

出典 *Original Material*

全訳

あなたはアメリカの大学生で，クリエイティブ・ライティングの夏期講座を受講しようと考えています。あなたはウェブサイトでそのような講座を見つけます。

YCW シアトル
1週間集中講座

毎年恒例の第5回 YCW クリエイティブ・ライティング集中講座にご参加ください。キャンプで他の若いライターたちと共に過ごし，出版歴のある作家や芸術家から学んでください。

日程：2023年8月20日から27日
場所：シアトル，ワシントン湖，キャンプ YCW
受講料：750ドル — 宿泊設備，食事は提供されます（キャンプ内での店舗で使用する現金を持参してください）
オプショナル・アクティビティ：ハイキング，湖のクルーズ

受講可能講座

◆**シェイクスピア・コース**：受賞歴のある脚本家に補佐してもらい，皆さんはシェイクスピアの戯曲2作品を分析します。また，小グループで寸劇制作に取り組み，講座最終日の午前中にキャンプ参加者の前でそれを上演します。

◆**ブロンテ・コース**：出版歴のある小説家，カレン・ネルソンがこの講座の講師です。彼女がライティングの基礎，ストーリーテリングの手法，作品の出版方法について指導します。あなたの短編は製本され，講座終了後1週間で郵送で届きます。

◆**リー・コース**：世界的に最も有名なコミックを複数制作しているスタン・リーの名前にちなんだコースで，コミック作りの基礎を指導します。また，出版歴のある漫画家，カナ・カガワから日本の漫画についても学習します。最後の夜には，皆さんの作品をスライド上映してキャンプの参加者に披露します。

▲**応募要項**

1. 2023年6月7日までに**オンラインの申込書**に記入してください。希望するコースを明記してください。
2. 6月8日以降，参加確認のメールが届きます。

＊各コースとも定員は学生20名ですので注意してください。1つのコースで応募者数が多すぎる場合は，参加者は無作為に選ばれます。希望コースに参加できなかった学生は，申し込みをキャンセルしても，希望者の少ないコースに参加しても構いません。

設問解説

問1 　1　 正解①

「キャンプの講師は全員，　1　」

① 作品が出版されたり高く評価された専門家だ
② 日本語に精通している
③ 資格のある文学の教師だ
④ 小説が受賞経験のある作家だ

　正解は①。冒頭の囲み枠内に「出版歴のある作家や芸術家から学んでください」とある。また，各コースの説明からも「受賞歴のある脚本家」，「出版歴のある小説家」，「出版歴のある漫画家」という，それぞれ専門家の講師だということがわかる。

問2 　2　 正解④

「キャンプ最終日の午前中に，参加者は　2　」

① 日本の漫画のスライド上映を楽しむ
② ワシントン湖へ釣りに出かける
③ ブロンテ・コースの学生が制作した本を読む
④ キャンプ中に書かれた劇を見る

　正解は④。最終日の午前中の活動に関しては，シェイクスピア・コースの説明に「小グループで寸劇制作に取り組み，講座最終日の午前中にキャンプ参加者の前でそれを上演します」とある。

　漫画のスライド上映は最後の夜に行われ，上映されるのはリー・コースの参加者の作品なので①は誤り。②や③のようなことも，本文からは読み取れない。

問3 　3　 正解①

「1つのコースの人気が高すぎる場合はどうなるか」　3　

① 各学生には選ばれるチャンスが平等にある。
② 各学生の文章能力がチェックされる。
③ 早く応募した学生が選ばれる。
④ 学生はクラス分けテストを受けなければならない。

　正解は①。最後のアステリスク（＊）のあとの第2文に，「1つのコースで応募者数が多すぎる場合は，参加者は無作為に選ばれます」と書かれている。「無作為に選ばれる」ということなので，参加できるかどうかのチャンスは平等だということになる。

主な語句・表現

［本文］

・問題冊子を参照のこと。

◇ annual 形「年1回の；毎年の」　　　　　　◇ intensive 形「集中した；徹底的な」
◇ accommodation 名「宿泊設備」　　　　　　◇ available 形「利用できる；手に入る」
◇ analyze 動「…を分析する」　　　　　　　◇ award-winning 形「受賞歴のある」
◇ screenwriter 名「シナリオライター；脚本家」
◇ perform 動「…を演じる；上演する」
◇ campmate 名「同じキャンプに寝泊まりする人」
◇ novelist 名「小説家」
◇ complete 動「〈書類など〉に（必要事項を）記入する」
◇ state 動「…を述べる；言明する」　　　　◇ confirmation 名「確認」
◇ note 動「…に注意する；気をつける」　　◇ at random「無作為に」

— 英 R 94 —

第2問

解答　問1 - ③　　問2 - ②　　問3 - ⑤　　問4 - ①　　問5 - ③　　（各2点）

出典　*Original Material*

全訳

あなたは学校の生徒会の一員です。あなたと他のメンバーは，学校の下級生たちがもっと活動的になるのを促すにはどうしたらよいかということを話し合っています。アイディアを得るために，あなたはアメリカのある学校が始めたスクール・フィットネス・プログラムについての記事を読んでいます。

徒歩通学プロジェクト

調査によって，生徒たちの活動レベルが年々下がっているということが明らかになっています。さらに，学校に徒歩，または自転車で通学している生徒の数もこれまでの年より減っています。このような運動不足は，生徒たちが不健康で肥満傾向にあることを意味します。

多くの親御さんは子どもたちには，往復とも徒歩で通学してほしいと思っていますが，安全面での不安があります。そのため，たとえ学校まで徒歩圏内に住んでいても，子どもたちを学校まで車で送ったり，スクールバスに乗せたりするのです。

当校は11月1日から試験的に徒歩通学プロジェクトを始めました。同じ地区に住む生徒たちが集団になって，監督役の大人の人といっしょに学校まで歩いてもらいました。各通学路につき大人のボランティアが2人付き添い，3つの徒歩通学路が決まりました。当初，1年生と2年生の75人の生徒が参加したのですが，12月の冬休みが始まる前には，この徒歩通学プログラムを利用していたのは60人だけでした。理由を調べるために生徒や保護者のフィードバックを見てみましょう。

生徒／保護者からのフィードバック

M.M.　このプロジェクトのおかげで，私の娘を含む多くの生徒に別のクラスの新しい友達ができました。それに，生徒たちは以前より運動を楽しみ始めました。これは成功だと私は思います。

K.J.　私は最初，この徒歩通学を楽しんでいたのですが，雨の日は嫌でした。冬は雨が多いので，雨の日はバスに乗ろうと思います。

R.B.　プロジェクトが始まって数週間後，息子の通学路にいたボランティアの方がお2人とも，ご家庭の事情で辞めなければならなくなりました。生徒たちだけで学校まで歩いて行かせることはできなかったので，息子を車で学校へ送ることを再開しました。そういう親御さんは他にもいらっしゃいました。

V.K.　私の友人も参加を希望したのですが，彼女はプロジェクトの対象エリア外に住んでいるのです。彼女も参加できればよいのにと思います。

W.L.　私は徒歩通学プロジェクトがとても気に入っていますが，理由は学校に着く前に友達とおしゃべりができるので，早起きをして時間通りに家を出ようという気持ちになるからです。

— 英 R 95 —

設問解説

問1　　4　　正解 ③

「徒歩通学プロジェクトの目的は　4　ことだった」

① 親に午前中自由な時間を与える
② 親の交通費の負担を減らす
❸ 生徒たちに運動の機会を与える
④ 生徒たちが学校に時間通りに着くことを手伝う

正解は ③。このプロジェクトを始めるきっかけは第1段落に書かれている。生徒たちの活動レベルの低下，運動不足がもたらす不健康，肥満傾向への対策としてプロジェクトがスタートした経緯が記されている。

①，②，④ のような記述はない。

問2　　5　　正解 ②

「徒歩通学プロジェクトについての1つの事実は　5　ということだ」

① 生徒全員が参加した
❷ 15人の生徒がプロジェクトを辞めた
③ 永続的なプロジェクトである
④ 雨の日は中止になった

正解は ②。第3段落第4文（Seventy-five students ...）を見ると，「当初の参加者数は75人だったが，12月の冬休み前には60人になった」，つまり参加した生徒数が15人減ったことがわかる。

第3段落第4文（Seventy-five students ...）に「1年生と2年生が参加した」とあり，また「生徒／保護者からのフィードバック」では4人目の V.K. が「対象エリア外に住んでいる友人が参加できない」と述べているので，① は誤り。第3段落第1文（Our school started ...）にはこのプロジェクトが「11月1日から試験的に始めた」とあるので，③ も誤り。フィードバックの中で K.J. が「雨の日は嫌でした」と述べていることから，このプロジェクトは雨の日にも行われたことがわかるので，④ も誤り。

問3　　6　　正解 ⑤

「フィードバックによると，　6　は生徒または保護者から報告された問題だった」

A：保護者の無関心
B：プロジェクトに含まれる限定された地域
C：冬の道路状況
D：ボランティアの不足

① A と B
② A と C
③ A と D
④ B と C
❺ B と D
⑥ C と D

正解は ⑤。V.K. は「友人はプロジェクトの対象エリア外に住んでいるので参加できなかった」という趣旨のフィードバックをしているので，「プロジェクトの対象地域が限定されていること」がもう1つの問題点であると考えられることから，B は一致する。また，R.B. のフィードバックに「ボランティアがプロジェクトの途中で辞めた」とあるので D も一致する。

A のようなフィードバックはない。K.J. は冬に雨が多いとは述べているが，道路状況が問題だとは述べていないので，C も不適切。

— 英 R 96 —

問4 ☐7☐ 正解 ①

「徒歩通学プロジェクトに対する意見の1つは ☐7☐ ということだ」

① 多くの生徒が他の生徒と知り合うのに役立った
② 朝の出発時間が早すぎた
③ バスに乗るよりも速かった
④ 親が子どもたちをさらに信頼し始めた

正解は ①。フィードバックに M.M. が,「このプロジェクトのおかげで,私の娘を含む多くの生徒に別のクラスの新しい友達ができました」と述べていることから,この内容と合っている ① が正解となる。

②,③,④ のような記述はない。

問5 ☐8☐ 正解 ③

「筆者の疑問に答えているのは ☐8☐ だった」

① K.J.
② M.M.
③ R.B.
④ V.K.
⑤ W.L.

正解は ③。筆者の疑問とは,第3段落第4,5文(Seventy-five students ... / Let's look at ...)で述べられている,「11月に75人でスタートしたプロジェクトが12月の冬休み前までに60人に減ってしまった理由」ということ。R.B. が「ボランティアの人が辞めたために,親たちは再び子どもを車で学校に送り始めた」と述べている。その結果プロジェクトを辞める生徒が生じたと考えられるので,これが疑問に対する答えになっている。

(主な語句・表現)

・問題冊子を参照のこと。

[リード文]
◇ student council「生徒会」

[本文]
◇ in addition「その上;さらに加えて」　◇ previous 形「前の;以前の」
◇ unhealthy 形「健康でない」　◇ overweight 形「太りすぎの」
◇ be worried about ...「…を心配している」　◇ safety 名「安全」
◇ on a trial basis「試験的に」　◇ supervisor 名「監督者;管理者」
◇ feedback 名「反応;意見」　◇ thanks to ...「…のおかげで;…のせいで」
◇ in the beginning「最初は」　◇ trust O to −「安心して O に − させる」
◇ motivate O to −「O を − する気にさせる」

第3問

解答	問1 - 9 ③, 10 ①, 11 ④, 12 ②	（完答で3点）
	問2 - ② 　　問3 - ③	（各3点）

出典 — *Original Material*

全訳 —
あなたは他の交換留学生たちとアパートをシェアしています。自分たちの台所が散らかっているので，掃除をして整理することに決めました。あなたはベテランのホームオーガナイザーが書いた次の記事を読みます。

キッチン効率の最大化

出産後，初めて仕事に復帰したとき，私は生活をできるだけ整理し効率的にして，物事を予定通りに進め，子どもたちと過ごせる時間を最大にする必要があると感じました。自分の時間のかなりの部分が食事の準備に関わっていることに気づいたので，まずキッチンを整理することに決めました。次のように，私はキッチンを使いやすくして，料理や片付けに使う時間を減らすことに成功しました。

キッチンを片付ける第一段階は，ごちゃごちゃしたものを処分することです。私は1年間使っていない平皿，大皿，なべなどは，どんなものでも売るかリサイクルするか捨てるかしてよいと決めました。これで収納スペースがたくさんできました。次に，いちばんよく使う器具は全部，私がそれを使う場所の近くに置きました。たとえば，私が毎日使うフライパンはコンロの右にある棚に入れました。私のような右利きの人は，こうすれば簡単に右手でフライパンを取り出し，すぐにコンロの上で使えることになります。コーヒーカップはコーヒーメーカーの隣に置き，一方で，収納容器は冷蔵庫の上の棚に入れました。

その後で，食料品に目を向けました。食料品が箱やパッケージに入っていると，どれくらい残っているのかわかりにくいことがあります。パッケージがほぼ空っぽで，新しいのを買っておくのを忘れていたことに気づいてがっかりすることがよくありました。その問題を解決するために，私は残りの量が簡単にわかるように，シリアル，小麦粉，パスタ，砂糖などを入れるための透明なガラスのびんを買いました。今では，買わなければいけないものをチェックしやすいように，お店に行く前にスマートフォンを使って棚の写真を撮ります。

最後に，自分の好きなレシピのバーチャル図書館を作りました。私はよく，紙の切れ端やメモ帳に料理のよいアイディアを書いていたのですが，これだと紙の山ができるだけでなく，自分が欲しいものをすぐに見つけるのが難しかったのです。その代わりに，私は自分のレシピを全部写真に撮って，タブレットに保存しました。古い紙は全部捨てて，今ではボタンをタッチすれば，どれでも見ることができるのです。夫が料理担当のときには，メールでそれを送ることもできます！

— 英 R 98 —

設問解説

問1　⊡ 9 ⊡ → ⊡ 10 ⊡ → ⊡ 11 ⊡ → ⊡ 12 ⊡　正解 ③ → ① → ④ → ②
「次の出来事（①～④）を起きた順番に並べよ」
① 筆者は道具の置き場所を変えた。
② 筆者は自分のレシピのデジタルコピーを作った。
③ 筆者は使っていない道具を処分した。
④ 筆者は透明な入れ物を買った。

　正解は ③ → ① → ④ → ②。キッチンの片付けについては時系列で書かれているので，順に追っていけばよい。第2段落第1，2文（The first step ... / I decided that ...）から，筆者はまず「1年間使っていないごちゃごちゃしたものを処分した」ことがわかる。続く第4文（Next, I put ...）以降には，道具を効率的に使えるように「置き場所を変えた」と書かれている。第3段落第4文（To solve that ...）では，中身が見えないために残りの量がわからない問題を解決するために「透明なガラスのびんを買った」とある。最終段落第1文（Finally, I made ...）では，「自分の好きなレシピのバーチャル図書館を作った」と書かれている。したがって，正解は ③ → ① → ④ → ② となる。

問2　⊡ 13 ⊡　正解 ②
「あなたが筆者のアドバイスに従って効率的なキッチンを作るなら，あなたは ⊡ 13 ⊡ べきだ」
① めったに使わないものを捨てるのはやめる
② ものは必ず合理的な場所に置く
③ 1年間使ってからものを捨てる
④ 食品はなくなるのを待ってから買う

　正解は ②。キッチンの効率性を高めることとして，第2段落第4文（Next, I put ...）に「いちばんよく使う器具は使う場所の近くに置く」とあり，そのあとに具体例が書かれている。

　① と ③ は第2段落第1，2文（The first step ... / I decided that ...）の「1年間使っていないごちゃごちゃしたものを処分した」に一致しない。④ のようなことも筆者は述べていない。

問3　⊡ 14 ⊡　正解 ③
「この記事から，あなたは筆者が ⊡ 14 ⊡ ことがわかる」
① 以前ほど食料品にお金を使わない
② 彼女の夫にもっと料理をしてほしいと思っている
③ 最近はキッチンで無駄に過ごす時間が減っている
④ 彼女の子どもたちに家事を手伝ってほしいと思っている

　正解は ③。記事のタイトルや第1段落最終文（Here is how ...）からもわかるように，この記事は「キッチンを使いやすくして，料理や片付けに使う時間を減らすことに成功した方法」について書いてある。したがって，そこから推測できる ③ が正解。

　① の食料品については第3段落（After that, I ...）で残りの量をわかりやすくするためにした工夫のことは書かれているが，それにより食料品にかかるお金が減ることには言及されていない。② は，最終段落最終文（I can even ...）で筆者の夫について触れられているが，夫にもっと料理をしてほしいとは述べていない。④ は，キッチンを効率化するきっかけとして第1段落第1文（When I first ...）に子どもたちのことが出てくるが，子どもたちに家事を手伝ってほしいとは書かれていない。

— 英 R 99 —

（主な語句・表現）　・問題冊子を参照のこと。

[リード文]　◇ messy 形「散らかって；汚い」　　　◇ organize 動「…を整理する」

[第1段落]　◇ maximize 動「…を最大限にする；…を最大限に利用する」
(When I first ...)　◇ on schedule「予定通りに；定刻に」　　◇ decrease 動「…を減らす」
　◇ tidy up「片付ける；整理する」

[第2段落]　◇ get rid of ...「…を処分する；取り除く」　◇ clutter 名「乱雑；散乱したもの」
(The first step ...)　◇ plate 名「（浅い）皿；平皿」　　　◇ dish 名「（深い）皿；大盛り皿」
　◇ pan 名「平なべ」　　　　　　　　　◇ free up ...「〈時間・場所など〉を空ける」
　◇ storage 名「保管；貯蔵」
　◇ frying pans（= O）that I use daily I（= S）put（= V）in ...「私は毎日使うフライパンを
　　…に入れた」
　◇ cooker 名「オーブン；コンロ」　　　◇ right-handed 形「右利きの」
　◇ coffee machine「コーヒーメーカー」

[第3段落]　◇ focus on ...「〈注意・関心〉を…に向ける」
(After that, I ...)　◇ replacement 名「置き換え；代用品」　◇ flour 名「小麦粉」

[最終段落]　◇ virtual 形「仮想の；バーチャルの」　◇ recipe 名「レシピ」
(Finally, I made　◇ scrap 名「断片；一片」　　　　　　◇ notepad 名「メモ帳」
　　　　...)　◇ a pile of ...「たくさんの…；山のような…」
　◇ photograph 動「…の写真を撮る；…を撮影する」
　◇ store 動「（データ）を記憶装置に保存する」
　◇ turn 名「順番」

— 英 R 100 —

第4問

解答　　問1 - ②　　問2 - ②　　問3 - ④　　問4 - ②　　　　　　　　（各3点）

出典　　*Original Material*

全訳　　英語の授業であなたは関心のある社会的および環境問題について書いています。これが最も新しい草稿です。あなたは今，先生からのコメントに基づいて，修正に取り組んでいます。

コンピューターゲームをすることの利点	コメント
テレビゲームは親や教師たちの間で悪評を買っています。彼らは，テレビゲームには利点がまったくなく，子どもの勉強と社会生活に対する悪影響である，と信じていることが多いのです。(1)∧ゲームをすることは若者たちにとってさまざまな利点があることを示している研究もあります。	⑴ ここの文章の主題を導入するつなぎとなる文を追加してください。
第一に，心理学者による研究は，ある種のテレビゲームをすることはゲームをする者たちの思考能力を向上させることを示しました。これらの思考能力にはナビゲーション能力や記憶力や論理的思考能力が含まれます。これは，プレーヤーが攻撃されることを避けようとしながら標的を見つけて撃つことを必要とするシューティングゲームに特に言えることです。実際，プレーヤーは，こうした技術を教えるために作られた現実生活の過程とまったく同じぐらい，テレビゲームをすることによってそうした技術を磨いていきます。	
第二に，ある長期的研究は，ゲームは問題解決能力を発達させる可能性があることを発見しました。ロールプレイングゲームはこうした能力を発達させるのに特に有益です。その研究が発見したところによると，生徒がロールプレイングのテレビゲームをする時間が長ければ長いほど，翌年の学校の成績が向上します。要するに，ロールプレイングゲームをすることは(2)学校の成績を向上させる可能性があるのです。	⑵ 前の文章で使った語句を避けて，別の表現を使ってみてください。
(3)∧プレイする時間が短く簡単なゲームは息抜きを促し，プレーヤーの気分がプレー前よりもよくなる可能性があります。簡単に言えば，テレビゲームをすると，若者たちの気分がよくなることがあり得るのです。これは，鬱や精神衛生に関する問題がより一般的になりつつある社会においては重要なことです。	⑶ この段落の主題文を入れてください。
要約すれば，テレビゲームには多くの利点があります。(4)∧もちろん，欠点もありますが，適度にゲームを行えば，ゲームは多くの点で人に利益をもたらす可能性があるのです。	⑷ ここで利点を要約してください。

先生のコメント
非常に興味深いです！　私も頭をよくするためにテレビゲームをした方がいいのでしょう！ ^^

設問解説

問1 | 15 | **正解②**

「コメント(1)に基づくと，追加するべき最も適切なつなぎとなる文はどれか」 | 15 |

① 実際のところ，おそらくこれは正しいのでしょう。

② **しかし，それが常に実情であるというわけではありません。**

③ 実際，ほとんどの研究はそのことを支持しています。

④ 手短に言えば，これはまったく支持されてはいません。

正解は**②**。コメント(1)には「ここの文章の主題を導入するつなぎとなる文を追加してください」とある。空所(1)の直前では，親や教師たちはテレビゲームには利点がまったくなく，子どもの勉強と社会生活に悪影響を及ぼすと信じている，と述べられ，空所(1)の直後には「ゲームをすることは若者たちにとってさまざまな利点があることを示している研究もあります」とある。つまり，空所(1)の前後ではテレビゲームの利点に関し，親や教師の思い込みと実際の研究では逆の内容が述べられている。また，この文章の主題は，第2段落（First, research by ...），第3段落（Second, a long-term ...），第4段落（Finally, video games ...）において述べられているように，テレビゲームのいくつかの利点である。以上から正解は**②**となる。

①，③，④はいずれも自然な文脈とはならないので不可。

問2 | 16 | **正解②**

「コメント(2)に基づくと，代わりに使うべき最も適切な表現はどれか」 | 16 |

① 学校の成績を下げる原因となる

② **よりよい学業成績の結果につながる**

③ 生徒により多くの学校の勉強をさせる

④ 結果として成績の下落を招く

正解は**②**。コメント(2)には「前の文章で使った語句を避けて，別の表現を使ってみてください」とある。下線部(2)を含む文の直前の文では，the greater the improvement in school grades the following year（翌年の学校の成績が向上します）という表現が用いられているが，下線部(2)には improve school grades（学校の成績を向上させる）とあり，improvement の動詞形と school grades が繰り返して用いられている。意味は変えずに表現の繰り返しを避けるように指示されているのだから，正解は**②**と判断できる。

①，③，④はいずれも下線部(2)と同様の意味を表していないので不可。

問3 | 17 | **正解④**

「コメント(3)に基づくと，追加するべき最も適切な主題文はどれか」 | 17 |

① 最後に，人の気分と精神衛生にとっては時間が長くかかる難しいテレビゲームをする方がよいのです。

② 最後に，テレビゲームをすることは人の幸福感や気分に対してどの方向にもほとんど影響を与えません。

③ 最後に，テレビゲームをする時間が長ければ長いほど，精神衛生は悪影響を受けます。

④ **最後に，テレビゲームは，人の気分を改善し，不安を感じることを防ぐのに役立ちます。**

正解は**④**。コメント(3)には「この段落の主題文を入れてください」とある。空所(3)を含む第4段落では，時間が短く簡単なテレビゲームは人の気分を改善させ，これは，鬱や精神的な健康問題がより一般的になりつつある社会においては重要なことであるということが述べられているので，その内容を簡潔にまとめた**④**が正解となる。

①，②，③はいずれもこの段落の内容を表してはいないので不可。

問4 　18　 正解②

「コメント(4)に基づくと，どの文を追加するべきか」 　18

① それは，設計したり，熱心に取り組んだり，他の若者たちと交際したりすることができる人の能力を発達させます。

② それは，認知能力を改善し，解決策を見つける能力を磨き，人によい気分を感じさせます。

③ それは，人の精神や勉強する能力を保護し，鬱を増大させます。

④ それは，プレーヤーのシューティング能力や集中力や活力レベルを向上させます。

　正解は②。コメント(4)には「ここで利点を要約してください」とある。空所(4)を含む段落の前までの段落構成は以下のようになっている（カッコ内の数字は段落番号を表す）。

　　[1] 序論　　「親や教師たちはテレビゲームには利点がまったくなく，子どもに悪影響を及ぼすと信じている」

　　[2] 主題　　「しかし，テレビゲームにはさまざまな利点がある」
　　　　　　　　例示1「思考能力の向上」

　　[3] 例示2「問題解決能力の発達とそれによる学業成績の向上」

　　[4] 例示3「精神面における効用」

　以上から，この文章全体の主題である「テレビゲームにおけるさまざまな利点」は第2段落から第4段落において「思考能力の向上」，「問題解決能力の発達とそれによる学業成績の向上」，「精神面における効用」として具体的に述べられていることがわかる。よってその3つの利点をまとめた②が正解とわかる。

　①，③，④はいずれもこの文章中で述べられているテレビゲームの利点の要約とはなっていないので不可。

（主な語句・表現）　・問題冊子を参照のこと。

[リード文]
◇ draft 名「草稿；下書き」　　　　　　　◇ work on ...「…に取り組む」
◇ revision 名「修正」　　　　　　　　　　◇ based on ...「…に基づいて［た］」

[タイトル]
◇ benefit 名「利点；利益」

[第1段落]
(Video games have ...)
◇ reputation 名「評判」　　　　　　　　　◇ influence on ...「…への影響」
◇ multiple 形「多数の；多様な」

[第2段落]
(First, research by ...)
◇ improve 動「…を改善する；…を向上させる」
◇ navigation skill「ナビゲーション能力（自身の位置を正確に把握し，ルートを計画し追跡するプロセスや活動に関する能力）」
◇ reasoning 名「論理的思考能力；推論力」　◇ be true for ...「…に当てはまる」
◇ target 名「標的」　　　　　　　　　　　◇ avoid －ing「－することを避ける」
◇ polish 動「…を磨く」
◇ just as much ... as 〜「〜とまったく同じぐらい（多く）」
◇ designed to －「－するために作られた」

[第3段落]
(Second, a long-term ...)
◇ role-playing game「ロールプレイングゲーム（各自に割り当てられたキャラクターを操作し，目的を達成するゲーム）」
◇ improvement 名「向上」　　　　　　　　◇ school grade「学校の成績」
◇ in short「要するに」

— 英 R 103 —

[第4段落]
(Finally, video games ...)

◇ encourage 動「…を促す」
◇ put simply「簡単に言えば」
◇ mental health「精神衛生」

◇ relaxation 名「息抜き」
◇ depression 名「鬱；意気消沈」

[最終段落]
(In summary, video ...)

◇ in summary「要約すれば」
◇ benefit 動「…に利益をもたらす」

◇ in moderation「適度に」
◇ in many ways「多くの点で」

[コメント]

◇ linking 形「つなぎとなる；接続する」
◇ insert 動「…を挿入する［入れる］」

◇ introduce 動「…を導入する」
◇ summarize 動「…を要約する」

[設問・選択肢]

◇ case 名「実情；事実」
◇ decline 動「下がる；低下する」
◇ achievement 名「達成；成績」
◇ have little effect on ...「…にほとんど影響を及ばさない」
◇ negatively affect ...「…に悪影響を及ぼす」
◇ prevent A from －ing「Aが－するのを防ぐ」
◇ anxious 形「不安な」
◇ cognitive ability「認知能力」

◇ school performance「学校の成績」
◇ academic result「学業成績の結果」

◇ socialize with ...「…と交際する」
◇ refine 動「…を向上させる」

第5問

解答

問1 – ④	問2 – ①	（各3点）
問3 ┃21┃ – ① ┃22┃ – ⑤		（各2点）
問4 – ③	問5 – ①	（各3点）

出典 （参考）https://archive.aessweb.com/index.php/5007/article/view/2596

全訳

あなたは来年，オーストラリアで日本語のアシスタント教師としてボランティアをすることに決めました。準備のために，あなたは語学教授法に関する2つの記事を読んでいます。

タスク中心学習
K. 松井
岩橋高校　英語教師

何年も前ですが，私が日本で高校生だったころ，私の授業はすべて「文法訳読法」を用いて教えられていました。実際，私自身が英語教師になったときでさえ，それは私が用いたやり方でした。私は生徒たちに英語の文法規則とその意味を日本語で教え，それから，この規則を用いて日本語から英語へ翻訳する練習をしました。生徒たちは文法をとても詳しく学び，試験に合格することができたのです。退屈でしたが，効果はありました。

しかし，仕事を一休みしてオーストラリアの語学学校で勉強したとき，私は語学学習には別の方法があることに気づきました。私の先生は「タスク中心学習」を用いました。これは文法規則に焦点を当てるのではなく，私たちは英語で完成させるタスクを与えられ，その後，タスクを終えてから言語をチェックしました。たとえば，私たちは友達の旅行スケジュールの計画を立てるタスクを与えられました。私たちは宿泊設備，アクティビティを調べ，ホテルに予約の電話をかけるロールプレイをし，それから友達にメールを書かなければなりませんでした。このタスクの間，私たちはリーディング，ライティング，スピーキング，そしてリスニングのスキルを使い，それが「課題」だと思わずに言語の訓練をしたのです。このプロジェクト，つまり「タスク」が終わると，先生は日本語を全く使わずに私たちの英語に対するアドバイスをくれました。

私は日本に帰ったらこの方法をもっと使おうと決めました。今，高校教師として，私は自分の英語の授業ではできるだけ多くタスク中心学習を使っています。生徒たちはより積極的に参加し，学習した言語を実際に使う能力が向上したことに私は気づきました。昔ながらの文法訳読法は終わりにしてもいいころだと思います。また，教室で英語の教師が日本語を使うことを推奨すべきではないとも考えます。

文法訳読法
M. 鈴木
関東言語大学　研究員

私は松井氏のタスク中心言語学習の体験を興味深く拝読し，それが言語学習の中級者にはとても有益になり得るという点で同意見です。それによりコミュニケーションが促され，生徒たちは，言語が日常生活を送るためのツールであることを理解することができます。

しかしながら，言語教授法として，特に初級者を指導する際は，文法訳読を全面的に排除するべきではないと思います。たとえば，12歳の日本人生徒のクラスを例に挙げましょ

う。彼らは英語に接する機会がきわめて限られているので，単語の知識はほぼありませんし，まして文法の知識はそれ以下です。彼らはいかなる種類の有意義なタスクも英語でやり遂げることはできないでしょう。彼らは教師の指示を理解できないでしょうから，英語で彼らにそのタスクについて説明することはさらに困難でしょう。初級者の段階では，私たちは彼らに語彙や文法というツールを与えて，彼らが理解できる言語でそれについて説明することが必要です。

　ヨルダンの学校で行われたある調査で，研究者たちは，英文法のポイントを起点言語（彼らの母語であるアラビア語）で教わった生徒のテストの結果と，目標言語（英語）だけで教わった生徒の結果を比較しました。彼らは同程度の学力の生徒たちを，ランダムに10人ずつの2つのグループに分けました。Aグループには，母語で指導して文法訳読法を用いて特定の文法項目を教えました。Bグループには，同じ文法項目を英語だけで多くの例文を用いて教えました。それから，2つのグループは同じ文法のテストを受けました。ご覧の通り，2つのグループにはテストの平均点に著しい差があります。

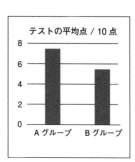

　したがって，タスク中心学習は優れた教授法であることに賛同はしますが，生徒たちが正確に英語の読み書きを学習し，極めて重要な大学入試に合格してほしいと願うなら，私たちは文法訳読をやめるべきではありません。よい英語の授業とは，数多くの多様な教授法を組み入れて，生徒たちには言語を徹底的に理解させ，文法訳読ではできないやり方で生徒たちにやる気を出させるものだと私は考えます。

設問解説

問1　19　正解 ④

「松井氏は　19　と考えている」
① 文法訳読は試験の準備には効果がない
② タスク中心学習は試験に合格するためには最良の方法だ
③ 文法を教えることは英語教師にとって退屈だ
④ **日本語で教えることは生徒たちには役に立たない**

　正解は④。松井氏は第2段落（However, when I ...）で自分が体験した「タスク中心学習」を紹介している。最終段落（I decided to ...）では，その効果を実感したうえで，第4文（I believe it ...）で「（日本語で教える）文法訳読法は終わりにしてもいいころだ」，最終文（I also think ...）では「教室で英語の教師が日本語を使うことを推奨すべきではない」と書いている。したがって，④が正解だと判断できる。

　松井氏の記事では第1段落で文法訳読法を紹介し，第4, 5文（The students learned ... / It was boring ...）で「生徒たちは文法をとても詳しく学び，試験に合格することができ，退屈だったが効果はあった」と書いている。「効果はあった」ので①は誤り。②のような記述はない。また，「退屈だった」と感じたのは当時の松井氏で，一般の英語教師にとって退屈だとは述べていないので③も誤り。

問2　20　正解 ①

「鈴木氏が紹介した調査で，生徒たちは　20　」
① **異なる教授法で学習した後で比較された**
② 異なる学力の2つのグループに分けられた
③ 実験後は前より良い結果を出すことができなかった
④ 母語で例文を教わった

　正解は①。調査に関しては鈴木氏の記事の第3段落に書かれている。第1文（In one study ...）で研究者たちは「英文法のポイントを母語で教わった生徒のテストの結果と，

目標言語（英語）だけで教わった生徒の結果を比較した」と書かれている。「母語で教わった」は文法訳読の教授法，「目標言語（英語）で教わった」はタスク中心学習の教授法なので，① が正解。

第3段落第2文（They randomly divided ...）から，生徒たちは「同程度の学力」の2つのグループだったことがわかるので，② は誤り。また，実験は2つのグループの比較であり，実験前と後の比較ではないので，③ は誤り。第3段落第3，4文（Group A was ... / Group B was ...）から両グループともに同じ英語の文法項目を学習する際，グループAは母語で，グループBは多くの例文を用いて英語だけで学習したことがわかるので，④ も誤り。

問3 　21　 正解①　 　22　 正解⑤
「鈴木氏は，タスク中心言語学習は中級の生徒たちの　21　スキルを向上させるのに効果的であるのに対し，文法訳読は生徒たちが正確に　22　言語を学ぶのを確実にするので，初級者を教える場合には重要な方法だと説明している（各空所に選択肢 ① ～ ⑥ のうちから最適なものを1つずつ選べ。）」
　　① コミュニケーション
　　② 仕事
　　③ 起点
　　④ 学習
　　⑤ 目標
　　⑥ ライティング
　鈴木氏はタスク中心言語学習について第1段落（I enjoyed reading ...）で，「中級者にはとても有益で，コミュニケーションを促す」と述べている。これは，中級の生徒たちのコミュニケーションスキルを向上させるのに有益だということなので，　21　には ① が入る。

　文法訳読については，初級者への指導法として，第2段落（However, I do ...）でその必要性を主張し，最終段落第1文（Therefore, while I ...）で「生徒たちが正確に英語の読み書きを学習し，大学入試に合格してほしいなら，文法訳読をやめるべきではない」と述べている。第3段落第1文（In one study ...）にあるように，ここでの英語とは生徒たちにとって目標言語なので，　22　には ⑤ が入るのが適切。

問4 　23　 正解③
「筆者は2人とも，文法訳読は　23　のに有益だという点で同意見だ」
　　① 創造的に書く方法を学ぶ
　　② 中級レベルの生徒たちのやる気を出させる
　　③ 試験で高得点を取る
　　④ 英語をツールとして見る
　正解は ③。文法訳読に関して，松井氏は第1段落第4，5文（The students learned ... / It was boring ...）で「生徒たちは文法を詳しく学び，試験に合格することができ，効果はあった」と述べている。また，鈴木氏は最終段落第1文（Therefore, while I ...）で「生徒たちが正確に英語の読み書きを学習し，極めて重要な大学入試に合格してほしいと願うなら，私たちは文法訳読をやめるべきではありません」と述べている。以上から，2人とも試験で高得点を取り入試に合格するには文法訳読は効果的だという点で意見が一致している。したがって，③ が正解。

　① のような記述はない。② のようなことは，松井氏の意見からは読み取れない。④ については，「英語をツールとして見る」という表現を松井氏は全く用いていない。また鈴木氏の記事の第1段落最終文（It encourages communication ...）に「それによりコミュニケーションが促され，生徒たちは，言語が日常生活を送るためのツールであることを理解する

— 英R 107 —

ことができます」とあるが，下線部の「それ（It）」は，タスク中心学習のことなので，④
は正解になれない。

問5 　24 　正解 ①
　　　「鈴木氏の主張をさらに裏付けるには，どの追加情報が最適か」 　24
　　　① 　タスク中心学習法と文法訳読法の最適な組み合わせ方
　　　② 　文法訳読学習が上級の生徒にとってより楽しくなるための方法
　　　③ 　外国語の教師が授業で母語を使うべきかどうか
　　　④ 　タスク中心の言語学習が初級段階で効果がある理由
　　正解は ①。鈴木氏の最終段落最終文（I believe a ...）「よい英語の授業とは，数多くの
多様な教授法を組み入れて，生徒たちには言語を徹底的に理解させ，文法訳読ではできな
いやり方で生徒たちにやる気を出させるものだ」に注目する。これは「生徒たちに言語を
徹底的に理解させる」文法訳読法と「文法訳読ではできないやり方で生徒たちにやる気を
出させる」タスク中心学習を組み合わせることが「よい英語の授業」につながることを示
唆している。したがって，① の「タスク中心学習と文法訳読法の最適な組み合わせ方」が
鈴木氏の主張の裏付けになる。

　　鈴木氏は文法訳読法を上級レベルの生徒に向けて行うべきだとは述べていないので，②
は鈴木氏の主張をさらに裏付ける情報とはならない。③ も，文法訳読法の利点を説く鈴木
氏の意見を裏付ける情報とは考えられない。また，鈴木氏は「タスク中心学習は初級段階
で効果がない」と考えているので，④ の「タスク中心の言語学習が初級段階で効果がある
理由」も鈴木氏の主張の裏付けにはならない。

主な語句・表現
・問題冊子を参照のこと。

[松井氏の記事]
[第1段落]　　◇ grammar 名「文法」　　　　　　　　　◇ translation 名「翻訳」
　　　　　　　◇ method 名「方法；方式」　　　　　　　◇ in detail「詳細に」
　　　　　　　◇ boring 形「退屈な；つまらない」　　　◇ effective 形「効果的な」

[第2段落]　　◇ take a break from ...「…をやめて休憩する；…を一休みする」
　　　　　　　◇ instead of ...「…の代わりに；…ではなくて」
　　　　　　　◇ complete 動「…を完成する；仕上げる；終える」
　　　　　　　◇ look at ...「…を調べる；検査する」　　◇ research 動「…を調べる」
　　　　　　　◇ accommodation 名「宿泊設備」　　　　◇ role-play 動「役割を演じる」
　　　　　　　◇ reservation 名「予約」

[最終段落]　　◇ engaged 形「没頭して；熱中して」
　　　　　　　◇ it is time that SV（＝過去形）「（そろそろ）S が V してもいい頃だ」
　　　　　　　◇ retire 動「…を引退させる」　　　　　　◇ encourage 動「…を奨励する；促進する」

[鈴木氏の記事]
[第1段落]　　◇ beneficial 形「…に有益な；ためになる」　　◇ intermediate 形「中級の；中程度の」

[第2段落]　　◇ get rid of ...「…を取り除く；…から脱する」
　　　　　　　◇ exposure 名「さらすこと；さらされること」
　　　　　　　◇ meaningful 形「意味のある；有意義な」　　◇ instruction 名「指示」

[第3段落]　　◇ conduct 動「…を行う」　　　　　　　　◇ Jordan 名「ヨルダン」
　　　　　　　◇ compare 動「…を比較する」　　　　　　◇ result 名「結果；（試験などの）成績」
　　　　　　　◇ source language「起点言語《翻訳における原文の言語》」

◇ target language「目標言語《学習・教授対象の言語》」
◇ randomly副「ランダムに；無作為に」　　◇ academic形「学業成績の」
◇ specific形「特定の；一定の」
◇ significant形「重大な；意味のある；かなり多い」

[**最終段落**]
◇ accurately副「正確に；精密に」　　　　◇ all-important形「極めて重要な」
◇ incorporate動「…を組み入れる；合体させる」
◇ thorough形「徹底的な；完全な」　　　◇ motivate動「…に動機［興味］を与える」

第6問

解答	

問1 － ④　　　問2 － ②　　　　　　　　　　　　　　　　　　　（各3点）

問3 － 27 ・ 28 － ① ・ ③　　　　　　　　（順不同・両方正解で3点）

　　　 29 － ②　　　　　　　　　　　　　　　　　　　　　　（3点）

問4 － ④　　　問5 － ④　　　　　　　　　　　　　　　　　　　（各3点）

出典 | *Original Material*

全訳 | あなたは路上で自動運転車が許可されるべきかどうかについてのエッセイに取り組んでいます。以下の各ステップに従っていきます。

　ステップ1：自動運転車に関するさまざまな見解を読んで理解する。
　ステップ2：自動運転車が許可されるべきかどうかについての判断を下す。
　ステップ3：追加の情報源を使って，エッセイの概要を作成する。

[ステップ1] さまざまな情報源を読む
筆者A（高齢者）
私はこの新しいテクノロジーにわくわくしています。歳をとるにつれて，私の反応は悪くなってきているので，今私が普通車を運転するのは危険すぎます。しかし，自動運転車があれば，私はさらにあと何年も自立を維持することができるでしょう。このテクノロジーは障害を持つ人たちにとっても非常に役に立つでしょう。高齢者や障害者が1人で安全に動き回ることを可能とするものは何であれ，よいものなのです。私が心配する唯一のことは，こうした車がどれだけ高額になるかということです！

筆者B（教習所教官）
私は自動運転車が増えることについて心配してはいません。むしろ，私が心配するのは，路上であまり車の運転には向いていない運転者をより多く見ることになるということです。車が自動運転から運転者による操作に切り替わる状況は確実にあり，私たちはいまだにすべての人が人工知能なしに十分に車の運転が上手であることを必要としています。一方，このテクノロジーは高齢者や障害者といった現在普通車を運転することができない人たちに利益をもたらします。そうした人たちはより長く自立を維持することができるでしょう。

筆者C（自動車エンジニア）
車会社のエンジニアとして，私は自動運転車の安全性についてまったく心配してはいません。実際，私たちはこうした車を人が運転する車よりも安全であるように特別に設計しています。我が国では，車の事故の85％が人の過失によって引き起こされています。もし人の過失を減らすことができれば，毎年数百もの命を救うことができます。もちろん，コンピューターの安全性に関しては，常に車内のコンピューターがハッキングされる可能性があるので，少し心配なところはありますが，私たちはそうしたことを迅速に処理する技術と知識を持っていると自負しております。

筆者D（警官）
私の毎日の業務の多くは，スピード違反や飲酒運転や危険な運転といった路上での違反のために人々に警告を与えたり，逮捕したりすることに関係しています。私は，この新しいテクノロジーが利用可能になると交通事故を減少させるかもしれない，と聞いたことがあ

— 英R 110 —

ります。しかし，私は実際のところ，誤ってより多くの事故を引き起こし得る非常に多くのことが存在するので，そうしたことは起こらないと思います。全般的に言うと，私はこの新しいテクノロジーを導入するのはよい考えではないと思います。私が言及した問題に対する解決策は，運転免許試験をより厳格化し，法律を改良することです。

筆者 E（タクシー運転手）
私はタクシー運転手として働き，私の業界は大きな影響を受けることになるので，この新しいテクノロジーを興味深く追っています。私は，個人の車ばかりでなくタクシーやバスも最終的には無人車に取って代わられることになるのではと懸念しています。最初は車自体は普通車より高額になるでしょうが，価格は安くなり始めるでしょう。その時点で，運送会社は運転手は不必要な出費であると判断することになるでしょう。私は，タクシーやバスの運転手が現在のように働けなくなるかもしれないと心配しています。

設 問 解 説

問1 　25 　正解④
「筆者 A と B は両者とも 　25 　と言及している」
① こうしたテクノロジーを備えた車は価格がより高額になるので，高齢者は使用することができない
② 各家庭は，祖父母がより助けてくれるので，自動運転車によい影響を受けるであろう
③ こうした新しい車は自ら運転を行うので，自動車教習を受ける人は減るだろう
④ **自動運転車はある特定の人々の集団が運転者となって自立を維持することを可能とするだろう**

正解は④。高齢者である筆者 A は第 3 文（However, if I ...）で「しかし，自動運転車があれば，私はさらにあと何年も自立を維持することができるでしょう」と述べている。また教習所教官の筆者 B は，第 4 文（On the other ...）以降で「一方，このテクノロジーは高齢者や障害者といった現在普通車を運転することができない人たちに利益をもたらします。そうした人たちはより長く自立を維持することができるでしょう」と述べている。両者とも自動運転車は高齢者や障害者といった特定の人々の自立を維持することになる，と言及していると判断できるので，正解は④。

①に関しては，筆者 A が最終文（The only thing ...）で自動運転車が高額になる可能性に触れているが，そのために高齢者は自動運転車を使用できないとは述べていないし，筆者 B は自動運転車の価格についてはまったく触れていないので不可。

②，③に関しては，いずれも筆者 A と B が述べている内容とはなっていないので不可。

問2 　26 　正解②
「筆者 C は 　26 　と示唆している」
① 多くの人々がこうした車の安全性について心配しているが，こうした車は普通車とまったく変わらない
② **人間の運転手の必要をなくすことによって，こうした新しい車は事故の数を減らすことに役立つだろう**
③ こうした車があると，操縦がはるかにしやすいので，人々は車の運転がさらに上手くなるだろう
④ こうした車は，事故の危険がある場合には車が運転手操作式に切り替わるよう設計されている

正解は②。自動車エンジニアである筆者 C は第 2 文（In fact, we ...）で，自分たちは自動運転車を人が運転する車よりも安全であるように設計している，と述べた後で，続く第 3 文（In my country, ...）～第 4 文（If we can ...）で，自分たちの国の車の事故の 85%

— 英 R 111 —

が人の過失によるものなので，それを減らすことができれば事故の数は大きく減少し，たくさんの命を救うことになる，と主張しているが，これは言い換えれば，<u>人間が運転する車に自動運転車が取って代わることで事故の数を減らすことができる</u>ということを意味しているので，正解は②となる。

①，③，④に関しては，いずれも筆者Cが述べている内容とはなっていないので不可。

[ステップ2] 判断を下す

問3 ⎡27⎤・⎡28⎤ 正解①・③ ⎡29⎤ 正解②

「さまざまな見解を理解したので，自動運転車の導入に関して判断を下し，それを以下のように書き出した。⎡27⎤，⎡28⎤，⎡29⎤を完成させるのにもっとも適切な選択肢を選びなさい」

あなたの判断：自動運転車は路上で許可されるべきだ。
・ 筆者⎡27⎤と⎡28⎤があなたの判断を支持している。
・ その2人の筆者の主要な論拠：⎡29⎤。

⎡27⎤と⎡28⎤に入る選択肢（順序は問わない）
① A
② B
③ C
④ D
⑤ E

正解は①と③。高齢者である筆者Aは上の**問1**の解説でも触れたように，第3文（However, if I ...）〜第4文（This technology will ...）において，<u>自動運転車は高齢者や障害者の自立を維持することで非常に有益だ</u>，と言及している。また自動車エンジニアである筆者Cは上の**問2**の解説でも触れたように，第2文（In fact, we ...）〜第4文（If we can ...）で，<u>自分たちエンジニアは自動運転車を人が運転する車よりも安全であるように設計しており，自動運転車が人間の過失を減らすことができれば車の事故は大幅に減少する</u>と言っている。以上から筆者AとCは「自動運転車は路上で許可されるべきだ」という「あなた」の判断を支持する意見を述べていることがわかるので，⎡27⎤と⎡28⎤には①と③が入ることになる。

⎡29⎤に入る選択肢
① 現在，事故は人間の運転手ではなく自動車製造業者の責任となるのだろう
② **自動運転の技術を導入することで，運転技能にかかわらず安全に車を運転することが可能になるだろう**
③ 自動運転車は普通車よりも危険人物によってハッキングされる可能性がはるかに少ない
④ アルコールを飲んで車を運転したために逮捕される人の数は劇的に減少するだろう

正解は②。筆者Aは今の自分にとって普通車を運転するのは危険である，と述べているが，第5文（Anything that allows ...）で「（自動運転車は）高齢者や障害者が1人で安全に動き回ることを可能とする」と述べている。また筆者Cも，自動運転車が人間の過失を減らすことができれば車の事故は大幅に減少すると述べている。以上から，「あなた」の判断を支持している筆者AとC共通の論拠は選択肢②の「自動運転の技術を導入することで，運転技量にかかわらず安全に車を運転することが可能になるだろう」ということだとわかる。

なお筆者Bは，「すべての人が人工知能なしに十分に車の運転が上手であることが必要」と述べているため選択肢②には当てはまらない。

— 英R 112 —

(全訳)　[ステップ３] 情報源ＡとＢを使って，概要を作成する。
あなたのエッセイの概要：

自動運転車が未来の姿だ

序論
　近年，自動運転車を開発する自動車製造業者が増えている。このテクノロジーに懸念を抱く人は多いが，自動運転車は路上において許可されるべきだ。

本論
　理由１：[ステップ２から]
　理由２：[情報源Ａに基づく]　……　30
　理由３：[情報源Ｂに基づく]　……　31

結論
　こうした理由で，人々は自動運転車を購入して使用することを許可されるべきだ。

情報源Ａ
　現在，車や小型トラックは世界の炭素排出量の約 10％ を占めている。したがって，この排出量を減らすためにあらゆる手段を講じることが非常に重要である。それを行う方法の１つは，自動運転車に移行することによるものである。今，車は高速で運転されるときやブレーキをかけるときやあまりに急速に加速するときにはたくさんのエネルギーを燃焼する。一方，自動運転車は，できる限り燃焼する燃料を少なくするために，スピードや加速を最適化することができるほどとても賢くなっている。また自動運転車は移動のために最も効率のよいルートを選ぶことができる。加えて，こうした車が最終的に完全な無人運転となれば，同じ車ですべての家族を自動で仕事場や学校へ送り届けることができるので別々の車で短い移動をたくさん行う必要がなく，各家庭が必要とする乗り物は少なくなるだろう。最後に，テクノロジーが向上するにつれて，そうした車の重量は減少し，燃料の燃焼量の一層の減少にさえつながるだろう。現在，バッテリーは重いが，時間をかけて軽くなっていく可能性が高い。

情報源Ｂ
　米国のある保険会社の研究が示しているところによると，自動運転車がより一般的になれば，私たちが保険に支払う金額は変わる可能性が高い。算定グラフは，車が自動運転になった場合の将来の見積りと比較した，さまざまな種類の車の保険に対して現在支払っている金額を示している。これは自動運転車が事故を起こす可能性がより低いという理由によるものである。

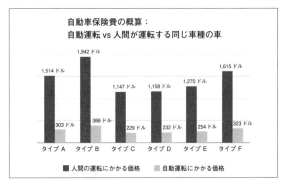

設問解説

問 4 | 30 | **正解 ④**

「**情報源 A に基づけば，以下のどれが理由 2 としてもっとも適切か**」 | 30 |

① 人間が運転する車は自動運転車よりも約 10％ 非効率的である。

② 新しい自動運転車は古い自動運転車よりバッテリーは軽く，より速くブレーキがかかるので，運転効率がよりよい。

③ 自動運転車は人間が運転する車よりも長い距離をより速く移動でき，バッテリーは軽いので，二酸化炭素を排出する燃料の使用量はより少ない。

④ **自動運転車は燃費がよく，車での移動数を削減できるので，環境にとってよりよいものかもしれない。**

正解は ④。情報源 A の第 5 文（Self-driving cars, on ...）では「一方，自動運転車は，できる限り燃焼する燃料を少なくするために，スピードや加速を最適化することができるほどとても賢くなっている」と，自動運転車の燃費がよい点が述べられ，さらに第 7 文（In addition, if ...）では「加えて，こうした車［自動運転車］が最終的に完全な無人運転となれば，さまざまな車で短い移動をたくさん行う必要がなく，同じ車ですべての家族を自動で仕事場や学校へ送り届けることができるので各家庭が必要とする乗り物は少なくなるだろう」と，自動運転車を使用すれば車での移動回数が少なくて済むことが述べられている。車での移動回数が少なくて済むということは，それだけ二酸化炭素の排出量を減らすことになるので，環境に対してよいものとなると推測できる。また第 8 文（Finally, as technology ...）では「最後に，テクノロジーが向上するにつれて，そうした車の重量は減少し，燃料の燃焼量の減少にさえつながるだろう」と今後のテクノロジーの発展により使用する燃料の減少につながることが述べられている。以上から，自動運転車は燃費がよく，車での移動回数が少なくて済み，テクノロジーの発展と相まって二酸化炭素の排出量を減らすことになるので，環境に対してよい自動車となる可能性が高いと推測できる。よって正解は ④ となる。

①，②，③ に関しては，いずれも情報源 A で述べられている内容ではないので不可。

問 5 | 31 | **正解 ④**

「**理由 3 として，あなたは『自動運転車は人々のお金を節約する可能性が高い』と書くことにした。情報源 B に基づけば，どの選択肢がこの記述をもっともよく支持しているか**」 | 31 |

① 自動運転車の約 50％ は，損傷を受けた場合の修理費が安く済むので，人間が運転する車よりも保険料が安くなるだろう。

② 自動車保険会社における変更により，自動運転車の保険料は人間が運転する車の半額となっている。

③ 小型車や自動運転車は両方とも普通車よりも自動車保険料が安いので，それらに切り替える人が増えるだろう。

④ **自動運転車は事故に巻き込まれる可能性が低いので，自動運転車の所有者は毎年保険料をおよそ 1,000 ドル節約できるかもしれない。**

正解は ④。情報源 B のグラフより，どの車種においても自動運転車の保険料は人間が運転する車よりも大体 1,000 ドルほど低くなっていることがわかる。情報源 B の最終文（This is because ...）には「これは自動運転車が事故を起こす可能性がより低いという理由によるものである」と述べられていることから，正解は ④ となる。

①，②，③ に関しては，いずれも情報源 B で述べられている内容およびグラフからわかる内容ではないので不可。

主な語句・表現	・問題冊子を参照のこと。

[リード文]
◇ work on ...「…に取り組む」　　　　　◇ self-driving car「自動運転車」
◇ permit 動「…を許可する」
◇ take a position about ...「…についての判断を下す」
◇ allow 動「…を許可する」　　　　　　◇ outline 名「概要」

[ステップ1]
◇ regular car「普通車」　　　　　　　　◇ independence 名「自立；独立」
◇ disabled people「障害者」
◇ elderly people「お年寄り；高齢者」= the elderly, senior citizen
◇ by oneself「1人で」　　　　　　　　◇ driving instructor「教習所教官」
◇ concern 名「懸念；心配」　　　　　　◇ unsuitable 形「不適切な；不向きな」
◇ switch from A to B「A から B に切り替わる」
◇ artificial intelligence「人工知能」　　◇ benefit 動「…に利益をもたらす」
◇ disability 名「障害」　　　　　　　　◇ vehicle 名「乗り物；車」
◇ security 名「安全性」
◇ a chance that ...「…という可能性」　 that はここでは同格の名詞節を導く接続詞。
◇ hack 動「(コンピューターシステム) に不正にアクセスする；…をハッキングする」
◇ be confident that ...「…に自信を持っている」
◇ involve −ing「−することに関係する」　◇ arrest 動「…を逮捕する」
◇ offense 名「違反」　　　　　　　　　◇ available 形「利用可能な」
◇ go wrong「間違う；誤る」　　　　　　◇ overall 副「全体として；全般的に」
◇ bring ... in「…を導入する」　　　　　◇ impact 動「…に影響を及ぼす」
◇ eventually 副「最終的に」　　　　　　◇ be replaced by ...「…に取って代わられる」
◇ driverless car「無人車」　　　　　　◇ at first「初めは；最初は」
◇ transportation company「運送会社」

[設問文・選択肢]
◇ mention that ...「…と言及している」
◇ be positively affected by ...「…によい影響を受ける」
◇ allow O to −「O が−することを許す [可能とする]」
◇ state that ...「…と述べる」　　　　　◇ remove 動「…を取り除く」
◇ so that S can ...「(目的を表して) S が…するために」
◇ mode 名「(様) 式」

[ステップ2]
◇ now that ...「(今や) …なので」　　　◇ introduction 名「導入」
◇ as below「以下のように」　　　　　　◇ car manufacturer「自動車製造業者」
◇ be likely to −「−する可能性が高い」

[ステップ3]
◇ van 名「小型トラック；バン」　　　　◇ account for ...「〈割合〉を占める」
◇ carbon emission「炭素排出量」
◇ take steps to −「−するための手段を講じる」　 本文では every step is taken to − と受動
　態で表現されている。
◇ accelerate 動「加速する」　　　　　　◇ smart 形「利口な；賢い」
◇ optimize 動「…を最適化する」　　　　◇ as ... as possible「できるだけ…」
◇ journey 名「旅程；移動」　　　　　　◇ insurance company「保険会社」
◇ currently 名「現在」　　　　　　　　◇ compared to ...「…と比較して [比較した]」

[設問文・選択肢]
◇ inefficient 形「非効率的な」
◇ CO_2-emitting fuel「二酸化炭素を排出する燃料」
◇ be involved in ...「…に巻き込まれる」

第7問

解答

問1 － ④　　問2 － ①　　　　　　　　　　　　　　　　　　　（各3点）

問3 － | 34 | ⑤, | 35 | ④, | 36 | ③, | 37 | ①　　（完答で3点）

問4 － ③　　　　　　　　　　　　　　　　　　　　　　　　　（3点）

問5 － ②・③　　　　　　　　　　　　　　　（順不同・両方正解で3点）

出典　*Original Material*

全訳

あなたの理科の先生は，科学の分野で重要な仕事をした女性について調べ，メモを使ってクラスで調査を発表するという課題を全員に出しました。あなたはアルベルト・アインシュタインの最初の妻であるミレヴァ・マリッチについての記事を見つけました。

ミレヴァ・マリッチの生涯

「アルベルト・アインシュタイン」という名前は誰もが知っている。彼は20世紀で最も重要な物理学者と見なされ，1921年にはノーベル物理学賞を獲得している。しかし，彼の最初の妻のセルビア人物理学者ミレヴァ・マリッチについて知る人はほとんどいない。彼女は2人が初めて会った1896年から，1919年に離婚するまでアインシュタインの伴侶だった。アインシュタインの成功のカギはミレヴァであったと，多くの人が信じている。

ミレヴァ・マリッチは1875年，セルビアの裕福な家庭に生まれた。大学以前の教育はすべて故国で受けた。当時，彼女の通っていた高校では物理の授業を受けられるのは男子だけだったが，父親は彼女の能力を認め，彼女が授業に参加できるよう特別に許可を取ってくれた。1886年，彼女はスイスのチューリッヒ工科大学に入った。アルベルト・アインシュタインと同時期に入学したのである。彼女はそのコースで唯一の女子学生で，そのことは彼女がいかに才能のある人であったかを示している。当時女性の科学者のための機会は非常に限られていたのだから。ミレヴァとアルベルトは長い年月をともに勉強して過ごした。彼らが当時交わしていた手紙からも，彼女が彼の研究に大きな影響を与えたことは明らかだ。ミレヴァとアルベルトは非常に似通った成績で大学を出たが，応用物理学だけは差があった。その科目ではミレヴァの方がアルベルトよりもずっとよい成績だったのだ。

アルベルトの両親は彼のミレヴァとの関係に，彼女の国籍と宗教と高い知性を理由に反対した。彼にとってふさわしい妻にはなれないと思ったのである。しかし，彼らは関係を続け1903年に結婚した。

結婚する前からすでに，彼らは協力して研究に取り組んでいた。1900年には彼らは最初の研究論文を提出したが，それにはアルベルト1人の署名しかなかった。それにも関わらず，彼らはお互いや友人たちに宛てた手紙の中でそれを「私たちの論文」と呼んでいた。ミレヴァはなぜ論文に自分の名を付け加えなかったのだろうか。主な理由は2つあると考えられている。第1に，ミレヴァはアルベルトの両親に2人の結婚を認めてもらえるように，彼に有名になってほしかった。第2に当時は女性に対する大きな偏見があったからだ。研究を男性の名前だけで発表することで，それが肯定的に受け取られる可能性がより大きかったのだ。

— 英 R 116 —

1905 年はアインシュタインにとって最も実りの多い年だった。その年，彼は 5 本の主要な論文を発表し，その 1 つは 1921 年のノーベル賞受賞につながった。ミレヴァは当時友人に，夫と 2 人で毎晩遅くまでこれらの論文の執筆に取り組んだものだと語っていた。それに加えて，アインシュタインの伝記の執筆者は，アインシュタインが休んでいる間にミレヴァが論文を点検しそれを送ったと述べた。アルベルト自身も友人に「僕には妻が必要だ。僕の数学的な問題はすべて彼女が解決してくれる」と語っていた。これにも関わらず，高名な物理学者になったのはアルベルトで，一方ミレヴァは裏方で静かに働いていたのだった。

1912 年，アルベルトはいとこのエルザ・ロウエンタールとひそかに関係を持ち始めた。また彼はこのころ仕事のためにヨーロッパのいろいろな都市に住んでいた。このため，ミレヴァとの結婚は破綻し，1919 年離婚に至った。離婚後のアルベルトとミレヴァの仲は良くなく，ミレヴァの死後に彼女の貢献の真相が暴露され「アインシュタインの神話」が破壊されてしまうことを，アルベルトの弁護士たちが心配していたという証拠がある。

ミレヴァ・マリッチは歴史の中でその仕事が隠されてきた多くの女性科学者の 1 人にすぎない。彼女のアインシュタインに与えた影響が認められたのは，やっと最近になってのことだ。当時の多くの女性の場合と同様に，彼女は夫の成功を支えるために自分自身の願いをあきらめたのである。実際，ミレヴァ・マリッチなくして，アルベルト・アインシュタインはおそらく今日のようなよく知られた名にはなっていなかっただろう。

あなたのメモ：

ミレヴァ・マリッチの生涯

ミレヴァ・マリッチについて
- 故国セルビアで若い時期を過ごした。
- スイスの大学でアルベルト・アインシュタインと出会った。
- 彼女の物理学の才能を証明するのは 32 ことである。

ミレヴァの人生に影響を与えた人々
- 父親。彼は彼女が男の子たちと並んで勉強できるように戦ってくれた。
- アルベルトの両親。彼らはアルベルトとの結婚に反対し，おそらくそのために彼女は 33 ことになった。

影響を与えた出来事
チューリッヒ工科大学に入学した → 34 → 35 → 36 → 37

ミレヴァとアルベルトの遺産
アルベルトの弁護士たちは 38 のではないかと心配した。

ミレヴァの物語から学ぶことができること
- 39
- 40

設問解説

問1 | 32 | 正解 ④

「| 32 | に入る最適な選択肢を選べ」

① チューリッヒ工科大学へ進学する奨学金を得た

② 高校で最優秀の成績だった

③ 大学でアインシュタインに認められた

④ 受講した大学のコースに入ることができた女性は彼女1人だけだった

正解は④。第2段落第5文 (She was the ...) に「彼女はそのコースで唯一の女子学生で，そのことは彼女がいかに才能のある人かを示している。当時女性の科学者のための機会は非常に限られていたのだから」とあることから，④ が正解。

その他の選択肢については，特に本文に記述はないので不適当。

問2 | 33 | 正解 ①

「| 33 | に入る最適な選択肢を選べ」

① 共著の研究論文に自分の名を書くのを避ける

② アルベルトのアドバイスは全くもらわずに彼女自身の研究を完成させる

③ アルベルトを伴わずさまざまなヨーロッパの都市に移り住む

④ アルベルトが物理学の研究論文を書く手伝いをするのをやめる

正解は①。第4段落第6文 (The first is ...) では，ミレヴァが論文に自分の名を付けなかった理由について，「第1に，ミレヴァはアルベルトの両親に2人の結婚を認めてもらえるように，彼に有名になってほしかった」と述べられている。つまり彼の両親に結婚を反対されていたために，論文に自分の名を付けずアルベルト1人の名前で発表したのだということがわかる。したがって正解は①。

②のミレヴァ自身の研究について述べた個所はないので不適当。③の「ヨーロッパ各地に住んだ」のはミレヴァではなくアルベルトなので不適当。④のように，アルベルトの両親から結婚に反対されたせいで彼の論文執筆の手伝いをやめたという記述はないので④は不適当。

問3 | 34 | → | 35 | → | 36 | → | 37 | 正解 ⑤ → ④ → ③ → ①

「5つの出来事 (①〜⑤) のうち4つを選び，起こった順に並べなさい」

① アルベルトと彼のいとこは秘密の恋愛関係を持ち始めた。

② アルベルトは応用物理学の成績がミレヴァよりよかった。

③ アルベルトはノーベル賞受賞につながる論文を発表した。

④ ミレヴァとアルベルトはついに結婚した。

⑤ ミレヴァとアルベルトは彼らの最初の論文を完成し発表した。

正解は ⑤ → ④ → ③ → ①。「チューリッヒ工科大学に入学した」に続く4つの出来事を並べる。まず，大学に入ってからのことを述べている ② についてみると，第2段落最終文 (Mileva and Albert ...) に「応用物理学だけは差があった。その科目ではミレヴァの方がアルベルトよりもずっとよい成績だったのだ」とあり，② は事実ではないため正解には含まれない。① は第6段落第1文 (In 1912, Albert ...) から1912年，③ は第5段落第1，2文 (1905 was Einstein's ... / He published five ...) から1905年，④ は第3段落最終文 (However, they continued ...) から1903年，⑤ は第4段落第2文 (In 1900, they ...) から1900年。したがって，これらを時系列に並べると ⑤ → ④ → ③ → ① の順になる。

問4 | 38 | 正解 ③

「| 38 | に最適な選択肢を選べ」

① ミレヴァが友人たちに語っていたほどはアルベルトを支えていなかった

② ミレヴァが自分の仕事に値する評価を受けられない

— 英 R 118 —

③ 論文へのミレヴァの貢献が知られて，アルベルトの名声が地に落ちる

④ 夫婦が共同で発表した論文は彼女の死後見つからない

正解は③。「アルベルトの弁護士たちは 38 と心配した」に入るものを選ぶ。ミレヴァの死後のことについては第6段落最終文（Albert and Mileva ...）に「…ミレヴァの死後に彼女の貢献の真相が暴露され『アインシュタインの神話』が破壊されてしまうことを，アルベルトの弁護士たちが心配していたという証拠がある」とあるので，これに一致する③が正解。

その他の選択肢についての記述はない。

問5 39 ・ 40 正解②・③

「 39 ・ 40 に最適な選択肢を選べ（順番は問わない）」

① アルベルトは，彼の両親の強い反対がなければより大きな成功を収めていただろう。

② アインシュタインは非常に重要な物理学者だったが，彼の妻の影響は信じられているよりも大きい可能性がある。

③ ミレヴァはその仕事が十分には認められていない女性科学者の一例である。

④ ノーベル賞は男性科学者よりも女性科学者に多く与えられるべきだ。

⑤ アルベルト・アインシュタインの仕事のほとんどが，彼自身ではなく妻によって完成された。

正解は②と③。②の「ミレヴァのアルベルトへの影響」については第5段落に書かれており，また，結論的に最終段落最終文（In fact, without ...）に「実際，ミレヴァ・マリッチなくして，アルベルト・アインシュタインはおそらく今日のようなよく知られた名にはなっていなかっただろう」とある。また，③については，最終段落第1文（Mileva Marić is ...）に「ミレヴァ・マリッチは歴史の中でその仕事が隠されてきた多くの女性科学者の1人にすぎない」とある。よって②と③が正解。

①のアルベルトの両親の反対については第3段落第1文（Albert's parents opposed ...）に「アルベルトの両親は彼のミレヴァとの関係に…反対した」とある。しかし「反対されなかったらより大きな成功を収めていただろう」と考える根拠はないので不適切。④については記述がない。⑤の，ミレヴァのアルベルトへの協力については第5段落に書かれている。第3文（Mileva mentioned to ...）には「ミレヴァは…夫と2人で毎晩遅くまでこれらの論文の執筆に取り組んだものだと語っている」とあるが，「ほとんど彼自身ではなくミレヴァが完成した」という記述はないので不適切。

（主な語句・表現）
[リード文]
・問題冊子を参照のこと。
◇ note 名「メモ」　　　　　　　　　　　◇ article 名「記事；論文」

[第1段落]　◇ physicist 名「物理学者」　　　　　　◇ physics 名「物理学」
（Everyone　◇ be associated with ...「…と一緒にいる；交際している」
knows the ...）　◇ divorce 動「離婚する」

[第2段落]　◇ Serbia 名「セルビア」　　　　　　　◇ wealthy 形「裕福な」
（Mileva Marić　◇ complete 動「…を仕上げる；終える」　◇ be allowed to −「−することを許される」
was ...）　　◇ lecture 名「講義」　　　　　　　　◇ recognize 動「…を認める；…だとわかる」
　　　　　　◇ obtain 動「…を獲得する」　　　　◇ permission 名「許可」
　　　　　　◇ participate 動「参加する」
　　　　　　◇ Zurich Polytechnic「チューリッヒ工科大学」
　　　　　　◇ enroll 動「入学する；登録する」　　◇ indicate 動「…を示す」

	◇ exchange 動「…を交換する」	◇ similar 形「同じような；よく似た」
	◇ grade 名「成績」	◇ applied physics「応用物理学」
	◇ achieve 動「…を獲得する；達成する」	

[第3段落]
(Albert's parents opposed ...)

	◇ oppose 動「…に反対する」	◇ relationship 名「関係」
	◇ nationality 名「国籍」	◇ religion 名「宗教」
	◇ intellect 名「知性」	◇ suitable 形「ふさわしい」

[第4段落]
(Even before their ...)

	◇ submit 動「…を提出する」	◇ refer to ...「…に言及する；触れる」
	◇ make a name for oneself「名を上げる；有名になる」	
	◇ prejudice against ...「…に対する偏見」	◇ positively 副「肯定的に；プラス方向に」

[第5段落]
(1905 was Einstein's ...)

	◇ mention 動「…のことを話に出す；…に言及する」	
	◇ stay up late「遅くまで起きている」	◇ biographer 名「伝記作家」
	◇ celebrated 形「名高い；高名な」	
	◇ in the background「目立たない所で；表には出ず」	

[第6段落]
(In 1912, Albert ...)

	◇ collapse 名「崩壊；破綻」	◇ be on good terms「仲が良い」
	◇ input 名「(提供された) 情報；アドバイス；助力；貢献」	
	◇ be revealed「曝露される」	◇ be destroyed「破壊される」

[最終段落]
(Mileva Marić is ...)

	◇ be acknowledged「認められる」	◇ as with ...「…の場合と同じように」
	◇ abandon 動「…をあきらめる」	◇ household 形「よく知られた」

[メモ]

	◇ evidence 名「証拠」	◇ influential 形「影響のあった」
	◇ alongside 前「…と並んで」	
	◇ be concerned that ...「…ということを心配する」	

[設問文・選択肢]

	◇ avoid －ing「－するのを避ける」	◇ joint research paper「共同執筆論文」
	◇ rearrange 動「…を並べ替える」	◇ recognition 名「評価」
	◇ deserve 動「…を受けるに値する」	◇ ruin 動「…を台なしにする；破滅させる」

第8問

解 答

問1 - ①		（2点）
問2 - ②・④		（順不同・完答で3点）
問3 - ④ 問4 - ① 問5 - ①		（各3点）

出典 *Original Material*

全訳

　あなたは大学の生物学の発表の準備をしている学生グループの一員です。役に立つウイルスについての発表の，自分の担当部分を作るために次の一節を利用しています。

　ウイルスと言えば，あなたはおそらく病気を思い浮かべるだろう。何といっても，ウイルスは頻繁に人間を襲う病気の多くの原因なのだ。インフルエンザや一般的な風邪，COVID-19やそのほか数えきれない病気が，特にヒトに伝染するウイルスによって引き起こされている。そのため多くの人が，すべてのウイルスは悪いもので何としても避けなくてはならないものだと信じている。しかし，それは厳密に言うと正しくない。私たちの体内にあって病気の原因にはまったくならないウイルスもたくさんある。実際，本当はその正反対なのである。なぜなら私たちの消化器系の中に住んでいる多くのウイルスは，有害な細菌を殺すことによって，実際には私たちの健康を保っていてくれるのだから。そういうウイルスは「バクテリオファージ［殺菌ウイルス］」と呼ばれ，ヒトの細胞を害することは全くない。さらに科学者たちは，がん細胞を殺せる他の種類のウイルスもずっと研究し続けている。これらの抗がんウイルスはすでに患者の皮膚がんを治療するために使われており，将来はこのような種類の治療がもっと開発されることが期待されているのだ。

　ウイルスについて興味深いことは，それらが本当は「生きて」などいないということだ。ウイルスは細胞でできているのではなく，エネルギーを作り出すことも自己増殖することもできない。簡単な言葉で言うと，それらはタンパク質の外被に囲まれた，DNAのような遺伝物質の小さなかけらにすぎない。ウイルスは非常に単純な構造をしているので，非常に小さい。実際，ほとんどのウイルスはヒトの細胞の100分の1の小ささだ。非常に小さいので通常の顕微鏡では見ることができない。しかし，ウイルスが宿主になる細胞の外側に付着してその遺伝子の指示を注入し，それから自分のコピーを作り出すために宿主細胞の機構を利用することができるのは，その小ささと構造のおかげなのだ。このようにしてウイルスが細胞を攻撃すると，その結果，たいてい宿主細胞は死んでしまう。

　研究者たちがウイルスを使ったがん治療を開発できたのは，宿主細胞を殺してしまうというウイルスの能力のおかげだ。2015年に初めて，ウイルスを使用したがん治療を患者に実施してよいという合衆国政府からの認可が得られた。科学者たちは，たいていヒトの口腔に炎症を作り出す原因となるヘルペスウイルスを使った。彼らはウイルスのタンパク質の外被を変異させ，ウイルスが健康な細胞を無視し，がん細胞の外側に取り付くようにした。またウイルスの遺伝子物質をも変異させ，ウイルスが抗原［アンチゲン］と呼ばれる分子を生産するようにした。抗原はヒトの免疫細胞をがんの患部へと引き寄せるのである。すると医師たちはこれらの変異したウイルスをがんの患部に1週間おきに注入できる。それらのウイルスは増殖するためにがん細胞を利用し，そしてその過程で宿主細胞を殺してしまうのである。人体の免疫システムもまた，自分自身でがん細胞を攻撃する。このようにして，大きな皮膚がんの腫瘍が破壊されてしまう。

　この治療法には普通の薬と比べて多くの良い点がある。第1に，ウイルスはがん細胞を攻撃するだけで健康な細胞には手を付けないので，悪い副作用が少ない。またそれは，外科手術では取り除けない皮膚腫瘍を治療するのにもよい方法だ。さらに，ウイルスは腫瘍

— 英R 121 —

にじかに注入されるので，治療は患部に的を絞って行われる。この治療法は病院に長く入院するのでなく，短時間通院すればよいので，患者にとっても楽だ。他方，熱や疲労感といった軽い副作用がある可能性がある。さらに，この治療法は免疫システムの弱い患者には使えない。

現在科学者たちは，視力が徐々に弱まっていく眼病の患者たちに同様の治療法を試みている。科学者たちはこの病気の患者の視力が失われるのを阻止するため，目に治療を届けられるように，ウイルスの中の遺伝子情報を変化させた。実験室のネズミについてはこの治療は成功しており，近い将来人間にも実施できると期待されている。しかし，このタイプの治療法に伴う最大の難問の1つは，ウイルスがその重要な内包物を，それを必要としている細胞に届けないうちに，人体自身の免疫システムがそのウイルスを見分けて殺してしまうのを防ぐことだ。

要約すると，ウイルスは善用できる。がんと闘い，遺伝子病の患部に重要な遺伝子を届けるために利用できる。将来は，その他の多くの人間の病気が，特別に改作されたウイルスによって治せるかもしれない。

あなたの発表用のスライド：

| 善玉ウイルス | 1．基本的情報
・多くの病気がウイルスによって引き起こされる
・多くの「善玉ウイルス」も私たちの体内には存在する
・
・ 41
・ |

| 2．皮膚がんの治療
・変異させたヘルペスウイルス
・腫瘍に注入される
・がん細胞は死滅
・患者の免疫システムの活性化 | 3．この治療法のよい点
・ 42
・ 43 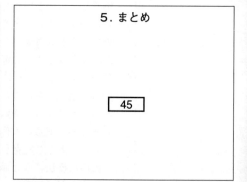 |

| 4．どのように治療法は働くのか
44 | 5．まとめ
45 |

設問解説

問1 　41　　正解①

「　41　に入れるべきでないのは次のうちどれか」

① ヒトの細胞の速やかな増殖を助ける
② ほとんどのウイルスはヒトの細胞の100分の1の大きさである
③ 宿主細胞がなければ増殖できない
④ 増殖するとたいてい宿主細胞を殺してしまう
⑤ たんぱく質の外被に包まれた単純な遺伝子物質

　正解は①。ウイルスについての基本的な情報は第2段落に書かれている。本文の内容と一致しないものを選ぶことに注意。1文ずつどの選択肢と一致するか見ていく。

　第2文（They are not ...）「ウイルスは細胞でできているのではなく，エネルギーを作りだすことも自己増殖することもできない」及び第7文（However, it's a ...）「…それから自分のコピーを作り出すために宿主細胞の機構を利用することができるのは，その小ささと構造のおかげなのだ」は③と一致する。第3文（In simple terms, ...）「…それらはタンパク質の外被に囲まれた，DNAのような遺伝物質の小さなかけらにすぎない」は⑤に一致する。第5文（In fact, most ...）「実際，ほとんどのウイルスはヒトの細胞の100分の1の小ささだ」は②と一致する。最終文（The attack on ...）「このようにしてウイルスが細胞を攻撃すると，その結果，たいてい宿主細胞は死んでしまう」は④と一致する。

　①はウイルスの特徴として本文に書かれていないので，これが正解。

問2 　42　・　43　　正解②・④

「スライドの『この治療法のよい点』に，この治療法の患者にとって利益となる側面を2つ選んで入れなさい（順番は問わない）」　42　・　43

① 変異ヘルペスウイルスを使うことで，患者は将来ヘルペスに感染しない免疫も獲得できる。
② 医師のところに短時間通院するだけでよいので患者の負担が少ない。
③ 外科手術で腫瘍を取り除くことをずっと楽で速くするために使われることが普通である。
④ 変異ヘルペスウイルスはがん細胞だけを攻撃するように改作されているので，健康な細胞は死なない。
⑤ 発熱を伴うがんの治療薬とは違い，この治療法には副作用がない。

　正解は②と④。ウイルスを使った治療法の特徴については第4段落に書かれている。第2文（First, there are ...）には「第1に，ウイルスはがん細胞を攻撃するだけで健康な細胞には手を付けないので，悪い副作用が少ない」とある。これは④に一致するので，正解。また第5文（This treatment is ...）に「この治療法は病院に長く入院するのでなく，短時間通院すればよいので，患者にとっても楽だ」とあるのに一致するのは②で，これがもう1つの正解である。

　①の「将来ヘルペスに感染しない」ということについての記述はないので誤り。「外科手術」については第4段落第3文（It is also ...）に「またそれは，外科手術では取り除けない皮膚腫瘍を治療するのにもよい方法だ」とあるが，「外科手術に使われる」とは述べていないので③は不適当。副作用については第6文（On the other ...）に「他方，熱や疲労感といった軽い副作用がある可能性がある」とあるので，⑤の「副作用がない」と矛盾する。

— 英R 123 —

問3　44　正解④

「スライド『どのように治療法は働くのか』の図に付けるラベルを完成させよ」　44

① (A) 抗原 (B) 免疫細胞
　 (C) 変異したウイルス

② (A) 抗原 (B) 変異したウイルス
　 (C) 免疫細胞

③ (A) 免疫細胞 (B) 変異したウイルス
　 (C) 抗原

④ (A) 変異したウイルス (B) 抗原
　 (C) 免疫細胞

⑤ (A) 変異したウイルス (B) 免疫細胞
　 (C) 抗原

　正解は④。この治療の仕組みについては第3段落に書かれている。まず，第4文（They modified the ...）「彼らはウイルスのタンパク質の外被を変異させ，ウイルスが健康な細胞を無視し，がん細胞の外側に取り付くようにした」とあるので，図の(A)はがん細胞に取り付く変異したウイルスだとわかる。そして，第5文（They also modified ...）に「またウイルスの遺伝子物質をも変異させ，ウイルスが抗原［アンチゲン］と呼ばれる分子を生産するようにした。抗原はヒトの免疫細胞をがんの患部へと引き寄せるのである」とあることから，右側の図はがん細胞に取り付いたウイルスから(B)の抗原が発生し，(C)の免疫細胞が引き寄せられている状況を表しているとわかる。これに一致する④が正解。

　がん細胞の図は，第7文（The viruses would ...）に「それらのウイルスは増殖するためにがん細胞を利用し，そしてその過程で宿主細胞を殺してしまう」とあるように，がん細胞を宿主として増殖した変異ウイルスによって細胞が破壊される過程を表している。

問4　45　正解①

「最後のスライドに最適な記述はどれか」　45

① 多くのウイルスが病気を引き起こすが，実は人間に恩恵をもたらすものもある。さらに，不健康な細胞に的を絞って殺すことができるように一部のウイルスを変異させることができる。

② 将来，ウイルスに関する私たちの知識ががんのような病気を治すのに役立つだろう。しかし，この科学技術が発達するまでは，ウイルスは人間にとって危険なものである。

③ 病気を治すウイルスの方が病気を引き起こすウイルスよりも数が多い。だからウイルスに対する否定的な評価はもはやふさわしくない。

④ 病気を引き起こすウイルスは，時にはがんのようなヒトの病気を治すように進化してきた。

　正解は①。ウイルスというものに関する評価は主に第1段落に書かれている。第7文（In fact, the ...）「実際，本当はその正反対なのである。なぜなら私たちの消化器系の中に住んでいる多くのウイルスは，有害な細菌を殺すことによって，実際には私たちの健康を保っていてくれるのだから」，および第3段落第4文（They modified the ...）「彼らはウイルスのタンパク質の外被を変異させ，ウイルスが健康な細胞を無視し，がん細胞の外側に取り付くようにした」の内容と合っている①が正解。

　②については，第1段落最終文（These cancer-killing viruses ...）「これらの抗がんウイルスはすでに患者の皮膚がんを治療するために使われており，将来はこのような種類の治療がもっと開発されることが期待されているのだ」と，「ウイルスは人間によって危険なもの」という評価は矛盾するので②は不適当。③の役に立つウイルスと役に立たないウイルスの数の比較については特に記述はないので不適当。④については，ウイルスがヒトの

— 英R 124 —

病気を治すように進化してきたという記述はないので誤りである。

問5 　46　 正解①

「人体自身の免疫システムがウイルスを使った治療法の効果にとって障害になるのはなぜか」　46

① 人体の免疫システムは，ウイルスが病気を治療する前にそれを見つけて殺してしまう可能性がある。
② ヒトの免役システムは体内に侵入してくるウイルスにうまく反応できない。
③ ヒトの免役システムはウイルスを認識できないので，その治療は役に立たない。
④ ウイルスが原因で，人体の免役システムが，がん細胞でなく健康な細胞を殺してしまう。

正解は①。ヒトの免役システムとウイルスを使った治療法との関係については第5段落に書かれている。最終文（However, one of ...）「しかし，このタイプの治療法に伴う最大の難問の1つは，ウイルスがその重要な内包物を，それを必要としている細胞に届けないうちに，人体自身の免疫システムがそのウイルスを見分けて殺してしまうのを防ぐことだ」と一致する①が正解。

本文のこの部分は，③の「ヒトの免役システムはウイルスを認識できない」と矛盾するので③は誤り。②の免役システムの欠点については記述がないので誤り。ウイルスが免疫システムに働きかけて健康な細胞を攻撃させるということは書いていないので④も誤り。

（主な語句・表現）　・問題冊子を参照のこと。
[リード文]　◇ biology 名「生物学」

[第1段落]
(When you think ...)

◇ after all「そもそも；何しろ」　　　◇ be responsible for ...「…の原因である」
◇ regularly 副「いつも；決まって」
◇ affect 動「〈病気などが〉…を襲う；…に影響を及ぼす」
◇ countless 形「無数の；数えきれない」
◇ are caused by ...「…によって引き起こされる」
◇ specifically 副「特に；とりわけ」　　◇ infect 動「…に伝染する」
◇ at all costs「どんな犠牲を払っても；ぜひとも」
◇ strictly 副「厳密に言うと」　　　　◇ opposite 形「正反対の」
◇ digestive 形「消化（器）の」　　　◇ harmful 形「有害な」
◇ bacteria 名「バクテリア；細菌」
◇ bacteriophage 名「バクテリオファージ；殺菌ウイルス」
◇ cell 名「細胞」　　　　　　　　　　◇ treatment 名「治療；手当」

[第2段落]
(The interesting thing ...)

◇ be made out of ...「…から作られて」　　◇ reproduce 動「再生する；増殖［繁殖］する」
◇ by oneself「ひとりで；独力で」　　　◇ in ... terms「…な言葉で」
◇ genetic 形「遺伝子の」　　　　　　　◇ material 名「物質」
◇ surround 動「…を取り囲む」　　　　◇ protein 名「タンパク質」
◇ case 名「外被；殻；容器」　　　　　◇ structure 名「構造（体）」
◇ standard 形「標準の；普通の；通常の」　◇ microscope 名「顕微鏡」
◇ bind to ...「…と化学結合する」　　　◇ host cell「宿主細胞」
◇ insert 動「…を差し込む；注入する」　◇ instruction 名「指示」
◇ machinery 名「機構；仕組み」　　　　◇ results in ...「…という結果になる」

— 英R 125 —

[第3段落]　◇ approve 動「…を認可する」　　　　　　　◇ sore 名「ただれ；傷」
(It is a ...)　◇ modify 動「…を修正する；変形する」　　◇ ignore 動「…を無視する」
　　　　　　　◇ molecule 名「分子；微分子；微片」
　　　　　　　◇ antigen 名「抗原」　免疫系にさまざまな免疫応答を引き起こす物質。
　　　　　　　◇ immune 形「免疫の」　　　　　　　　◇ site 名「場所；部位」
　　　　　　　◇ every two weeks「1 週おきに」

[第4段落]　◇ benefit 名「恩恵；利益；良い点」　　　◇ compared to ...「…に比べると」
(There are many　◇ side effect「副作用」
　　　...)　◇ leaves ... alone「…に手をつけずにおく；…に被害を与えない」
　　　　　　　◇ remove 動「…を取り除く」　　　　　◇ surgery 名「外科手術」
　　　　　　　◇ directly 副「直接に」　　　　　　　◇ location 名「場所；部位」
　　　　　　　◇ involve 動「…を巻き込む」　　　　　◇ instead of ...「…でなく；…の代わりに」
　　　　　　　◇ tiredness 名「疲労（感）」

[第5段落]　◇ currently 副「現在」　　　　　　　　◇ vision 名「視力」
(Currently,　◇ gradually 副「徐々に；次第に」　　　◇ decline 動「衰える」
scientists are ...)　◇ alter 動「…を変える」　　　　　　　◇ laboratory 名「実験室」
　　　　　　　◇ associated with ...「…に伴う」　　　◇ therapy 名「療法」
　　　　　　　◇ prevent ... from －ing「…が－するのを防ぐ」
　　　　　　　◇ identify 動「…を見分ける；認識する」

[最終段落]　◇ in summary「要約すると」　　　　　◇ gene 名「遺伝子」
(In summary,　◇ cure 動「…を治す」　　　　　　　　◇ adapt 動「…を改作する；変える」
viruses ...)

第４回　実戦問題　解答・解説

第４回　解答・解説

英語（リーディング） 第4回 （100点満点）

（解答・配点）

問題番号（配点）	設問	解答番号	正解	配点	自己採点欄
第1問（6）	1	1	②	2	
	2	2	③	2	
	3	3	③	2	
小計					
第2問（10）	1	4	⑤	2	
	2	5	③	2	
	3	6	①	2	
	4	7	③	2	
	5	8	③	2	
小計					
第3問（9）	1	9	①	3*	
		10	②		
		11	④		
		12	③		
	2	13	②	3	
	3	14	③	3	
小計					
第4問（12）	1	15	①	3	
	2	16	③	3	
	3	17	②	3	
	4	18	④	3	
小計					
第5問（16）	1	19	①	3	
	2	20	①	3	
	3	21	②	3	
	4	22	③	3	
	5	23	①	2	
		24	②	2	
小計					

問題番号（配点）	設問	解答番号	正解	配点	自己採点欄
第6問（18）	1	25	③	3	
	2	26	②	3	
	3	27 － 28	① － ⑤	3*	
		29	④	3	
	4	30	④	3	
	5	31	④	3	
小計					
第7問（15）	1	32	②	3	
	2	33 － 34	① － ⑤	3*	
	3	35	⑤	3*	
		36	④		
		37	①		
		38	③		
	4	39	③	3	
	5	40	②	3	
小計					
第8問（14）	1	41	②	4	
	2	42	①	3	
		43	④	3	
	3	44 － 45	① － ③	4*	
小計					

（注）
1 ＊は，全部正解の場合のみ点を与える。
2 －（ハイフン）でつながれた正解は，順序を問わない。

第1問

解答

| 問1 - ② | 問2 - ③ | 問3 - ③ | (各2点) |

出典 *Original Material*

全訳

あなたはニュージーランドのウェリントンにある美術館の広告を見ており，大学生向けのコンクールに関する知らせに注目します。あなたは参加を検討しています。

大学生よ，ごみを一変させよ！

部屋をきれいにしてごみを処分する時では？　以下を一読あれ！

課題は，大掃除をして出たごみすべてについて7日間の日記をつけ，「クール」なものや実用品を作ること！

参加規則

◆4月1日から5月19日までのうちの1週間，毎日ごみの記録を残してください。
◆ごみを使ってアート作品か実用品を作ってください。
◆7日間経った後に作品の写真を3枚から5枚撮って，5月26日23時59分までにごみの日誌と一緒に，対応するリンクにアップロードしてください。

> → **アートをアップロード**
> → **実用品をアップロード**

◆30語未満であなたの出品作の作製理由を説明してください。

最高作品に投票を！

◆各カテゴリーに1回のみ投票可で，自作への投票は不可とします。出品作すべてを見るにはリンクをクリックし，5月27日から5月の末日の20時までに投票してください。

> → **投票**

◆投票ごとにかかる1.5ニュージーランド・ドルは，リサイクル意識の向上のために役立てられます。

優勝者

「アート」カテゴリーの優勝者は，来年1月5日まで作品を当館で展示します！
「実用品」カテゴリーの優勝者は，作品を地元のプロのアーティストが複製して当館のギフトショップで売り出します！
1等，2等，3等入賞者にはそれぞれ，当館の夏の「それってごみなの？」展の無料入場券2枚をお贈りします！

設問解説

問1　　1　　正解 ②

「作品は　1　の間にアップロードできる」

① 4月1日から5月19日
② **4月8日から5月26日**
③ 5月27日から5月31日
④ 6月1日から1月5日

— 英 R 129 —

正解は②。Rules of Entry（参加規則）の第1文（Record your trash ...）～第3文（Take 3 to ...）に「4月1日から5月19日までのうちの1週間，毎日ごみの記録を残し」，「アート作品か実用品を作って」，「7日間経った後に作品の写真を3枚から5枚撮って，5月26日23時59分までにごみの日誌と一緒に，対応するリンクにアップロード」するように，とある。最も早くアップロードするには4月1日から7日までごみの記録を残した後で翌8日に行うことになり，締め切りは5月26日であるため，②が正解。

問2 　2　 正解③

「このコンクールに参加する際には，　2　ならない」

① ギフトショップで何か欲しい物を買わなければ
② さまざまな種類のごみを集めなければ
③ **自分の要らない物で何かを作らなければ**
④ 2つの違う出品作に投票しなければ

正解は③。コンクールに出品する作品は，本文冒頭の1文（Your task is ...）にあるように「大掃除をして出たごみ」つまり「自分にとって要らない物」で作ることを求められているため，③が正解。

他の選択肢の内容は広告に含まれない。

問3 　3　 正解③

「2等や3等に入賞すると　3　ことができる」

① ウェリントンで働くアーティストに会う
② ギフトショップで何か選ぶ
③ **夏の展覧会を見に誰かを連れて行く**
④ 1月までならいつでも美術館を訪ねる

正解は③。Winners（優勝者）の第3文（Those in first, ...）に「1等，2等，3等入賞者にはそれぞれ，当館の夏の『それってごみなの？』展の無料入場券2枚を」贈るとあるので，夏の展覧会に連れを1人伴って行くことができることになるため，③が正解。

他の選択肢の内容は広告に含まれない。

(主な語句・表現)
・問題冊子を参照のこと。

[リード文] ◇ consider － ing「－することを検討する」

[本文] ◇ get rid of ...「…を片付ける［処分する］」　◇ read on「読み続ける」
◇ clean-up图「（大）掃除」　◇ cool形「すてきな；かっこいい」
◇ entry图「参加者［物］；出品作」　◇ relevant形「対応する；適切な」
◇ NZD图「ニュージーランド・ドル」　New Zealand dollar の略。
◇ donate動「…を寄付する」　◇ reproduce動「…を複製［模造］する」

第2問

解答

| 問1 - ⑤ | 問2 - ③ | 問3 - ① | 問4 - ③ | 問5 - ③ | （各2点） |

出典 | *Original Material*

全訳 | あなたはあなたの学校の英語雑誌のスタッフの一員です。イギリスから来た助教員のポーラが記事を投稿しました。

宇宙人の存在を信じますか。最近の調査によれば，メキシコの人々はとりわけ信じがちですが，約70％の人々が我々人類だけが知的な生命体であるわけではないと信じているロシアほどではありません。これに対し，中国でそう考えている人々は半分弱で，オランダで同意するのは4人に1人ほどのようです。

では，宇宙についての研究にさらに時間をかけるべきなのでしょうか。

よく知られた科学雑誌が宇宙探索の良い点と悪い点を述べています。

宇宙探索の利点とは：
➤ 我々の宇宙行きを可能にするための多くのテクノロジーが，今や地球での我々の生活を向上させている。
➤ 我々の研究の大部分は地球でなされているので，我々は地球外へと飛行する必要さえない。
➤ 地球の資源のすべてを使ってしまった後で，人類が生き延びることのできる別の惑星を見つけるために重要である。

しかし，宇宙に関する調査には途方もない費用がかかり，多くの天然資源を燃料として使用する必要がある。さらに我々は宇宙を，そこに我々が残すことになるあらゆるごみの入った巨大なごみ箱にしようとしている。

男性や若い世代が宇宙人の存在を信じる傾向が最も強いのですが，これは彼らが，宇宙人の映画やとてもリアルな印象の今日のハイテクによる特殊効果を非常に好むためかもしれません。信心深い人々は往々にして，神によって創造されたがゆえに人類はかけがえがない，と信じています。我々の半数以上が地球外に生命が存在するに違いないと考えてはいますが，私を含めて5人に3人以上が，人類と同じくらい知能が高いものがいそうだとは思っていません。真理を探り出そうと努める価値はあるのでしょうか。

— 英R 131 —

設問解説

問1 ┃ 4 ┃ 正解 ⑤

「宇宙人の存在を信じる人々の比率に関して，最高から最低までの国別の順位を示すものはどれか」┃ 4 ┃
　　① 中国－オランダ－ロシア
　　② 中国－ロシア－オランダ
　　③ オランダ－中国－ロシア
　　④ オランダ－ロシア－中国
　　⑤ ロシア－中国－オランダ
　　⑥ ロシア－オランダ－中国

　　正解は ⑤。ポーラの記事の第1段落第2文（A recent survey ...）から，宇宙人の存在を信じるロシア人は約70%，最終文（Whereas just under ...）から，中国人では半分をわずかに下回り，オランダ人では4人に1人ほどとわかるので，⑤ が正解。

問2 ┃ 5 ┃ 正解 ③

「よく知られたその科学雑誌によれば，宇宙探索の利点の1つは ┃ 5 ┃ ということである」
　　① 我々は人生をより刺激的にできる
　　② 我々は宇宙空間によりたやすく行く
　　③ 我々がより進歩した科学技術を手にしている
　　④ 我々は健康により良い惑星を見つける

　　正解は ③。ポーラの記事に記載された科学記事からの引用の1つめの➤（Many technologies designed ...）に，「我々の宇宙行きを可能にするための多くのテクノロジーが，今や地球での我々の生活を向上させている」とあるので，③ が正解。
　　他の選択肢は引用部分に含まれない内容。

問3 ┃ 6 ┃ 正解 ①

「ポーラの記事内で言及されているある考え方が，┃ 6 ┃ というものである」
　　① 「神によって創られた人類は特別な生命形態である」
　　② 「男性は SF 映画を最も好む」
　　③ 「我々自身の惑星をさらに研究することが必要である」
　　④ 「宇宙はごみを捨てるのに適した場所である」

　　正解は ①。ポーラの記事の最終段落第2文（Religious people often ...）に，信心深い人々について「神によって創造されたがゆえに人類はかけがえがない」という見解を取る場合が多いことが述べられているので，① が正解。
　　② は最終段落第1文（Men and younger ...）に「彼ら［＝男性や若い世代］が，宇宙人の映画や…を非常に好む」とは書かれているが，「SF 映画全般を」「最も」好むという内容とはずれがあるため不適。③ は本文に書かれていない内容。④ の宇宙へのごみ投棄について書かれているのは，科学記事からの引用の最終文（We are also ...）に見られる「我々は宇宙を…巨大なごみ箱にしようとしている」という懸念であるため，不適。

問4 ┃ 7 ┃ 正解 ③

「宇宙人についてのポーラの意見を最も正しく要約したものはどれか」┃ 7 ┃
　　① それらは存在しそうにない。
　　② 人々が真理を知ることは決してないかもしれない。
　　③ 実際の宇宙人はあまり知的ではありそうにない。
　　④ 信じるか否かはその人の文化にはよらない。

　　正解は ③。ポーラの記事の最終段落第3文（Though more than ...）に「私を含めて5人に3人以上が，人類と同じくらい知能が高いものがいそうだとは思っていない」と書か

れているので，③ が正解。

　他の選択肢は本文に見られない内容。

問5　　8　　正解 ③
　「記事に対する最も適切な題名はどれか」　　8
　　① 神かそれとも科学か
　　② 我が惑星を守ること
　　③ 宇宙―我々はさらに多くを知るべきか
　　④ 人間の想像力

　正解は ③。ポーラの記事の第2段落（So, should we ...）の「宇宙についての研究にさらに時間をかけるべきなのでしょうか」という問いかけや，最終段落最終文（I wonder if ...）の「真理を探り出そうと努める価値はあるのでしょうか」という疑問から，彼女が宇宙研究に対していささか懐疑的な立場を取っていることがわかるため，③ が最も適切であると言える。

　他の選択肢は，それぞれポーラの記事といくらかは関連があるが，その全体の内容を表す題名としては不適切。

（主な語句・表現）
　　　　[本文]

・問題冊子を参照のこと。
◇ believe in ...「…の存在を信じる」
◇ in particular「とりわけ；特に」
◇ pros and cons「良い点と悪い点；賛否両論」
◇ design O to –「O を–するよう計画［意図］する」　ここでは受動態の be designed to – に由来する designed to –が，直前の Many technologies を修飾する形容詞句として用いられている。
◇ at home「地元で（の）」　ここでは「宇宙での（in space）」と対比された「地球での」の意味で用いられている。
◇ with all the garbage we are leaving up there「我々が上空のそこに残そうとするあらゆるごみのある」　we are leaving up there は形容詞節として all the garbage を修飾しており，直前には関係代名詞の that を補うことができる。up there は副詞が2つ重ねられた副詞句。　（例）It's too hot *in here*.（この室内は暑すぎる）
◇ myself included「私自身を含めて」「〈名詞〉＋ included」は「…を含めて」という意味の，独立分詞構文に由来する表現。

[設問文・選択肢]
◇ in terms of ...「…に関して」
◇ outer space「（大気圏外の）宇宙空間」

— 英R 133 —

第3問

解 答	問1 - ⑨ ①, ⑩ ②, ⑪ ④, ⑫ ③	（完答で3点）
	問2 - ②　　問3 - ③	（各3点）

出典　*Original Material*

全訳　あなたはやりがいのある事業への参加に興味を持ち，ボランティア活動のカタログに載っているある話を見つけました。

未来に向けた建設

　昨年の7月，私は同じ学校の他の7人の生徒に加え昨年の卒業生2人と共に，ルーマニアの小さな町へと向かった。我々が目指したのはこの発展途上国の貧困地域の田舎町で，目的は「人類のすみか」のためのボランティアとして支援することだった。奮闘中の共同体に恒久的永続的変化をもたらすことを目指す事業の一部として，我々は2週間を過ごすことになっていた。私は塗装を除いては建築の経験は皆無だったが，その塗装はルーマニアを発つ前日にようやく行った。

　短時間飛行機に乗ってから，狭い道でヒツジの群れが追いたてられているの以外には足止めされることなく，美しい田園地帯を長いことバスに揺られた後，我々は到着した。滞在することになる簡素な宿泊設備を案内されて間もなく，我々は頑丈な防護用のヘルメットとスケジュール表を手渡された。そこには世界各地から約200人が数週間あるいは数日間滞在しており，新参者にすべきことを教えていた。

　現場に到着してみると，穴が地面に整然と掘られ，仕事に必要な道具類と共に建築資材が整えて並べられており，休憩用のテントもあった。初日の私のチームの仕事は，木材を決まった大きさに切った後レンガを使って家の外壁を作ることだった。ほどなく私が意欲を失ってしまったのは，チームのあるメンバーが私を怒鳴りつけ始めたときだった。私は木材の測り方を間違えて小さく切り過ぎてしまったのである。なお悪いことに，私は暑さに対して準備ができていなくて，具合が悪くなってから午前中に長い休憩を取らざるを得なかったのである。

　やめることも考えていたが，初日から腹を立てた女性に，どんな過ちでも家の完成を待ち望んでいる人々にとってはそれを遅らせることにもつながるのだ，と冷静に説明されて，あらためてやる気が湧いてきた。もっと真剣にならなければ，と気づかされたのである。働き始める前夜に，家の1軒に住まうことになっている十代の姉妹に我々は紹介されていたが，我々の仕事が完了したときに私は彼女たちと話をした。彼女たちは，小さい時に両親を農作業中の事故で亡くして，金を稼ぐために学校を辞めざるを得ず，孤児であふれるホームに住んでいたのだ，と説明された。きつい2週間だったが，彼女たちのうれし涙を見たとき十分に報われた。

— 英R 134 —

設問解説

問1　⑨ → ⑩ → ⑪ → ⑫　正解 ① → ② → ④ → ③

「次の出来事（①～④）を起こった順番に並べよ」

① ヒツジがグループを遅らせた。
② チームが，家を手に入れる姉妹に初めて会った。
③ 筆者が塗装を行った。
④ 筆者が暑い気候のために具合が悪くなった。

正解は① → ② → ④ → ③。①は第2段落第1文（After a short ...）より，筆者のグループが目的地の村に向かう移動中での出来事。②は第4段落第3文（On the night ...）より，筆者が働き始める前夜のこと。③は第1段落最終文（I had absolutely ...）より，筆者がルーマニアを発つ前日のこと。④は第3段落第2文（The first day ...）および最終文（To make matters ...）より，筆者が働き始めた日のこと。以上より，① → ② → ④ → ③が正解。

問2　13　正解②

「なぜチームのメンバーの1人は，それほどまでに筆者に腹を立てたのか」　13

① 筆者があまりにも不愛想な態度を取った。
② 筆者が木材を正しい大きさに切らなかった。
③ 筆者が健康管理に失敗した。
④ 筆者が建築の経験について嘘をついた。

正解は②。第3段落第3文（My motivation was ...），第4文（I'd measured the ...）より，このメンバーが筆者を怒鳴りつけたのは，筆者が「木材の測り方を間違えて小さく切り過ぎてしまった」ことが理由であったため，②が正解。

①，④については本文に言及のない内容。③については，第3段落最終文（To make matters ...）に「なお悪いことに，私は暑さに対して準備ができていなくて，具合が悪くなってから午前中に長い休憩を取らざるを得なかった」とあるが，冒頭の「なお悪いことに」の含意は「怒鳴られて筆者が意欲を失ったことに加えて」ということであって，「筆者が体調を崩した」と「メンバーの1人の立腹」とは別のこととして描かれており，両者の間に因果関係はない。

問3　14　正解③

「この話から，事業の目標は　14　ことであったことがわかった」

① 孤児のためのセンターを建設する
② 質素な家をより快適にすることに助力する
③ 人々に長期にわたる住居を供給する
④ わずかな教育しか受けていない人々に新たな技能を教える

正解は③。第1段落第2文（Our destination was ...）の「目的は『人類のすみか』のためのボランティアとして支援すること」，同段落第3文（We would spend ...）の「奮闘中の共同体に恒久的永続的変化をもたらすことを目指す事業」，最終段落第1文（Considering quitting, I ...）の「家の完成を待ち望んでいる人々」といった表現が見られることなどから総合的に判断して，③が正解であるとわかる。

他の選択肢については，事業がそれらを目指していることを示す記述は特に見られず，いずれも不適。

主な語句・表現　・問題冊子を参照のこと。

［リード文］　◇ worthwhile 形「時間や労力をかける価値がある；やりがいのある」

［第1段落］　◇ habitat 名「居住地；すみか」
（Last July, I ...）　◇ design O to – 「O を–するよう計画［意図］する」　ここでは受動態の be designed to –

— 英 R 135 —

に由来する designed to − が，直前の a project を修飾する形容詞句として用いられている。

◇ struggling 形「苦闘［奮闘］する」

◇ painting, which I finally put into practice「塗装，それをようやく私は実行した」 ここでは「塗装」の意味で用いられている painting の補足説明となる節を，非制限用法の関係代名詞 which が導いている。put O into practice は「O を実行［実施］する」という意味。

[第2段落]
(After a short ...)

◇ interrupted only by a group of sheep being driven along a narrow road「狭い道に沿ってヒツジの群れが追い立てられるのにだけさえぎられて」 分詞構文。前置詞 by の目的語は受動態の動名詞 being driven で，直前の a group of sheep はその意味上の主語を示している。

◇ not long after ...「…の後まもなく［すぐ］」

◇ basic 形「必要最小限の；質素な」

◇ accommodation 名「宿泊［収容］設備」

◇ would tell newcomers what to do「新参者に何をすべきかを教えるのだった」 would は「繰り返された動作」を表す用法。what to do は「疑問詞 + to 不定詞」からなる名詞句で，「何をすべきか」という意味。

[第3段落]
(I arrived at ...)

◇ I arrived at the site to find neat holes dug in the ground, building materials organized and laid out with the necessary tools for the job「私は現場に到着し，地面に整然とした穴が掘られ，仕事に必要な道具と共に建築資材が整理され配列されているのを見つけた」 to find は「結果」を表す副詞用法の to 不定詞。find O p.p. は「O が−されているのを見つける［のがわかる］」の意味で，ここでは neat holes dug と building materials organized and laid out という 2 組の O p.p. が and でつながれ，後者ではさらに organized と laid という 2 組の p.p. が and でつながれている。lay ... out / lay out ... は「…を配列する［並べる］」という意味。

◇ and a tent for breaks「そして休憩用のテント」 この a tent は find の目的語となっている。

◇ The first day「最初の日には」 ここでは副詞句として働いている。

◇ to make matters worse「(その上) さらに悪いことには」

[最終段落]
(Considering quitting, I ...)

◇ Considering quitting「やめることを考えたが」 分詞構文。consider −ing は「−することを検討する」という意味。

◇ drive 名「意欲；やる気」

◇ drop out of ...「…から離脱［中退］する」

◇ pack O with ...「O に…をいっぱいに入れる［ぎっしり詰め込む］」 ここでは受動態の be packed with ... に由来する packed with ... が直前の a home を修飾する形容詞句として用いられている。

◇ Though a tough two weeks「厳しい 2 週間だったが」 接続詞 though の後に，it was (it はいわゆる「状況」を表す用法) などが省略されていると考えられる。

◇ it was all worth it「それは十分に価値があった」 主語の it は，「状況」を表す用法とも，a tough two weeks を指すとも取れる。ここでの all は，「まったく；すっかり」などというニュアンスの副詞。worth it は worthwhile (時間や労力をかける価値がある；やりがいのある) とほぼ同じ内容。

[設問文・選択肢]

◇ put O into the order「O を整理する［並べる］」

— 英 R 136 —

第4問

解答				
問1 - ①	問2 - ③	問3 - ②	問4 - ④	（各3点）

出典 | *Original Material*

全訳

英語の授業であなたは関心のある IT 問題についてのエッセイを書いています。これが最も新しい草稿です。あなたは今，先生からのコメントに基づいて，修正に取り組んでいます。

画像生成 AI は適切に用いるべきだ	先生のコメント
近年，人工知能（AI）が急速に発達してきました。AI は，音楽を生成したり，外国語を翻訳したり，データを分析したりといった多くのことに用いられます。AI は多くの建設的な形で使用することが可能です。しかし，多くの美術家が美術作品を生成する AI プログラムに懸念を抱いています。彼らはこうしたプログラムは制限されるか規制されるべきであると考えているのです。	
第一に，画像生成 AI は実在する美術家の作品を盗用します。こうしたプログラムは，人間の美術家によって制作された数千にも及ぶ本物の美術作品の実例をもとにして学習しなければなりません。(1)∧多くの美術家は，AI プログラムがそのようにして自分たちの美術作品を利用することを承諾していません。彼らは自分たちの作品が盗まれ，不法に利用されていると考えているのです。	⑴ AI プログラムがどのようにしてそれを行うのかを私に教えてくれませんか？ここにさらに情報を追加してください。
第二に，AI 画像は実在する美術家の仕事を奪ってしまいます。画像生成 AI は，人間の美術家よりもはるかに安い価格で，しかもはるかに少ない時間で写真や絵を作成することができます。こうしたことは実在する美術家に対する需要(2)を変化させ，彼らの仕事を減らしてしまいます。将来的には，たとえ美術家が高度な技術を有し，数年かけて自分の技術を完成させてきたのだとしても，そうしたことが原因で美術家は仕事を失ってしまうかもしれないのです。	⑵ どのように需要を変化させるのですか。もっと具体化してください。
最後に，(3)美術の学習について考えてみましょう。線画や絵画や写真はみな創造的な表現形態であり，私たち人間にとって重要なものです。美術の練習は手の小さな筋肉を発達させ，想像力と創造性を促します。もし美術がボタンをクリックすることで作ることができるものになってしまうならば，私たちの文化におけるこの重要な要素を失うことになるでしょう。	⑶ 主題文は論点を適切に要約していません。書き直してください。
結論として，AI プログラムは許諾なしに美術家の作品の見本を取り，美術家の仕事の機会を減少させ，人々が自分で美術作品を制作しようとする気持ちをなくさせてしまいます。多くの美術家は，AI 画像の利点にもかかわらず，それは私たちの文化全般に悪影響をもたらしていると考えています。(4)∧	⑷ ここに結論となる文を追加してください。
全体的なコメント これは非常に興味深いものです。私はこれまで画像生成 AI について考えたことはありませんでした。よく頑張りました！	

設問解説

問1　15　正解①

「コメント(1)に基づくと，ここにどの文を入れるべきか」　15

① AIプログラムはこれらの画像を分析し，それらの見本を取って新しい画像を作ります。

② AIプログラムは他者の画像を使用することなく，オリジナルの美術作品を制作することができます。

③ AIプログラムはプロの美術家から購入した美術作品や写真を利用します。

④ AIプログラムは人間の美術家から無料で寄付された絵画を利用します。

　正解は①。コメント(1)には，「AIプログラムがどのようにしてそれを行うのかを私に教えてくれませんか？　ここにさらに情報を追加してください」とあるが，「それ」とは直前の2つの文で述べられている，人間の美術家によって制作された本物の美術作品をもとにして学習することで実在する美術家の作品を盗用することを指している。よってそのことを簡潔に言い換えた選択肢①「AIプログラムはこれらの画像を分析し，それらの見本を取って新しい画像を作ります」が空所(1)に追加されるべきであると判断できるので，正解は①となる。

　②，③，④はいずれもそうした内容とはなっていないので不可。

問2　16　正解③

「コメント(2)に基づくと，どの語あるいは表現をここで代わりに用いるべきか」　16

① を拡張させ

② を拡大させ

③ **を減少させ**

④ に取って代わり

　正解は③。コメント(2)には，「どのように需要を変化させるのですか。もっと具体化してください」とある。下線部(2)を含む文では「こうしたこと［画像生成AIが人間の美術家よりもはるかに安価かつはるかに少ない時間で写真や絵を作成することができること］は実在する美術家に対する需要(2)を変化させ，彼らの仕事を減らしてしまいます」とあることから，下線部(2)をより具体的に言い換えれば「実在する美術家に対する需要を減少させる」ことだと判断できる。よって正解は③となる。

　①，②，④はいずれもそうした意味にはなっていないので不可。

問3　17　正解②

「コメント(3)に基づくと，ここにどの主題文を入れるべきか」　17

① 画像生成AIの絵や写真を制作する能力は人間を上回っています

② **AI画像が増加していくと，人々は美術作品を研究したり，練習したりする気をなくしてしまうでしょう**

③ AI画像を使用する子どもは，美術家とは違う方法で自分の想像力を使います

④ AI画像を使用することは異なる種類の創造性であるので，それは奨励されるべきです

　正解は②。コメント(3)には，「主題文は論点を適切に要約していません。書き直してください」とある。この段落の主題は，下線部(3)の後で述べられているように，美術は人間の想像力と創造性を促すが，画像生成AIの利用によってそうした人間の文化の重要な要素を失ってしまうことになるということだが，それは言い換えれば人間が美術作品を自分の力で研究したり制作したりする機会や動機を奪ってしまうと捉えることができる。よって正解は②となる。

　①，③，④はいずれもこの段落で述べられている内容ではないので不可。

— 英R 138 —

問4 　18　 正解④

「コメント(4)に基づくと，どの文を追加するべきか」　18

① 結果として，美術家は画像生成 AI をもっと注意して利用するべきです。
② その結果，AI テクノロジーはまだ十分に効果的ではありません。
③ 要約すると，AI をもっと発達させるべきです。
④ **したがって，画像生成 AI の使用は制限されるべきです。**

　正解は④。コメント(4)には，「ここに結論となる文を追加してください」とある。空所(4)の前には，多くの美術家は AI プログラムは私たちの文化全般に悪影響をもたらすと考えている，と述べられている。したがって，そうした悪影響をもたらす AI プログラムは制限されるべきである，と続ければ，結論として自然な内容となると判断できる。よって正解は④となる。ちなみに，第 1 段落（In recent years, ...）最終文でも「彼ら［多くの美術家］はこうしたプログラムは制限されるか規制されるべきであると考えているのです」という同じ趣旨のことが述べられている。

　①，②，③はいずれも自然な文脈とはならないので不可。

主な語句・表現

・問題冊子を参照のこと。

[リード文]
◇ draft 名「草稿；下書き」　　　　　　◇ work on ...「…に取り組む」
◇ revision 名「修正」　　　　　　　　　◇ based on ...「…に基づいて［た］」

[タイトル]
◇ AI art generator「画像生成 AI」　　◇ properly 形「適切に」

[第 1 段落]
（In recent years,
...）
◇ artificial intelligence (AI)「人工知能」　◇ AI program「AI プログラム」
◇ generate 動「…を生成する」　　　　◇ art 名「美術（作品）」
◇ restrict 動「…を規制する」

[第 2 段落]
（First, AI art ...）
◇ consent to ...「…を承諾する；…に同意する」
◇ illegally 副「不法に」

[第 3 段落]
（Second, AI art
...）
◇ demand for ...「…の需要」　　　　　◇ leave A with B「A に B を残す」
◇ cause O to -「O が-する原因となる」　◇ even though 接「たとえ…としても」
◇ highly skilled「高度な技術を持っている」

[最終段落]
（In conclusion,
AI ...）
◇ in conclusion「結論として」　　　　◇ sample 動「…の見本を取る」
◇ without permission「許可［許諾］なしに」
◇ discourage A from - ing「A に-することを思い止まらせる［-する気をなくさせる］」
◇ negative influence on ...「…への悪影響」

[先生のコメント]
◇ in what way 疑「どのようにして…か」　◇ specific 形「具体的な」
◇ adequately 副「適切に」　　　　　　◇ summarize 動「…を要約する」
◇ point 名「要点」

[設問文・選択肢]
◇ insert 動「…を入れる［挿入する］」　◇ analyze 動「…を分析する」
◇ image 名「画像」　　　　　　　　　◇ donate 動「…を寄付する」
◇ for free「ただで；無料で」　　　　　◇ be good at ...「…が得意だ」
◇ consequently 副「その結果；したがって」　◇ in summary「要約すると」

— 英 R 139 —

第5問

解答

| 問1 - ① | 問2 - ① | 問3 - ② | 問4 - ③ | (各3点) |

問5 | 23 - ① | 24 - ② | (各2点)

出典   *Original Material*

全訳

あなたは9月からアメリカのワイアット大学で勉強することになっていて，住まいが必要です。どのような選択肢があるかを確かめるために，オリビアとロブという2人の学生のブログを見ています。

ワイアット大学で会いましょう！
投稿者：オリビア　2022年7月17日午後3時32分

　大学での新生活のために住まいが必要ですか？　考えるべきことの1つが，家賃には何が含まれているのかとその他の出費です。今年度に学生が家賃に含まれない必需品に使った平均金額をご覧ください。

追加の費用 ― ご注意を！

日用食料品	電気	インターネット	交通	洗濯
月110ドル	月20ドル	月15ドル	月20〜30ドル	月38ドル

　当然，住まいの所在地や部屋の種類によって違いがあります。キャンパス内の寮や個室に住めば，移動は不要です。家庭に下宿すれば，普通は作りたての食事が込みですが，1つ問題なのは必ずしもプライバシーを期待できないことです。私なら，食事付きより月に95ドル割安な，キャンパス内の個室の食事無しのプランを選ぶことを勧めます。バスは学割が利かないので，私なら授業に歩いて行けるようゾーン1の部屋を推奨します。

　ところで，目に付かないところで節約できたり出費がかさんだりすることを忘れないように！　アパート，下宿ともキャンパス外の住まいには，キャンパス内の個室の住まいと比べて少なくとも倍の敷金がかかります。キャンパス内の寮に住む場合は夏の間は引き払わなくてはならないのですが，それでお金は節約できます。

我がワイアットにようこそ！
投稿者：ロブ　2022年7月18日午前11時3分

　ワイアット大学での生活を始めるとき，住まい探しに苦労したのを覚えています。
　僕は1年生の時は，洗濯代金以外全部込みのキャンパス内の個室で過ごしましたが，たぶん食事のサービスは別で支払うようにする方が良いでしょう。僕は友達と一緒に勉強したりぶらついたりして食事に間に合わないことがよくあったんです。それから，僕の部屋からは授業にすぐ行けましたけれど，ゾーン2や3のバスの便も良いです。ゾーン3からの通学の方が時間はかかりますし，バス代も余計にかかることと2つの地域の家賃の差が比較的少ないことを考えるなら，私なら町の中心部に近い方に住む方を選ぶでしょう。

服を洗うたびに支払っていては，お金がすぐになくなってしまいます！　でも1軒のアパートに他の3人の学生と暮らすとしたら，洗濯機は1人あたり120ドルくらい払えば手に入れられて，洗濯代のほぼ全額を節約できます。キャンパス内の寮では食事と洗濯以外は何でも込みですが，1人の時間を楽しむ人には絶対向きません！

タイプ	月の家賃		
	ゾーン1 (市の中心地)	ゾーン2	ゾーン3
家庭A，B，Cに下宿	240 ドル (A)	198 ドル (B)	182 ドル (C)
キャンパス内の寮	66 ドル		
キャンパス内の食事付きの個室	270 ドル		
キャンパス外の学生用アパート X，Y，Z	220 ドル (X)	170 ドル (Y)	150 ドル (Z)

https://helpwithaccommodationwu.example.com

敷金のことを忘れないでください！　キャンパス内に住むには，寮では150ドル，個室では300ドル入居時にかかります。

設問解説

問1　19　正解①

「オリビアが大学の近くに住むことを勧めるのは　19　からである」

① 市バスは学生料金を提供していない
② 市バスの便はあてにならない
③ 授業に歩いて行くのは良い運動になる
④ 歩いて通学すると時間の節約になる

　正解は①。オリビアはブログの第2段落最終文（There aren't student …）で，「バスは学割が利かないので，私なら授業に歩いて行けるようゾーン1の部屋を推奨」すると書いているため，①が正解。

　他の選択肢の内容はいずれも，彼女のブログには見られない。

問2　20　正解①

「ロブは　20　買うよう勧めている」

① できれば他の学生たちと共同で洗濯機を
② キャンパスの食事は少ないので追加の食料を
③ インターネットへのアクセスを速めるために何かしらの wi-fi ルーターを
④ 勉強しやすくするために自分専用の机を

　正解は①。ロブはブログの第3段落第1文（If you pay …）と第2文（But if you …）で，「服を洗うたびに支払っていては，お金がすぐになくなって」しまうが「1軒のアパートに他の3人の学生と暮らすとしたら，洗濯機は1人あたり120ドルくらい払えば手に入れられて，洗濯代のほぼ全額を節約」できると，洗濯機を共同購入するメリットを強調しているので，①が正解。

　他の選択肢の内容はいずれも，ロブのブログには見られない。

— 英R 141 —

問3　21　正解②

「オリビアとロブは共に　21　を勧めている」

① ゾーン2の住まいを選ぶこと

② 食事込みではない住まいを選ぶこと

③ 可能なら家庭に下宿すること

④ うまくやっていけるルームメイトと暮らすこと

正解は②。オリビアはブログの第2段落第4文（I'd advise selecting ...）に「食事付きより月に95ドル割安な，キャンパス内の個室の食事無しのプランを選ぶこと」を勧めると書いている。またロブのブログの第2段落第1文（I spent my ...）には，彼が「1年生の時は，洗濯代金以外全部込みのキャンパス内の個室で過ごし」たが「たぶん食事のサービスは別で支払うようにする方が良い」とあり，続く第2文（I often missed ...）には，彼が「食事に間に合わないことがよくあった」ことがその理由として挙げられている。以上より②が正解。

①については，ロブはブログの第2段落最終文（The journey from ...）で「私なら（ゾーン2とゾーン3のうちで）町の中心部に近い方（であるゾーン2）に住む方を選ぶでしょう」と書いているが，オリビアはゾーン2を推すコメントは特に書いていないので不適。③については，オリビアのブログの第2段落第3文（If you stay ...）に，「普通は作りたての食事が込み」だが「1つ問題なのは必ずしもプライバシーを期待できない」と，メリットとデメリットの両方が挙げてあり，一概に彼女によって勧められているとは言い難い。また，ロブのブログには一切言及がないため，やはり不適。④は2人のブログいずれにも見られない内容。

問4　22　正解③

「もしあなたが自分のプライバシーを確保したいが，月々の家賃は最も安くしたいなら，4つの選択肢のうちで　22　ことを選ぶべきである」

① キャンパス内の寮に住む

② 食事無しでキャンパス内の個室に住む

③ キャンパス外の学生用アパートYに住む

④ 家庭Cに下宿する

正解は③。①については，ロブのブログの第3段落最終文（In the on-campus ...）に「1人の時間を楽しむ人には絶対」向かないとあるように，また④についても，オリビアのブログの第2段落3文（If you stay ...）に「必ずしもプライバシーを期待できない」とあるように，それぞれプライバシーの確保は難しいため，これらは候補から外れる。②については，ロブのブログの表とオリビアのブログの第2段落第4文（I'd advise selecting ...）の「食事付きより月に95ドル割安な，キャンパス内の個室の食事無しのプラン」という記述より，家賃は 270 − 95 = 175（ドル）となる。これに対し③の家賃はロブのブログの表より170ドルなので，これが正解となる。

問5　23　正解①　24　正解②

「4つの選択肢のうちで，払う敷金を一番安くしたければ　23　を選ぶことになりそうである。また，ゾーン1にある部屋に丸1年住む必要があるなら，　24　に住むことで月々の家賃が最も廉価になりそうである（各空所に選択肢①～④のうちから1つ選べ。）」

① キャンパス内の寮

② キャンパス外の学生用アパートX

③ 食事付きのキャンパス内の個室

④ 家庭Aでの下宿

23　　正解は①。敷金については，ロブのブログの最終段落最終文（If you live ...）に「キャンパス内に住むには，寮では150ドル，個室では300ドル」必要になることが，オリビアのブログの最終段落第2文（In off-campus accommodation, ...）に「キャンパス外の住まいには，キャンパス内の個室の住まいと比べて少なくとも倍」かかることが書かれているため，①が正解。

　　24　　正解は②。ゾーン1にある住まいの月々の家賃は，ロブのブログの表を見れば①が66ドルで最も安いことがわかるが，オリビアのブログの最終段落最終文（If you live ...）に「キャンパス内の寮に住む場合は夏の間は引き払わなくてはならない」とあり「丸1年住む必要」を満たさないことになるので，次に安い220ドルの②が正解。

主な語句・表現
［リード文］
・問題冊子を参照のこと。
◇ accommodation 名「宿泊［収容］設備［施設］」
◇ option 名「選択肢」

［オリビアの
ブログ］
◇ adventure 名「珍しい経験」
◇ hidden 形「隠れた；気がつきにくい」
◇ deposit 名「敷金；保証金」
◇ double those「それらの2倍」　double の直後に of を補って考えることができる。　**(例)** The population of this city is more than *double* (*of*) what it was twenty years ago.（この都市の人口は，20年前の2倍以上である）　those は既出の語の繰り返しを避けて用いられる指示代名詞で，ここでは the deposits の代用。

［ロブのブログ］
◇ the tough time I had finding ...「…を見つけるのにした苦労」　I had finding ... は形容詞節として the tough time を修飾しており，直前に関係代名詞の which または that を補うことができる。have a tough time −ing で「−するのに辛い思い［苦労］をする」という意味。
◇ bus service「バスの運行［便］」
◇ pick ... up / pick up ...「…を（安く）手に入れる」

［設問文・選択肢］
◇ router 名「ルーター」　ネットワークの伝送経路を制御する機器。
◇ without food included「食事が含まれていない」「without +〈名詞〉+ p.p.」は「〈名詞〉が−されていなくて［いない］」という意味で，ここでは形容詞句として直前の accommodation を修飾している。　**(例)** Perhaps there is no way to cough *without* your mouth *closed*.（ことによると，口を閉じない咳のし方というのはないのかもしれない）
◇ roommates you can get along well with「一緒にうまくやっていけるルームメイト」you can get along well with は形容詞節として roommates を修飾しており，直前に関係代名詞の who などを補うことができる。get along well with ... は「…とうまくやっていく」という意味。
◇ ensure 動「…を確実にする［確保］する」　ここでは過去分詞が want O C（O が C であることを望む）の C の位置に用いられている。

― 英 R 143 ―

第6問

解答

問1 − ③	問2 − ②	（各3点）
問3 − 27 ・ 28 − ① · ⑤		（順不同・両方正解で3点）
29 − ④		（3点）
問4 − ④	問5 − ④	（各3点）

出典 *Original Material*

全訳

あなたは金融教育（個人的財政に関する知識）の授業が学校で教えられるべきかどうかについてのエッセイに取り組んでいます。以下の各ステップに従っていきます。

　ステップ1：金融教育に関するさまざまな見解を読んで理解する。
　ステップ2：金融教育が学校で教えられるべきかどうかについての判断を下す。
　ステップ3：追加の情報源を使って，エッセイの概要を作成する。

[ステップ1] さまざまな情報源を読む
筆者A（生徒）
私の学校が個人的財政の授業を導入する予定であると聞いた時，私たちにはすでに非常に多くの学業が課されているので，私は苛立ちを覚えました。それにもかかわらず，何回か授業を受けた後で気持ちが変わり始めました。私は，将来私の役に立つことになる非常に多くの重要な情報を学んだのです。私の両親は南米からの移民で懸命に働いていますが，それほど多くのお金を持ってはいません。私は自分でよりよい将来を築きたいと思っており，この授業は私に自分のお金に関する賢明な決断をするための知識を与えてくれたのです。

筆者B（高等学校校長）
私は，この地域の一部の学校と同様に，カリキュラムに個人的財政の授業を加えることを考えていました。しかし，私たちにはそれを適切に行うための十分な時間はなく，教える資格を取得していて，時間の空いている教師も十分にはいません。私は，個人的財政といった，生きていく上での技術は家庭で教えられるべきだと考えています。生徒の中には家族からこうした能力を学ぶ機会を持っていない者もいることは理解しています。そういうわけで，私たちは財政的な問題を含めた個人的な問題について生徒たちに話すことができるカウンセラーを置くことになるでしょう。

筆者C（親）
私は自分の子どもたちにお金の管理の仕方についてずっと教えてきました。幼い年齢からでさえ，私は子どもたちにお小遣いを与え，子どもたちのために普通預金口座を開設しました。子どもたちが大学生活を始めるときに，私は彼らがもっともよい奨学金の契約を獲得する力になるつもりですし，子どもたちがアルバイトをすることを勧めます。したがって，私は学校での個人的財政の授業は必要ないと思っています。また私は誰がその教科を教えることになるのかということについて懸念を持っています。一般に今のところ教師は財政問題について話をする資格を取得してはいないと思っています。

筆者D（金融ジャーナリスト）
この質問に答える前に，「金融教育」とは何かということを問わねばなりません。学校は何

— 英R 144 —

を教えるつもりなのでしょうか。これは非常に広範囲にわたる科目であり，基本原理の多くは常識なのです。私は，幼い子どもたちでさえお金を貯め，返すことができないお金は借りない必要があることは理解していると思います。もちろん，私の仕事は年金や投資について書くことですが，そうした情報は絶えず変化しています。自分のお金をどこに預けるべきかを知りたいと思うなら，学校の教師に訊くのではなく，新聞の金融欄を読むことを勧めます。

筆者E（大学のカウンセラー）

仕事柄，私は，どの奨学金を利用するかということに関して間違った判断をしたために，多くの学生がひどい財政状態で大学生活を始めていることを知っています。もちろん，一部の学生には非常に見識のある親や裕福な親がいるために，そのように困ったことにはなりません。一方，非常に頭のよい学生の中には，単に親が準備をしてくれなかったがゆえに困ったことになってしまう者もいます。私は，彼らに親や家族が与えることができない知識を学校が与えることによってこうした学生を援助するべきだと思います。

設問解説

問1　25　正解③

「筆者CとDは両者とも　25　と言及している」

① 年金や投資についての情報を教えることはあまりに難しいので，生徒は専門家に相談するべきである

② 生徒は大学に行きアルバイトでお金を稼ぐことによって，財政に関してもっと多くのことを学ぶことができる

③ **教師は，個人的財政についての授業を教えるのに必要な知識や経験を持っていないかもしれない**

④ 生徒のスケジュールが忙しいので，学校で個人的財政を教えるための十分な時間がない

　正解は③。親である筆者Cは最終文（I think teachers ...）で「一般に今のところ教師は財政問題について話をする資格を取得してはいないと思っています」と述べており，金融ジャーナリストである筆者Dは最終文（If you want ...）で「自分のお金をどこに預けるべきかを知りたいと思うなら，学校の教師に訊くのではなく，新聞の金融欄を読むことを勧めます」と述べていることから，両者とも選択肢③の「教師は，個人的財政についての授業を教えるのに必要な知識や経験を持っていないかもしれない」ということに言及しているとみなすことができる。よって正解は③となる。

　①，②，④に関しては，いずれも筆者CとDが述べている内容とはなっていないので不可。

問2　26　正解②

「筆者Bは　26　と示唆している」

① 彼女は個人的財政の授業を時間割に加えたいと思っているが，教師と生徒が反対している

② **生徒の中には，家族が個人的財政について教えていないために，不利な立場に置かれている者もいる**

③ 生徒たちは個人的財政の授業を受けたいと思っているが，教師たちがそれを教えるための知識を持っていない

④ 若者は大人よりもリスクを伴う決断をしてしまう可能性が高いので，若い頃はお金を扱うべきではない

　正解は②。高等学校校長である筆者Bは第3文（I believe life ...）～第4文（I understand that ...）で，個人的財政は家庭で教えられるべきものであると考えているが，

— 英R 145 —

生徒の中にはそうした能力を家庭では学べない者もいることも理解している，と述べている。続く最終文（That is why ...）における「そういうわけで，私たちは財政的な問題を含めた個人的な問題について生徒たちに話すことができるカウンセラーを置くことになるでしょう」という発言は，個人的財政を家庭で学ぶ生徒に比べて，そうしたことを家庭で学べない生徒が不利な立場に置かれてしまいかねないことに対する対応策を考えてのことであると判断できる。以上から正解は②となる。

　①に関しては，後半の「教師と生徒が反対している」ということが筆者Ｂが述べている内容とはなっていないので不可。

　③に関しては，前半の「生徒は個人的財政の授業を受けたいと思っている」ということが筆者Ｂが述べている内容とはなっていないので不可。

　④に関しては，筆者Ｂが述べている内容とはなっていないので不可。

[ステップ2] 判断を下す
問3 　27 ・ 28 　正解①・⑤　 29 　正解④
　「さまざまな見解を理解したので，学校で個人的財政を教えることに関して判断を下し，それを以下のように書き出した。 27 ， 28 ， 29 を完成させるのにもっとも適切な選択肢を選びなさい」

あなたの判断：高校で個人的財政に関する授業は教えられるべきだ。
　・　筆者 27 と 28 があなたの判断を支持している。
　・　その2人の筆者の主要な論拠： 29 。

　 27 と 28 に入る選択肢（順序は問わない）
　①　A
　②　B
　③　C
　④　D
　⑤　E

　正解は①と⑤。生徒である筆者Ａは第1文（When I heard ...）〜第3文（I learned so ...）で，学校で個人的財政の授業が導入された時，最初はすでに多くの授業があることから苛立ちを覚えたが，何回か財政の授業を受けた後で気持ちが変わり，将来に役立つ重要なことを学んだ，と述べ，最終文（I want to ...）後半でも「この授業は私に自分のお金に関する賢明な決断をするための知識を与えてくれたのです」と結論づけることで，学校で財政の授業を受けることの重要性を強調している。また大学のカウンセラーである筆者Ｅは第1文（Due to my ...）や第3文（On the other ...）で，学生の中にはお金の面で困った状況に陥っている者がいる，と述べ，その対応策として最終文（I think that ...）で「私は，彼らに親や家族が与えることができない知識を学校が与えることによってこうした学生を援助するべきだと思います」と提言している。

　以上から筆者ＡとＥは「高校で個人的財政に関する授業は教えられるべきだ」というあなたの判断を支持する意見を述べていることがわかるので， 27 と 28 には①と⑤が入ることになる。

　 29 に入る選択肢
　①　高校時代にお金について学ぶことで，生徒は将来よりよい仕事を手にすることができるだろう
　②　貧しい親は財政やお金について子どもから学ぶことができ，それが親の生活を改善していく

— 英 R 146 —

③　学校で財政について学ぶ生徒は，自分の将来の見込みを向上させるために一生懸命勉強しようという動機が高くなる

④　学校で個人的財政を教えることはさまざまな背景を持つ生徒間の不平等を減少させるだろう

　正解は④。筆者Aは第4文（My parents are ...）で，自分の両親が南米からの移民で経済的に苦労していることを述べ，続く最終文（I want to...）で，自分は自分の力でよりよい将来を築きたいと考えており，そうしたお金に関する懸命な決断をするための知識を高校の財政の授業が与えてくれた，と述べていることから，経済的に不利な背景を持っていても高校の授業がそうした状況を克服することに役立ち，生徒間の不平等を減少させることにつながると考えていると推測できる。また筆者Eは第1文（Due to my ...）～第2文（Of course, some ...）で，家庭でのお金に関する教育の有無によって大学生活において経済的不均衡が存在することを指摘し，上でも述べたように，その対応策として最終文（I think that ...）で「私は，彼らに親や家族が与えることができない知識を学校が与えることによってこうした学生を援助するべきだと思います」と述べることで，学生間の経済的不均衡を減少させるための提言を行っていると考えることができる。

　以上から，あなたの判断を支持している筆者AとEの論拠は選択肢④の「学校で個人的財政を教えることはさまざまな背景を持つ生徒間の不平等を減少させるだろう」ということだとわかる。

（全訳）

[ステップ3]　情報源AとBを使って，概要を作成する。
あなたのエッセイの概要：

学校は生徒に向けた個人的財政の授業を導入するべきだ

序論

　近年，世界中のより多くの学校でさまざまな国で生徒に向けた個人的財政に関する授業が導入されている。これは以下の理由ですぐれた案である。

本論

　理由1：（ステップ2から）
　理由2：（情報源Aに基づく）　……　| 30 |
　理由3：（情報源Bに基づく）　……　| 31 |

結論

　高校の教師はお金と個人的財政に関して生徒たちに教えるべきだ。

情報源A

高校生に個人的財政に関する授業を提供する1つの利点は，のちの人生においてリスクを伴う経済活動に従事する可能性が減少するということだ。その目安の1つとなるものは，給料日ローンを借りる可能性である。給料日ローンとは，非常に高い金利で，数週間といった短い期間内にすぐ返済することを必要とするローンである。こうしたローンを借りて返却できない人々は，法律上の問題に陥るか，必要なお金を手に入れるために犯罪に巻き込まれてしまうことさえある。しかし，さまざまな研究は，学生時代に個人的財政の教育に参加した若者は給料日ローンを借りることに関わる可能性がはるかに低いことを示している。またそうした学生は，クレジットカードによる借り入れといった借金の返済を遅らせる可能性も低かった。これは，こうした生徒が大人になって自分の財政的決断に対する責任を持つようになったときに，法律上の問題が減少し，犯罪に巻き込まれる可能性が減る

— 英R 147 —

ことにつながると想定することができる。

情報源 B
米国における最近の研究は，3つの州における，高校で個人的財政の授業を受けた学生のクレジットスコアを追跡した。クレジットスコアは，それが銀行やそれ以外の機関が，ある人がお金に関してどれだけ信用できるかを特定するのに役立つために，重要なものである。クレジットスコアが高い人はローンやクレジットカードでよい金利を得る可能性が高くなり，住宅ローンの認可を受ける可能性が高くなる。

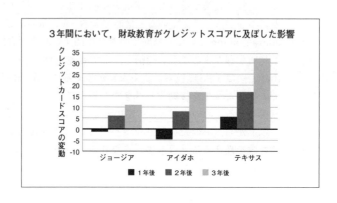

設問解説

問4　30　正解 ④

「情報源Aに基づけば，以下のどれが理由2としてもっとも適切か」　30

① 高校で財政の授業を受けた学生はより多くのお金を稼いだため，そうした学生間で犯罪率は下降した。
② 学生は高校で個人的財政の授業を受けた後では，クレジットカードやローンを利用する可能性が低くなった。
③ 法律や金融に関わる仕事に入っていく学生は，高校で財政の授業を受けた可能性が高かった。
④ 学校で財政教育を受けた若者は，リスクの高い財政上の決断をする可能性が低かった。

正解は④。情報源Aの第1文（One advantage of ...）で「高校生に個人的財政に関する授業を提供する1つの利点は，のちの人生においてリスクを伴う経済活動に従事する可能性が減少するということだ」という主張がなされ，その後で具体例として給料日ローンやクレジットカードローンの状況を述べて，最終文（We can assume...）で「これ［個人的財政教育を受けた者は借金などの問題に巻き込まれる可能性が低くなったこと］は，こうした生徒が大人になって自分の財政的決断に対する責任を持つようになったときに，法律上の問題が減少し，犯罪に巻き込まれる可能性が減ることにつながると想定することができる」と最初に述べられた主張を繰り返すことでその内容を強調している。よって正解は④となる。

①，③に関しては，いずれも情報源Aで述べている内容とはなっていないので不可。

②に関しては，情報源Aの第5文（However, studies show ...）で「しかし，さまざまな研究は，学生時代に個人的財政の教育に参加した若者は給料日ローンを借りることに関わる可能性がはるかに低いことを示している」とは述べられているが，クレジットカード自体の利用の可能性については言及されていないので不可。

問5　31　正解④

「理由3として，あなたは『個人的財政の授業を受けると，学生は財政に関しより責任を持つようになる』と書くことにした。情報源Bに基づけば，どの選択肢がこの記述をもっともよく支持しているか」　31

① 3つの州における学生のすべてが，3年後に何とかクレジットスコアを上昇させることができた。しかし，財政教育を教えるという点ではアイダホはもっともうまくいっていない州だった。

② 一部の州では，財政の授業を受けた1年後にクレジットスコアが下がった。これはつまり，若者は常に，自分の長期的未来に影響を及ぼすまずい財政的決断をしているということである。

③ 2つの州において，財政の授業を受けたことによる，クレジットスコアに対する悪影響があった。その後，それらのクレジットスコアは上昇したのだが，それはクレジットスコアは時間の経過と共に常に上昇するということを示している。

④ 学校で財政の授業を受けた3年後，3つの州すべての学生たちはクレジットスコアをかなり向上させた。このことは，彼らが適切な財政的決断を行っていることを示している。

正解は④。グラフから3つの州すべてにおいて，高校で個人的財政の授業を受けた1年後から3年後にかけてクレジットカードスコアは劇的に上昇していることがわかるので，正解は④となる。

①，②，③に関しては，いずれも情報源Bで述べられている内容およびグラフからわかる内容ではないので不可。

【主な語句・表現】

[リード文]
・問題冊子を参照のこと。
◇ work on ...「…に取り組む」　　　　　　◇ financial education「金融［財政］教育」
◇ take a position about ...「…についての判断を下す」
◇ outline 图「概要」

[ステップ1]
◇ introduce 動「…を導入する」　　　　　◇ annoyed 形「苛立って」
◇ immigrant 图「移民」　　　　　　　　　◇ principal 图「校長」
◇ district 图「地域；地区」　　　　　　　◇ qualified 形「資格のある」
◇ that [this] is why ...「そういうわけで…；したがって…」
◇ pocket money「お小遣い」　　　　　　　◇ savings account「普通預金口座」
◇ deal 图「契約」　　　　　　　　　　　　◇ student loan「奨学金」
◇ encourage O to -「O に - するよう勧める」
◇ be concerned about ...「…について心配している」
◇ basics 图「基本原理」　　　　　　　　　◇ pay ... back「…を返す」
◇ pension 图「年金」　　　　　　　　　　◇ investment 图「投資」
◇ recommend -ing「- することを勧める」　◇ which 图 to -「どの 图 を - するべきか」
◇ take out ...「〈ローンなど〉を組む」　　◇ help ... out「〈経済的に〉…を援助する」

[設問文・選択肢]
◇ mention that ...「…と言及している」　　◇ consult 動「…に相談する」
◇ expert 图「専門家」　　　　　　　　　　◇ imply that ...「…と示唆している」

[ステップ2]
◇ now that ...「（今や）…なので」　　　　◇ as below「以下のように」
◇ be motivated to -「- するよう動機づけられる」
◇ prospect 图「将来の見込み」　　　　　　◇ inequality 图「不平等」
◇ background 图「背景；経歴」

[ステップ3]　◇ engage in ...「…に従事する」　　　　◇ one measure of ...「…の１つの目安」
　　　　　　　◇ likelihood 名「可能性」
　　　　　　　◇ payday loan「給料日ローン」　次の給料を担保に貸し出される小口の短期ローン。
　　　　　　　◇ interest rate「金利」　　　　　　　　◇ repay 動「…を返済する」
　　　　　　　◇ legal 形「法的な」
　　　　　　　◇ get [become] involved in ...「…に巻き込まれる」
　　　　　　　◇ take part in ...「…に参加する」　　　◇ debt 名「借金」
　　　　　　　◇ assume that ...「…と想定［推定］する」
　　　　　　　◇ track 動「…を追跡する」
　　　　　　　◇ credit score「クレジットスコア；信用スコア」　個人のクレジットカードの支払い（また
　　　　　　　　は返済）の履歴に基づいて，その人の財政面の信用度を数値化したもの。
　　　　　　　◇ undergo 動「…を受ける［経験する］」　　◇ trustworthy 形「信頼［信用］できる」
　　　　　　　◇ regarding 前「…に関して」　　　　　　◇ approve 動「…を認可する」
[設問文・選択肢]　◇ manage to −「何とか−する（ことができる）」
　　　　　　　◇ in terms of ...「…の観点から；…の点で」
　　　　　　　◇ affect 動「…に影響を及ぼす」
　　　　　　　◇ a negative effect on ...「…への悪影響」
　　　　　　　◇ over time「時間（の経過）と共に」

第7問

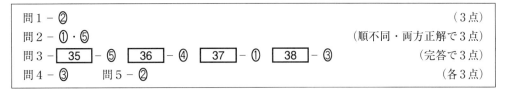

解 答

問1 — ②　　　　　　　　　　　　　　　　　　　　　　　　　　　　（3点）
問2 — ①・⑤　　　　　　　　　　　　　　　　　　（順不同・両方正解で3点）
問3 — 35 — ⑤　 36 — ④　 37 — ①　 38 — ③　　　　（完答で3点）
問4 — ③　　問5 — ②　　　　　　　　　　　　　　　　　　　（各3点）

出 典

Original Material

全 訳

あなたは英語の授業で、プロの発明家について発表することになっています。以下の記事を見つけて、発表用の草案を準備しました。

> 　海で多くの人々が救命ボート、つまり海難に遭った人々を救助する目的のボートに救われてきた。1790年に、イングランド沿岸近くで一隻の船が沈んだ後、その惨事を目撃した地元のある実業家が何事かをなさなければ、と決断した。彼は一部が軽い木材で出来た、転覆しにくい救命ボートを設計した。それは実際に多くの人々を救ったが、1つ大きな問題があった。陸地近くの事故にしか役立たなかったのである。
> 　1840年頃にアメリカでマリア・ビーズリーが水車屋、つまり小麦粉の製造業者の元に生まれた。彼女は父親の持つ機械に大いに興味を持ち、それらがどのように作動するのかを繰り返し検証した。13歳の時に、彼女は湖を帆走する船の設計と製作に成功したが、これが後の1880年に救命ボートの設計を改良するきっかけになったのかもしれない。
> 　酒造りの工場を所有していた祖父のうちの1人の元を学校の夏休みに訪れた彼女は、輸送用の木製の樽に関心をひきつけられ、樽の製造機について学んだ。この興味が元になって後年、彼女は樽の製造過程を速める道具を発明し、1881年と1882年にその特許を取得した。樽の製造量を増やすことと、それにより当然ながら製品の販売高を上げることとが可能になったため、各地の事業者がこの機械を手に入れたがった。数年越しにさまざまな改良を機械に加えつつ彼女の事業は繁盛し、彼女が死の10年ほど前にそれを売却した際には約140万ドルを手にした。今日で言えば、何と4千万ドル以上になる。
> 　息子たちの教育のためにフィラデルフィア市に引っ越した時、おそらくビーズリーは工学技術への愛着で身を立てる決心をしたのだろう。この都市で1876年に、世界の国々が最新の業績を誇示する万国博覧会が開かれた。彼女は頻繁に訪れて、1870年代の終わりに足温器やロースト用鉄板を発明する着想を得た。
> 　1895年にビーズリーはシカゴに住んでいたが、鉄道によりアメリカの東西海岸をシカゴ経由で結ぶ一大鉄道事業が発表された。ビーズリーもこれに携わることになり、列車の速度と、さらに重要なこととしては安全性を向上させる方法を探求した。ビーズリーは、速度の上昇を可能にしつつ、高速での脱線の可能性を低減する形状の新たな列車の主要な設計者として承認を受けた。運転手の視野をより鮮明化できる窓を備えたその列車は、従来型と比べて安全性の高い輸送形態となった。
> 　しかしながら、ビーズリーが最も人の記憶に残っているのは、その救命ボートの設計によってである。彼女のボートは荒海にあって堅牢であり、明らかに耐火性を備えていた。折り畳み可能であるため、船への収納ははるかに容易になった。1800年代の終わりから1900年代の初めにかけて、生活の向上を求める人々による船でのアメリカへの移住が急増しており、ビーズリーの救命ボートと列車の改良によって何百人もの命が救われたことは間違いない。

マリア・ビーズリーの家族は彼女の強力な支えとなった。妻の収入や所有物が法的には夫に帰属した時代にあって，夫のジョンは功績を我が物にすることを拒んだ。息子は1913年に彼女が亡くなるまでは身近で一緒に働いた。人生を一変させる機械を作るという彼女の決意は並外れたものであり，その作品は1893年のシカゴ万国博覧会で展示された。彼女が初めは洋裁師だったということは信じ難いことである。

あなたの発表の草案：

マリア・ビーズリー（1840 年頃〜 1913 年）
― 32 ―

誕生から学生時代
　ー水車屋の元に生まれる
　ー 33
　ー 34

人生における重要な出来事の順序

↓　　　　万国博覧会が彼女に工学的興味を引き起こした。
　　　　　　　 35
　　　　　ビーズリーは樽の製造機の特許を獲得した。
　　　　　　　 36
　　　　　　　 37
　　　　　　　 38

列車の設計
　ービーズリーの設計した列車は， 39 。

救命ボートの設計
　ー初期の救命ボートは陸地近くの事故にしか役立たなかった。
　ー 40

設 問 解 説

問 1　 32 　正解 ②

「あなたの発表の最も良い副題はどれか」 32
　① 驚嘆すべき家族と人生を一変させる設計
　② 人命救助のための工学設計
　③ さまざまな形や大きさの発明品
　④ 利己的な女性実業家にして発明家

　正解は②。第 6 段落第 1 文（Nevertheless, Beasley is ...）にあるように，ビーズリーは何より救命ボートの設計者として名高く，また第 5 段落第 3 文（Beasley was acknowledged ...），最終文（Built with windows ...）にあるように，その列車の設計の改善も安全性の向上に寄与したため，第 6 段落最終文（In the late ...）の「ビーズリーの救命ボートと列車の改良によって何百人もの命が救われたことは間違いない」といった評価が下されているので，②が正解。

　①は最終段落第 4 文（Her determination to ...）に「人生を一変させる機械を作るという彼女の決意」という表現が見られ，本文全体の内容から彼女がそれを成し遂げたと評価できるが，その家族に関しては最終段落第 1 文（Maria Beasley's family ...）〜第 3 文（Her son worked ...）に，「彼女の強力な支えとなった」ことに関しての記述があるのみで，「驚

― 英 R 152 ―

嘆すべき」という評価につながる内容は見当たらない。③については，ボート，樽の製造機，足温器，ロースト用鉄板，列車，という本文に挙げられている彼女の発明品の形や大きさが多様であることに間違いはないが，そのこと自体が重要な意味を持つ，というニュアンスは本文のどこにも感じられず，副題に相応しいとは決して言えない。④は，「利己的な」の1語が本文からはまったく読み取れないため，やはり不適である。

問2 　33 ・ 34 　正解①・⑤
「誕生から学生時代を完成させるために， 33 と 34 に最も適した2つの選択肢を選べ（順序は問わない。）」
　① 湖を帆走するための自分自身のボートを作製した
　② 国家規模の発明コンクールに参加し優勝した
　③ 面倒に遭っている船員たちに助力した
　④ 小麦粉を精製する全く新しい方法を思いついた
　❺ 親類の会社で機械を研究した

　正解は①と⑤。①は第2段落最終文（When she was ...）の「13歳の時に，彼女は湖を帆走する船の設計と製作に成功した」という内容に，⑤は第3段落第1文（Visiting one of ...）の「工場を所有していた祖父のうちの1人の元を学校の夏休みに訪れた彼女は，…樽の製造機について学んだ」という内容に，それぞれ合っているため，①・⑤が正解。
　他の選択肢の内容は，いずれも本文に見られない。

問3 　35 → 36 → 37 → 38 　正解⑤ → ④ → ① → ③
「人生における重要な出来事の順序を完成させるために，5つの出来事（①～⑤）のうち4つを起きた順に選べ」
　① ある鉄道の事業が列車の設計を改善するためにビーズリーを雇った。
　② ビーズリーは息子の教育をフィラデルフィアで行うために当地に引っ越した。
　③ ビーズリーは大金と引き換えに自分の事業を売却した。
　④ ビーズリーの発明品のいくつかが万国博覧会で展示された。
　⑤ 救命ボートの設計がビーズリーによって改良された。

　正解は⑤ → ④ → ① → ③。人生における重要な出来事の順序の空所になっていない2つの出来事と，ここでの選択肢5つを時系列に沿って並べると，以下のようになる。

1．第4段落第1文（Beasley probably decided ...）に「息子たちの教育のためにフィラデルフィア市に引っ越した」と記述のある②。

2．第4段落第2文（This city held ...），最終文（She was a ...）の「この都市［＝フィラデルフィア］で1876年に，世界の国々が最新の業績を誇示する万国博覧会が開かれた」，「彼女は頻繁に訪れて，1870年代の終わりに足温器やロースト用鉄板を発明する着想を得た」という記述に当たる，「万国博覧会が彼女に工学的興味を引き起こした」。

3．第2段落最終文（When she was ...）に「1880年に救命ボートの設計を改良する」と記述のある⑤。→ 35

4．第3段落第2文（This curiosity later ...）に「彼女は樽の製造過程を速める道具を発明し，1881年と1882年にその特許を取得した」と記述のある「ビーズリーは樽の製造機の特許を獲得した」。

5．最終段落第4文（Her determination to ...）に「その作品は1893年のシカゴ万国博覧会で展示された」という記述のある④。→ 36

6．第5段落第1文（In 1895, Beasley ...），第2文（Beasley became involved, ...）「1895年に…一大鉄道事業が発表された。ビーズリーもこれに携わることに」なった，という記述の内容に当たる①。→ 37

— 英R 153 —

7．第3段落第4文（Making various improvements ...）の「彼女が死の10年ほど前にそれ［＝樽の製造業］を売却した」，最終段落第3文（Her son worked ...）の「1913年に彼女が亡くなる」との記述から，<u>1903年頃</u>のことと推定できる③。→　38

よって⑤→④→①→③が正解。

問4　　39　　正解③

「列車の設計を完成させるために，　39　に最も適した選択肢を選べ」
① 長時間使用した後で過熱しない，より良いエンジンを備えていた
② 何かが当たってもほとんど割れることのない，より強度の高い窓を備えていた
③ **高速で運転中に線路にしっかり留まることができた**
④ 他の種類の公共交通と比べてはるかに危険度が低かった

正解は③。彼女が設計したのは，第5段落第3文（Beasley was acknowledged ...）に述べられている「高速での脱線の可能性を低減する形状の新たな列車」であったため，③が正解。

他の選択肢のうち①，②は本文中に関連する記述はなく，④の「危険度」に関しては，第5段落最終文（Built with windows ...）に「従来型と比べて安全性の高い輸送形態となった」という記述はあるが「他の種類の公共交通」との比較はなされていない。

問5　　40　　正解②

「救命ボートの設計を完成させるために，　40　に最も適した選択肢を選べ」
① 彼女のボートは消火を手助けするのにも使えた。
② **彼女のボートは保管用に小さくできた。**
③ 新たなアメリカ市民が彼女のボートで到着した。
④ 彼女の救命ボートの設計は今日まで変更されていない。

正解は②。第6段落第3文（They could be ...）の「折り畳み可能であるため，船への収納ははるかに容易になった」という記述内容に合っているため，②が正解。

①については，第6段落第2文（Her boats were ...）に「耐火性を備えていた」との記述はあるが，「耐火性」と「消火にとっての有効性」は別物である。③は，彼女が設計したのは海難が起きた際という非常時用の救命ボートであって，航海用ではないため，不適。④のような内容の記述も本文中に見られない。

主な語句・表現
・問題冊子を参照のこと。

[第1段落]
(Many people at ...)
◇ made partly of a light wood「一部が軽い木材で出来た」 make O of ...（〈材料〉でOを作る）の受動態である be made of ... に由来する made of ... に副詞の partly（部分的に）が組み合わされ，直前の a rescue boat を修飾する形容詞句として用いられている。
◇ which would be difficult to turn upside-down「それはひっくり返されにくくなる」 非制限用法の関係代名詞 which がまとめる，a rescue boat <made partly of a light wood> の補足説明となる節。upside-down は「さかさまの；ひっくり返った」という意味の形容詞で，turn O upside-down は「Oをさかさまにする［ひっくり返す］」という意味。ここでは which が turn の意味上の目的語となっている。

[第2段落]
(Around 1840, Maria ...)
◇ be born in ... to ～「…（の地）に～を親として［～の元に］生まれる」
◇ miller图「水車屋；製粉業者」
◇ would examine ...「（繰り返し）…を調べたものだった」 would は「繰り返された動作」を表す用法。
◇ inspire O to －「Oを促して－させる［－するよう駆り立てる］」

— 英R 154 —

[第3段落] (Visiting one of ...)	◇ barrel 名「樽」 ◇ patent 動「…の特許を取得する」 名「特許」
[第4段落] (Beasley probably decided ...)	◇ make a career of ...「…で身を立てる；…を生業とする」 ◇ show ... off / show off ...「…を見せびらかす［誇示する］」 ◇ foot warmer「足温器」 ◇ roasting pan「ロースト用鉄板；天パン」 ◇ decade 名「十年間」 1870 – 1879 年，あるいは 1871 – 1880 年といった 10 年間。
[第5段落] (In 1895, Beasley ...)	◇ acknowledge O as ...「O を…（である）と認める［承認する］」 ここでは受動態で用いられている。 ◇ allow O to – 「O が – することを可能にする」 ◇ come off the rails「〈電車が〉脱線する」 ◇ Built with ...「…がついた形で作られて」 分詞構文。
[第6段落] (Nevertheless, Beasley is ...)	◇ fireproof 形「防火［耐火］性の」 ◇ boom 動「急増する」 ◇ there is no doubt that ...「…ということに対して疑いの余地はない；…ということは間違いない」 that ... は接続詞 that が導く，doubt と同格関係の名詞節。
[最終段落] (Maria Beasley's ...)	◇ take credit「功績［手柄］を横取りする」 ◇ start out「人生［仕事］を始める」
[設問文・選択肢]	◇ in the order they happened「それらが起きた順番に」 they happened は形容詞節として the order を修飾しており，直前には「前置詞＋関係代名詞」の in which などが省略されていると考えられる。 ◇ put ... out / put out ...「〈火事など〉を消火する」

第8問

解答

問1 − ②　　　　　　　　　　　　　　　　　　　　　　　　（4点）

問2 | 42 | − ①　　　| 43 | − ④　　　　　　　　　　　　（各3点）

問3 − ① · ③　　　　　　　　　　　　　　（順不同・両方正解で4点）

出典　*Reading Explorer 5* (Cengage Learning), 2016 edition, UNIT 3

全訳

あなたは「社会における健康に関する一般的な懸念事項」というテーマの発表コンテストにむけたポスターを準備する生徒のグループの一員です。ポスターを作成するのに以下の文章を使用してきました。

アレルギーと戦う
～今日の健康に関する一般的懸念～

　今日，何百万もの人々がアレルギーに苦しんでいる。実際，アレルギーは現代的な現象であり，化学物質，植物性，食品性，薬品のいずれに関連するかを問わず，対処に迫られる人の数は，都市の拡大や産業の進展につれて増加している。アフリカや南米の辺鄙な地域では，アレルギーを持つ人は今でも滅多に見られない。アレルギーが生命にかかわる場合は稀だが，我々は悲惨な状態に追い込まれることもある。アメリカの幼い子どもの6％ほどに食品アレルギーが見られ，今日では食品が我々の多くに対して害を及ぼす材料，つまりナッツやミルク，玉子，魚類，大豆，小麦を含む場合は，包装に印刷するよう製造業者は法的に要求されている。深刻なアレルギーを持つ子どもは，他の子どもの昼食に含まれる品目が原因で不調をきたすことを避けるために，クラスメートとは別のテーブルで食事をしたり，さらには家庭で教育を受けたりせざるを得ない。

　では，ありふれた物質に対してなぜアレルギーが出てしまうのだろうか。原因は残念ながら明確ではない。ある日，身体がケーキの中の小麦のような無害な食材に出会い，何らかの理由でそれに敵の印を付ける。最初は何も起きないが，身体はこれを覚えていて，戦闘を行うべく計画を練り始める。我々を毒や病気から保護する免疫系が，細胞に付着して攻撃的物質が再び身体に侵入するのを待ち受ける「兵隊」を製造し始める。実際に侵入が起きると，数ヵ月経ってからであっても「兵隊」は化学物質で応戦するのだが，実際には我々の皮膚に炎症が起きたり，咳や鼻水が出たりする。戦闘と我々の肉体的反応は，時を経て激しさを増すこともある。

　アレルギーは親から遺伝する場合もあるが，患者数の増加がこれほど急速なのだからこれが唯一の原因ではないのは明らかである。我々の環境や行動が，この増加と何らかの関係があるに違いないのである。工場生産されたミルクの代替品で育てられた乳児は，母乳を飲む乳児と比べてアレルギーにかかる危険性が高い可能性がある，という仮説がある。同様なことが，果物や野菜などの天然の食材よりも多くの調整された食材を消費する場合にもあてはまる可能性がある。交通量の多い道路近くに住んでいる子どもの方が，おそらくは往来する車両が空中に放出する物質が原因で，アレルギーは酷くなる場合がある，と論じる科学者もいる。

— 英 R 156 —

皮肉なことだが，あまりに清潔過ぎることもおそらく一因となるのである。科学技術は，我々に有効な薬品と清潔な病院，寒さや悪天候を排除するばかりか，我々を汚れから防御もする堅牢な住宅をもたらしている。自然の中で遊んだり汚れたりしないということは，子どもの発育期の身体が我々の健康を害するものを攻撃する練習の機会を失い，怠惰になって十分な準備が叶わない，ということにもなりかねない。植物関連のアレルギーを持つ人々の症例が1819年に初めて表面化したとき，無学の貧しい者は1人として含まれなかった。今日では，先進国の富裕ではない家族でも清潔な生活を送ることが可能であり，畑の土壌や動物の排泄物など我々が出会う必要のある汚れは，都市部ではほとんどどこにも見られなくなっている。

　子どもを然るべき種類の汚れに幼い時期にさらすことが重要な解決法になり得る，と考える科学者もいるが，進化と絶えず変化する我々の身体のことを考えれば，年齢を重ねて清潔に暮らすときには，それによってもたらされる害が増える可能性もある。防御機構を身につけさせるために，子どもを幼い時に小麦粉など一般的なアレルギー源にできるだけ多くさらすべきであると考える専門家もいる一方で，そうしたものから子どもを完全に遠ざけるべきだと考える専門家もいる。我々の知識が未だに不十分であることは明らかなのである。しかし現在，我々のアレルギーへの意識は高まっており，空気中の埃を除去する特殊な換気扇を備えた部屋を提供し，皮膚を傷めやすい物質を含まない製品でシーツを洗うホテルも多い。遺伝子操作を行うことで，味を変えずに食品からいくつかの成分を取り除くことも可能である。しかし我々は，科学を用いてどこまで自然に手を加えるべきなのだろうか。そして手を加えたとしても，将来いかなる新たな物質を我々の身体が拒絶するようになるのだろうか。

あなたの発表用ポスターの草案：

なぜアレルギーが起きるのか？

41

さまざまなアレルギーの原因とおぼしきもの

タイプ	原因	仮説	起源
1	食事	加工食品を消費し，　42　子どもは危険が大きい可能性がある。	食品，飲料など
2	交通	交通量の多い地域では，子どものアレルギーが悪化する可能性がある。	ガソリンに含まれる化学物質など
3	自然	汚れや排泄物との接触の欠如は　43　可能性がある。	土壌，動物など

アレルギーの解決策の候補：

44

45

設問解説

問1 　41　 **正解②**

「あなたのグループは，ポスターの最初の見出しの下に，アレルギーがなぜ起きるかの理由を本文で説明されているように紹介したい。以下のうち最も適切なのはどれか」 　41　

① 　それらは，現代の生活にはより多くの新たに開発された薬品が使われているために起きる。

② 　**それらは我々の身体による，おそらくは安全なものに対する説明のつかない激しい反応である。**

③ 　それらは，我々が生活環境に突然完全な変化をもたらすときに始まる。

④ 　それらは，テクノロジーがあまりにも大きく進歩して我々の脳内に変化をもたらす際に起きる。

正解は②。問われているのは「なぜアレルギーが起きるのか」の「理由」に当たるもの。文章の第2段落第2文（The reason is, ...）～第6文（When it does, ...）の，アレルギーの「原因は残念ながら明確ではない」が，「身体が…無害な食材に出会い，何らかの理由でそれに敵の印を付け」，その物質が再び身体に侵入した場合，それに備えて身体が製造した「兵隊」が「化学物質で応戦する」という内容に一致するため，②が正解。

①は，第1段落第2文（Indeed, allergies are ...）から薬品関係のアレルギーが存在することは読み取れるが，「新たに開発された」薬品の増加とアレルギーとの関連についての記述は見られない。③，④も本文に見られない内容。

問2 　42　 **正解①** 　43　 **正解④**

「あなたは，アレルギーの原因となり得るタイプ1と3に対する仮説を書くことを求められた。 　42　 と 　43　 に対する最も適切な選択肢を選べ」

タイプ1 　42　

① 　**また調整された乳幼児用ミルクを飲む**

② 　また多くの甘い菓子を食べる

③ 　しかし栄養価の高いジュースは避ける

④ 　しかしナッツや魚はまったく食べない

正解は①。空所に入れるべきものは，食事を原因とするアレルギーの仮説を完成させるのに最も適切な選択肢。第3段落第3文（There are theories ...），第4文（The same could ...）の「工場生産されたミルクの代替品で育てられた乳児は，母乳を飲む乳児と比べてアレルギーにかかる危険性が高い可能性がある，という仮説がある」，「同様なことが，果物や野菜などの天然の食材よりも多くの調整された食材を消費する場合にもあてはまる可能性がある」という内容に一致するため，①が正解。

②の「甘い菓子」や③の「ジュース」についての記述は見られない。④の「ナッツ」，「魚類」については，第1段落第5文（Around 6% of ...）で「包装に印刷するよう製造業者は法的に要求されている」食材として挙げられているが，幼児期に摂取しないことがアレルギーの危険性を高める可能性があるとは述べられていない。

タイプ3 　43　

① 　我々をそれらの危険に気づかなくする

② 　我々を新鮮な郊外の空気に十分に触れられなくする

③ 　我々が低い気温に耐えることを困難にする

④ 　**我々を健康に悪い要素に対して脆くする**

正解は④。空所に入れるべきものは，自然を原因とするアレルギーの仮説を完成させるのに最も適切な選択肢。第4段落第3文（Not playing in ...）の「自然の中で遊んだり汚れたりしないということは，子どもの発育期の身体が我々の健康を害するものを攻撃する

— 英 R 158 —

練習の機会を失い，怠惰になって十分な準備が叶わない，ということにもなりかねない」という内容に一致すると言えるため，④が正解。

他の選択肢の内容に相当する記述は，本文に見られない。

問3　44 ・ 45 　正解①・③

「あなたはアレルギーに立ち向かい得る方法となり得るものについて記述している。記事によれば以下のうちどの2つが適切か（順序は問わない）」

44 ・ 45

　① 子どもは，アレルギー源になることの多い食品から遠ざけられるべきだ。
　② 幼い子どものいる家庭は，寝室に空気清浄機を備えるべきだ。
　③ 人々は，幼い時期に適切な種類の汚いものに出会う機会を持つべきだ。
　④ 一般に子どもが具合を悪くする植物や食品は，科学的に改変すべきだ。
　⑤ 天然素材でできた特別なベッドシーツが，子ども向けに売られるべきだ。
　⑥ 子どもの健康な発達を促すビタミンが，ある種の食品に加えられるべきだ。

正解は①・③。最終段落第2文（While some professionals ...）には，「そうしたもの［＝一般的なアレルギー源］から子どもを完全に遠ざけるべきだと考える」専門家が存在すると書かれているので，①は正解。また第4段落最終文（Today even families ...）の「畑の土壌や動物の排泄物など我々が出会う必要のある汚れ」という表現や，最終段落第1文（Some scientists believe ...）に「子どもを然るべき種類の汚れに幼い時期にさらすことが重要な解決法になり得る，と考える科学者」もいることが述べられていることなどから，③も正解。

②の「空気清浄機」，⑤の「特別なベッドシーツ」については，最終段落第4文（We are more ...）に「現在，…空気中の埃を除去する特殊な換気扇を備えた部屋を提供し，皮膚を傷めやすい物質を含まない製品でシーツを洗うホテルも多い」と述べられているが，「子どものいる家庭」や「子ども向け」という内容につながる記述はない。④の「食品の科学的改変」については，最終段落第5文（Through engineering genetics, ...）に「遺伝子操作を行うことで，味を変えずに食品からいくつかの成分を取り除くことも可能である」と述べられているが，やはり「子ども」との関連性について触れられてはいないし，改変が推奨されるという方向での記述も見られない。⑥の「ビタミンの添加」については，本文に関連する記述はない。

（主な語句・表現）　・問題冊子を参照のこと。
［タイトル］　◇allergy图「アレルギー」

［第1段落］　◇life-threatening圈「生命を脅かす；生命にかかわる」
（Nowadays　◇packaging图「パッケージ；包装紙」
millions of ...）　◇ingredient图「成分；原料」
　◇namely ...「すなわち…」
　◇avoid them getting sick「彼らの具合が悪くなるのを避ける」　avoid - ing は「－することを避ける」という意味で，ここでの them は動名詞 getting の意味上の主語を示している。

［第2段落］　◇flag動「…に印をつける」
（So why are ...）　◇remembering it「それを覚えていて」　分詞構文。
　◇immune system「免疫系；免疫機構」
　◇'soldiers' that attach to cells and wait for the offensive material to enter the body again「細胞に付着して攻撃的物質が再び身体に入るのを待つ『兵士たち』」　免疫反応における抗原に対抗する抗体が，「兵士」にたとえられている。

◇ When it does「それが実際に起きると」 ここでの it は代名詞として the offensive material の，does は代動詞として enters the body again の代用となっている。

◇ which actually irritate our skin, or make us cough or our noses run「それは実際には，我々の皮膚に炎症を起こさせたり，我々に咳をさせたり我々の鼻水を流れさせたりする」 非制限用法の関係代名詞 which が導く，chemicals の補足説明となる節。irritate は「…に炎症を起こさせる」という意味。or でつながれた us cough と our noses run は，それぞれ「make O +〈原形〉」の「O +〈原形〉」にあたり，noses run とは「鼻水が出る」ことを意味する。

[第3段落]
(Though allergies can ...)

◇ have something to do with ...「…といくらか関係がある」
◇ milk-substitute 图「ミルクの代用品［代替品］」
◇ be at risk of −ing「−する危険がある」
◇ process 動「〈食品〉を加工［調整］する」

[第4段落]
(Being too clean, ...)

◇ presumably 副「おそらくは；たぶん」
◇ spotless 形「清浄［清潔］な」
◇ keep ... out / keep out ...「…を中に入れない［締め出す］」
◇ Not playing in nature or getting dirty can mean ...「自然の中で遊んだり汚れたりしないことは…を意味し得る」 Not に続く playing と getting が and でつながれた否定形の動名詞が can mean の主語として働いており，mean の直後には，その目的語となる名詞節を導く接続詞の that が省略されている。
◇ children's developing bodies lose the chance ... and therefore grow lazy and become insufficiently prepared「子どもの発達中の身体は…機会を失い，したがって怠惰になり十分に準備ができなくなる」 lose, grow, become という3つの現在形の動詞が，2つの and によってつながれている。
◇ surface 動「表面化する；明るみに出る」
◇ waste 图「排泄物」

[最終段落]
(Some scientists believe ...)

◇ do harm「害を与える」
◇ defense 图「防衛機構」 病原菌に抵抗する防衛反応のこと。
◇ distance O from ...「O を…から遠ざける」
◇ fan 图「送風機；換気扇」
◇ engineer 動「〈遺伝子〉を操作する」

[ポスター]

◇ manufactured 形「（工業的に）生産された；加工された」
◇ possible 形 ［後ろの名詞を修飾して］「…の候補になる［…となる可能性のある］もの」

[設問文・選択肢]

◇ as explained in the passage「本文で説明されているように」 接続詞の as の直後には it ［= the reason］is を補うことができる。
◇ supposedly 副「おそらくは；たぶん」
◇ vulnerable 形「脆い；脆弱な」
◇ tackle 動「〈問題など〉に取り組む［立ち向かう］」

第 5 回　実戦問題　解答・解説

第5回　解答・解説

英語（リーディング） 第5回 （100点満点）

（解答・配点）

問題番号（配点）	設問	解答番号	正解	配点	自己採点欄
第1問（6）	1	1	②	2	
	2	2	③	2	
	3	3	④	2	
小計					
第2問（10）	1	4	⑤	2	
	2	5	③	2	
	3	6	②	2	
	4	7	①	2	
	5	8	②	2	
小計					
第3問（9）	1	9	③	3*	
		10	①		
		11	④		
		12	②		
	2	13	③	3	
	3	14	①	3	
小計					
第4問（12）	1	15	④	3	
	2	16	④	3	
	3	17	①	3	
	4	18	①	3	
小計					
第5問（16）	1	19	①	3	
	2	20	②	3	
	3	21	④	3	
	4	22	①	3	
	5	23	④	2	
		24	②	2	
小計					

問題番号（配点）	設問	解答番号	正解	配点	自己採点欄
第6問（18）	1	25	①	3	
	2	26	④	3	
	3	27 － 28	② － ⑤	3*	
		29	③	3	
	4	30	①	3	
	5	31	③	3	
小計					
第7問（15）	1	32	①	3	
	2	33	⑤	3*	
		34	③		
	3	35	②	3*	
		36	①		
		37	⑤		
		38	③		
	4	39	④	3	
	5	40	①	3	
小計					
第8問（14）	1	41	③	4	
	2	42	④	3	
		43	④	3	
	3	44 － 45	① － ②	4*	
小計					

（注）
1 ＊は，全部正解の場合のみ点を与える。
2 －（ハイフン）でつながれた正解は，順序を問わない。

— 英R 162 —

第 1 問

| 解 答 | 問 1 － ②　　　問 2 － ③　　　問 3 － ④ | （各 2 点） |

出典　　*Original Material*

全訳

あなたは学校の英語クラブの部長であり，クラブは次のようにチラシで説明されているコンテストに参加する予定です。

第 1 回青年英語演劇コンテスト

　青年英語演劇協会は，最初となるコンテストを開催します。最高のエンターテインメントとしての形のひとつである演劇を通して，日本人の若者に積極的に英語を学んでもらうことをねらいとしています。

　このコンテストには 3 つのステージ（段階）があります。各ステージで勝者が選出され，3 つのステージすべてに合格すると，グランドファイナル（本選）に参加することができます。

| グランドファイナル | 会場：センチュリーホール
日時：2023 年 2 月 5 日 |

大賞賞品

優勝チームは，2023 年 3 月にオーストラリアのキャンベラで開催されるインターナショナル・イングリッシュ・キャンプに参加できます。

コンテストについての情報：

ステージ	アップロードするもの 及びイベント	詳細	2022 年の締切 及び日程
ステージ 1	アンケートへの回答及び英語のエッセイ	エッセイの語数：150 - 200 語	8 月 13 日昼 12 時までにアップロードすること
ステージ 2	あなたのチームが演じている様子を撮影した動画	（演技）時間：25 - 30 分	10 月 25 日昼 12 時までにアップロードすること
ステージ 3	地域予選	このサイト上に，グランドファイナルへ進出する勝者（チーム）を発表します。	12 月 23 日開催

グランドファイナルでの評価基準に関する情報

発音及び イントネーションなど	ジェスチャー及び パフォーマンス	発声及び アイコンタクト	チームワーク	審査員からの 質問への返答
40%	10%	10%	30%	10%

— 英 R 163 —

◆アンケート，英語のエッセイのタイトル，演劇用の台本をオンラインでダウンロードする必要があります。

<u>ここをクリック</u>してください。

◆資料はオンラインでアップロードする必要があります。すべての日時は日本標準時（JST）です。
◆ステージ1とステージ2の結果は，各ステージの締め切りから7日後にウェブサイトで知ることができます。

詳細については，<u>ここをクリック</u>してください。

設問解説

問1　　1　　正解②

「ステージ1に参加するには，　1　ことが必要である」
① 質問に答えて，パフォーマンスの動画を作成する
② 質問に答え，英語でエッセイを書く
③ 英語のエッセイを書いて，パフォーマンスの動画を作成する
④ 英語のエッセイを書いて，演劇（の台本）を書く

　正解は②。Contest information（コンテストについての情報）を記した一覧表を読み取る。各ステージに参加するための要件は，表の中の "Things to Upload & Events" の欄で示されており，ステージ1に参加するための要件としては，Answers to a questionnaire, and an English essay「アンケートへの回答及び英語のエッセイ」という記載がある。よって，②が正解。

問2　　2　　正解③

「ステージ1の結果はいつから確認できるか」　2
① 8月6日
② 8月13日
③ 8月20日
④ 8月27日

　正解は③。チラシの最後の◆（You can get ...）に，「ステージ1とステージ2の結果は，各ステージの締め切りから7日後にウェブサイトで知ることができます」とある。ステージ1の締め切り日は8月13日であり，それから7日後なので8月20日からステージ1の結果を確認することができるということになる。よって，③が正解。

問3　　3　　正解④

「グランドファイナルで高得点を得るためには，自然な英語を話すことと　3　に最大の努力を注ぐ必要がある」
① 声や表情をコントロールすること
② 審査員にストーリーを丁寧に説明すること
③ ドラマチックなジェスチャーをすること
④ グループとしてよりうまく機能すること

　正解は④。Grand Final Grading Information（グランドファイナルでの評価基準に関する情報）の図表を見ると，Pronunciation & Intonation, etc.（発音及びイントネーションなど）の評価項目に最も重い40%の比重が置かれていて，これが「自然な英語を話すこと」に該当するとわかる。次に重い比重が置かれているのはTeamwork（チームワーク）で，30%であるが，チームワークに関わる内容としては，選択肢の④「グループとしてよりうまく機能すること」が当てはまると考えられる。よって，正解は④。

— 英 R 164 —

主な語句・表現

[リード文]
・問題冊子を参照のこと。
◇ chief 形「〈階級・重要度などにおいて〉最高の」
◇ flyer 名「（折り込み）チラシ」　　　　　◇ as follows「以下の通り」

[チラシ]
◇ aim to -「-することをねらいとする」
◇ encourage A to -「Aが-するように勧める［励ます］；Aを励まして-させる［してもらう］」
◇ form 名「形；形態」　　　　　　　　　　◇ competition 名「競争；試合；コンテスト」
◇ participate in ...「…に参加する」（= take part in ...）
◇ Grand Final「グランドファイナル；（最終）本選」
◇ questionnaire 名「アンケート」　　　　　◇ video 名「動画；ビデオ」
◇ regional 形「地域の；地方の」　　　　　◇ detail 名「詳細；詳しい内容」
◇ deadline 名「締切（日）」　　　　　　　◇ script 名「〈演劇などの〉台本」
◇ play 名「演劇；戯曲」　　　　　　　　　◇ material 名「資料」

[設問文・選択肢]
◇ expression 名「表情；表現」　　　　　　◇ dramatic 形「ドラマチックな；劇的な」

第2問

解答

| 問1 - ⑤ | 問2 - ③ | 問3 - ② | 問4 - ① | 問5 - ② | （各2点） |

出典　*Original Material*

全訳　あなたと英国からの交換留学生であるジョンは，学校の英字新聞の編集者です。彼はその新聞に，ある記事を書きました。

授業でタブレットを使うのは好きですか？　英国はICT（情報通信技術）教育を推進してきていますが，順調に進んでいるとは言えないと思います。日本ではどうでしょうか？　日本の高校に関するいくつかの調査結果は，私たちにいくつかの答えを与えてくれています。

> ➤ 2018年時点では，各々の生徒にタブレットを提供しなかった学校の数は，提供した学校の約5倍でした。
>
> 2020年の状況は次のとおりでした：
> ➤ タブレットの導入を考えていなかった学校の数は，考えていた学校の3倍以上でした。
> ➤ 私立高校の43.8％は，生徒ごとにめいめいがタブレットを持っていましたが，一方，公立高校においてはわずか5.4％の学校だけが各生徒につき1台を提供していました。
> ➤ すべての生徒にタブレットを提供することを計画している高校は，公立高校よりも私立高校にずっと多くありました。

ご存知のように，私たちの学校では幸運にも個別のタブレットが提供されています。ただ，各生徒がきちんとかつ十分に使いこなしているかどうか，私はいぶかしく思っています。先生方はタブレットを使うのに十分熟練しているでしょうか？　先生方は，各生徒に日ごろの授業で自分の持つタブレットを最大限に活用させようとしているでしょうか？　私は校長先生からある情報を得ました。数学の教師の10人に4人は，ICT教育の推進に熱心に取り組んでいます。これは英語教師の数よりも多いです。彼らの11人に3人は，生徒にタブレットを使用させています。そして，最も低い割合は国語の教師です。

実際，今後，このような電子ツールに，私たちはより依存する必要がはたしてあるのかどうかと私は思います。私たちの学校の生徒や先生方にアンケートなどをやらなくてはいけないと思いますし，そうすれば，現状の改善につながるであろうタブレットの使い方についてヒントを得ることになるかもしれません。

— 英R 166 —

設問解説

問1　　4　　正解⑤

「ICT 教育に熱心に取り組んでいるあなたたちの学校の先生方の比率の点で，次のどれが教科の先生の順位を<u>高いものから低いものへと</u>表しているか」　　4

① 英語教師 — 国語教師 — 数学教師
② 英語教師 — 数学教師 — 国語教師
③ 国語教師 — 英語教師 — 数学教師
④ 国語教師 — 数学教師 — 英語教師
⑤ **数学教師 — 英語教師 — 国語教師**
⑥ 数学教師 — 国語教師 — 英語教師

　正解は⑤。記事内の囲みの下の段落の第 5 文（I've got some ...）以降に，「数学の教師の 10 人に 4 人は，ICT 教育の推進に熱心に取り組んでいます。これは英語教師の数よりも多いです。彼らの 11 人に 3 人は，生徒にタブレットを使用させています。そして，最も低い割合は国語の教師です」という記述がある。したがって，⑤が正解。

問2　　5　　正解③

「ジョンの学校での現在の ICT 教育に関する彼のコメントは，　5　ということを表している」

① 彼は自国の ICT 教育は劣っていると感じている
② 彼は学校でのタブレットの効果的な使い方に満足している
③ **彼は学校でタブレットが有効に活用されているかどうか懐疑的である**
④ 彼はもっと多くの種類のオンライン学習を見たいと思っている

　正解は③。記事内の囲みの下の段落の前半（As you know, ...）に，「ご存知のように，私たちの学校では幸運にも個別のタブレットが提供されています。ただ，各生徒がきちんとかつ十分に使いこなしているかどうか，私はいぶかしく思っています。先生方はタブレットを使うのに十分熟練しているでしょうか？　先生方は，各生徒に日ごろの授業で自分の持つタブレットを最大限に活用させようとしているでしょうか？」とある。ICT 教育の一環として，生徒にはめいめいに 1 台ずつタブレットが配布されているが，果たして有効に活用されているかどうか疑わしいというジョンの気持ちが表れる文章になっている。よって，正解は③。

　①について，ジョンは記事の冒頭で「英国は ICT（情報通信技術）教育を推進してきていますが，順調に進んでいるとは言えないと思います」とは述べているが，自国の英国が「劣っている」（inferior）と言っているわけではない。②については，「満足している」（satisfied）ということが読み取れる個所は本文中にはない。同様に，④についても，その内容を裏付ける記述は本文中にない。

問3　　6　　正解②

「調査結果からわかることを最もよく反映している陳述は　6　である」

① 「自分のタブレットを手に入れることができるのだから，私は公立学校の生徒だったらいいのに」
② **「私の学校は公立です。そして，現時点では ICT 教育を推進する予定はありません」**
③ 「2018 年には，3 校に 1 校の学校が各生徒めいめいにタブレットを提供しました」
④ 「大多数の学校は，自校の ICT 教育を実践する授業を改善するつもりです」

　正解は②。記事内の囲みの最後の➤（There were many ...）に「すべての生徒にタブレットを提供することを計画している高校は，公立高校よりも私立高校にずっと多くありました」とある。逆に言うと，公立高校は私立高校に比べて，将来の ICT 教育推進については消極的である，ということである。よって，正解は②。

— 英 R 167 —

他の選択肢については，タブレットが生徒1人につき1台行き渡っている高校は，公立よりも私立の方が多いので，① は誤りとなる。③ については，囲みの最初で「2018年時点では，各々の生徒にタブレットを提供しなかった学校の数は，提供した学校の約5倍でした」とあることから，約5校に1校の割合でしか生徒めいめいにタブレットが提供されていなかったということがわかるので誤りとなる。④ を正解とする根拠となる記述は調査結果には見当たらない。

問4　　7　　正解 ①
「ジョンの学校でのICT教育についての彼の意見を最もよく要約しているのはどれか」
　　7
　　① 状況を改善するためには，いくつかの調査が必要である。
　　② タブレットは思ったほど役に立たない。
　　③ タブレットの使い方を教える先生向けの講座を実施する必要がある。
　　④ 生徒がタブレットを使いやすくする必要がある。
　正解は ①。記事の最終文（I think we've ...）に，「私たちの学校の生徒や先生方にアンケートなどをやらなくてはいけないと思いますし，そうすれば，現状の改善につながるであろうタブレットの使い方についてヒントを得ることになるかもしれません」とある。よって，正解は ①。
　他の選択肢を正解とする根拠となる内容は本文中には書かれていない。

問5　　8　　正解 ②
「この記事に最もふさわしいタイトルはどれか」　　8
　　① タブレットのコストと性能
　　② タブレットの導入とその未来
　　③ タブレットの公立学校への配布戦略
　　④ タブレットの有用性と問題点
　正解は ②。この記事は，まず，日本の高校におけるタブレット端末の生徒1人1台の配置の現状について，調査結果をまとめている。言い換えれば，タブレットの導入に関する現状を述べている。その後，ジョンは自校におけるタブレットの生徒への配布状況の現実を確認し，また，教師も含む学校全体の教育や授業におけるタブレットの活用状況について現状とコメントをまとめ，最後に，それらの現状に基づいて将来自校においてどのようなICT教育が図られるべきかを探るために，アンケート調査などが必要なのではないかと問題提起している。よって，正解は ②。
　他の選択肢については，それらに関わる直接的な内容は本文中には見当たらない。③ については，本文にはタブレットの配布に関する事実が調査結果により示されているが，その配布に関する「戦略」が述べられているわけではない。

主な語句・表現　・問題冊子を参照のこと。
[リード文]　◇ an exchange student「交換留学生」
◇ UK = United Kingdom (of Great Britain and Northern Ireland)「連邦王国；イギリス」
◇ editor 图「編集者」　　　　　　　　◇ paper 图「新聞」(= newspaper)
◇ article 图「〈新聞・雑誌・ネットなどの〉記事」

[本文]　◇ tablet 图「タブレット端末」(= tablet PC)
◇ promote 動「…を推進する」　　　　　◇ smoothly 副「順調に；円滑に」
◇ How about ...?「…はどうでしょうか；…はいかがでしょうか」
◇ survey 图「調査」

— 英 R 168 —

◇ provide A for B「A を B に供給する［与える］」（= provide B with A）

◇ five times as large as that of schools which did in 2018　that = the number, which did = which provided a tablet for each student

◇ three times as large as that of schools which did　that = the number, which did = which thought of introducing tablets

◇ while接「（…である）一方, ～」 対照を表す。

◇ with one　one = a tablet

◇ many more private than public high schools「公立高校よりもはるかに多くの私立高校」

◇ individual形「個々の；個別の」　　　　◇ properly副「適切に；しっかりと」

◇ fully副「十分に」

◇ skillful形「技術［技能］のある；熟練［熟達］した」

◇ use one　one = a tablet

◇ make the most of ...「〈有利な条件など〉を最大限に活用する」

◇ head teacher「《英》校長」《米》では principal。

◇ eager形「熱心な；熱意のある」

◇ Three in eleven of them　them = English teachers

◇ depend on ...「…に頼る［依存する］」　　◇ electronic形「電子の；電子工学の」

◇ we've［= we have］got to give ...　have got to は have to -「-しなければならない」の口語的な表現。

◇ questionnaire名「アンケート（調査）；質問表」

◇ ... or something「…か何か」 表現を柔らかくしてぼかす言い方。

◇ usage名「使用（方法）；使うこと；使い方」

◇ lead to ...「…につながる；…へと導かれる」

◇ improvement名「改善；改良；向上」

◇ present形「現在の；現状の；今の」（= current）

◇ situation名「状況；状態」

[設問文・選択肢]
◇ in terms of ...「…の点において；…という観点から」

◇ ratio名「割合」　　　　　　　　　　　◇ eagerly副「熱心に」

◇ inferior形「劣っている」 ⇔ superior形「優れている」

◇ effective形「効果的な」 副詞形は effectively「効果的に」。

◇ skeptical形「懐疑的な；疑い深い」　　◇ statement名「陳述；述べること［内容］」

◇ reflect動「…を反映する；映し出す」　◇ finding名「発見；所見」

◇ majority名「大多数；大半」 ⇔ minority名「少数（派）」

◇ intend to -「-しようとする；-しようと意図する」

◇ summarise動「…を要約する；まとめる」《米》の綴りでは summarize となる。

◇ hold動「…を催す；開催する」　　　　◇ suitable形「適する；適合する」

◇ strategy名「戦略；（戦略的）計画」　◇ distribute動「配布する」

第3問

解答

問1 - 　9　③，　10　①，　11　④，　12　②　　　　　　　　　　　（完答で3点）

問2 - ③　　　問3 - ①　　　　　　　　　　　　　　　　　　　　（各3点）

出典 （参考）https://www.myenglishpages.com/english/reading-bob-marley.php

全訳

アメリカの友達が，彼のお気に入りのミュージシャンを紹介してくれました。あなたはもっと知りたいと思い，ある音楽雑誌で次の記事を見つけました。

レゲエの魂，ボブ・マーリー

　ボブ・マーリーは1945年2月6日に生まれました。彼はジャマイカのレゲエ歌手であり，また，ソングライター，ミュージシャン，ギタリストでもあり，国際的な名声を獲得し，熱狂的なファンからは今なお高い評価を得ています。1963年にグループ *The Wailers*（ウェイラーズ）でスタートし，彼は独特の作詞作曲とボーカルスタイルを作り出して，すぐにそれは世界中の聴衆に賞賛を持って受けとめられました。1974年にウェイラーズが解散した後，マーリーはソロとして活躍し，1977年6月のアルバム『エクソダス』のリリースでそのピークを迎えました。そのアルバムが彼の世界的な評価を確立し，また，7,500万枚以上のレコード販売数を伴う，歴史に残る世界最高の売り上げを誇るアーティストの1人としての彼の地位につながったということは疑う余地もありません。

　ボブ・マーリーは，1930年代にジャマイカで発展したアブラハムの宗教である（ラスタファリを信奉する），献身的なラスタファリアンでした。この宗教は彼にインスピレーションを与え，彼の音楽を精神的な感性で満たしました。ラスタファリ運動はレゲエの発展における重要な要素でした。ラスタファリ（運動）の熱情的な支持者として，ボブ・マーリーはレゲエ音楽を，ジャマイカの社会的に恵まれない地域から国際的な音楽シーンへと持ち上げました。

　1977年7月，マーリーは足の1本の指の爪の下が，ある種の致命的な病気にかかっていることが判明しました。彼の医者たちは彼に手術をするよう強く勧めました。しかし，マーリーは彼の宗教的信念を持ち出して，彼らのアドバイスをはねのけました。その病気にもかかわらず，彼は癌が彼の体全体に広がり，健康が悪化するまでツアーを続けました。彼は，1981年5月11日にマイアミのシダーズ・オブ・レバノン病院（現在のマイアミ大学病院）で36歳で亡くなりました。彼の肺と脳への癌の広がりが彼の死を引き起こしました。彼の息子ジギーへの彼の最後の言葉は，「お金は命を買えない」でした。

設問解説

問1　　9　　正解 ③,　　10　　正解 ①,　　11　　正解 ④,　　12　　正解 ②

「以下の出来事（①～④）を起きた順に並べなさい」

①　マーリーはソロで歌い始めた。
②　マーリーは自分の病気を発見した後，ツアーを止めなかった。
③　マーリーは *The Wailers* というグループの一員になった。
④　アルバム『エクソダス』がリリースされた。

　まず，第1段落第3文（Starting out in ...）に「1963年にグループ *The Wailers*（ウェイラーズ）でスタートし，彼は独特の作詞作曲とボーカルスタイルを作り出して，すぐにそれは世界中の聴衆に賞賛を持って受けとめられました」とある。

　続けて第4文（After *The Wailers* ...）に「1974年にウェイラーズが解散した後，マーリーはソロとして活躍し，1977年6月のアルバム『エクソダス』のリリースでそのピークを迎えました」とある。

　そして，最終段落第1文（In July, 1977, ...）以降に「1977年7月，マーリーは足の1本の指の爪の下が，ある種の致命的な病気にかかっていることが判明しました。... その病気にもかかわらず，彼は癌が彼の体全体に広がり，健康が悪化するまでツアーを続けました」とある。

　以上のことを，具体的な年号や月なども手掛かりにして時系列でまとめると，③→①→④→②の順番になるとわかる。

問2　　13　　正解 ③

「マーリーは　13　という理由で，医者からの治療を受けることを拒否した」

①　手術をするには遅すぎると思った
②　コンサートツアーで忙しかった
③　**自分の信仰に従っていた**
④　彼の癌は初期段階だった

　正解は③。最終段落第2文から第3文（His doctors strongly ....　However, Marley turned ...）に，「彼の医者たちは彼に手術をするよう強く勧めました。しかし，マーリーは彼の宗教的信念を持ち出して，彼らのアドバイスをはねのけました」とある。マーリーが自らが信じるところのラスタファリ運動の主義や信条に従う形で，手術を断ったことがわかる。よって，正解は③。

問3　　14　　正解 ①

「この話から，あなたは　14　ということがわかった」

①　**宗教はマーリーの音楽に影響を与えた**
②　宗教によってマーリーはジャマイカに移住した
③　マーリーは彼のバンドメンバーとは反りが合わなかった
④　マーリーの音楽は彼の国からお金を奪った

　正解は①。第2段落全体の内容を読むと，マーリーの信じるラスタファリが彼にいかに大きな影響を及ぼしていたかがわかる。とりわけ，第2文（This religion inspired ...）の「この宗教は彼にインスピレーションを与え，彼の音楽を精神的な感性で満たしました」という1文は，宗教がマーリーの音楽に影響を与えたということを明確に述べている。よって，正解は①。

　②と④については，それらが言及されている箇所は見当たらない。また，③については，確かにマーリーが最初に所属した *The Wailers*（ウェイラーズ）というバンドは解散したが，「メンバーと反りが合わなかった」というような記述はどこにも見当たらない。

|主な語句・表現| ・問題冊子を参照のこと。

[第1段落]
(Bob Marley was born ...)

◇ Reggae 名「レゲエ」 狭義においては 1960 年代後半ジャマイカで発祥し，1980 年代前半まで流行したポピュラー音楽。広義においてはジャマイカで成立したポピュラー音楽全般のことをいう。2018 年にはユネスコの無形文化遺産に登録された。

◇ achieve 動「〈地位や名声など〉を得る；獲得する」

◇ fame 名「名声」　　　　　　　　　◇ praise 動「…を称賛する；褒め称える」

◇ enthusiastic 形「熱心な；熱情的な」

◇ distinctive 形「卓越した；傑出した；特筆に値する」

◇ admiration 名「称賛；褒めること」

◇ break up「〈グループなどが〉解散する；〈ペアなどが〉別れる」

◇ pursue 動「…を追い求める；追求する」　◇ establish 動「…を確立する；打ち立てる」

◇ reputation 名「評判；評価」

[第2段落]
(Bob Marley was a ...)

◇ committed 形「献身的な；傾倒している」

◇ Rastafarian 名「ラスタファリアン（ラスタファリ運動の実践者）」 ラスタファリ運動（Rastafari movement）は，1930 年代にジャマイカの労働者階級と農民を中心にして発生した宗教的思想運動である。

◇ Abrahamic religion「アブラハムの宗教」 アブラハムの神の崇拝を支持する一神教のグループ。ユダヤ教，キリスト教，イスラム教などが含まれる。

◇ inspire 動「…を鼓舞する；刺激する；霊感を与える」

◇ fill A with B「A を B で満たす［一杯にする］」

◇ spirituality 名「霊性；霊的なこと；精神性」

◇ passionate 形「熱心な；情熱的な」　　　◇ deprived 形「恵まれない；貧困の」

[第3段落]
(In July, 1977, ...)

◇ suffer from ...「〈病気など〉で苦しむ；…を患う」

◇ fatal 形「死に至る；致命的な；極めて重大な」

◇ operation 名「手術」

◇ turn down ...「…を断る［拒絶する］」（＝ decline）

◇ cite 動「…を引用する」　　　　　　　◇ in spite of ...「…にもかかわらず」

◇ spread 動「広がる；拡大する」 名詞形も spread「拡大；広がり」である。

◇ lung 名「肺」　　　　　　　　　　　◇ brain 名「脳」

[設問文・選択肢]

◇ refuse 動「拒否する；拒絶する」　　　◇ influence 名「影響（力）」

◇ get along with ...「…とうまく［仲良く］やっていく［付き合う］」

◇ deprive A of B「A から B を奪う」

第４問

解答

| 問１－④ | 問２－④ | 問３－① | 問４－① | （各３点） |

出典　*Original Material*

全訳

英語の授業であなたは関心のある社会問題についてのエッセイを書いています。これが最も新しい草稿です。あなたは今，先生からのコメントに基づいて，修正に取り組んでいます。

高糖度飲料に課税する利点	先生のコメント
果汁飲料や炭酸清涼飲料といった甘い飲み物は世界中の若者たちに非常に人気があります。しかし，こうした飲み物を消費することは健康に悪いということがわかっています。糖分を摂取しすぎると肥満や，心臓病や糖尿病といったその他の健康上の問題を引き起こす可能性があるのです。(1)たとえば，世界中の多くの政府が，甘い飲み物にいわゆる「砂糖税」を付加することによって市民の糖分摂取を減らそうとしています。この新しい税はいくつかの好ましい結果を生み出してきました。	⑴ ここには正しくない語が用いられています。別の語あるいは表現を選んでください。
第一に，甘い飲み物に対する税は消費を減らします。アメリカの５つの都市において甘い飲み物に税が付加されると，(2)それは33%減少しました。つまり，人々は甘い飲み物を買うことをやめて，その代わりにより健康にいいものを購入しました。貧困地域において，これが特に重要な効果となっているのは，貧困地域の人々は健康的ではなく，より糖分の多い飲み物を消費する傾向にあるからです。	⑵ ここの「それ」は何を意味していますか。完全な形で文を書き出しなさい。
第二に，甘い飲み物の価格を上げると肥満を減らし(3)＾ます。小学校に通う年齢の子どもたちがこのことによって最も恩恵を受けています。イギリスで販売されている飲み物に砂糖税が付加されると，小学校高学年において肥満になっている子どもたちの数が大きく減少したのです。さらに，抜歯のために病院へ行く子どもたちの数が減りました。	⑶ あなたの主題文はこの一節においてあなたが言及している他の効果をまとめていません。それを追加してください。
最後に，砂糖税は政府が健康管理にあてるお金を節約することに役立ちます。人々がより健康的になると，公立病院を利用する回数が減り，より長生きし，仕事をする時間が増えます。それは，政府が健康管理や失業給付にあてるお金を少なくするに違いないことを意味します。そのお金は，教育に投資したり都市を改善したりするといった他の多くの方法において，社会に利益をもたらすために使うことができるのです。	
結論として，甘い飲み物に税を加えることには多くの利益があります。それによって，人々が飲む甘味飲料が減り，子どもの健康を改善し，(4)病院を助けます。市民の健康と幸福を増進させるために，世界中のもっと多くの国々がこうしたことを行うべきです。	⑷ ここは実際のところ，第４段落で書かれていたことをまとめていません。書き直してください。

設問解説

問1　15　正解④

「コメント(1)に基づくと，代わりに使う最もよい語はどれか」　15

① 加えて
② 対照的に
③ それどころか
④ したがって

正解は④。下線部(1)の前文では，糖分の摂取過多が健康上の問題を引き起こす可能性があることが述べられ，下線部(1)に続く文では，砂糖税によって市民の糖分摂取を減らそうとしていることが述べられているが，これは前文の例示ではなく結果であることから，④の Therefore「ゆえに；したがって」に変えると自然な文脈となる。

①，②，③ はいずれも自然な文脈とはならないので不可。

問2　16　正解④

「コメント(2)に基づくと，ここで使うべき最もよい表現はどれか」　16

① 納税額
② 人々が食べる量
③ 納税する人の数
④ こうした飲料の購入

正解は④。下線部(2)を含む文の前文には「第一に，甘い飲み物に対する税は消費を減らします」とあり，下線部(2)を含む文ではそのことを言い換えて「甘い飲み物に税が付加されると，それは33%減少しました」と述べられていることから，下線部(2)"it"「それ」が指す内容は前文の甘い飲み物の消費であると推測でき，それは「こうした飲料の購入」と言い換えられることから，正解は④とわかる。

①，②，③ はいずれも自然な文脈とはならないので不可。

問3　17　正解①

「コメント(3)に基づくと，ここにはどの表現が追加されるべきか」　17

① 子どもが歯の問題を避けるのに役立ち
② 学業成績を伸ばし
③ 子どもたちにもっと一生懸命に勉強させ
④ 学校への出席を向上させ

正解は①。コメント(3)には「あなたの主題文はこの一節においてあなたが言及している他の効果をまとめていません。それを追加してください」とある。この一節とは，この段落のことだが，第3文（When a sugar ...）で，イギリスにおいて飲み物に砂糖税が付加されると，肥満になっている小学校高学年の子どもたちの数が減少したことが述べられ，続く第4文（In addition, the ...）では，抜歯のために病院へ入る子どもの数が減少したことが述べられている。主題文に追加するべき内容はこの第4文で述べられている子どもたちの歯の問題が減少したことであるとわかるので，正解は①となる。

②，③，④ はいずれもこの段落で述べられている内容とは関係がないので不可。

問4　18　正解①

「コメント(4)に基づくと，置き換えたものとしてどれが最適か」　18

① 社会に利益をもたらす計画に政府がお金をあてることを可能にします
② 学校が政府から教育のためのより多くのお金を受け取ることに役立ちます
③ インフラを改善することによって自分たちの都市をより住みやすくします
④ 病院や学校が不必要なことにお金を浪費することをやめさせます

正解は①。コメント(4)では，下線部(4)には第4段落で書かれていたことがまとめられて

いないので書き直しなさい，と述べられている。第4段落では砂糖税がもたらす効果の最後のものとして，健康管理にあてるお金が節約され，それを社会に利益をもたらすために用いることができることが述べられているので，正解は ① とわかる。

②，③，④ はいずれも第4段落で述べられている内容ではないので不可。

(主な語句・表現)

・問題冊子を参照のこと。

[リード文]
◇ draft 名「草稿；下書き」　　　　　　　◇ work on ...「…に取り組む」
◇ revision 名「修正」　　　　　　　　　　◇ based on ...「…に基づいて［た］」

[タイトル]
◇ benefit 名「利点；利益」　　　　　　　◇ tax 動「…に課税する」
◇ high-sugar 形「高糖度の」

[第1段落]
(Sweet drinks such ...)
◇ soda 名「炭酸清涼飲料」
◇ be popular with ...「…の間で人気のある」　◇ consume 動「…を消費する」
◇ take in ...「…を摂取する」　　　　　　◇ obesity 名「肥満」
◇ diabetes 名「糖尿病」　　　　　　　　◇ get O to -「O に - させる」
◇ reduce 動「…を減らす」　　　　　　　◇ intake 名「摂取」
◇ so-called 形「いわゆる」　　　　　　　◇ sugar tax「砂糖税」

[第2段落]
(First, a tax ...)
◇ consumption 名「消費」　　　　　　　◇ be added to ...「…に付加される」
◇ decline 動「減少する」
◇ by 33%「33%（分）」 by はここでは差を表す前置詞。
◇ alternative 名「代わりのもの」

[第3段落]
(Second, raising the ...)
◇ raise 動「…を（引き）上げる」　　　　◇ benefit from ...「…から利益を得る」
◇ obese 形「肥満の」　　　　　　　　　◇ grade 名「学年」
◇ in addition「さらに；加えて」　　　　◇ removal of teeth「抜歯」

[第4段落]
(Finally, sugar taxes ...)
◇ help O 原形「O が - するのに役立つ［- するのを助ける］」
◇ healthcare 名「健康管理；医療」
◇ spend A on B「A〈お金や時間〉を B にあてる」
◇ unemployment benefit「失業給付」　　◇ be used to -「- するために使われる」
◇ benefit 動「…に利益を与える」　　　　◇ invest in ...「…に投資する」

[最終段落]
(In conclusion, applying ...)
◇ in conclusion「結論として」　　　　　◇ apply 動「…を適用する」
◇ beverage 名「飲料」　　　　　　　　　◇ well-being 名「幸福」

[先生のコメント]
◇ incorrect 形「不正確な；間違った」　　◇ write out ...「…を書き出す」
◇ in full「完全な形で」　　　　　　　　◇ topic sentence「主題文」
◇ summarize 動「…を要約する［まとめる］」◇ mention 動「…に言及する」
◇ passage 名「一節」

第5問

解 答	問1 − ① 問2 − ② 問3 − ④ 問4 − ①	(各3点)
	問4 [23] − ④ [24] − ②	(各2点)

出 典　（参考）https://www.slicktext.com/blog/2019/10/smartphone-addiction-statistics/
　　　　　https://financesonline.com/smartphone-addiction-statistics/

全 訳　あなたは現在，米国のロバート大学で勉強しています。社会科の授業で，スマートフォン
が人々に与える影響についてレポートするよう求められています。あなたは，スマートフォ
ンの使い方について考察している2人の学生ポールとリンダのブログを見つけました。

スマートフォン依存症では？
2022年9月5日午後4時52分にポールによって投稿されました。

　2007年に世界で最初のiPhoneが登場して以来，スマートフォンの使用は着実に私
たちの日常生活の一部として受け入れられるようになりました ― そして，スマート
フォン依存症の統計はそれを証明しています。2022年の今，私たちは私たちのスマー
トフォンにべったりとへばり付けられています。私たちは通信と接続を私たちのスマー
トフォンに依存しているため，スマートフォンの過度の使用がいつ中毒になるかを判
断するのは難しいかもしれません。しかしながら，次の統計は知っておく必要があり
ます。

> 10代の若者の52%は，友人とぶら
> ぶらしている間，スマートフォンを見
> ながら長時間黙って座って過ごしてい
> ます。

> 調査対象の親の47%は，子どもが
> スマートフォンに「病みつき」になっ
> ていると考えています。

> 調査対象の教師のうち，67%が，生徒
> たちはモバイルデバイスに集中力を削が
> れていることに気付いていました。

> 89%の親が，自分の子どものスマー
> トフォンの使用に対する責任を感じて
> います。

> 英国で調査された親のうち，46%
> が自分はモバイルデバイスに「病みつ
> きになっている」と答えました。

　実際，私はかつて，おそらくスマートフォンが原因で，睡眠不足やストレスレベル
の上昇，うつ症状や不安感に悩まされていました。それで，私はスマートフォンを使
うのをやめました。デジタルデバイスへの依存症は，他の種類の依存症ほど深刻な健
康への悪影響を及ぼしませんが，実際には確かに精神的健康面だけでなく身体的健康
にも影響を及ぼします。ここで立ち止まって，「あなたの」スマートフォンの使い方に
ついてよく考えてみませんか？

― 英 R 176 ―

> 学校でのスマートフォンの（過剰）使用
> 2022年9月6日午前11時22分にリンダによって投稿されました。

　現代における人間の一番の親友であると主張するに最も値するものがあるとすれば，それは間違いなくスマートフォンでしょう。モバイルデバイスは，あらゆる種類の人間の活動に浸透しています。ほぼすべての人々が，自宅，学校，職場，および余暇の時間にスマートフォンを使用します。携帯電話にアクセスできないことが「ノモフォビア」，すなわち携帯電話との接触がなくなることへの恐れへの道を開いたほどです。そのため，現在のスマートフォン依存症に関する統計を理解することは，それが実際にどれほど深刻であるかを把握するために重要です。

　ここでは，学校におけるスマートフォンの使い方や使う習慣に光を当てたいと思います。スマートフォンは小さなコンピュータであることを考えれば，それは授業で役立つさまざまな機能を担うことができます。これにより，ユーザーはさまざまな方法でデバイスを楽しむことができます。残念なことに，楽しみが多すぎると非生産的になる可能性があります。スマートフォン依存症に関する統計が示唆しているように，携帯電話は学校においては学業の大きな妨げになることがわかっています。このことは，生産性の低下を引き起こしてしまうことになるのです。

パーセンテージ	（それぞれの）パーセンテージは何を示していますか？
20%	生徒がテキストメッセージのやり取りをしたり，ソーシャルメディアのチェックをしたりすることに費やした時間の授業に占める割合
45%	常にオンラインになっている生徒の割合。これには，彼らが授業に参加している時間が含まれる。
46%	教育者に，スマートフォンの使用と授業とをより融合する方法を見つけてもらいたいと思っている保護者の割合
49%	授業中にスマートフォンやその他のデジタルガジェットに気を取られている生徒の割合
80%	授業中の携帯電話の使用を制限する方針を持っている学校の割合

　もしあなたが今のあなたのスマートフォンとの深い関係性に不安感を持っているとしたら，あなたの生活におけるテクノロジーとのより健康的な関係を築く方法があります。毎日の使用状況を追跡し，ログオフを促すリマインダーを送信するアプリを使用して，スマートフォンに費やす時間を制限してみてください。携帯電話の設定によって，画面使用の平均時間にアクセスすることもできます。スマートフォンの使用を制限するのに役立つもう1つのやり方は，（画面の）カラー設定を白黒に変えることです。深夜の（暗い中での）画面スクロールでは，白黒の画面は（カラー画面ほど）視覚的には刺激がありません。そして，そうすることであなたはデバイスの使用をやめやすくなるのです。

設問解説

問1　　19　　正解 ①

「ポールは　19　という理由で，スマートフォンの使用をやめることを勧めている」

① スマートフォンは私たちの健康に有害である
② スマートフォンは人間関係を損なう可能性がある
③ スマートフォンは多額の費用がかかる
④ スマートフォンは対面でのコミュニケーションを妨げる

　正解は①。ポールのブログの最終段落第3文後半（it does indeed ...）に「（デジタルデバイスに依存していることは，）実際には確かに精神的健康面だけでなく身体的健康にも影響を及ぼします」とある。実際，ポール自身，スマートフォンが原因でさまざまな健康被

— 英R 177 —

害を被り，自分はスマートフォンの使用をやめたと言っている。したがって，正解は①。

他の選択肢（②，③，④）については，それらの内容に関わる記述はポールのブログには見当たらない。

問2　20　正解②

「リンダは　20　ということを示唆している」

① スマートフォンの影響による身体面の健康に注意する必要がある

② スマートフォンの画面の色を変更してみるべきである

③ スマートフォンの電源を自動的に切るアプリをインストールするべきである

④ 他のデジタルガジェットを使って，スマートフォンを使う時間を制限すべきである

正解は②。リンダのブログの最終段落第4文（Another trick that ...）に「スマートフォンの使用を制限するのに役立つもう1つのやり方は，（画面の）カラー設定を白黒に変えることです」とある。その理由として，続く最終文（Late night scrolling ...）で「深夜の（暗い中での）画面スクロールでは，白黒の画面は（カラー画面ほど）視覚的には刺激がありません。そして，そうすることであなたはデバイスの使用をやめやすくなるのです」と述べている。したがって，正解は②。

他の選択肢（①，③，④）については，それらの内容に関わる記述はリンダのブログには見当たらない。

問3　21　正解④

「ポールとリンダの両方が，あなたが　21　ことを勧めている」

① 通信技術の進歩に感謝する

② スマートフォンが人々によってどれほど効果的に利用されているかを調べる

③ SNS（ソーシャル・ネットワーキング・サービス）の使用がいかに危険であるかを理解する

④ 統計を通して，人々がスマートフォンによってどれほど影響を受けているかを把握する

正解は④。ポールはブログの最初で，以下のように述べている。

Since the world saw the first iPhone in 2007, smartphone usage has steadily become an accepted part of our daily lives — and the smartphone addiction statistics prove it. ... However, it's necessary to know the following statistics:「2007年に世界で最初のiPhoneが登場して以来，スマートフォンの使用は着実に私たちの日常生活の一部として受け入れられるようになりました — そして，スマートフォン依存症の統計はそれを証明しています。…しかしながら，次の統計は知っておく必要があります」

また，同じくリンダも，ブログの冒頭で次のように述べている。

If there's anything that most deserves the claim to being a man's best friend in the modern age, it has got to be the smartphone. ... As such, understanding the current smartphone addiction statistics is important to get a grasp of how serious it really is.「現代における人間の一番の親友であると主張するに最も値するものがあるとすれば，それは間違いなくスマートフォンでしょう。…そのため，現在のスマートフォン依存症に関する統計を理解することは，それが実際にどれほど深刻であるかを把握するために重要です」

特に，それぞれの下線部は，統計を通して人々がスマートフォンによっていかに影響を被るかを把握することの重要性を指摘し，読者に統計を通して理解することを勧めていると読み取ることができる。よって，正解は④。

他の選択肢（①，②，③）については，それらの内容に関わる記述は2人のブログには見当たらない。

問4　22　正解①

「授業中にデジタルガジェットに気を取られている生徒の割合は，22　生徒の割合よりも高くなっている」

① 常にインターネットに接続している
② 自分のスマートフォンを適切に使用している
③ 携帯電話の使用を制限するアプリを使用している
④ 深夜にスマートフォンを使う

正解は①。授業中にデジタルガジェットに気を取られている生徒の割合については，リンダのブログの中にある統計結果のひとつである Students who are distracted by smartphones and other digital gadgets in class「授業中にスマートフォンやその他のデジタルガジェットに気を取られている生徒の割合」を見れば，それが49%であることがわかる。一方，選択肢の①にある，常にインターネットに接続している生徒の割合については，同じくリンダのブログの Students who are constantly online. This includes the time that they are in class.「常にオンラインになっている生徒の割合。これには，彼らが授業に参加している時間が含まれる」を見れば，それが45%であることがわかる。両者を比較すると，前者の割合の方が後者よりも高いことがわかる。よって，正解は①となる。

他の選択肢（②，③，④）それぞれの内容を表す割合の数値は，2人のブログのどちらにも示されていない。

問5　23　正解④　24　正解②

「23　ブログから，24　保護者は半数未満であることがわかる（選択肢①〜④から，それぞれ空所ごとに最も適切なものを1つ選択しなさい。）」

① 学校でのスマートフォンの使用方法に満足している
② 自分の子どもがスマートフォンを使いすぎていると考えている
③ リンダの
④ ポールの

選択肢の①の内容に関わる個所として，リンダのブログに Parents who want educators to find ways to integrate the use of smartphones into lessons more「教育者に，スマートフォンの使用と授業とをより融合する方法を見つけてもらいたいと思っている保護者の割合」とあり，それが46%であることが示されている。これは，言い換えれば，学校でのスマートフォンの使用方法に満足していない保護者が半数未満ということであり，①の内容を示すものではない。一方，選択肢②の内容に関わる個所としては，ポールのブログに 47% of parents surveyed believe their children are "addicted" to their smartphones「調査対象の親の47%は，子どもがスマートフォンに『病みつき』になっていると考えています」とある。これは，まさに②の内容である「自分の子どもがスマートフォンを使いすぎていると考えている」保護者は半数未満，ということを示すものである。

よって，23　の正解は④，24　の正解は②となる。

【主な語句・表現】

・問題冊子を参照のこと。

［リード文］　◇ social studies「（教科としての）社会科」　◇ affect 動「…に影響を与える［及ぼす］」

［ポールのブログ］
◇ addiction 名「常用癖；依存症；中毒」　◇ steadily 副「着実に；どんどん；しっかりと」
◇ statistics 名「統計；統計学」　◇ prove 動「…を証明する」
◇ be glued to ...「…に（はりついたように）熱中している；夢中になっている」
◇ rely on ...「…に頼る；依存する」　◇ determine 動「…を決定する；決心する」
◇ excessive 形「過度の；行き過ぎた」　◇ teen 名「10（歳）代の少年少女」
◇ hang out「（…で）うろうろする；ぶらぶらする」

— 英 R 179 —

◇ survey 動「…を調査する」
◇ addict 動「〈人に〉（麻薬などを）常習させる；中毒にさせる」「〈人を〉（…に）ふけらせる（to ...）」 通例過去分詞で形容詞的に用いる（⇒ addicted）。
◇ distract 動「（…の）気持ちをそらす［散らす］；混乱させる」
◇ mobile device「モバイル機器」 携帯電話・スマートフォンや小型パソコンなど。
◇ device 名「器具；装置」
◇ take responsibility for ...「…に責任を負う；請負う」
◇ deprivation 名「はく奪；喪失；欠乏（状態）」
◇ depression 名「気分の落ち込み；うつ（状態）；憂うつ」
◇ anxiety 名「心配（事）；不安」　　　　◇ while 接「…である一方；…とは言え」
◇ impact 動「〈…に〉強い影響を与える」　◇ indeed 副「実に；実際に；本当に」
◇ not only A but (also) B「AのみならずBも（また）；Aだけでなく Bも」
◇ physical 形「体の；肉体的な」　　　　◇ wellbeing 名「健康（な状態）」

[リンダのブログ]　◇ claim 名「権利（の主張）；資格」
◇ penetrate 動「…を貫く；染み込む；浸透する」
◇ nearly 副「ほとんど」
◇ Nearly everyone uses one at home, ...　one = a mobile device
◇ So much so that ...「そのような状況［程度］であるので，（結果として）…である」
◇ pave the way for ...「…への道を開く；…を容易にする」
◇ nomophobia 名　"no-mobile-phone phobia" の縮約形。phobia とは「恐怖症；病的恐怖」という意味の名詞で，nomophobia は「スマートフォンや携帯電話での連絡が取れなくなることへの病的な恐れ・不安感」という意味。
◇ as such「そのため；そのような状態であるので」
◇ current 形「今の；現在の」　　　　　◇ get a grasp of ...「…を把握する；理解する」
◇ how serious it really is　it = nomophobia
◇ shine a light on ...「…に光を当てる」　◇ habit 名「習慣」
◇ Given that ...「…ならば；…を考えれば」　◇ take on ...「…を持つようになる；帯びる」
◇ counterproductive 形「逆効果の；非生産的な」
◇ prove to be ...「（結局）…となる；…であることがわかる」（= turn out to be ...）
◇ distraction 名「気を散らすもの［こと］」　◇ dip 名「窪み；へこみ；低下」
◇ productivity 名「生産性」
◇ texting 名　主にスマートフォンや携帯電話などに備わる SMS（ショートメッセージサービス）などを利用してテキストメッセージのやりとりを行うこと，あるいは特にテキストメッセージの作成・送信をすること。
◇ constantly 副「常に；常時」　　　　　◇ include 動「…を含む」
◇ educator 名「教育者」
◇ integrate 動「…を統合する；調和させる；まとめる」
◇ gadget 名「気のきいた小物；ちょっとした機械装置」
◇ policy 名「方針；方策」　　　　　　　◇ restrict 動「…を制限する」
◇ attachment 名「付着；愛着；愛情」　　◇ cultivate 動「…を培う；求める；深める」
◇ app = application 名　スマートフォンなどの「アプリ」のこと。
◇ track 動「…を追跡する；探知する」
◇ reminder 名「〈思い出させるための〉注意；合図」
◇ trick 名「〈物事を上手にする〉やり方；こつ；要領；秘訣」
◇ stimulating 形「刺激する」
◇ visual 名「〈通例複数形で〉映像」 音声に対して写真・画面など。

— 英 R 180 —

◇ encourage 動「(…を) 促進する；助長する；奨励する」
◇ put down「(…を) 下に置く；(…を) 抑える；静める；やめる」

[設問文・選択肢]　◇ install 動「〈装置などを〉〈…に〉取り [据え] 付ける」
◇ automatically 副「自動的に」　　　　　◇ appreciate 動「…を感謝する」
◇ advance 名「進歩；前進；発展」　　　　◇ look into ...「…を調べる；研究する」
◇ utilize 動「…を利用する；活用する」　　◇ properly 副「適切に；正しく」

第6問

解答

問1 － ①	問2 － ④	(各3点)
問3 － 27 ・ 28 － ②・⑤		(順不同・両方正解で3点)
29 － ③		(3点)
問4 － ①	問5 － ③	(各3点)

出典 *Original Material*

全訳 あなたは地元で栽培あるいは生産された食品を食べるよう奨励されるべきかどうかについてのエッセイに取り組んでいます。以下の各ステップに従っていきます。

ステップ1：地元産の食品に関するさまざまな見解を読んで理解する。
ステップ2：地元で生産された食品を食べるよう努めるべきかどうかについての判断を下す。
ステップ3：追加の情報源を使って，エッセイの概要を作成する。

[ステップ1] さまざまな情報源を読む
筆者A（環境運動家）
2005年，サンフランシスコの一部の食品活動家が，人々に1ヵ月間地元で栽培された食品しか食べないということに挑んでもらいました。私はその挑戦に参加しましたが，それは実に難しいことでした。私たちは，どれほど私たちが輸入食品に依存しているかということを常に認識しているわけではありません。しかし，私は輸入食品ではなく，地元の生産物を積極的に探すべきだと判断しました。地元の生産物の方が新鮮だし，地元の農家を支援することができるし，食品輸送の間に排出される温室効果ガスの量が減少します。みんなが試しにこのことをやってみるべきです。

筆者B（科学者）
私は，地元産の食品を買う方が環境にやさしい，と信じていました。しかし，その考えはデータによって常に裏づけられるわけではありません。食品の周期に関するデータを見ると，温室効果ガスの大部分は輸送段階の間ではなく，生産段階の間において排出されているのです。したがって，私の意見では，自分の食べるものが環境に及ぼしている影響について心配であるならば，食品がどこからやってくるかではなく，どのように生産されるかということを心配するべきなのです。

筆者C（小規模食料雑貨店所有者）
私には，地元の地域に農場を所有する家族がいるので，地元産の食品を自分の店に置いておくことで彼らを支援することは私にとっては容易なことです。もちろん，新鮮な食品は非常に季節に特有な面を持っているので，1年中そうすることは可能ではありません。しかし，私の店のお客さんは新鮮な地元の食品に少し余分にお金を払うことをいとわないので，私はお客さんたちの望むものを提供しようと努めています。店の在庫の中には輸入されたものもありますが，私はできるだけそうしたものは制限しようとしています。私は輸入食品が環境に及ぼす影響について心配しているので，できる限り地元で栽培された果実や野菜を購入したいと思っています。

— 英R 182 —

筆者D（農業従事者）

私が栽培している食品の多くは大手スーパーマーケットチェーン店に低価格で売られていきます。スーパーマーケットは非常に大きな勢力なので，実際のところ自分の食品の値段を上げる交渉をすることはできません。しかし，私は自分のところの野菜を地元の直売所でもよく販売しています。そうすることによって，私はより高額な価格を請求できるし，私は自分の住む地域社会の地元の人々に販売することを好みますが，それはそうした人たちは私が質の高い食品を生産することに向けている仕事を評価してくれるからです。私としては，より多くの人が自分が住んでいる地域の農業従事者から買うことで地元の地域社会を支援することを間違いなく奨励するでしょう。

筆者E（母親）

地元産の食品を買うことはすばらしい考えであるように思われますが，それは非常に偏った食事につながる可能性があります。私は国の北部に住んでいて，気候は芳しくないので，輸入食品に頼らずには十分な食品を手に入れることができません。加えて，地元の直売所は非常に質の高い地元の農産物を販売していますが，それはかなり高額になることもあります。ほとんどの家庭はそれを買えるほど十分なお金を持っていません。私は，人々の中には輸入食品がもたらす環境面での負担を心配している者もいることを知っていますが，食糧生産において，輸送は温室効果ガスの排出のほんのわずかな割合しか占めていないと読んだことがあります。

設問解説

問1　　25　　正解①

「筆者DとEは両者とも　25　と言及している」

① 地元で栽培された食品は他の場所から輸入された食品よりも高額になることが多い

② 大手スーパーマーケットで売られている食品は，市場で売られている食品に比べると，質がよくない

③ もし地元で栽培されたものを買うように制約されたならば，さまざまな食品を食べることは難しい

④ 食品が自分たちが住んでいる場所の近くで栽培されたものならば，人々は農業従事者の仕事をより評価してくれる

　正解は①。農業従事者である筆者Dは第1文（A lot of ...）〜第2文（Supermarkets are very ...）で，大手スーパーマーケットチェーン店では自分が栽培した食品は安値で売られているが，大手スーパーの勢力は強いので値段を上げる交渉はできないということが語られているが，その後に続く第3文（However, I often ...）〜第4文（By doing this, ...）では「しかし，私は自分のところの野菜を地元の直売所でもよく販売しています。そうすることによって，私はより高額な価格を請求できるし，私は自分の住む地域社会の地元の人々に販売することを好みますが，それはそうした人たちは私が質の高い食品を生産することに向けている仕事を評価してくれるからです」と述べられており，こうしたことからは，地元で食品を栽培すると費用が多くかかることが推測できる。また母親である筆者Eは第3文（In addition, local ...）で「加えて，地元の直売所は非常に質の高い地元の農産物を販売していますが，それはかなり高額になることもあります」と述べていることから，両者とも選択肢①の「地元で栽培された食品は他の場所で生産された食品よりも高額になることが多い」ということに言及していると判断できる。よって正解は①となる。

　②，④に関しては，いずれも筆者DとEが述べている内容とはなっていないので不可。

　③に関しては，筆者Eが第1文（Buying locally-produced food ...）で述べている内容からうかがえることであるが，筆者Dが述べている内容ではないので不可。

— 英R 183 —

問2 26 正解 ④

「筆者Bは 26 と示唆している」

① 食品の生産は，多くの人たちが信じているほど環境にとって悪いものではない

② もし大規模な組織が人々に何かするように勧めるのであれば，それは研究に基づいているに違いない

③ 環境にとってもっとも悪い食糧生産の段階は輸送である

④ 科学者によって徹底的に研究されると，正しいと思われることが間違っていると示されることもあるかもしれない

正解は④。科学者である筆者Bは第1文（I had believed ...）で，自分が地元産の食品を買う方が環境にやさしいという考えを持っていたと述べているが，それは地元産の食品は輸送距離が短くて済むのでそのために排出される温室効果ガスの量が少ないという理由によるものであると推測できる。しかし第3文（When I looked ...）では「食品の周期に関するデータを見ると，温室効果ガスの大部分は輸送段階の間ではなく，生産段階の間において排出されているのです」とデータの裏づけから以前に考えていたことは間違っていたことを認めている。よって正解は④となる。

①，②，③に関しては，いずれも筆者Bが述べている内容とはなっていないので不可。

[ステップ2] 判断を下す

問3 27 ・ 28 正解 ②・⑤ 29 正解 ③

「さまざまな見解を理解したので，地元産の食品だけを買うことが奨励されるべきかどうかに関して判断を下し，それを以下のように書き出した。 27 , 28 , 29 を完成させるのにもっとも適切な選択肢を選びなさい」

あなたの判断：人々は地元産の食品だけを買うように奨励されるべきではない。

・ 筆者 27 と 28 があなたの判断を支持している。

・ その2人の筆者の主要な論拠： 29 。

27 と 28 に入る選択肢（順序は問わない）

① A

② B

③ C

④ D

⑤ E

正解は②と⑤。科学者である筆者Bは問2の解説でも触れたように，第1文で（I had believed ...）地元産の食品を買う方が環境にやさしいと信じていたと述べているが，第3文（When I looked ...）で温室効果ガスの大部分は輸送段階の間ではなく，生産段階の間において排出されているというデータの裏づけにより，その考えが誤っていたことを認めているので，筆者Bは「人々は地元産の食品だけを買うように奨励されるべきではない」というあなたの判断を支持していることがわかる。また母親である筆者Eは第1文（Buying locally-produced food ...）で「地元産の食品を買うことはすばらしい考えであるように思われますが，それは非常に偏った食事につながる可能性があります」と，地元産の食品だけを利用することの健康面におけるデメリットを述べ，第3文（In addition, local ...）〜第4文（Most families don't ...）で，地元の農産物はかなり高額になることがあり，ほとんどの家庭にはそれを購入するほどの経済的余裕がないと，地元産の食品だけを利用することの経済面でのデメリットを述べていることから，筆者Eも「人々は地元産の食品だけを買うように奨励されるべきではない」というあなたの判断を支持していることがわかる。以上から筆者BとEがあなたの判断を支持していることになるので， 27 と 28 に

— 英R 184 —

は②と⑤が入ることになる。

　　29　に入る選択肢
　　①　気候が芳しくない地域では，地元で栽培された食品を食べることは不可能だ
　　②　一般的に人々はあまりにも肉を食べすぎており，それは環境にとって悪いことだ
　　❸　**食品を輸送することは多くの人々が信じているほど環境にとって悪いことではない**
　　④　国家間で輸送される食品はほとんどないので，それは環境にまったく影響を及ぼすことはない

　正解は③。筆者Bは上でも触れたように，第3文（When I looked ...）で「食品の周期に関するデータを見ると，温室効果ガスの大部分は輸送段階の間ではなく，生産段階の間において排出されているのです」と指摘し，筆者Eは最終文（I know some ...）で「私は，人々の中には輸入食品が環境面での代償を心配している者もいることを知っていますが，食糧生産において，輸送は温室効果ガスの排出のほんのわずかな割合しか占めていないと読んだことがあります」と述べている。以上から，あなたの判断を支持している筆者BとEの論拠は選択肢③の「食品を輸送することは多くの人々が信じているほど環境にとって悪いことではない」ということだとわかる。

全訳

[ステップ3] 情報源AとBを使って，概要を作成する。
あなたのエッセイの概要：

> **我々は人々が地元産の食品だけを食べるよう奨励するべきではない**
>
> **序論**
> 　最近，多くの人々が輸入食品を避けて，環境を救済し健康を改善するために，地元産の食品を購入しようとしている。しかし，この考えには多くの問題がある。
>
> **本論**
> 　理由1：（ステップ2から）
> 　理由2：（情報源Aに基づく）　……　　30
> 　理由3：（情報源Bに基づく）　……　　31
>
> **結論**
> 　人々は地元産の食品だけを買って食べるよう奨励されるべきではない。

情報源A
食糧生産は非常に季節に特有な面を持っており，各種果実や野菜の収穫時期は非常に短い。それはつまり，もし我々が地元の食品だけを食べようとするならば，生産過剰と生産過少の時期が存在することになるということだ。生産過剰期には，食品をできるだけ長い期間にわたって使用し，無駄にしてしまわないように，食品を貯蔵しなければならない。例えば，イギリスのリンゴの旬となる時期は秋にピークを迎える。毎年，その季節にはイギリスでは最大61万トンのリンゴが生産される。これらのリンゴが1年中鮮度を保ち，顧客の需要を満たすために，リンゴは冷蔵されなければならない。ある研究は，地元のイギリス産リンゴを10ヵ月間冷蔵しておくには，必要なときに南米からイギリスへ船でリンゴを輸入するよりも多くの費用がかかり，2倍の水準のガスの排出を生み出すことを示した。食品を輸入することによって国の食糧必要量を満たす方が，大量の食品を貯蔵して鮮度を保つよりもはるかに持続可能であり，エネルギー効率がよくなる。

— 英R 185 —

情報源 B

ある農業関連の雑誌が行った研究は，店舗での入手可能な総供給量と比較した，イギリスで生産される食品の生産量に目を向けた。下のグラフはその研究によってわかったことを示している。こうした食品の多くは地元の気候状況で生産することは困難であり，温室で栽培されなければならず，そのためにそうした食品は輸入食品より高額になるのである。

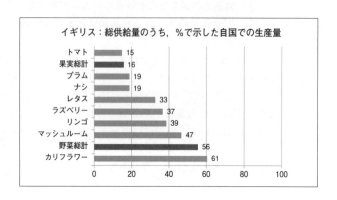

設問解説

問4　30　正解①

「情報源Aに基づけば，以下のどれが理由2としてもっとも適切か」　30

①　ほとんどの食品は季節に特有なものなので，それを貯蔵するよりも必要なときに外国から運んだ方がよりエネルギー効率がよい。

②　食品は約10ヵ月ほどしか貯蔵できないので，食品を冷蔵するよりも輸入した方が我々の健康にとってはよい。

③　果実はたいてい長期間にわたって貯蔵することはできないので，外国から輸入すれば，より新鮮でおいしい果実を手に入れることができる。

④　南米はリンゴの栽培においてはイギリスよりも効率がよいので，イギリス人は輸入リンゴを食べるように努めるべきだ。

正解は①。情報源Aの第1文（Food production is ...）では「食糧生産は非常に季節に特有な面を持っており，各種果実や野菜の収穫時期は非常に短い」と述べられ，最終文（It is far ...）では直前で示された研究結果をまとめて，「食品を輸入することによって国の食糧必要量を満たす方が，大量の食品を貯蔵して鮮度を保つよりもはるかに持続可能であり，エネルギー効率がよくなる」と指摘されている。以上から，正解は①となる。

②，③，④に関しては，いずれも情報源Aが述べている内容とはなっていないので不可。

問5　31　正解③

「理由3として，あなたは『ある国々の人たちは，地元産の食品だけを購入することによって健康的な食事をすることは可能ではないだろう』と書くことにした。情報源Bに基づけば，どの選択肢がこの記述をもっともよく支持しているか」　31

①　地元で栽培される食品のほとんどが多くの成人および子どもに好まれていないので，はるかに安価であるという理由で彼らは不健康な食品を購入する可能性が高い。

②　トマトやその他の果実といったもっとも健康的な食品は地元で生産されると最大で15％も値段が高くなるので，ほとんどの人々はそれらを購入する経済的余裕がない。

③　イギリスで購入するのに入手可能な野菜の約半分と果実の6分の1だけが自国で生産されていた。輸入食品を避けることで，より多くの費用がかかり，おそらく偏った食事につながることだろう。

④　イギリスの人々は主として地元で栽培された果実を食べることができるが，地元で栽培された野菜を食べることはそれよりもはるかに難しく高額なものとなるので，

偏った食事につながることだろう。

　正解は ③。グラフより，イギリスで供給される「野菜総計」の自国での生産量は56%と約半分となっており，「果実総計」の方は16%と約6分の1となっていることがわかる。また情報源 B の最終文（Many of these ...）で「こうした食品［イギリスで生産される食品］の多くは地元の気候状況で生産することは困難であり，温室で栽培されなければならず，そのためにそうした食品は輸入食品より高額になるのである」と述べられているが，このことから，輸入食品を利用しなければ購入できる地元産の食品が限られたものだけになってしまい，それが偏った食事につながりうることも推測可能である。よって正解は ③ となる。

　①，②，④ に関しては，いずれも情報源 B が述べている内容およびグラフからわかる内容とはなっていないので不可。

主な語句・表現

［リード文］
・問題冊子を参照のこと。
◇ work on ...「…に取り組む」
◇ encourage O to –「O に – するよう奨励する［勧める］」
◇ locally-produced 形「地元産の」
◇ take a position about ...「…についての判断を下す」
◇ outline 名「概要」

［ステップ1］
◇ campaigner 名「運動家」　　　　　　◇ activist 名「活動［運動］家」
◇ challenge O to –「O に – するよう挑む；O を – する気にさせる」
◇ join in ...「…に参加する」
◇ decide that ...「…と判断する；…と決断する」
◇ greenhouse gas「温室効果ガス」　　◇ transportation 名「輸送」
◇ try – ing「試しに – してみる」　　　◇ back up ...「…を裏づける［実証する］」
◇ related to ...「…に関連した」　　　　◇ life cycle「過程；周期」
◇ not A but B「A ではなく B」　　　　◇ phase 名「段階」
◇ be concerned about ...「…を心配する」
◇ if ..., then ～「もし…ならば，～」　then（その時には）は if との呼応を表しているだけ
　なので，訳に出す必要はない。
◇ impact 名「影響」　　　　　　　　　◇ worry about ...「…について心配する」
◇ grocery store「食料雑貨店」
◇ stock 動「〈商品など〉を置いておく［在庫として持っている］」
◇ all year round「1 年中」　　　　　　◇ seasonal 形「季節に特有な」
◇ the impact imported food has on ...「輸入食品が…に及ぼす影響」　imported food has
　on ... は直前の the impact を先行詞とする関係代名詞（関係代名詞の which [that] は目的
　格のため省略されている）。
◇ negotiate 動「…について交渉する」　◇ farmers market「直売所」
◇ charge 動「…を請求する」　　　　　◇ produce 名「農産物」
◇ account for ...「〈割合〉を占める」　◇ proportion 名「割合」
◇ emission 名「排出」

［設問文・選択肢］
◇ mention that ...「…と言及している」　◇ of poor quality「質が悪い」
◇ compared to ...「…と比べると」　　　◇ appreciate 動「…を評価する［認める］」
◇ imply that ...「…と示唆している」
◇ recommend O to –「O に – するよう勧める」
◇ be proved ...「…と示される」　　　　◇ in depth「徹底的に」

［ステップ2］　◇ now that ...「(今や) …なので」　　　　◇ as below「以下のように」
　　　　　　　◇ have an impact on ...「…に影響を及ぼす」

［ステップ3］　◇ harvesting season「収穫時期」
　　　　　　　◇ over-production 名「生産過剰」　⇔ under-production 名「生産過少」
　　　　　　　◇ so that S can ...「〈目的を表して〉S が…するために」
　　　　　　　◇ up to ...「最大［最高］で…」　　　◇ meet demand「需要を満たす」
　　　　　　　◇ cold storage「冷蔵」　　　　　　◇ by sea「船で」
　　　　　　　◇ far 副「〈後の比較級を強調して〉はるかに；ずっと」　= much
　　　　　　　◇ sustainable 形「(環境破壊せず) 持続可能な」
［設問文・選択肢］◇ refrigerate 動「…を冷蔵する」　　　◇ tasty 形「おいしい」
　　　　　　　◇ be likely to −「−する可能性が高い」
　　　　　　　◇ can afford to −「−する (経済的) 余裕がある；−できる」

— 英 R 188 —

第7問

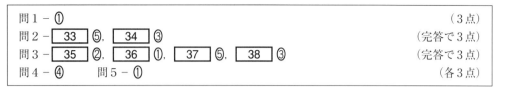

出典　（参考）https://www.myenglishpages.com/english/reading-edgar-allan-poe-biography.php

全訳

あなたは英語の授業で，世界の優れた作家についてのプレゼンテーションを行います。あなたは次の記事を見つけて，プレゼンテーション用のメモを用意しました。

　エドガー・アラン・ポーは，1809年1月19日にマサチューセッツ州ボストンで生まれました。彼はアメリカ人の作家，詩人，編集者，そして文芸評論家でした。彼は，米国のロマン主義とアメリカ文学の中心的な人物として広く認められています。ポーはミステリーの物語で最もよく知られています。彼は最も初期のアメリカ人短編小説家の1人であり，一般的に探偵小説のジャンルの創始者と見なされています。

　ポーの父と母はどちらもプロの俳優でした。彼らはその詩人（＝ポー）が3歳になる前に亡くなりました。ジョン・アランとフランシス・アランは正式に彼を養子にすることはありませんでしたが，バージニア州リッチモンドで里子として彼を育てました。ポーはバージニア大学に1学期間通いましたが，お金がなかったために大学を去りました。ポーは彼の教育資金とギャンブルの借金のことでジョンと喧嘩（けんか）をしました。1827年に，彼は偽名でアメリカ陸軍に入隊しました。この時，彼の執筆活動は彼の最初の出版物で始まりましたが，それは，謙虚に，「ある1人のボストン市民」の作とのみ記された匿名の詩集である『タマレーン，その他の詩集』（1827年）という作品での始まりでした。1829年にフランシス・アランが亡くなると，ポーとジョン・アランは一時的に良好な関係を再構築しました。（しかし，）ポーは後にウェスト・ポイントで軍の士官の訓練生として失敗を犯してしまいました。彼は詩人兼作家になりたいという強い願いを固く表明し，そして，ジョン・アランと決別しました。

　詩人として真剣にそのキャリアをスタートさせようとし始めたポーでしたが，そうするためには彼は困難な時期を選んでしまったことになります。アメリカの出版業界は，1837年恐慌，つまり，アメリカの金融危機によって特に大きな打撃を受けていました。利益，価格，賃金が下がったのです。失業率が上昇し，悲観論が広まりました。出版社はしばしば作家への支払いを拒否したり，約束の時よりもはるかに遅れて支払いをしたりしました。ポーは苦労したに違いありません。彼の初期における詩の試みの後，ポーは散文に注意を向けました。彼はその後の数年間，文学の雑誌や定期刊行物の業界で働いていました。彼は，彼独自の手法による文学評論家として活動し，有名になりました。彼は仕事によって，ボルチモア，フィラデルフィア，ニューヨーク市を含むいくつかの都市の間を行ったり来たりしなければなりませんでした。1835年，ボルチモアで，彼はいとこのヴァージニア・クレムと結婚しました。そしてこのことが，彼の著作の一部に影響を与えた可能性があります。

1845年1月，ポーは『大鴉』という詩を出版し，人気を博しました。ポーはその出版に対してたったの9ドルしか支払われませんでしたが，それはポーという名をほぼ一瞬の間に一般に馴染みのあるものにしました。彼の妻はその出版の2年後に結核で亡くなりました。何年もの間，彼は彼自身のジャーナル，『ペン』（後に『スタイラス』と改名）を作成することを計画していましたが，それが出版されないうちに彼は亡くなりました。1849年10月7日，40歳で，ポーはボルチモアで亡くなりました。彼の死因は不明であり，アルコール，脳疾患，コレラ，薬物，心臓病，自殺，結核，およびその他の原因など，さまざまな要因と結びつけられてきています。

　エドガー・アラン・ポーと彼の作品は，米国および世界中の文学に影響を与えると同時に，執筆の専門分野の草分けとしてもその役割を果たしました。彼はホラー及び探偵小説の両方の創始者の1人として見なされています。彼はまた，現代の短編小説の「構築者」としても認められています。評論家として，彼は（文学の）スタイルと構造の効果というものを強調した最初の作家の1人でした。したがって，彼は「芸術のための芸術」運動の先駆者でした。ポーは，シャルル・ボードレールによる初期の翻訳のおかげもあって，とりわけフランスで尊敬されています。ボードレールの翻訳は，その芸術的な出来栄えにより，ヨーロッパ全体でポーの作品の決定版となりました。

　ポーと彼の作品は，文学，音楽，映画，そしてテレビにおける大衆文化全体に登場します。彼の住んだ家の多くは今日，博物館として寄贈されています。米ミステリー作家協会は，ミステリージャンルの傑出した作品に対して，エドガー賞として知られる毎年恒例の賞を授与しています。

プレゼンテーションのためのメモ：

エドガー・アラン・ポー

彼は1809年1月19日に生まれ，探偵小説のジャンルの創始者と考えられている。

若齢期
　－ジョンとフランシス・アランに世話を受けた。
　－彼はジョンと口論になったが，後に彼と仲直りした。
　－ 32

新しい人生と結婚
　－彼は自身の関心の中心を 33 に切り替えた。
　－彼は 34 における彼自身のスタイルで有名になった。
　－彼はいとこであるヴァージニア・クレムと結婚した。

成功と死
　│　 35
　│　彼は偽名を使って陸軍に入隊した。
　│　 36
　│　 37
　│　 38
　↓　彼は原因不明のままボルチモアで亡くなった。

— 英 R 190 —

影響
- 彼と彼の作品は，文学，音楽，映画，テレビにおける大衆文化全般に登場する。
- ⌜ 39 ⌟

業績及び評価
- 彼はホラーと探偵小説の分野を創始した。
- 彼は（文学の）スタイルと構造が物語にどのような影響を与えるかについて，最初に焦点を当てた。
- ⌜ 40 ⌟

設問解説

問1 ⌜ 32 ⌟ 正解 ①

「⌜ 32 ⌟に最適な文を選びなさい」
① 彼は，詩人兼作家になると宣言して，ジョンとの接触を断ち切った。
② 彼の父親は家族を捨てて家を出た。
③ 彼の最初の詩集によって，彼の名前は人々によく知られるようになった。
④ ポーは軍に入隊した直後，再びジョンと険悪な関係となった。

正解は①。第2段落第10文（He firmly stated ...）に「彼は詩人兼作家になりたいという強い願いを固く表明し，そして，ジョン・アランと決別しました」とあることから，①が正解とわかる。

②については，父親はポーが3歳になる前に亡くなったという記述があるだけで，「家族を捨てて家を出た」ということがわかる記述はない。③については，彼の最初の詩集は『タマレーン，その他の詩集』であり，それは匿名の詩集であったので，ポーの名前が明らかになることはなかった。④については，ポーが陸軍に入隊した2年後に（フランシスが亡くなって）2人は良好な関係を再構築した，とあるので，誤りである。

問2 ⌜ 33 ⌟ 正解 ⑤ ⌜ 34 ⌟ 正解 ③

「新しい人生と結婚を完成させるのに，⌜ 33 ⌟と⌜ 34 ⌟に入る最適なものを選びなさい」
① 探偵小説
② 雑誌の編集
③ 文芸批評
④ ミステリーの筋立て
⑤ 散文の著述

⌜ 33 ⌟については，第3段落第6文（After his early ...）に「彼の初期における詩の試みの後，ポーは散文に注意を向けました」とあることから，⑤が入る。

⌜ 34 ⌟については，同じ第3段落第8文（He became well-known, ...）に「彼は，彼独自の手法による文学評論家として活動し，有名になりました」とある。よって，③が正解。

問3 ⌜ 35 ⌟ 正解 ②，⌜ 36 ⌟ 正解 ①，⌜ 37 ⌟ 正解 ⑤，⌜ 38 ⌟ 正解 ③

「5つの出来事（① ～ ⑤）の中から4つを起こった順序で選び，成功と死を完成しなさい」
① 匿名の詩集が出版された。
② 彼はバージニア大学に入学した。
③ 妻が病気で亡くなった。
④ 『ペン』が創刊された。
⑤ 『大鴉』が出版され，大ヒットした。

まず，第4段落に「『ペン』が出版される前にポーは亡くなった」（... he died before it could be published）とあるので，彼の生前のことについてまとめている⌜ 35 ⌟～

— 英 R 191 —

38 の中には入らない。よって，④ は正解から除外されることになる。

35 は，ポーが陸軍に入隊する以前の出来事である。残された選択肢で当てはまるのは，第2段落より ② しかない。次に，36 ～ 38 については，本文を時系列で整理して考える。まず，陸軍入隊中にポーは最初の匿名の詩集『タマレーン，その他の詩集』を 1827 年に出版した。その後，第4段落によると 1845 年 1 月に，ポーは『大鴉』という詩を出版して人気を博し，その出版の 2 年後にポーの妻は結核で亡くなった。以上のことを読み取れれば，正解は 36 – ①，37 – ⑤，38 – ③ となることがわかる。

問4 39 正解 ④

「影響を完成させるのに，39 に入る最も適切な選択肢を選びなさい」

① 当時流行していた小説のスタイルや構造を改良した。
② 彼はボードレールにインスピレーションを与え，その作品はポーによって翻訳された。
③ 短編小説に対する彼の文芸批評は，ミステリー小説に影響を与えた。
④ 彼の作品はフランス語に翻訳され，ヨーロッパで高く評価されるようになった。

正解は ④。第5段落第6文（Poe is particularly ...）に「ポーは，シャルル・ボードレールによる初期の翻訳のおかげもあって，とりわけフランスで尊敬されています。ボードレールの翻訳は，その芸術的な出来栄えにより，ヨーロッパ全体でポーの作品の決定版となりました」とある。ポーの作品が，シャルル・ボードレールによってフランス語に翻訳され，その翻訳がヨーロッパ中で読まれて，高い評価を得るようになったということが読み取れ，これは，選択肢 ④ の内容を表している。

選択肢 ① については，同じ第5段落第4文（As a critic he ...）に「評論家として，彼は（文学の）スタイルと構造の効果というものを強調した最初の作家の 1 人でした」とあるが，① の中の「当時流行していた」や「改良した」の部分が本文からは読み取れない。選択肢 ② については，ボードレールがポーの作品を翻訳したわけであり，ポーがボードレールの作品を翻訳したわけではない。また，選択肢 ③ の内容については，本文のどこにも触れられていない。

問5 40 正解 ①

「業績及び評価を完成させるのに，40 に入る最も適切な選択肢を選びなさい」

① 毎年，著名なミステリー作家がポーの名のもとに表彰される。
② 彼は建築家として，自分の家を博物館に変えた。
③ 彼は米ミステリー作家協会を設立した。
④ 彼はミステリーを芸術的に批判する傾向に反対した。

正解は ①。最終段落最終文（The Mystery Writers ...）に，「米ミステリー作家協会は，ミステリージャンルの傑出した作品に対して，エドガー賞として知られる毎年恒例の賞を授与しています」とある。これは，選択肢 ① の内容と一致する。

選択肢 ② については，同じ最終段落第2文（A number of ...）に「彼の住んだ家の多くは今日，博物館として寄贈されています」とあるが，「彼が建築家であった」という記述は本文のどこにもない。また，選択肢 ③ についても，米ミステリー作家協会を「設立した」という記述は本文にはなく，選択肢 ④ については，第5段落第5文に，He was thus a forerunner in the "art for art's sake" movement.「したがって，彼は『芸術のための芸術』運動の先駆者でした」という記述はあるが，「ミステリーを芸術的に批判する傾向に反対した」という内容を表す記述は見当たらない。

— 英 R 192 —

主な語句・表現	・問題冊子を参照のこと。

[第1段落]
(Edgar Allan
Poe was ...)

◇ critic 名「批評家」　　　　　　　　　　◇ figure 名「人物」
◇ literature 名「文学」　　　　　　　　　　◇ tale 名「物語」
◇ practitioner 名「実践者」　　　　　　　◇ detective fiction「探偵［推理］小説」
◇ genre 名「〈芸術作品の〉ジャンル；様式」

[第2段落]
(Both Poe's
father ...)

◇ adopt 動「…を養子として引き取る」　　◇ raise 動「…を育てる」
◇ foster child「養子；里子」
◇ semester 名「（2学期制度での）1学期；半学年」
◇ due to ...「…のせいで」（= because of ...）
◇ lack 名「欠乏；不足」　　　　　　　　　◇ quarrel 動「口げんかする；口論する」
◇ fund 名「資金」　　　　　　　　　　　　◇ debt 名「借金；負債」
◇ enlist 動「（軍隊に）入る」　　　　　　◇ humbly 副「謙虚に；慎み深く；遠慮して」
◇ anonymous 形「匿名の；作者不明の」
◇ credit 動「（…に）帰する」　**(例)** an invention *credited* to Edison（エジソンに権利のある発明）
◇ temporary 形「一時の；一時的な」　　　◇ trainee 名「訓練生」
◇ firmly 副「固く；しっかりと」　　　　　◇ state 動「…を述べる」
◇ part ways with ...「…とは離れて行く；…と決別する」

[第3段落]
(Although Poe
began ...)

◇ attempt 名「試み；企て」　　　　　　　◇ pessimism 名「悲観主義；悲観論」
◇ prevail 動「広がる；広まる」　　　　　　◇ prose 名「散文」
◇ periodical 名「定期刊行物」

[第4段落]
(In January
1845 ...)

◇ raven 名「大鴉;ワタリガラス」　crow よりも大きいカラスで、不吉な鳥とされる。
◇ sensation 名「大評判；センセーション」
◇ household name「よく知られている人物や物の名前；おなじみの名前」
◇ tuberculosis 名「結核」　　　　　　　　◇ attribute 動「（…に）帰する」
◇ cholera 名「（病気の）コレラ」　　　　◇ suicide 名「自殺；自死」

[第5段落]
(Edgar Allan
Poe and ...)

◇ originator 名「創始者；創設者；開祖」　◇ architect 名「建築家」
◇ forerunner 名「先駆者；先祖」
◇ sake 名〈for the *sake* of ... ／ for ...'s *sake* で〉「…のための［に］」
◇ definitive 形「決定的な；最も信頼のおける」

[最終段落]
(Poe and his ...)

◇ dedicate 動「（…に）ささげる；寄贈する」
◇ annual 形「年々の；例年の；毎年の」　◇ distinguished 形「抜群の；すぐれた」

[メモ]

◇ make up with ...「〈人と〉仲直りする」　◇ affect 動「…に影響を与える［及ぼす］」

[設問文・選択肢]

◇ statement 名「陳述」　　　　　　　　　◇ abandon 動「…を捨てる；見捨てる」
◇ become on bad terms with ...「…と仲が悪くなる；険悪な関係となる」
◇ plot 動「〈演劇や文学作品など〉の筋立てを行う；プロットを作る」
◇ pass away「〈人が〉亡くなる；死ぬ」　die の婉曲表現。
◇ prominent 形「傑出した；卓越した」　　◇ honor 動「〈名誉賞など〉を与える［授与する］」
◇ in the name of ...「…の名において；…の権威のもとに」
◇ trend 名「傾向；趨勢；流行（のスタイル）」

第8問

解答

問1 - ③		（4点）
問2　42 - ④　　43 - ④		（各3点）
問3 - ①・②		（順不同・両方正解で4点）

出典

（参考）https://www.ccohs.ca/oshanswers/chemicals/whmis_ghs/pictograms.html
https://www.vumc.org/safety/sites/vumc.org.safety/files/public_files/osha/
what-pictograms-mean.pdf

全訳

あなたは，「メッセージを送る方法」というタイトルでのポスタープレゼンテーションの準備をしているグループにいます。あなたのグループは，絵文字でメッセージを伝える方法であるピクトグラムに興味があり，次の文章を使用してポスターを作成することを計画しています。

ハザード・ピクトグラム
―メッセージをすばやく伝えることのできる記号―

　ここで紹介するピクトグラムとは，危険物を扱うユーザーに，どのような種類の危険性が存在するかを即座に示すグラフィック画像のことです。たとえば，（そのピクトグラムを用いれば）一目で，その製品が可燃性（すぐに燃焼する可能性がある）であるかどうか，あるいは別の点で健康に害を及ぼす可能性があるかどうかを確認できます。

　その中に，ひし型をしているピクトグラムがあります。そして，このひし形の中には，潜在的な危険（たとえば，火事を引き起こす，食べた場合に有害である，強酸性である，など）を表す記号が書かれています。その記号とひし型のデザインの両方を併せて，ピクトグラムと呼びます。ピクトグラムには，特定の危険等級あるいはカテゴリーが割り当てられています。

　ハザード・ピクトグラムは，国際的な「化学品の分類および表示に関する世界調和システム（GHS）」の一部を形成しています。GHSには2つのセットのピクトグラムが含まれています。1つは容器のラベル付けと職場での危険警告用に用いるもので，2つめのセットは危険物の輸送中に使用するためのものです。対象となる相手に応じてどちらか一方が選択されますが，2つを一緒には使用しません。ピクトグラムのこの2つのセットは，同じ危険性に対して同じ記号を使用しますが，輸送用のピクトグラムには用いる必要のない記号もあります。輸送用のピクトグラムにはよりさまざまな色があり，サブカテゴリー（下位の分類）を表す番号などの追加情報が含まれている場合もあります。

　ハザード・ピクトグラムは，GHSに基づく容器のラベル付けの重要な要素の1つであり，次のような他の情報を伴います。

・その製品の説明
・必要に応じて，「危険」または「警告」のいずれかの注意喚起のことば
・その製品によってもたらされるリスクの性質や程度を示す「危険性通告」
・ユーザー（及び他の人や一般的な環境）へのリスクを最小限に抑えるために，その製品をどのように取り扱うべきかを示す「予防措置的通告」

— 英R 194 —

・（その製品の）供給元（それは製造業者あるいは輸入業者であるかもしれません）の身元

　化学物質のGHSハザード・ピクトグラムは，（各国に対して）ハザード・ピクトグラムの国内システムについての基盤を提供したり，あるいは，それに取って代わることを目的としています。実際，GHS輸送ピクトグラムは，多くの国の国内規制で広く実施されている「危険物輸送に関する国連勧告」で推奨されているものと同じものです。

　下の図は，ハザード・ピクトグラムの例をいくつか示したものです。

図1　ハザード・ピクトグラム

　各ピクトグラムの意味を推測できますか？　それらは2つのグループに分けられます。1つのグループ（番号1及び2）は，上で述べたピクトグラムの最初のセットである，物理的危険性を示すピクトグラムを表しています。他方，もう1つのグループ（番号3，4，5，6及び7）には，2番目のセットである輸送用のピクトグラムが含まれています。それでは，最初のグループから始めて，それぞれを見ていきましょう。

　最初のグループのピクトグラムには，それぞれ独自の名前があります。No. 1は「Flame（火炎）」，No. 2は「Flame over Circle（サークル上の炎）」と呼ばれています。前者は，水や空気にさらされたときに自ら発火しやすい，または可燃性ガスを放出して他の原料の燃焼を引き起こす可燃性の原料または物質を意味し，一方，後者は，何かが燃えるのを助ける，または火をより熱く，より長く持続させるような化学物質である酸化剤を意味します。

　次に，2番目のグループに移りましょう。No. 3は，可燃性の固体，あるいは自己反応性物質を示しています。これらは，輸送中に遭遇する条件下で，発火したり，あるいは摩擦によって火災を引き起こしたりその一因となったり，注意深く取り扱わないと爆発する可能性があります。No. 4は，引火性液体，すなわち，引火点が60℃未満で，燃焼を維持し続けることができる液体を意味します。No. 5は，自然燃焼しやすい物質，すなわち，輸送中に遭遇する通常の状態で自然に熱くなったり，空気との接触により熱くなることから，発火しやすい物質を意味します。No. 6は，他への影響力のある物質を示しています。これらの物質は，それ自体は必ずしも可燃性ではありませんが，一般には酸素を放出することにより，他の物質の燃焼を引き起こしたり，その一因となる可能性があります。最後に，No. 7は有機毒を意味します。これは，ある特定の化学構造を持つ有害物質や危険物質を含む有機物質です。

　それぞれのピクトグラムは特定の種類の危険を表し，危険物を扱う人なら誰でもすぐに認知できるように作られています。もっとも，これらのピクトグラムは一般の人々が理解するにはそれほど簡単なものではありませんが。

あなたのプレゼンテーション・ポスターの草案：

ハザード・ピクトグラムを知っていますか？

ハザード・ピクトグラムとは何か

・それは，製品にどのような種類の危険性が存在しているかを示すグラフィック画像です。

・ 41

何種類かのハザード・ピクトグラム

No.	ピクトグラム	危険性の内容	一般的な意味
1		・可燃性の原料または物質	それらは，燃焼または 42 可能性のある原料または物質です。
2		・酸化剤	43 化学物質です。
3		・可燃性固形物 ・自己反応性を有する物質	摩擦により発火しやすい原料または物質です。

共通のメッセージを持つピクトグラム

44
45

設問解説

問 1 　 41 　 正解 ③

「ポスターの最初の見出しの下で，あなたのグループは，文章で説明されている通り，ハザード・ピクトグラムを紹介したいと考えている。次のうちのどれが最も適切か」

41

① 同じ危険が異なる記号で表されることがあります。

② 2つのセットがあり，同時に両方を使用できます。

③ **製品に関するその他の情報がそれに添えられます。**

④ 国連によって発明され，世界中で広く受け入れられています。

正解は ③。第4段落第1文（Hazard pictograms are ...）に「ハザード・ピクトグラムは，GHS に基づく容器のラベル付けの重要な要素の1つであり，次のような他の情報を伴います」という記述があり，その後，何点か具体的な表記の例が箇条書きで示されている。つまり，製品にはピクトグラムだけでなく，普通その他の情報も添えられて，注意喚起されることになるということである。このことは，選択肢 ③ の内容と一致する。

選択肢 ① と ② については，本文の第3段落に次のような記述があることに注意する。

— 英 R 196 —

第3文～第4文（Either one or ... ～ The two sets ...）「対象となる相手に応じてどちらか一方が選択されますが，2つを一緒には使用しません。ピクトグラムのこの2つのセットは，同じ危険性に対して同じ記号を使用しますが，輸送用のピクトグラムには用いる必要のない記号もあります」

「同じ危険性に対して同じ記号を使用」する，とあるので，選択肢の ① は誤りと見なされる。また，「2つを一緒には使用しません」とあるので，② についても誤りであることがわかる。

また，選択肢 ④ については，第5段落第2文（In fact, GHS ...）に「実際，GHS 輸送ピクトグラムは，多くの国の国内規制で広く実施されている『危険物輸送に関する国連勧告』で推奨されているものと同じものです」という記述があるが，「国連によって発明され」という内容は本文からは読み取れない。よって，④ も不正解である。

以上のことにより，正解は ③ となる。

問2 　42 　正解 ④ 　　43 　正解 ④
「あなたは No. 1 と No. 2 のピクトグラムの一般的な意味を書くように頼まれた。
　42 　と 　43 　に入る最も適切な選択肢をそれぞれ選びなさい」
　No. 1 　42
　　① 　猛毒を含んでいる
　　② 　火の近くで爆発する
　　③ 　低温下でも溶ける
　　④ 　燃焼性のガスを放出する

　No. 2 　43
　　① 　適切な制御をしないと活性化し，発火する可能性がある
　　② 　原料が爆発するのにかかる時間を短縮できる
　　③ 　酸素を吸収できる物質が含まれている
　　④ 　火の温度を上げたり，燃焼時間をより長くする

No. 1 と No. 2 のピクトグラムについては，第8段落を見ると「No. 1 は『Flame（火炎）』，No. 2 は『Flame over Circle（サークル上の炎）』と呼ばれています。前者は，水や空気にさらされたときに自ら発火しやすい，または可燃性ガスを放出するような可燃性原料または物質を意味し，一方，後者は，何かを燃やすのを助ける，または火をより熱く，より長く持続させるような化学物質である酸化剤を意味します」とある。

よって，No. 1 　42 　については ④，No. 2 　43 　については ④ が選ばれることになる。

問3 　44 　・ 　45 　正解 ① ・ ②
「あなたは共通のメッセージを共有するいくつかのピクトグラムについて記述している。この記事によると，次の選択肢のうち，どの2つが適切か（順番は問わない。）」
　44 　・ 　45

　　① 　No. 1 と No. 5 は，空気と接触させると危険になりうる。
　　② 　No. 1 と No. 6 は，発火の原因となりうるガスを放出する。
　　③ 　No. 1, 6, 7 は，有毒ガスが発生する可能性があることを意味している。
　　④ 　No. 1 と No. 7 は，燃焼しやすく有害ガスを生み出すことを意味している。
　　⑤ 　No. 2 と No. 6 は，可燃性であり，大火災の原因となりえることがあることを示している。
　　⑥ 　No. 3, 4, 6 は，低温で燃焼し始めることを示している。

選択肢①：第8段落第2文（The former means ...）に，「前者（= No. 1）は，水や空気にさらされたときに自ら発火しやすい，または可燃性ガスを放出して他の原料の燃焼を引き起こす可燃性の原料または物質を意味し…」とあることから，No. 1は①の内容と合っているとわかる。また，第9段落第5文（No. 5 means ...）に，「No. 5は，自然燃焼しやすい物質，すなわち，輸送中に遭遇する通常の状態で自然に熱くなったり，空気との接触により熱くなることから，発火しやすい物質を意味します」とあることから，No. 5も①の内容と合っている。したがって①は正しい。

選択肢②：上に引用した第8段落第2文に，「前者（= No. 1）は，水や空気にさらされたときに自ら発火しやすい，または可燃性ガスを放出して他の原料の燃焼を引き起こす可燃性の原料または物質を意味し…」とあることから，No. 1は②の内容と合っている。また，第9段落第6文（No.6 shows ...）に，「No. 6は，他への影響力のある物質を示しています。これらの物質は，それ自体は必ずしも可燃性ではありませんが，一般には酸素を放出することにより，他の物質の燃焼を引き起こしたり，その一因となる可能性があります」とあることから，No. 6も②と合っている。したがって②は正しい。

選択肢③：No. 1とNo. 6は「毒」とは関係ない。

選択肢④：No. 7には「燃焼しやすい」という性質はない。

選択肢⑤：No. 2もNo. 6もそれ自体は必ずしも「可燃性がある」わけではない。

選択肢⑥：No. 3とNo. 6については，「低温で」燃焼し始めるということは書かれていない。

以上より，正解は①と②で，選択肢③〜⑥はすべて誤り。

主な語句・表現

・問題冊子を参照のこと。

[リード文]
◇ pictogram 名「ピクトグラム」 グラフィック・シンボルの典型。意味するものの形状などを使って，その意味概念を理解させる記号。
◇ pictorial 形「絵の；絵を用いた」

[第1段落]
(Pictograms introduced here ...)
◇ hazard 名「危険；ハザード」 形容詞は hazardous（危険な）。
◇ graphic 形「図表による；記号上の」
◇ glance 名「ちらっと見ること；一目；一瞥」
◇ flammable 形「可燃性の；燃えやすい」

[第2段落]
(Some pictograms have ...)
◇ represent 動「…を表す；表現する；表出する」
◇ potential 形「潜在的な；内に潜む」　◇ acid 名「酸；酸性のもの」
◇ be referred to as ...「…と呼ばれる；…と称される」
◇ assign 動「…を与える；あてがう」　◇ specific 形「（ある）特定の」
◇ class 名「等級」

[第3段落]
(Hazard pictograms form ...)
◇ form 動「…を形成する；形作る」　◇ classification 名「分類」
◇ chemical 名「化学物質［製品；薬品］」　◇ container 名「容器；コンテナ」
◇ require 動「…を要求する；求める」

[第4段落]
(Hazard pictograms are ...)
◇ nature 名「性質；本質」　◇ precautionary 形「予防の；用心の」
◇ supplier 名「供給者」
◇ manufacturer 名「（大規模な）製造業者；メーカー」
◇ importer 名「輸入者；輸入業者」

[第5～7段落]	◇ UN = United Nations「国際連合」　　◇ regulation 图「規則；規制；ルール」 ◇ physical 形「物理的な」
[第8段落] (The pictograms of ...)	◇ the former「前者」 ⇔ the latter「後者」　◇ material 图「原料；材料；素材」 ◇ substance 图「物質；物体」 ◇ (be) liable to −「−しやすい；容易に−してしまう」 ◇ emit 動「…を放出する；(外に) 出す」 ◇ identify 動「(…と) 同一であると見なす；同一視する」 ◇ oxidizer 图「酸化剤；酸化性物質」
[第9段落] (Next, let us ...)	◇ solid 图「固体」　　　　　　　　　◇ self-reactive 形「自己反応性の」 ◇ friction 图「摩擦」　　　　　　　　◇ liquid 图「液体」 ◇ flash point「引火点；引火温度」 ◇ be capable of −ing「−することができる [可能である]」 ◇ sustain 動「…を維持する；保持する」　◇ spontaneously 副「自然に；自然発生的に」 ◇ in themselves　in oneself で「それ自体」という意味。 ◇ oxygen 图「酸素」　　　　　　　　◇ organic 形「有機の；有機体の」
[最終段落] (Each pictogram ...)	◇ recognizable 形「認知 [認識] することのできる」 ◇ handle 動「…を扱う；取り扱う」
[ポスター]	◇ common 形「共通の；共有の」
[設問文・選択肢]	◇ heading 图「見出し；表題」　　　　◇ accompany 動「…に伴う；同時に起こる」 ◇ shorten 動「…を短くする；短縮する」　◇ absorb 動「…を吸収する」 ◇ length 图「長さ」 ＜ long 形「長い」　◇ order 图「順序；順番」 ◇ matter 動「問題となる；重要である」　◇ poisonous 形「毒 (性) のある」

2022 年度 大学入試センター公表

令和 7 年度（2025 年度）大学入学共通テスト
試作問題
英語（リーディング）

解答・解説

英語（リーディング）　試作問題A・B　（30点満点）

（解答・配点）

問題番号（配点）	設問	解答番号	正解	配点	自己採点欄	問題番号（配点）	設問	解答番号	正解	配点	自己採点欄
第A問（18）	1	1	②	3		第B問（12）	1	1	①	3	
	2	2	②	3			2	2	②	3	
	3	3 － 4	②－⑤	3			3	3	③	3	
		5	④	3			4	4	①	3	
	4	6	②	3		小　計					
	5	7	②	3		合　計					
小　計						（注）　－（ハイフン）でつながれた正解は，順序を問わない。					

— 英 R 202 —

第A問
〈全訳〉
あなたは高校生が授業中にスマートフォンを使うのを許されるべきかどうかについてのエッセイを作成中で，以下のステップを踏もうとしています。

ステップ1：スマートフォンの使用についてのさまざまな見解を読んで理解する。
ステップ2：高校生が授業中にスマートフォンを使用することについて1つの立場をとる。
ステップ3：さらにいろいろな情報源を利用して，エッセイのアウトラインを作成する。

[ステップ1]　さまざまな情報源を読む

著者A（教員）
私の同僚たちはしばしば，スマートフォンが生涯あせない知識や技術を生徒が身につけるのに役立つのかどうか疑います。私は，使い方をよく考えれば役に立つと思っています。スマートフォンは，学習効果を高めることのできる授業中のさまざまな活動を支援してくれます。例えば，学習課題のために調査をしたり，学んだことを他の人と共有したりできます。もう1つの利点として，生徒に機器を供与する必要がなくなります。生徒は自分のスマホを使えるのですから！　学校は，生徒が持つ強力なコンピューター機器を最大限に活用するべきです。

著者B（心理学者）
スマートフォンが生徒の学習を促すことができるという意見は広く受け入れられています。けれども，多くの人に信じられているからといって，それが正しい意見だと言えるわけではありません。最近の研究によって，高校生が授業中にスマートフォンの使用を許されると，学習に集中することができなくなることがわかりました。それどころか，生徒は自分のスマートフォンを使っていなくても，クラスメートがスマートフォンを使っているのを見ると気が散ってしまいました。学校が教室を，スマートフォンによる干渉のない場所にするべきであるのは明らかです。

著者C（親）
私は最近，高校生の息子にスマートフォンを買ってあげました。その理由は，学校が私たちの町から離れたところにあるからです。息子はたいてい朝早くに出かけて，遅い時間に帰ってきます。今では，息子は困ったことがあれば私に連絡を取ったり，必要な情報を手に入れることができます。その一方で，息子が時々スマートフォンを見ながら歩いているのを見かけます。注意していないと，事故に遭うかもしれません。一般的には，高校生はスマートフォンを持つ方が安全ですが，それでも親はそのリスクを認識しておく必要があると私は思います。息子が授業中にどのように利用しているのかも気になります。

著者D（高校生）
私たちは学校で授業中にスマホを使うことを許されています。ほとんどの生徒がスマートフォンを持っているので，私たちの学校がその使用を許可するのは理にかなっています。授業中，私たちはスマートフォンの外国語学習のアプリを利用していて，これは私には本当に役に立ちます。今では学ぶことへの興味が昔よりも増して，テストの点数も上がりました。けれども先日，私は授業中にオンラインの漫画を読んでいたのを先生に見つかって，怒られてしまいました。こういったことが時折起こりますが，全体的に見て，スマートフォンは私の学習を改善してくれました。

著者E（学校長）
私の学校の先生たちは，生徒たちが授業中にスマートフォンを使って友達と遊ぶだろうと考えていたので，当初はスマートフォンに対して懐疑的でした。こういうわけで，私たちはスマートフォンを禁止しました。しかしながら，ますます多くの教育用アプリが利用できるようになると，私たちはスマートフォンを教室での学習用機器として利用できるのではないかと考えるようになりました。昨年私たちは授業中のスマートフォン利用を許すことにしました。残念ながら，私たちが望んでいた結果は得られませんでした。スマートフォンは生徒の気を散らしてしまうことが私たちにはわかったのです。ただし利用のためのルールを整備して，生徒たちがそれに従った場合は例外でした。とは言えこれは，言うのは簡単ですが実行するのは難しいことでした。

〈設問解説〉

「教室でのスマートフォン使用についての是非」がトピックで，各著者の基本的な立場と，主な主張をまとめると，以下のようになる。

著者	基本的な立場	主な主張
A	賛成	・さまざまな学習活動を支援。 ・学校が生徒に機器を供与する必要がない。
B	反対	・学習に集中できなくなる。
C	賛成	・非常時の連絡や情報取得に役立つ。 ・ただし歩行中の使用は危険。教室での使用法も気になる。
D	賛成	・学習への興味の増加。 ・テストの成績の向上。
E	反対	・生徒の気を散らす。 ・ルール作りの難しさ。

問1　1　正解－②

「著者AとDはいずれも　1　と述べている」

① スマートフォンの学習用アプリは，生徒が試験の成績を上げるのに役立てられる

② 教育の道具としてスマートフォンを使う理由の1つは，ほとんどの生徒がそれを持っているということだ

③ スマートフォンは学校でも家庭でも，学習活動を支援するために使うことができる

④ スマートフォンは，生徒が自分の考えをクラスメートと共有するのを可能にする

　正解は②。著者Aは，第5文（Another advantage is ...）で，「もう1つの利点として，生徒に機器を供与する必要がなくなります。生徒は自分のスマホを使えるのですから」と述べており，下線部分は②の内容と合っている。また著者Dは，第2文(It makes sense ...)で「ほとんどの生徒がスマートフォンを持っているので，私たちの学校がその使用を許可するのは理にかなっています」と述べていて，これも②の内容と合う。したがって②が正解となる。

　①の「スマートフォンの学習用アプリは，生徒が試験の成績を上げるのに役立てられる」については，著者Dは言及していると考えられるが，著者Aははっきりと言及していないので，正解にはなれない。③の「スマートフォンは学校でも家庭でも，学習活動を支援するために使うことができる」のようなことは，著者AもDも述べていない。④については，著者Aは言及しているが，著者Dは言及していない。

問2　2　正解－②

「著者Bは　2　ということを示唆している」

① デジタル機器から離れて時間を過ごすことは，生徒の学習意欲を妨げる

② 一般に抱かれている考えが，研究が明らかにする事実とは異なることが時にありうる

③ スマートフォンを持っていない生徒は，自分のことを学習能力がより高いとみなす可能性が高い

④ 教室は，生徒が教師に干渉されずに学ぶことのできる場であるべきだ

　正解は②。著者Bの意見の第2文（Being believed by many, ...）に「けれども，多くの人に信じられることが，意見を正しいものにするわけではない（多くの人に信じられているからといって，それが正しい意見だと言えるわけではない）」とある。この中の「多くの人に信じられること（Being believed by many）」が②の中の「一般に抱かれている（commonly held）」とほぼ同内容であり，「意見を正しいものにするわけではない（does not make an opinion correct）」が②の中の「考えが…事実とは異なる（beliefs can be different from the facts）」とほぼ同内容であることがわかればよい。

　①は，学習にデジタル機器を利用することに賛成する内容であり，著者Bの主張とは根本的に異なる。③のように，スマートフォンを持たない学生が「自分のことを学習能力がより高いとみなす」とも著者Bは述べていない。④は「教師」を「スマートフォン」に置き換えないと，著者Bの主張と合わない。

〈主な語句・表現〉

take a position「ある立場をとる」／ additional 形「追加の」／ source 名「情報源；資料」／ colleague 名「同僚」／ as long as ...「…する限り［間］は」／ enhance 動「…を高める；増す」／ share A with B「AをBと共有する；AをBに伝える」／ provide A with B「AにBを供給する」／ device 名「機器；デバイス」／ take full advantage of ...「…を十分に利用する」／ widespread 形「広く行き渡った」／ encourage 動「…を奨励する」／ Being believed by many「多くの人々に信じられること」 Being は動名詞。／ make (V) an opinion (O) correct (C)「意見を正しいものにする」／ concentrate on ...「…に集中［専念］する」／ distraction 名「気を散らすもの」／ be free from ...「…がない」／ interference 名「邪魔；妨害；干渉」／ be located「位置している；ある」／ contact 動「連絡を取る」／ access 動「…に接続する；…を入手する」／

— 英 R 204 —

make sense「理にかなう」／ make use of ...「…を利用［活用］する」／ app 图「アプリ（ケーション）」／ catch O －ing「O が－しているのを見つける」／ overall 副「概して；全体としては」／ initially 副「初めのうちは」／ be skeptical of ...「…について懐疑的だ」／ socialize 動「交際［おしゃべり］する」／ ban 動「…を禁止する」／ learning aid「学習補助機器」／ smartphone use「スマートフォンの使用」／ distract 動「…の気をそらす」／ in place「整って；施行されて」／ easier said than done「〈ことわざ〉言うは易く行うは難し」

〈全訳〉
［ステップ２〕　１つの立場をとる
　問３　正解　　 3 ・ 4 －②・⑤, 5 －④
「あなたはさまざまな見解を理解したので，高校生の授業でのスマートフォンの使用に関する立場を決めて，それを以下のように書き出してみた。 3 ， 4 ， 5 を埋めるのに最適な選択肢を選びなさい」

あなたの立場：高校生は授業中のスマートフォンの使用を許されるべきではない。
　・著者 3 と 4 はあなたの立場を支持している。
　・この２人の著者の主要な論点： 5 。

〈設問解説〉
　 3 と 4 の選択肢（順序は問わない）
① A
② B
③ C
④ D
⑤ E

　 5 の選択肢
① 授業中のスマートフォン使用の実際的なルールを作るのは学校の教師にとって難しい
② 教育用アプリは使いづらいので，スマートフォンは学習の邪魔になるかもしれない
③ スマートフォンはコミュニケーション用に作られていて，教室での学習には向いていない
④ 生徒が授業中にスマートフォンを利用できる間は，勉強に集中できない
　 3 と 4 には，「あなた」の立場と合う主張をしている著者を選ぶ。「あなたの立場」は「高校生は授業中のスマートフォンの使用を許されるべきではない」ということであるから，解説冒頭の表に示したように，基本的な立場が「反対」である②Bと⑤Eが正解となる。

　 5 には，著者BとEに共通する主要な論点として適切なものを選ぶ。表の中の「主な主張」からわかるように，Bは「学習に集中できなくなる（第３文：A recent study ...／第４文：In fact, ...）」こと，そしてEは「生徒の気を散らす（第６文：We found that ...）」ことを，授業中のスマートフォンの使用に反対の主な理由として挙げている。したがってこれらとほぼ同内容の記述を含む②か④が正解の候補となるが，②の中の「教育用アプリは使いづらい」については，著者BもEも述べていないことから，正解にはなれない。したがって正解は④に決まる。
　①の「ルール作りの難しさ」については，表からもわかるように，著者Eが触れている（第６文：We found that ...／第７（最終）文：This was easier ...）と考えることはできるが，著者Bはこのことについて触れていないので，本問の正解にはなれない。③のような主張は，２人の著者のいずれもしていない。

〈主な語句・表現〉
　now that ...「（今や）…なので」／ as below「以下のように」／ argument 图「論拠；論点；主張」／ option 图「選択肢」／ practical 形「実際［実用］的な」／ focus on ...「…に集中する」／ have access to ...「…を利用できる」

— 英 R 205 —

〈全訳〉
[ステップ3] 情報源AとBを利用してアウトラインを作成する

あなたのエッセイのアウトライン：

授業中にスマートフォンを使うのは良い考えではない

序論
スマートフォンは現代生活には欠かせないものとなったが，生徒が授業中に自分のスマートフォンを使うのは禁止するべきだ。

本論
　理由1：[ステップ2から]
　理由2：[情報源Aを根拠に]　……　6
　理由3：[情報源Bに根拠に]　……　7

結論
高校は，生徒が授業でスマートフォンを使用するのを許すべきではない。

情報源A
モバイル機器には学習に役立つ利点があります。例えば，大学生が双方向型のモバイルアプリを利用した際には，デジタル教科書と比較して，心理学の習得度が上がったことをある研究が示しました。情報は同じだったものの，アプリが持つ3D画像などの追加機能が，学生たちの学習効果を高めたのです。しかしながら，デジタル機器が全て同等に効果的ではないことに注意するのは大事です。別の研究では，学生はスマートフォンを使うよりもノートパソコンを使う方が，画面がより大きいことから，内容への理解度が高まることがわかりました。学校は学生の学習効果を最大限に高める種類のデジタル機器を選択しなければならないし，学校が学生にスマートフォンを使わせるのではなく，コンピューターやタブレットを供与すべきだとする強力な論拠もあります。すべての学生に同じアプリがインストールされたコンピューターかタブレットが供与されれば，技術上の問題も少なくなり，教師も授業を行いやすくなるでしょう。これにより，自分のスマートフォンを持っていない学生が，授業でのすべての活動に参加することも可能となります。

情報源B
米国で行われたある研究によって，多くのティーンエイジャーがスマートフォン依存症になっていることがわかった。この研究は，13歳から18歳の約1,000人の学生を調べた。下のグラフは，自分のスマートフォンの使い方を述べたものとして合っていると答えた学生の比率を示している。

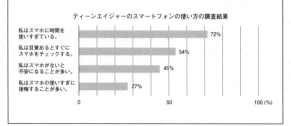

〈設問解説〉
問4　6　正解ー②
「情報源Aに基づくと，理由2に最もふさわしいものは次のどれか」　6
①　3D画像を表示するアプリは学習には必要不可欠だが，すべての学生がこういったアプリをスマートフォンに入れているわけではない。
②　ある種のデジタル機器は教育効果を高めることができるが，スマートフォンは最適ではない。
③　学生は大学への準備として，スマートフォンだけでなく他のデジタル機器も扱う技術を身につけるべきだ。
④　心理学研究では，デジタル機器が学習に好ましい影響を及ぼすことが示されていないので，私たちは教科書を使い続けるべきだ。

正解は②。空所には，高校の授業でスマートフォンを使用すべきでない理由としてふさわしいもので，かつ情報源A（Source A）の中で述べられているものを入れる。情報源Aの第4文（It is important ...）から第6文（Schools must select ...）に，「しかしながら，デジタル機器がすべて同等に効果的ではないことに注意するのは大事です。別の研究では，学生はスマートフォンを使うよりもノートパソコンを使う方が，画面がより大きいことから，内容への理解度が高まることがわかりました。学校は学生の学習効果を最大限に高める種類のデジタル機器を選択しなければならないし，学校が学生にスマートフォンを使わせるのではなく，コンピューターやタブレットを供与すべきだとする強力な論拠もあります」とあることから，下線部の内容と合っていて，授業でスマートフォンを使用すべきでない理由として妥当な内容でもあることから，②が正解となる。

①については、「3D画像を表示するアプリは学習には必要不可欠（essential）だ」や「すべての学生がこういったアプリをスマートフォンに入れているわけではない」といったことは情報源Aでは述べられていないので誤りである。③は「大学への準備として（to prepare for university）」の部分が、本文からは読み取れないので正解にはなれない。④のようなことも本文からは読み取れない。

問5　正解―②

「あなたは理由3として、『若い学生はスマートフォン依存症になる危険に直面している』と書くことにした。情報源Bに基づけば、この発言を最も適切に支持する選択肢はどれか」

① 半数以上のティーンエイジャーが、スマートフォンを使いすぎていると報告したが、実際にそのことを後悔している人は4分の1に満たない。このことは、依存症の問題が認識されていないことを示すのかもしれない。

② ティーンエイジャーの4人に3人近くは、スマホに時間を使いすぎている。実際に、目覚めた後すぐにスマホをチェックする人は50パーセントを超えている。ティーンエイジャーの多くは、スマホを使わずにいることができない。

③ 70パーセントを超えるティーンエイジャーが、スマホを使う時間が多すぎると考えていて、半数以上がスマホがないと不安を感じてしまう。この種の依存は、彼らの日常生活に悪影響を及ぼすことがある。

④ ティーンエイジャーはいつもスマホを使っている。実際に、4分の3を上回る人々が、スマホを使いすぎだと認めている。彼らの生活は、朝から晩までスマートフォンに支配されている。

正解は②。情報源Bの内容と合っている選択肢を選ぶ。②の第1文の「4人中3人に近いティーンエイジャーは、スマホに時間を使いすぎている」は、情報源Bの棒グラフの一番上にある「私はスマホに時間を使いすぎている（I spend too much time ...）」が、72パーセントであることと合っている。また、②の第2文の「実際に、目覚めた後すぐにスマホをチェックする人は50パーセントを超えている」は、情報源Bの棒グラフの2番目にある「私は目覚めるとすぐにスマホをチェックする（I check my phone ...）」が54パーセントであることと合っている。したがって②は情報源Bの内容を正しく反映していることから、これが正解となる。

①は、第1文の「半数以上のティーンエイジャーが、スマートフォンを使いすぎていると報告したが、実際にそのことを後悔している人は4分の1に満たない」の下線部分が、情報源Bの棒グラフの一番下にある「私はスマホの使いすぎに後悔することが多い（I often feel regret ...）」が27パーセントであることと合わない。③は、第1文の「70パーセントを超えるティーンエイジャーが、スマホを使う時間が多すぎると考えていて、半数以上がスマホがないと不安を感じてしまう」の下線部分が、情報源Bの棒グラフの3番目にある「私はスマホがないと不安になることが多い（I often feel anxious ...）」が45パーセントであることと合わない。④は、第2文の「実際に、4分の3を上回る人々が、スマホを使いすぎだと認めている」の下線部分が、情報源Bの棒グラフの一番上にある「私はスマホに時間を使いすぎている」が、72パーセントであることと合わない。

〈主な語句・表現〉

essential形「必要不可欠な」／ prohibit O from －ing「Oが－するのを禁止する」／ body名「本文；本論」／ based on ...「…に基づく」／ conclusion名「結論」／ advantage名「利点」／ psychology名「心理学」／ interactive形「双方向型の」／ compared with ...「…と比べると」／ extra形「追加の；特別の」／ feature名「特徴」／ not all equally effective「すべてが同程度に効果的というわけではない」／ maximize動「…を最大にする」／ with the same apps installed「同じアプリがインストールされた状態で」／ enable O to －「Oが－するのを可能にする」／ conduct動「…を行う」／ participate in ...「…に参加する」／ be addicted to ...「…への依存症［中毒］である」／ anxious形「不安な」／ regret名「残念な気持ち；後悔」

第 B 問

〈全訳〉

英語の授業であなたは関心のある社会問題についてのエッセイを書いています。これが最も新しい草稿です。あなたは今，先生からのコメントに基づいて，修正を行っています。

ファッションに関する環境に優しい行動

多くの人はファッションを愛しています。衣服は自己表現にとって大切ですが，ファッションは環境に有害となることがあります。日本では，毎年約48万トンもの衣服が捨てられていると言われています。これは1日に大型トラック約130台の分量に相当します。私たちはこの「投げ捨て」行為を改める必要があるのです。このエッセイでは，より持続可能になるための3つの方法を取りあげます。

第1に，買い物をする時は，無計画に物を買うのは避けましょう。政府の調査によると，買い物客のおよそ64パーセントは，何がすでにクローゼットの中にあるのかを考えません。(1)∧ですから，買い物をする時にはよく計画を立てた上で物を選ぶようにしましょう。

加えて，通例ならより長持ちする質の高い衣服を買ってください。値段は高めかもしれませんが，数年間着ることができる服はお値打ち品です。(2)∧より安価な布は脱色したり，すぐに古く見え始めることがあるので，より早く捨てる必要があるのです。

最後に，(3)自分の服のことを考えましょう。たとえば，それらを中古衣料店に売却してください。そうすることで，他の人がそれを喜んで着てくれます。服を必要とする人のためにチャリティーに寄付してもよいでしょう。服の新しい用途を見つけるのも1つの方法です。衣類をキルトやバッグなどの役に立つ物に作り変えるいろいろな方法があります。

結論としては，ライフスタイルを変えるべき時が来ているのです。これからは，買い物に出かける前にクローゼットを調べる，(4)より良い品物を選ぶ，そして最後に，自分の衣服を再び生かすようにしましょう。このようにすれば，私たちはみなファッションに関してより持続可能になれるのです。

コメント

(1) ここは何かが足りません。2つの文をつなぐために，間にさらに情報を追加してください。

(2) ここにつなぎの表現を挿入してください。

(3) この主題文はこの段落とあまり合っていません。書き直してください。

(4) 下線部の表現はあなたのエッセイの内容を十分にまとめきれていません。変更してください。

総評：

あなたのエッセイは良くなっています。この調子で頑張ってください。（あなたは自分のクローゼットをチェックしましたか。私はしましたよ！ ☺）

〈設問解説〉

問1　1　正解ー①

「コメント(1)に基づくと，どの文を加えるのが最も良いか」

① その結果，人々は必要のない似た品物をたくさん買ってしまうのです。

② このために，お客さんは衣服のショッピングを楽しむことができません。

③ このせいで，店員はお客さんが何を必要としているかを知りたいのです。

④ この状況では，消費者は買い物に行くのを避ける傾向があります。

正解は①。①の文を加えれば，下に示すように，①の中の「その結果（As a result）」が表す因果関係や，続く文の冒頭の「ですから（So）」が表す順接関係が，いずれも内容の上で適切なものとなる。なお，①の直前に来る文（According to a government survey, ...）の中の「何がすでにクローゼットの中にあるのか（what is already in their closet）」とは，「何をすでに買ってあるか」という意味を比喩的に言い表したものである。

②や③を選ぶと，これらの中の「このために（Because of this）」や「このせいで（Due to this）」が論理上うまく働かない。④を選んでも，この文の内容が前後の文と適切につながらない。

「政府の調査によると，買い物客のおよそ64パーセントは，何がすでにクローゼットの中にあるのかを考えません（According to a government survey, ...）」

↓

「その結果（As a result）」〈結果を導く〉

「人々は必要のない似た品物をたくさん買ってしまうのです（(1)）」

↓

「ですから（So）」〈結論を導く〉

「買い物をする時にはよく計画を立てた上で物を選ぶようにしましょう（try to plan ...）」

問2　[2]　正解－②
「コメント(2)に基づくと，どの表現を加えるのが最適か」

① たとえば
② 対照的に
③ にもかかわらず
④ それゆえ

正解は②。(2)の前にある文（Even though the price ...）は，「値段は高めかもしれませんが，数年着ることができる服はお値打ち品です」という内容で，「値段の高い服の利点」を述べている。そして(2)の後に来る文（Cheaper fabrics can ...）は，「より安価な布は脱色したり，すぐに古く見え始めることがあるので，より早く捨てる必要があるのです」という内容で，「安価な服の欠点」が述べられている。つまりこの2つの文は対照的な内容になっていることから，②の「対照的に［これに対して］」を選ぶのが最適である。

他の選択肢はいずれも(2)の前後の文の論理関係を適切に表していない。

問3　[3]　正解－③
「コメント(3)に基づくと，この主題文の最適な書き直し方はどれか」

① 新しい服を買う数を減らしましょう
② 古い服を処分しましょう
③ 服を再利用する方法を見つけましょう
④ 要らなくなった服を寄付しましょう

正解は③。この段落の内容を端的に表す主題文として最適なものを選ぶ。続く文は，「たとえば（For example）」で始まり，主題文の具体例が示される。この具体例は，以下の3つに分けることができる。

・具体例1「中古衣料店に売却する（For example, sell them ...）」
・具体例2「チャリティーに寄付する（You could also donate ...）」
・具体例3「服の新しい用途を見つける（Another way is ...）」

この3つの具体例を一般的な表現で簡潔に言い表したものを，主題文とするのが適切である。3つの具体

例はいずれも，「服の再利用」の方法を示していると考えられることから，正解は③に決まる。なお，最終段落第2文（From now on, ...）の中の「自分の衣服を再び生かす（give your clothes a second life）」が，第4段落（Finally, ...）の内容を端的にまとめた表現であることにも注意したい。

①は3つの具体例とは全く無関係な内容である。②で用いられている dispose of ... は，「…を処分する」という意味だが，具体的には「廃棄・譲渡・売却」といった方法による処分を表す。これを選んだ場合，具体例3の「服の新しい用途を見つける」が適切な例とは言えなくなるので，②は正解になれない。④を選んだ場合，具体例1と3が適切な例にならない。

問4　[4]　正解－①
「コメント(4)に基づくと，置き換えた表現としてどれが最適か」

① 状態が悪くならない品物を買う
② 安価でファッショナブルな服を選ぶ
③ 作り変えることのできる品物を選ぶ
④ 中古の服を買う

正解は①。本文の段落構成は以下のようになっている（カッコ内の数字は段落番号を表す）。
[1] 序論　「持続可能なファッションの必要性」
[2] 本論1「計画性のある買い物をする」
[3] 本論2「長持ちする質の高い衣服を選択する」
[4] 本論3「古い服を再利用する」
[5] 結論　「ライフスタイルを変えるべき時」

そして「結論」に当たる最終第5段落の第2文（From now on, ...）で提案されている3つの事項は，以下に示すように，「本論」である第2・3・4段落の要点をそれぞれ表していることに注意したい。

・本論1→「買い物に出かける前にクローゼットを調べる（check your closet ...）」
・本論2→「(4)より良い品物を選ぶ（select better things）」
・本論3→「自分の衣服を再び生かす（give your clothes ...）」

つまり，先生のコメント(4)は，下線部(4)の表現が本論2の要点として適切なものではない，という意味である。したがって，下線部(4)には，本論2の趣旨である「長持ちする質の高い衣服を選択する」の意味に最も近いものを入れるのが最適なので，正解は①に決まる。①の中の「状態が悪くならない品物（items that maintain their condition）」が，「長持ちする衣服」と同内容であるとわかればよい。他の選択肢は，いずれも本論2の内容とは無関係なので，正解にはなれない。

〈主な語句・表現〉

social issue「社会問題」／ draft 名「草稿」／ work on ...「…に取り組む」／ revision 名「改訂；修正」／ eco-friendly 形「環境に優しい」／ self-expression 名「自己表現」／ harmful 形「有害な」／ throw O away「Oを捨てる」／ be equal to ...「…に等しい［匹敵する］」／ highlight 動「…を強調する；際立たせる」／ sustainable 形「持続可能な」／ unplanned purchase「無計画な購入」／ approximately 副「約；およそ」／ in addition「加えて；さらに」／ last long「長持ちする」／ good value「十分な価値；お値打ち品」／ fabric 名「布地」／ used clothing store「中古衣料店」／ that way「その方法で；そのようにすれば」／ donate 動「…を寄付する」／ transform A into B「A を B に変化させる」／ outfit 名「服装一式」／ quilt 名「キルト；ベッドカバー」／ in conclusion「結論として」／ from now on「今からずっと」／ miss 動「…を抜かす；省略する」／ insert 動「…を挿入する」／ match 動「…と合う；調和する」／ summarize 動「…を要約する」／ content 名「内容」／ Keep up the good work.「その調子だ；がんばれ」

2024 年度
大学入学共通テスト 本試験
英語（リーディング）

解答・解説

■ 2024 年度（令和６年度）本試験「英語（リーディング）」得点別偏差値表
下記の表は大学入試センター公表の平均点と標準偏差をもとに作成したものです。

平均点　51.54　　　標準偏差　19.94　　　　　　　　受験者数　449,328

得 点	偏差値	得 点	偏差値
100	74.3	50	49.2
99	73.8	49	48.7
98	73.3	48	48.2
97	72.8	47	47.7
96	72.3	46	47.2
95	71.8	45	46.7
94	71.3	44	46.2
93	70.8	43	45.7
92	70.3	42	45.2
91	69.8	41	44.7
90	69.3	40	44.2
89	68.8	39	43.7
88	68.3	38	43.2
87	67.8	37	42.7
86	67.3	36	42.2
85	66.8	35	41.7
84	66.3	34	41.2
83	65.8	33	40.7
82	65.3	32	40.2
81	64.8	31	39.7
80	64.3	30	39.2
79	63.8	29	38.7
78	63.3	28	38.2
77	62.8	27	37.7
76	62.3	26	37.2
75	61.8	25	36.7
74	61.3	24	36.2
73	60.8	23	35.7
72	60.3	22	35.2
71	59.8	21	34.7
70	59.3	20	34.2
69	58.8	19	33.7
68	58.3	18	33.2
67	57.8	17	32.7
66	57.3	16	32.2
65	56.8	15	31.7
64	56.2	14	31.2
63	55.7	13	30.7
62	55.2	12	30.2
61	54.7	11	29.7
60	54.2	10	29.2
59	53.7	9	28.7
58	53.2	8	28.2
57	52.7	7	27.7
56	52.2	6	27.2
55	51.7	5	26.7
54	51.2	4	26.2
53	50.7	3	25.7
52	50.2	2	25.2
51	49.7	1	24.7
		0	24.2

英語（リーディング）　2024年度　本試験　（100点満点）

（解答・配点）

問題番号（配点）	設問		解答番号	正解	配点	自己採点欄
第1問（10）	A	1	1	④	2	
		2	2	①	2	
	B	1	3	④	2	
		2	4	③	2	
		3	5	①	2	
小計						
第2問（20）	A	1	6	①	2	
		2	7	②	2	
		3	8	①	2	
		4	9	④	2	
		5	10	②	2	
	B	1	11	①	2	
		2	12	①	2	
		3	13	①	2	
		4	14	③	2	
		5	15	②	2	
小計						
第3問（15）	A	1	16	②	3	
		2	17	②	3	
	B	1	18	①	3*	
			19	②		
			20	③		
			21	④		
		2	22	③	3	
		3	23	②	3	
小計						

問題番号（配点）	設問		解答番号	正解	配点	自己採点欄
第4問（16）		1	24	③	3	
		2	25	④	3	
		3	26	④	2	
		4	27	⑤	2	
			28	④	3	
		5	29	③	3	
小計						
第5問（15）		1	30	④	3*	
			31	⑤		
			32	①		
			33	②		
		2	34	②	3	
		3	35	①	3*	
			36	②		
		4	37	③	3	
		5	38	②	3	
小計						
第6問（24）	A	1	39	⑥	3*	
			40	②		
		2	41	①	3	
		3	42	③	3	
		4	43	①	3	
	B	1	44	④	2	
		2	45	④	2	
		3	46 － 47	② － ③	3*	
		4	48	③	3	
		5	49	⑤	2	
小計						
合計						

（注）
1　＊は，全部正解の場合のみ点を与える。
2　－（ハイフン）でつながれた正解は，順序を問わない。

— 英 R 212 —

第1問

A

〈全訳〉

　あなたは米国のある語学学校で英語を学んでいます。学校はあるイベントを計画中です。あなたは参加したいので，案内広告を読んでいます。

ソープ英語学校
インターナショナルな夕べ
5月24日金曜日　午後5時から8時
入場料：5ドル

ソープ英語学校（TELS）はインターナショナルな交流イベントを計画しています。TELSの学生は入場料を支払う必要はありません。学生ロビーの受付で学生証を提示してください。

● **世界の様々な地域の食べ物を味わおう**
　中東のフムスの味をご存知ですか？　メキシコのタコスはどうですか？　北アフリカのクスクスは？　すべて試食できますよ。

● **色々な言語や新しいコミュニケーションの仕方を体験しよう**
　"hello" や "thank you" などの基本的な表現をアラビア語，イタリア語，日本語，スペイン語で書いてみましょう。こういった文化圏の人々がコミュニケーションをとるために，表情や手をどのように用いるのかを学びましょう。

● **ダンスの実演を見学しよう**
　午後7時から舞台で行われるフラメンコ，フラダンス，サンバのダンスショーを見てください！それぞれのダンスの後で，実演者が基本のステップを教えます。どうぞ参加してください。

ホールでは，たくさんの写真，旗，地図，織物，手工芸品，ゲームが展示されます。あなたの出身国の写真や物品で，イベントで展示できるものをお持ちでしたら，5月17日までに学校職員にお知らせくださいね！

〈設問解説〉

問1　1　正解―④

「このイベントに無料で参加するには，1しなければならない」

① 出身国の写真を持参
② ショーのことでスタッフに相談する
③ 学生ロビーにある用紙に記入
④ **TELSの学生であることを証明するものを提示**

　正解は④。案内広告の冒頭付近の説明文中に，「TELSの学生は入場料を支払う必要はありません（TELS students don't need ...）。学生ロビーの受付で学生証を提示してください（Please present ...）」とあることから，下線部の内容と合っている④が正解となる。

　他の選択肢は，「このイベントに無料で参加する」条件とは関係がない。

問2　2　正解―①

「このイベントでは，2ことができる」

① **様々な文化のジェスチャーを学ぶ**
② ダンス競技会に参加する
③ 外国語で短い物語を読む
④ 国際的な料理を作ってみる

　正解は①。案内広告の中程にある2つ目の丸印（●）の項目（Experience different languages ...）の最終文（Learn how people ...）に，「こういった文化圏の人々がコミュニケーションをとるために，表情や手をどのように用いるのかを学びましょう」とある。①の中の「ジェスチャー（gestures）」は，下線部と同内容と考えられることから，①が正解となる。

　②のように「ダンス競技会（competition）に参加する」や，④のように「国際的な料理を作って（cooking）みる」ことができるとは，本文中では述べられていない。③に相当することも本文では述べられていない。

〈主な語句・表現〉

flyer 名「ちらし；ビラ」／ entrance fee「入場料」／ organize 動「〈行事などを〉準備［計画］する」／ present 動「…を提示する」／ reception desk「受付」／ facial 形「顔の」／ steps 名「（ダンスの）ステップ」／ textile 名「織物」／ crafts 名「手工芸品」／ display 動「…を展示する」

B

〈全訳〉

　あなたは米国にいる交換留学生で，来週あなたのクラスは日帰り旅行に出かけます。先生が情報を提供してくれました。

イエントンビルのツアー
イエントンビル旅行案内所は，
3つの市内観光ツアーを提供しています。

歴史ツアー
ツアーの1日は，聖パトリック教会の訪問から始まります。この教会は1800年代の半ばに市が設立された時に建てられたものです。教会の向かい側には，20世紀初めの市長舎があります。市長舎とその美しい庭園のツアーが行われます。最後に，公共バスで市を横断して，平和公園を訪れましょう。ここは第二次世界大戦のすぐ後に開園し，1960年代にはここで数多くのデモ活動が行われました。

芸術ツアー
午前中はイエントンビル芸術地区で過ごします。最初に訪れるのは，数多くのヨーロッパや米国の絵画がある美術館です。昼食後は通りの向かい側に行き，ブルートン音楽堂でコンサートを楽しんでから，少し歩いて芸術家通りに行きます。この区域は数年前，新しい芸術家たちのアトリエと近隣にある彫刻公園が造られた時に開発されました。芸術家たちのアトリエでの制作活動を見た後は，公園を散策して，木々の中に彫刻を見つけてください。

スポーツツアー
朝一番で，イエントンビル・ライオンズというフットボールチームがトレーニングしているのを，郊外にある屋外施設で見学できます。午後は，昨秋に完成したイエントンビルホッケー競技場まで地下鉄で移動します。この競技場の独特のデザインについて知るために，展示ホールでしばらく時間を過ごしてください。最後に，競技場でプロによるホッケーの試合を楽しみましょう。

2024年1月，イエントンビル旅行案内所

〈設問解説〉

問1　　3　　正解ー④

「イエントンビルには　3　がある」
① 市が建設された250年前に建てられた教会
② 町の中心部にある独特なフットボールのトレーニング施設
③ 訪問客が独自の芸術作品を作ることができるアトリエ
④ **美術館と音楽堂の両方がある芸術地区**

　正解は④。イエントンビルのツアー案内の「芸術ツアー（The Arts Tour）」の項の第1文（The morning will ...）から第3文（After lunch, ...）に，「午前中はイエントンビル芸術地区で過ごします。最初に訪れるのは，数多くのヨーロッパや米国の絵画がある美術館です。昼食後は通りの向かい側に行き，ブルートン音楽堂でコンサートを楽しんでから，少し歩いて芸術家通りに行きます」とあることから，④は正しいとわかる。
　①については，「教会（church）」に関する記述は本文中では「歴史ツアー（The History Tour）」の中にあるのみで，そこでは教会は「1800年代の半ばに（in the mid-1800s）」に設立されたと述べられている。一方①の中では教会は「250年前（250 years ago）」に建てられたとある。この2つの記述が合わないことから，①は誤りとなる（ちなみに本文の最下部にあるように，このツアーの案内文が作成されたのは2024年1月である）。②の中の「フットボールのトレーニング施設」については，本文中の「スポーツツアー（The Sports Tour）」の項に記述があるが，本文中ではトレーニング施設は「郊外にある（in the suburbs）」と述べられていて，これが②の中の「町の中心部にある（in the center of the town）」と明らかに合わない。③については，「訪問客が独自の芸術作品を作ることができる」の部分が本文中では述べられていない。

問2　　4　　正解ー③

「3つのツアーすべてにおいて，あなたは　4　だろう」
① 市の歴史的な事件について学ぶ
② 人々が自分の技術を披露しているのを見る
③ **屋内と屋外の両方で時間を過ごす**
④ 公共交通を利用して動き回る

　正解は③。下の表に示すように，3つのツアーすべてが，屋内と屋外の両方の活動を含んでいると考えられることから，③が正解となる。

— 英 R 214 —

	屋内での活動と考えられるもの	屋外での活動と考えられるもの
歴史ツアー	・教会の見学 ・市長舎の見学	・市長舎の庭園の見学 ・平和公園の見学
芸術ツアー	・美術館の見学 ・音楽堂でのコンサートに参加 ・アトリエ見学	・芸術家通りまでの徒歩移動 ・彫刻公園の散策
スポーツツアー	・ホッケー競技場内の展示ホールの見学 ・ホッケー競技場で試合の見学	・屋外施設でのトレーニング見学

①については，芸術ツアーやスポーツツアーの項に明確な記述がないため，正解にはなれない。②については，芸術ツアーで行われる「芸術家の制作活動の見学」や，スポーツツアーで行われる「プロのホッケーチームの練習や試合の見学」が，これに該当すると考えることはできるが，歴史ツアーにはこれに該当する活動がないので，②は正解になれない。④については，芸術ツアーの項に該当する記述がない。

問3　5　正解－①

「ツアーで訪れることのできる，イエントンビルの中の最も新しい場所はどれか」

① ホッケー競技場
② 市長舎
③ 平和公園
④ 彫刻公園

正解は①。①の「ホッケー競技場」については，スポーツツアーの項の第2文（In the afternoon, ...）に「午後は，昨秋に（last fall）完成したイエントンビルホッケー競技場まで地下鉄で移動します」とある。②の「市長舎」については，歴史ツアーの項の第2文（Opposite the church ...）に「教会の向かい側には，20世紀初めの（early-20th-century）市長舎があります」とある。③の「平和公園」については，歴史ツアーの項の最終文（Opened soon after ...）に「ここは第二次世界大戦のすぐ後に（soon after World War II）開園し，1960年代にはここで数多くのデモ活動が行われました」とある。④の「彫刻公園」については，芸術ツアーの項の第4文（This part of the district ...）に「この区域は数年前（several years ago），新しい芸術家たちのアトリエと近隣にある彫刻公園が造られた時に開発され

ました」とある。これら下線部の表現を比較することで，最も新しい場所は①のホッケー競技場であることがわかる。

〈主な語句・表現〉

Opposite the church is ...「教会の向かい側には…がある」／ soon after ...「…のすぐ後に」／ site 图「場所；現場」／ district 图「地域；地区」／ art gallery「美術館」／ sculpture 图「彫刻」／ at work「活動［仕事］中で」／ first thing in the morning「朝一番に」／ open-air 形「野外の」／ facility 图「施設」／ arena 图「競技場」／ exhibition 图「展示」

第2問

A

〈全訳〉

　あなたは英国の高校の交換留学生で，次のようなチラシを見つけます。

戦略ゲーム部へのお誘い

　チェスや将棋や碁などの戦略ゲームを覚えたいと思ったことはありませんか。これらは実際はただのゲームではないのです。気を散らすことなく論理的に深く考えるといった技術を身につけることができます。加えて，これらのゲームは本当に楽しいのです！　この部は我が校のすべての生徒に開かれています。上手下手に関係なく，入部を歓迎します。

私たちは一緒に戦略ゲームをプレーして…

● 部員による実演から基本的な動きを学びます
● 部の仲間とオンラインで対戦します
● 部のウェブページで秘訣を共有します
● それぞれのゲームの歴史や作法を学びます
● コンピューターのソフトを使ってゲームを分析します
● 地元や全国のトーナメントに参加します

定例会：水曜日の午後，スチューデントセンターの301号室にて

- -

部員のコメント

－ 授業中に頭がよりはっきりして，落ち着いて，集中できています。
－ 一部のゲームにある種の類似点があることを学べるのってすごいです。
－ トーナメントでは，他の参加者と戦略について話し合うのが私は好きです。
－ 部員たちはチェスの実際的な戦略を説明するインターネット動画を共有しています。
－ 碁についての良いアドバイスをしてくれる友達を持ててうれしいです。
－ 私は入部した時まったくの初心者でしたが，全然問題ありませんでした！

〈設問解説〉

　問1　　6　　正解－①

「チラシによると，この部について言えることはどれか」

① **完全な初心者も歓迎される。**
② 部員はコンピュータープログラムを編集する。
③ プロのプレーヤーが正式な対戦を披露する。
④ 他校の生徒も入部できる。

　正解は①。チラシ上部にある勧誘文の第1段落最終文（Regardless of skill level, ...）に「上手下手に関係なく，入部を歓迎します」とあり，「部員のコメント（Member Comments）」の最後のコメント（I was a complete beginner ...）にも「私は入部した時まったくの初心者でしたが，全然問題ありませんでした！」とあることから，①は正しいと言える。

　②の「コンピュータープログラムの編集（edit）」や，③の「プロの（professional）プレーヤー」については，本文中では述べられていない。④のような，「他校の生徒が入部できる」という記述もない。

　問2　　7　　正解－②

「次の中で，部の活動として述べられて<u>いない</u>ものはどれか」

① 部員でない人たちと対戦すること
② **コンピューターと対戦すること**
③ ゲームのプレーに関するアイディアをインターネット上で共有すること
④ 戦略ゲームの背景を調べること

　正解は②。②の「コンピューターとの対戦（Playing matches）」については，本文中に記述がないので，これが正解となる。

　①については，チラシの勧誘文の中で，部の活動内容について丸印（●）付きの箇条書き形式で説明している最後の項目（participate in ...）に「地元や全国のトーナメントに参加します」とあることなどから，部員でない人々とも対戦をすると考えられるので，正解にはなれない。③の「ゲームのプレーに関するアイディア（game-playing ideas）をインターネット上で共有すること」については，丸印の3つ目の項目（share tips on ...）に「部のウェブページで秘訣（tips）を共有します」とあり，「部員のコメント」の4つ目（Members share ...）に「部員たちはチェスの実際的な戦略を説明するインターネット動画（Internet videos that explain practical strategies）を共有しています」とある。3つの下線部は，ほぼ同内容と考えられることから，③も正解にはなれない。④の「戦略ゲームの背景（backgrounds）を調べること」については，

丸印の4つ目（learn the history ...）に「それぞれのゲームの歴史（history）や作法を学びます」とあり，2つの下線部はほぼ同内容と考えられることから，④も正解にはなれない。

問3　**8**　正解－①

「ある部員が述べた1つの**意見**は，**8**ということだ」

① **異なるゲームを比較するのは面白い**
② 碁に関する多くの動画は役に立つ
③ 部員たちは競技会で秘訣を学ぶ
④ 定例会は学外で開かれる

正解は①。「部員のコメント」の2つ目（It's cool to ...）に，「一部のゲームにある種の類似点があることを学べるのってすごいです」とあることから，これとほぼ同内容と考えられる①が正解となる。

②の「碁に関する多くの動画は役に立つ」という意見を述べている部員はいないので，これは正解にはなれない。③や④は，「意見（opinion）」とみなすことはできないので，正解にはなり得ない。

問4　**9**　正解－④

「部からの勧誘文とある部員のコメントはどちらも**9**ということに触れている」

① 新しい部員は経験があることを見せなければならない
② 良いプレーヤーになるにはオンラインによるサポートが必要だ
③ 将棋は論理的で刺激的なゲームだ
④ **戦略ゲームは集中力を高めるのに役立つ**

正解は④。勧誘文の第1段落第3文（You can learn ...）に「気を散らすことなく（without distractions）論理的に深く考えるといった技術を身につけることができます」とあり，部員のコメントの1番目（My mind is ...）に「授業中に頭がよりはっきりして，より落ち着いて，より集中できています（more focused）」とある。2つの下線部は，いずれも④の中の「集中力を高める（improve concentration）」とほぼ同内容と考えられることから，④が正解となる。

①や②のようなことは，本文では述べられていない。③のようなことをコメントとして述べている部員もいない。

問5　**10**　正解－②

「この部は，**10**ことを望んでいる生徒に最も適している可能性が高い」

① 自分独自のコンピューター戦略ゲームを作り出す
② **戦略ゲームをプレーする技術レベルを上げる**
③ 戦略ゲームのプレーを通じて，英国の適切な作法を学ぶ
④ 部室で戦略ゲームをプレーして週末を過ごす

正解は②。消去法で考えるとわかりやすい。戦略ゲーム部は，チェスや将棋や碁を楽しむクラブであって，①のように「自分独自のコンピューター戦略ゲームを作り出す」ことについては全く述べられていないので，これは誤りとなる。また，部の活動内容として，勧誘文中の第2段落の丸印の4つ目の項（learn the history ...）に「それぞれのゲームの歴史や作法を学びます」とあるが，③のように「英国の適切な作法を学ぶ」とは述べられていないので，これも誤りである。また④のように「週末に」部室が利用できるとも本文には書かれていない。

これに対して②の「戦略ゲームをプレーする技術レベルを上げる」ことについては，本文中にこれと合わない記述はなく，逆に勧誘文の第2段落の活動内容の説明の中の「部員による実演から基本的な動きを学びます（learn basic moves ...）」，「部のウェブページで秘訣を共有します（share tips on ...）」，「コンピューターのソフトを使ってゲームを分析します（analyse games using ...）」などの活動は，②のようなことを希望する生徒にとっては有益なことと考えられるので②が正解となる。

〈主な語句・表現〉

strategy 图「戦略」／ logically 副「論理的に」／ distraction 图「気を散らすこと」／ regardless of ...「…に関係なく」／ demonstration 图「実演」／ tip 图「秘訣」／ etiquette 图「エチケット；作法」／ analyse 動「…を分析する」／ participate in ...「…に参加する」／ cool 形「かっこいい；すごい」／ participant 图「参加者」／ practical 形「実際的な；実用性のある」

— 英 R 217 —

B

〈全訳〉

　あなたは米国へ留学することになっている大学生で，旅行保険を必要としています。米国で6ヵ月間勉強した女性の留学生が書いた，以下のような保険プランについてのレビューを見つけます。

　外国旅行をする前には，考えるべきことがたくさんあります。ふさわしい衣服を荷物として詰め，旅行の費用を準備し，それから（必要ならば）薬も忘れてはいけません。さらに，旅行保険も購入するのがよいでしょう。

　私はカリフォルニアにあるフェアビル大学に留学した時，トラブセイファー・インターナショナルの旅行保険を購入しました。オンラインでの申し込みは15分もかからず，すぐに加入できました。どんな支払い方法も受け入れられ，普通は月単位です。3種類のプランがありました。すべてのプランに，1回の健康診断が含まれています。

　プレミアムプランは，月100ドルです。このプランは，スマートフォンのアプリや電話による24時間の医療サポートを提供します。入院が必要な場合は，直ちに金銭的援助が受けられます。

　スタンダードプランは私に最適でした。これには24時間の電話案内が含まれ，外国で健康に過ごすための秘訣が書かれた電子メールが毎週送られてきました。月75ドルで，安くはありませんでした。けれども，保険料を6ヵ月分前払いしたため，オプションの15パーセント割引を受けられたのは嬉しいことでした。

　予算が限られている方は，月25ドルのエコノミープランを選ぶこともできます。他のプランと同様に24時間の電話サポートが付いていますが，救急医療のみをカバーします。また，サポートセンターが必要と判断した場合は，病院までのタクシーを割引料金で手配してくれます。

　私は一度も病気や怪我をしなかったので，保険に入ったのはお金の無駄だと思っていました。するとブラジルから来た友人がサッカーをしている時に足を骨折して，数日間入院が必要となりました。彼はプレミアムプランを選んでいたので，すべてが保険でカバーされたんです！　私は保険がいかに大切かに気づきました。

困った時にサポートしてもらえるとわかっていることの大切さに。

〈設問解説〉

　問1　□11□　正解－①

「このレビューによると，次の中で正しいのはどれか」

① 最も高価なプランでは，昼夜を問わない医療扶助が受けられる。

② 最も安価なプランでは，いかなる理由であれ無料で入院できる。

③ 中間レベルのプランには，1回の健康診断は含まれない。

④ 筆者のプランの負担額は毎月100ドルを超えた。

　正解は①。①の中の「最も高価なプラン（the most expensive plan）」とは，本文中の「プレミアムプラン（the Premium Plan）」のことだが，これについて説明している第3段落第2文（The plan provides ...）に，「このプランは，スマートフォンのアプリや電話による24時間の医療サポート（24-hour medical support）を提供します」とある。下線部の表現は，①の中の「昼夜を問わない医療扶助（Day and night medical assistance）」と同内容と考えられることから，①が正解となる。

　②のようなことは，本文からは読み取れない。③は，第2段落最終文（All plans include ...）の「すべてのプランに，1回の健康診断が含まれています」という記述と合わない。第4段落第1文（The Standard Plan ...）に，「スタンダードプランは私に最適でした」とあることなどから，④の中の「筆者のプラン（The writer's plan）」とは，スタンダードプランであることがわかる。このプランは月額75ドル（同段落第3文：It wasn't cheap: ...）だが，筆者は半年分を前払いすることで15パーセントの割引を受けた（同段落最終文：However, it was nice ...）とあるので，④が誤りであることは明らかである。

　問2　□12□　正解－①

「最も安価な選択プランに含まれていないものはどれか」

① 電子メールによるサポート

② 緊急治療

③ 電話による問い合わせ窓口

④ 交通機関の補助

　正解は①。「最も安価な選択プラン（the cheapest option）」とは，「エコノミープラン（the Economy Plan）」のことである。このプランについて述べている第5段落（If your budget is ...）を参照すると，「予算

が限られている方は，月25ドルのエコノミープランを選ぶこともできます。他のプランと同様に24時間の電話サポート（telephone support → ③）が付いていますが，救急治療（emergency care → ②）のみをカバーします。また，サポートセンターが必要と判断した場合は，病院までのタクシーを割引料金で手配してくれます（arrange a taxi to a hospital at a reuduced cost → ④）」とあり，下線部の表現が，カッコ内に示した選択肢の内容に対応していることから，②や③や④は正解になれない。①については言及されていないので，これが正解となる。

問3　13　正解─①

「トラブセイファー・インターナショナルの説明として最適なのはどの組み合わせか」
A：ひと月ごとの支払いが可能である。
B：学生のための奨学金プランを計画している。
C：服薬を忘れないよう助けてくれる。
D：インターネットを用いた**登録システムを提供し**ている。
E：申請書を処理するのに数日間要する。

① ＡとＤ
② ＡとＥ
③ ＢとＤ
④ ＢとＥ
⑤ ＣとＤ

正解は①。Aについては，第2段落第3文（They accept any form ...）に「どんな支払い方法も受け入れられ，普通は月単位（on a monthly basis）です」とあることから正しい。BやCのようなことは本文中では触れられていない。Dについては，第2段落第2文（I signed up ...）に「オンラインでの申し込み（signed up online）は15分もかからず，すぐに加入できました」とあることから考えて正しい。Eについては，上の文の中に「申し込みは15分もかからず（signed up ... in less than 15 minutes）」とあるのと合わない。以上により，正解は①の「ＡとＤ」に決まる。

問4　14　正解─③

「筆者は自分の選んだプランについて　14　という**意見**を持っている」
① それは自分が健康を志向するのを妨げた
② 電話による案内に満足しなかった
③ **費用削減のためのオプションは魅力的だった**
④ 自分の足の骨折の治療費がカバーされた
正解は③。③は第4段落最終文（However, it was

nice ...）に，「けれども，保険料を6ヵ月分前払いしたため，オプションの15パーセント割引を受けられたのは嬉しいことでした（it was nice to get the optional 15% discount）」とあるのと合っている。
①のようなことは本文からは読み取れない。筆者が実際に電話サポートを受けたという記述もないので，②も誤りである。④は「自分の足の骨折（her broken leg）」が誤りであるし，「意見（opinion）」と見なすこともできないので，これも誤りである。

問5　15　正解─②

「筆者の態度を最も適切に説明しているのは次のどれか」
① スマートフォンのアプリは役に立つと信じている。
② **旅行の準備は大切だと考えている。**
③ 米国の医療制度は世界でも独特だと感じている。
④ 違う病院に行く方が友達にとっては良かっただろうと思っている。

正解は②。第1段落第1文（There are many things ...）に「外国旅行をする前には，考えるべきことがたくさんあります。…」とあり，最終段落最終文（I realized how ...）に「私は保険がいかに大切かに気づきました。…」とあることなどから，筆者は旅行をする際，旅行保険への加入などをはじめとする事前の準備が大切であると考えていることがわかるので，②が正解となる。他の選択肢を正解とするような記述は，本文中にはない。

〈主な語句・表現〉

insurance 图「保険」／ female 形「女性の」／ pack 動「〈荷物を〉詰める」／ appropriate 形「適切な」／ expenses 图「経費；支出金」／ medication 图「薬剤（治療）」／ sign up「申し込みをする」／ cover 動「…を補償する」／ payment 图「支払い」／ on a monthly basis「1ヵ月ごとに」／ health check-up「健康診断」／ app 图「アプリ（ケーション）」／ financial 形「金銭的な」／ authorize 動「…を認可［許可］する」／ work 動「機能する；うまくいく」／ optional 形「自分で選べる」／ discount 图「割引」／ coverage 图「保険の範囲」／ in advance「あらかじめ」／ budget 图「予算」／ emergency 图「緊急事態」／ at a reduced cost「割引価格で」／ in trouble「困った事態に」

— 英 R 219 —

第3問

A

〈全訳〉

　あなたの英語指導補助教員の姉妹であるスーザンが，先月あなたのクラスを訪れました。彼女は今は英国に戻っていて，ブログに自分が参加したイベントについて書きました。

こんにちは！

　私は友人たちと一緒に外国人旅行者のためのフォトラリーに参加しました。右のルールを見てください。私たちはフォトラリーの初心者だったので，チェックポイントの中の5つだけを目指すことにしました。私たちは3分で最初の目標である市立美術館に到着しました。たて続けに私たちは第2，第3，第4の目標に到達しました。万事順調！　ところが最後の目標であるこの市出身の有名な侍の像の所へ行く途中で，私たちは道に迷ってしまいました。時間はなくなってくるし，私の足は2時間以上歩いたせいで痛みました。私たちはペットの猿を連れた男性を呼び止めて助けを求めましたが，私たちの日本語も彼の英語もあまり上手ではありませんでした。彼が身振りを用いて行き方を説明してくれた後で，私たちはそこへ行く十分な時間がなく，諦めなければならないことに気づきました。私たちは彼と写真を撮って，さよならを言いました。サクラ市役所に戻った私たちは，優勝チームが19ものチェックポイントを制覇したことを聞いて驚きました。私たちの写真の1枚が選ばれて，イベントのウェブサイト上で公開されています（ここをクリック）。この写真を見ると，私は例の男性の温かさと優しさを思い出します。これは私たちだけの「金メダル」です。

サクラ市フォトラリーのルール

・各グループは**カメラ**と**紙の地図**しか使うことができません。どちらも私たちが提供します

・（観光スポットに指定されている）**25のチェックポイント**の写真をできるだけたくさん撮ってください

・制限時間は**3時間**

・写真には**3人のチームメンバー全員**が写っていないといけません

・メンバーは全員**一緒に**移動しなければなりません

・携帯電話は**禁止**

・交通機関の利用は**禁止**

〈設問解説〉

問1　16　正解—②

　「あなたはブログの中のリンクをクリックする。どの写真が出てくるだろうか」

　正解は②。本文の最後の2つの文（One of our photos ... ／ It reminds me ...）に，「私たちの写真の1枚が選ばれて，イベントのウェブサイト上で公開されています（ここをクリック）。この写真を見ると，私は例の男性の温かさと優しさを思い出します。これは私たちだけの『金メダル』です」とある。これらの文から，リンク先の写真には「例の男性（the man）」が写っていると考えられる。この男性は，ブログ本文第8文（We stopped a man ...）の中に出てくる「ペットの猿を連れた男性（a man with a pet monkey）」のことであるから，この男性が写っている選択肢②か③が正解となる。また，第10文（We took a photo ...）と第11文（When we got back ...）に，「私たちは彼と写真を撮って，さよならを言いました。サクラ市役所に戻った私たちは，優勝チームが19ものチェックポイントを制覇したことを聞いて驚きました」とある。下線部の記述から，写真はサクラ市役所に戻る前に撮られていたことがわかる。サクラ市役所はこのラリーのゴール地点と考えられることから，「ゴール！（GOAL！）」と記されている③も誤りである。したがって正解は②に決まる。

問2　17　正解—②

　「あなたはスーザンのブログにコメントすることを求められる。彼女へのコメントとして適切なものはどれか」

　① あなたが金メダルをつけている写真を見たいな。

　② あなたは最善を尽くしたね。日本へ戻ってきてもう一度やってみて！

　③ 19のチェックポイントに3時間で到達したの？本当？　うわー！！

　④ あなたの写真はすばらしいね！　電話をアップグレードしたの？

　正解は②。消去法で考えるとわかりやすい。①については，スーザンは実際には金メダルを獲得していないことから，コメントとして不適切である。なお，最終文（It reminds me ...）に「この写真を見ると，私は例の男性の温かさと優しさを思い出します。これは私たちだけの『金メダル』です」とあるが，下線部の「金メダル」とは，「貴重なもの」といった意味を表す比喩表現であって，実際の金メダルのことではない。③については，「19のチェックポイントに3時間で到達した」のは，優勝チームであって（第11文：When we got ...），スーザンのチームではないので，やはり誤り

— 英 R 220 —

である。④は，スーザンがラリー中に携帯電話で写真を撮ったことを前提とするコメントだが，「サクラ市フォトラリーのルール（Sakura City Photo Rally Rules）」の6つ目の項目に，「携帯電話は禁止（No mobile phones）」とあることから，ラリー中にスーザンが携帯電話で写真を撮ることはありえないので，これも正解になれない。

これに対して②は本文の内容と合わない点を含んでいないので，これが正解となる。冒頭の状況説明文の第2文（Now back in the UK, ...）に，「（スーザンは）今は英国に戻っていて，ブログに自分が参加したイベントについて書きました」とあるので，②の第2文（Come back to ...）の「日本へ戻ってきてもう一度やってみて！」も現状に合ったコメントとなる。

〈主な語句・表現〉
ALT图「外国語指導補助教員（Assistant Language Teacher）」／ take part [participate] in ...「…に参加する」／ aim for ...「…を目指す」／ in quick succession「たて続けに」／ on the way to ...「…へ行く途中で」／ statue图「像」／ get lost「道に迷う」／ run out「〈時間が〉なくなる」／ for help「助けを求めて」／ neither A nor B「AもBも…しない」／ remind A of B「AにBを思い出させる」／ as many ... as possible「できるだけ多くの…」／ designate動「…を指定する」／ sightseeing spot「観光地［名所］」／ transport图「交通機関」

B
〈全訳〉
あなたはイングリッシュデーに参加することにしています。あなたはその準備として，昨年それに参加したユズが書いた学校新聞の記事を読んでいます。

サウスシーアイランドへのバーチャル野外旅行

今年，イングリッシュデーとして，私たちはバーチャルサイエンスツアーに参加しました。冬の天気がひどかったので，私たちはスクリーンに投影される火山島の熱帯の景色を見てワクワクしました。

まず最初に私たちは，島の地形について学ぶため，ルートを見るためのナビソフトを利用して，「自動車旅行に出かけました」。私たちは「車に乗り込み」ましたが，窓の外を見て熱帯雨林の様子がより良くわかるようにと（→問1①），担任のリーチ先生は時々車を止めてく

れました。それが終わると，私たちはリーチ先生に，見たものについて質問をしました。

その後，私たちは「海に飛び込んで」，海洋生物の多様性について学びました。私たちはライブカメラを通して，サンゴ礁を観察しました。リーチ先生は私たちに，生き物の数を数えられますかと聞いてきましたが，数が多すぎました！　それから先生は10年前の海のイメージを見せてくれました。カメラを通して見たサンゴ礁は活動的でしたが，写真で見るとさらに生き生きしていました。10年経っただけでまったく違うように見えました（→問1②）。リーチ先生は私たちに，人間の活動が海に影響を及ぼしていて，私たちが今すぐ行動しなければ海は台無しになるだろうとおっしゃいました。

夜になると，私たちは「完璧な星空」の下で天文学を勉強しました。体育館にテントを張って，プロジェクターを使って天井に臨時のプラネタリウムを作りました（→問1③）。私たちは星座，流れ星，天の川が空いっぱいに広がっているのに魅了されました（→問1④）。誰かが一番明るく光るものの1つを指し示して，リーチ先生にあれが地球に近い惑星である金星ですかと尋ねました。先生はうなずいて，人間は人工的な光をたくさん作り出してしまったために，私たちの市の夜空にはほとんど何も見えないと説明されました。

学校が終わり家路に着いた頃には，天気は回復していて空にはもう雲はありませんでした。私は月の無い空を見上げて，リーチ先生が私たちにおっしゃったことは本当であることに気づきました。

〈設問解説〉
問1　正解　18 －①，19 －②
　　　　　　20 －③，21 －④
「ユズの投稿記事には，バーチャルツアーのイベントについて述べている生徒のコメントも含まれていた。これらのコメントを，イベントが起きた順に並べなさい」
①　私は島がどれほど危険なのかなと思っていました。美しい鳥やとても大きな蛇がジャングルにいました。
②　以前ははるかに多くの生物がいたということには本当にびっくりしました。私たちは美しい海を保護するべきです！
③　体育館にキャンプ場を設置するのはやや奇妙でしたが，とても楽しいことでした！　虫に噛まれることがなかったので，外でやるよりもいいですね！

— 英 R 221 —

④ 宇宙ショーの間，私たちは言葉を失い，そこにあるのにしばしば存在に気づかないものがあることを知りました。

正解は①→②→③→④。本文は，バーチャルサイエンスツアーのイベントについて，それらが行われた順序通りに述べているので，各選択肢に対応するイベントを本文中に見つけて，出て来る順序通りに並べればよい。

①については，この中の「ジャングル（the jungle）」が，「全訳」の第2段落中の下線部の中の「熱帯雨林（the rainforest）」を言い換えたものであることに気づけば，①は第2段落のバーチャルな「自動車旅行（a road trip）」について述べたものであるとわかる。

②については，これが「海（oceans）」を話題にしていること，そしてこの中の「以前は（before）」が，全訳の第3段落中の下線部内の「10年前（ten years ago）」を言い換えたものであることに気づけば，②は第3段落のバーチャルな「ダイビング」について述べたものであるとわかる。

③については，「体育館にキャンプ場を設置する（Setting up a camping site in the gymnasium）」とあり，これが全訳の第4段落の最初の下線部内の「体育館にテントを張って（put up tents in the gymnasium）」の言い換えと考えられるので，③はバーチャルな天体観測の準備としての「臨時のプラネタリウム（a temporary planetarium）」について述べているものだとわかる。

④については，前半の「宇宙ショーの間，私たちは言葉を失い」の部分が，全訳の第4段落の2つ目の下線部とほぼ同内容と考えられる。また後半の「そこにあるのにしばしば存在に気づかないものがあることを知りました」という意見も，同段落最終文（He nodded and explained ...）にあるリーチ先生の説明と合う内容である。したがって④は，最後のイベントであるバーチャルな「完璧な星空」の観測についてのコメントだとわかる。なおこのイベントは，「臨時のプラネタリウム」の設営後でないと行えないので，③の後に来る必要がある。以上により，正しい順序は①→②→③→④に決まる。

問2 　22 　正解－③
「このツアーから，ユズはサウスシーアイランドの 22 については学ばなかった」
① 海洋生態系
② 夜間の空
❸ 季節特有の天候
④ 木や植物

正解は③。このツアーでは，「季節特有の天候」に関するイベントは特に行われなかったので，③が正解となる。なお，第1段落第2文（The winter weather ...）に「冬の天気がひどかったので，私たちはスクリーンに投影される火山島の熱帯の景色を見てワクワクしました」とあり，最終段落第1文（On my way home ...）に「学校が終わり家路に着いた頃には，天気は回復していて空にはもう雲はありませんでした」とあるが，これらにおいて筆者はツアー前後の天気を話題にしているだけであり，ツアー自体から学んだことを述べているのではないことに注意。

①の「海洋生態系」については，第3段落第1文(Later, we "dived into the ocean" ...)に「その後，私たちは『海に飛び込んで』，海洋生物の多様性について学びました」とあることなどから考えて，ユズは海洋生態系についてある程度学んだと考えることができるので，①は正解になれない。②の「夜間の空」については，第4段落第1文（In the evening, ...）に「夜になると，私たちは『完璧な星空』の下で天文学を勉強しました」とあることと合っているので，やはり正解になれない。④の「木や植物」については，第2段落第2文（We "got into the car," ...）に「私たちは『車に乗り込み』ましたが，窓の外を見て熱帯雨林の様子がより良くわかるようにと，担任のリーチ先生は時々車を止めてくれました」とあり，ユズは（主に木や植物からなる）熱帯雨林の観察をしたことがわかるので，④もユズが学んだことに含まれると考えられる。

問3 　23 　正解－②
「帰宅途中で，ユズは上空を見ておそらく夜空の中の 23 を見たであろう」
① 流れ星
❷ ごく少数の星
③ 満月
④ 天の川

正解は②。最終段落最終文（I looked up ...）に「私は月の無い空を見上げて，リーチ先生が私たちにおっしゃったことは本当であることに気づきました」とあることから，下線部の「リーチ先生が私たちにおっしゃったこと（what Mr Leach had told us）」と合うものが正解となる。第4段落最終文（He nodded and explained ...）に，「（リーチ）先生はうなずいて，人間は人工的な光をたくさん作り出してしまったために，私たちの市の夜空にはほとんど何も見えないと説明されました」とあることから，下線部の内容に最も近い②が正解となる。他の選択肢は，いずれもリーチ先生の言葉とは無関係なので，正解にはなれない。

〈主な語句・表現〉

第1段落（This year, ...）
　virtual 形「仮想の；バーチャルな」／ tropical 形「熱帯の」／ scenery 名「風景」／ volcanic 形「火山のある」／ project 動「…を映写［投影］する」

第2段落（First, we ...）
　road trip「自動車旅行」／ geography 名「地形」／ navigation 名「航行；誘導」／ get a sense of ...「…を感じ取る；…の見当をつける」／ rainforest 名「熱帯雨林」

第3段落（Later, we ...）
　dive 動「飛び込む」／ diversity 名「多様性」／ marine 形「海の」／ coral reef「サンゴ礁」／ dynamic 形「活動的な」／ affect 動「…に影響する」／ ocean 名「海（洋）」／ ruin 動「…を台無しにする」

第4段落（In the evening, ...）
　astronomy 名「天文学」／ starry 形「星の多い」／ put up「…を建てる」／ gymnasium 名「体育館」／ temporary 形「一時的な」／ planetarium 名「プラネタリウム」／ ceiling 名「天井」／ fascinate 動「…を魅了する」／ constellation 名「星座」／ shooting star「流れ星」／ the Milky Way「天の川」／ Venus 名「金星」／ planet 名「惑星」／ nod 動「うなずく」／ artificial 形「人工的な」／ hardly anything「ほとんど何も…しない（≒ almost nothing）」／ visible 形「目に見える」

最終段落（On my way home ...　）
　on one's way home「家へ帰る途中で」／ improve 動「回復する」／ moonless 形「月のない」／ realise (that) ...「…ということをはっきりと理解する［に気づく］」

第4問

〈全訳〉

あなたの大学の英語クラブの部室にはいくつかの問題があり，あなたは部室を改装したいと思っています。以下の記事と部員を対象としたアンケート結果に基づいて，あなたはグループ討論のための資料を作成します。

良い教室には何が必要か？

ダイアナ・バッシュワース，

Trends in Education ライター

　多くの学校が教室の改善に取り組んでいる今，デザインについての決定を行うためのアイディアをいくつか持っておくのは大事なことです。SIN とは「刺激（Stimulation）」，「個別化（Individualization）」，「自然らしさ（Naturalness）」を表し，これは教室のデザインを考える時に考慮に入れると役に立つかもしれないフレームワークです。

　第1の「刺激」には2つの面があります。色と複雑さです。これは天井，床，壁，内装と関係があります。例えば，色合いに乏しい教室は退屈に感じるかもしれません。その一方で，教室は華やかになりすぎてもいけません。明るい色を1枚の壁や，床や，窓おおいや，家具に用いるのはよいかもしれません。加えて，壁にあまりに多くのものを飾っておくと，目を奪われて気が散ることがあります。壁面空間の20から30パーセントは空けておくことが勧められています。

　このフレームワークの次の項目は「個別化」ですが，ここにおいて考慮されるのは，オーナーシップとフレキシビリティの2点です。オーナーシップとは，教室が一人一人に合わせて作られていると感じるかどうかを指します。この例に含まれるのは，生徒の体の大きさや年齢に適した椅子や机があること，収納スペースや生徒の作品や学習課題を展示するための場所を備えていることなどです。フレキシビリティとは要するに，様々な種類の活動を可能にする教室があるということです。

　「自然らしさ」とは，自然光と人工的な光の両方の質と量，そして教室の温度に関わるものです。自然光が多すぎると，スクリーンやボードが見えづらくなり，光が乏しいと，生徒たちは読み書きがしづらいかもしれません。また，暑い夏の教室は効果的な学習を促しません。学校は光と温度の両方の調節を可能にする設備を導入するべきです。

　「自然らしさ」は私たちにより馴染みがあり，それゆ

えしばしば優先事項と考えられますが，他の要素も同じくらい重要なのです。こういった考え方により，皆さんの取り組みが最終的に成功することを望んでいます。

アンケートの結果

質問１：あなたの英語クラブの部室の利用法に合っている項目を選んでください。

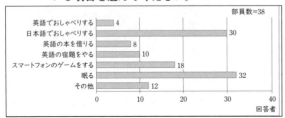

質問２：現在の英語クラブの部室についてどう思いますか。

主なコメント：

生徒１（S1）：天気の良い日には，プロジェクターのスクリーンやホワイトボードがよく見えません。また，温度を調節する方法もありません。

S2：窓際では，日光のせいで読むのに苦労します。教室の反対側だと十分な光量が得られません。また，本は整理されていなくて，壁はポスターだらけです。そのせいで居心地が悪く感じます。

S3：椅子はあまり自分に合わず，小さなグループで活動する時には机を動かすのが大変です。また，ここは英語クラブなのに，多くの部員は日本語を話しています。

S4：壁に貼ってある外国の写真を見ると，英語を話したくなります。みんなソファが好きです。ソファはとても快適で，眠るために部室を利用することもよくあります。

S5：部室はとても遠いので，私はめったに行きません！他に利用できる部屋はないのでしょうか？

S6：部室は灰色の部分が多いですね。私は好きではありません。でも壁に日常の英語のフレーズがたくさん掲げられているのはいいですね！

あなたの討論用資料：

部室改善プロジェクト

■ SIN フレームワーク
- どういうものか： 24
- SIN =「刺激(Stimulation)」,「個別化(Individualization)」,「自然らしさ(Naturalness)」

■ SIN とアンケート結果に基づくデザインの推奨案
-「刺激」：
  床に色彩豊かな絨毯を敷いて， 25 。

-「個別化」：
  部室の家具類を取り替える。
  （キャスター付きのテーブル→移動が簡単）

-「自然らしさ」：
  26
  A．窓に日除けを取り付ける。
  B．温度調節を可能にする。
  C．プロジェクターのスクリーンを窓から離す。
  D．ソファを壁の近くに置く。
  E．暗い方のコーナーにフロアランプを置く。

■ その他の議論すべき問題
- 28 のコメントが触れているように，部員の大多数が部室 27 。これはどうすれば改善できるか？
- グラフと 29 のコメントに基づいて，部員たちに英語をもっと話そうという気にさせるため，部室内での言葉に関するルールを定める方がよいだろうか？
- S5 は部室の場所が好きではないが，部室を変更することはできないので，部員が部室をより頻繁に訪れるのを促す方法を考えよう。

〈設問解説〉

問１　正解　24 ― ③

「 24 に入れるのに最適な選択肢を選びなさい」

① どの色が教室で使うのに適しているかを示してくれる指標
② 教室での生徒と先生の必要に優先順位をつける方法
③ 教室環境を設計する際に従うべきモデル
④ 教室が生徒の成績にどのように影響を及ぼすかを理解するためのシステム

正解は③。空所 24 には，SIN Framework の一般的

特徴を的確に言い表したもの（What it is）が入る。冒頭の記事の第1段落第2文（SIN, which stands for ...）に、「SIN とは『刺激（Stimulation）』、『個別化（Individualization）』、『自然らしさ（Naturalness）』を表し、これは教室のデザインを考える時に考慮に入れると役に立つかもしれないフレームワークです」とあることから、下線部の内容に最も近い③が正解となる。③の中の「教室環境（classroom environments）」とは、「教室内での学習活動に影響を及ぼす事物・状況」を表している。このように SIN は、教室のデザインを考える際の指標として適しているものであり、SIN によって、教室が生徒の成績にどのようにして影響を及ぼすかが理解できる、とは述べられていない。したがって④は、SIN の一般的特徴を表しているとは言えない。また SIN は「教室の色」のみに関するものではないので、①も誤りである。②のようなことも本文では述べられていない。

問2 　25　 正解－④

「25に入れるのに最適な選択肢を選びなさい」

① スクリーンをより良い場所に移動する
② それぞれの壁を違う色に塗る
③ 本を棚にしまう
④ 展示［掲示］されている物を減らす

正解は④。空所25を含む文（Cover the floor ...）の内容を、SIN における「刺激（Stimulation）」に関して述べられていることと、アンケート結果で述べられていることの両方から考えて「推奨されること（Recommendations）」にすることが求められている。まず SIN における「刺激（Stimulation）」について述べられているのは、冒頭記事中の第2段落（The first, Stimulation, ...）なので、この段落の中で述べられていることと合う選択肢が正解の候補となる。第6文（In addition, ...）に、「加えて、壁にあまりに多くのものを飾ると、目を奪われて気が散ることがあります」とある。④は下線部と反対のことを述べているので、④は「刺激」の面から推奨されることであると考えられる。さらに、アンケート結果の質問2（Q2）に対する主なコメントの中でも、S2 が「また、本は整理されていなくて、壁はポスターだらけです（Also, the books ...）。そのせいで居心地が悪く感じます（It makes me ...）」と述べている。この文の下線部も、やはり④の内容と反対のことを述べているので、④はアンケート結果に基づいても推奨されることと考えることができる。以上により④が正解に決まる。

①の「スクリーン（の位置）」や、③の「本の整理」については、記事中で「刺激（Stimulation）」について述べている第2段落中に該当する記述がないので、

いずれも正解にはなりえない。②については、第2段落第4文（On the other hand, ...）と第5文（A bright color ...）に、「その一方で、教室は華やかになりすぎてもいけません（should not be too colorful）。明るい色を1枚の壁（one wall）や、床や、窓おおいや、家具に用いるのはよいかもしれません」とある。下線部に注意することで、②の「それぞれの壁を違う色に塗る」は、記事の内容と合わないことがわかる。

問3 　26　 正解－④

「あなたは資料をチェックしていて、『自然らしさ』の項にある推奨案の中の誤りに気づく。次の中で、取り除くべきものはどれか」

① A
② B
③ C
④ D
⑤ E

正解は④。冒頭記事の中で、「自然らしさ（Naturalness）」について述べられているのは第4段落（Naturalness relates to ...）なので、この段落の内容と合わない、あるいは無関係なものが正解となる。同段落第2文（Too much natural light ...）に「(1)自然光が多すぎると、スクリーンやボードが見えづらくなり、(2)光が乏しいと、生徒たちは読み書きがしづらいかもしれません」とある。A の「窓に日除けを取り付ける」と、C の「プロジェクターのスクリーンを窓から離す」は、いずれも下線部(1)の事態を解決するための推奨案として、適切な内容である。また、E の「暗い方のコーナーにフロアランプを置く」は、下線部(2)の事態に対する推奨案として適切である。そして B の「温度調節を可能にする」は、同段落最終文（Schools should install ...）に「学校は光と温度の両方の調節を可能にする設備を導入するべきです」とあることから考えて、やはり適切である。これに対して、D の「ソファを壁の近くに置く」は、第4段落中に対応する記述がないことから、「自然らしさ」との関係性が乏しいため、これが正解となる。

問4 　正解　27－⑤、28－④

「27と28に入れるのに最適な選択肢を選びなさい」
27

① から本を借りる
② に簡単に行けない
③ で日本語を使わない
④ で不安を感じる
⑤ で仮眠をとる

— 英 R 225 —

28

① S1
② S2
③ S3
④ **S4**
⑤ S5
⑥ S6

正解は 27 が ⑤，28 が ④。部員の大多数（The majority of members）が部室に関して行っていることが 27 に入り，それについてコメントしている人物が 28 に入る。「部員の大多数が行っていること」と考えられるのは，「アンケートの結果（Results of the Questionnaire）」の「質問 1（Q1）」の項にあるグラフを参照することで，38 人中 30 人がしている「日本語でおしゃべりする（Chatting in Japanese）」と，32 人がしている「眠る（Sleeping）」であるとわかる。この 2 つのうち，「日本語でおしゃべりする」は，選択肢に該当するものがなく，「眠る」は ⑤ の「仮眠（naps）をとる」に該当することから，27 は ⑤ が正解となる。そして，「アンケートの結果」の「質問 2（Q2）」の中の S4 のコメントの第 2 文（Everyone likes the sofas ...）に，「みんなソファが好きです。ソファはとても快適で，眠るために（for sleeping）部室を利用することもよくあります」とあることから，28 は ④ が正解となる。

問 5　正解　29 － ③

「29 に入れるのに最適な選択肢を選びなさい」

① S1
② S2
③ **S3**
④ S4
⑤ S5
⑥ S6

正解は ③。29 を含む文（Based on both ...）の内容から，「部員が英語をもっと話す気にさせる（motivate members to speak English more）」ためのルール作りの必要性に関連するコメントをしている生徒が正解となる。S3 のコメントの第 2 文（Also, lots of members ...）に「また，ここは英語クラブなのに，多くの部員は日本語を話しています」とあり，S3 は英語を話す部員が少ないことを問題視していることが読み取れるので，③ が正解となる。他の部員のコメントからは，このような問題意識は感じ取れないので，③ 以外は正解になれない。

〈主な語句・表現〉

リード文

based on ...「…に基づいて」／ following 形「次に来る；下記の」／ questionnaire 名「アンケート」／ handout 名「プリント；資料」

記事

framework 名「枠組み；フレームワーク」／ aspect 名「側面」／ complexity 名「複雑さ」／ have to do with ...「…と関係がある」／ furnishings 名「備え付け家具；備品」／ uninteresting 形「面白くない；退屈な」／ on the other hand「他方；それに対して」／ in addition「加えて；さらに」／ visually 副「視覚的に」／ distracting 形「気を散らせる」／ display 動「…を展示［掲示］する」／ item 名「項目；事項」／ consideration 名「考慮すべきこと」／ ownership 名「所有（者であること）；オーナーシップ」／ flexibility 名「柔軟性；フレキシビリティ」／ refer to ...「…のことを言う；…を表す［示す］」／ personalized 形「個人向けにした」／ suitable 形「適した」／ storage space「収納スペース」／ allow for ...「…を考慮に入れる；…を可能にさせる」／ relate to ...「…に関係がある」／ quality 名「質」／ quantity 名「量」／ artificial 形「人工の」／ temperature 名「温度」／ have difficulty － ing「－するのに苦労する」／ lack 名「不足；欠乏」／ promote 動「…を促進する」／ effective 形「効果的な」／ install 動「…を取り付ける」／ adjustment 名「調節」／ be familiar to ...「…に馴染みがある」／ priority 名「優先事項」／ component 名「（構成）要素」／ equally 副「同様に」／ hopefully 副「願わくば；できれば」

アンケートの結果

match 動「…と合う」／ chat 動「おしゃべりする」／ check out「（本を）借りる」／ respondent 名「回答者」／ current 形「現在の」／ disorganized 形「乱雑な」／ uncomfortable 形「心地よくない」／ hardly ever「めったに…しない」／ available 形「利用可能な」／ phrase 名「言い回し；表現」

資料

improvement 名「改善」／ recommendation 名「勧め；提案」／ cover A with B「A を B でおおう」／ rug 名「じゅうたん」／ replace 動「…を取り替える」／ place 動「…を置く」／ issue 名「問題」／ majority 名「大多数」／ mention 動「…を話に出す；…に触れる」／ motivate O to －「O を励まして－させる」／ location 名「位置；所在地」

第5問
〈全訳〉
あなたは英語の討論グループに入っていて，ストーリーを紹介する番になりました。あなたは日本の英語雑誌の中にあるストーリーを見つけました。あなたは発表のためにメモを作成しています。

マキのキッチン

「いらっしゃいませ」とマキが声をかけるなか，2人のお客さんが彼女のレストランである「マキのキッチン」に入ってきました。マキは，父親が病気になった19歳の時に，家族でやっているお店の経営に加わりました。父親が回復した後も，マキは仕事を続けることにしました。やがてマキの両親は身を引いて，彼女がオーナーになりました。マキには常連のお客さんがたくさんいて，彼らはおいしいものを食べに来るだけではなく，カウンターに座って彼女とおしゃべりするためにやって来ました。お店はとてもうまくいっていましたが，時折マキは違うことをしている空想にふけることがありました。

「カウンターに座ってもいいですか？」という声を彼女は聞きました。そこには長年の友人であるタクヤとカスミがいました。数週間前にカスミがタクヤに電話をした時に，彼らはマキを尋ねて驚かそうと思いついたのでした。

タクヤの電話が振動して，カスミという馴染みのある名前が目に入りました。
「カスミ！」
「こんにちは，タクヤ，新聞にあなたが出ているのを見たわ。おめでとう！」
「ありがとう。ねえ，君は先月の20回目の高校の同窓会にいなかったね」
「ええ，行けなかったの。卒業から20年経ったなんて信じられないわ。実はね，あなたが最近マキに会ったかどうか聞きたくて電話してみたの」

タクヤの家族は，彼が高校に入る少し前に川中町に引っ越して来ました。彼は演劇部に入り，そこでマキやカスミと出会いました。3人は親友になりました。卒業後，タクヤは俳優になるため川中を離れましたが，マキとカスミは残りました。マキは大学で勉強したいという気持ちを固め，予備校に入学しました。一方カスミは就職しました。タクヤはいろいろな役柄に応募したものの，いつも不採用とされ，結局辞めてしまいました。

卒業からちょうど1年後に，タクヤは夢破れて川中に戻って来ました。彼がマキに電話すると，マキは同情してくれました。マキが家族でやっているレストランの経営をしなければならないので大学へ通う計画を断念したことを知って，タクヤは驚きました。彼女が仕事を始めた日が，彼が電話をした日でした。どういうわけか，タクヤはマキに助言せずにはいられませんでした。

「マキ，お宅のレストランで出しているコーヒーは変える方がいいと僕はいつも思っていたんだ。川中の人たちはもっと強い風味を望んでいると思うんだ。よかったらお勧めの別の銘柄を教えるよ」と彼は言いました。

「タクヤ，あなたは本当にコーヒー通ね。そういえば，カフェ・カワナカの前を通ったら，求人の掲示があったわ。あなたは応募するべきよ！」とマキは答えました。

タクヤはカフェ・カワナカに雇われて，コーヒー作りの技術に魅了されました。タクヤは仕事を始めてから1年目の記念日に，マキのレストランで彼女と話していました。

「マキ，僕の夢が何だか知っているかい？」と彼は言いました。
「きっとコーヒーに関係のあることね」
「その通り！ 自分のコーヒー店を持つことさ」
「あなたに勝る人はいないわ。何をぐずぐずしているの？」

マキに励まされてタクヤには意欲が出てきました。彼は仕事を辞め，コーヒー豆の焙煎機を買い，豆の焙煎を始めました。マキがレストランに「当店自慢のタクヤのコーヒーをご賞味あれ」という看板を出すと，この宣伝が役に立って，このコーヒーは川中で人気となりました。タクヤはコーヒー豆の販売でお金が儲かるようになりました。ついに彼は，自分のカフェを開店して，経営者として成功を収めたのです。

カスミが新聞を読んでいると，次のような見出しが目に入りました。「タクヤのカフェを求めて旅行者が川中に」。「タクヤがこんなに成功するなんて誰が考えたかしら？」とカスミは昔を振り返りながら心の中で思いました。

高校の演劇部でカスミは，演技をする部員たちのメイクを担当していました。彼女より上手な人はいませんでした。マキはこれに気づいて，ビューテラという化粧品会社が販売員の募集広告を出していることを知りました。彼女はカスミに応募するよう後押しして，卒業後カスミはビューテラの社員になりました。

仕事はきつく，カスミは一件一件回って化粧品を売りました。うまくいかない日に，彼女がマキに電話す

ると，マキは彼女を元気づけてくれました。ある日マキに1つのアイディアが浮かびました。「ビューテラはお化粧の講習会をやらないの？ そちらの方があなたに向いていると思うわ。化粧品の使い方を人に教えてあげるのよ。みんな自分の顔が気に入って，化粧品をたくさん買ってくれるわ！」

カスミの会社は彼女に講習会をやらせることに同意して，それはヒットしました！ カスミの売り上げ成績はとても良かったので，高校を卒業して8ヵ月経った時には，彼女は昇進していて，大都会の石島へ転居しました。それ以来，彼女は着実に会社の出世階段を上っていき，ついに今年副社長に任命されたのです。

「マキがいなかったら私は今副社長になれていないわ」と彼女は思いました。「彼女は私が苦労している時に助けてくれたのに，私は石島での仕事に没頭するあまり，彼女が予備校を辞めなければならない時に支えてあげられなかった」彼女は新聞をもう一度ちらりと見て，タクヤに電話することにしました。

「マキは同窓会にいなかったよ。もう長い間会っていないんだ」とタクヤは言いました。

「私も同じよ。残念だわ。彼女がいなかったら私たちはどうなっているのかしら」とカスミは問いかけました。

会話は途切れましたが，2人は無言で後ろめたい気持ちを伝えていました。その時，カスミはあることを思いつきました。

◆◆◆◆◆

3人の友人たちがおしゃべりをして笑っていると，「ところで，あなたたち2人に会えて本当にうれしいけど，なぜここへ来たの？」とマキは尋ねました。

「お返しだよ」とタクヤは言いました。

「わたし何か悪いことをしたかしら」とマキは尋ねました。

「いや。正反対さ。君は信じられないくらい人をよく理解できるね。人の長所を見極めて，それをどう生かすか教えてくれるんだ。僕たちがその証拠さ。君のおかげで僕たちは自分の才能に気づいたんだ」とタクヤは言いました。

「皮肉なことに，あなたは自分に対して同じことができなかったのよ」とカスミは付け加えました。

「君には石島大学がぴったりだと思うな。社会人を対象にしたカウンセリングの学位修得課程を提供しているんだ」とタクヤは言いました。

「月に数回通学しなければならないけど，わたしのところに泊まればいいわ。それに，レストランのスタッフを探す手助けはタクヤがしてくれるわ」とカスミは言いました。

マキは目を閉じて，川中に「マキのキッチン」と「マキのカウンセリング」の両方があるのを想像しました。彼女はそのアイディアが気に入りました。

あなたのノート：

マキのキッチン

ストーリーのアウトライン

マキ，タクヤ，カスミが高校を卒業する。
↓
　30
　31
　32
　33
↓
マキは第2のキャリアについて考え始める。

マキについて

・年齢：34
・職業：レストランのオーナー
・彼女はどうやって友人を支えたか：
　タクヤには励ましを与え，35。
　カスミには 〃 〃 36。

重要な節目の解釈

・カスミとタクヤは37ので，通話中に気まずい沈黙を経験する。
・最後の場面で，カスミはマキについて「皮肉」という言葉を使う。皮肉とは，マキが38ないということだ。

〈設問解説〉

問1　正解　　30 － ④，　31 － ⑤
　　　　　　　32 － ①，　33 － ②

「5つの出来事（①～⑤）の中から4つを選び，それらが起こった順に並べ直しなさい」

① カスミが会社の副社長になる。
② カスミがタクヤと連絡をとる。
③ マキが大学の学位を取得する。
④ マキが家族でやっている店で働き始める。
⑤ タクヤが自分で店を始めるよう励まされる。

　正解は④→⑤→①→②。本文のストーリーは，「◆◆◆◆◆」によって6つのセクション（以下「§」で表す）に区切られている。各セクションの内容を端的に示すと，以下のようになる。

　§1（"Irasshai-mase," said Maki ...）：マキのレストランにタクヤとカスミが訪れてきた場面
　§2（Takuya's phone vibrated, ...）：その数週間前に，カスミがタクヤに連絡をとった場面
　§3（Takuya's family had ...）：タクヤの歩み（高校入学前からカフェ開店まで）
　§4（Kasumi was reading ...）：カスミの歩み（高校時代から副社長就任まで）
　§5（"Maki wasn't at ...）：タクヤとカスミの会話
　§6（The three frinds ...）：マキのレストランでの3人の会話

　注意すべきは，全ての出来事が起こった順序通りに語られているわけではなく，§3と§4を除く4つのセクションは，時系列に沿って並べると，基本的に「§2→§5→§1→§6」という順序になる。この点に注意しつつ，各選択肢と本文の対応箇所を確認すると，以下のようになる。

　①の「カスミが会社の副社長になる」は，§4の第4段落最終文（Since then, ...）に「それ以来，彼女は着実に会社の出世階段を上っていき，ついに今年副社長に任命されたのです」とあることから，このストーリーが語られている「今年」の出来事であるとわかる。「今年」とは，§2の最後にあるカスミの発言中に，「卒業から20年経ったなんて信じられないわ（I can't believe ...）」とあることから，「卒業20年目の年」であるとわかる。

　②の「カスミがタクヤと連絡をとる」については，§4の最終段落（"I wouldn't be vice-president ...）に，「『マキがいなかったら私は今副社長になれていないわ』と彼女は思いました。『彼女は私が苦労している時に助けてくれたのに，私は石島での仕事に没頭するあまり，彼女が予備校を辞めなければならない時に支えてあげられなかった』彼女は新聞をもう一度ちらりと見て，

タクヤに電話することにしました」とある。2つの下線部に注意することで，カスミは副社長になった後で，タクヤに連絡をとることに決めたことがわかるので，「①→②」の順序になることがわかる。

　③の「マキが大学の学位を取得する」については，本文中に該当する記述がない。

　④の「マキが家族でやっている店で働き始める」については，§1の第1段落第2文（Maki had joined ...）に，「マキは，父親が病気になった19歳の時に，家族でやっているお店の経営に加わりました」とある。また，§3の第2段落第1文（Exaclty one year after ...）と第2文（He called Maki, ...）に，「卒業からちょうど1年後に，タクヤは夢破れて川中に戻って来ました。彼がマキに電話すると，マキは同情してくれました」とあり，第4文（Her first day ...）には「彼女が仕事を始めた日が，彼が電話をした日でした」とある。したがって④は，マキが19歳で，卒業から1年経った時の出来事であることがわかる。これは明らかに①より前の出来事なので，「④→①→②」の順序になることがわかる。

　⑤の「タクヤが自分の店を始めるよう励まされる」に対応するのは，§3の最終段落第1文（Maki's encouragement inspired ...）の「マキに励まされてタクヤには意欲が出てきました」などの記述である（マキがタクヤにカフェ・カワナカへの就職を勧めた§3の中ほどにある "Takuya, you really know ..." という言葉ではないことに注意）。この場面は，§3の後半部に「タクヤは（カフェ・カワナカでの）仕事を始めてから1年目の記念日に，マキのレストランで彼女と話していました（On the one-year anniversary ...）」とあることから，④の約1年後の出来事である。つまり高校を卒業して約2年後のことになるので，卒業から20年後の出来事である①よりも前に来る。以上により，「④→⑤→①→②」という順序に決まる。そして§1の最終文（A phone call ...）からわかるように，②の数週間後に，カスミとタクヤはマキの店を訪れる。店での再会の場面は最後の§6で描かれ，そこでカスミとタクヤは，マキに大学へ進学してカウンセリングの勉強をすることを勧める。そして本文の最後から2つ目の文（Maki closed her eyes ...）に，マキは「目を閉じて，川中に『マキのキッチン』と『マキのカウンセリング』の両方があるのを想像しました」とあるが，これに対応するのが，「ストーリーのアウトライン」の最後に与えられている「マキは第2のキャリアについて考え始める」である。まとめると以下のようになる。

— 英 R 229 —

３人が高校を卒業する。

↓

④　マキがレストランの仕事を始める。

↓

⑤　タクヤは自分の店を始めるよう励まされる。

↓

①　カスミが副社長に就任する。

↓

②　カスミがタクヤに連絡を取る。

↓

マキは第２のキャリアについて考え始める。

問２　正解　34 － ②

「 34 に入れるのに最適な選択肢を選びなさい」

①　30代前半

②　30代後半

③　40代前半

④　40代後半

正解は②。マキの「（このストーリーが語られている）現在」の年齢として正しいものを選ぶ。以下の３点が主な手がかりとなる。

⑴　マキは19歳の時に店の仕事を始めた（§１の第２文：Maki had joined ...）。

⑵　マキが店の仕事を始めたのは，卒業して１年後である（問１の④の解説を参照）。

⑶　「現在」では，３人が高校を卒業して20年経っている（§２の最後にあるカスミの発言中の "I can't believe it's been 20 years since we graduated."）。

以上の手がかりから，「現在」のマキの年齢は38歳と推測できるので，②が正解となる。

問３　正解　35 － ①，36 － ②

「 35 と 36 に入れるのに最適な選択肢を選びなさい」

①　製品を人々に知らせた

②　ビジネスで成功するアイディアを提案した

③　ビジネス用の設備を購入した

④　より大きな都市へ引っ越すことを提案した

⑤　成功に必要な技術を教えた

35 の正解は①。ここにはマキがタクヤを支援した方法を表すものが入る。§３の最後から３つ目の文（Maki had a sign ...）に，「マキがレストランに『当店自慢のタクヤのコーヒーをご賞味あれ』という<u>看板</u>を出すと，この宣伝が役に立って，このコーヒーは川中で人気となりました」とあることから，この内容と合っている①が正解となる。

36 の正解は②。ここにはマキがカスミを支援した方法を表すものが入る。マキがカスミにかけた言葉として，§４の第３段落第３文（One day, Maki ...）に，「ある日マキに１つのアイディアが浮かびました。『ビューテラはお化粧の講習会をやらないの？　そちらの方があなたに向いていると思うわ。化粧品の使い方を人に教えてあげるのよ。みんな自分の顔が気に入って，化粧品をたくさん買ってくれるわ！』」とある。この中のマキの言葉は，カスミが化粧品販売の仕事で成功するアイディアを提案していると考えられることから，②が正解となる。

他の選択肢のようなことをマキはタクヤにもカスミにもしていないので，これらは正解になれない。

問４　37　正解－③

「 37 に入れるのに最適な選択肢を選びなさい」

①　彼らの成功について話し合いたくない

②　長い間話していない

③　彼らの友人のありがたみがもっとわかっていなかったことを後悔している

④　マキが彼らの成し遂げたことをねたんだと思う

正解は③。 37 には，カスミとタクヤの間に気まずい沈黙が訪れた理由を表す表現が入る。§５の最後から２つ目の文（The conversation became ...）に「会話は途切れましたが，２人は無言で後ろめたい気持ちを伝えていました」とあることから，沈黙が訪れた理由は，２人が何らかの「後ろめたい気持ち（guilt）」を抱いたからだと考えられる。この「後ろめたい気持ち」が最も具体的に表現されているのは，§４の最終段落第１文（"I wouldn't be ..."）の中の「彼女（＝マキ）は私が苦労している時に助けてくれたのに，私は石島での仕事に没頭するあまり，彼女が予備校を辞めなければならない時に支えてあげられなかった」というカスミの言葉である。これはカスミが，自分の仕事に没頭することで大切な友人マキのありがたみを忘れていたことを後悔している言葉と理解することができるので，選択肢の中でこの言葉の内容に最も近い③が正解となる。

問５　38　正解－②

「 38 に入れるのに最適な選択肢を選びなさい」

①　いろいろなことを試みるのが好きでは（ない）

②　自分の才能が何かわかってい（ない）

③　自分に欠けている能力を理解してい（ない）

④　自分の夢を追いかけたいと思ってい（ない）

正解は②。本文中の「皮肉（irony）」の内容として適切なものを選ぶ。最終セクション（§６）の第５文

― 英 R 230 ―

("The irony is that ...) に，「『皮肉なことに，あなた
は自分に対して同じことができなかったのよ』とカス
ミは付け加えました」とあることから，皮肉の内容は「あ
なたは自分に対して同じことができなかった」という
ことであるが，この中の「同じこと」とは，その直前
の文 ("No. The opposite. ...) に「『いや。正反対さ。
君は信じられないくらい人をよく理解できるね。他の
人の長所を見極めて，それをどう生かすか教えてくれ
るんだ。僕たちがその証拠さ。君のおかげで僕たちは
自分の才能に気づいたんだ』とタクヤは言いました」
とあることから，この中の下線部であると考えられる。
つまり「皮肉」とは，下線部の中の「(他の) 人」を「自
分」に置き換えることができない，ということになる
ので，結局「自分をよく理解できない」，そして「自分
の長所を見極めて，それをどう生かすかがわからない」
ということになる。したがって，これらの意味に最も
近い ② が正解となる。

〈主な語句・表現〉

§ 1 ("*Irasshai-mase*," said Maki ...)

family business「家族経営の事業；家業」／
recover 動「回復する」／ eventually 副「結局；ついに」／
retire 動「引退する；身を引く」／ regular customer「常
連客」／ occasionally 副「時折」／ daydream 動「空
想する」

§ 2 (Takuya's phone vibrated, ...)

vibrate 動「振動する」／ Congratulations!「おめで
とう」／ reunion 名「同窓会」／ make it「出席する；
来る」／ graduate 動「卒業する」

§ 3 (Takuya's family had ...)

shortly before ...「…する少し前に」／ drama club「演
劇部」／ inseparable 形「離れていられない」／ enroll
in ...「…に入学する」／ preparatory school「予備校」／
on the other hand「他方」／ career 名「仕事」／ try
out for ...「…の選考試験を受ける」／ acting role「芝
居の役」／ reject 動「…を却下する」／ offer one's
sympathy「同情の気持ちを表す」／ abandon 動「…
を捨てる」／ cannot resist －ing「－することを我慢
できない」／ serve 動「〈飲食物を〉出す」／ bold 形「はっ
きりした；強い」／ flavor 名「風味」／
recommend 動「…を勧める」／ brand 名「銘柄」／
help-wanted 形「求人広告の」／ apply 動「応募する」／
hire 動「…を雇う」／ become fascinated by ...「…に
魅了される」／ anniversary 名「記念日」／
employment 名「雇用」／ have something to do with
...「…と関係がある」／ What are you waiting for?「何
をぐずぐずしているの；さっさと始めたら」／

encouragement 名「励まし」／ inspire 動「…を鼓舞
する」／ roaster 名「焙煎機」／ proudly 副「誇りを持っ
て」／ publicity 名「広告；宣伝」

§ 4 (Kasumi was reading ...)

headline 名「見出し」／ reflect on ...「…を熟考す
る」／ make-up 名「化粧（品）」／ cosmetics 名「化
粧品」／ advertise for ...「…を求めて広告を出す」／
employee 名「社員；従業員」／ tough 形「難しい；
つらい」／ door to door「家から家へ；戸別に」／ lift
her spirits「彼女を元気づける」／ workshop 名「講
習会」／ be suited for ...「…に適している」／
promote 動「…を昇進させる」／ steadily 副「着実に」／
climb one's way up the company ladder「会社の出世
の階段を登る」／ vice-president 名「副社長」／
struggle 動「格闘する；もがく」／ be absorbed「熱
中している」／ glance 動「ちらっと見る」／
article 名「記事」

§ 5 ("Maki wasn't at ...)

in ages「長い間」／ Same here.「私も同じだ」／
pity 名「残念なこと」／ wordlessly 副「言葉を用いず
に」／ guilt 名「罪悪感；うしろめたさ」

§ 6 (The three friends ...)

payback 名「お返し；仕返し」／ incredibly 副「信
じられないくらい」／ identify 動「…を特定する」／
strength 名「強み；長所」／ make use of ...「…を利
用［活用］する」／ proof 名「証拠」／ gift 名「（天賦の）
才能」／ irony 名「皮肉」／ ideal 形「理想的な」／
degree 名「学位」

第6問

A

〈全訳〉

　あなたの英語の先生は，この記事をあなたに割り当てました。あなたは短い話をするためにノートを用意しなければなりません。

時間の知覚

　「時間」という言葉を聞くと，すぐに思い浮かぶのはおそらく時間，分，秒でしょう。しかし19世紀後半に，哲学者アンリ・ベルクソンは，人は普通，時計によって測定されるような時間（**クロックタイム**）を経験しないことを説明しました。人間はクロックタイムを測定するための，既知の生物学的メカニズムを持っていないので，代わりに心理作用を用いるのです。これは**心理的時間**と呼ばれ，人によって知覚の仕方が異なるのです。

　宿題を終えるのにどのくらいかかりましたかと問われても，おそらく正確にはわからないでしょう。思い返して，概算をするでしょう。1975年に行われたある実験で，参加者たちは一定の時間，単純あるいは複雑な形を見せられ，それらを覚えるよう求められました。その後，彼らはどのくらいの間それらの形を見ていたかを問われました。彼らは答えるために，**追想的時間評価**と呼ばれる心理作用を用いました。これは記憶から取り出される情報に基づいて時間を見積もることです。複雑な形を見せられた参加者は時間をより長く感じましたが，単純な形を見た人たちは正反対の経験をしました。

　心理的時間を測定する別の方法に，**予期的時間評価**と呼ばれるものがあります。これは何かをしながら能動的に時間を計り続ける時に用いられます。想起される情報の量ではなく，活動中に時間に向けられる注意の度合いが活用されます。いくつかの研究では，参加者は課題をこなしながら，それを完成するのにかかる時間を推定しました。時間よりも課題に集中しなければならない，より負荷の高い心理的活動をしている人たちには，時間はより短く感じられました。より簡単な課題をこなした参加者には時間はより長く感じられ，待っていたり何もしていなかった人たちには最も長く感じられました。

　感情の状態も時間の意識に影響を及ぼすことがあります。例えばコンサートが楽しいあまり，時間を忘れてしまうことがあります。後になって，数時間が瞬く間に過ぎてしまったように思えてショックを受けます。これを説明するために私たちはしばしば「楽しい時間はあっという間に過ぎる」と言うのです。退屈な時には正反対のことが起こります。活動に集中する代わりに，時間の存在に気づくのです。退屈が終わるのが待ちきれないため，時はとてもゆっくり進むように思えます。恐れもまた時間の知覚に影響を及ぼします。2006年の研究では，60人を超える人々が初めてスカイダイビングを経験しました。不快な感情のレベルが高い参加者は，スカイダイビングに費やす時間を実際よりもずっと長いと思いました。

　心理的時間は，ライフステージにおいても異なる動きをするようです。子供は絶えず新しい情報に遭遇して新しい経験をしますが，これによって1日1日が記憶に残り，思い出すときにはより長く感じられるのです。さらに，誕生日や旅行など近づいてくる行事を楽しみに待つ時には時間は子供にとってゆっくりと過ぎるのです。ほとんどの大人にとっては，未知の情報に出会うことは稀で，新しい経験をすることはより少なくなるので，精神を集中する必要は減り，1日1日はより記憶に残らないものとなります。しかしながら，これはいつも正しいわけではありません。転職や新しい場所への転勤など劇的な変化が起こると，毎日の決まり事は一新されます。そのような場合には，こういった人たちにとっての時間の経過は，子供にとっての時間の経過と似ています。しかし一般的に言えば，大人になるにつれて時間は加速するようです。

　心理的時間についての知識は，退屈感に対処する一助となるかもしれないので，日常生活で役に立つ可能性があります。精神が集中していなくて時間のことを考えている時には，時間はゆっくりと過ぎるので，読書などのより興味をかき立てる活動に切り替えるのは，退屈を和らげて時間を速めるのに役立つでしょう。この次に「楽しい時間はあっという間に過ぎる」という言葉を聞いた時には，このことが思い出されるでしょう。

あなたのノート：

時間の知覚

段落別のアウトライン
1. 39
2. 追想的時間評価
3. 予期的時間評価
4. 40
   ➤ スカイダイビング
5. 年齢の影響
   ➤ 時間は歳をとるにつれて速く過ぎるが，41 。
6. 実用的な助言

聞き手を助けるための私の独自の例
A. 追想的時間評価
   例：42
B. 予期的時間評価
   例：43

〈設問解説〉

問1　正解　39 － ⑥，40 － ②

「39 と 40 に入れるのに最適な選択肢を選びなさい」

① 生物学的メカニズム
② 私たちの気持ちの影響
③ 記憶の種類
④ ライフステージ
⑤ 進行中の調査
⑥ 時間の種類

39 には，第1段落（When you hear ...）の内容を端的に示す表現が入る。この段落では，時計によって計測される時間を表す「クロックタイム（clock time）」に対して，人間が時計を用いずに感知する時間を表す「心理的時間（psychological time）」が紹介されている。つまり時間は複数の種類に分けて考えられるという趣旨であることから，⑥ の「時間の種類」が正解となる。① の「生物学的メカニズム（biological mechanism）」については，本段落第3文（Humans do not ...）の中で言及されているものの，これは人間が時間計測の手段として持ち合わせていないものとして紹介されているもので，本段落の中心となる事項ではない。

40 には，第4段落（Your emotional state ...）の内容を端的に示す表現が入る。第1文に「感情の状態（emotional state）も時間の意識に影響を及ぼす（influence）ことがあります」とあり，この後ではいろ

いろな感情の状態（コンサートでの興奮状態，退屈，恐れ）が時間の知覚の仕方に影響を及ぼす例が紹介されている。したがって下線部の意味にほぼ等しい ② の「私たちの気持ちの影響」が正解となる。

問2　41　正解－①

「41 に入れるのに最適な選択肢を選びなさい」

① あらゆる年齢における大きな生活様式の変化は，おそらく時間の進みを遅くするだろう
② 年齢に関係ない大きな生活様式の変化は，おそらく時間の進みを速めるだろう
③ 大人にとっての小さな生活様式の変化は，おそらく時間の進みを遅くするだろう
④ 子供にとっての小さな生活様式の変化は，おそらく時間の進みを速めるだろう

正解は①。第5段落の内容を要約した文を完成する。同段落第6文（Daily routines are ...）と第7文（In such cases, ...）に，「転職や新しい場所への転勤など劇的な変化が起こると，毎日の決まり事は一新されます。そのような場合には，こういった人たちにとっての時間の経過は，子供にとっての時間の経過と似ています」とある。この中の「劇的な変化（drastic changes）」は，① の中の「大きな生活様式の変化（major lifestyle change）」と同内容である。また，「こういった人たち（those people）」とは，劇的な変化を経験した大人のことである。そして「子供にとっての時間の経過（that for children）」とは，同段落第3文（Also, time creeps ...）などにあるように，「ゆっくりと過ぎる（creeps by）」ことである。以上の点から選択肢① は，上に引用した第6・7文の内容と合っているので，これが正解となる。

問3　42　正解－③

「42 に入れるのに最適な選択肢を選びなさい」

① クラスメートからのメッセージを予想すること
② 母親の携帯電話の番号を暗記すること
③ 今日何時間働いたかを思い起こすこと
④ 明日会議があることを思い出すこと

正解は③。「追想的時間評価（Retrospective timing）」の例として適切なものを選ぶ。このタイプの時間評価については，第2段落第5文（To answer, they ...）に，「彼らは答えるために，**追想的時間評価**と呼ばれる心理作用を用いました。これは記憶から取り出される情報に基づいて時間を見積もることです」とある。選択肢の中で，下線部中の「時間を見積もること（estimating time）」に対応するものを探せば，③ の「今日何時間働いたかを思い起こすこと」しかなく，

— 英 R 233 —

この行為は，下線部の内容と合っている。したがって③が正解となる。

問4　正解　43 －①

「43 に入れるのに最適な選択肢を選びなさい」

① 自分が今までどのくらいジョギングをしてきているかを推測すること
② バスケットボールチームの夏季合宿の予定を立てること
③ 鉄道の駅で自分のテニスのコーチに偶然出会うこと
④ この前の家族温泉旅行について考えること

正解は①。予期的時間評価（Prospective timing）の例として適切なものを選ぶ。第3段落第1文（Another process to measure ...）と第2文（It is used ...）に，「心理的時間を測定する別の方法に，**予期的時間評価**と呼ばれるものがあります。これは何かをしながら能動的に時間を計り続ける時に用いられます」とある。選択肢の①は，言い換えれば「ジョギングをしながら現在までのジョギング時間を推測する」ことに等しいので，下線部の例として適切である。

その他の選択肢はいずれも「時間を計り続ける」こととは関係のない行為なので，正解にはなれない。

〈主な語句・表現〉

第1段落（When you hear ...）

come to mind「思い浮かぶ」／ philosopher 名「哲学者」／ measure 動「…を測定する」／ known 形「既知の」／ biological 形「生物学的な」／ mental process「心理作用；精神過程」／ instead 副「代わりに」／ psychological 形「心理的な」／ perceive 動「知覚する」

第2段落（If you were asked ...）

estimate 名「見積もり」動「…を見積もる」／ participant 名「参加者」／ fixed 形「一定の」／ memorize 動「…を記憶する」／ afterwards 副「後になって」／ based on ...「…に基づいて」／ retrieve 動「取り戻す；回収する」／ the opposite「正反対のこと」

第3段落（Another process to measure ...）

actively 副「積極的に；能動的に」／ keep track of ...「…の経過を追う；…の記録をつける」／ instead of ...「…の代わりに」／ recall 動「…を思い出す」／ perform 動「…を遂行する」／ complete 動「…を完成する」／ challenging 形「やりがいのある；きつい」／ focus 名「焦点；集中」

第4段落（Your emotional state ...）

emotional 形「感情の」／ state 名「状態」／ influence 動「…に影響を及ぼす」／ awareness 名「意識；認識」／ pass by「過ぎ去る」／ in what seemed to be the blink of an eye「目の瞬き［一瞬］と思える（短い）時間のうちに」／ be focused on ...「…に集中している」／ wait for O to－「O が－するのを待つ」／ boredom 名「退屈」／ affect 動「…に影響する」／ perception 名「知覚」／ unpleasant 形「不快な」／ perceive O to be ...「O が…であるのに気づく」／ in reality「実際に」

第5段落（Psychological time also ...）

constantly 副「絶えず」／ encounter 動「…に遭遇する」／ memorable 形「記憶に残る」／ creep by「徐々に過ぎる」／ anticipate 動「…を予期する；心待ちにする」／ upcoming 形「まもなくやって来る」／ rarely 副「めったに…しない」／ frequent 形「頻繁に起こる」／ be the case「真相［事実］である」／ routine 名「決まってすること」／ shake up「再編［刷新］する」／ drastic 形「徹底的な」／ relocate 動「（新しい場所に）移転［移住］する」／ passage 名「（時の）経過」／ generally speaking「一般的に言って」／ accelerate 動「加速する」／ mature 動「成長する；大人になる」

最終段落（Knowledge of psychological time ...）

knowledge 名「知識」／ deal with ...「…を扱う［処理する］」／ engaging 形「興味をそそる」／ ease 動「…を和らげる」／ occasion 名「時；場合」／ be reminded of ...「…が思い出される」

— 英 R 234 —

B

〈全訳〉

　あなたは科学クラブのための発表を準備していて、ある科学のウェブサイトから引用した以下の文章を利用しています。

チリ・ペッパー：生活のスパイス

　チリ・チキンの中の赤い香辛料の小さな粒は、素敵な色味をちょっと添えてくれますが、小さな1粒を噛みつぶすだけで、口は火がついたようにひりひりと痛みます。これが大好きな人もいますが、痛い感覚を避けたがる人たちもいます。しかしその反面、その人たちはワサビを付けて刺身を食べることはできます。このことから、ピリッとした辛さとは実は何なのかと疑問に思い、チリとワサビの違いはどこから来るのか問いたくなるかもしれません。

　甘さや塩辛さや酸っぱさとは異なり、辛さは味ではありません。実は、私たちは辛いものを食べる時に、実際にはヒリヒリとした感覚、つまり辛さを味わってはいないのです。チリ・ペッパーやワサビを食べることから感じる辛さは、異なる種類の化合物から生じます。チリ・ペッパーのピリッとした辛みは、カプサイシンと呼ばれるより重くて油に似た成分に由来します。カプサイシンはTRPV1と呼ばれる受容体を始動させるため、口の中になかなか収まらない炎症のような感覚を残します。何かが口をヒリヒリさせている時に、TRPV1はストレスを誘発して私たちに知らせます。面白いことに、チリ・ペッパーの様々な種類に応じて、ピリッとした辛みにも広い幅があり、その度合いはカプサイシンの含有量によって決まります。これはスコビル値、別名スコビル辛味単位（SHU）を用いて測定されます。SHUの値の範囲は、甘くてマイルドなシシトウガラシの50–200から、キャロライナ・リーパー・ペッパーの220万に及びます。

　ワサビは根であって、ペッパーではないと考えられていて、カプサイシンを含んでいません。このため、ワサビはスコビル値でランク付けされてはいないのです。しかしながら、人々はそれに含まれる香辛料のレベルを、およそ1000SHUのチリと同程度とみなしましたが、それはこの尺度の下端に位置します。チリの香辛料には耐えられないのにワサビで味付けされたものは食べられる人がいる理由は、その中の香辛料の化合物が低密度であるからです。ワサビに含まれる化合物は容易に気化するので、食べた時に鼻にツーンとくるのです。

　チリ・ペッパーの摂取は、健康に良い効果を及ぼしうるので、カプサイシンの効用について多くの研究が

なされてきました。カプサイシンが体内のTRPV1受容体を活性化させる時に起こることは、人がストレスや負傷によって痛みを経験する時に起こることと似ています。奇妙なことに、カプサイシンは痛みを消すこともできます。科学者たちは、TRPV1はチリ・ペッパーに長時間さらされると活性化されなくなり、それで一時的に痛みの感覚が和らぐのです。このため、カプサイシンを含むスキンクリームは、筋肉痛を患っている人に効き目があるかもしれません。

　チリ・ペッパーを食べるもう1つの利点が、それが新陳代謝を促進することです。ある研究者のグループは、カプサイシンと体重に関する90の研究を分析して、人は辛いものを食べると食欲が減退することを発見しました。その理由は、辛い食べ物は心拍数を上げて、筋肉に送るエネルギーを増やし、脂肪をエネルギーに変えるためです。最近ワイオミング大学の科学者たちは、カプサイシンを主成分とする減量薬を開発しました。

　チリ・ペッパーは食の安全と関係があるとも考えられていて、このことがより健康な生活をもたらすかもしれません。食べ物は冷やされた環境の外に置かれていると、微生物が繁殖し、食べると病気になるかもしれません。研究によると、チリ・ペッパーに含まれるカプサイシンなどの化学物質には抗菌性があり、微生物の成長を遅らせたり、止めることさえできるのです。その結果、食べ物はより長持ちして、食物に起因する病気が減ります。このことにより、気候の暑い地域の人々はチリ・ペッパーを使う量がより多く、それゆえ、繰り返しさらされることでより辛い食べ物への耐性が高まる傾向があるのかもしれません。また、かつて冷蔵庫がなかった時は、彼らはより涼しい気候の地域の人々よりも食中毒にかかる可能性が低かったのです。

　チリ・ペッパーには健康上の利点があるようですが、健康に悪いこともあるのでしょうか？　スコビル値の高いペッパーは、大量に食べると身体的苦痛を引き起こすことがあります。世界で最も辛いチリのいくつかを短時間で食べた人々は、胃の不調、下痢、手の痺れ、心臓麻痺に似た症状を経験したと報告しています。100万のSHUを含むゴースト・ペッパーに触れると、人の皮膚が焼けることさえあるのです。

　幸いなことに、辛いものを食べた後で一部の人々が感じる不快感は、すぐに（普通は数時間以内に）消え去ることが多いのです。いくつかのマイナスの副作用はあるものの、辛い食べ物は依然として世界中で人気があり、食卓に香味を添えてくれます。覚えておいていただきたいのは、辛いものを食べるのは安全ですが、料理に加えるペッパーの量は注意する方が良いかもしれないということです。

発表用スライド：

**チリ・ペッパー：
生活のスパイス**

1

特徴

チリ・ペッパー	ワサビ
・油に似た成分	・ 44
・TRPV1 を始動	・蒸気に変化
・消えにくい感覚	・辛味が吹き抜ける

2

プラス効果

カプサイシンは…ことができる。 45
  A. 痛みを減らす
  B. より多くのエネルギーを体に与える
  C. 新陳代謝の速度を上げる
  D. 人が感じるストレスの量を減らす
  E. 食中毒を減らす

3

マイナス効果

短時間で強いチリ・ペッパーを食べすぎると，

  ・ 46
  ・ 47

4

香辛料への耐性

48

5

最後に

49

6

〈設問解説〉
　問1　 44 　正解－④
「スライド2の中のワサビの第1の特徴は何か」
　① ヒリヒリする味
　② 炎症のような感覚
　③ 長続きする感じ
　④ 軽い化合物
　正解は④。第2段落第3文（The bite we feel ...）と第4文（Chili peppers get ...）に，「チリ・ペッパーやワサビを食べることから感じる辛さは，異なる種類の化合物から生じます。チリ・ペッパーのピリッとした辛みは，カプサイシンと呼ばれるより重くて（heavier）油に似た成分に由来します」とある。これらの記述から，ワサビを形成する化合物は，チリ・ペッパーを形成する化合物よりも軽い（lighter）ことがわかるので，④が正解となる。
　他の選択肢は，いずれも本文中でワサビの特徴として述べられていない。

　問2　正解　 45 　正解－④
「スライド3の中にあなたが見つけた誤りはどれか」
　① A
　② B
　③ C
　④ D
　⑤ E
　正解は④。カプサイシンのプラス効果として不適切なものを選ぶ。Dに「人が感じるストレスの量を減らす」とあるが，カプサイシンとストレスの関係については，第2段落第5文（Capsaicin leaves ...）と第6文（TRPV1 induces stress ...）に，「カプサイシンは TRPV1 と呼ばれる受容体を始動させるため，口の中になかなか収まらない炎症のような感覚を残します。何かが口をヒリヒリさせている時に，TRPV1 はストレスを誘発して私たちに知らせます」とある。また，第4段落第2文（When capsaicin activates ...）には，「カプサイシンが体内の TRPV1 受容体を活性化させる時に起こることは，人がストレスや負傷によって痛みを経験する時に起こることと似ています」とある。これらはいずれも，カプサイシンはストレスやそれに似た症状を発現させるという内容であり，Dのようにカプサイシンが「人が感じるストレスの量を減らす」ということではないので，④が正解となる。
　Aの「痛みを減らす」については，第4段落第3文（Strangely, capsaicin can ...）に「奇妙なことに，カプサイシンは痛みを消すこともできます」とあることなどと合っている。Bの「より多くのエネルギーを体に

与える」については，カプサイシンと体重に関する研究の分析結果について述べている第5段落第3文（This is because ...）に，「その理由は，辛い食べ物は心拍数を上げて，筋肉に送るエネルギーを増やし，脂肪をエネルギーに変えるためです」とあることと合っている。Cの「新陳代謝の速度を上げる」については，第5段落第1文（Another benefit of ...）に「チリ・ペッパーを食べるもう1つの利点は，それが新陳代謝を促進することです」とあるのと合っている。Eの「食中毒を減らす」は，第6段落最終文（Also, in the past, ...）に「また，かつて冷蔵庫がなかった時は，彼ら（＝辛い食べ物を通じてカプサイシンを頻繁に摂取している暑い地域の人々）はより涼しい気候の地域の人々よりも食中毒にかかる可能性が低かったのです」とあることと合っている。

問3　46・47　正解－②・③

「スライド4に合う選択肢を2つ選びなさい（順序は問わない）」

① 有害なバクテリアを活性化させるかもしれない。
② 腹痛を起こすかもしれない。
③ 手の感覚を失うかもしれない。
④ 指に火がついたように感じるかもしれない。
⑤ 鼻が痛み出すかもしれない。

　正解は②と③。短時間で強いチリ・ペッパーを食べすぎた時に起こるマイナス効果を表すものを選ぶ。これについては第7段落（Chili peppers seem ...）で述べられている。第3文（People who have eaten ...）に，「世界で最も辛いチリのいくつかを短時間で食べた人々は，胃の不調（upset stomachs），下痢，手の痺れ（numb hands），心臓麻痺に似た症状を経験したと報告しています」とあり，②と③は下線部の内容と合っている。

　他の選択肢のようなことは，チリ・ペッパーの食べすぎによって起こるとは本文中では述べられていない。

問4　48　正解－③

「スライド5の香辛料への耐性についてどんなことが推論できるか」

① チリ・ペッパーへの耐性が高い人は，自分が食べるものに使われる香辛料に注意を払う。
② ワサビへの耐性が高い人は，チリ・ペッパーのマイナス効果をこわがる。
③ チリ・ペッパーへの耐性が低い人は，その辛さに慣れることができる。
④ ワサビへの耐性が低い人は，高レベルのSHUに耐えることができない。

　正解は③。香辛料への耐性に関して，第6段落第5

文（This may explain ...）に「このことにより，気候の暑い地域の人々はチリ・ペッパーを使う量がより多く，それゆえ，繰り返しさらされることでより辛い食べ物への耐性が高まる傾向があるのかもしれません」とある。下線部の中の「繰り返しさらされること（repeated exposure）」とは，この文脈では「辛いものを繰り返し食べること」を表している。このことから，③のように，最初はチリ・ペッパーが苦手でも，繰り返し食べていくうちにその辛さに慣れることがあると推論することが可能なので，③が正解となる。

　①や②のようなことは，本文からは読み取れない。④については，SHU値はカプサイシンの含有量によって決まる（第2段落第8文：This is measured ...）が，ワサビはカプサイシンを含んでいない（第3段落第1文：Wasabi is considered ...）ので，ワサビへの耐性とSHU値への耐性を直接関連づけることはできないことから，④は正解になれない。

問5　49　正解－⑤

「スライド6に最も適切な言葉を選びなさい」

① こわがらないで。辛いものを食べると自信が高まります。
② この次チリ・チキンを食べる時には，辛さはほんのわずかしか続かないことを思い出してください。
③ 香辛料の好みにおいては個性が大きな役割を果たすので，心配する必要はありません。
④ 残念なことに，ワサビへの耐性が低いことへの治療法はありません。
⑤ 辛い物を食べませんかと言われたら，それにはいくつかの利点があることを思い出してください。

　正解は⑤。チリ・ペッパーについての発表の最後の言葉として適切なものを選ぶ。消去法で考えるとわかりやすい。①の中の「辛いものを食べると自信が高まります」や，③の中の「香辛料の好みにおいては個性が大きな役割を果たす」という指摘は，発表内容の中に該当するものがないので，正解にはなれない。また，②の中の「辛さはほんのわずかしか続かない」は，最終段落第1文（Luckily the discomfort ...）の「幸いなことに，辛いものを食べた後で一部の人々が感じる不快感は，すぐに（普通は数時間以内に）消え去ることが多いのです」という記述を誤解したものなので，やはり正解にはなれない。また，この発表の表題は「チリ・ペッパー：生活のスパイス」なので，④のようにワサビについてのコメントで発表を結ぶのも不自然であるし，ワサビの耐性の低さへの治療法がないとも本文で

— 英 R 237 —

は述べられていない。したがって正解になりうるもの
は⑤のみである。⑤の中の「それ（＝辛い食べ物）に
はいくつかの利点がある」ことについては，第4段落
（Consuming chili peppers ...）から第6段落（It is
also believed ...）を中心に述べられており，発表内容
との矛盾点はなく，またこの発表の主旨と考えること
もできるので，これが正解として最適である。

〈主な語句・表現〉
第1段落（Tiny pieces of ...）
　touch 图「ちょっと手を加えること」／ bite into ...「…
をかじる」／ burn 動「ヒリヒリする」／ on fire「火
がついて」／ sensation 图「感覚；感じ」／ at the
same time「同時に；その反面」／ spiciness 图
＜ spicy 形「香辛料のきいた；ピリッとした」
第2段落（Unlike sweetness, saltiness, ...）
　unlike 前「…とは違って」／ saltiness 图＜ salty 形「塩
気のある；塩辛い」／ sourness 图＜ sour 形「酸っぱい」／
heat 图「熱；辛さ」／ bite 图「辛さ」／ be derived
from ...「…に由来する」／ compound 图「化合物」／
element 图「要素；成分」／ lingering 形「なかなか消
えない」／ trigger 動「…を誘発する；始動させる」／
receptor 图「受容器［体］」／ induce 動「…を誘発する」／
interestingly 副「興味深いことに」／ variety 图「種類」／
depend on ...「…によって決まる」／ measure 動「…
を測定する」／ range from A to B「A から B にわた
る」／ up to ...「最大［最高］…」
第3段落（Wasabi is considered ...）
　root 图「根」／ rank 動「…をランクづけする」／
compare A to B「A を B になぞらえる」／ tolerate 動「…
を許容する；…への耐性がある」／ flavored with ...「…
で味付けされた［風味を添えた］」／ density 图「密度；
濃度」／ vaporize 動「蒸発［気化］する」／ deliver
A to B「A〈打撃・攻撃など〉を B に加える」／
blast 图「強いひと吹き」
第4段落（Consuming chili peppers ...）
　consume 動「…を消費する；食べる」／ positive 形「肯
定的な；プラスの」／ effect 图「影響；効果」／
benefit 图「恩恵；利点」／ activate 動「…を活性化す
る」／ injury 图「負傷；けが」／ strangely 副「奇妙
なことに」／ go away「消えていく」／ cease to −「−
しなくなる」／ turn on「スイッチを入れる；刺激する」／
long-term 形「長期の」／ exposure to ...「…にさらさ
れる［触れる］こと」／ temporarily 副「一時的に」／
ease 動「…を和らげる」／ muscle ache「筋肉痛」

第5段落（Another benefit of ...）
　accelerate 動「…を加速する」／ metabolism 图「新
陳代謝」／ analyze 動「…を分析する」／ reduced 形「減
少した」／ appetite 图「食欲」／ heart rate「心拍数」／
convert A into B「A を B に変える」／ fat 图「脂肪」／
weight-loss 形「減量の」／ ingredient 图「成分」
第6段落（It is also believed ...）
　be connected with ...「…と関係［関連］がある」／
food safety「食の安全」／ refrigerated 形「冷蔵され
た」／ microorganism 图「微生物」／ multiply 動「繁
殖する」／ chemical 图「化学物質」／ antibacterial 形
「抗菌性の」／ property 图「特性」／ as a result「そ
の結果」／ last 動「〈ある期間〉もつ」／ food-
borne 形「食物が媒介する」／ have a tendency to −「−
する傾向がある」／ be tolerant of ...「…に対して耐性
がある」／ due to ...「…のせいで」／ refrigerator 图「冷
蔵庫」／ be likely to −「−しそうだ；−する可能性が
高い」／ food poisoning「食中毒」
第7段落（Chili peppers seem ...）
　discomfort 图「苦痛（からくる不快感）」／ in large
quantities「大量に」／ upset 形「不調な」／
diarrhea 图「下痢」／ numb 形「感覚のない；麻痺した」／
symptom 图「症状」／ heart attack「心臓麻痺」
最終段落（Luckily the discomfort ...）
　go away「消えゆく」／ despite 前「…にもかかわら
ず」／ negative 形「否定的な；マイナスの」／
flavorful 形「風味に富む」／ you might want to −「−
する方がいい」

— 英 R 238 —

2023 年度

大学入学共通テスト 本試験
英語（リーディング）

解答・解説

■ 2023 年度（令和 5 年度）本試験「英語（リーディング）」得点別偏差値表
下記の表は大学入試センター公表の平均点と標準偏差をもとに作成したものです。

平均点　53.81　　標準偏差　20.99　　　　　受験者数　463,985

得 点	偏差値	得 点	偏差値
100	72.0	50	48.2
99	71.5	49	47.7
98	71.1	48	47.2
97	70.6	47	46.8
96	70.1	46	46.3
95	69.6	45	45.8
94	69.1	44	45.3
93	68.7	43	44.8
92	68.2	42	44.4
91	67.7	41	43.9
90	67.2	40	43.4
89	66.8	39	42.9
88	66.3	38	42.5
87	65.8	37	42.0
86	65.3	36	41.5
85	64.9	35	41.0
84	64.4	34	40.6
83	63.9	33	40.1
82	63.4	32	39.6
81	63.0	31	39.1
80	62.5	30	38.7
79	62.0	29	38.2
78	61.5	28	37.7
77	61.0	27	37.2
76	60.6	26	36.8
75	60.1	25	36.3
74	59.6	24	35.8
73	59.1	23	35.3
72	58.7	22	34.8
71	58.2	21	34.4
70	57.7	20	33.9
69	57.2	19	33.4
68	56.8	18	32.9
67	56.3	17	32.5
66	55.8	16	32.0
65	55.3	15	31.5
64	54.9	14	31.0
63	54.4	13	30.6
62	53.9	12	30.1
61	53.4	11	29.6
60	52.9	10	29.1
59	52.5	9	28.7
58	52.0	8	28.2
57	51.5	7	27.7
56	51.0	6	27.2
55	50.6	5	26.7
54	50.1	4	26.3
53	49.6	3	25.8
52	49.1	2	25.3
51	48.7	1	24.8
		0	24.4

英語（リーディング） 2023年度　本試験　（100点満点）

（解答・配点）

問題番号（配点）	設問		解答番号	正解	配点	自己採点欄
第1問（10）	A	1	1	①	2	
		2	2	④	2	
	B	1	3	③	2	
		2	4	④	2	
		3	5	③	2	
小　計						
第2問（20）	A	1	6	②	2	
		2	7	②	2	
		3	8	②	2	
		4	9	④	2	
		5	10	①	2	
	B	1	11	④	2	
		2	12	①	2	
		3	13	①	2	
		4	14	①	2	
		5	15	②	2	
小　計						
第3問（15）	A	1	16	②	3	
		2	17	③	3	
	B	1	18	③	3*	
			19	④		
			20	②		
			21	①		
		2	22	③	3	
		3	23	②	3	
小　計						

問題番号（配点）	設問		解答番号	正解	配点	自己採点欄
第4問（16）		1	24	①	3	
		2	25	①	3	
		3	26	②	2	
			27	⑤	2	
		4	28	①	3	
		5	29	②	3	
小　計						
第5問（15）		1	30	④	3	
		2	31	③	3	
		3	32	②	3*	
			33	④		
			34	⑤		
			35	③		
		4	36	③	3	
		5	37 － 38	① － ⑤	3*	
小　計						
第6問（24）	A	1	39	③	3	
		2	40	④	3	
		3	41 － 42	④ － ⑥	3*	
		4	43	①	3	
	B	1	44	④	2	
		2	45 － 46	① － ⑤	3*	
		3	47	③	2	
		4	48	④	2	
		5	49	④	3	
小　計						
合　計						

（注）
1　＊は，全部正解の場合のみ点を与える。
2　－（ハイフン）でつながれた正解は，順序を問わない。

第1問

A

〈全訳〉

　あなたは米国で勉強中で，午後の活動として2つの公演のうち1つを選んで見に行く必要があります。担任の先生から次のようなプリントをもらいます。

金曜日の公演

パレス劇場 「どこでも一緒に」	グランド劇場 「ギター・クイーン」
笑いあり涙ありの恋愛劇	華やかな衣装が特徴のロックミュージカル
▸午後2時から（休憩はなく，上演時間は1時間45分） ▸上演後にロビーで俳優たちと話ができます ▸飲食物は販売していません ▸幸運な方5名にTシャツをプレゼントします	▸午後1時開演（2度の15分休憩を含めて3時間の上演） ▸開演前に衣装を着た出演者たちを迎える機会があります ▸軽い飲食物（スナックやドリンク）や，特製Tシャツなどのグッズをロビーで販売します

申込方法：どちらの公演を見に行きたいですか。下の書式に記入して担任の先生に今日中に提出してください。

- - - - - - - - - - - - - - - - - - -

1つ選んでください（✔）：
「どこでも一緒に」□　　「ギター・クイーン」□

氏名：＿＿＿＿＿＿＿＿＿＿＿＿

〈設問解説〉

　問1　[1]　正解─①

「あなたはプリントを読んだ後で何をしなさいと言われているか」

① 一番下の部分に記入してそれを提出する。
② 2つの公演についてより多くのことを調べる。
③ 自分が決めたことを担任の先生に話す。
④ 自分の名前を書いて自分の選択を説明する。

　正解は①。本文下部のInstructionsの第2文（Fill in the ...）に，「下の書式に記入して担任の先生に今日中に提出してください」とあり，①はこの内容と合っている。

　他の選択肢のようなことは本文からは読み取れない（④は「自分の選択を説明する」が誤り）。

　問2　[2]　正解─④

「2つの公演のどちらについても言えることはどれか」

① 上演前に飲み物を購入することはできない。
② 数枚のTシャツがおみやげにもらえる。
③ どちらも同じ時刻に終演する。
④ 劇場で俳優たちに会うことができる。

　正解は④。「パレス劇場（Palace Theater）」での公演についての説明の中に「上演後にロビーで俳優たちと話ができます（Actors available to ...）」とあり，「グランド劇場（Grand Theater）」での公演についての説明の中に「開演前に衣装を着た出演者たちを迎える機会があります（Opportunity to greet ...）」とあり，④はこれらの内容と合っている。

　①や②は，グランド劇場に当てはまらない。③については，パレス劇場の公演は，「午後2時から（休憩はなく，上演時間は1時間45分）（From 2:00 p.m. ...）」とあることから，終演時間は3時45分であり，グランド劇場の公演は，「午後1時開演（2度の15分休憩を含めて3時間の上演）（Starts at 1:00 p.m. ...）」とあることから，終演時間は午後4時であるとわかるので，③も誤りである。

〈主な語句・表現〉

　performance 名「（音楽・演劇などの）催し物」／handout 名「刷り物；プリント」／break 名「小休止；休憩」／running time「上演時間」／free 形「無料の」／feature 動「…を特徴［呼び物］とする」／two 15-minute breaks「2度の15分休憩」／greet 動「…に挨拶する；…を歓迎する」／cast 名「出演者（全員）」／light refreshments「軽い飲食物」／instructions 名「指示；命令」／fill in ...「…を埋める；…に記入する」／the form below「下の書式」／hand ... in「…を提出する」

B

〈全訳〉

あなたは夏休みに英語の力を伸ばしたいと思っている高校3年生です。あるインターナショナルスクールが提供する夏期集中英語キャンプのウェブサイトを見つけます。

夏期集中英語キャンプ
ギャリー・インターナショナルスクール（GIS）は，1989年から日本の高校3年生に夏期集中英語キャンプを提供してきました。2週間英語だけの環境で過ごしてみませんか！

日程：2023年8月1-14日
場所：山梨県・河口湖青年の家
費用：食事と宿泊代込みで12万円（カヤッキングやカヌーイングなどの自由選択活動は別料金）

コース設定

◆**フォレスト**：基本的な文法構造をマスターし，簡単なトピックについての短いスピーチを行い，発音のコツを身につけます。指導教官は数ヵ国で20年以上の英語の指導経験があります。キャンプの最終日にはスピーチコンテストに参加して，他のキャンプ参加者全員に聞いてもらいます。

◆**マウンテン**：グループで作業をして，英語の寸劇を書いて演じます。このコースの指導教官はニューヨーク市，ロンドン，シドニーの演劇学校で働いた経験があります。8月14日に寸劇を演じて，キャンプ参加者全員に楽しんでもらいます。

◆**スカイ**：このコースではディベート力と批判的思考法を身につけます。指導教官は多くの国でディベートチームを指導した経験を持ち，このテーマでベストセラーになったテキストを出版した人たちもいます。最終日には他のキャンプ参加者全員の前で短いディベートを行います。（注：受講を認められるのは上級レベルの英語力を持つ人に限られます）

▲**申し込み**
ステップ1：2023年5月20日までにここにあるオンライン申込書に記入してください。
ステップ2：あなたの英語力を評価したり希望のコースを尋ねるための面接を設定するため，私たちからあなたに連絡をします。
ステップ3：あなたにコースが割り当てられます。

〈設問解説〉

問1　3　正解ー③

「GISのすべての指導教官は　3　」

① 1989年以来ずっと日本にいる
② 国際大会で優勝したことがある
③ **他の国々で働いたことがある**
④ 人気のある本を何冊か書いたことがある

正解は③。GISは3つのコースを提供しているが，FORESTコースの説明には「指導教官は数ヵ国で20年以上の英語の教授経験があります（Your instructors have taught ...）」とあり，MOUNTAINコースの説明には「このコースの指導教官はニューヨーク市，ロンドン，シドニーの演劇学校で働いた経験があります（Instructors for this course ...）」とあり，SKYコースの説明には「指導教官は多くの国でディベートチームを指導した経験を持ち…（Your instructors have been to ...）」とある。これらの記述から③は正しいとわかる。

他の選択肢はいずれも，GISの指導教官全員に当てはまることとは考えられない。

問2　4　正解ー④

「キャンプの最終日にキャンプ参加者たちは　4　」

① お互いの成果を評価し合う
② 最優秀賞をもらうために競い合う
③ 将来についてのプレゼンを行う
④ **キャンプで身につけたことを披露する**

正解は④。キャンプで提供される3つのコースのうち，FORESTについては「キャンプの最終日にはスピーチコンテストに参加して，他のキャンプ参加者全員に聞いてもらいます（On the final day ...）」とあり，MOUNTAINについては「8月14日（つまりキャンプの最終日）に寸劇を演じて，キャンプ参加者全員に楽しんでもらいます（You'll perform your skit ...）」とあり，SKYについては「最終日には他のキャンプ参加者全員の前で短いディベートを行います（You'll do a short debate ...）」とある。これらの内容と合っている④が正解となる。

①については，お互いの成果を「評価し合う」とは本文では述べられていないので，正解にはなれない。②や③のようなことも，本文からは読み取れない。

問3　5　正解ー③

「あなたがキャンプの申込書を提出するとどうなるか」

① あなたは英語の指導教官たちに電話をする。
② あなたは英語の筆記試験を受ける。
③ **あなたの英語のレベルが調べられる。**

④ あなたの英語のスピーチのトピックが送られてくる。

正解は③。本文の「申し込み(Application)」のステップ2に,「あなたの英語力を評価したり希望のコースを尋ねるための面接を設定するため,私たちからあなたに連絡をします(We'll contact you ...)」とあることから,下線部の内容と合っている③が正解となる。

他の選択肢のようなことは,本文では述べられていない。

〈主な語句・表現〉

senior 形「最高学年の」／ intensive 形「集中的な」／ run 動「…を運営〔提供〕する」／ provide A for B「AをBに提供する」／ location 名「場所；所在地」／ prefecture 名「県」／ accommodation 名「宿泊(施設)」／ additional fees「追加料金」／ optional 形「選択の；任意の」／ Courses Offered「提供されるコース」／ grammar structure「文法構造」／ tip 名「ヒント；秘訣」／ take part in ...「…に参加する」／ skit 名「寸劇」／ debating skills「ディベート〔討論〕の技術」／ critical thinking「批判的思考(法)」／ have been to ...「…に行ったことがある」／ subject 名「主題；学科」／ those with ...「…を伴う〔持っている〕人々」／ advanced 形「上級の」／ accept 動「〈受講を〉認める」／ application 名「申し込み(書)」／ set up「…を設定する」／ assess 動「…を評価する」／ course preference「コースについての好み」／ assign 動「…を割り当てる」

第2問
A
〈全訳〉

あなたは長い距離を歩いて学校へ通っていて,しばしば足が痛くなることから,良い靴を1足買いたいと思っている。英国のあるウェブサイトで探していると,このような広告を見つける。

ナビ55が提供する新しいシューズ
スマートサポート

スマートサポート・シューズは丈夫で長持ち,しかもお手頃な価格です。3つのカラーとスタイルの中からお求めになれます。

ナノチップ

特徴

スマートサポート・シューズに組み込まれたナノチップは,iSupportアプリに接続するとあなたの足の形を調べます。このアプリをあなたのスマートフォン,パソコン,タブレット,スマートウォッチのいずれか,あるいはすべてにダウンロードしてください。それからシューズを履いている間に,あなたの足のデータをチップに収集させると,シューズの内側が自動的に調節されて,インソールが正確でパーソナライズされたものとなります。ナビ55の他の製品と同様に,このシューズにも定評あるルートメモリー機能が搭載されています。

優れた点

より良いバランス：パーソナライズされたインソールが,あなたの立ち方を調節することによって,足,脚部,背中が痛むのを防ぎます。

運動の促進：とても履き心地がいいので,定期的に歩こうという気持ちになります。

ルートメモリー：歩いている間,チップがあなたの毎日のルート,距離,ペースを記録します。

ルートオプション：デバイスで現在地を見たり,道案内の音声を自動的にイヤホンで流したり,スマートウォッチで道案内を読むことができます。

お客様の声

● 私は道案内の方法を選べるのが気に入っていますが,ビジュアルガイダンスよりオーディオガイダンスの方が好きです。

● 1ヵ月で2キロもやせました！

- 今は自分のシューズをとても気に入っていますが，履き慣れるのに数日かかりました。
- 雨でも滑らないので，一年中履いています。
- 軽くて履き心地がいいので，自転車に乗る時も履いています。
- あちこち簡単に出かけられます！ 道に迷う心配は無用です。
- とてもかっこいいです。アプリの基本機能は使いやすいですが，お金を払ってオプションの上級機能を利用することはないと思います。

〈設問解説〉

問1 ⑥ 正解－②

「メーカーの説明によれば，この新しいシューズを最も適切に言い表しているものはどれか」

① 安価な夏向きのシューズ
② **ハイテクなふだん履きのシューズ**
③ 軽くて快適なスポーツシューズ
④ スタイリッシュでカラフルなサイクリングシューズ

正解は②。広告中の Advantages の項には，「運動の促進：とても履き心地がいいので，定期的に歩こうという気持ちになります（Promotes Exercise: ...）」，「ルートメモリー：歩いている間，チップがあなたの毎日のルート，距離，ペースを記録します（Route Memory: ...）」といった記述がある。これらの中の下線部の表現から，これは「ふだん履きのシューズ（everyday shoes）」と考えることができる。また，ナノチップが組み込まれていて，使用者がアプリを使って様々な機能を利用できると述べられていることから，このシューズは「ハイテク（high-tech）」であると考えることもできる。したがって②が正解として最適である。

このシューズが「夏向き（①）」であるとか，「スポーツ（③）」や「サイクリング（④）」に向いているとは，メーカーの説明からは読み取れないので，他の選択肢はいずれも誤りとなる（この問いでは「メーカーの説明（the maker's statements）」として正しいものを選ぶことが求められているので，「お客様の声（Customers' Comments）」の項にある内容を正解の根拠にすることはできない）。

問2 ⑦ 正解－②

「このシューズが提供する利点の中で，あなたが気に入る可能性が最も高いものはどれか」

① 定期的な運動をよりたくさんすること［より規則正しい運動をすること］
② **パーソナライズされたインソールを備えている**

こと
③ あなたの歩く速さを知っていること
④ 履くとかっこよく見えること

正解は②。問題の冒頭文（You want to ...）に，「あなたは長い距離を歩いて学校へ通っていて，しばしば足が痛くなることから，良い靴を1足買いたいと思っている」とあることに注意する。下線部から，足が痛くならない機能が「あなた」が最も気に入る利点となると考えることができる。その利点とは，Advantages の最初の項に「より良いバランス：パーソナライズされたインソールが，あなたの立ち方を調節することによって，足，脚部，背中が痛むのを防ぎます（Better Balance: ...）」とあることから，「パーソナライズされたインソール（the personalised support）」が「あなたが気に入る可能性が最も高い利点」であることになる。したがって正解は②に決まる。

他の選択肢を正解とする根拠はない。

問3 ⑧ 正解－②

「利用客が述べた意見の1つに，⑧というのがある」

① アプリは早歩きを促す
② **アプリの無料機能は利用しやすい**
③ このシューズはお買い得だ
④ このシューズはサイクリングの速度を上げる

正解は②。「お客様の声（Customers' Comments）」の内容と合っているものが正解となる。最後の意見（They look great. ...）に「とてもかっこいいです。アプリの基本機能は使いやすいですが，お金を払ってオプションの上級機能を利用することはないと思います」とあることから，この内容と合っている②が正解となる（アプリの基本機能が無料であることは，後半の「お金を払って…」という記述からわかる）。

①のように「アプリが早歩きを促す」や，④のように「シューズがサイクリングの速度を上げる」という意見を述べた利用客はいない。③のようなことも「お客様の声」の中では述べられていない。

問4 ⑨ 正解－④

「ある利用客は，オーディオ機器の利用についてコメントしている。このコメントは次のどの利点に基づくものか」

① より良いバランス
② 運動の促進
③ ルートメモリー
④ **ルートオプション**

正解は④。「オーディオ機器の利用」について触れているのは，「お客様の声」の最初の意見（I like the ...）

— 英 R 244 —

のみである。そこには「私は道案内の方法を選べるの が気に入っていますが，ビジュアルガイダンスよりオー ディオガイダンスの方が好きです」とあることから， このコメントは「道案内（directions）」に関する利点 に基づくものである。4つの選択肢の中で，「道案内」 と関連があるのはルートオプション（これについては， 「デバイスで現在地を見たり，道案内の音声を自動的に イヤホンで流したり，スマートウォッチで道案内を読 むことができます」と述べられている）のみなので， ④が正解となる。

問5 ⑩ 正解ー①
「ある利用客の意見では，⑩が勧められている」
① シューズを履き慣れるのにかかる時間を見込ん でおくこと
② 体重を減らすのに役立つ時計を買うこと
③ シューズを履く前にアプリに接続すること
④ お金を払って iSupport の上級機能を利用するこ と

　正解は①。「お客様の声（Customers' Comments）」 の3つ目のコメント（I love my ...）に，「今は自分の シューズをとても気に入っていますが，履き慣れるの に数日かかりました」とある。このコメントは，この シューズを履き慣れるにはある程度時間がかかるので， 最初は自分に合わないと感じても，しばらく様子を見 るのが良いと勧めている，つまり靴を履き慣れるまで 「時間を見込んでおくこと（allowing time）」を勧めて いると考えられることから，①は適切な内容である。
　②のように「時計」を買うことを勧めているコメン トはない。③や④のようなことを勧めているコメント もない。

〈主な語句・表現〉
sore形「痛い」／ advertisement名「広告」／ line 名「製品の種類；製品群」／ long-lasting形「長持ち する」／ reasonably priced「手頃な価格の」／ feature名「特徴」／ nano-［接頭辞］「10億分の1」／ chip名「チップ；半導体（の小片）」／ analyse動「… を分析する」／ application名「アプリ」／ A, B, C, and/or D「A, B, C, D のすべてまたはそのどれか」／ personalised形「個人向けにした；パーソナライズさ れた」／ foot support「靴底［足裏］サポート；インソー ル」／ as with ...「…と同様に」／ function名「機能」／ help (to) 原形「－するのに役立つ」／ keep ... free from pain「…が痛くならないようにし続ける」／ back名「背中」／ promote動「…を促す」／ be willing to－「－するのをいとわない」／ directions名「行

き方；道順」／ prefer A to B「B よりも A を好む」／ get used to them「シューズに慣れる」 them は my pair (of shoes) を指している。／ all year round「一年 中」／ They are so light and comfortable (that) ... 「それはとても軽くて快適なので…」／ get around「あ ちこち動き回る」／ get lost「道に迷う」／ cool形「かっ こいい」／ be based on ...「…に基づいている」／ recommend動「…を勧める」／ put ... on「…を身に つける」

B

〈全訳〉

　あなたは生徒会の委員です。委員たちは生徒が時間を効率よく使うのに役立つ生徒プロジェクトについて議論してきました。あなたはアイディアを得ようとして，あるスクール・チャレンジについてのレポートを読んでいます。それは日本の他の学校で学んでいた交換学生が書いたものでした。

通学チャレンジ

　私の学校では，ほとんどの生徒はバスか列車で通学しています。多くの生徒が携帯電話でゲームをしたり，おしゃべりしているのをよく見かけます。けれども，この時間を読書や宿題に使うこともできるはずです。私たちは生徒たちが通学時間をより有効に使うのを助けるためにこの活動を始めました。生徒たちには1月17日から2月17日までの通学時の活動のチャートを完成させることが求められました。合計300人の生徒が参加しましたが，その3分の2以上は2年生で，およそ4分の1は3年生でした。1年生で参加したのはわずか15名でした。1年生の参加者がこんなに少なかったのはなぜでしょう。（以下に示す）参加者たちの感想によれば，どうやらこの問題には答えがあるようです。

参加者たちの感想

HS：このプロジェクトのおかげで，私は英語の単語テストで過去最高点を取ることができました。小さな目標をいくつも設定して，それをクリアしながら通学するのは楽でした。

KF：私の友人は参加できなかったので残念そうでした。彼女は家が近いので，歩いて通学しています。他の参加方法もあったらよかったのですが。

SS：私の乗る列車はいつも混んでいて立っていなければならないので，本やタブレットを開けるスペースはありません。耳で聞く教材しか利用できませんでしたが，量が全然足りませんでした。

JH：私は学習日誌を作りましたが，このおかげで自分が時間をどう使っているのかに気づきました。どういうわけか，私の1年生のクラスメートのほとんどは，このチャレンジについて知らなかったようでした。

MN：私はバスに乗っている時間はほとんど，ビデオを見て過ごしていて，それは授業をより理解するのに役立ちました。時間がとても速く流れるように感じました。

〈設問解説〉

問1　11　正解─④

「通学チャレンジの目的は，生徒たちが11のを助けることだった」

① より敏速に通学する

② 試験の点数を上げる

③ 英語の授業によりうまく対処する

④ 時間をよりうまく使う

　正解は④。本文中の「通学チャレンジ（Commuting Challenge）」に関する説明文の第4文（We started this ...）に，「私たちは生徒たちが通学時間をより有効に使うのを助けるためにこの活動を始めました」とあることから，下線部の内容に最も近い④が正解となる。

　他の選択肢は，このチャレンジの目的とは考えられない。

問2　12　正解─①

「通学チャレンジに関する1つの**事実**は，12ということである」

① **1年生の参加者は10パーセント未満だった**

② 冬季に2ヵ月間行われた

③ 生徒たちはバスの中で携帯機器を使わなければならなかった

④ 参加者の大多数は列車で通った

　正解は①。「通学チャレンジ（Commuting Challenge）」に関する説明文の第6文（A total of ...）以降に，「合計300人の生徒が参加しましたが，その3分の2以上は2年生で，およそ4分の1は3年生でした。1年生で参加したのはわずか15名でした」とある。下線部の内容から①は正しいとわかる。

　②は「2ヵ月」を「1ヵ月」に直さないと，第5文（Students had to ...）の内容と合わない。③のようなことは本文からは読み取れない。④は「列車」を「バスか列車」に直さないと，第1文（Most students come ...）の内容と合わない。

問3　13　正解─①

「参加者たちの感想によると，13が参加者たちが報告した活動の中にあった」

A：学習記録をとること

B：言語を学ぶこと

C：タブレットでメモを取ること

D：授業ノートを携帯電話で読むこと

　正解は①。本文中の「参加者たちの感想（Feedback from participants）」の内容に合うものを選ぶ。AはJHの感想（私は学習日誌を作りましたが…）と合っている。BはHSの感想（このプロジェクトのおかげで，

私は英語の単語テストで過去最高点を取ることができました…）と合っている。

CやDのようなことを述べた生徒はいない。

問4　14　正解ー①

「通学チャレンジに関する参加者の意見の1つに，14というのがある」

① それは徒歩で通学する生徒たちを含むこともできたであろうに
② 列車内は本を読むには良い場所だった
③ 勉強のためのオーディオ教材は豊富にあった
④ 娯楽のためにビデオを見ることは，時間の経過を早めるのに役立った

正解は①。本文中の「参加者たちの感想（Feedback from participants）」を参照する。KF の感想に「私の友人は参加できなかったので残念そうでした。彼女は家が近いので，歩いて通学しています。他の参加方法もあったらよかったのですが」とある。この感想は，徒歩で通学する生徒たちもチャレンジに参加できるようにするべきだったという意味に解せることから，①が正解となる（①の中の could have p.p. は「（その気になれば）…することもできたであろう（がしなかった）」という意味を表している）。

②や③のような感想を述べた生徒はいない。④は「娯楽のために（for fun）」が MN の感想と合わない。

問5　15　正解ー②

「筆者の疑問は15によって答えられている」

① HS
② JH
③ KF
④ MN
⑤ SS

正解は②。「筆者の疑問」とは，「通学チャレンジ（Commuting Challenge）」に関する説明文の下から3行目にある「1年生の参加者がこんなに少なかったのはなぜでしょう（How come ...?）」である。この疑問に答えていると考えられるのは，JH の感想の第2文（For some reason ...）の「どういうわけか，私の1年生のクラスメートのほとんどは，このチャレンジについて知らなかったようでした」である。この発言は，「1年生の参加が少なかったのは，彼らへの告知不足が原因」と解せる発言であるから，上の疑問の答えに相当する発言と考えられる。したがって②が正解に決まる。

他の生徒の感想の中に，上の疑問への答えと考えられるものは含まれていない。

〈主な語句・表現〉

　student council「生徒会」／ efficiently 副「効率よく」／ challenge 名「難題；チャレンジ」／ commute 動「通学する」／ they could also use ...「彼らは（その気になれば）…を使うこともできるだろう」／ effectively 副「効果的に；有効に」／ complete 動「…を完成させる；記入する」／ chart 名「図表；グラフ；チャート」／ participate 動「参加する」／ two thirds「3分の2」／ first [second; third] -years「1［2；3］年生の生徒たち」／ a quarter「4分の1」／ How come ... ?「どうして…なのか」／ based on ...「…に基づくと」／ feedback 名「反応；意見；感想」／ the highest score ever「今までで最高の得点」／ goals to complete「達成すべき目標」／ on my way「途中で」／ There should have been ...「…がある方が良かった」／ take part「参加する」／ audio materials「オーディオ［耳で聞く］教材」／ not nearly ...「…に近いどころではない；全然…でない」／ enough = enough materials「十分な量の教材」／ keep a log「記録をとる；日誌をつける」／ for some reason「何らかの理由で；どういうわけか」／ spend O -ing「O を -ing して過ごす」

第3問
A
〈全訳〉

　あなたはシドニーのキャンバーフォード大学で勉強しています。クラスのキャンプ旅行に行くことになっていて、準備のためにキャンプクラブの会報を読んでいます。

　　　　キャンプに行くのなら、読んでください！

　こんにちは、私はケイトリンです。私が最近行ったクラブ旅行から得た2つの実用的なキャンプの教訓をお話ししたいと思います。1つ目は、バックパックを大きく3つの部分に分けて、一番重いものを中間部に入れ、バックパックのバランスを取ることです。次に、より頻繁に使う日常必需品は、上部に入れるのが良いです。つまり、寝袋は下部に入れて、食べ物や料理器具やテントは中間部に、服は上部に入れるのです。良いバックパックにはたいてい、すぐに取り出せる小物を入れておくための「ブレーン（補助ポーチ）」が付いています。

　去年、私たちは晩に屋外で楽しく料理を作って食べました。私はキャンプファイアーの近くに座っていましたが、テントに戻る頃には、寒さでこごえていました。寝る前に何枚も重ね着をしましたが、それでも寒く感じました。すると友達が私に、上に着ている重ね着を脱いで、それを寝袋に詰め込んですき間を少しふさいでみなさいと言いました。この詰め方方式は私には初めてでしたが、一晩中暖かく過ごせたので驚きました！

　私のアドバイスが、あなたが暖かく快適に過ごすのに役立てば幸いです。キャンプ旅行を楽しんでくださいね。

〈設問解説〉

問1　16　正解―②

「ケイトリンのアドバイスに従えば、バックパックをどのように詰めるべきか」

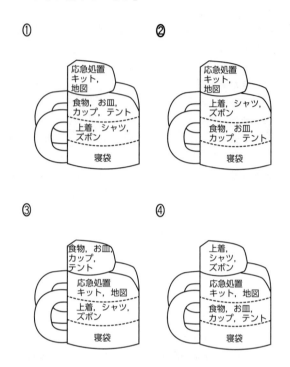

　正解は②。ケイトリンが書いた会報記事の中で、バックパックの詰め方に関するアドバイスは、第1段落第3文（The first thing ...）以降の「1つ目は、バックパックを大きく3つの部分に分けて、一番重いものを中間部に入れ、バックパックのバランスを取ることです。次に、より頻繁に使う日常必需品は、上部に入れるのが良いです。つまり、寝袋は下部に入れて、(A)食べ物や料理器具やテントは中間部に、(B)服は上部に入れるのです。良いバックパックにはたいてい、すぐに出せる小物を入れておくための『ブレーン（補助ポーチ）』が付いています」という部分である。下線部(A)から、図中の「中間部（middle section）」に「食べ物や料理器具やテント（food, plates, cups, tent）」が入っている②か④が正解だとわかる。次に下線部(B)から、「服（clothes）」、つまり「上着やシャツやズボン（jackets, shirts, trousers）」が、「上部（top section）」に入っている②が正解に決まる。②は上記のアドバイスの他の内容とも矛盾しない。

問2　17　正解―③

「ケイトリンの話によると、17が、夜通し暖かくして過ごすのに最適な方法である」

① テントから出るのを避けること
② キャンプファイアーのそばで温かいものを食べること
③ 寝袋の中のすき間をふさぐこと
④ 着替えをすべて身につけること

正解は③。ケイトリンが書いた記事の第2段落最終文（This stuffing method ...）に，「この詰め物方式 (stuffing method) は私には初めてでしたが，一晩中暖かく過ごせたので驚きました！」とあることから，下線部に相当するものが正解となる。「この詰め物方式」とは，直前にある「すると友達が私に，上に着ている重ね着を脱いで，それを寝袋に詰め込んですき間を少しふさいでみなさいと言いました（Then, my friend ...）」という文の中の下線部分に相当するので，この内容と合っている③が正解となる。

〈主な語句・表現〉

newsletter 图「会報」／ practical 圏「実用的な」／ divide A into B「A を B に分ける」／ frequently used「頻繁に使われる」／ daily necessities「日常必需品」／ place 働「置く」／ sleeping bag「寝袋」／ cookware 图「料理器具」／ come with ...「…が付いてくる」／ additional 圏「追加の；補助的な」／ easy-to-reach「簡単に手が届く」／ have fun －ing「－して楽しむ」／ close to ...「…の近くに」／ by the time I got back to ...「私が…に戻るまでには」／ freeze 働「凍るほど寒く感じる」／ put on ...「…を身につける」／ extra 圏「余分の；追加の」／ layers of ...「何重もの…」／ take off ...「…を脱ぐ」／ outer 圏「外側の」／ stuff A into B「A を B に詰め込む」／ fill up ...「…を埋める［ふさぐ］」

B

〈全訳〉

あなたの英語クラブは学校祭のために「アドベンチャールーム」を作ります。あなたはアイディアを得るために，ある英国人男性が作ったルームについてのブログを読んでいます。

──────────────

自分だけの「ホームアドベンチャー」を作ってみよう。

去年，私は「アドベンチャールーム」の体験会に参加しました。本当に楽しかったので，私は子どもたちのためにルームを作ってみました。あなたが自分独自のルームを作る際のヒントを紹介しましょう。

┌─────────────────────┐
│ **アドベンチャーを作るための重要な手順** │
│ テーマ→筋書き→パズル→衣装 │
└─────────────────────┘

まず最初に，テーマを選びます。私の息子たちはシャーロック・ホームズの大ファンなので，私は探偵推理ものに決めました。私は居間の家具の配置を変えたり，持っていた古い絵やランプを加えてシーン設定をしました（→問1③）。

次に，物語の筋書き作りをします。私たちは，「消えたチョコレート事件」という筋書きにしました。子どもたちが探偵になって，行方不明になったお菓子を見つける手がかりを探すというものです。

3つめのステップは，パズルや難問を考案することです。ここで役に立つ発想は，解答からさかのぼりながら作業することです。たとえば課題が，3けたの数字でロックされた南京錠の付いた箱を開けることだとしたら，3けたの番号を隠す方法を考えてください。古い本は，メッセージの隠し場所としてぴったりです。いろいろなページの語にアンダーラインをして謎めいた文章を作り上げる作業はとても楽しいものでした。忘れてはいけないのは，最終ゴールが近づくにつれて，パズルをますます難しくするべきだということです。雰囲気を出すために，私はそれから子どもたちに衣装を着せました（→問1④）。私が虫メガネを渡すと長男はとても興奮して，ただちにシャーロック・ホームズのように振る舞い出しました。その後子どもたちは，第1の手がかりを探し始めました（→問1②）。

この「アドベンチャールーム」は，私の家族向けに特別にデザインされたので，難問の中には我が家独自の

── 英 R 249 ──

ものを含めました。最後の課題として，私は２つの小さなカップを持ってきてそれぞれにプラスチックのステッカーを貼り，それからヨーグルトをたっぷりと入れました。「探偵たち」が手がかりを明らかにするには，ヨーグルトをカップの底まで食べ進めなければなりませんでした（→問１①）。子どもたちはどちらもヨーグルトを食べたがらないので，これは本当に彼らには辛いものでした。アドベンチャーをしている間，子どもたちは完全に集中してとても楽しめたので，私たちは来月また別のものをやることにします。

〈設問解説〉

問１　正解　18 －③，19 －④
**　　　　　　 20 －②，21 －①**

「次の出来事（①〜④）を，それらが起こった順に並べなさい」

①　子どもたちは好きではないものを食べた。
②　子どもたちはお菓子を探し始めた。
③　父親は家の居間の飾り付けをした。
④　父親は息子たちに着る物を与えた。

正解は③→④→②→①である。各選択肢に相当する本文中の記述は，「全訳」中の下線部を参照のこと。本文は基本的に出来事が起こった順序通りに述べられているので，本文の記述の順序通りに並べればよい。

問２　22　正解－③

「この父親のアドバイスに従って，あなた独自の『アドベンチャールーム』を作ろうとするならば，あなたは 22 べきである」

①　３文字の単語に集中する
②　ランプの下に秘密のメッセージを残しておく
③　チャレンジを少しずつ難しくする
④　シャーロック・ホームズのように振る舞う練習をする

正解は③。ブログ本文の第４段落第６文（Remember that the …）に，「忘れてはいけないのは，最終ゴールが近づくにつれて，パズルをますます難しくするべきだということです」とあり，③はこの内容と合っているので正解となる。

他の選択肢の内容は，「あなた独自の『アドベンチャールーム』を作ろうとする」場合に，従うべきアドバイスとは考えられない。

問３　23　正解－②

「この話から，この父親は 23 ことがわかる」

①　お菓子を探すことに集中するようになった
②　特に自分の子どもに体験してほしいものを作った

③　アドベンチャーゲームを準備するのにある程度苦労した
④　部屋の装飾にたくさんのお金を費やした

正解は②。ブログ本文の最終段落第１文（This "adventure room" …）に，「この『アドベンチャールーム』は，私の家族向けに特別にデザインされたので，難問の中には我が家独自のものを含めました」とある。下線部中の「家族（family）」とは，「子どもたち」のことと考えられることから，下線部の内容と合っている②が正解となる。他の選択肢の内容は，本文からは読み取れない。

〈主な語句・表現〉

take part in …「…に参加する」／ tip 图「ヒント；秘訣」／ storyline 图「筋立て」／ rearrange 動「…を配列し直す」／ some old paintings and lamps (that) I had「私が持っていたいくつかの古い絵やランプ」／ to set the scene「状況を設定するために〈…を加えた〉」／ missing 形「あるべきところにない」／ clue 图「手がかり；かぎ」／ locate 動「…を捜し出す」／ challenge 图「難題；チャレンジ」／ backwards 副「後ろ向きに；逆さに」／ three-digit「３けたの」／ padlock 图「南京錠」／ code 图「暗号；番号」／ Old books are fantastic for hiding messages in「古い本は（その中に）メッセージを隠すにはすばらしい」／ have fun －ing「－して楽しむ」／ progressively 副「次第に；ますます」／ get into the spirit「熱中する」／ magnifying glass「拡大鏡；虫メガネ」／ specifically 副「明確に；とりわけ」／ made some of … personal「…の一部をパーソナル［私的］なものにした」／ fill A with B「AをBで満たす」／ eat one's way to …「どんどん食べて…まで進む」／ reveal 動「…を明らかにする」／ be focused「集中している」／ concentrate on …「…に集中する」／ have trouble －ing「－するのに苦労する」／ spend O －ing「－するのにOを費やす」

第4問
〈全訳〉
あなたは先生から，効果的な勉強法についての2つの投稿記事を読むように求められました。あなたは次の授業で，学んだことを議論します。

効果的な学習法とは：文脈学習です！
ティム・オックスフォード
ストーンシティ中学校　理科教諭

理科の教師である私は，学習に苦労している生徒をどうやって助けたらよいかいつも気にかけています。最近私が知ったのは，生徒たちの主な学習法は，新しい情報を全部思い出せるようになるまで繰り返し学習するというものでした。たとえば試験勉強をする時には，下の例のようなワークブックを利用して，空欄に入る用語を繰り返し唱えようとするのです。「黒曜石は火成岩で，黒っぽくて，ガラス質で… 黒曜石は火成岩で，黒っぽくて，ガラス質で…」 こういった生徒たちは，その情報を覚えたと感じるでしょうが，すぐに忘れて，試験で低い点数を取るでしょう。また，このような反復式の学習は退屈で，やる気がそがれます。

生徒たちの学習の役に立つようにと，私は「文脈学習」を応用してみました。この種の学習では，新しい知識は生徒自身の経験を通じて積み上げられていきます。私の理科の授業のために，生徒たちはさまざまな種類の石の特徴を学びました。私は生徒たちにワークブックにある用語を暗記させるのではなく，いろいろな石の入った大きな箱をクラスに持っていきました。生徒たちは石を調べて，観察した特徴に基づいて名前を特定しました。

この経験のおかげで，これらの生徒たちは学習した石の特徴をいつでも説明できるようになると思います。しかし1つ問題なのは，私たちにはいつも文脈学習をする時間があるとは限らないので，生徒はやはりドリル方式で勉強するだろうということです。私はこれが最良の方法だとは思いません。今でも生徒の学習を改善する方法を模索しています。

石の名前	黒曜石
石の種類	火成岩
色	黒っぽい
質感	ガラス質
画像	

反復学習を効果的に行う方法
チェン・リー
ストーンシティー大学教授

オックスフォード先生の文脈学習に関するお考えはとても鋭いものでした。それが有益になりうることには私も賛成です。けれども反復も役に立つことがあります。しかしながら，先生が話題にされた反復的学習法は「集中学習」と呼ばれるもので，これは効果的ではありません。別の種類の反復学習に，「分散学習」と呼ばれるものがあります。これは学習者が新しい情報を記憶したら，より長い間隔をあけて復習するというものです。

学習の間隔が重要な差となります。オックスフォード先生の例では，生徒たちはおそらくワークブックを使って短期間で勉強しようとしたのでしょう。この場合，生徒は復習を続けるにつれて，内容に注意が向かなくなっていったのかもしれません。こうなる理由は，内容がもはや新しくないので，おそらく無視されるだろうからです。これに対して，間隔がより長いと，内容についての生徒の記憶は弱くなります。それゆえ，生徒は前に覚えたことを思い出すのにより大きな努力を払わなければならないので，より大きな注意を払うのです。たとえば，生徒がワークブックを使って勉強して，3日間置いてからまた勉強すれば，おそらく教材をよりよく覚えられるでしょう。

これまでの研究で，分散学習の利点を支持する証拠が得られています。ある実験では，AとBのグループに分けられた生徒たちが，50の動物の名前を覚えようとしました。どちらのグループも4回学習しましたが，グループAは1日間隔で学習し，グループBは1週間間隔で学習しました。右の図が示すように，最後の学習セッションから28日たつと，テストにおいて想起される名前の平均的割合は，分散学習のグループの方が高かったのです。

生徒はしばしば短期間でたくさんの情報を覚える必要があり，学習の間に長い休止期間を設けるのは現実的ではないかもしれません。しかし理解していただきたいのは，集中学習が長期の想起力にとっては良くないかもしれないということです。

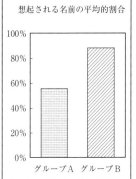

〈設問解説〉

本文を読み，効果的な学習法に関する2人の投稿者の評価について，基本的に以下のように理解できればよい。

	オックスフォード氏	リー氏
反復学習 (repetitive learning)	(A)否定的	(B)集中型（massed）には否定的 (C)分散型（spaced）には肯定的
文脈学習 (contextual learning)	(D)肯定的	(E)肯定的

これらの点を踏まえた上で，問いに取り組むことが大事である。

問1　正解　24 － ①

「オックスフォード氏は 24 と考えている」

① 連続する反復学習は退屈だ
② 用語の説明を読むのは役に立つ
③ 生徒たちは科学に興味がない
④ ワークブックで勉強すればうまくいく

　正解は①。表中の(A)に関する問題。オックスフォード氏の投稿記事の第1段落最終文（Also, this sort ...）に「また，このような反復式の学習は退屈で，やる気がそがれます」とあり，この内容と合っている①が正解となる。本文中の「このような反復式の学習（this sort of repetitive learning）」と①の中の「連続する反復学習（continuous drilling）」がほぼ同じ意味であることがわかればよい。

　他の選択肢を正解とする根拠はない。

問2　25　正解－①

「リー氏によって論じられた研究においては，生徒たちは最後のセッションの 25 後にテストを受けた」

① 4週間
② すぐ
③ 1日
④ 1週間

　正解は①。リー氏の投稿記事の第3段落最終文（As the figure ...）に，「右の図が示すように，最後の学習セッションから 28 日たつと，テストにおいて想起される名前の平均的割合は，分散学習のグループの方が高かったのです」とあることから，下線部と同じ意味である①が正解となる。

問3　26　正解－②，27 － ⑤

「オックスフォード氏が論じた 27 学習の不利な点を克服するために，リー氏は 26 間隔での学習を伴う分

散学習を紹介している（① ～ ⑥ の中からそれぞれの空所に最適なものを選びなさい）」

① 文脈の
② 長期の
③ 固定された
④ 不規則な
⑤ 集中した
⑥ 実用的な

　26 には，表中の(C)にあるように，リー氏が推奨する分散学習の特徴を表す語が入る。リー氏の投稿記事の第1段落最終文（There is another ...）に，「別の種類の反復学習に，『分散学習』と呼ばれるものがあります。これは学習者が新しい情報を記憶したら，より長い間隔をあけて復習するというものです」とあることから，26 には「より長い（longer）」に等しい意味の語が入ることがわかる。選択肢の中でこの意味に最も近いのは，②の extended（延長された；長期の）である。

　リー氏が分散学習を紹介した目的は，表中の(B)にあるように，集中型の反復学習に対しては否定的，つまり集中型には不利な点があると考えるためである。このことはリー氏の投稿の第1段落第4文以降（However, the repetitive ...）の「しかしながら，（オックスフォード）先生が話題にされた反復的学習法は『集中学習』と呼ばれるもので，これは効果的ではありません。別の種類の反復学習に，『分散学習』と呼ばれるものがあります。（以下略）」などの記述から明らかである（この集中型の持つ「不利な点（disadvantages）」とは，具体的には「内容に注意が向かなくなるかもしれないこと（リー氏投稿文の第2段落第3文：In this case, ...）」，「長期の想起力にとって良くないかもしれないこと（同最終段落最終文：You should understand, ...）」などが挙げられている）。したがって 27 には⑤の「集中した（massed）」が入る。

問4　正解　28 － ①

「2人の投稿者は，28 は新しい情報を覚えるのに役に立つことで意見が合っている」

① 経験に基づく学習
② 適切な休息をとること
③ 長期間の注意
④ ワークブックを使った学習

　正解は①。表中の(D)と(E)に示されているように，2人の投稿者の両方が肯定的に評価している学習法は文脈学習（contextual learning）である。このことは，オックスフォード氏の投稿記事の第2段落第1・2文（To help them ... ・In this kind ...）に，「生徒たちの学習の役に立つようにと，私は『文脈学習』を応用してみ

— 英 R 252 —

ました。この種の学習では，新しい知識は生徒自身の経験を通じて積み上げられていきます」とあり，リー氏の投稿記事の第1段落第1・2文（Mr. Oxford's thoughts ...・I agree that ...）に，「オックスフォード先生の文脈学習に関するお考えはとても鋭いものでした。それが有益になりうることには私も賛成です」とあることからわかる。また，上に引用した文から，文脈学習とは，新しい知識が生徒自身の「経験（experience）」を通じて積み上げられるということもわかる。したがって2人の投稿者はいずれも，「経験に基づく（experiential）」学習の有用性を支持していることになるので，①が正解に決まる。

②の「適切な休息」については，リー氏が紹介した「分散型の反復学習」のことを指すと考えることはできるが，オックスフォード氏はこれについては何も述べていないので，②は正解になれない。③については，両者とも触れていない。④については，オックスフォード氏の投稿文の第1段落（As a science ...）から，彼が否定的な立場をとっていることがわかるので，やはり正解になれない。

問5　正解　29 ─②

「分散学習に賛成するリー氏の主張をさらに支持するには，次のどの情報を追加するのが最適だろうか」

① 理科の授業を魅力的にする主な要因
② 分散学習にとって最も効果的な間隔の長さ
③ 生徒のワークブックに視覚資料が含まれているかどうか
④ オックスフォード氏の生徒たちはなぜ情報をよく覚えられなかったのか

正解は②。リー氏の投稿の第3段落（Previous research has ...）においては，長時間の間隔を置いて学習を行う分散学習に効果があることを示唆する実験結果が紹介されているが，具体的に「どのくらい長さの間隔を置くのが最も効果的か」ということについては明らかにされていない。したがって②の情報は，この学習法をさらに支持する有力な追加情報となりうることから，②が正解となる。

①や③は，分散学習とは無関係なことなので，正解にはなれない。④については，すでにリー氏の投稿記事の第2段落（The interval between ...）の中で考察がなされていることから，これがリー氏の主張をさらに支持する最適な追加情報になるとは考えられない。

〈主な語句・表現〉
リード文
effective 形「効果的な」
オックスフォード氏の投稿文
contextual 形「文脈上の；状況の」／ be concerned about ...「…を気にかけている」／ term 名「用語」／ obsidian 名「黒曜石」／ igneous 形「火成の」／ glassy 形「ガラス状の」／ repetitive 形「繰り返しの」／ dull 形「退屈な」／ demotivating 形「やる気をそぐ」／ apply 動「…を適用［応用］する」／ construct 動「…を構築する」／ property 名「特徴；特性」／ rather than having them memorize ...「彼らに…を暗記させるのではなく」／ examine 動「…を調べる」／ identify 動「…を特定する」／ based on ...「…に基づいて」／ characteristic 名「特徴」／ thanks to ...「…のおかげで」／ describe 動「…を記述［説明］する」／ issue 名「問題」／ drill 名「練習；ドリル」／ improve 動「…を改善する」／ texture 名「感触；質感」
リー氏の投稿文
insightful 形「洞察に富む」／ beneficial 形「有益な」／ repetition 名「反復；繰り返し」／ work well「うまく機能する」／ strategy 名「戦略；方策」／ massed 形「ひとかたまりになった；集中した」／ spaced 形「一定の間隔を置いた」／ review 動「…を見直す；復習する」／ interval 名「（時間的）間隔」／ key 形「重要な」／ pay attention to ...「…に注意を払う」／ content 名「内容」／ no longer「もはや…でない」／ could easily「おそらく…だろう」／ in contrast「対照的に」／ effort 名「努力」／ recall 動「…を思い出す」，名「想起（力）」／ be likely to ‐「‐しそうである」／ previous 形「以前の」／ evidence 名「証拠」／ advantage 名「利点」／ experiment 名「実験」／ memorize 動「…を暗記する」／ at one-day intervals「1日の間隔を置いて」／ the figure to the right「右側の図」／ 28 days after ...「…の28日後に」／ session 名「集団活動；セッション」／ ratio 名「比率」／ practical 形「実用的な；現実的な」

─ 英 R 253 ─

第5問
〈全訳〉
（全訳中の下線部については，設問解説の問3を参照のこと）

あなたの英語の先生はクラスの全員に，気持ちを高めてくれるストーリーを見つけて，メモを使ってそれを討論グループに発表するよう指示しました。あなたは英国の高校生が書いたストーリーを見つけました。

卓球が教えてくれたこと
ベン・カーター

球は電光のような速さで僕のバックハンド側に飛んできた。それは全く予想外で，僕には反応する時間がなかった。僕はポイント，そして試合を落とした。敗北…またか！　僕が卓球をやり始めて最初の数ヵ月間はこんな感じでした。イライラがつのりましたが，このスポーツは僕に，単により優れた運動選手になる方法以上のものを教えてくれたことが，今の自分にはわかっています。

僕は中学時代はサッカーが大好きでした。僕は得点王の1人でしたが，チームメートとはうまくいきませんでした。コーチからはよく，もっとチームプレーヤーになりなさいと言われました。この問題に取り組まなければならないことはわかっていましたが，僕はコミュニケーションをとるのが決して得意ではありませんでした。

我が家が新しい町に引っ越す時に，僕はサッカー部を去らなければなりませんでした。いずれにせよサッカーはやめることにしていたので，動揺はしませんでした。新しい学校には，体育のトレント先生がコーチをしている卓球部があったので，僕は入部しました。正直に言うと，僕が卓球を選んだ理由は，自分には個人競技の方が楽だと思ったからです。

最初の頃は，負け試合の数が勝ち試合を上回っていました。僕は欲求不満で，練習が終わると誰とも口を聞かずにまっすぐ帰宅することもよくありました。ところがある日のこと，トレント先生は僕に，「ベン，君はいい選手になれるかもしれないが，もっと試合のことを考える必要があるね。自分では何をする必要があると思うかい？」と言いました。「わかりません」と僕は答えました。「もっと球に集中することですか？」「そうだよ」とトレント先生は続けました。「だが相手の動きをよく見て，それに応じて自分のプレーを変えていくことも必要だね。いいかい，相手は人間なんだ。球じゃないんだよ」。（→問3②）この言葉は僕に強い印象を

残しました。

僕は相手の動きにより細かく注意して，自分のプレースタイルを意図的に修正しました。（→問3④）これは易しくはなく，多大な集中力を必要としました。けれども努力の甲斐あって，僕のプレーは上達しました。自信が深まり，僕は練習の後で居残りをするようになりました。僕はスタープレーヤーに変わりつつあり，クラスメートたちは以前よりも僕に話しかけようとしました。僕は人気者になりつつあると思いましたが，本当の会話が始まらないうちに僕たちは話すのをやめていました。僕のプレーは上達したかもしれませんが，会話術が上達していないのは明らかでした。

兄のパトリックは，僕がうまく会話ができる数少ない人々の中の1人でした。ある日，僕はコミュニケーションの問題を彼に説明しようとしましたが，理解させることができませんでした。僕たちは話題を卓球に変えました。「実際には卓球のどこが面白いんだい？」と彼は興味ありげに僕に聞きました。僕は相手の動きを分析して次の動きを瞬時に判断するのが楽しいと言いました。（→問3⑤）パトリックは考え込んだ様子でした。「人がコミュニケーションをする時も，それと同じような技術を使うんじゃないかな」と彼は言いました。

その時はわかりませんでしたが，兄と話した後すぐに，僕はある卓球のトーナメントで銀メダルを獲得しました。クラスメートたちは本当に喜んでいるようでした。その中の1人だったジョージが駆け寄ってきました。「やあ，ベン！」と彼は言いました。「お祝いのパーティーをやろうよ！」　僕は何も考えずに，「ダメだよ。練習があるんだ」と答えました。（→問3③）彼は少し傷ついたようで，他には何も言わずに立ち去りました。

なぜ彼は気を悪くしたのだろう。僕はこの出来事についてしばらく考えました。なぜ彼はパーティーをしないかと言ったのだろう。僕は何か違うことを言うべきだったのか。たくさんの問いが頭に浮かびましたが，その後で僕は，彼はただ親切にしてくれただけなんだということに気づきました。もし僕が「それはいいね。ありがとう！　トレント先生と話して，練習を少し休めるかどうか調べてみるよ」と言っていたら，結果はもっと良くなっていたかもしれません。その時，パトリックの言葉の意味がわかりました。相手の意図を把握しようと試みることがなければ，自分がどう反応すればいいかがわかることはないでしょう。

僕はまだ，コミュニケーションが世界一上手だというわけではありませんが，今は以前よりも自分のコミュニケーション術に自信を持っていることには間違いありません。来年には，僕は友人たちと一緒に，他校との卓球リーグの編成の仕事をすることになっています。

あなたのメモ：

卓球が教えてくれたこと

著者（ベン・カーター）について
・中学ではサッカーをしていた。
・新しい学校で卓球を始めたのは，彼は　30　からだった。

他の重要人物
・トレント先生：ベンの卓球コーチで，彼のプレーが上達するのを助けた。
・パトリック：ベンの兄で，　31　。
・ジョージ：ベンのクラスメートで，彼の勝利を祝いたいと思った。

ベンのコミュニケーションが上達する道のりにおいて影響を及ぼした出来事
卓球を始めた→　32　→　33　→　34　→　35

ジョージとの会話の後でベンが気づいたこと
彼は　36　べきだった。

このストーリーから私たちが学べること
・　37
・　38

〈設問解説〉
問1　正解　　30　－④
「　30　に最適な選択肢を選びなさい」
① それが彼がコミュニケーションをとるのに役立つだろうと考えた
② 学校で人気者になることを望んだ
③ 試合に簡単に勝てると思った
❹ チームスポーツをするの避けたいと思った

正解は④。空所には，ベンが新しい学校で卓球を始めた理由として正しいものが入る。ベンのストーリーの第3段落最終文（To be honest, ...）に，「正直に言うと，僕が卓球を選んだ理由は，自分には個人競技の方が楽だと思ったからです」とあることから，下線部とほぼ同じ内容である④が正解となる。

他の選択肢を正解とする根拠はない。

問2　正解　　31　－③
「　31　に最適な選択肢を選びなさい」
① コミュニケーションの何が楽しいのかを彼に聞いた
② もっと自信を持つようにと彼を励ました
❸ 彼が必要としている，人と付き合う技術を彼が

身につけるのを助けた
④ 彼が学校の友人たちに何を言うべきだったかを教えた

正解は③。ベンの兄パトリックの役割として適切なものを選ぶ。第6段落第4文（"What do you ..."）以降にある「『実際には卓球のどこが面白いんだい？』と彼は興味ありげに僕に聞きました。僕は相手の動きを分析して次の動きを瞬時に判断するのが楽しいと言いました。パトリックは考え込んだ様子でした。『人がコミュニケーションをする時も，それと同じような技術を使うんじゃないかな』と彼は言いました」というベンとパトリックのやり取りから，パトリックは下線部の発言において，人とうまくコミュニケーションをとるコツをベンに示唆したと考えられることから，③が正解となる。③の中の「人と付き合う技術（social skills）」とは，本文における「コミュニケーション術（communication skills）」を言い換えたものだと考えられればよい。

①は上に引用した記述の中の「実際には卓球のどこが面白いんだい？」を誤解したものなので誤り。②や④のようなことは，ベンとパトリックのやり取りからは読み取れない。

問3　正解　　32　－②，　33　－④
　　　　　　　　　34　－⑤，　35　－③
「5つの選択肢（①～⑤）の中から4つを選び，それらを起こった順序通りに並べ替えなさい」
① 卓球のチャンピオンになった
② 先生とうまくプレーする方法について話し合った
③ 自分のことを祝うパーティーを拒んだ
④ 相手の動きを観察するようになった
⑤ 兄と卓球について話した

正解は②→④→⑤→③。各選択肢の本文における対応箇所は，全訳中の下線部を参照のこと。①については，（ベンは銀メダルを獲得したことはあるものの）本文中に該当する記述がない。

問4　　36　正解－③
「　36　に最適な選択肢を選びなさい」
① 友人に彼の動機についてもっと多くのことを知るために質問をする
② トレント先生と他のクラスメートをパーティーに招待して感謝の気持ちを表す
❸ 適切に振る舞うために友人の視点を理解しようと試みる
④ うまくコミュニケーションをとるためによりよいチームプレーヤーになるよう懸命に努力する

— 英 R 255 —

正解は ③。ジョージとの会話の後で，ベンが気づいたこととして適切なものを選ぶ。ジョージとの会話の後でベンが考えたことは，第8段落（Why was he ...）に書かれている。この段落の最終文（Without attempting to ...）に「相手の意図を把握しようと試みることがなければ，自分がどう反応すればいいかがわかることはないでしょう」とある。選択肢 ③ の中の「友人の視点を理解しようとする（tried to understand his friend's point of view）」が，上の文の中の「相手の意図を把握しようと試みる（attempting to grasp someone's intention）」とほぼ同内容で，③ の中の「適切に振る舞う（act appropriately）」が，上の文の中の「自分がどう反応すればいいかがわかる（know how to respond）」に対応していると考えられれば，③ が正しいとわかる。

他の選択肢のようなことに，ベンがジョージとの会話の後で気づいたとは，本文では述べられていない。

問5 　37 ・ 38 　正解—① ・ ⑤
「37 と 38 に最適な2つの選択肢を選びなさい（順序は問わない）」
① 周囲の人々のアドバイスが私たちを変えるのに役立つことがある。
② コミュニケーションが上手くなるには自信が大切だ。
③ 友人に自分の意図をはっきりと伝えることが大切だ。
④ チームメートが互いに与え合う支えは助けになる。
⑤ あることから学んだことを別のことに応用することができる。
　正解は ① と ⑤。このストーリーから得られる教訓として適切なものを2つ選ぶ。① については，「周囲の人々」とはストーリー中のトレント先生や兄のパトリックのことで，「私たちを変える」とは，ベンが人々とのコミュニケーションが上手にとれるようになることを指していると考えれば，本文から得られる教訓の1つと考えることができる。⑤ については，「あることから学んだこと」を「卓球から学んだこと」，つまり「相手の動きを瞬時に読んで自分の反応を決めること」と考えて，「別のこと」を「人とのコミュニケーション」と考えれば，本文の内容に合ったものとなるので，これがもう1つの正解となる。
　② については，ベンは「コミュニケーションが上手くなって自信がついた」とは言える（最終段落第1文：I'm still not the best ...）が，本文の内容から「コミュニケーションが上手くなるには自信が大切だ」と考え

ることはできない。③ については，本文の内容から「友人の意図をはっきりと理解することが大切だ」ということは言える（第8段落最終文：Without attempting to grasp ...）が，「友人に自分の意図をはっきりと伝えることが大切だ」と考えることはできない。④ のように，チームメートと支え合うことの重要性も，本文では述べられていない。

〈主な語句・表現〉
リード文
　inspirational 形「インスピレーションを与える；気持ちを高めてくれる」
第1段落（The ball flew ...）
　at lightning speed「電光石火の速さで」／ unexpected 形「予期しない」／ This is how it was in the first few months「最初の数ヵ月間はこのような有様だった」 it は漠然と「状況」を表す。／ frustrating 形「挫折感を起こすような」／ athlete 名「運動選手」
第2段落（In middle school, ...）
　middle school「中学校」／ get along with ...「…とうまくやっていく」／ work on ...「…に取り組む」／ strong point「長所；得意」
第3段落（I had to ...）
　be upset「動揺する；気分を害する」／ PE「体育（physical education）」／ to be honest「正直に言うと」／ individually 副「個人で」
第4段落（At first, I ...）
　at first「最初の頃は」／ focus on ...「…に集中する」／ opponent 名「対戦相手」／ adjust 動「…を調整する」／ accordingly 副「それに応じて」／ impression 名「印象」
第5段落（I deliberately modified ...）
　deliberately 副「意図的に」／ modify 動「…を修正する」／ concentration 名「集中（力）」／ pay off「利益を産む；引き合う」／ confidence 名「自信」／ stay behind「居残る」／ turn into ...「…に変わる」／ get started「始まる」／ obviously 副「明らかに」
第6段落（My older brother ...）
　communicate with ...「…と気持ちを伝え合う」／ problem with ...「…に関する問題」／ switch to ...「…へ切り換える」／ analyse 動「…を分析する」／ instant 形「瞬時の」／ thoughtful 形「考え込んだ」／ That sounds like ...「それは…のように聞こえる」
第7段落（At that time, ...）
　seem pleased「喜んでいるようだ」／ come running over「駆け寄ってくる」／ celebrate 動「お祝いする」／ look a bit hurt「少し傷ついたように見える」／ walk off「歩き去る」

第8段落（Why was he ...）

incident 图「出来事」／ should have p.p.「…すべきだった」／ was just being kind「ただ親切にしているだけだった」／ get some time off practice「練習をしばらく休む」／ outcome 图「結果」／ make sense「意味をなす」／ grasp 動「…を把握［理解］する」／ intention 图「意図」／ respond 動「応答する」

最終段落（I'm still not ...）

definitely 副「確かに；絶対に」／ feel confident in ...「…に自信がある」／ co-ordinate 動「…を組織する；まとめ上げる」

第6問

A

〈全訳〉

　あなたは学校で討論のグループに入っています。あなたは次の記事を要約するよう頼まれました。あなたはメモだけを使ってそれについて話します。

コレクション活動

　コレクション活動は昔から，社会のあらゆる層で，文化や年齢集団の壁を越えて行われてきました。博物館は，物が集められ，保管され，将来の世代に伝えられてきたことの証です。コレクションを始める理由は様々です。例えば女性のＡさんは，毎週土曜日の朝に子どもたちと一緒にヤードセールへ行くのが楽しみです。ヤードセールでは，不用品が人の家の前で売られます。ある日のこと，彼女は骨董品のお皿を見ていると，珍しい絵に目が釘付けになり，それをわずか数ドルで買いました。彼女は時間をかけて心に残る同じような物をいくつも見つけて，今ではささやかな美術品のコレクションを所有しています。その中のいくつかには，支払った金額以上の価値があるかもしれません。ある人にとってのガラクタは，別の人にとっては宝物になることがあるのです。人がどのようにしてコレクションを始めるのであろうと，物を集めるのは人間の性なのです。

　1988 年に，ブレンダ・ダネットとタマール・カトリエルという研究者が，10 歳未満の子どもたちについての 80 年にわたる数々の研究を分析して，約 90 パーセントの子どもが何かを集めていたことを知りました。このことは，人は幼時から物を集めるのが好きであることを私たちに示しています。大人になった後でも，人は物を集め続けます。この分野の研究者たちは一般に，大人のおよそ 3 分の 1 がこういった行動を続けるということで意見が一致しています。これはどうしてなのでしょう。最も代表的な説明は情緒と関連しています。友人や家族からもらったグリーティングカードや，特別な行事で使ったドライフラワー，海岸で過ごした日に拾った貝殻，古い写真などをとっておく人がいます。人によっては，コレクションが若かった日々への架け橋となるのです。子どもの頃から集めた野球カードや，漫画本，人形，ミニカーを持っているかもしれません。また歴史への愛着を持っている人もいて，歴史的な文書や，有名な人の署名の入った手紙やサインなどを探し求めてずっととっておくのです。

　人によっては，社交的な理由もあります。分けてあげたり，見せたり，さらには交換するためのピンなど

— 英 R 257 —

を集め，これによって新しい友達を作るのです。他にも，一部のギネス世界記録保持者のように，独特のコレクションをすることで勝ち取る名声を享受する人たちもいます。カード，ステッカー，切手，コイン，玩具が「普通の」コレクションのリストの上位を占めてきましたが，一部のコレクターは，もっと意外な物に傾いていきます。2014年の9月に，ギネス世界記録はドイツのハリー・スパールさんを，3,724点にものぼるハンバーガー関連の世界最大級のコレクション保持者として表彰しました。Tシャツから枕，犬の玩具に至るまで，スパールさんの部屋は「ハンバーガー」関連のありとあらゆる物でいっぱいでした。同様に，中国のリウ・フーチャンさんはトランプのコレクターです。彼は異なる種類の11,087組ものトランプを持っています。

最も理解しやすい動機は，喜びかもしれません。純粋に楽しむためにコレクションを始める人たちがいます。しばしば眺めるためだけの絵画を買って掛けておくこともあれば，お気に入りの音楽を聴くために録音素材や古風なアナログレコードを集めることもあります。こういった種類のコレクターは，宝のように大切な音楽の金銭的価値にはあまり関心を持ちそうにありませんが，明確に投資対象として物を集める人もいます。ある特定の名作ゲームは無料でダウンロードできますが，同じゲームを未開封のまま最初の包装状態，つまり「ミントコンディション」で持っていると，ゲームに大きな値打ちが出ることがあります。さまざまな価値ある「コレクターアイテム」を所有すれば，経済的な安全性が保証されるかもしれないのです。

このようなコレクション活動は，遠い未来まで続くことは間違いありません。人が物を持ち続ける理由はおそらく変わらないでしょうが，テクノロジーの進歩はコレクションに影響を及ぼすでしょう。テクノロジーは物理的な制約を取り除くことができるため，今や個人が30年前は考えられなかったような膨大な音楽や芸術のデジタルコレクションを持つことが可能となっています。けれども，テクノロジーがコレクションにそれ以外のどんな影響を及ぼすかははっきりしません。次の世代のコレクションがどんな形や規模のものになるか想像することさえ大変です。

あなたのメモ：

コレクション活動

導入部
- ◆コレクション活動は昔から人間の経験の一部となっている。
- ◆ヤードセールの話は私たちに 39 ということを教えてくれる。

諸事実
- ◆ 40
- ◆ギネス世界記録
  - ◇スパール：ハンバーガーに関するものが3,724点
  - ◇リウ：11,087組のトランプ

コレクションをする理由
- ◆コレクションをする動機は情緒的なものも，社交的なものもある。
- ◆次のような様々な理由が挙げられている。 41 ， 42 ，歴史への興味，子ども時代の熱中，有名になること，分け合うことなど。

将来のコレクション
- ◆ 43

〈設問解説〉
問1 39 正解－③
「39 に最適な選択肢を選びなさい」
① 人々がコレクターに物を高い値段で売るのにぴったりの場所はヤードセールだ
② 人々は物を不正確に評価し，その結果ジャンク品に法外なお金を払ってしまうことがある
③ **ある人にとって大事でない物が，別の人には価値ある物になるかもしれない**
④ かつて収集されて別の人の庭に捨てられた物は，他の人々には価値があるかもしれない

正解は③。ヤードセールの話が教えてくれることとして適切なものを選ぶ。ヤードセールについては，本文第1段落で述べられているが，その第8文（One person's trash ...）に「ある人にとってのガラクタは，別の人にとっては宝物になることがあるのです」とあることから，この内容と合っている③が正解となる。

他の選択肢のようなことは，本文からは読み取れない。

問2　40　正解−④

「40に最適な選択肢を選びなさい」

① 子どもの約3分の2は，普通の物を集めない。
② 大人のほぼ3分の1が，娯楽で物を集め始める。
③ 子どものおよそ10パーセントが，友達と同じようなコレクションを持っている。
④ 人々のだいたい30パーセントが，大人になるまでコレクション活動を続ける。

　正解は④。本文中で述べられている事実として正しいものを選ぶ。第2段落第1文（In 1988, researchers ...）から第4文（Researchers in the ...）に，「1988年に，ブレンダ・ダネットとタマール・カトリエルという研究者が，10歳未満の子どもたちについての80年にわたる数々の研究を分析して，約90パーセントの子どもが何かを集めていたことを知りました。このことは，人は幼時から物を集めるのが好きであることを私たちに示しています。大人になった後でも，人は物を集め続けます。この分野の研究者たちは一般に，大人のおよそ3分の1がこういった行動を続けるということで意見が一致しています」とあり，下線部の内容と合っている④が正解となる。

　他の選択肢はいずれも上の引用部分の一部を誤解したものであり，正解にはなれない。

問3　41・42　正解−④・⑥

「41と42に最適な選択肢を選びなさい（順序は問わない）」

① テクノロジーを進歩させたいという願望
② 予期せぬ機会を逃すことへの恐れ
③ 空虚感を埋め合わせること
④ 大切な出来事の記念
⑤ 将来のために物を再利用すること
⑥ 何らかの種類の利潤を求めること

　正解は④と⑥。コレクション活動を行う理由として本文中に挙げられているものを2つ選ぶ。④については，コレクション活動を続ける大人が多い理由を説明している第2段落第6・7文（The primary explanation ...）に「最も代表的な説明は情緒と関連しています。友人や家族からもらったグリーティングカードや，特別な行事で使ったドライフラワー，海岸で過ごした日に拾った貝殻，古い写真などをとっておく人がいます」とあり，④の「大切な出来事の記念」は，この部分を一般的に表したものと考えられるため，正解の1つとなる。

　⑥については，第4段落第4文（This type of ...）に，「こういった種類のコレクターは，宝のように大切な音楽の金銭的価値にはあまり関心を持ちそうにありませんが，明確に投資対象として物を集める人もいます」

とあることなどと合っている。

　他の選択肢のようなことは，コレクション活動を行う理由として挙げられていない。

問4　正解　43−①

「43に最適な選択肢を選びなさい」

① コレクションはおそらく規模や形態を変え続けるだろう。
② 新品状態のゲームのコレクターは，より多くのデジタルコピーを持つようになるだろう。
③ コレクション活動への情熱を失った人々が，再びコレクションを始めるだろう。
④ テクノロジーの進歩のせいで，コレクション活動をする理由は変わるだろう。

　正解は①。コレクション活動の未来について当てはまるものを選ぶ。これについて述べられているのは最終段落だが，その最終文に，Can you even imagine the form and scale that the next generation's collections will take? とある。これはいわゆる修辞疑問文で，文字通りには「あなたは次の世代のコレクションがとる形や規模を想像することさえできるだろうか」という意味だが，実質的には「あなたは次の世代のコレクションがとる形や規模を想像することとさえできないだろう」，つまり「次の世代のコレクションは形や規模が大きく変化する」ことを示唆している。したがってこの内容と合っている①が正解となる。

　②や③のようなことは本文では述べられていない。④は，最終段落第2文（Although the reasons ...）に「人が物を持ち続ける理由はおそらく変わらないでしょうが，テクノロジーの進歩はコレクションに影響を及ぼすでしょう」とあるのと合わない。

〈主な語句・表現〉

第1段落（Collecting has existed ...）
　age group「年齢集団」／ proof that ...「…という証拠」／ pass down ...「…を（次の世代へ）渡す」／ unwanted 形「不必要な」／ antique 形「骨董品の」／ ... catch one's eye「…に目が釘付けになる」／ buy A for B「A（＝品物）を B（＝金額）で買う」／ over time「長い期間にわたって」／ impression on ...「…への印象」／ modest 形「適度な；ささやかな」／ be worth more than ...「…以上の価値がある」／ trash 名「ゴミ」／ treasure 名「宝物」／ regardless of ...「…に関係なく」／ it is human nature to −「−するのは人間の性質［本質］だ」

第2段落（In 1988, researchers ...）
　analyze 動「…を分析する」／ stuff 名「もの」／

— 英 R 259 —

approximately 副「およそ」／ one third「3分の1」／ primary 形「主要な」／ be related to ...「…と関係がある」／ emotion 名「感情；情緒」／ seashell 名「貝殻」／ ... and so on [forth]「…など」／ connection to ...「…とのつながり」／ youth 名「青春時代；若さ」／ miniature car「ミニカー」／ attachment to ...「…への愛着」／ hold onto ...「…を手放さない［取っておく］」／ autograph 名「サイン」

第3段落（For some individuals ...）

appreciate 動「…をありがたく思う」／ fame 名「名声」／ top 動「…のトップに載っている」／ lean toward ...「…の方に（心が）傾く」／ the more unexpected「より意外なもの」／ recognize A for B「A を B のことでたたえる」／ hamburger-related 形「ハンバーガー関連の」／ be filled with ...「…で満たされている」／ all things "hamburger"「ハンバーガーに関するあらゆるもの」／ playing card「トランプ」／ set 名「（トランプの）組」

第4段落（Perhaps the easiest ...）

the easiest motivation to understand「最も理解しやすい動機づけ」／ pleasure 名「喜び」／ pure enjoyment「純粋な楽しみ」／ put up「（絵画を）掛ける」／ paintings just to gaze at frequently「しばしば眺めるためだけの絵画」／ vinyl record「アナログレコード」／ be unlikely to -「-しそうにない」／ monetary value「金銭的価値」／ treasured 形「宝のように大切な」／ specifically 副「とりわけ；はっきりと」／ investment 名「投資（の対象）」／ certain 形「ある特定の」／ for free「無料で」／ packaging 名「包装（材料）」／ mint condition「新品状態；ミントコンディション」／ ensure 動「…を保証する」／ financial security「経済的な安全性」

最終段落（This behavior of ...）

definitely 副「確かに」／ likely 副「おそらく」／ have an influence on ...「…に影響を及ぼす」／ remove 動「…を取り除く」／ physical constraint「物理的制約」／ unimaginable 形「想像できない」／ what other impacts「他のどんな影響」 what は疑問形容詞。／ have an impact on ...「…に影響を与える」／ take 動「（ある形を）とる」

B

〈全訳〉

　あなたは生徒たちのあるグループに入っていて，国際科学プレゼンテーションコンテストの準備をしています。あなたは次の文章を利用して，珍しい生き物についてのプレゼンテーションの自分の担当箇所を作成しています。

　世界で最も強靭な動物の名前を挙げてくださいと誰かに言えば，その人は摂氏50度の高温でも生きられるからフタコブラクダだとか，マイナス58度以下の低温でも生きられるからホッキョクギツネだと言うかもしれません。ところが，緩歩動物が地球で最も強靭な生き物と広く考えられていることから，上の答えはどちらも間違いとなるでしょう。

　緩歩動物は，クマムシという名でも知られている微生物で，体長は0.1ミリから1.5ミリです。6,000メートルの高山から，4,600メートルの海底まで，ほぼあらゆる場所に生息しています。厚い氷の下や，熱い温泉の中でも見つけることができます。緩歩動物のほとんどは水中に生息していますが，地球で最も乾燥した土地の一部に見られることもあります。ある研究者は，緩歩動物が25年間降水記録のない砂漠の中の岩の下に生息しているのを見つけたことを報告しました。それが必要とするのは，生活の場となる数滴の水あるいは薄く張った水だけです。水が干上がると，それらも干上がります。それらは水分の大半を失って3パーセントのみを残し，新陳代謝のスピードは通常の0.01パーセントに落ちます。干上がった緩歩動物は今や「タン（樽）」と呼ばれる一種の熟睡状態に入ります。この状態は再び水に浸されるまで続きます。するとそれはスポンジのように水を吸収して，まるで何事も起こらなかったかのように復元するのです。緩歩動物のタンの期間が1週間なのか10年間なのかは，あまり大事な問題ではありません。水に囲まれた瞬間に，それは再び元気になるのです。緩歩動物はタンの状態ではとても強靭で，摂氏マイナス272度の低温，そして151度の高温の中でも生きることができます。一体どうやってこれを成し遂げるのかは，完全にはわかっていません。

　緩歩動物の地球上での生存能力（約5億4千万年前から地球にいるのです）よりもさらに驚くべきは，その宇宙における生存能力かもしれません。2007年に，ヨーロッパの研究者のチームが，何匹もの生きている緩歩動物を宇宙空間に送り出し，ロケットの外側に10日間放置しました。地球に戻る際，68パーセントがまだ生きているのを研究者たちは知って驚きました。つ

まり大部分は10日の間，この地球上よりも1,000倍強烈なX線や紫外線に耐え抜くことができたのです。その後2019年に，イスラエルの宇宙船が月面に衝突し，タン状態にあった非常に多くの緩歩動物が月面に放り出されました。誰もこれらを回収しに行った人がいないので，これらがまだ生きているかどうかはわかりません。残念なことです。

緩歩動物は短いキュウリのような形をしています。胴体のそれぞれの側に4本の短い足があります。それぞれの足先に付着盤が付いている種もあれば，爪が付いている種もあります。爪には16の変種があることがわかっていて，それは爪を持っている種を区別するのに役立ちます。すべての緩歩動物には眼窩（がんか）がありますが，すべての種が眼を持っているわけではありません。眼は単純な作りで，全部で5つの細胞しかなく，光を感知するのはその中の1つだけです。

緩歩動物は基本的に，植物を食べるものと，他の生き物を食べるものとに分けることができます。植物を食べる種には，腹口（サメのように，頭の下部に付いている口）があります。他の生き物を食べる種には終端口があります。つまりマグロのように，口は頭の最先端に付いているのです。緩歩動物の口には歯はありません。しかし吻針（ふんしん）と呼ばれる2本の鋭い針を持っていて，それで植物の細胞やより小さな生き物の体を突き刺し，中身を吸い出せるのです。

どちらのタイプの緩歩動物も，消化器系はかなり単純です。口は咽頭（のど）につながり，そこで消化液と食物が混ぜ合わされます。咽頭の上方には唾液腺があります。これは口の中へ流れ込んで消化を助ける液体を分泌します。咽頭を過ぎると，食物を消化器官に運ぶ管があります。この管は食道と呼ばれます。中腸は，簡単な胃や腸に当たる器官ですが，これは食物を消化して栄養分を吸収します。それから残存物はそこを通り抜けて最終的に肛門まで移動します。

あなたのプレゼンテーションのスライド：

緩歩動物：

極限まで生き残る地球の生物

1．基本情報

・体長0.1ミリから1.5ミリ
・短いキュウリのような形
・
・
44
・
・

2．生息地

・ほぼあらゆる場所に生息する
・以下のような過酷な環境
　✓ 海抜6キロメートル
　✓ 海底4.6キロメートル
　✓ 砂漠の中
　✓ －272度から151度まで
　✓ （おそらく）宇宙空間

3．生き延びる秘訣

 ⇔
「タン」　　　　活動状態

・ 45
・ 46

4．消化器系 47

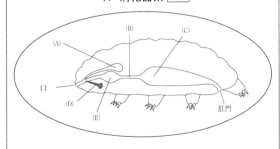

5．最後に

48

〈設問解説〉

問1 44 **正解一④**

「次の中で, 44 に含めるべきで**ないもの**はどれか」

① 8本の短い足
② 目が見えないものと見えるもの
③ 植物を食べるものと生き物を食べるもの
④ **16の異なる足の種類**
⑤ 歯の代わりに2本の吻針

正解は④。緩歩動物の基本情報として正しくないものを選ぶ。この生物の基本的特徴については, 本文の第4・5段落に, 次のように述べられている。

・第4段落 (Tardigrades are shaped ...):緩歩動物は短いキュウリのような形をしています。胴体のそれぞれの側に4本の短い足があります (→①)。それぞれの足先に付着盤が付いている種もあれば, 爪が付いている種もあります。爪には16の変種があることがわかっていて (→×④), それは爪を持っている種を区別するのに役立ちます。すべての緩歩動物には眼窩(がんか)がありますが, すべての種が眼を持っているわけではありません (→②)。眼は単純な作りで, 全部で5つの細胞しかなく, 光を感知するのはその中の1つだけです。

・第5段落 (Basically, tardigrades can ...):緩歩動物は基本的に, 植物を食べるものと, 他の生き物を食べるものとに分けることができます (→③)。植物を食べる種には, 腹口 (サメのように, 頭の下部に付いている口) があります。他の生き物を食べる種には終端口があります。つまりマグロのように, 口は頭の最先端に付いているのです。緩歩動物の口には歯はありません。しかし吻針と呼ばれる2本の鋭い針を持っていて (→⑤), それで植物の細胞やより小さな生き物の体を突き刺し, 中身を吸い出せるのです。

それぞれの下線部の後に, 対応する選択肢の番号を示してある。これらの内容から, ④の「16の異なる足の種類」が誤りだとわかるので, これが正解となる。

問2 正解 45 ・ 46 **一①・⑤**

「『生き延びる秘訣』のスライドに入れるために, 緩歩動物が生き延びるのに最も役立つ2つの特徴を選びなさい (順序は問わない。)」

① **乾燥した状況では, その新陳代謝は通常の1パーセント未満まで低下する。**
② タンの状態にある緩歩動物は摂氏151度を超える温度の中で生き延びることができる。
③ 緩歩動物の体内の水分が0.01パーセントを超えるとタンの状態は止まる。

④ そのサメのような口によって, より簡単に他の生き物を食べることができる。
⑤ **極度の放射線レベルに耐える能力を持っている。**

正解は①と⑤。①については, 第2段落第7・8文 (When the water ...・They lose all ...) に「水が干上がると, それらも干上がります。それらは水分の大半を失って3パーセントのみを残し, 新陳代謝のスピードは通常の0.01パーセントに落ちます」とあるのと合っている。⑤については, 第3段落第4文 (This means that ...) に「つまり大部分は10日の間, この地球上よりも1,000倍強烈なX線や紫外線に耐え抜くことができたのです」とあるのと合っている。

②は第2段落第14文 (When tardigrades are ...) に「緩歩動物はタンの状態ではとても強靭で, 摂氏マイナス272度の低温, そして151度の高温の中でも生きることができます」を誤解したもので, 下線部の内容から②のように「摂氏151度を超える温度の中で生き延びることができる」と考えることはできない。③は上に引用した第2段落第7・8文の内容を誤解したもので, ③のようなことは本文からは読み取れない。④は第5段落第2文 (Those that eat ...) に「植物を食べる種には, 腹口 (サメのように, 頭の下部に付いている口) があります」とあるのと合わない。

問3 正解 47 **一③**

「『消化器系』のスライドにある緩歩動物のイラスト上の空欄を埋めなさい」

① (A) 食道　　(B) 咽頭　　(C) 中腸
　 (D) 吻針　　(E) 唾液腺
② (A) 咽頭　　(B) 吻針　　(C) 唾液腺
　 (D) 食道　　(E) 中腸
③ **(A) 唾液腺　(B) 食道　　(C) 中腸**
　 (D) 吻針　　(E) 咽頭
④ (A) 唾液腺　(B) 中腸　　(C) 吻針
　 (D) 食道　　(E) 咽頭
⑤ (A) 吻針　　(B) 唾液腺　(C) 咽頭
　 (D) 中腸　　(E) 食道

正解は③。緩歩動物の消化器系については, 最終段落 (Both types of ...) で次のように述べられている。「どちらのタイプの緩歩動物も, 消化器系はかなり単純です。(ア) 口 (mouth) は咽頭 (のど) につながり, そこで消化液と食物が混ぜ合わされます。咽頭の上方には唾液腺があります。これは口の中へ流れ込んで消化を助ける液体を分泌します。(イ) 咽頭を過ぎると, 食物を消化器官に運ぶ管があります。この管は食道と呼ばれます。(ウ) 中腸は, 簡単な胃や腸に当たる器官ですが, これは食物を消化して栄養分を吸収します。それから

— 英 R 262 —

残存物はそこを通り抜けて最終的に肛門（Anus）まで移動します」。下線部(ア)の記述から，スライドの中の(E)が咽頭（Pharynx）で，その上方にある(A)が唾液腺（Salivary gland）であることがわかる。さらに下線部(イ)の記述から，(B)が食道（Esophagus）であるとわかる（この時点で正解は③に決まる）。そして下線部(ウ)の記述から，(C)が中腸（Middle gut）であることがわかる。また，第5段落第4文と5文（The mouths of ... / They do, however, ...）に「緩歩動物の口には歯はありません。しかし吻針と呼ばれる2本の鋭い針を持っていて，それで植物の細胞やより小さな生き物の体を突き刺し，中身を吸い出せるのです」とあることから，通常の動物の歯の位置と考えられる(D)が吻針（Stylets）であるとわかる。

問4 　48 　正解－④
「最後のスライドに最もふさわしい言葉はどれか」
① 何千何万年もの間，緩歩動物は地球や宇宙の最も過酷な環境のいくつかを生き抜いてきた。この生き物は人類よりも長生きするだろう。
② 緩歩動物は宇宙から来て，ホッキョクギツネやフタコブラクダの限界を超える温度下で生きることができるので，この生き物はきっと人間よりも強い。
③ 緩歩動物は間違いなく地球で最も強靭な生き物である。それは山の頂上でも，海の底でも，温泉の中でも生き延びることができる。そして月面にも生息することができるのだ。
④ 緩歩動物は地球上の最も過酷な状況のいくつか，そして少なくとも一度の宇宙旅行を生き抜いてきた。この驚くべき生き物は，人間よりも長く生きながらえるかもしれない。

　正解は④。プレゼンテーションを締めくくる結びの言葉として適切なものを選ぶ。④の第1文の「緩歩動物は地球上の最も過酷な状況のいくつか，そして少なくとも一度の宇宙旅行を生き抜いてきた」は，本文第2段落（Tardigrades, also known ...）や第3段落（Perhaps even more ...）の内容と合っている。そして④の第2文の「この驚くべき生き物は，人間よりも長く生きながらえるかもしれない」は，この文章に基づく推量として適切な内容である。したがって④が正解となる。

　①については，本文第3段落第1文（Perhaps even more ...）に，「緩歩動物の地球上での生存能力（約5億4千万年から地球にいるのです）よりもさらに驚くべきは…」とあるので，①の第1文中の「何千何万年もの間（For thousands of years）」という表現は正

確とは言えない。また，本文では緩歩動物の未来についての考察は基本的になされていないため，本文の内容から第2文のように「この生き物は人類よりも長生きするだろう（will live）」と結論づけるのも無理がある（正解の④は，第2文の中で「この驚くべき生き物は，人間よりも長く生きながらえるかもしれない（might outlive）」という，①よりも非断定的な推量の表現を用いていることに注意）。②については，「緩歩動物は宇宙から来て」の部分が本文からは読み取れないので誤りである。③については，宇宙船から月面に放出された緩歩動物に関して本文第3段落最終文（Whether these are ...）に「誰もこれらを回収しに行った人がいないので，これらがまだ生きているかどうかはわかりません。残念なことです」とあることから，③の第2文のように「そして月面でも生息することができるのだ」と考えることはできない。

問5 　49 　正解－④
「緩歩動物を宇宙に送り出すことに関して推測できることは何か」
① 緩歩動物が宇宙で生き延びることができるかどうかは，重要と考えられことが一度もなかった。
② 緩歩動物は，何百万年もの間地球上にいる他の生物と同様に，X線や紫外線放射に耐えることができる。
③ イスラエルの研究者たちは，あんなにも多くの緩歩動物が宇宙の過酷な環境で生き延びるとは予想しなかった。
④ 緩歩動物が月面で生き延びることができるかどうかを誰も見に行ってきていない理由が，筆者の注意を引きつけた。

　正解は④。問4の解説でも引用した第3段落最終文（Whether these are ...）の「誰もこれらを回収しに行った人がいないので，これらがまだ生きているかどうかはわかりません。残念なことです」という記述は，月面に残された緩歩動物を誰も調べに行っていないのはなぜかと筆者は疑問に思ったことだろう（つまりその理由が筆者の注意を引きつけただろう），と推測するのに十分な根拠となりうることから，④が正解となる。

　①のように推測する根拠は本文中にはない。②についても，「何百万年もの間地球上にいる緩歩動物以外の生物も，X線や紫外線放射に耐えることができるだろう」と推測する根拠は本文中にはないので，やはり誤りとなる。③については，「イスラエル」を「ヨーロッパ」に変えれば正しいが，「イスラエル」のままでは適切な内容にならない（第3段落参照）。

— 英 R 263 —

〈主な語句・表現〉

第1段落 (Ask someone to ...)

 tough 形「丈夫な」／ Bactrian camel「フタコブラクダ」／ Arctic fox「ホッキョクギツネ」

第2段落 (Tardigrades, also known ...)

 tardigrade 名「緩歩動物」／ water bear「クマムシ」／ microscopic creature「微生物」／ length 名「長さ；全長」／ hot spring「温泉」／ desert 名「砂漠」／ All they need are ...「彼らが必要とするものは…だけだ」／ layer 名「層」／ so do they = they dry up, too「それらも干上がる」／ all but ...「…を除く全て」／ metabolism 名「新陳代謝」／ dried-out 形「乾燥した」／ state 名「状態」／ soak 動「…を漬ける；浸す」／ absorb 動「…を吸収する」／ spring back to life「復活する；息を吹き返す」／ as if ...「まるで…ように」／ the moment ...「…するとすぐに」／ come alive「生き生きとする」

第3段落 (Perhaps even more ...)

 more amazing（= C）than ... is（= V）their ability（= S）to －「…よりも驚くべきは，それらが－する能力だ」／ a number of ...「数多くの…」／ ultraviolet radiation「紫外線（放射）」／ intense 形「強烈な」／ spacecraft 名「宇宙船」／ crash 動「衝突する」／ spill 動「こぼす；吐き出す」／ pity 名「残念なこと」

第4段落 (Tardigrades are shaped ...)

 be shaped like ...「…のような形をしている」／ cucumber 名「キュウリ」／ species 名「（生物学上の）種」／ sticky pad「付着盤」／ claw 名「爪」／ variation 名「変異体」／ identify 動「…を特定する」／ primitive 形「原始的な；単純な」／ cell 名「細胞」／ light sensitive「光を感知する」

第5段落 (Basically, tardigrades can ...)

 basically 副「基本的には」／ divide A into B「A を B に分ける」／ plant matter「植物」／ creature 名「生き物；動物」／ vegetation 名「植物」／ ventral 形「腹の」／ located in ...「…の中に位置する［ある］」／ shark 名「サメ」／ terminal 形「終端の」／ tuna 名「マグロ」／ do ... have ～「（確かに；実際に）～を持つ」do は強調の助動詞。／ needle 名「針」／ stylet 名「吻針」／ pierce 動「…を突き刺す；突き通す」／ so the contents can be sucked out「中身を吸い出すことができるように」

最終段落 (Both types of ...)

 digestive system「消化器系」／ lead to ...「…につながる」／ pharynx 名「咽頭」／ digestive juice「消化液」／ Located（= C）above ... is（= V）a salivary gland（= S）「…の上方に位置しているのは唾液腺である」／ digestion 名「消化」／ tube 名「管」／ transport 動「運ぶ」／ gut 名「消化器官；腸」／ esophagus 名「食道」／ stomach 名「胃」／ intestine 名「腸」／ organ 名「臓器；器官」／ digest 動「…を消化する」／ nutrient 名「栄養素」／ leftovers 名「残り物」／ eventually 副「結局は；最後には」／ anus 名「肛門」

① 20240711